Little Lulu®

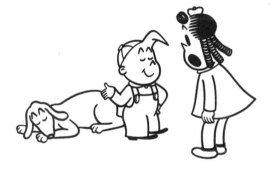

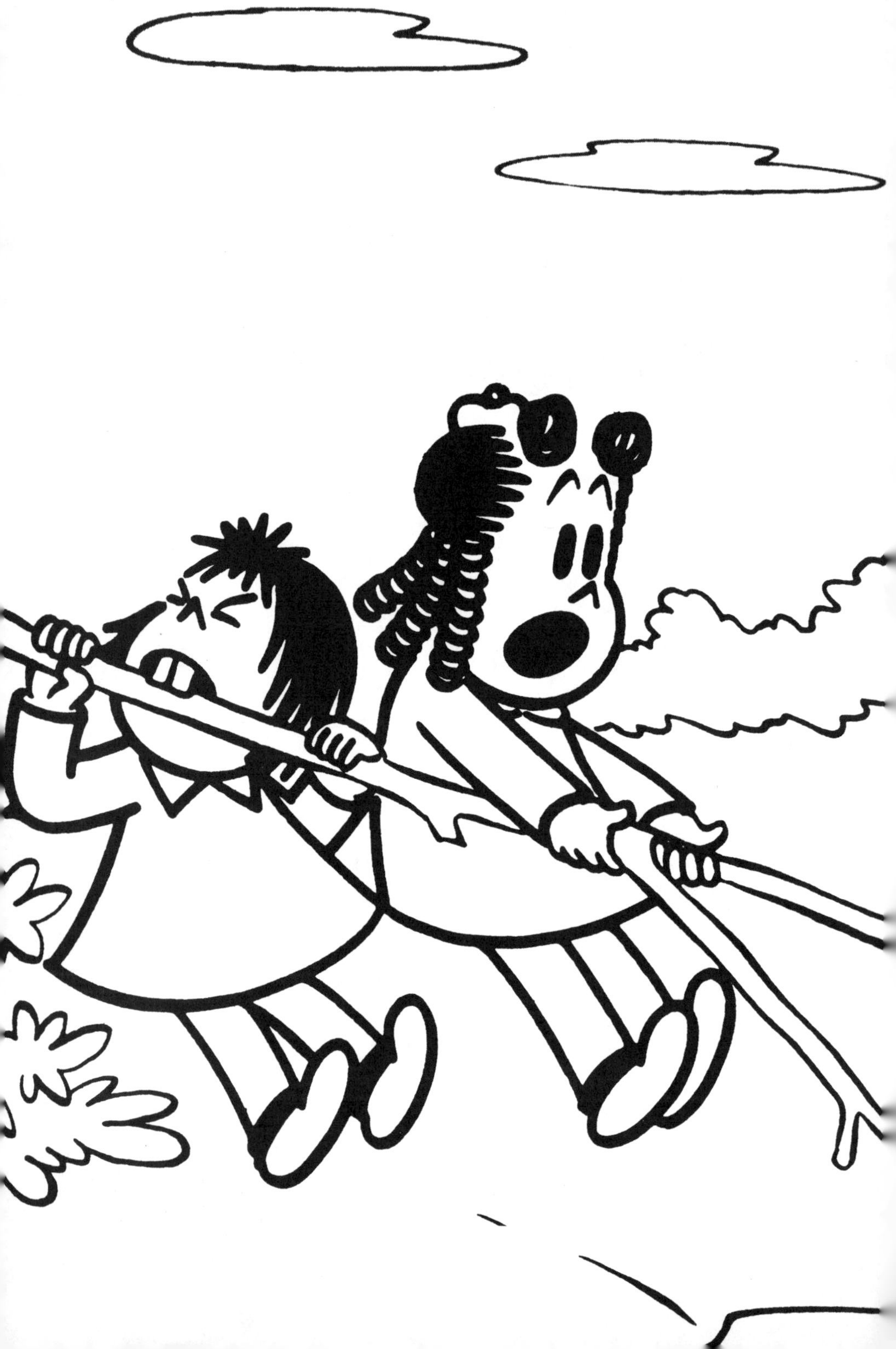

Little Lulu®

A Handy Kid

Story and Art

John Stanley

and

Irving Tripp

Based on the character

created by

Marge Buell

DARK HORSE BOOKS®

Publisher
Mike Richardson

Editor
Dave Marshall

Collection Designer
Krystal Hennes

Art Director
Lia Ribacchi

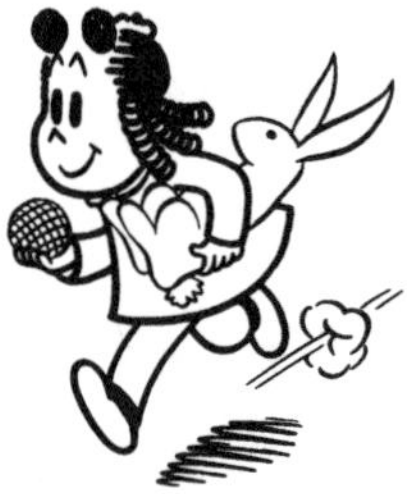

Published by
Dark Horse Books
A division of Dark Horse Comics, Inc.
10956 SE Main Street
Milwaukie, OR 97222

darkhorse.com

Little Lulu ® Vol. 16: A Handy Kid

First edition: July 2007
ISBN-10: 1-59307-685-1
ISBN-13: 978-1-59307-685-6

1 3 5 7 9 10 8 6 4 2
Printed in the United States of America

A note about Lulu

Little Lulu came into the world through the pen of cartoonist Marjorie "Marge" Henderson Buell in 1935. Originally commissioned as a series of single-panel cartoons by *The Saturday Evening Post*, Lulu took the world by storm with her charm, smarts, and sass. Within ten years, she not only was the star of her own cartoon series, but a celebrity spokesgirl for a variety of high-profile commercial products.

Little Lulu truly hit her stride as America's sweetheart in the comic books published by Dell Comics starting in 1945. While Buell was solely responsible for Lulu's original single-panel shenanigans, the comic-book stories were put into the able hands of comics legend John Stanley. Stanley wrote and laid out the comics while artist Irving Tripp provided the finished drawings. After a number of trial appearances in Dell Comics, Lulu's appeal was undeniable, and she was granted her very own comic-book series, called *Marge's Little Lulu*, which was published regularly through 1984.

This volume contains every comic from issues sixty-nine through seventy-four of *Marge's Little Lulu*.

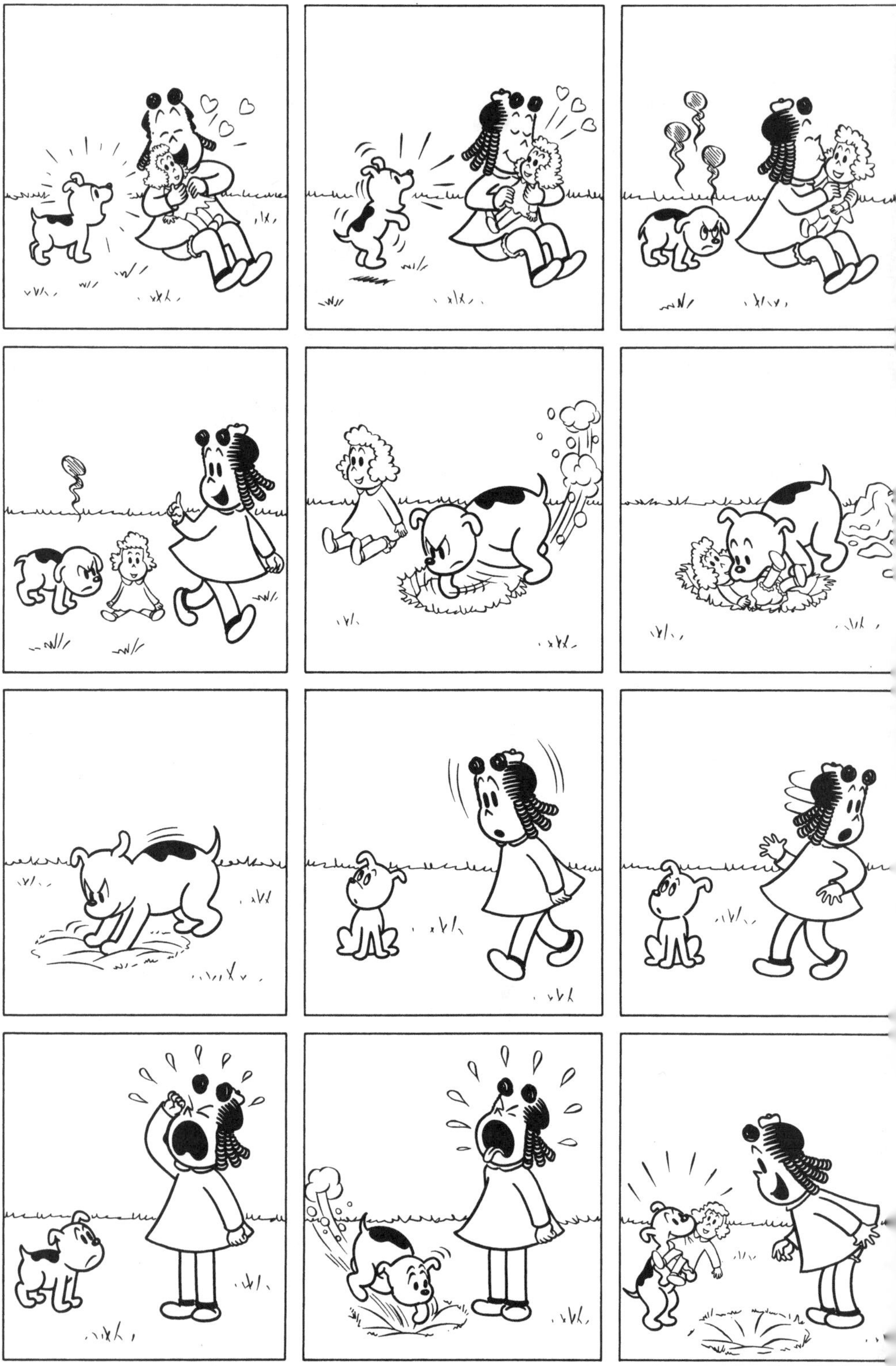

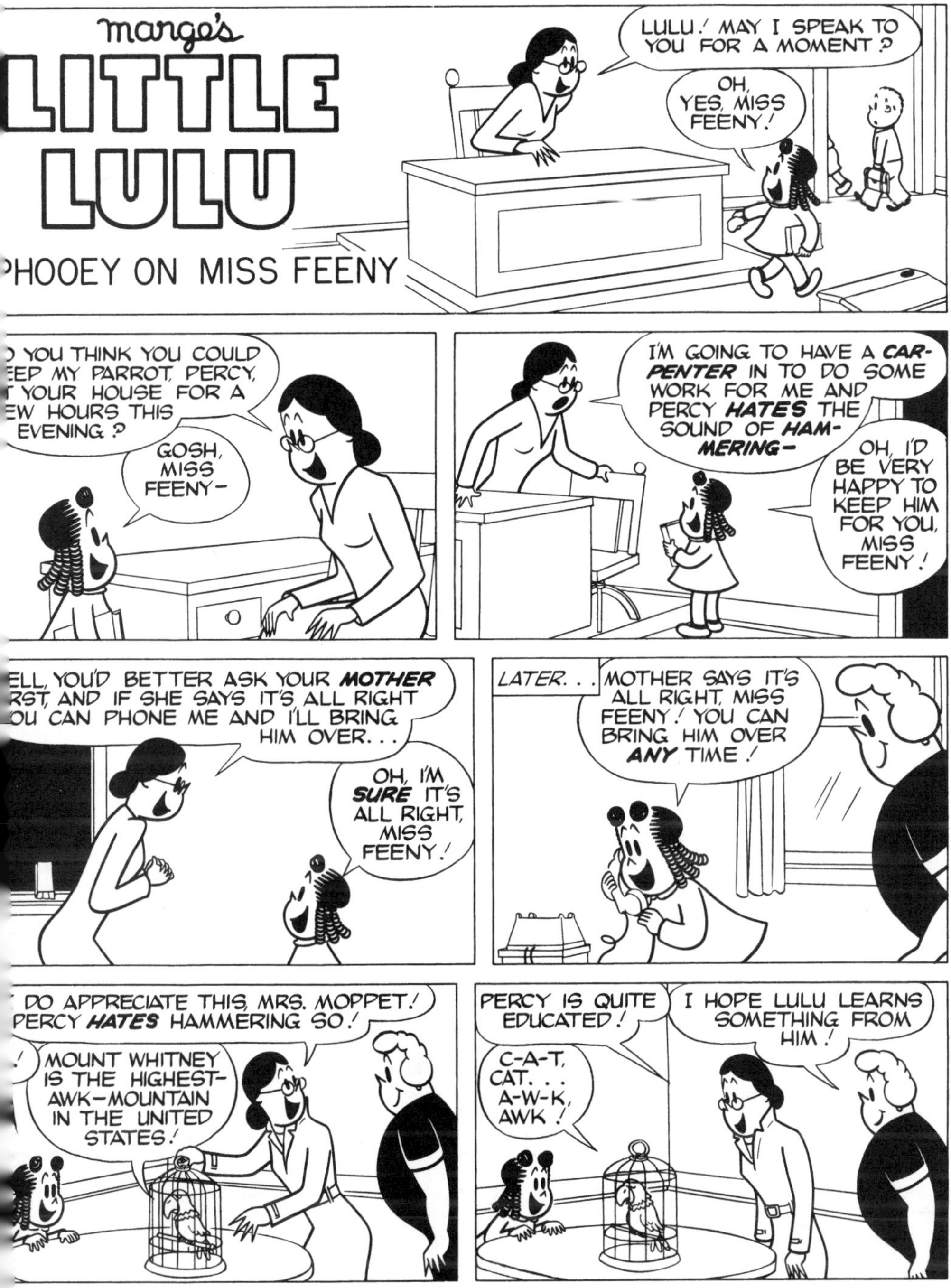
marge's
LITTLE LULU
PHOOEY ON MISS FEENY
LULU! MAY I SPEAK TO YOU FOR A MOMENT?
OH, YES, MISS FEENY!
YOU THINK YOU COULD EEP MY PARROT, PERCY, T YOUR HOUSE FOR A EW HOURS THIS EVENING?
GOSH, MISS FEENY—
I'M GOING TO HAVE A CARPENTER IN TO DO SOME WORK FOR ME AND PERCY HATES THE SOUND OF HAMMERING—
OH, I'D BE VERY HAPPY TO KEEP HIM FOR YOU, MISS FEENY!
ELL, YOU'D BETTER ASK YOUR MOTHER RST, AND IF SHE SAYS IT'S ALL RIGHT OU CAN PHONE ME AND I'LL BRING HIM OVER...
OH, I'M SURE IT'S ALL RIGHT, MISS FEENY!
LATER...
MOTHER SAYS IT'S ALL RIGHT, MISS FEENY! YOU CAN BRING HIM OVER ANY TIME!
DO APPRECIATE THIS, MRS. MOPPET! PERCY HATES HAMMERING SO!
MOUNT WHITNEY IS THE HIGHEST—AWK—MOUNTAIN IN THE UNITED STATES!
PERCY IS QUITE EDUCATED!
I HOPE LULU LEARNS SOMETHING FROM HIM!
C-A-T, CAT... A-W-K, AWK!

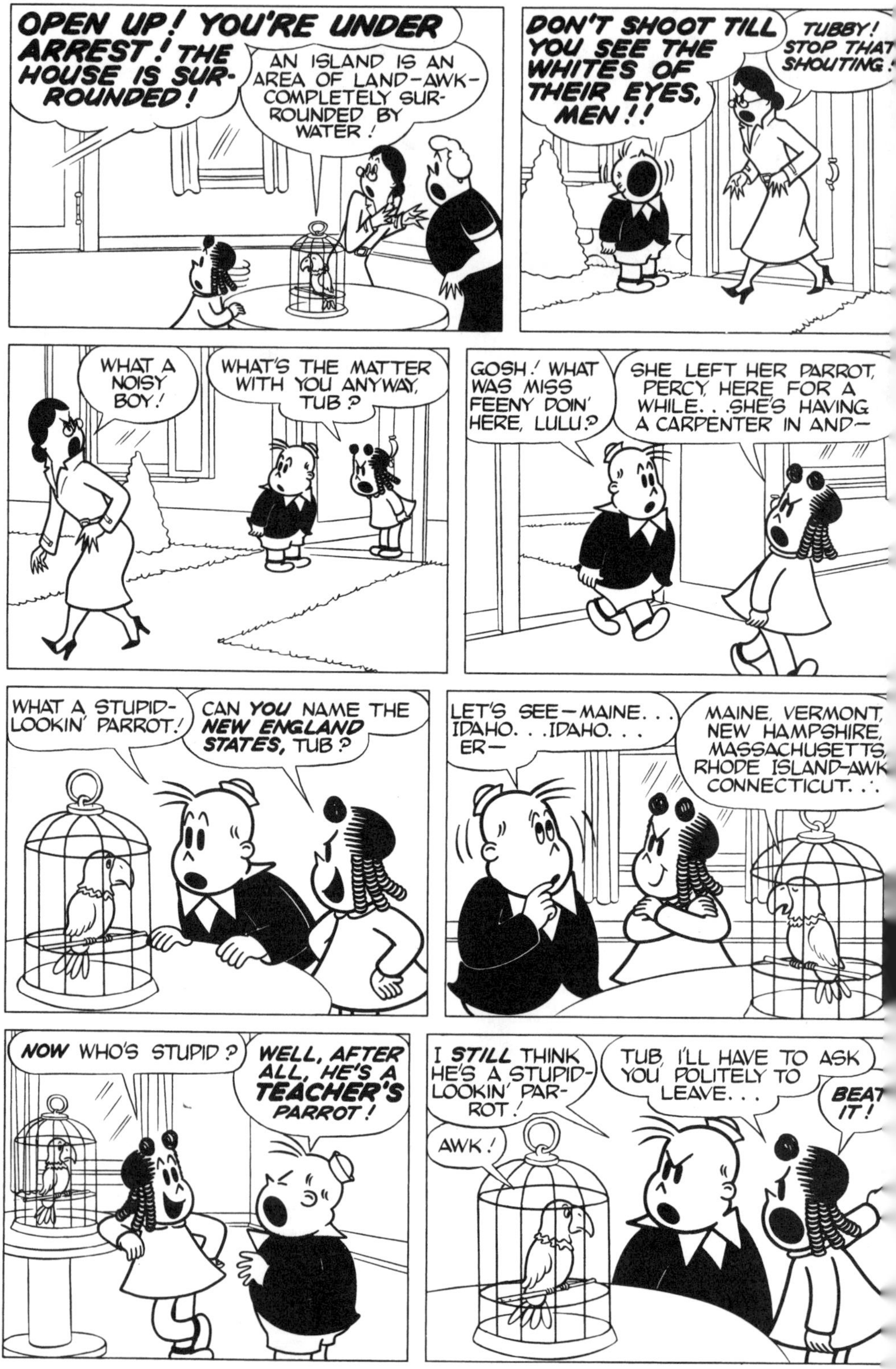
OPEN UP! YOU'RE UNDER ARREST! THE HOUSE IS SURROUNDED!
AN ISLAND IS AN AREA OF LAND-AWK-COMPLETELY SURROUNDED BY WATER!
DON'T SHOOT TILL YOU SEE THE WHITES OF THEIR EYES, MEN!!
TUBBY! STOP THAT SHOUTING!
WHAT A NOISY BOY!
WHAT'S THE MATTER WITH YOU ANYWAY, TUB?
GOSH! WHAT WAS MISS FEENY DOIN' HERE, LULU?
SHE LEFT HER PARROT, PERCY, HERE FOR A WHILE. . .SHE'S HAVING A CARPENTER IN AND—
WHAT A STUPID-LOOKIN' PARROT!
CAN YOU NAME THE NEW ENGLAND STATES, TUB?
LET'S SEE—MAINE. . . IDAHO. . .IDAHO. . . ER—
MAINE, VERMONT, NEW HAMPSHIRE, MASSACHUSETTS, RHODE ISLAND-AWK-CONNECTICUT. . .
NOW WHO'S STUPID?
WELL, AFTER ALL, HE'S A TEACHER'S PARROT!
I STILL THINK HE'S A STUPID-LOOKIN' PAR-ROT!
AWK!
TUB, I'LL HAVE TO ASK YOU POLITELY TO LEAVE. . .
BEAT IT!

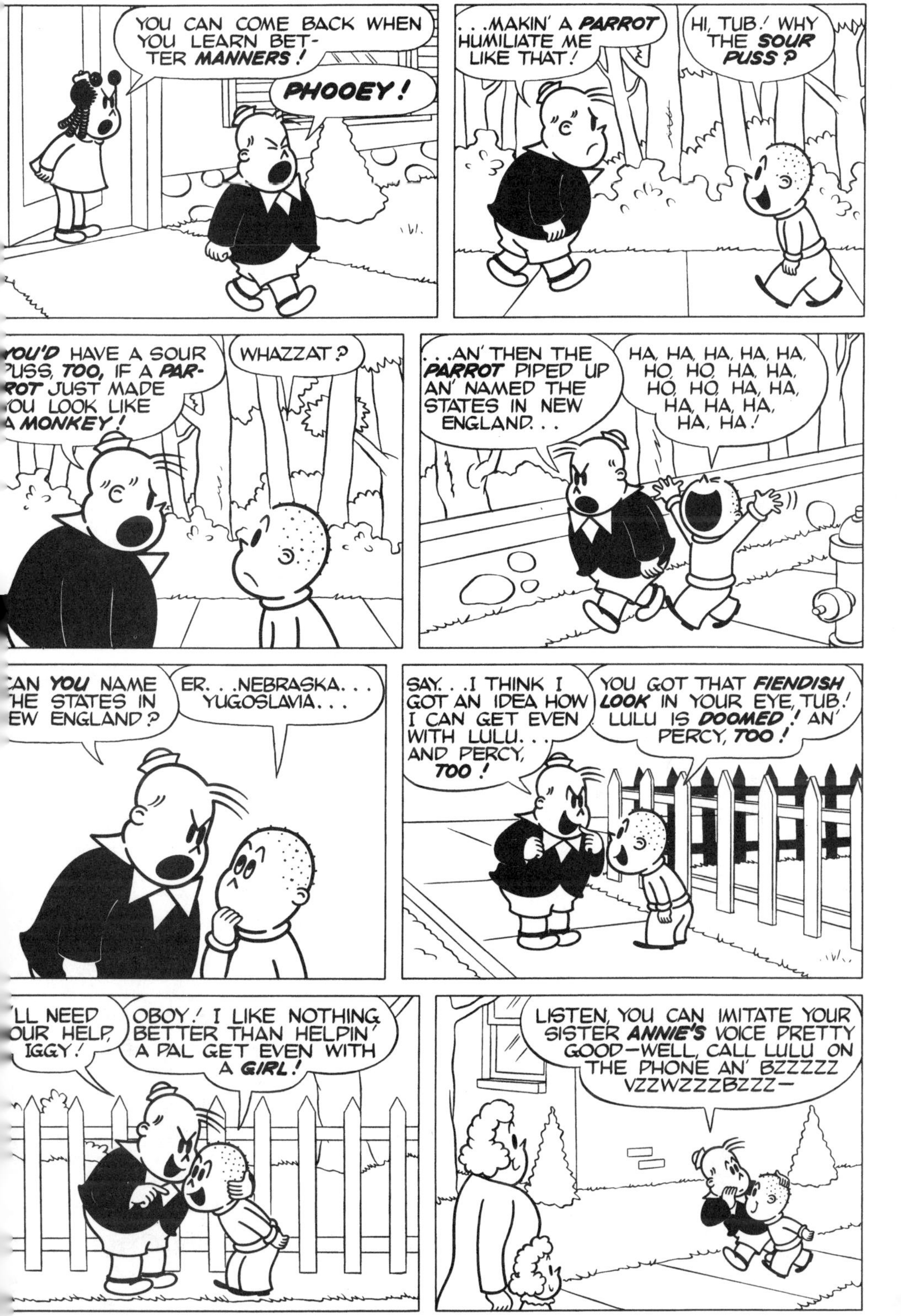
YOU CAN COME BACK WHEN YOU LEARN BET-TER MANNERS!
PHOOEY!
...MAKIN' A PARROT HUMILIATE ME LIKE THAT!
HI, TUB! WHY THE SOUR PUSS?
YOU'D HAVE A SOUR PUSS, TOO, IF A PAR-ROT JUST MADE YOU LOOK LIKE A MONKEY!
WHAZZAT?
...AN' THEN THE PARROT PIPED UP AN' NAMED THE STATES IN NEW ENGLAND...
HA, HA, HA, HA, HA, HO, HO, HA, HA, HO, HO, HA, HA, HA, HA, HA, HA, HA!
CAN YOU NAME THE STATES IN NEW ENGLAND?
ER...NEBRASKA... YUGOSLAVIA...
SAY...I THINK I GOT AN IDEA HOW I CAN GET EVEN WITH LULU... AND PERCY, TOO!
YOU GOT THAT FIENDISH LOOK IN YOUR EYE, TUB! LULU IS DOOMED! AN' PERCY, TOO!
I'LL NEED YOUR HELP, IGGY!
OBOY! I LIKE NOTHING BETTER THAN HELPIN' A PAL GET EVEN WITH A GIRL!
LISTEN, YOU CAN IMITATE YOUR SISTER ANNIE'S VOICE PRETTY GOOD—WELL, CALL LULU ON THE PHONE AN' BZZZZZ VZZWZZZBZZZ—

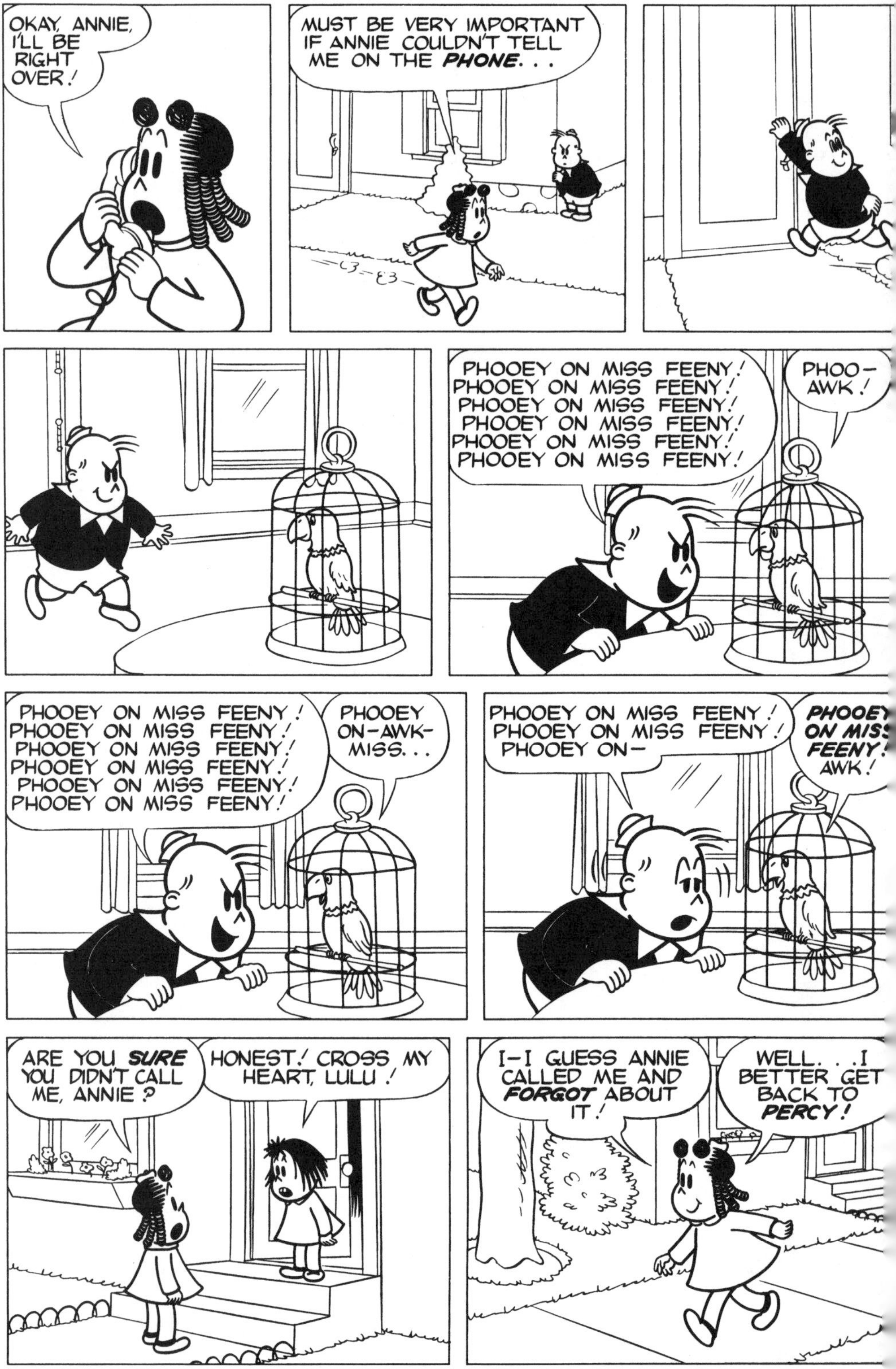
OKAY, ANNIE, I'LL BE RIGHT OVER!
MUST BE VERY IMPORTANT IF ANNIE COULDN'T TELL ME ON THE PHONE...
PHOOEY ON MISS FEENY! PHOOEY ON MISS FEENY! PHOOEY ON MISS FEENY! PHOOEY ON MISS FEENY! PHOOEY ON MISS FEENY! PHOOEY ON MISS FEENY!
PHOO-AWK!
PHOOEY ON MISS FEENY! PHOOEY ON MISS FEENY! PHOOEY ON MISS FEENY! PHOOEY ON MISS FEENY! PHOOEY ON MISS FEENY! PHOOEY ON MISS FEENY!
PHOOEY ON-AWK-MISS...
PHOOEY ON MISS FEENY! PHOOEY ON MISS FEENY! PHOOEY ON-
PHOOEY ON MISS FEENY! AWK!
ARE YOU SURE YOU DIDN'T CALL ME, ANNIE?
HONEST! CROSS MY HEART, LULU!
I-I GUESS ANNIE CALLED ME AND FORGOT ABOUT IT!
WELL...I BETTER GET BACK TO PERCY!

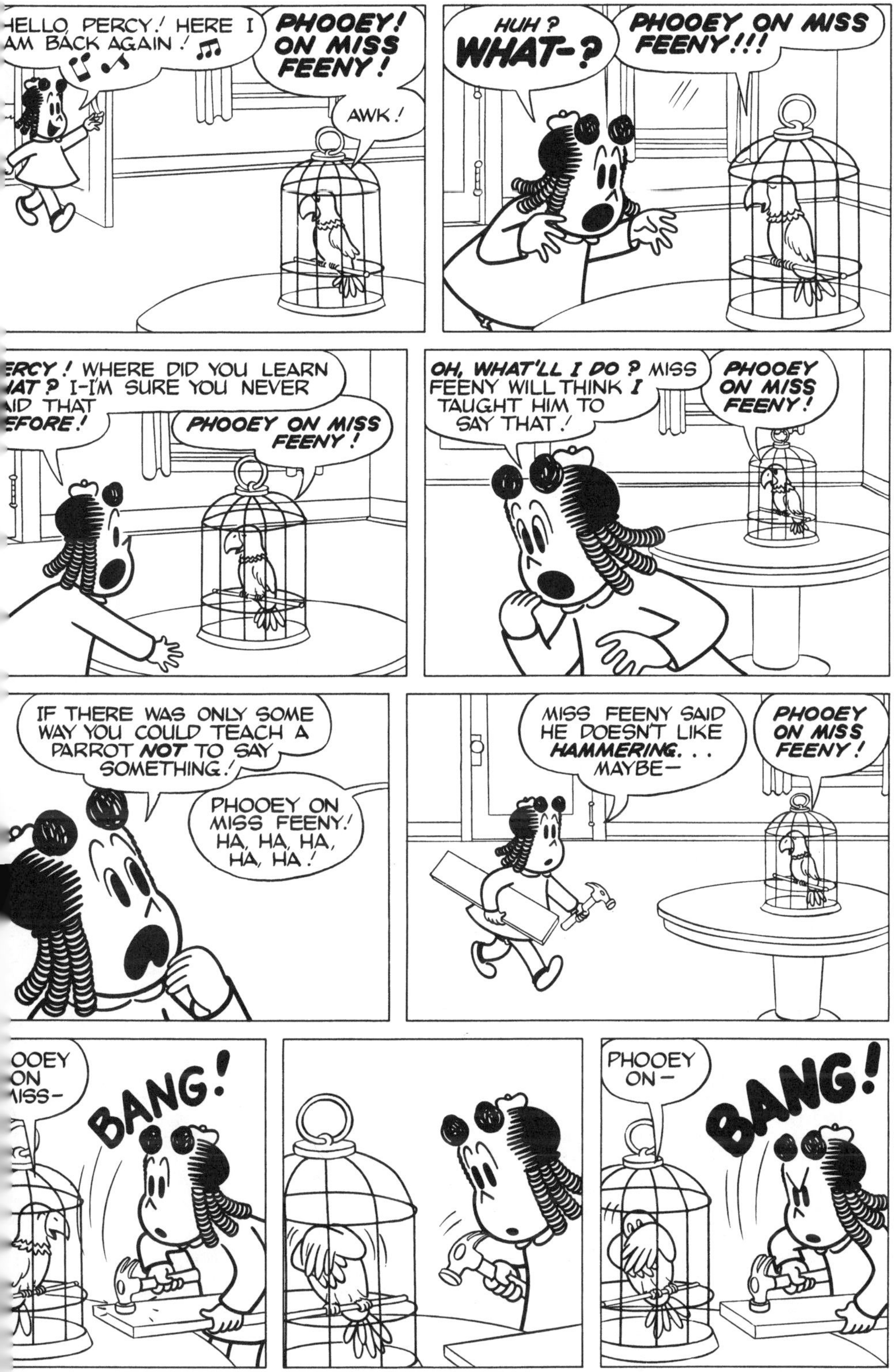
HELLO, PERCY! HERE I AM BACK AGAIN!
PHOOEY! ON MISS FEENY!
AWK!
HUH? WHAT-?
PHOOEY ON MISS FEENY!!!
ERCY! WHERE DID YOU LEARN AT? I-I'M SURE YOU NEVER ID THAT EFORE!
PHOOEY ON MISS FEENY!
OH, WHAT'LL I DO? MISS FEENY WILL THINK I TAUGHT HIM TO SAY THAT!
PHOOEY ON MISS FEENY!
IF THERE WAS ONLY SOME WAY YOU COULD TEACH A PARROT NOT TO SAY SOMETHING!
PHOOEY ON MISS FEENY! HA, HA, HA, HA, HA!
MISS FEENY SAID HE DOESN'T LIKE HAMMERING... MAYBE-
PHOOEY ON MISS FEENY!
OOEY ON ISS-
BANG!
PHOOEY ON-
BANG!

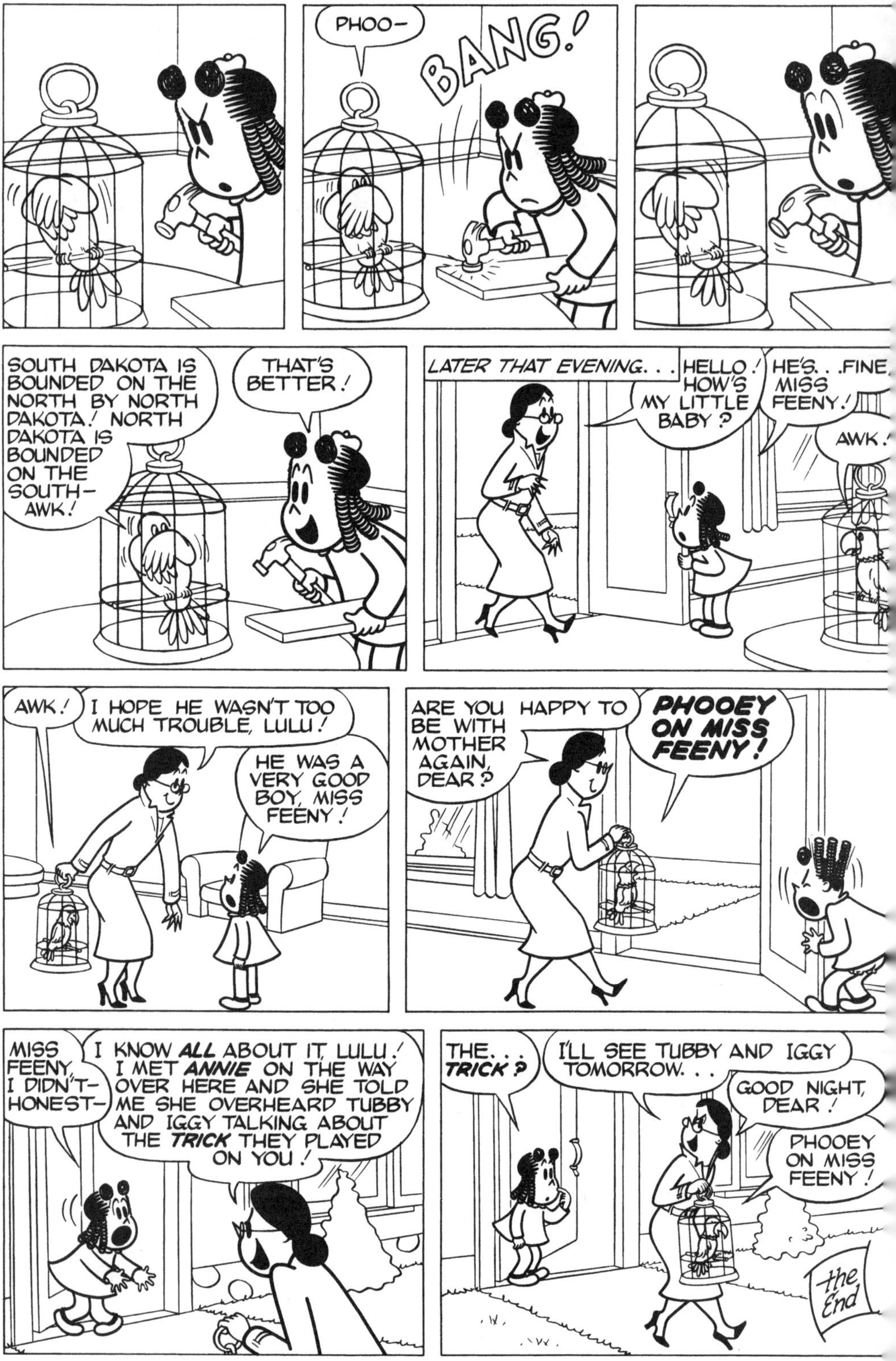

PHOO—
BANG!
SOUTH DAKOTA IS BOUNDED ON THE NORTH BY NORTH DAKOTA! NORTH DAKOTA IS BOUNDED ON THE SOUTH— AWK!
THAT'S BETTER!
LATER THAT EVENING. . .
HELLO! HOW'S MY LITTLE BABY?
HE'S. . .FINE, MISS FEENY!
AWK!
AWK!
I HOPE HE WASN'T TOO MUCH TROUBLE, LULU!
HE WAS A VERY GOOD BOY, MISS FEENY!
ARE YOU HAPPY TO BE WITH MOTHER AGAIN, DEAR?
PHOOEY ON MISS FEENY!
MISS FEENY, I DIDN'T— HONEST—
I KNOW ALL ABOUT IT, LULU! I MET ANNIE ON THE WAY OVER HERE AND SHE TOLD ME SHE OVERHEARD TUBBY AND IGGY TALKING ABOUT THE TRICK THEY PLAYED ON YOU!
THE. . . TRICK?
I'LL SEE TUBBY AND IGGY TOMORROW. . .
GOOD NIGHT, DEAR!
PHOOEY ON MISS FEENY!
the End

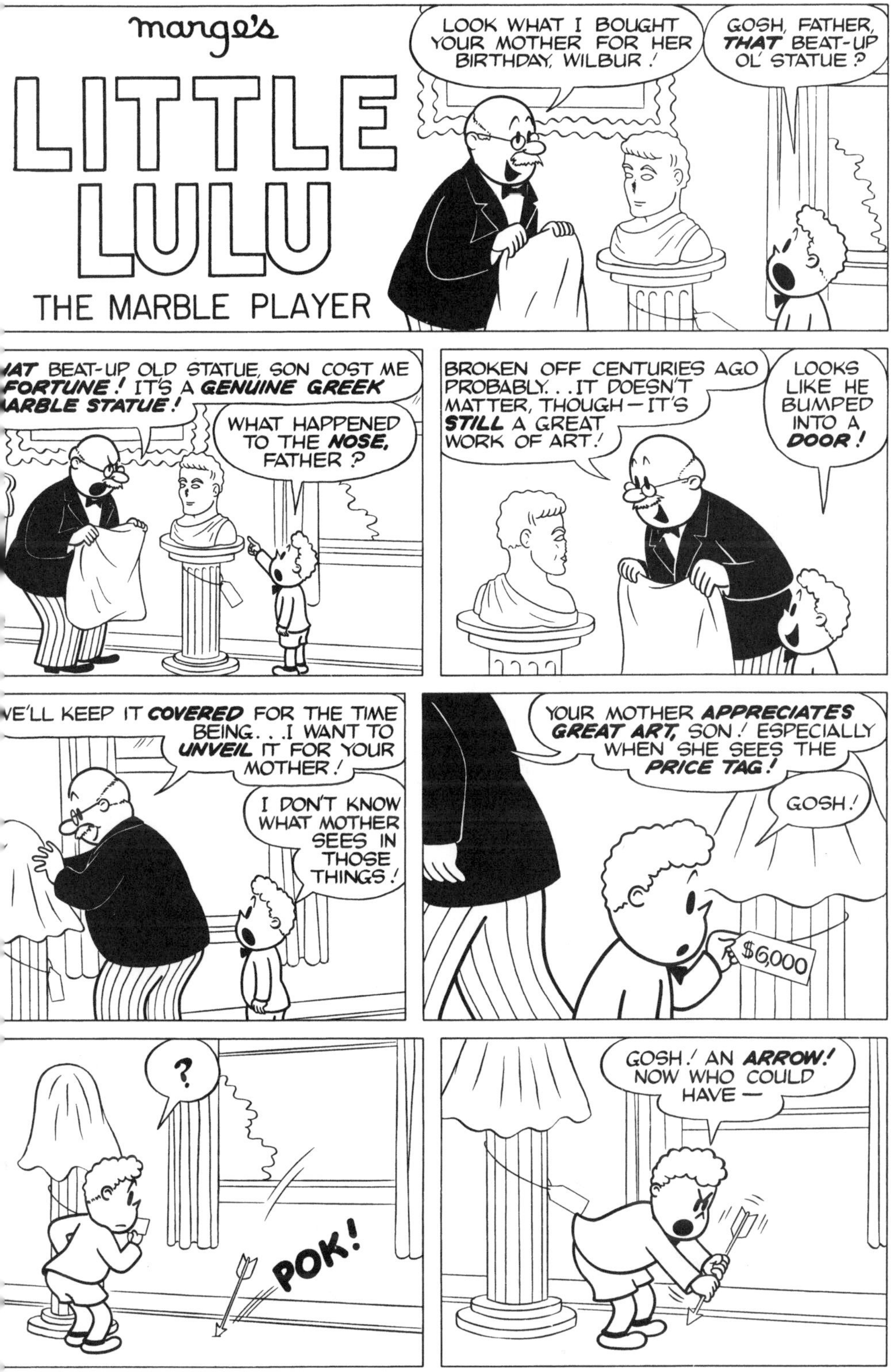
marge's
LITTLE LULU
THE MARBLE PLAYER
LOOK WHAT I BOUGHT YOUR MOTHER FOR HER BIRTHDAY, WILBUR!
GOSH, FATHER, THAT BEAT-UP OL' STATUE?
AT BEAT-UP OLD STATUE, SON COST ME FORTUNE! IT'S A GENUINE GREEK ARBLE STATUE!
WHAT HAPPENED TO THE NOSE, FATHER?
BROKEN OFF CENTURIES AGO PROBABLY. . .IT DOESN'T MATTER, THOUGH—IT'S STILL A GREAT WORK OF ART!
LOOKS LIKE HE BUMPED INTO A DOOR!
E'LL KEEP IT COVERED FOR THE TIME BEING. . .I WANT TO UNVEIL IT FOR YOUR MOTHER!
I DON'T KNOW WHAT MOTHER SEES IN THOSE THINGS!
YOUR MOTHER APPRECIATES GREAT ART, SON! ESPECIALLY WHEN SHE SEES THE PRICE TAG!
GOSH!
$6,000
?
POK!
GOSH! AN ARROW! NOW WHO COULD HAVE —

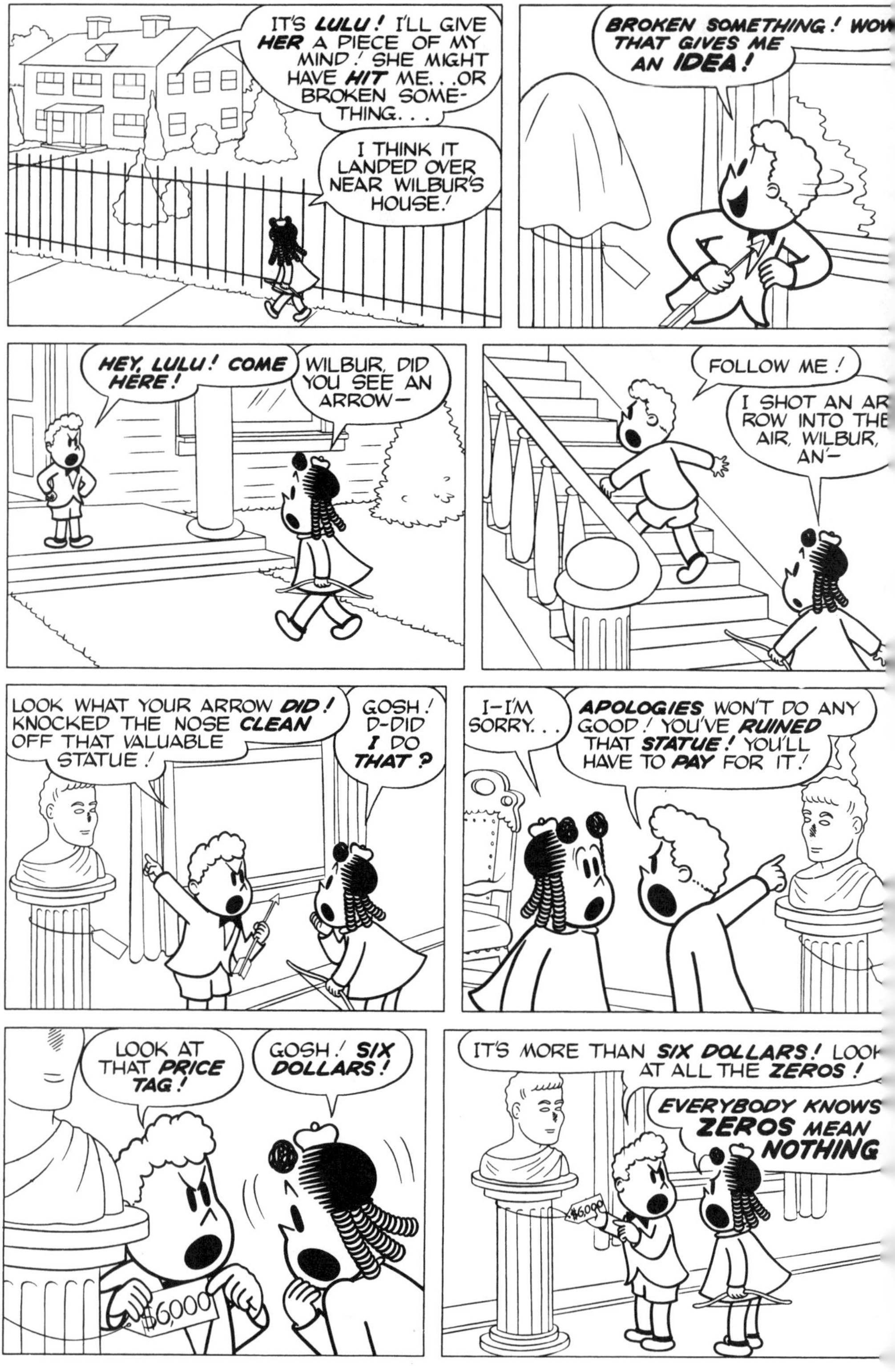
IT'S LULU! I'LL GIVE HER A PIECE OF MY MIND! SHE MIGHT HAVE HIT ME...OR BROKEN SOMETHING...
I THINK IT LANDED OVER NEAR WILBUR'S HOUSE!
BROKEN SOMETHING! WOW THAT GIVES ME AN IDEA!
HEY, LULU! COME HERE!
WILBUR, DID YOU SEE AN ARROW—
FOLLOW ME!
I SHOT AN AR ROW INTO THE AIR, WILBUR, AN'—
LOOK WHAT YOUR ARROW DID! KNOCKED THE NOSE CLEAN OFF THAT VALUABLE STATUE!
GOSH! D-DID I DO THAT?
I-I'M SORRY...
APOLOGIES WON'T DO ANY GOOD! YOU'VE RUINED THAT STATUE! YOU'LL HAVE TO PAY FOR IT!
LOOK AT THAT PRICE TAG!
GOSH! SIX DOLLARS!
$6,000
IT'S MORE THAN SIX DOLLARS! LOOK AT ALL THE ZEROS!
EVERYBODY KNOWS ZEROS MEAN NOTHING
$6,000

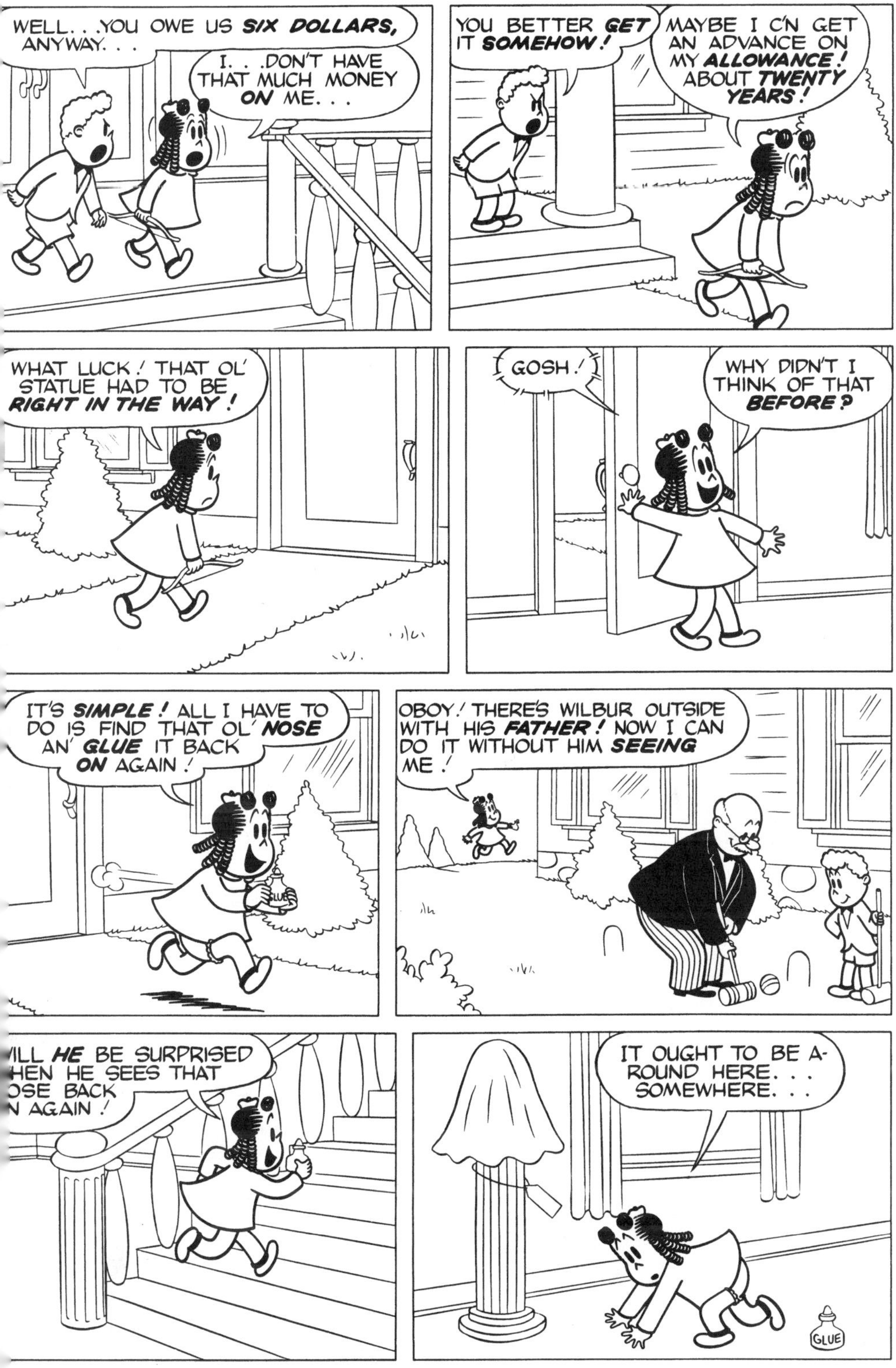
WELL. . .YOU OWE US SIX DOLLARS, ANYWAY. . .
I. . .DON'T HAVE THAT MUCH MONEY ON ME. . .
YOU BETTER GET IT SOMEHOW!
MAYBE I C'N GET AN ADVANCE ON MY ALLOWANCE! ABOUT TWENTY YEARS!
WHAT LUCK! THAT OL' STATUE HAD TO BE RIGHT IN THE WAY!
GOSH!
WHY DIDN'T I THINK OF THAT BEFORE?
IT'S SIMPLE! ALL I HAVE TO DO IS FIND THAT OL' NOSE AN' GLUE IT BACK ON AGAIN!
GLUE
OBOY! THERE'S WILBUR OUTSIDE WITH HIS FATHER! NOW I CAN DO IT WITHOUT HIM SEEING ME!
ILL HE BE SURPRISED HEN HE SEES THAT OSE BACK N AGAIN!
IT OUGHT TO BE A-ROUND HERE. . . SOMEWHERE. . .
GLUE

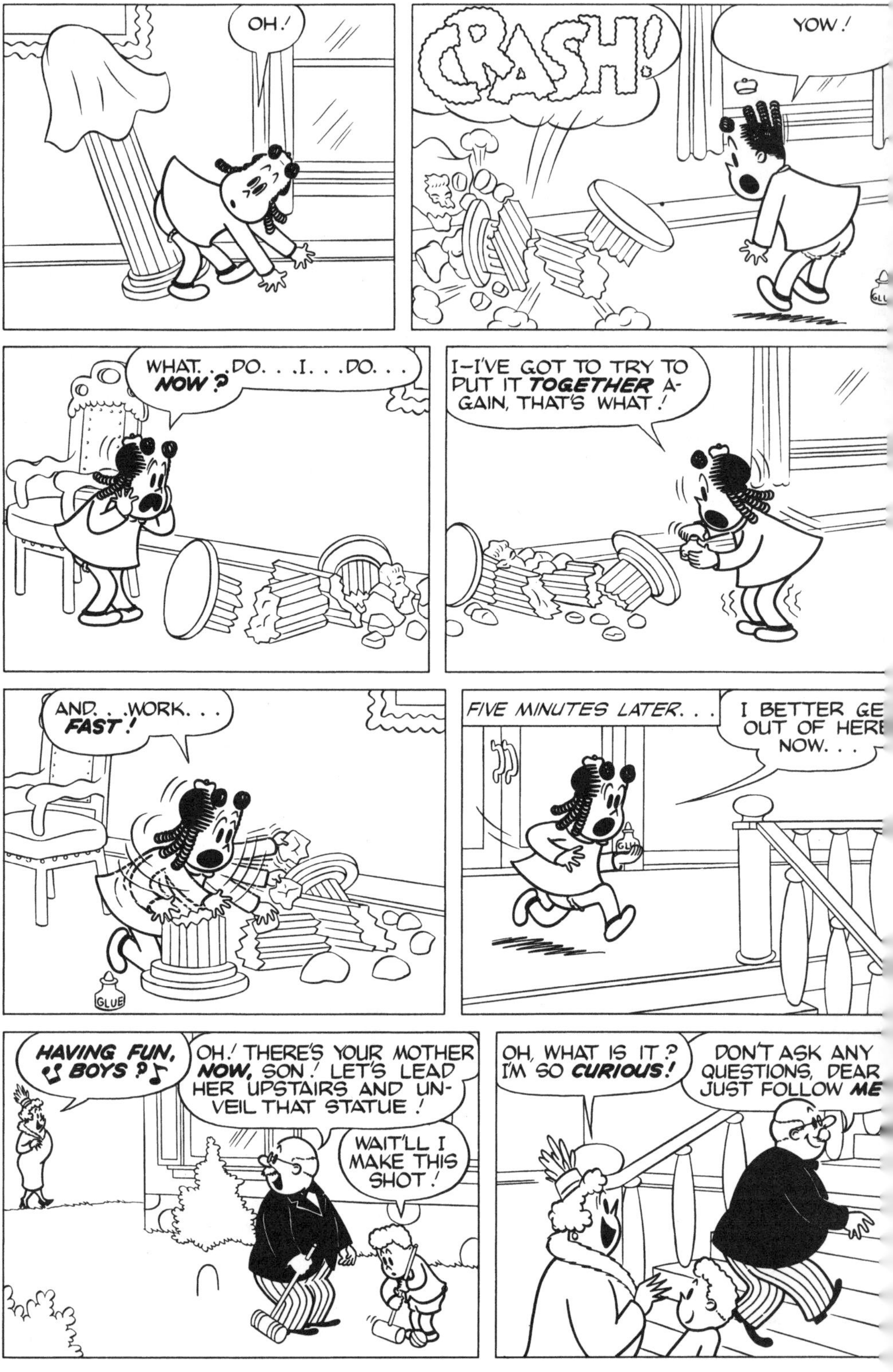
OH.!
CRASH!
YOW.!
WHAT. . .DO. . .I. . .DO. . . NOW?
I—I'VE GOT TO TRY TO PUT IT TOGETHER A-GAIN, THAT'S WHAT.!
AND. . .WORK. . . FAST.!
FIVE MINUTES LATER. . .
I BETTER GE OUT OF HERE NOW. . .
GLUE
HAVING FUN, BOYS?
OH.! THERE'S YOUR MOTHER NOW, SON.! LET'S LEAD HER UPSTAIRS AND UN-VEIL THAT STATUE.!
WAIT'LL I MAKE THIS SHOT.!
OH, WHAT IS IT? I'M SO CURIOUS!
DON'T ASK ANY QUESTIONS, DEAR JUST FOLLOW ME

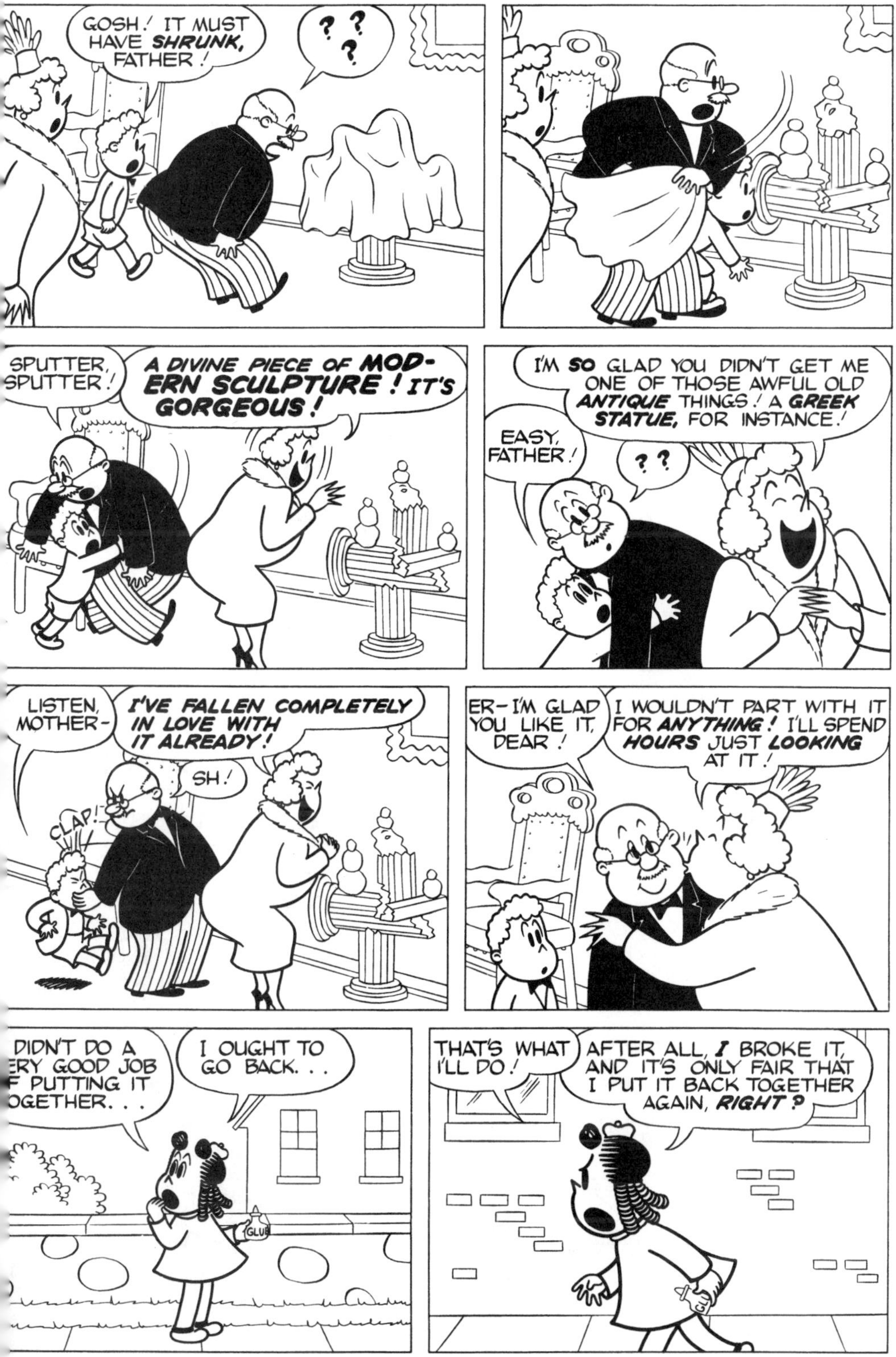

GOSH! IT MUST HAVE SHRUNK, FATHER!
? ? ?
SPUTTER, SPUTTER!
A DIVINE PIECE OF MODERN SCULPTURE! IT'S GORGEOUS!
I'M SO GLAD YOU DIDN'T GET ME ONE OF THOSE AWFUL OLD ANTIQUE THINGS! A GREEK STATUE, FOR INSTANCE!
EASY, FATHER!
? ?
LISTEN, MOTHER-
I'VE FALLEN COMPLETELY IN LOVE WITH IT ALREADY!
SH!
CLAP!
ER- I'M GLAD YOU LIKE IT, DEAR!
I WOULDN'T PART WITH IT FOR ANYTHING! I'LL SPEND HOURS JUST LOOKING AT IT!
DIDN'T DO A ERY GOOD JOB F PUTTING IT OGETHER. . .
I OUGHT TO GO BACK. . .
GLUE
THAT'S WHAT I'LL DO!
AFTER ALL, I BROKE IT, AND IT'S ONLY FAIR THAT I PUT IT BACK TOGETHER AGAIN, RIGHT?

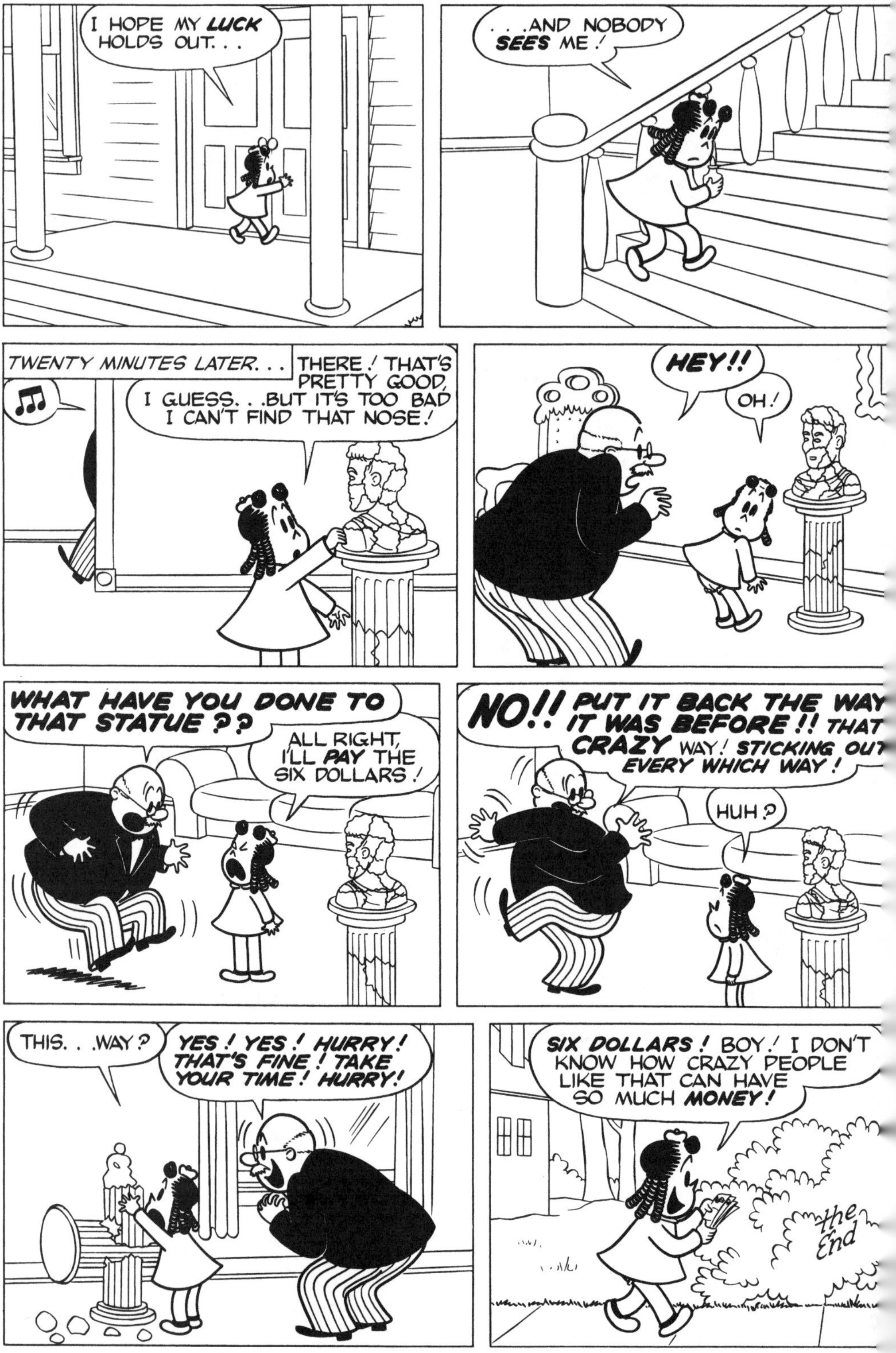
I HOPE MY LUCK HOLDS OUT. . .
. . .AND NOBODY SEES ME.!
TWENTY MINUTES LATER. . .
THERE.! THAT'S PRETTY GOOD, I GUESS. . .BUT IT'S TOO BAD I CAN'T FIND THAT NOSE.!
HEY!!
OH.!
WHAT HAVE YOU DONE TO THAT STATUE ??
ALL RIGHT, I'LL PAY THE SIX DOLLARS.!
NO!! PUT IT BACK THE WAY IT WAS BEFORE!! THAT CRAZY WAY.! STICKING OUT EVERY WHICH WAY!
HUH?
THIS. . .WAY?
YES! YES! HURRY! THAT'S FINE! TAKE YOUR TIME! HURRY!
SIX DOLLARS! BOY.! I DON'T KNOW HOW CRAZY PEOPLE LIKE THAT CAN HAVE SO MUCH MONEY!
the End

marge's
LITTLE LULU
THE SUBSTITUTE

I'M SORRY YOU GOT A BAD REPORT CARD, TUB!

I'D HATE TO BE IN *YOUR* PANTS WHEN YOUR FATHER SEES THAT *REPORT CARD,* TUB!

BETCHA YOU [W]ON'T BE ABLE [T]O *SIT DOWN* [F]OR A *MONTH!*

MISS FEENY, OUR TEACHER, IS THE ONE WHO OUGHT TO GET THE SPANKIN'!

GOSH, *WHY,* TUB?

IT ISN'T *MY* FAULT THAT SHE'S TOO STU-PID TO *TEACH* ME ANYTHING!

HA, HA, HA! *MISS FEENY* IS STUPID, HE SAYS!

I-I'M AFRAID TO FACE MY *FATHER* WITH THIS REPORT CARD...

HE'LL BE PRETTY MAD, HUH?

HE'S GOT A *TERRIBLE TEMPER!* HE'LL BLOW UP! HE'LL HIT THE CEILIN'! AND WHAT'S *WORSE,* HE'LL HIT *ME!!*

HE'LL CALM DOWN AFTER AWHILE, TUB!

[OH,] SURE! BUT LOOK [W]HAT'LL HAPPEN TO [M]E IN THE [ME]ANTIME!

WELL...THERE'S NOTHING YOU CAN DO ABOUT IT NOW, TUB...

HMM...SAY MAYBE THERE *IS* SOMETHING YOU CAN DO ABOUT IT, LULU...

ME?

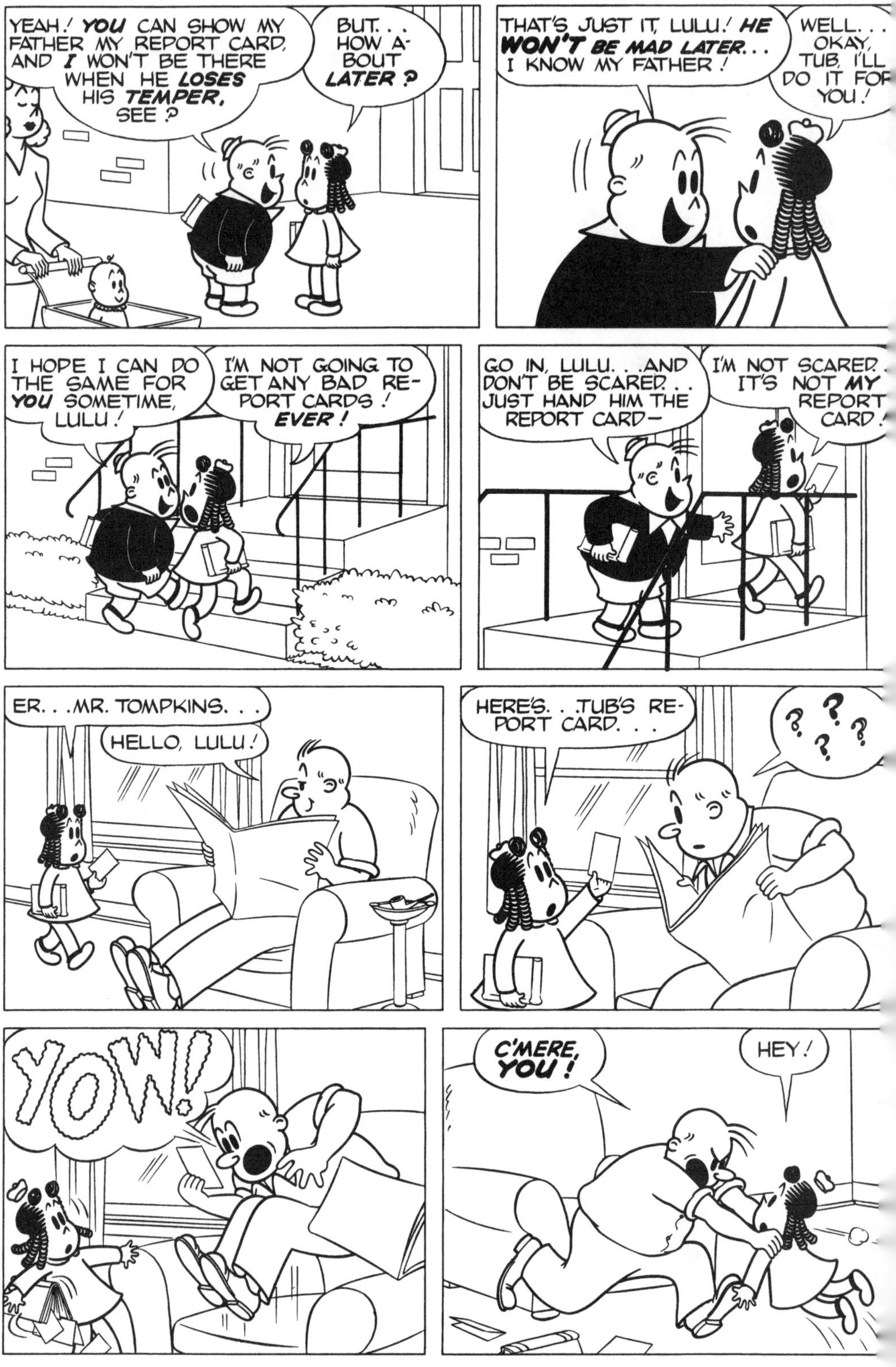
YEAH! YOU CAN SHOW MY FATHER MY REPORT CARD, AND I WON'T BE THERE WHEN HE LOSES HIS TEMPER, SEE?
BUT. . . HOW A-BOUT LATER?
THAT'S JUST IT, LULU! HE WON'T BE MAD LATER. . . I KNOW MY FATHER!
WELL. . . OKAY, TUB, I'LL DO IT FOR YOU!
I HOPE I CAN DO THE SAME FOR YOU SOMETIME, LULU!
I'M NOT GOING TO GET ANY BAD RE-PORT CARDS! EVER!
GO IN, LULU. . .AND DON'T BE SCARED. . . JUST HAND HIM THE REPORT CARD—
I'M NOT SCARED. . IT'S NOT MY REPORT CARD!
ER. . .MR. TOMPKINS. . .
HELLO, LULU!
HERE'S. . .TUB'S RE-PORT CARD. . .
? ? ? ?
YOW!
C'MERE, YOU!
HEY!

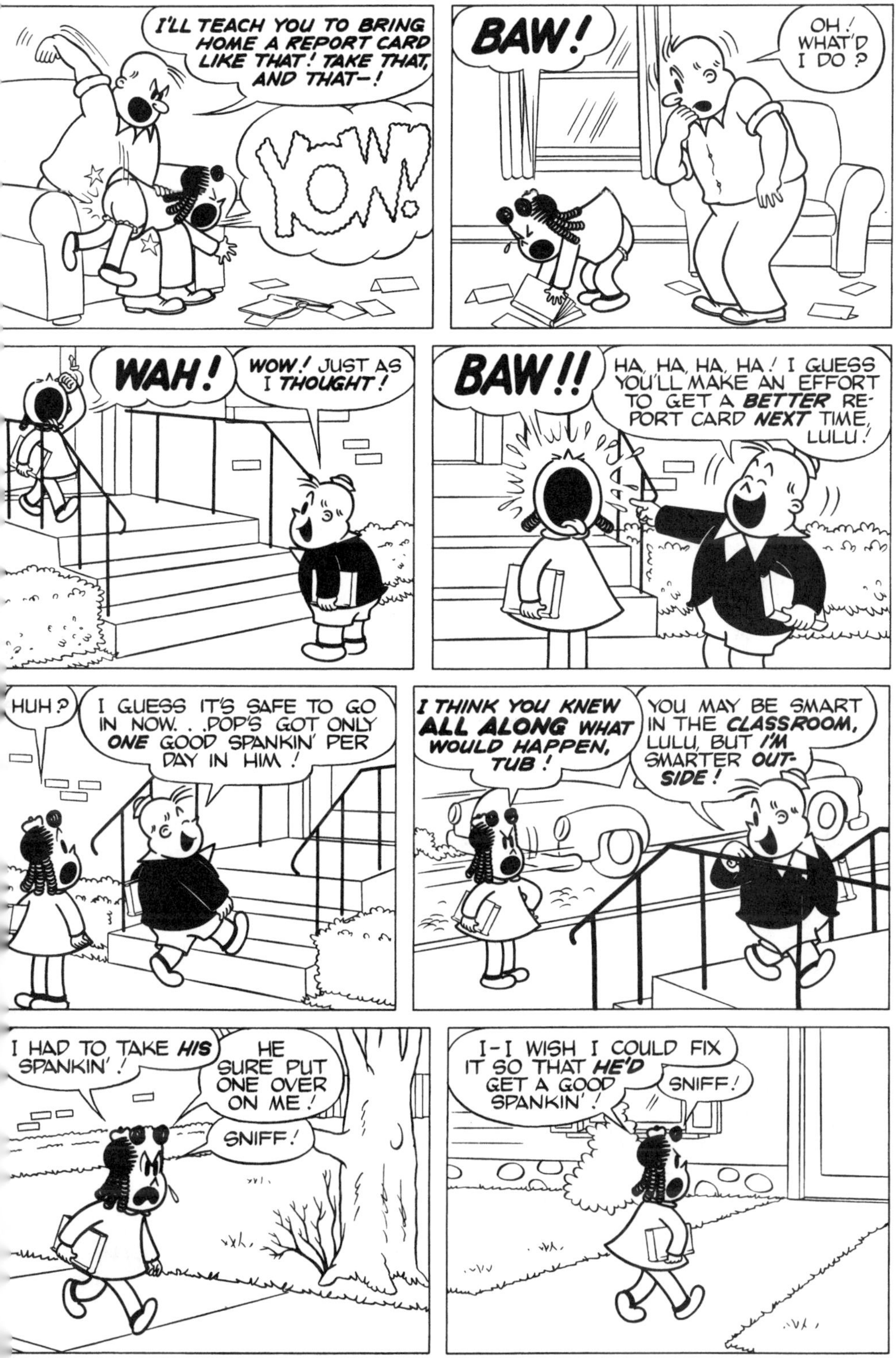

I'LL TEACH YOU TO BRING HOME A REPORT CARD LIKE THAT! TAKE THAT, AND THAT—!
YOW!
BAW!
OH! WHAT'D I DO?
WAH!
WOW! JUST AS I THOUGHT!
BAW!!
HA, HA, HA, HA! I GUESS YOU'LL MAKE AN EFFORT TO GET A BETTER REPORT CARD NEXT TIME, LULU!
HUH?
I GUESS IT'S SAFE TO GO IN NOW. . .POP'S GOT ONLY ONE GOOD SPANKIN' PER DAY IN HIM!
I THINK YOU KNEW ALL ALONG WHAT WOULD HAPPEN, TUB!
YOU MAY BE SMART IN THE CLASSROOM, LULU, BUT I'M SMARTER OUTSIDE!
I HAD TO TAKE HIS SPANKIN'!
HE SURE PUT ONE OVER ON ME!
SNIFF!
I-I WISH I COULD FIX IT SO THAT HE'D GET A GOOD SPANKIN'!
SNIFF!

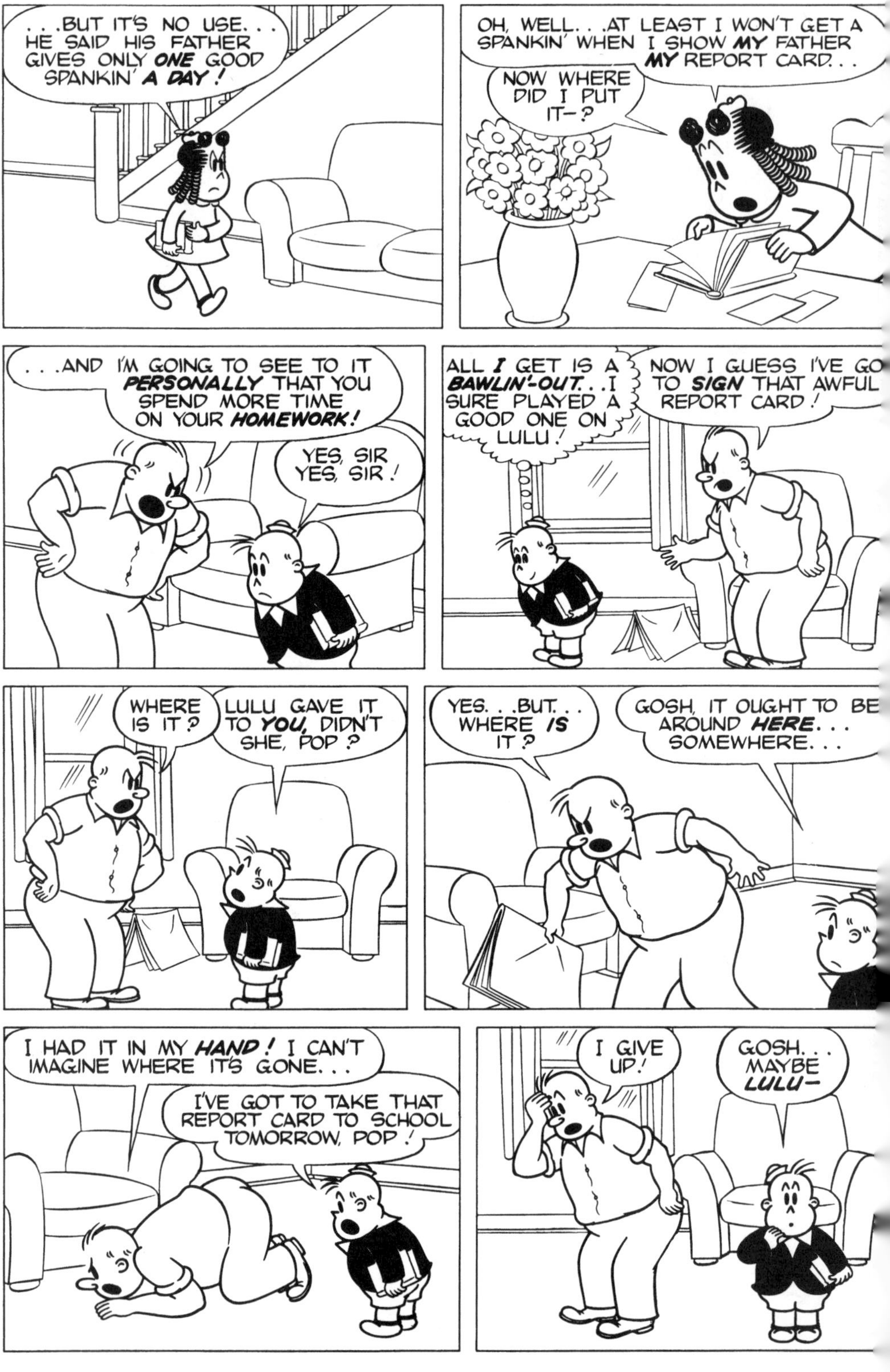

. . .BUT IT'S NO USE. . . HE SAID HIS FATHER GIVES ONLY ONE GOOD SPANKIN' A DAY!
OH, WELL. . .AT LEAST I WON'T GET A SPANKIN' WHEN I SHOW MY FATHER MY REPORT CARD. . .
NOW WHERE DID I PUT IT—?
. . .AND I'M GOING TO SEE TO IT PERSONALLY THAT YOU SPEND MORE TIME ON YOUR HOMEWORK!
YES, SIR YES, SIR!
ALL I GET IS A BAWLIN'-OUT. . .I SURE PLAYED A GOOD ONE ON LULU!
NOW I GUESS I'VE GO TO SIGN THAT AWFUL REPORT CARD!
WHERE IS IT?
LULU GAVE IT TO YOU, DIDN'T SHE, POP?
YES. . .BUT. . . WHERE IS IT?
GOSH, IT OUGHT TO BE AROUND HERE. . . SOMEWHERE. . .
I HAD IT IN MY HAND! I CAN'T IMAGINE WHERE IT'S GONE. . .
I'VE GOT TO TAKE THAT REPORT CARD TO SCHOOL TOMORROW, POP!
I GIVE UP!
GOSH. . . MAYBE LULU—

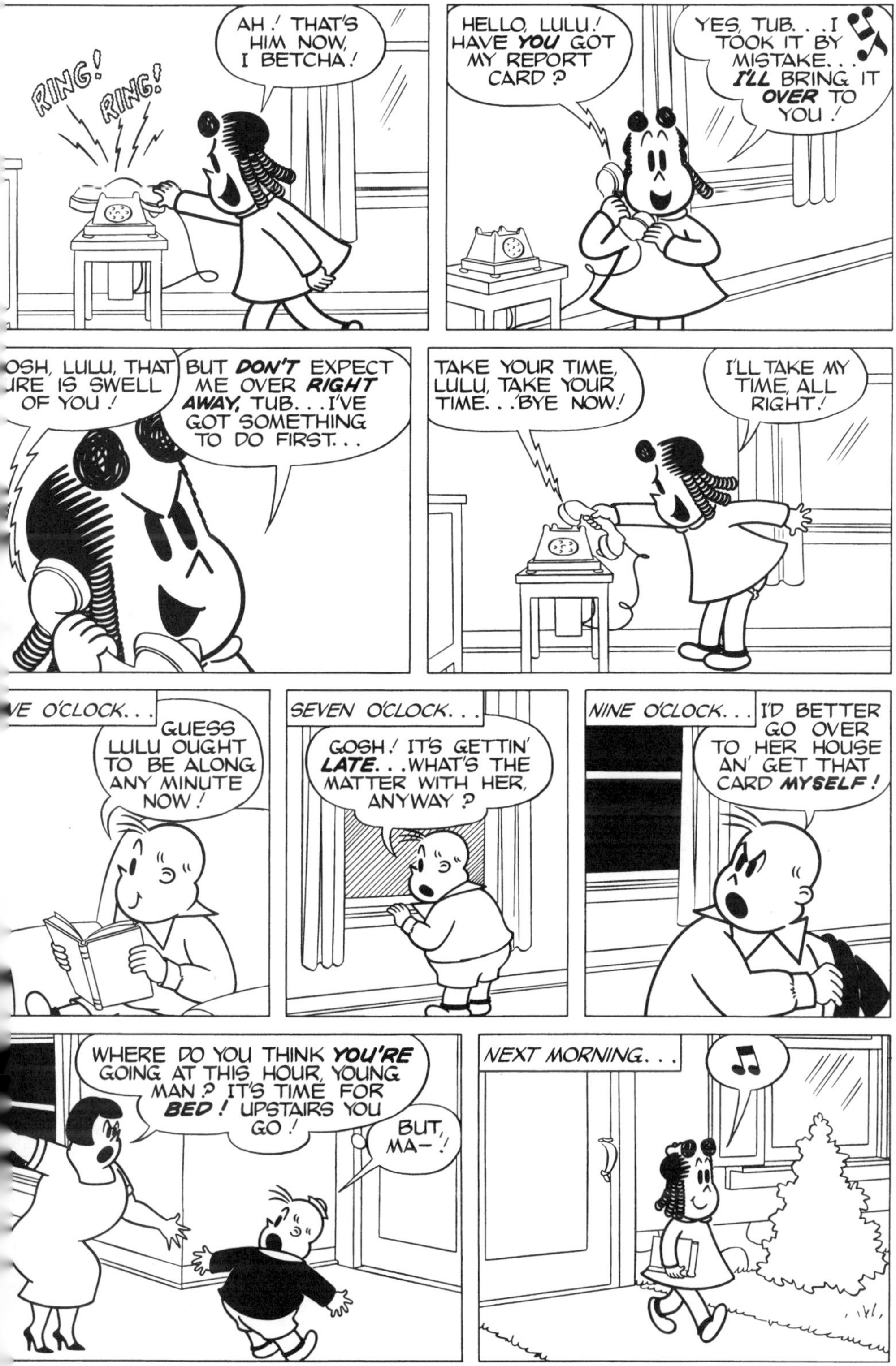
RING! RING!
AH! THAT'S HIM NOW, I BETCHA!
HELLO, LULU! HAVE YOU GOT MY REPORT CARD?
YES, TUB. . . I TOOK IT BY MISTAKE. . . I'LL BRING IT OVER TO YOU!
OSH, LULU, THAT URE IS SWELL OF YOU!
BUT DON'T EXPECT ME OVER RIGHT AWAY, TUB. . . I'VE GOT SOMETHING TO DO FIRST. . .
TAKE YOUR TIME, LULU, TAKE YOUR TIME. . . BYE NOW!
I'LL TAKE MY TIME, ALL RIGHT!
VE O'CLOCK. . .
GUESS LULU OUGHT TO BE ALONG ANY MINUTE NOW!
SEVEN O'CLOCK. . .
GOSH! IT'S GETTIN' LATE. . . WHAT'S THE MATTER WITH HER, ANYWAY?
NINE O'CLOCK. . .
I'D BETTER GO OVER TO HER HOUSE AN' GET THAT CARD MYSELF!
WHERE DO YOU THINK YOU'RE GOING AT THIS HOUR, YOUNG MAN? IT'S TIME FOR BED! UPSTAIRS YOU GO!
BUT, MA—!
NEXT MORNING. . .

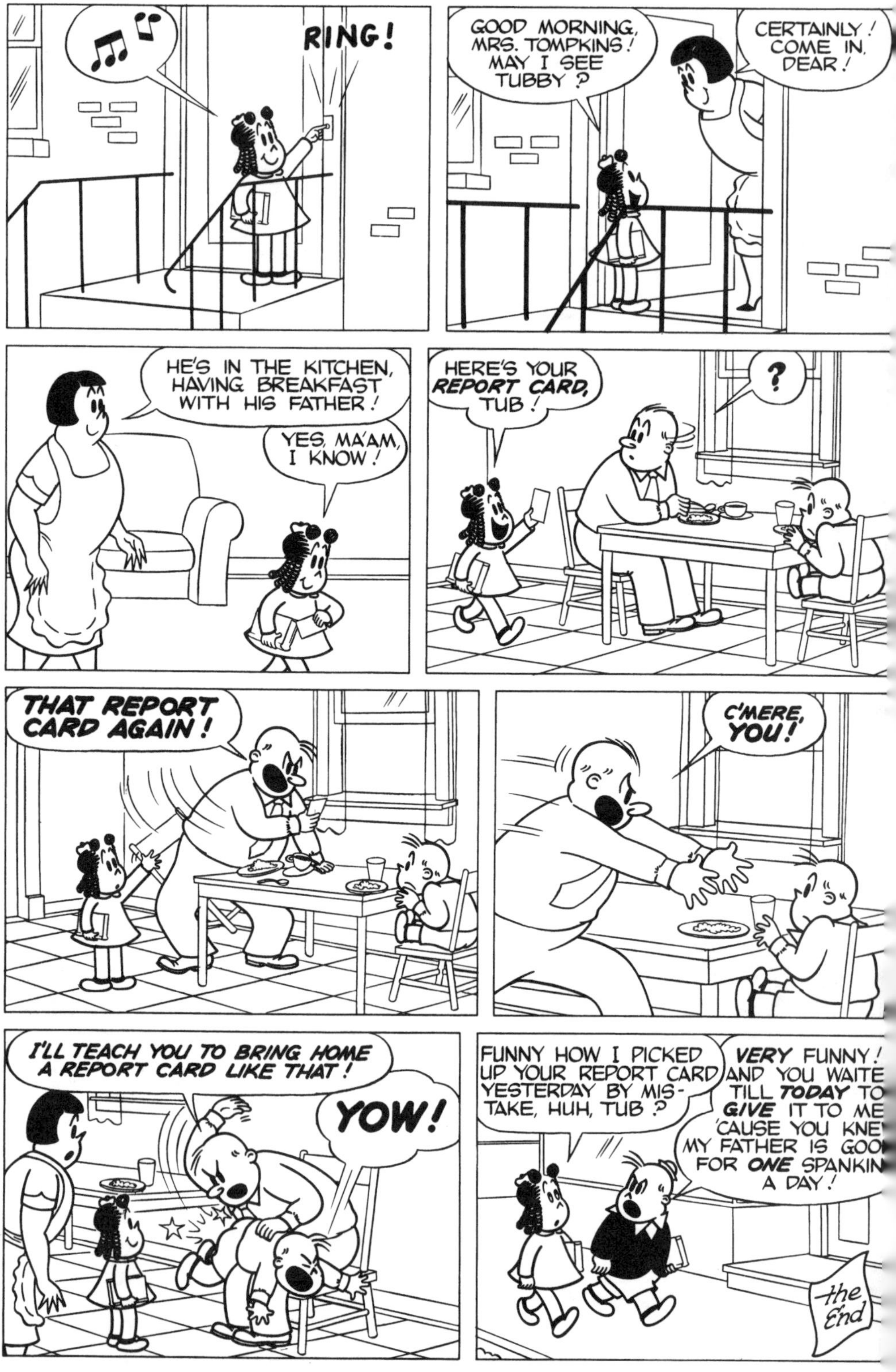

RING!
GOOD MORNING, MRS. TOMPKINS! MAY I SEE TUBBY?
CERTAINLY! COME IN, DEAR!
HE'S IN THE KITCHEN, HAVING BREAKFAST WITH HIS FATHER!
YES, MA'AM, I KNOW!
HERE'S YOUR REPORT CARD, TUB!
?
THAT REPORT CARD AGAIN!
C'MERE, YOU!
I'LL TEACH YOU TO BRING HOME A REPORT CARD LIKE THAT!
YOW!
FUNNY HOW I PICKED UP YOUR REPORT CARD YESTERDAY BY MIS-TAKE, HUH, TUB?
VERY FUNNY! AND YOU WAITE TILL TODAY TO GIVE IT TO ME 'CAUSE YOU KNE MY FATHER IS GOO FOR ONE SPANKIN A DAY!
the End

marge's Little Lulu

THE CASE OF THE FACEPRINT ON THE TOWEL

GOSH, TUB, WHAT ARE YOU UP TO NOW?

LULU, I JUST INVENTED SOMETHING THAT'LL DO AWAY WITH *FINGER-PRINTING!*

WHAT? *FACEPRINTING!* LOOK! I GOT A *PRINT* OF *CHUBBY'S FACE* IN THIS *MUD!*

WHEN CHUBBY GROWS UP AN' DOES SOMETHIN' *BAD,* HE'LL PROB'LY LEAVE A *PRINT* OF HIS *FACE* AT THE *SCENE* OF THE CRIME...

HOW DO YOU KNOW CHUBBY WILL *DO* SOMETHING BAD?

CHUBBY IS GONNA BE A *BURGLAR* WHEN HE GROWS UP! AREN'T YOU, CHUB, OL' BOY?

YES!

WHAT'S A BURGLAR, CHUBBY?

I DUNNO!

AS I WAS SAYIN'—CHUB WILL PROB'LY LEAVE A FACEPRINT AT THE SCENE OF THE CRIME, AND THE POLICE WILL MATCH IT UP WITH *THIS* ONE!

WHAT MAKES YOU THINK BURGLARS GO AROUND *LEAVING FACEPRINTS?*

THAT'S THE SILLIEST THING I EVER HEARD! HA, HA, HA, HA, HO, HO!

THEY LAUGHED AT COLUMBUS!

COLUMBUS INVENTED AMERICA!

25

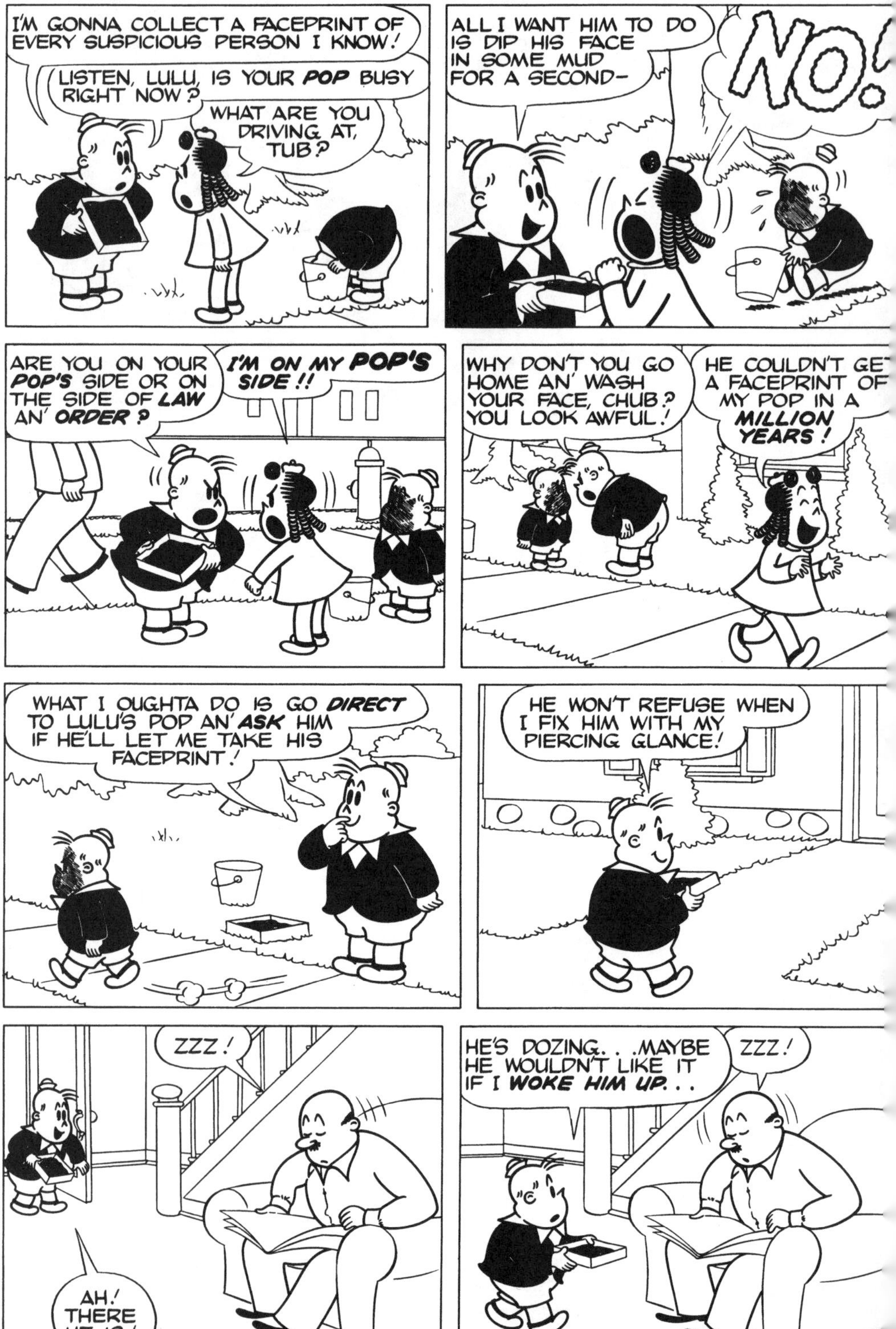

I'M GONNA COLLECT A FACEPRINT OF EVERY SUSPICIOUS PERSON I KNOW!
LISTEN, LULU, IS YOUR POP BUSY RIGHT NOW?
WHAT ARE YOU DRIVING AT, TUB?
ALL I WANT HIM TO DO IS DIP HIS FACE IN SOME MUD FOR A SECOND–
NO!
ARE YOU ON YOUR POP'S SIDE OR ON THE SIDE OF LAW AN' ORDER?
I'M ON MY POP'S SIDE!!
WHY DON'T YOU GO HOME AN' WASH YOUR FACE, CHUB? YOU LOOK AWFUL!
HE COULDN'T GET A FACEPRINT OF MY POP IN A MILLION YEARS!
WHAT I OUGHTA DO IS GO DIRECT TO LULU'S POP AN' ASK HIM IF HE'LL LET ME TAKE HIS FACEPRINT!
HE WON'T REFUSE WHEN I FIX HIM WITH MY PIERCING GLANCE!
ZZZ!
AH! THERE HE IS!
HE'S DOZING. . .MAYBE HE WOULDN'T LIKE IT IF I WOKE HIM UP. . .
ZZZ!

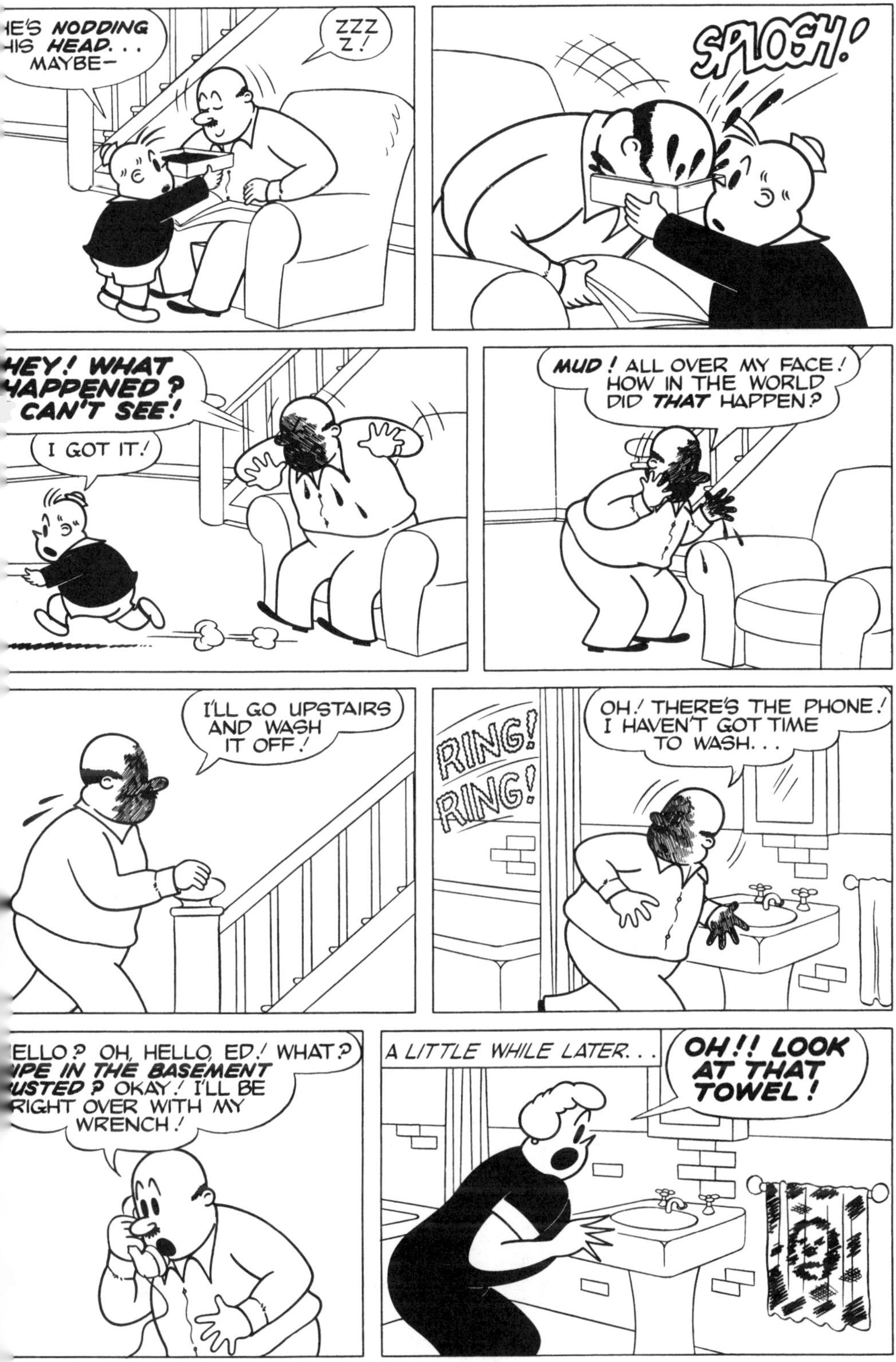

HE'S NODDING HIS HEAD. . . MAYBE–
ZZZ Z!
SPLOSH!
HEY! WHAT HAPPENED? CAN'T SEE!
I GOT IT!
MUD! ALL OVER MY FACE! HOW IN THE WORLD DID THAT HAPPEN?
I'LL GO UPSTAIRS AND WASH IT OFF!
RING! RING!
OH! THERE'S THE PHONE! I HAVEN'T GOT TIME TO WASH. . .
HELLO? OH, HELLO, ED! WHAT? PIPE IN THE BASEMENT BUSTED? OKAY! I'LL BE RIGHT OVER WITH MY WRENCH!
A LITTLE WHILE LATER. . .
OH!! LOOK AT THAT TOWEL!

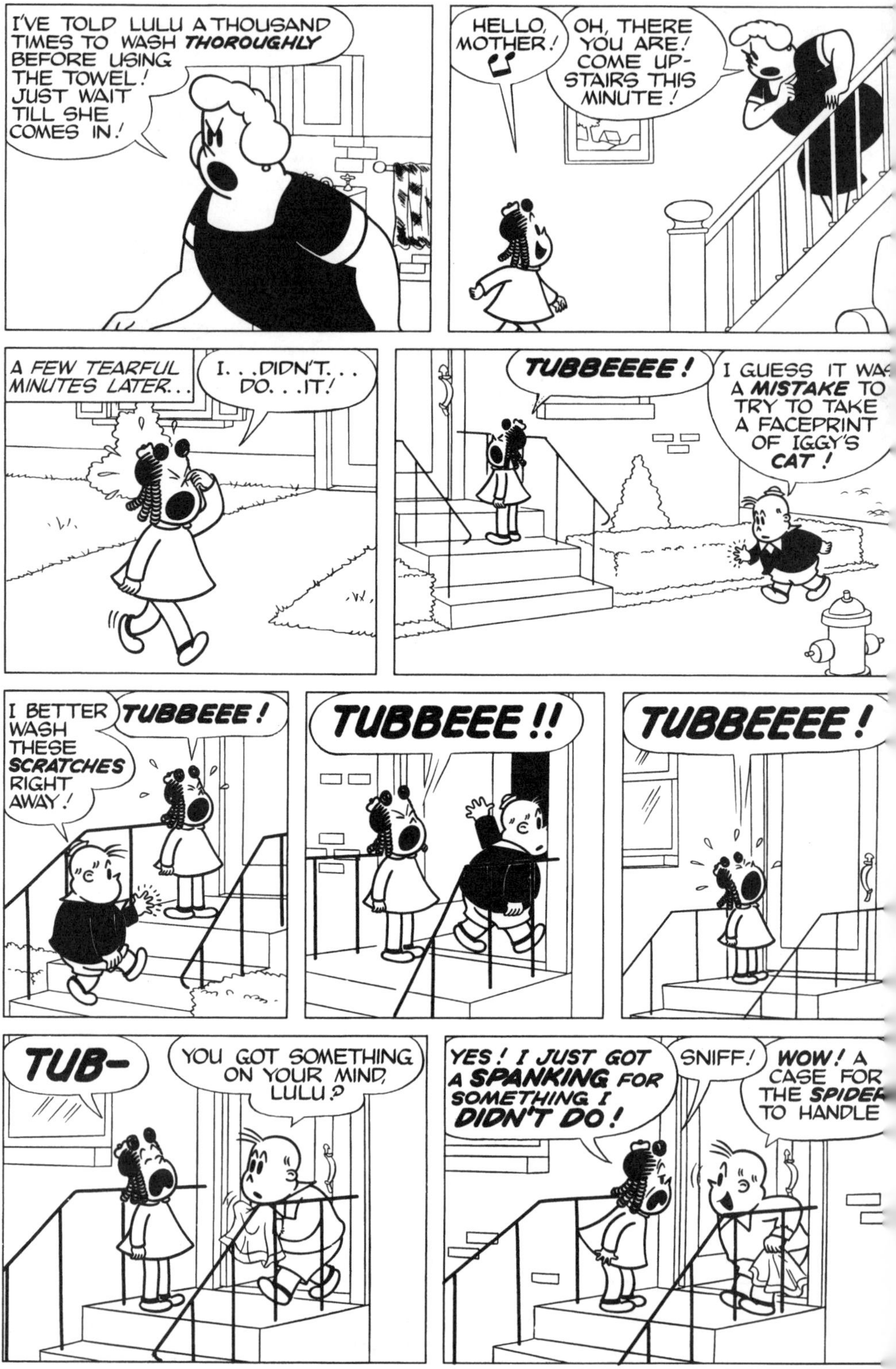
I'VE TOLD LULU A THOUSAND TIMES TO WASH **THOROUGHLY** BEFORE USING THE TOWEL! JUST WAIT TILL SHE COMES IN!
HELLO, MOTHER!
OH, THERE YOU ARE! COME UP-STAIRS THIS MINUTE!
A FEW TEARFUL MINUTES LATER...
I...DIDN'T... DO...IT!
TUBBEEEE!
I GUESS IT WAS A **MISTAKE** TO TRY TO TAKE A FACEPRINT OF IGGY'S **CAT**!
I BETTER WASH THESE **SCRATCHES** RIGHT AWAY!
TUBBEEE!
TUBBEEE!!
TUBBEEEE!
TUB-
YOU GOT SOMETHING ON YOUR MIND, LULU?
YES! I JUST GOT A **SPANKING** FOR SOMETHING I **DIDN'T DO**!
SNIFF!
WOW! A CASE FOR THE **SPIDER** TO HANDLE

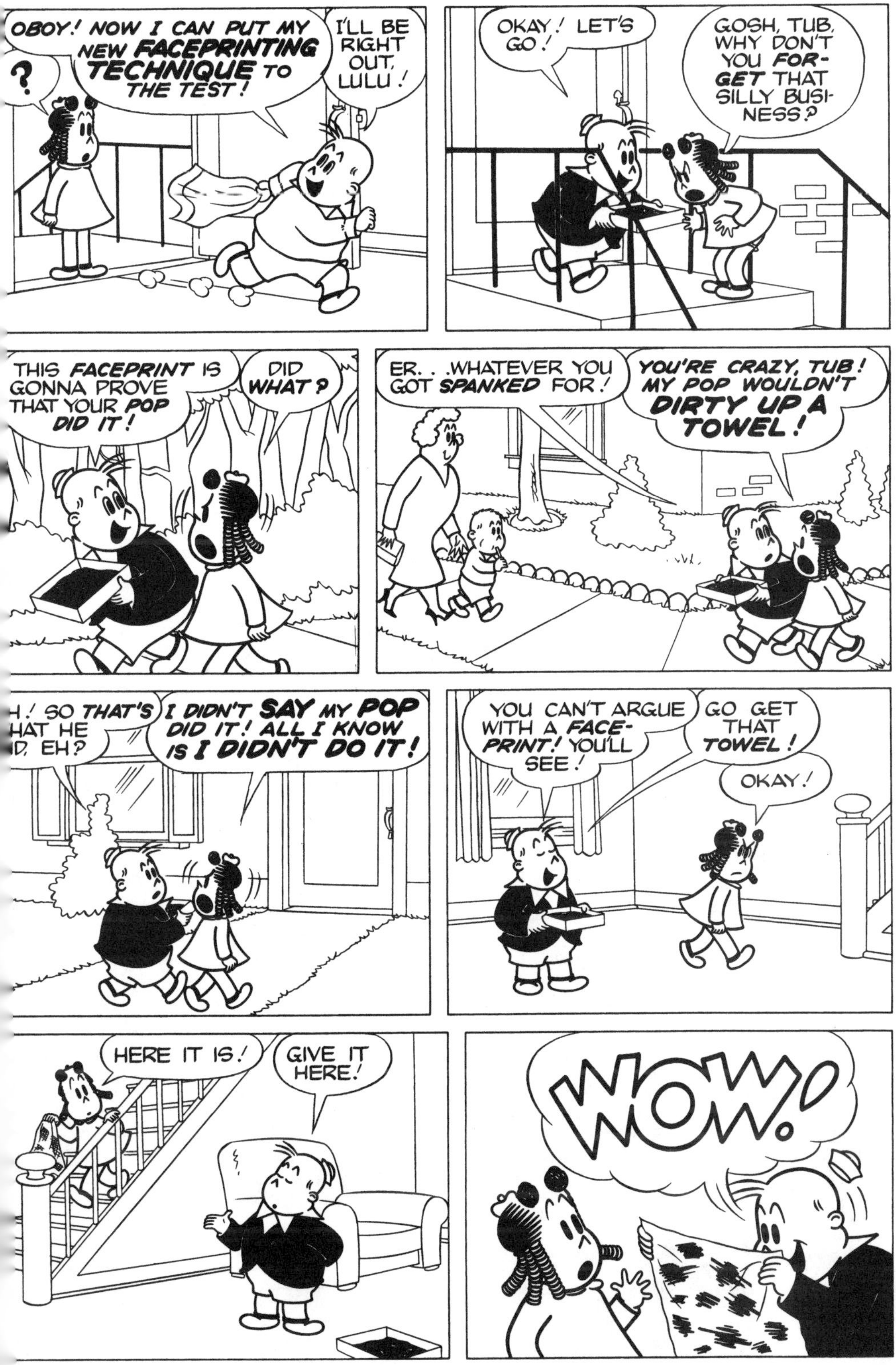
?
OBOY! NOW I CAN PUT MY NEW FACEPRINTING TECHNIQUE TO THE TEST!
I'LL BE RIGHT OUT, LULU!
OKAY! LET'S GO!
GOSH, TUB, WHY DON'T YOU FORGET THAT SILLY BUSINESS?
THIS FACEPRINT IS GONNA PROVE THAT YOUR POP DID IT!
DID WHAT?
ER. . .WHATEVER YOU GOT SPANKED FOR!
YOU'RE CRAZY, TUB! MY POP WOULDN'T DIRTY UP A TOWEL!
H! SO THAT'S HAT HE D, EH?
I DIDN'T SAY MY POP DID IT! ALL I KNOW IS I DIDN'T DO IT!
YOU CAN'T ARGUE WITH A FACEPRINT! YOU'LL SEE!
GO GET THAT TOWEL!
OKAY!
HERE IT IS!
GIVE IT HERE!
WOW!

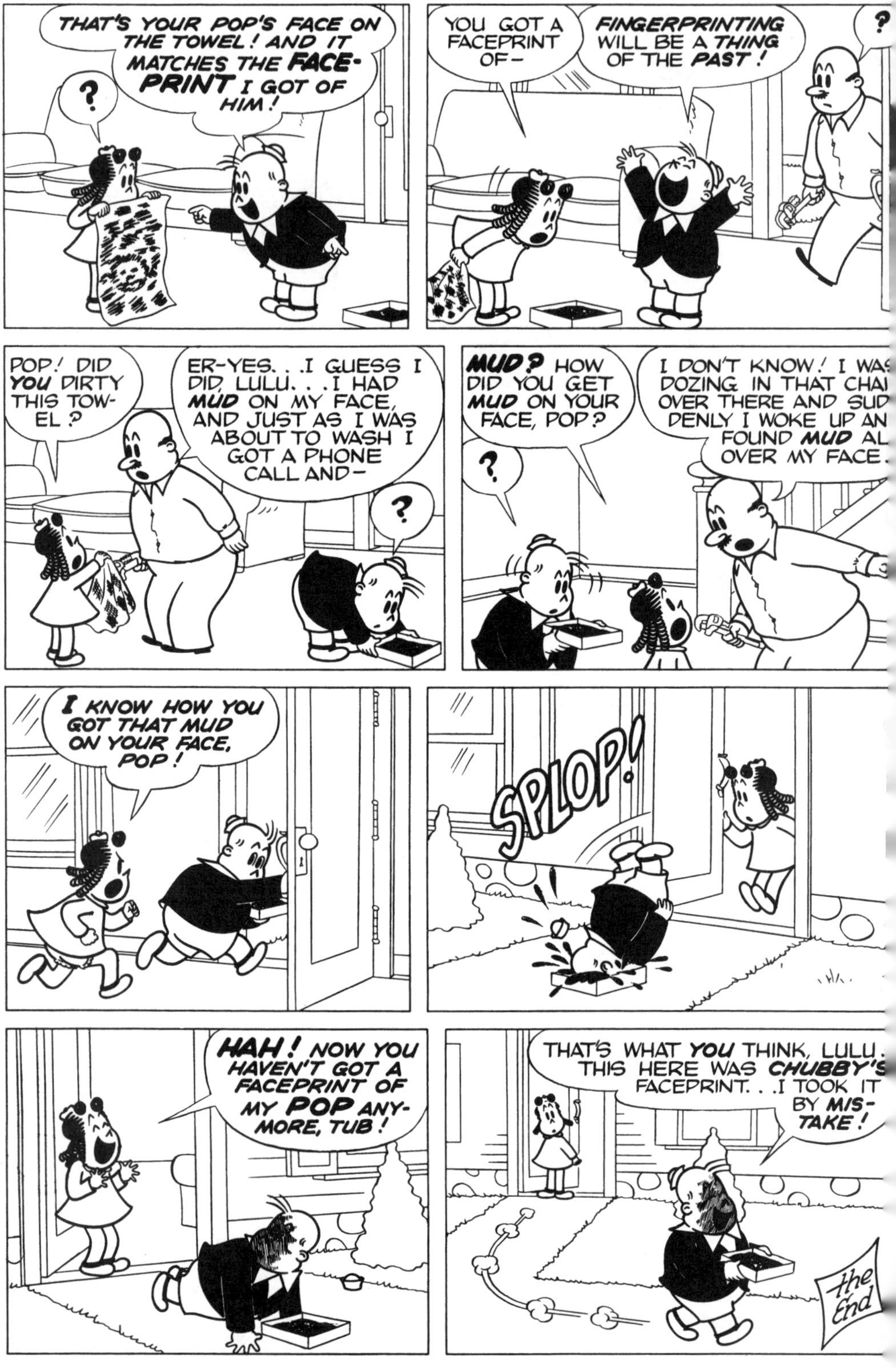
THAT'S YOUR POP'S FACE ON THE TOWEL! AND IT MATCHES THE FACE-PRINT I GOT OF HIM!
?
YOU GOT A FACEPRINT OF–
FINGERPRINTING WILL BE A THING OF THE PAST!
?
POP! DID YOU DIRTY THIS TOW-EL?
ER-YES...I GUESS I DID, LULU...I HAD MUD ON MY FACE, AND JUST AS I WAS ABOUT TO WASH I GOT A PHONE CALL AND–
?
MUD? HOW DID YOU GET MUD ON YOUR FACE, POP?
?
I DON'T KNOW! I WA DOZING IN THAT CHAI OVER THERE AND SUD DENLY I WOKE UP AN FOUND MUD AL OVER MY FACE.
I KNOW HOW YOU GOT THAT MUD ON YOUR FACE, POP!
SPLOP!
HAH! NOW YOU HAVEN'T GOT A FACEPRINT OF MY POP ANY-MORE, TUB!
THAT'S WHAT YOU THINK, LULU. THIS HERE WAS CHUBBY'S FACEPRINT...I TOOK IT BY MIS-TAKE!
the End

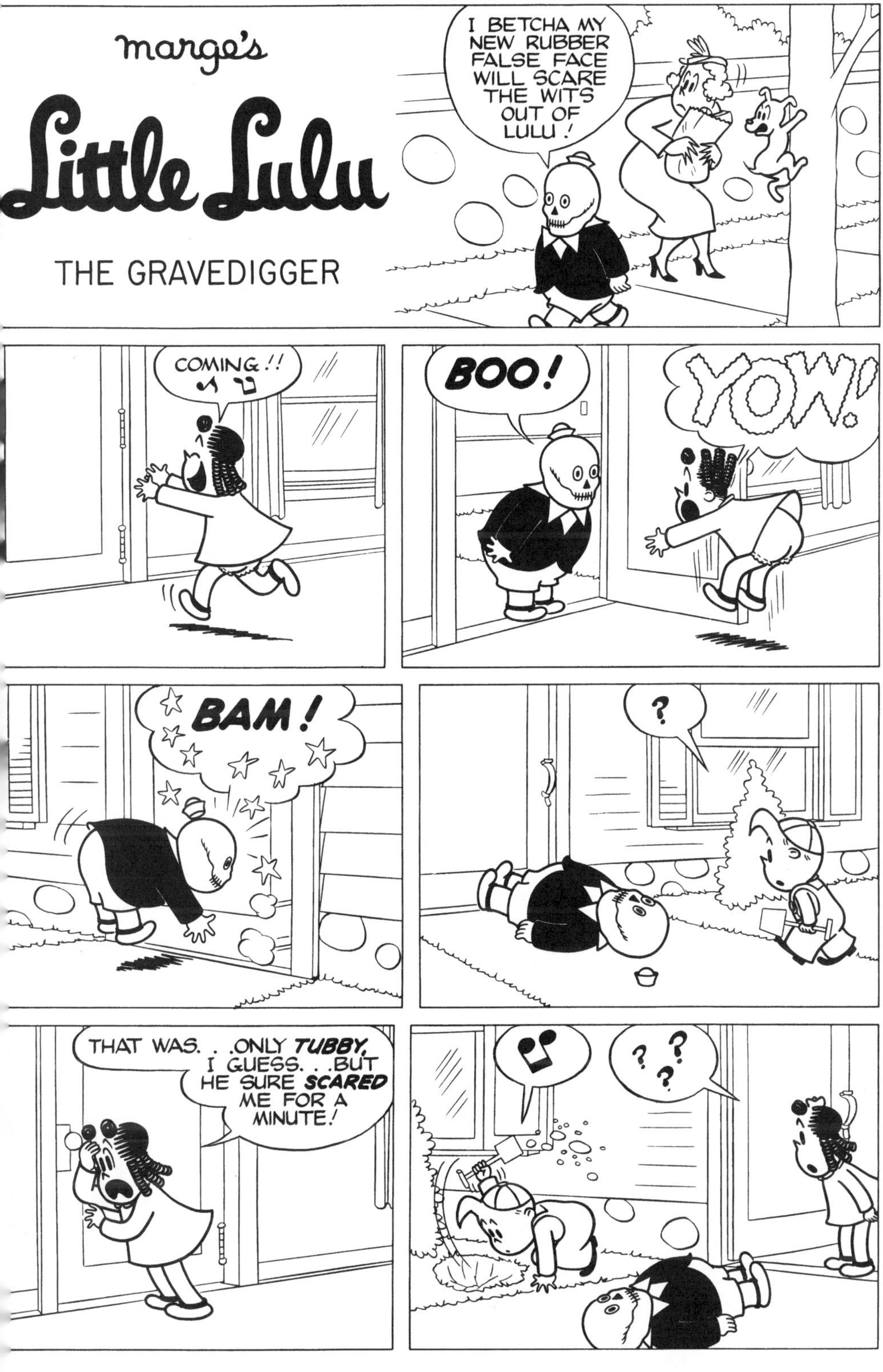
marge's
Little Lulu
THE GRAVEDIGGER
I BETCHA MY NEW RUBBER FALSE FACE WILL SCARE THE WITS OUT OF LULU!
COMING!!
BOO!
YOW!
BAM!
?
THAT WAS. . .ONLY TUBBY, I GUESS. . .BUT HE SURE SCARED ME FOR A MINUTE!
? ? ?

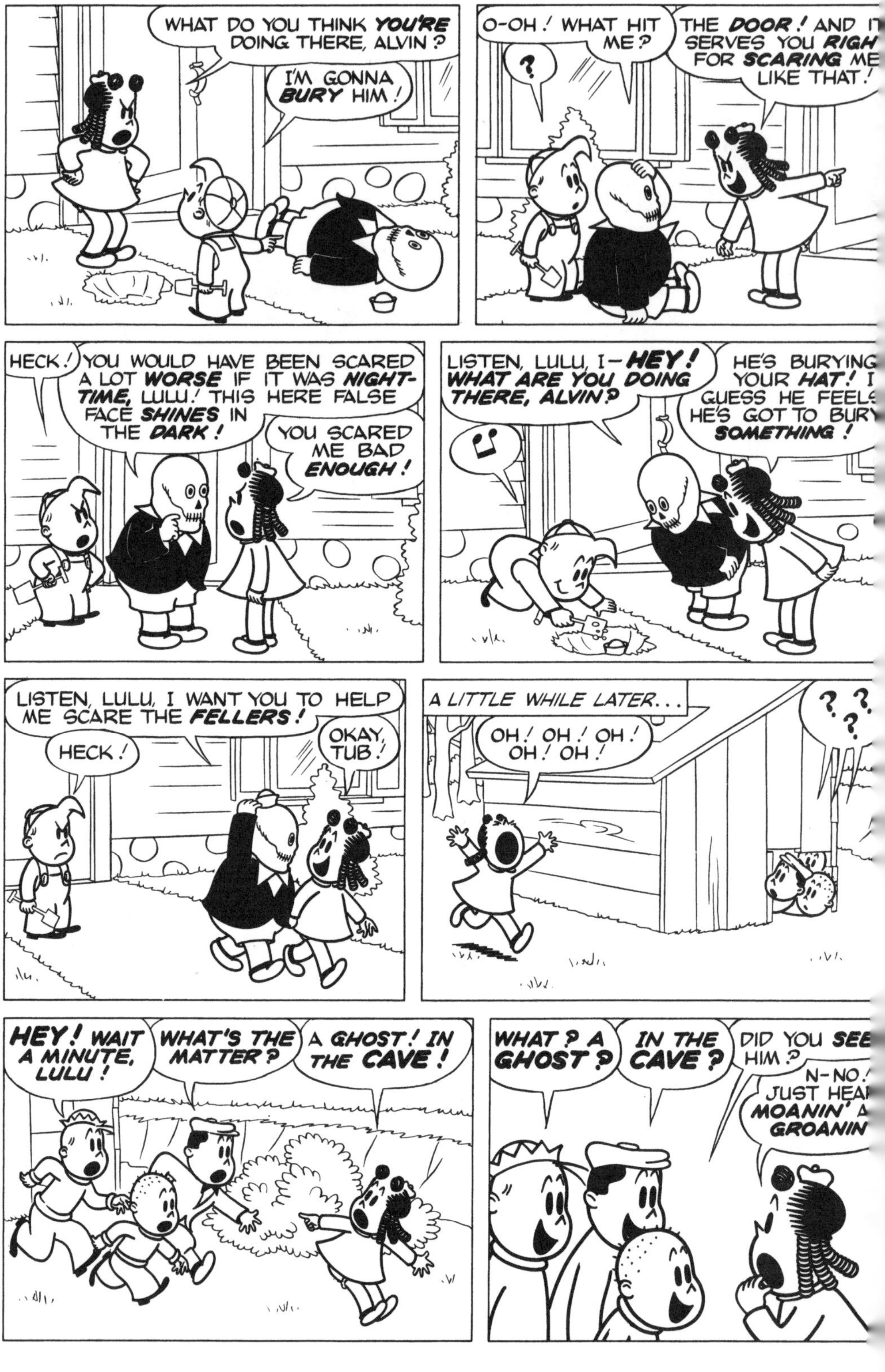

WHAT DO YOU THINK YOU'RE DOING THERE, ALVIN?
I'M GONNA BURY HIM!
O-OH! WHAT HIT ME?
?
THE DOOR! AND IT SERVES YOU RIGH FOR SCARING ME LIKE THAT!
HECK!
YOU WOULD HAVE BEEN SCARED A LOT WORSE IF IT WAS NIGHT-TIME, LULU! THIS HERE FALSE FACE SHINES IN THE DARK!
YOU SCARED ME BAD ENOUGH!
LISTEN, LULU, I—HEY! WHAT ARE YOU DOING THERE, ALVIN?
HE'S BURYING YOUR HAT! I GUESS HE FEELS HE'S GOT TO BURY SOMETHING!
LISTEN, LULU, I WANT YOU TO HELP ME SCARE THE FELLERS!
HECK!
OKAY, TUB!
A LITTLE WHILE LATER...
OH! OH! OH! OH! OH!
? ? ?
HEY! WAIT A MINUTE, LULU!
WHAT'S THE MATTER?
A GHOST! IN THE CAVE!
WHAT? A GHOST?
IN THE CAVE?
DID YOU SEE HIM?
N-NO! JUST HEAR MOANIN' A GROANIN

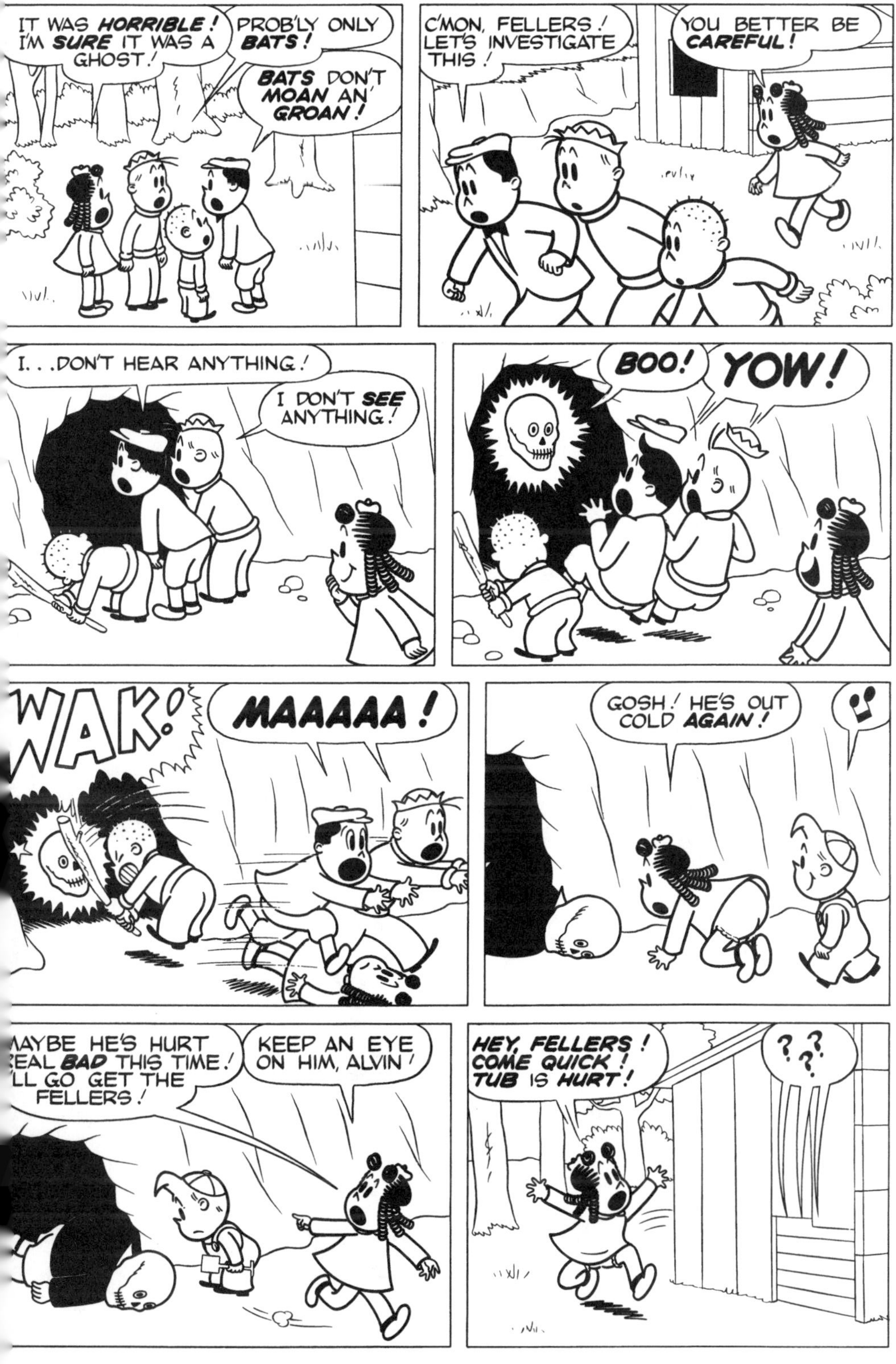
IT WAS HORRIBLE! I'M SURE IT WAS A GHOST!
PROB'LY ONLY BATS!
BATS DON'T MOAN AN' GROAN!
C'MON, FELLERS! LET'S INVESTIGATE THIS!
YOU BETTER BE CAREFUL!
I...DON'T HEAR ANYTHING!
I DON'T SEE ANYTHING!
BOO!
YOW!
WAK!
MAAAAA!
GOSH! HE'S OUT COLD AGAIN!
AYBE HE'S HURT
EAL BAD THIS TIME!
'LL GO GET THE FELLERS!
KEEP AN EYE ON HIM, ALVIN!
HEY, FELLERS! COME QUICK! TUB IS HURT!
? ? ?

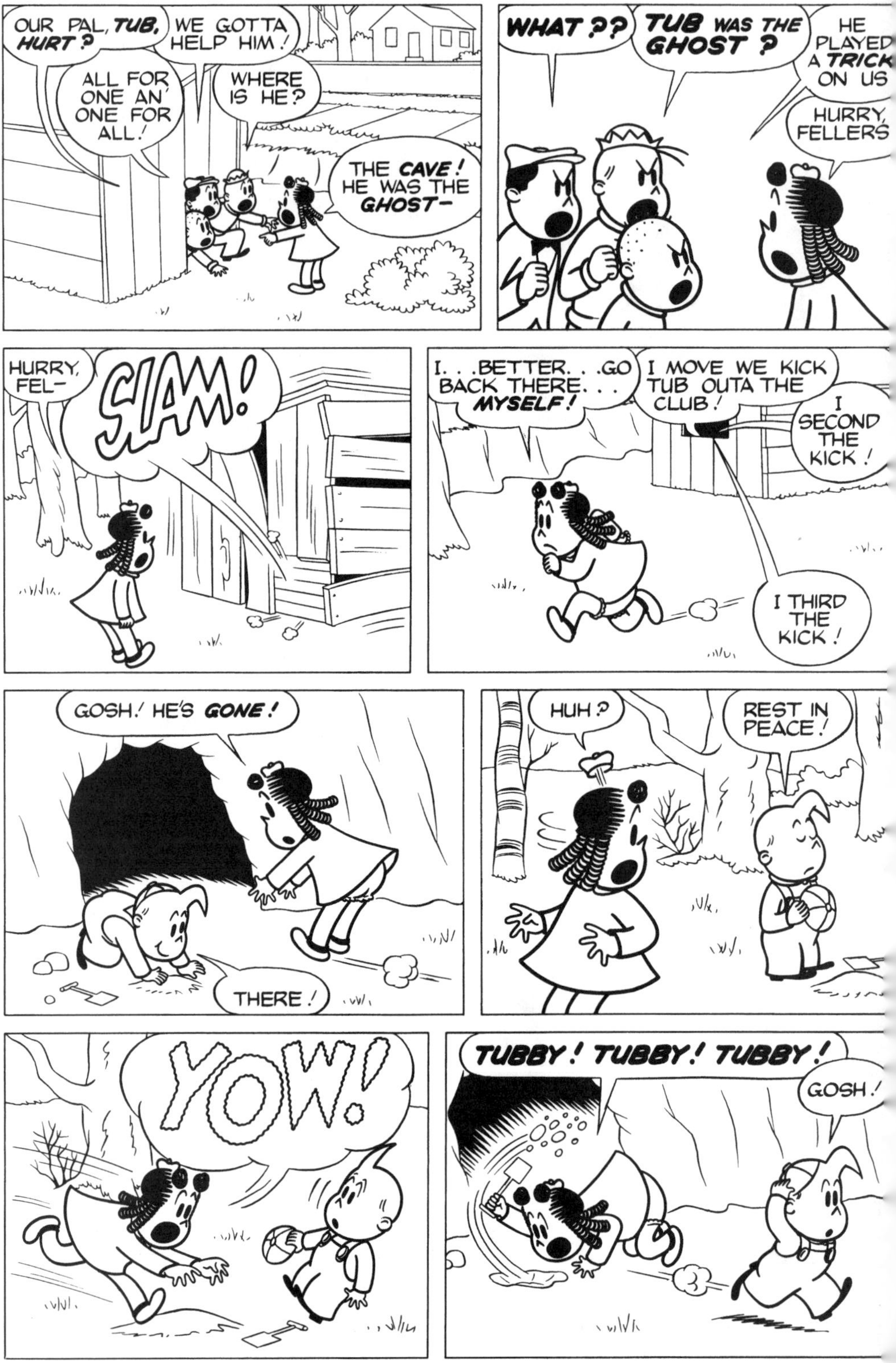
OUR PAL, TUB, HURT?
WE GOTTA HELP HIM!
ALL FOR ONE AN' ONE FOR ALL!
WHERE IS HE?
THE CAVE! HE WAS THE GHOST-
WHAT??
TUB WAS THE GHOST?
HE PLAYED A TRICK ON US
HURRY, FELLERS
HURRY, FEL-
SLAM!
I. . .BETTER. . .GO BACK THERE. . . MYSELF!
I MOVE WE KICK TUB OUTA THE CLUB!
I SECOND THE KICK!
I THIRD THE KICK!
GOSH! HE'S GONE!
THERE!
HUH?
REST IN PEACE!
YOW!
TUBBY! TUBBY! TUBBY!
GOSH!

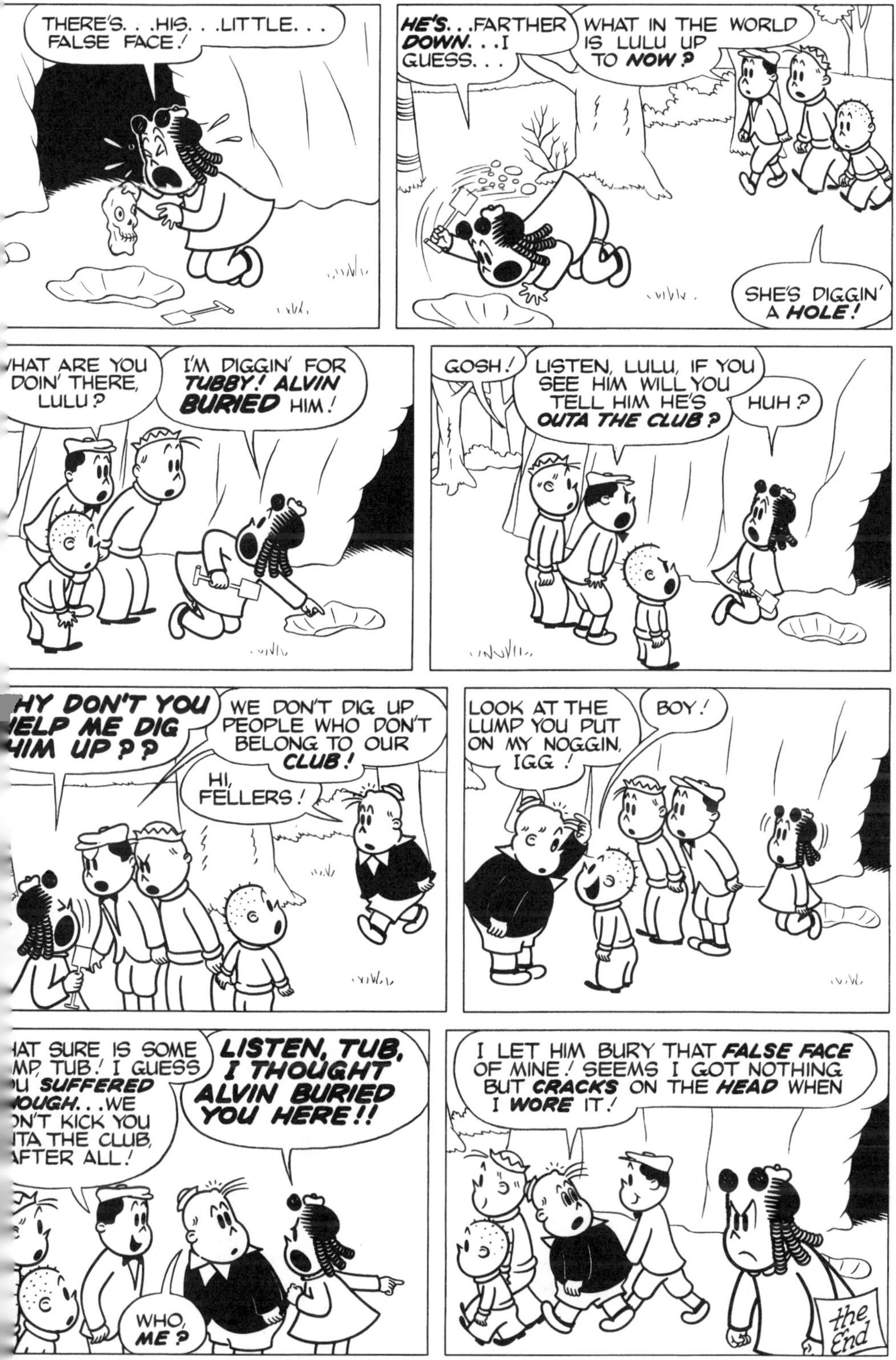

THERE'S. . .HIS. . .LITTLE. . . FALSE FACE!
HE'S. . .FARTHER DOWN. . .I GUESS. . .
WHAT IN THE WORLD IS LULU UP TO NOW?
SHE'S DIGGIN' A HOLE!
HAT ARE YOU DOIN' THERE, LULU?
I'M DIGGIN' FOR TUBBY! ALVIN BURIED HIM!
GOSH!
LISTEN, LULU, IF YOU SEE HIM WILL YOU TELL HIM HE'S OUTA THE CLUB?
HUH?
HY DON'T YOU ELP ME DIG HIM UP??
WE DON'T DIG UP PEOPLE WHO DON'T BELONG TO OUR CLUB!
HI, FELLERS!
LOOK AT THE LUMP YOU PUT ON MY NOGGIN, IGG!
BOY!
HAT SURE IS SOME MP, TUB! I GUESS U SUFFERED OUGH. . .WE N'T KICK YOU ITA THE CLUB, AFTER ALL!
LISTEN, TUB, I THOUGHT ALVIN BURIED YOU HERE!!
WHO, ME?
I LET HIM BURY THAT FALSE FACE OF MINE! SEEMS I GOT NOTHING BUT CRACKS ON THE HEAD WHEN I WORE IT!
the End

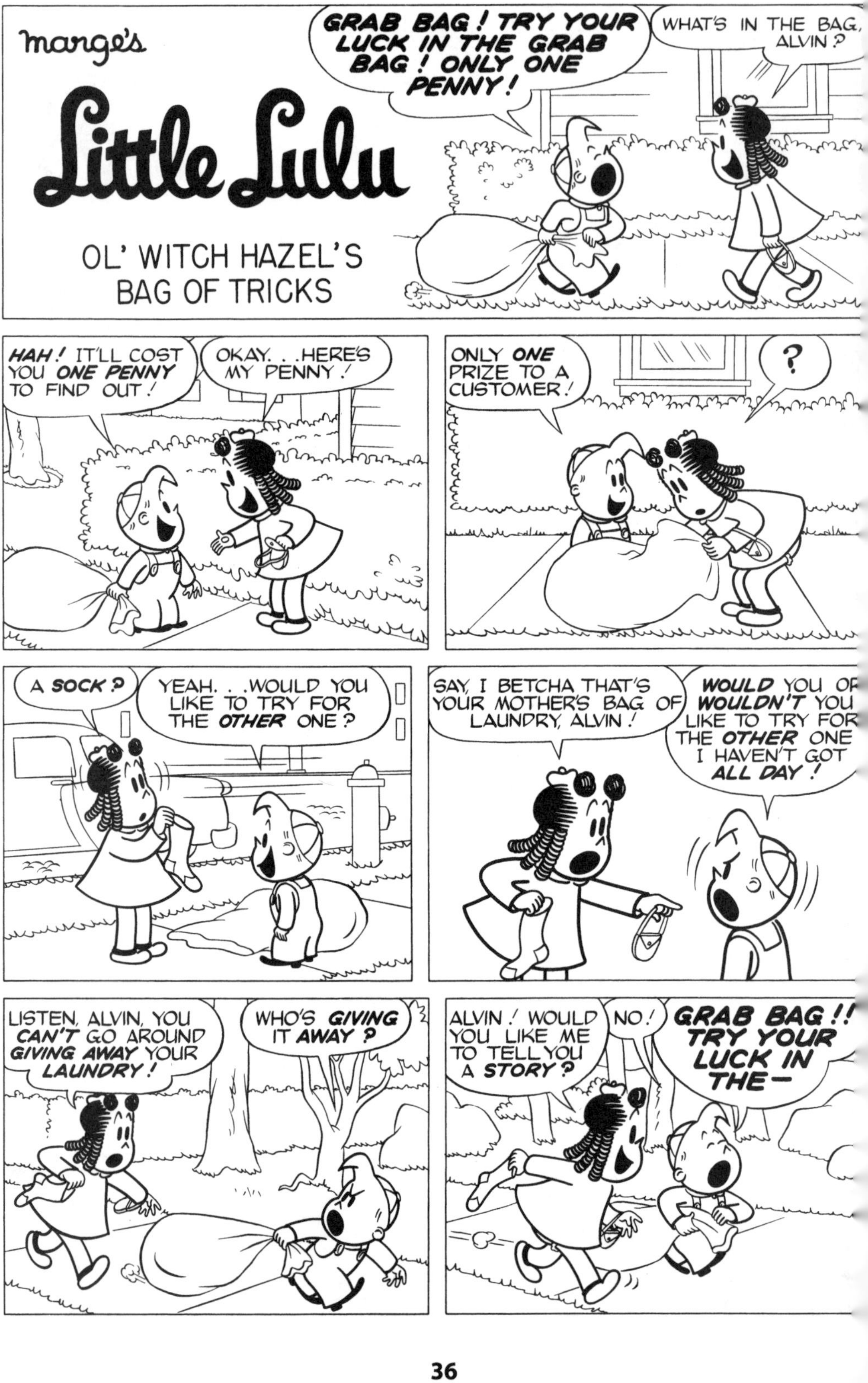
marge's
Little Lulu
OL' WITCH HAZEL'S BAG OF TRICKS
GRAB BAG! TRY YOUR LUCK IN THE GRAB BAG! ONLY ONE PENNY!
WHAT'S IN THE BAG, ALVIN?
HAH! IT'LL COST YOU ONE PENNY TO FIND OUT!
OKAY. . .HERE'S MY PENNY!
ONLY ONE PRIZE TO A CUSTOMER!
?
A SOCK?
YEAH. . .WOULD YOU LIKE TO TRY FOR THE OTHER ONE?
SAY, I BETCHA THAT'S YOUR MOTHER'S BAG OF LAUNDRY, ALVIN!
WOULD YOU OR WOULDN'T YOU LIKE TO TRY FOR THE OTHER ONE I HAVEN'T GOT ALL DAY!
LISTEN, ALVIN, YOU CAN'T GO AROUND GIVING AWAY YOUR LAUNDRY!
WHO'S GIVING IT AWAY?
ALVIN! WOULD YOU LIKE ME TO TELL YOU A STORY?
NO!
GRAB BAG!! TRY YOUR LUCK IN THE—

ONCE UPON A TIME THERE WAS A LITTLE TOWN CALLED HAPPY HOLLOW. . .

EVERYBODY IN THE TOWN OF HAPPY HOLLOW SHOULD HAVE BEEN VERY HAPPY. . . BUT NOBODY WAS. . .

THEY WEREN'T HAPPY BECAUSE OL' WITCH HAZEL, WHO LIVED IN THE WOODS OUTSIDE OF TOWN, HAD BEEN MAKING EVERYBODY MISERABLE.'

NOW LET'S SEE. . .WHAT'LL I DO TO 'EM *TODAY?*

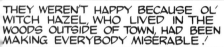

HAZEL HAD A BIG BLACK BAG OF TRICKS, AND EVERY DAY SHE WOULD DO SOMETHING TO MAKE EVERYBODY UNHAPPY!

CACKLE, CACKLE, CACKLE!

A LITTLE OF THIS MAGIC SAND SPRINKLED ON THEIR SIDEWALKS. . .

ONE DAY SHE'D TURN THE STREETS OF HAPPY HOLLOW INTO *QUICKSAND*. . .

WHAT'LL SHE DO NEXT?

ISN'T IT *AWFUL?*

THAT *WITCH!*

THE NEXT DAY THERE WOULDN'T *BE* ANY DAY. . .HAZEL HAD TURNED DAY INTO NIGHT. . .

TEN O'CLOCK IN THE *MORNING* AND IT'S AS BLACK AS *MIDNIGHT!*

IT'S THAT *WITCH* AGAIN!

OW!

WHY DON'T YOU LOOK WHERE YOU'RE GOING?

THE POOR UNHAPPY PEOPLE OF HAPPY HOLLOW COULDN'T EVEN *MOVE AWAY.* . . HAZEL WOULD FIX IT SO THAT THEIR FURNITURE STUCK TO THE FLOOR!

UGH! UGH!

IT'S NO USE. . .I GUESS WE'LL *HAVE* TO STAY!

MEANWHILE, THERE WAS A LITTLE GIRL IN HAPPY HOLLOW WHO HAD TROUBLES OF HER OWN. . .

I'VE GOT TO MAKE MY OWN WAY IN THE WORLD. . .

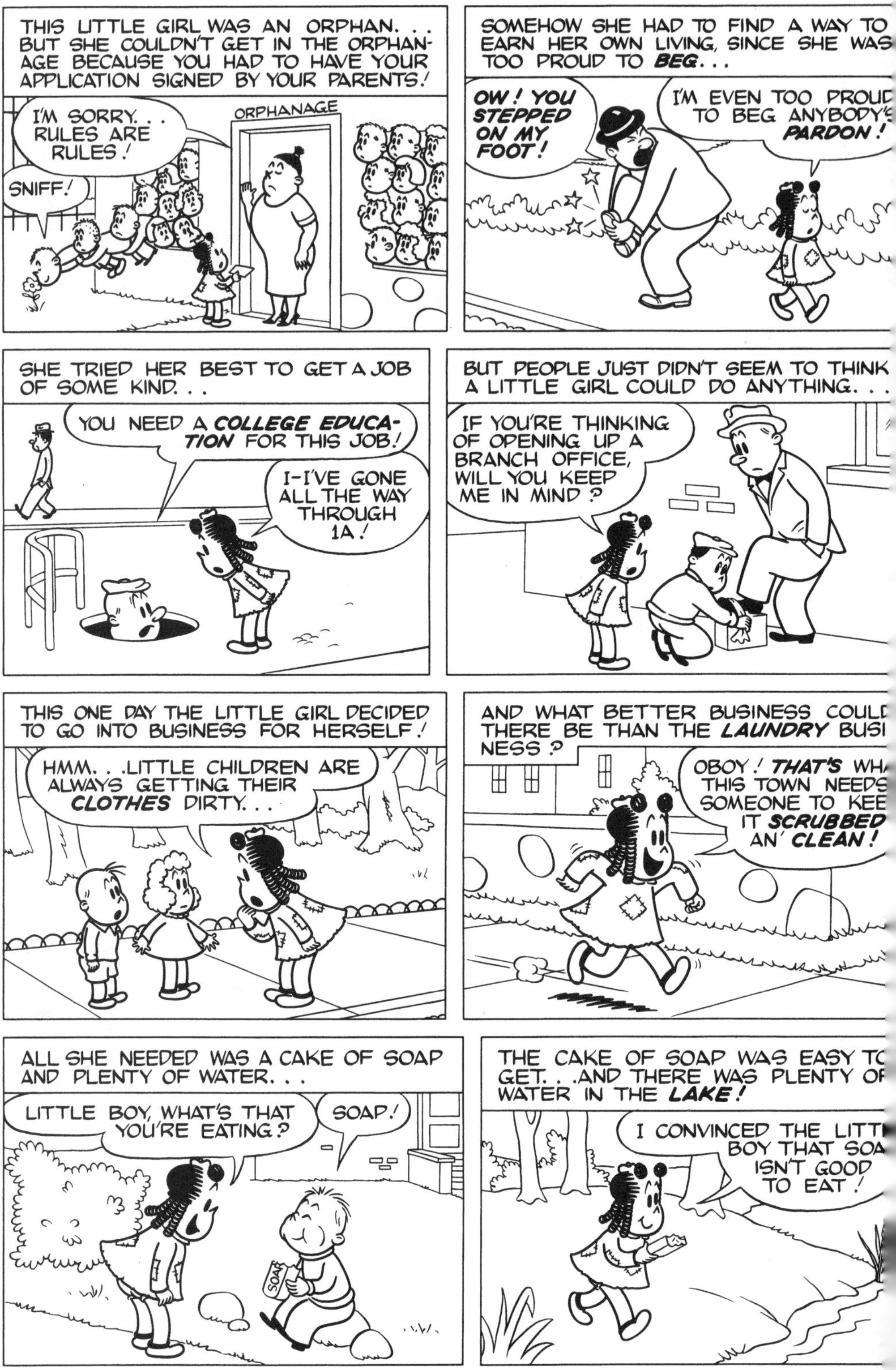
THIS LITTLE GIRL WAS AN ORPHAN. . . BUT SHE COULDN'T GET IN THE ORPHANAGE BECAUSE YOU HAD TO HAVE YOUR APPLICATION SIGNED BY YOUR PARENTS!
I'M SORRY. . . RULES ARE RULES!
ORPHANAGE
SNIFF!
SOMEHOW SHE HAD TO FIND A WAY TO EARN HER OWN LIVING, SINCE SHE WAS TOO PROUD TO BEG. . .
OW! YOU STEPPED ON MY FOOT!
I'M EVEN TOO PROUD TO BEG ANYBODY'S PARDON!
SHE TRIED HER BEST TO GET A JOB OF SOME KIND. . .
YOU NEED A COLLEGE EDUCATION FOR THIS JOB!
I-I'VE GONE ALL THE WAY THROUGH 1A!
BUT PEOPLE JUST DIDN'T SEEM TO THINK A LITTLE GIRL COULD DO ANYTHING. . .
IF YOU'RE THINKING OF OPENING UP A BRANCH OFFICE, WILL YOU KEEP ME IN MIND?
THIS ONE DAY THE LITTLE GIRL DECIDED TO GO INTO BUSINESS FOR HERSELF!
HMM. . .LITTLE CHILDREN ARE ALWAYS GETTING THEIR CLOTHES DIRTY. . .
AND WHAT BETTER BUSINESS COULD THERE BE THAN THE LAUNDRY BUSINESS?
OBOY! THAT'S WHAT THIS TOWN NEEDS SOMEONE TO KEEP IT SCRUBBED AN' CLEAN!
ALL SHE NEEDED WAS A CAKE OF SOAP AND PLENTY OF WATER. . .
LITTLE BOY, WHAT'S THAT YOU'RE EATING?
SOAP!
SOAP
THE CAKE OF SOAP WAS EASY TO GET. . .AND THERE WAS PLENTY OF WATER IN THE LAKE!
I CONVINCED THE LITTLE BOY THAT SOAP ISN'T GOOD TO EAT!

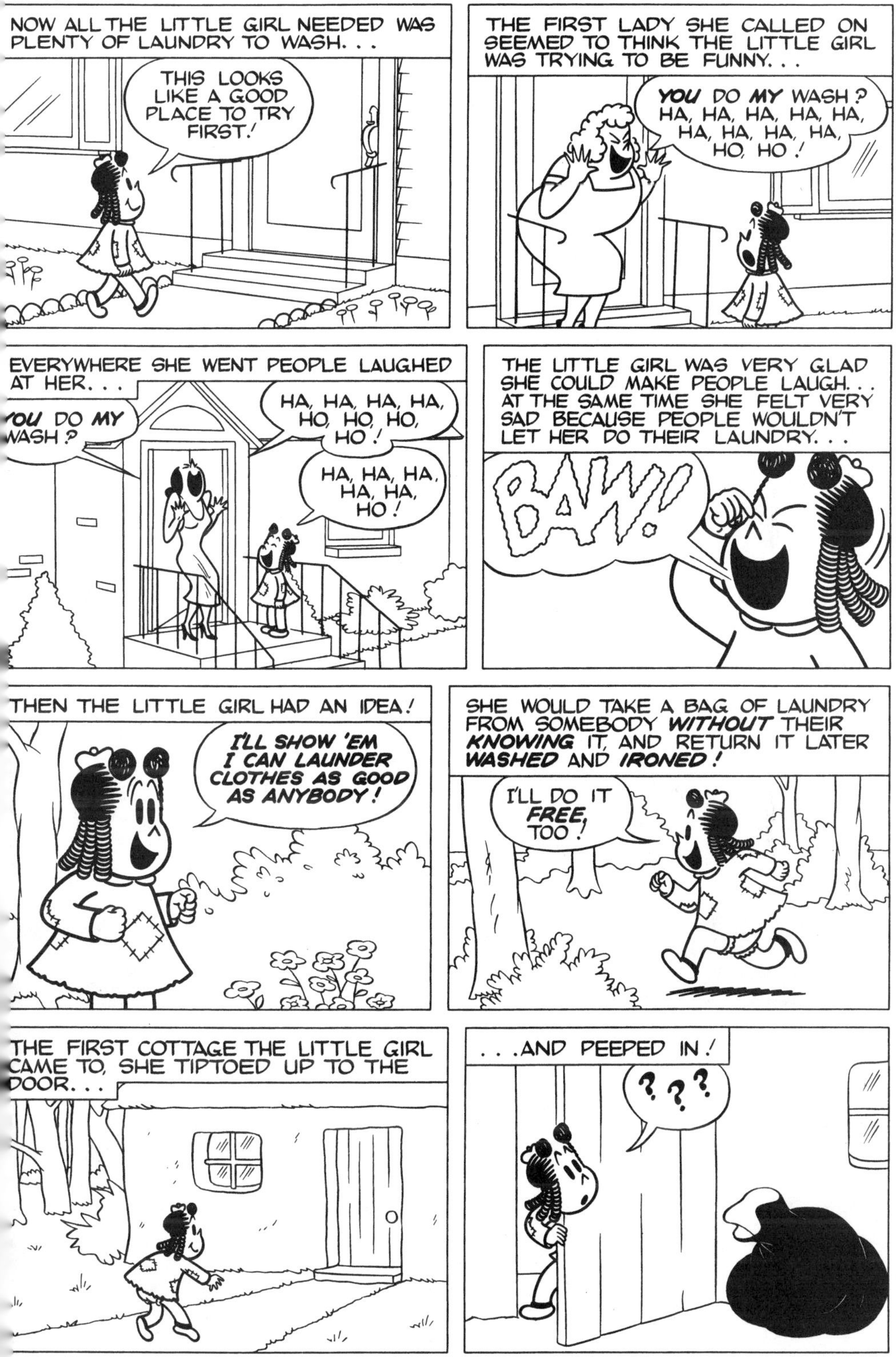
NOW ALL THE LITTLE GIRL NEEDED WAS PLENTY OF LAUNDRY TO WASH. . .
THIS LOOKS LIKE A GOOD PLACE TO TRY FIRST!
THE FIRST LADY SHE CALLED ON SEEMED TO THINK THE LITTLE GIRL WAS TRYING TO BE FUNNY. . .
YOU DO MY WASH? HA, HA, HA, HA, HA, HA, HA, HA, HA, HO, HO!
EVERYWHERE SHE WENT PEOPLE LAUGHED AT HER. . .
YOU DO MY WASH?
HA, HA, HA, HA, HO, HO, HO, HO!
HA, HA, HA, HA, HA, HO!
THE LITTLE GIRL WAS VERY GLAD SHE COULD MAKE PEOPLE LAUGH. . . AT THE SAME TIME SHE FELT VERY SAD BECAUSE PEOPLE WOULDN'T LET HER DO THEIR LAUNDRY. . .
BAW!
THEN THE LITTLE GIRL HAD AN IDEA!
I'LL SHOW 'EM I CAN LAUNDER CLOTHES AS GOOD AS ANYBODY!
SHE WOULD TAKE A BAG OF LAUNDRY FROM SOMEBODY WITHOUT THEIR KNOWING IT, AND RETURN IT LATER WASHED AND IRONED!
I'LL DO IT FREE, TOO!
THE FIRST COTTAGE THE LITTLE GIRL CAME TO, SHE TIPTOED UP TO THE DOOR. . .
. . .AND PEEPED IN!
???

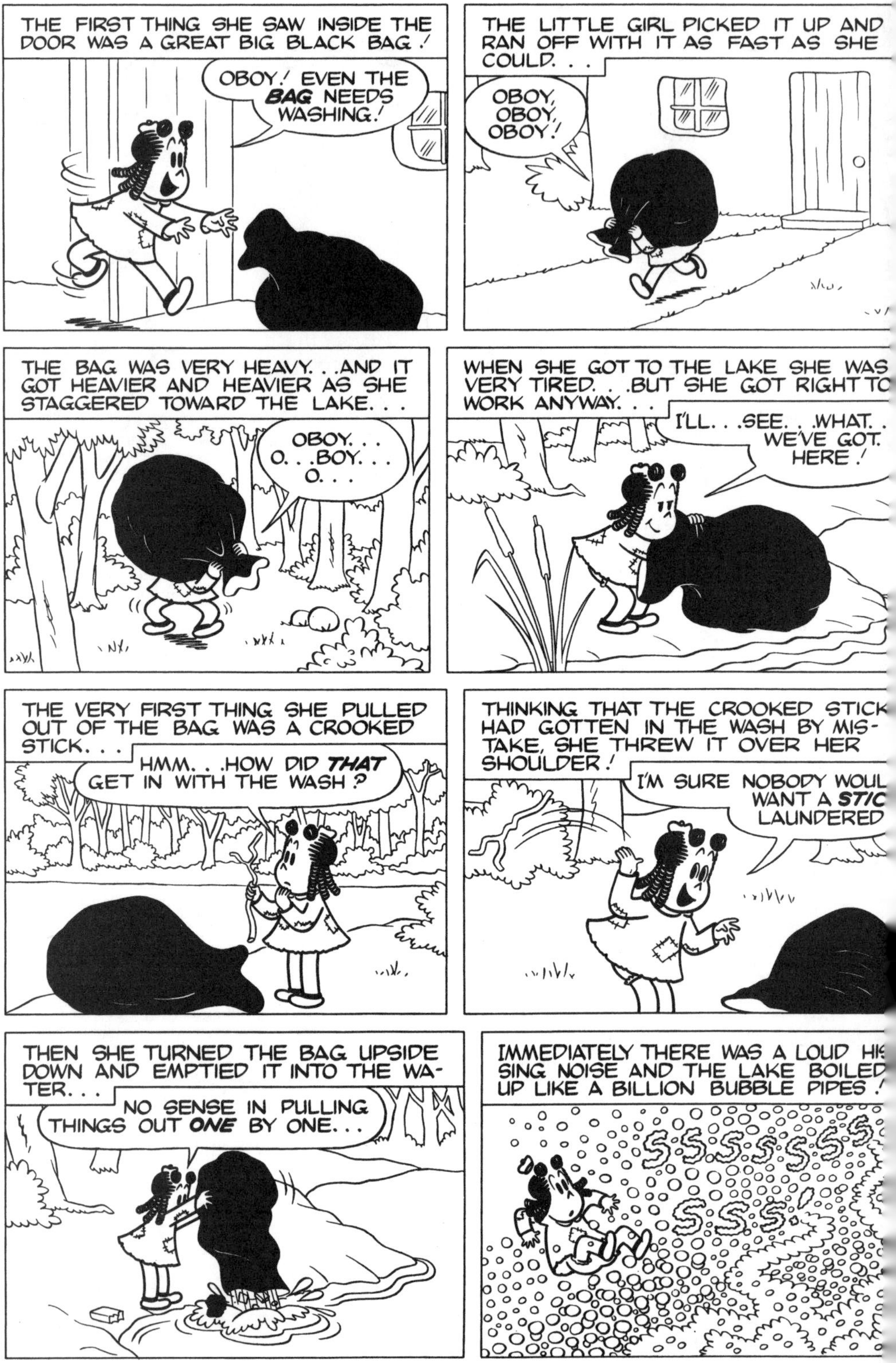
THE FIRST THING SHE SAW INSIDE THE DOOR WAS A GREAT BIG BLACK BAG!
OBOY! EVEN THE BAG NEEDS WASHING!
THE LITTLE GIRL PICKED IT UP AND RAN OFF WITH IT AS FAST AS SHE COULD. . .
OBOY, OBOY, OBOY!
THE BAG WAS VERY HEAVY. . .AND IT GOT HEAVIER AND HEAVIER AS SHE STAGGERED TOWARD THE LAKE. . .
OBOY. . . O. . .BOY. . . O. . .
WHEN SHE GOT TO THE LAKE SHE WAS VERY TIRED. . .BUT SHE GOT RIGHT TO WORK ANYWAY. . .
I'LL. . .SEE. . .WHAT. . WE'VE GOT HERE!
THE VERY FIRST THING SHE PULLED OUT OF THE BAG WAS A CROOKED STICK. . .
HMM. . .HOW DID THAT GET IN WITH THE WASH?
THINKING THAT THE CROOKED STICK HAD GOTTEN IN THE WASH BY MISTAKE, SHE THREW IT OVER HER SHOULDER!
I'M SURE NOBODY WOUL WANT A STIC LAUNDERED
THEN SHE TURNED THE BAG UPSIDE DOWN AND EMPTIED IT INTO THE WATER. . .
NO SENSE IN PULLING THINGS OUT ONE BY ONE. . .
IMMEDIATELY THERE WAS A LOUD HISSING NOISE AND THE LAKE BOILED UP LIKE A BILLION BUBBLE PIPES!
SSSSSSSS
SSSS!

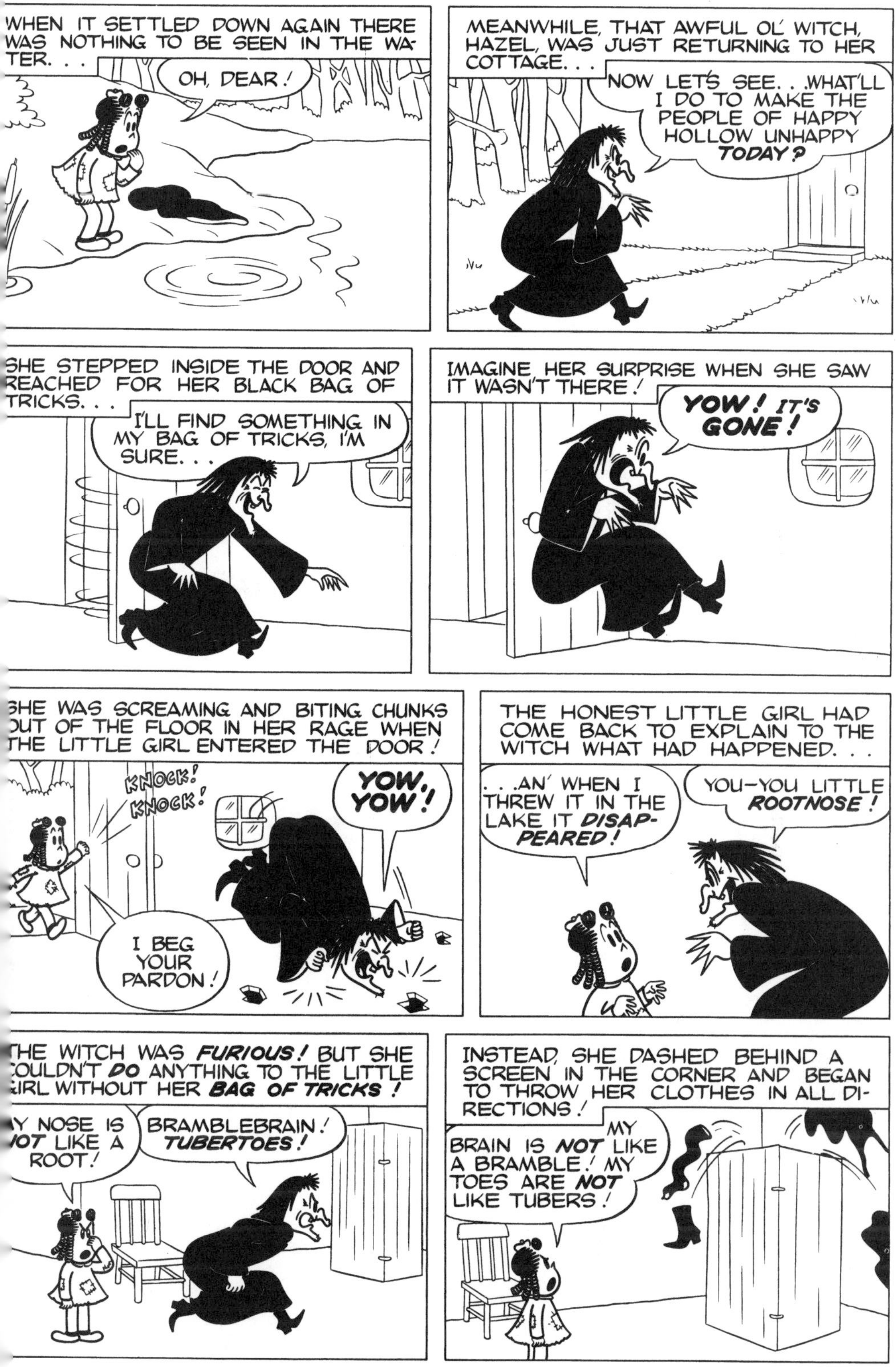
WHEN IT SETTLED DOWN AGAIN THERE WAS NOTHING TO BE SEEN IN THE WATER. . .
OH, DEAR!
MEANWHILE, THAT AWFUL OL' WITCH, HAZEL, WAS JUST RETURNING TO HER COTTAGE. . .
NOW LET'S SEE. . WHAT'LL I DO TO MAKE THE PEOPLE OF HAPPY HOLLOW UNHAPPY TODAY?
SHE STEPPED INSIDE THE DOOR AND REACHED FOR HER BLACK BAG OF TRICKS. . .
I'LL FIND SOMETHING IN MY BAG OF TRICKS, I'M SURE. . .
IMAGINE HER SURPRISE WHEN SHE SAW IT WASN'T THERE!
YOW! IT'S GONE!
SHE WAS SCREAMING AND BITING CHUNKS OUT OF THE FLOOR IN HER RAGE WHEN THE LITTLE GIRL ENTERED THE DOOR!
KNOCK! KNOCK!
YOW, YOW!
I BEG YOUR PARDON!
THE HONEST LITTLE GIRL HAD COME BACK TO EXPLAIN TO THE WITCH WHAT HAD HAPPENED. . .
. . .AN' WHEN I THREW IT IN THE LAKE IT DISAPPEARED!
YOU—YOU LITTLE ROOTNOSE!
THE WITCH WAS FURIOUS! BUT SHE COULDN'T DO ANYTHING TO THE LITTLE GIRL WITHOUT HER BAG OF TRICKS!
MY NOSE IS NOT LIKE A ROOT!
BRAMBLEBRAIN! TUBERTOES!
INSTEAD, SHE DASHED BEHIND A SCREEN IN THE CORNER AND BEGAN TO THROW HER CLOTHES IN ALL DIRECTIONS!
MY BRAIN IS NOT LIKE A BRAMBLE! MY TOES ARE NOT LIKE TUBERS!

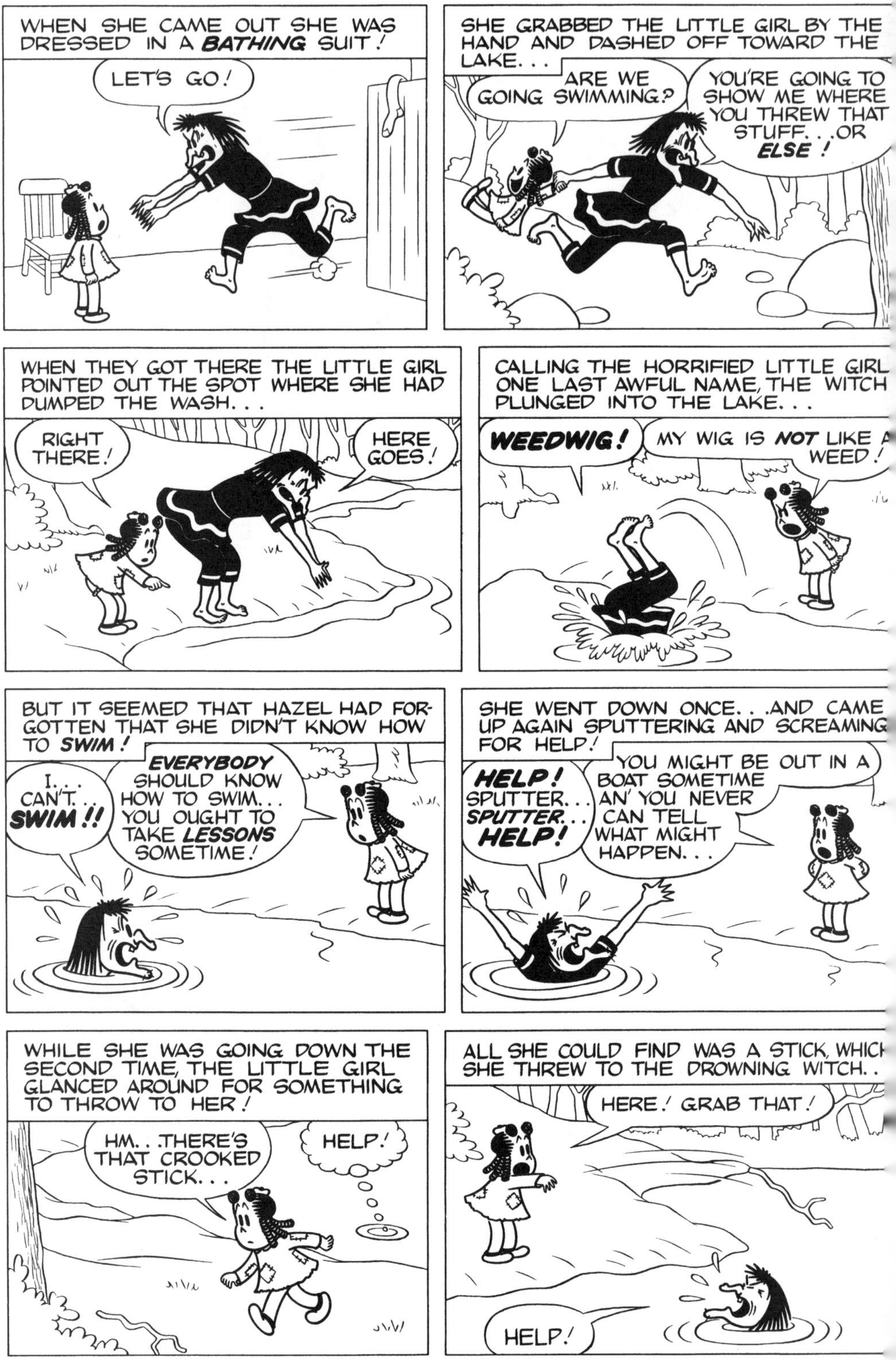
WHEN SHE CAME OUT SHE WAS DRESSED IN A BATHING SUIT!
LET'S GO!
SHE GRABBED THE LITTLE GIRL BY THE HAND AND DASHED OFF TOWARD THE LAKE...
ARE WE GOING SWIMMING?
YOU'RE GOING TO SHOW ME WHERE YOU THREW THAT STUFF...OR ELSE!
WHEN THEY GOT THERE THE LITTLE GIRL POINTED OUT THE SPOT WHERE SHE HAD DUMPED THE WASH...
RIGHT THERE!
HERE GOES!
CALLING THE HORRIFIED LITTLE GIRL ONE LAST AWFUL NAME, THE WITCH PLUNGED INTO THE LAKE...
WEEDWIG!
MY WIG IS NOT LIKE A WEED!
BUT IT SEEMED THAT HAZEL HAD FORGOTTEN THAT SHE DIDN'T KNOW HOW TO SWIM!
I... CAN'T... SWIM!!
EVERYBODY SHOULD KNOW HOW TO SWIM... YOU OUGHT TO TAKE LESSONS SOMETIME!
SHE WENT DOWN ONCE...AND CAME UP AGAIN SPUTTERING AND SCREAMING FOR HELP!
HELP! SPUTTER... SPUTTER... HELP!
YOU MIGHT BE OUT IN A BOAT SOMETIME AN' YOU NEVER CAN TELL WHAT MIGHT HAPPEN...
WHILE SHE WAS GOING DOWN THE SECOND TIME, THE LITTLE GIRL GLANCED AROUND FOR SOMETHING TO THROW TO HER!
HM.. THERE'S THAT CROOKED STICK...
HELP!
ALL SHE COULD FIND WAS A STICK, WHICH SHE THREW TO THE DROWNING WITCH...
HERE! GRAB THAT!
HELP!

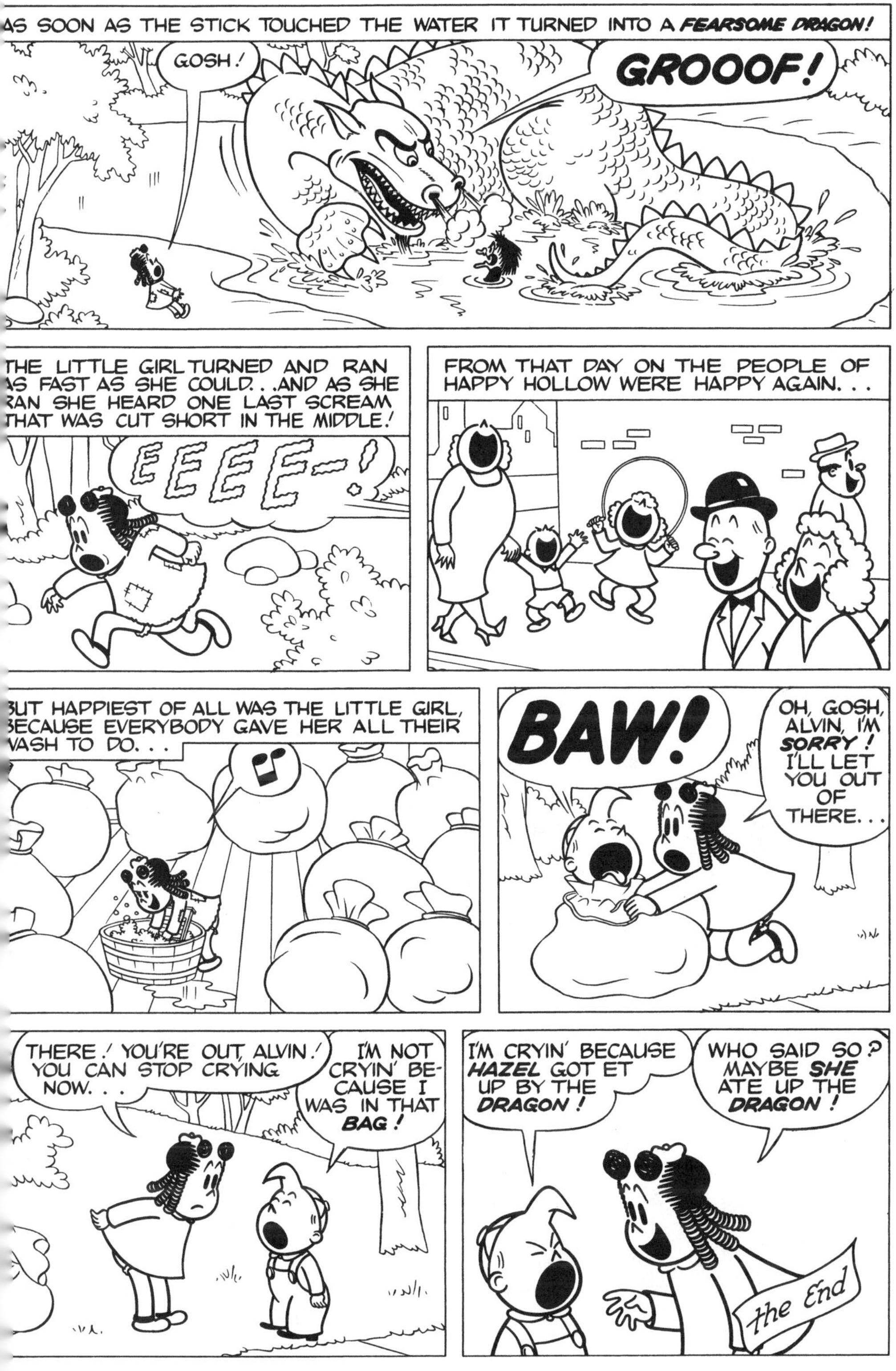
AS SOON AS THE STICK TOUCHED THE WATER IT TURNED INTO A FEARSOME DRAGON!
GOSH!
GROOOF!
THE LITTLE GIRL TURNED AND RAN AS FAST AS SHE COULD. . .AND AS SHE RAN SHE HEARD ONE LAST SCREAM THAT WAS CUT SHORT IN THE MIDDLE!
EEEE-!
FROM THAT DAY ON THE PEOPLE OF HAPPY HOLLOW WERE HAPPY AGAIN. . .
BUT HAPPIEST OF ALL WAS THE LITTLE GIRL, BECAUSE EVERYBODY GAVE HER ALL THEIR WASH TO DO. . .
BAW!
OH, GOSH, ALVIN, I'M SORRY! I'LL LET YOU OUT OF THERE. . .
THERE! YOU'RE OUT, ALVIN! YOU CAN STOP CRYING NOW. . .
I'M NOT CRYIN' BE-CAUSE I WAS IN THAT BAG!
I'M CRYIN' BECAUSE HAZEL GOT ET UP BY THE DRAGON!
WHO SAID SO? MAYBE SHE ATE UP THE DRAGON!
the End

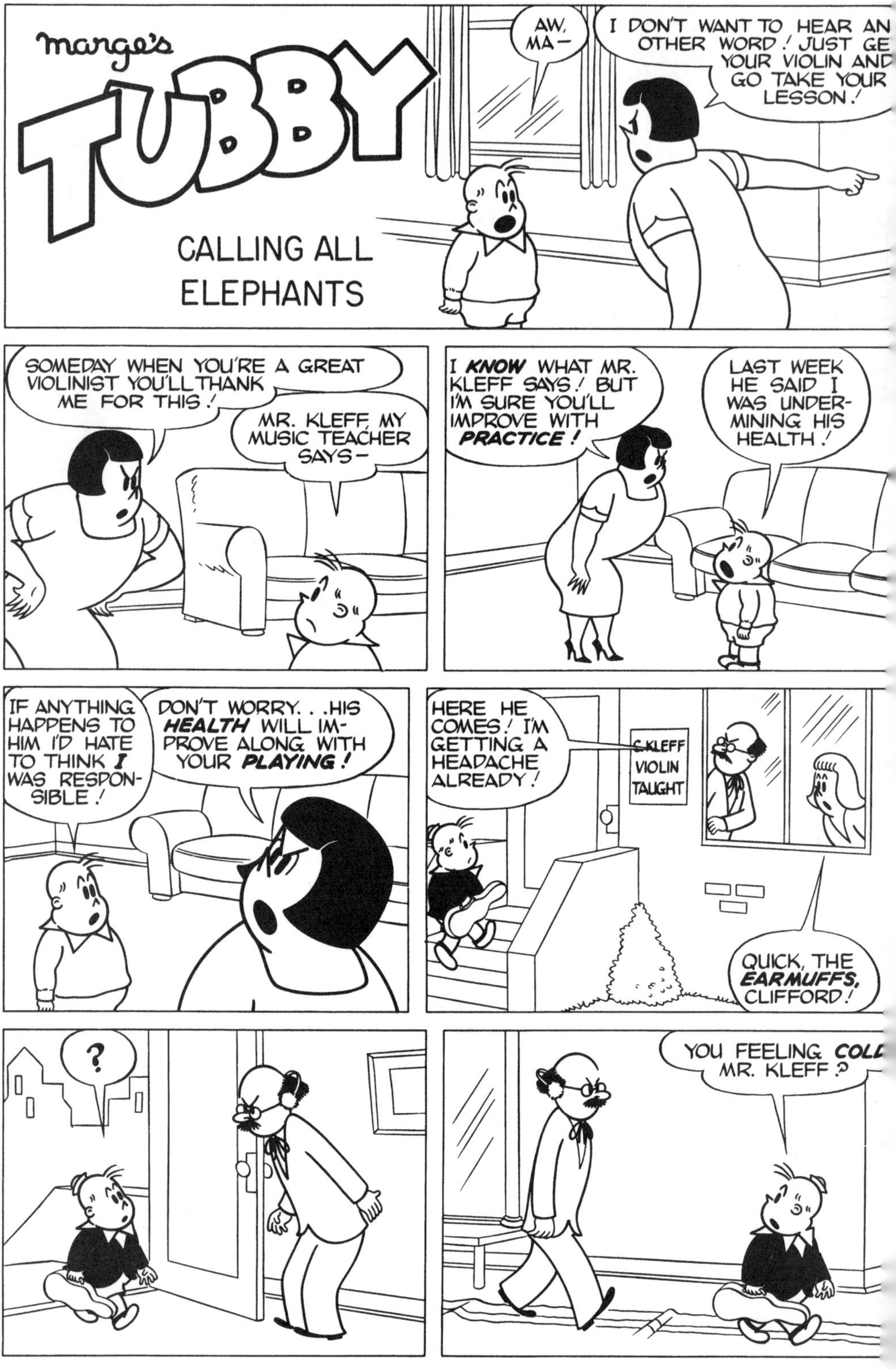

marge's
TUBBY
CALLING ALL ELEPHANTS
AW, MA—
I DON'T WANT TO HEAR AN OTHER WORD! JUST GE YOUR VIOLIN AND GO TAKE YOUR LESSON!
SOMEDAY WHEN YOU'RE A GREAT VIOLINIST YOU'LL THANK ME FOR THIS!
MR. KLEFF, MY MUSIC TEACHER SAYS—
I KNOW WHAT MR. KLEFF SAYS! BUT I'M SURE YOU'LL IMPROVE WITH PRACTICE!
LAST WEEK HE SAID I WAS UNDERMINING HIS HEALTH!
IF ANYTHING HAPPENS TO HIM I'D HATE TO THINK I WAS RESPONSIBLE!
DON'T WORRY. . .HIS HEALTH WILL IMPROVE ALONG WITH YOUR PLAYING!
HERE HE COMES! I'M GETTING A HEADACHE ALREADY!
C.KLEFF VIOLIN TAUGHT
QUICK, THE EARMUFFS, CLIFFORD!
?
YOU FEELING COLD MR. KLEFF?

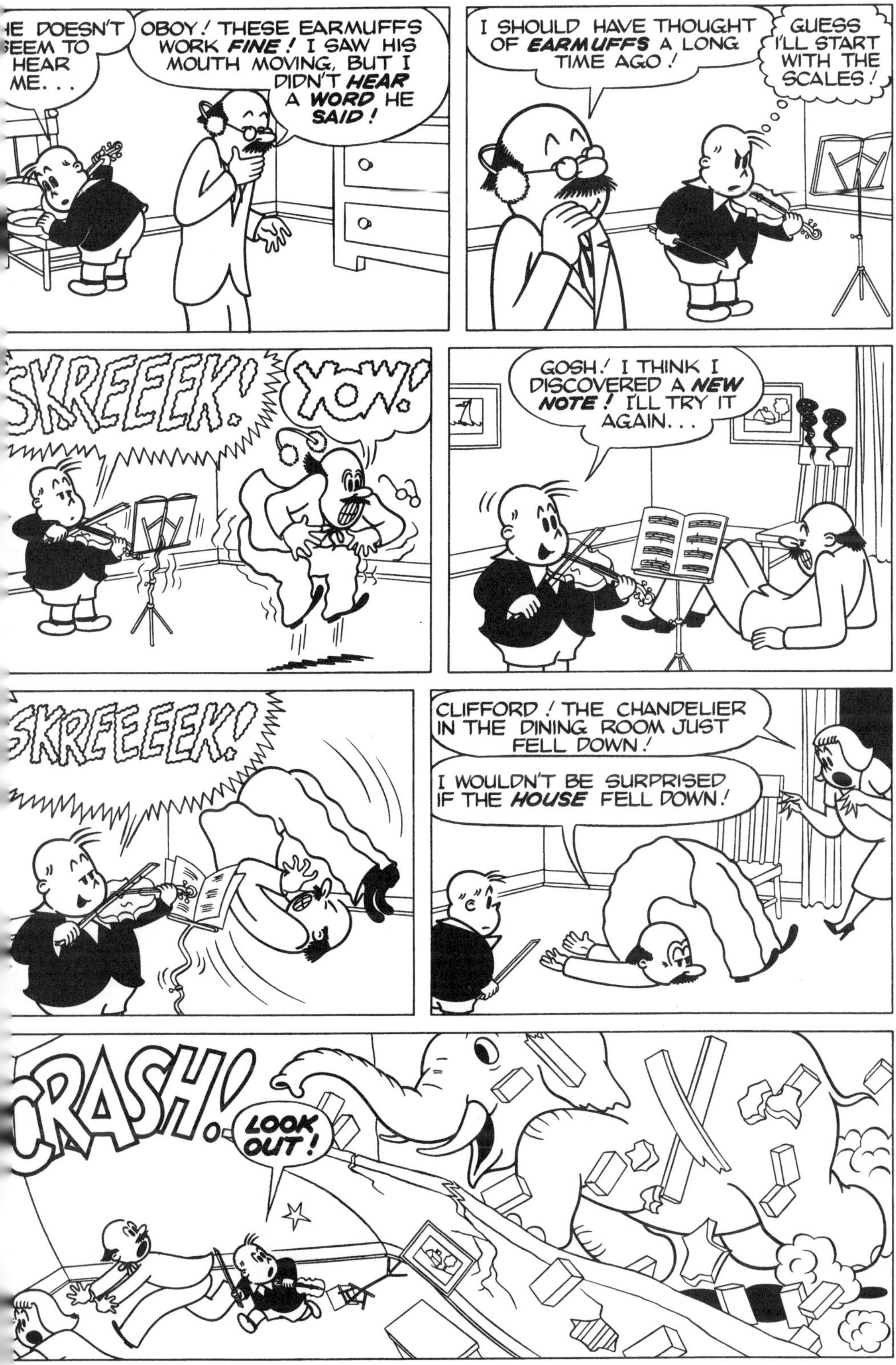
HE DOESN'T SEEM TO HEAR ME...
OBOY! THESE EARMUFFS WORK FINE! I SAW HIS MOUTH MOVING, BUT I DIDN'T HEAR A WORD HE SAID!
I SHOULD HAVE THOUGHT OF EARMUFFS A LONG TIME AGO!
GUESS I'LL START WITH THE SCALES!
SKREEEK!
YOW!
GOSH! I THINK I DISCOVERED A NEW NOTE! I'LL TRY IT AGAIN...
SKREEEEK!
CLIFFORD! THE CHANDELIER IN THE DINING ROOM JUST FELL DOWN!
I WOULDN'T BE SURPRISED IF THE HOUSE FELL DOWN!
CRASH!
LOOK OUT!

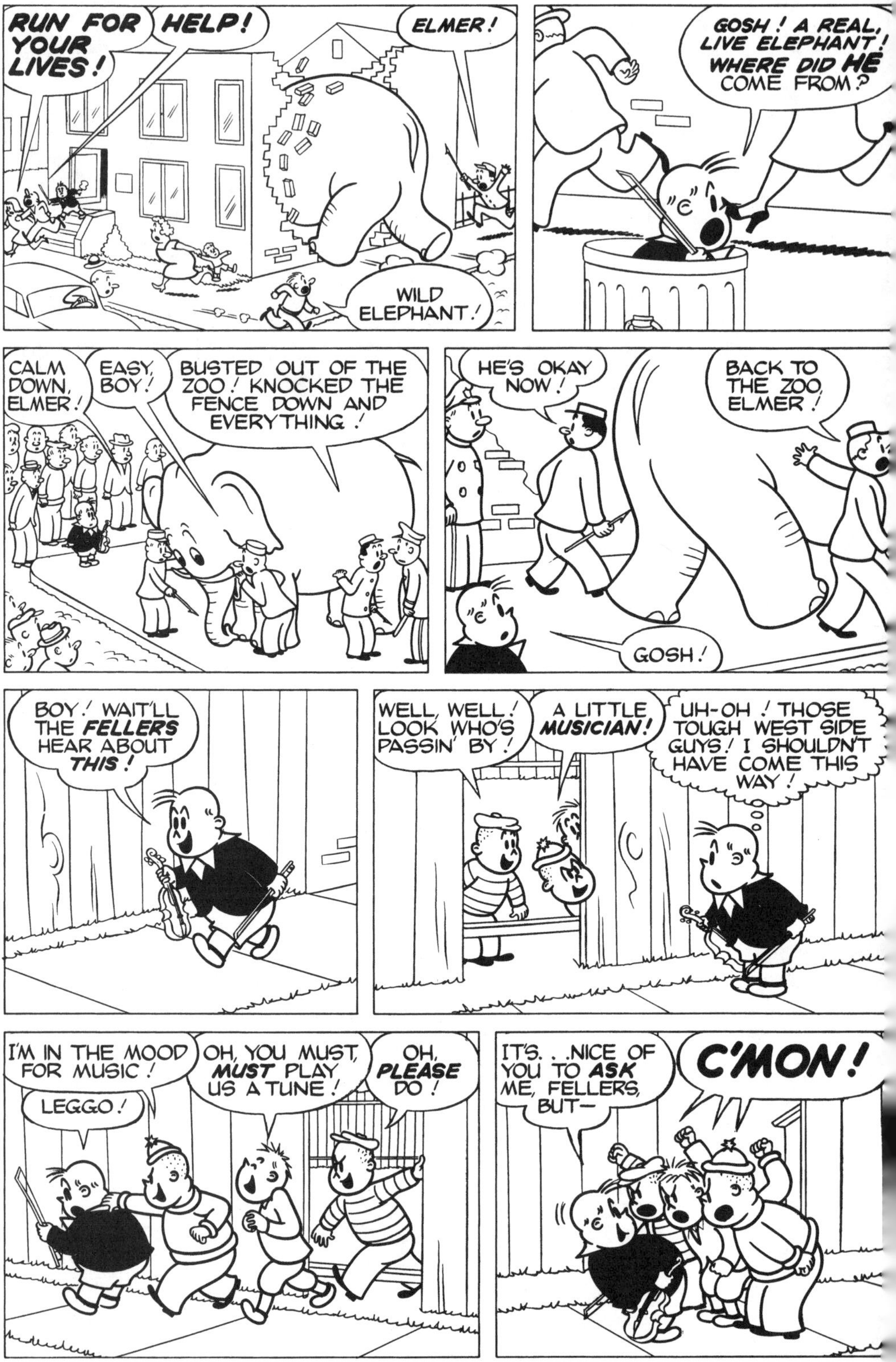
RUN FOR YOUR LIVES!
HELP!
ELMER!
WILD ELEPHANT!
GOSH! A REAL, LIVE ELEPHANT! WHERE DID HE COME FROM?
CALM DOWN, ELMER!
EASY, BOY!
BUSTED OUT OF THE ZOO! KNOCKED THE FENCE DOWN AND EVERYTHING!
HE'S OKAY NOW!
BACK TO THE ZOO, ELMER!
GOSH!
BOY! WAIT'LL THE FELLERS HEAR ABOUT THIS!
WELL, WELL! LOOK WHO'S PASSIN' BY!
A LITTLE MUSICIAN!
UH-OH! THOSE TOUGH WEST SIDE GUYS! I SHOULDN'T HAVE COME THIS WAY!
I'M IN THE MOOD FOR MUSIC!
LEGGO!
OH, YOU MUST, MUST PLAY US A TUNE!
OH, PLEASE DO!
IT'S. . .NICE OF YOU TO ASK ME, FELLERS, BUT—
C'MON!

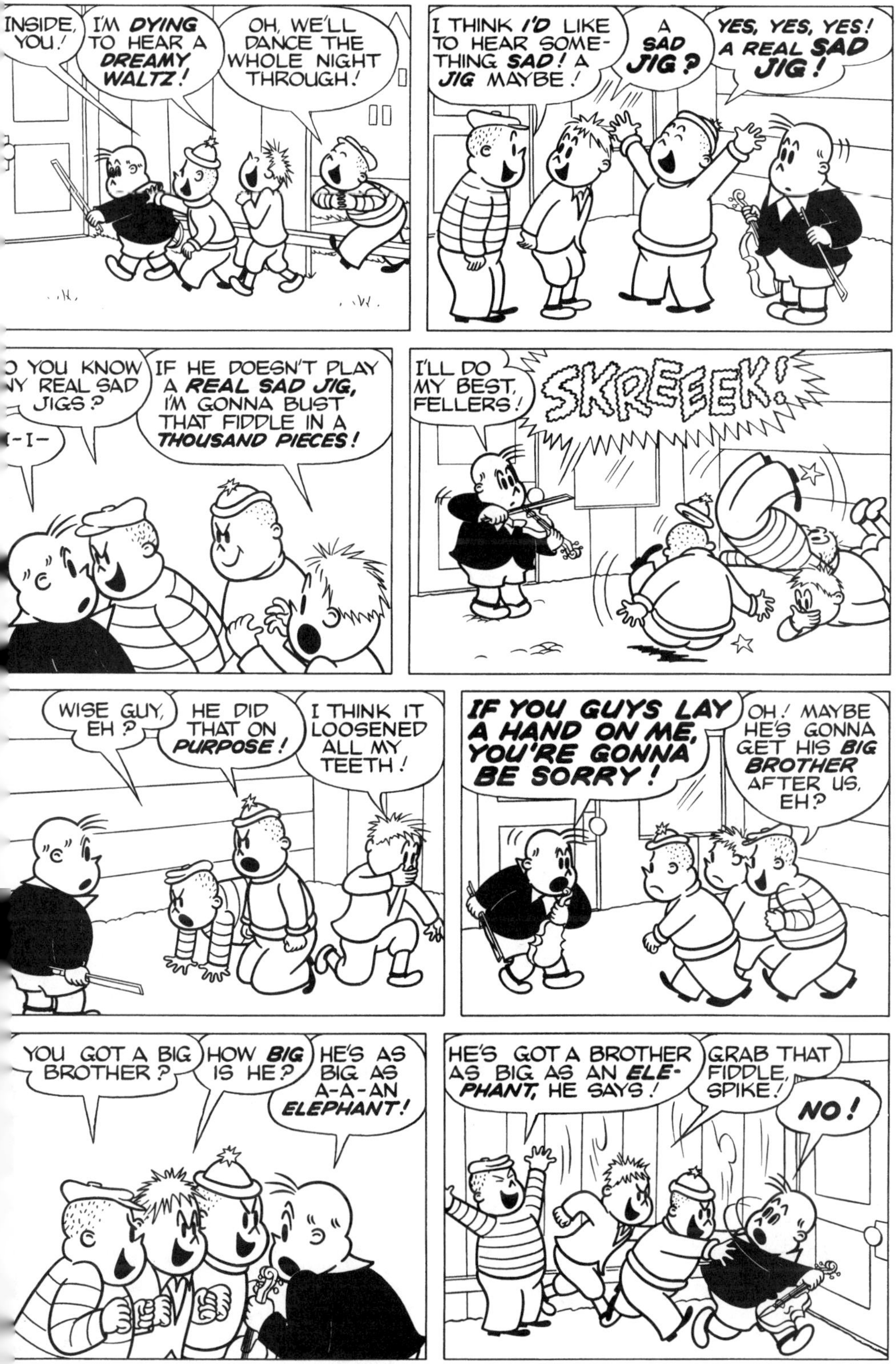
INSIDE, YOU!
I'M DYING TO HEAR A DREAMY WALTZ!
OH, WE'LL DANCE THE WHOLE NIGHT THROUGH!
I THINK I'D LIKE TO HEAR SOMETHING SAD! A JIG MAYBE!
A SAD JIG?
YES, YES, YES! A REAL SAD JIG!
O YOU KNOW NY REAL SAD JIGS?
I-I-
IF HE DOESN'T PLAY A REAL SAD JIG, I'M GONNA BUST THAT FIDDLE IN A THOUSAND PIECES!
I'LL DO MY BEST, FELLERS!
SKREEEK!
WISE GUY, EH?
HE DID THAT ON PURPOSE!
I THINK IT LOOSENED ALL MY TEETH!
IF YOU GUYS LAY A HAND ON ME, YOU'RE GONNA BE SORRY!
OH! MAYBE HE'S GONNA GET HIS BIG BROTHER AFTER US, EH?
YOU GOT A BIG BROTHER?
HOW BIG IS HE?
HE'S AS BIG AS A-A-AN ELEPHANT!
HE'S GOT A BROTHER AS BIG AS AN ELEPHANT, HE SAYS!
GRAB THAT FIDDLE, SPIKE!
NO!

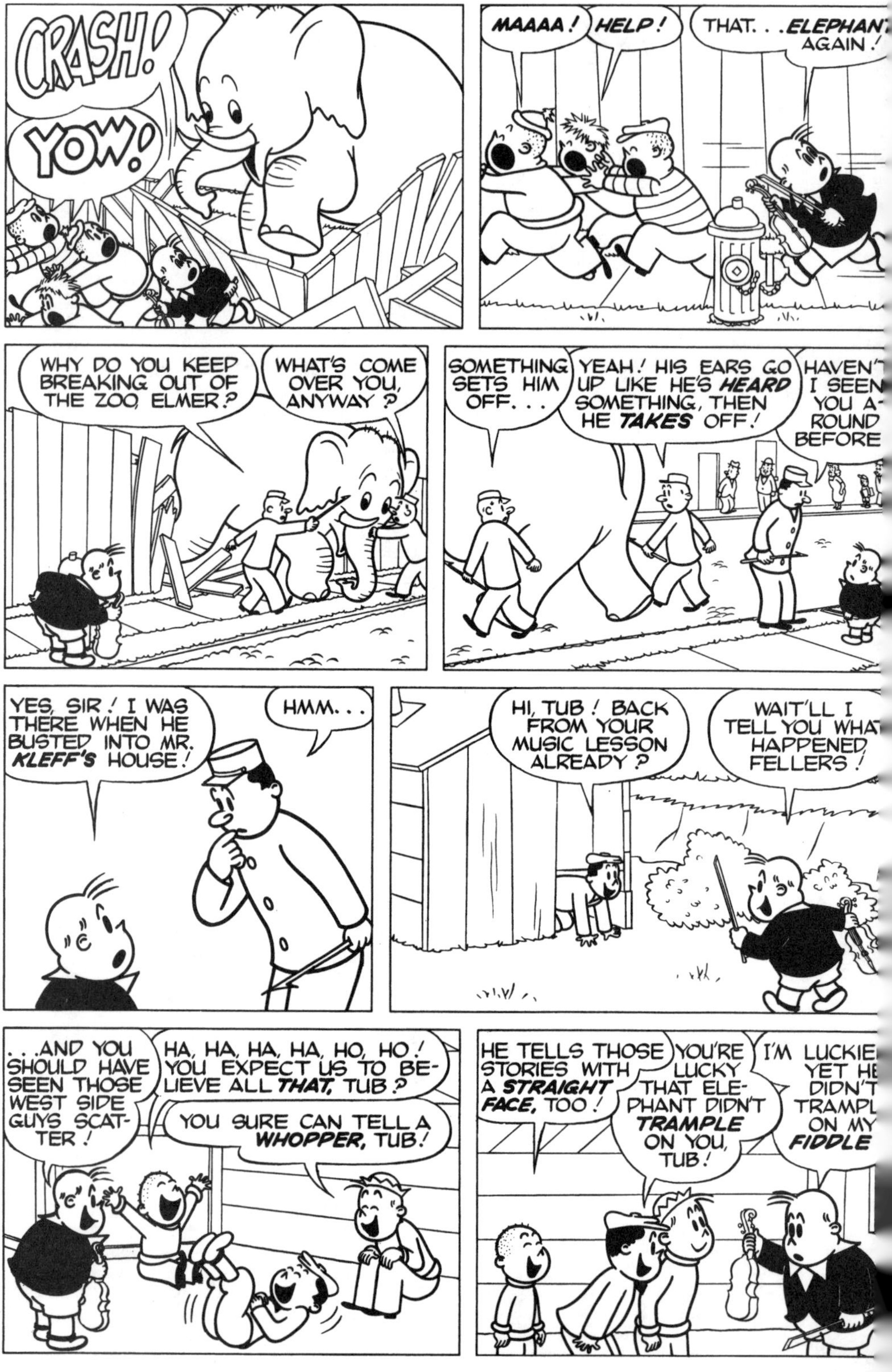
CRASH!
YOW!
MAAAA!
HELP!
THAT. . .ELEPHANT AGAIN!
WHY DO YOU KEEP BREAKING OUT OF THE ZOO, ELMER?
WHAT'S COME OVER YOU, ANYWAY?
SOMETHING SETS HIM OFF. . .
YEAH! HIS EARS GO UP LIKE HE'S HEARD SOMETHING, THEN HE TAKES OFF!
HAVEN'T I SEEN YOU A-ROUND BEFORE
YES, SIR! I WAS THERE WHEN HE BUSTED INTO MR. KLEFF'S HOUSE!
HMM. . .
HI, TUB! BACK FROM YOUR MUSIC LESSON ALREADY?
WAIT'LL I TELL YOU WHAT HAPPENED, FELLERS!
. . .AND YOU SHOULD HAVE SEEN THOSE WEST SIDE GUYS SCAT-TER!
HA, HA, HA, HA, HO, HO! YOU EXPECT US TO BE-LIEVE ALL THAT, TUB?
YOU SURE CAN TELL A WHOPPER, TUB!
HE TELLS THOSE STORIES WITH A STRAIGHT FACE, TOO!
YOU'RE LUCKY THAT ELE-PHANT DIDN'T TRAMPLE ON YOU, TUB!
I'M LUCKIE YET HE DIDN'T TRAMPL ON MY FIDDLE

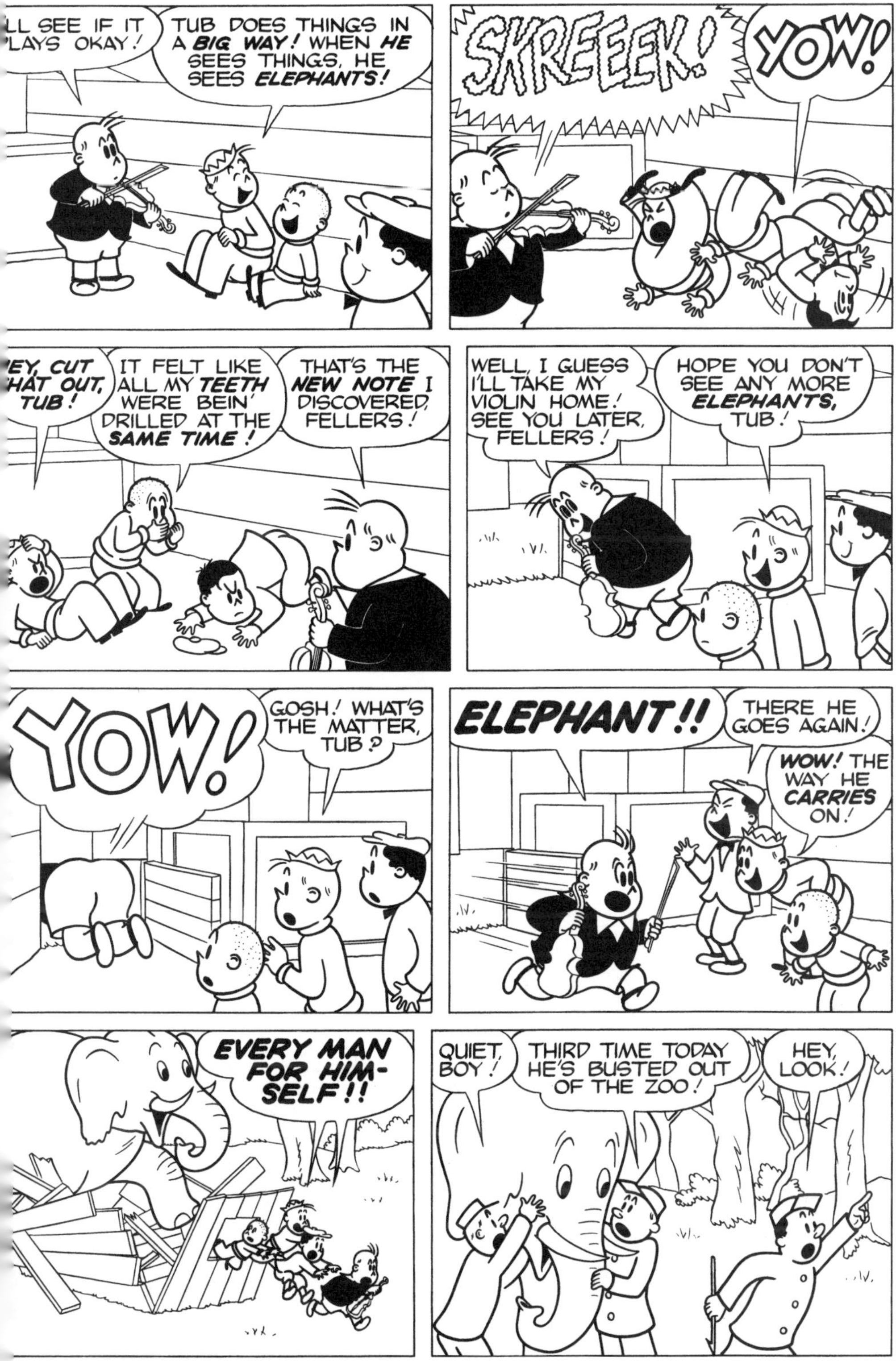
LL SEE IF IT
PLAYS OKAY!
TUB DOES THINGS IN A BIG WAY! WHEN HE SEES THINGS, HE SEES ELEPHANTS!
SKREEEK!
YOW!
EY, CUT HAT OUT, TUB!
IT FELT LIKE ALL MY TEETH WERE BEIN' DRILLED AT THE SAME TIME!
THAT'S THE NEW NOTE I DISCOVERED, FELLERS!
WELL, I GUESS I'LL TAKE MY VIOLIN HOME! SEE YOU LATER, FELLERS!
HOPE YOU DON'T SEE ANY MORE ELEPHANTS, TUB!
YOW!
GOSH! WHAT'S THE MATTER, TUB?
ELEPHANT!!
THERE HE GOES AGAIN!
WOW! THE WAY HE CARRIES ON!
EVERY MAN FOR HIM-SELF!!
QUIET, BOY!
THIRD TIME TODAY HE'S BUSTED OUT OF THE ZOO!
HEY, LOOK!

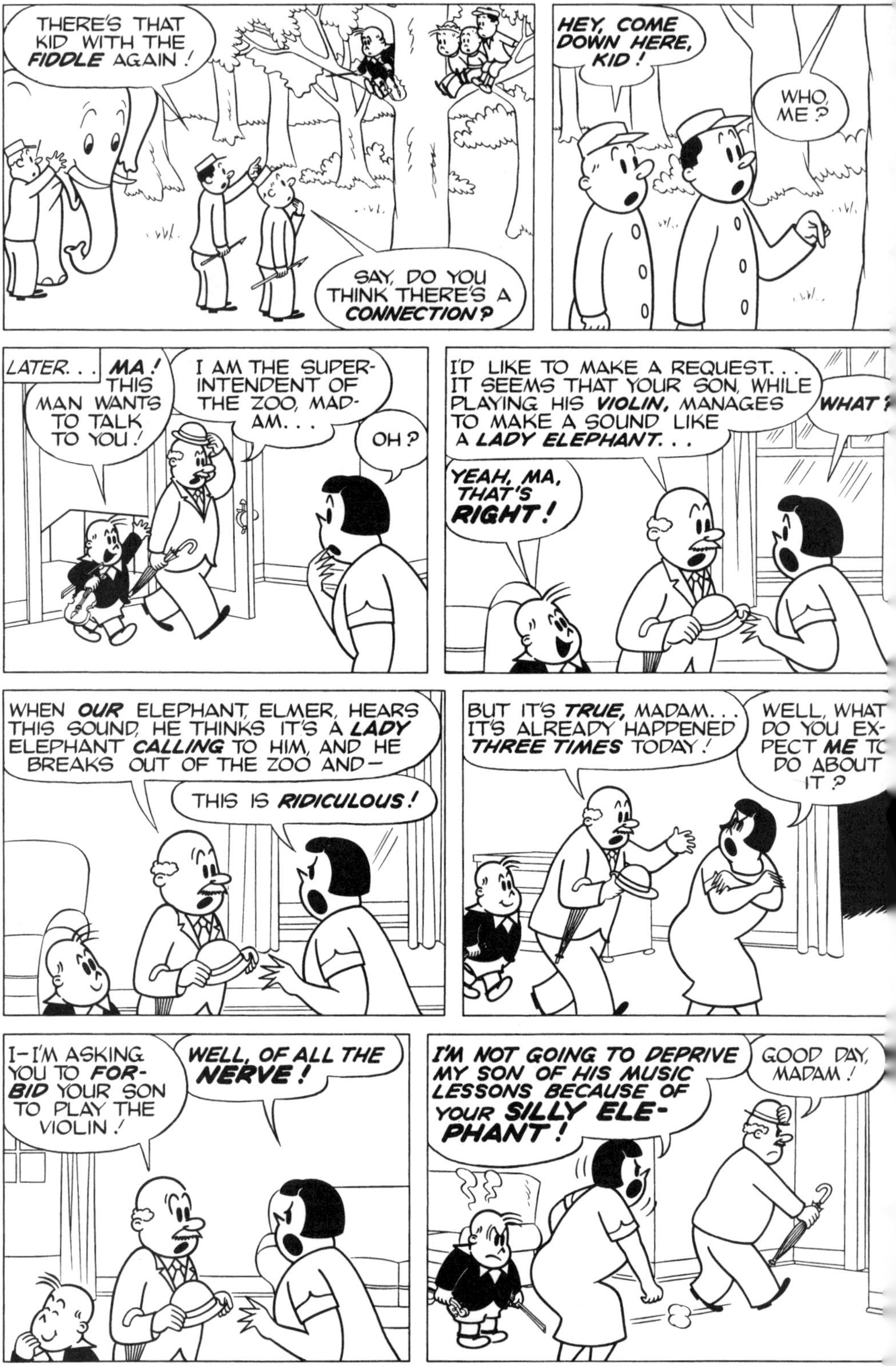
THERE'S THAT KID WITH THE FIDDLE AGAIN!
SAY, DO YOU THINK THERE'S A CONNECTION?
HEY, COME DOWN HERE, KID!
WHO, ME?
LATER...
MA! THIS MAN WANTS TO TALK TO YOU!
I AM THE SUPER-INTENDENT OF THE ZOO, MAD-AM...
OH?
I'D LIKE TO MAKE A REQUEST... IT SEEMS THAT YOUR SON, WHILE PLAYING HIS VIOLIN, MANAGES TO MAKE A SOUND LIKE A LADY ELEPHANT...
WHAT?
YEAH, MA, THAT'S RIGHT!
WHEN OUR ELEPHANT, ELMER, HEARS THIS SOUND, HE THINKS IT'S A LADY ELEPHANT CALLING TO HIM, AND HE BREAKS OUT OF THE ZOO AND—
THIS IS RIDICULOUS!
BUT IT'S TRUE, MADAM... IT'S ALREADY HAPPENED THREE TIMES TODAY!
WELL, WHAT DO YOU EX-PECT ME TO DO ABOUT IT?
I—I'M ASKING YOU TO FOR-BID YOUR SON TO PLAY THE VIOLIN!
WELL, OF ALL THE NERVE!
I'M NOT GOING TO DEPRIVE MY SON OF HIS MUSIC LESSONS BECAUSE OF YOUR SILLY ELE-PHANT!
GOOD DAY, MADAM!

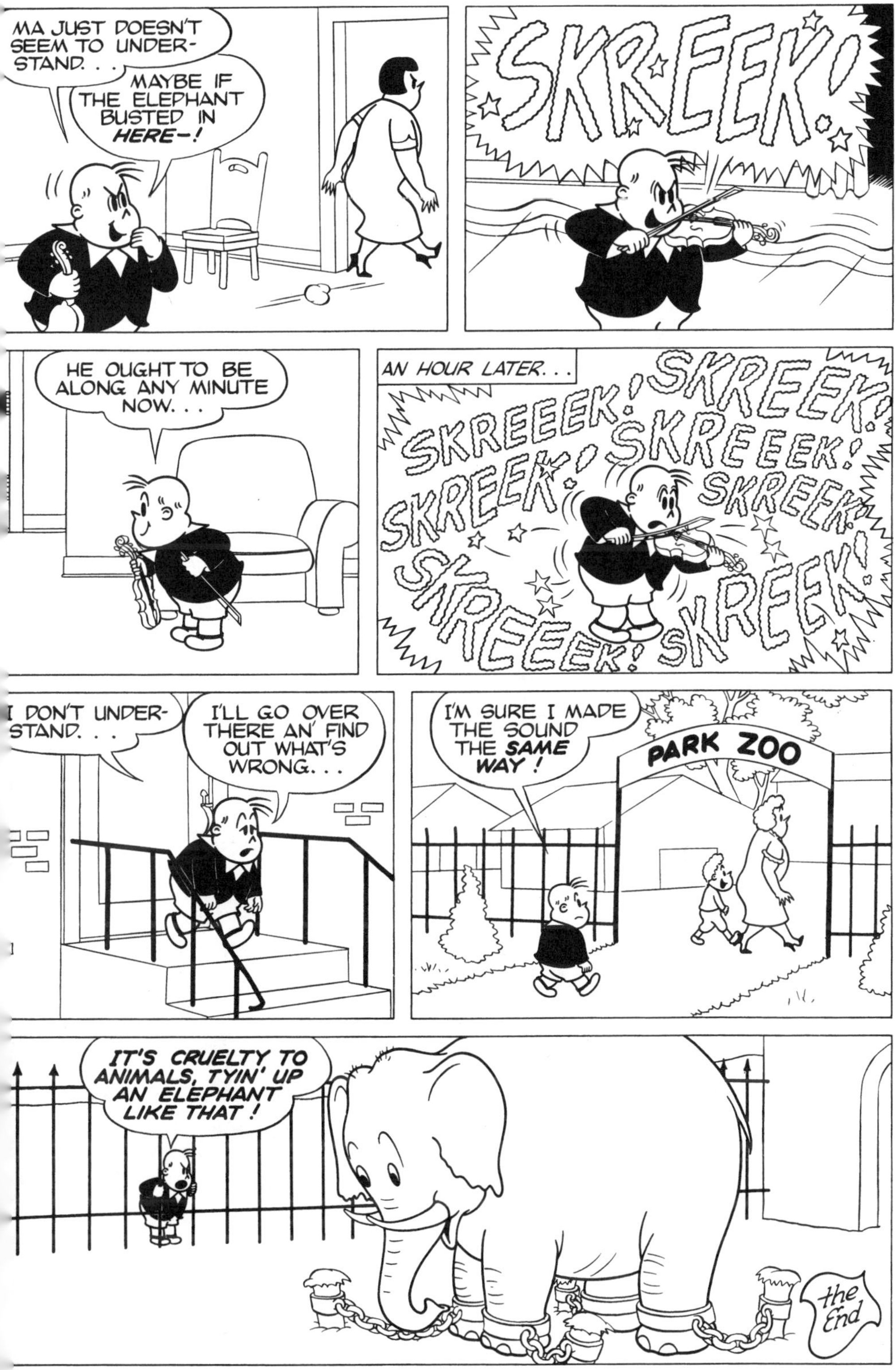

MA JUST DOESN'T SEEM TO UNDER-STAND. . .
MAYBE IF THE ELEPHANT BUSTED IN HERE–!
SKR-EEK!
HE OUGHT TO BE ALONG ANY MINUTE NOW. . .
AN HOUR LATER. . .
SKREEEK! SKREEK! SKREEK! SKREEEK! SKREEK! SKREEK! SKREEEK! SKREEK!
I DON'T UNDER-STAND. . .
I'LL GO OVER THERE AN' FIND OUT WHAT'S WRONG. . .
I'M SURE I MADE THE SOUND THE SAME WAY!
PARK ZOO
IT'S CRUELTY TO ANIMALS, TYIN' UP AN ELEPHANT LIKE THAT!
the End

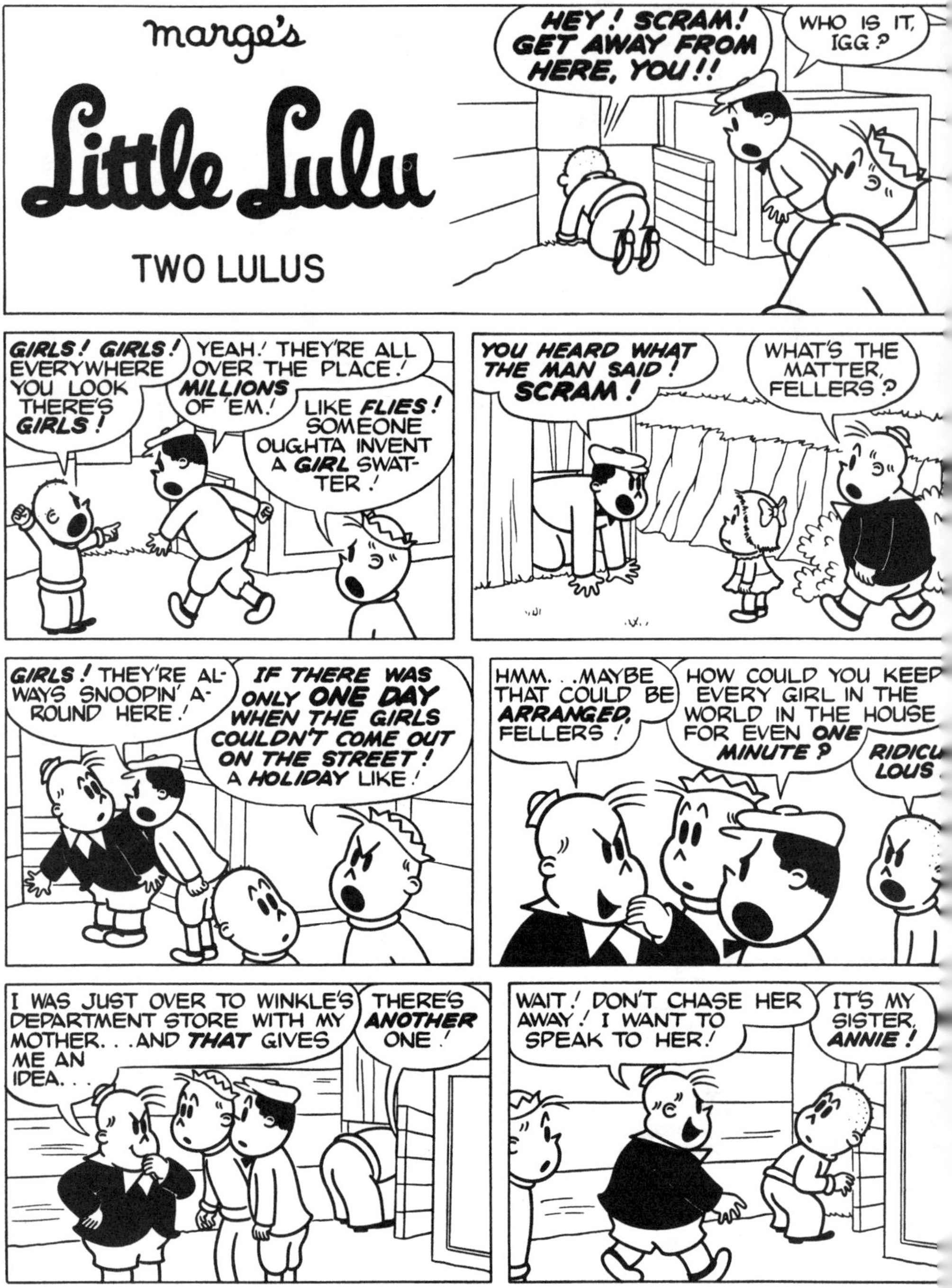
marge's
Little Lulu
TWO LULUS
HEY! SCRAM! GET AWAY FROM HERE, YOU!!
WHO IS IT, IGG?
GIRLS! GIRLS! EVERYWHERE YOU LOOK THERE'S GIRLS!
YEAH! THEY'RE ALL OVER THE PLACE! MILLIONS OF 'EM!
LIKE FLIES! SOMEONE OUGHTA INVENT A GIRL SWATTER!
YOU HEARD WHAT THE MAN SAID! SCRAM!
WHAT'S THE MATTER, FELLERS?
GIRLS! THEY'RE ALWAYS SNOOPIN' AROUND HERE!
IF THERE WAS ONLY ONE DAY WHEN THE GIRLS COULDN'T COME OUT ON THE STREET! A HOLIDAY LIKE!
HMM...MAYBE THAT COULD BE ARRANGED, FELLERS!
HOW COULD YOU KEEP EVERY GIRL IN THE WORLD IN THE HOUSE FOR EVEN ONE MINUTE?
RIDICULOUS
I WAS JUST OVER TO WINKLE'S DEPARTMENT STORE WITH MY MOTHER...AND THAT GIVES ME AN IDEA...
THERE'S ANOTHER ONE!
WAIT! DON'T CHASE HER AWAY! I WANT TO SPEAK TO HER!
IT'S MY SISTER, ANNIE!

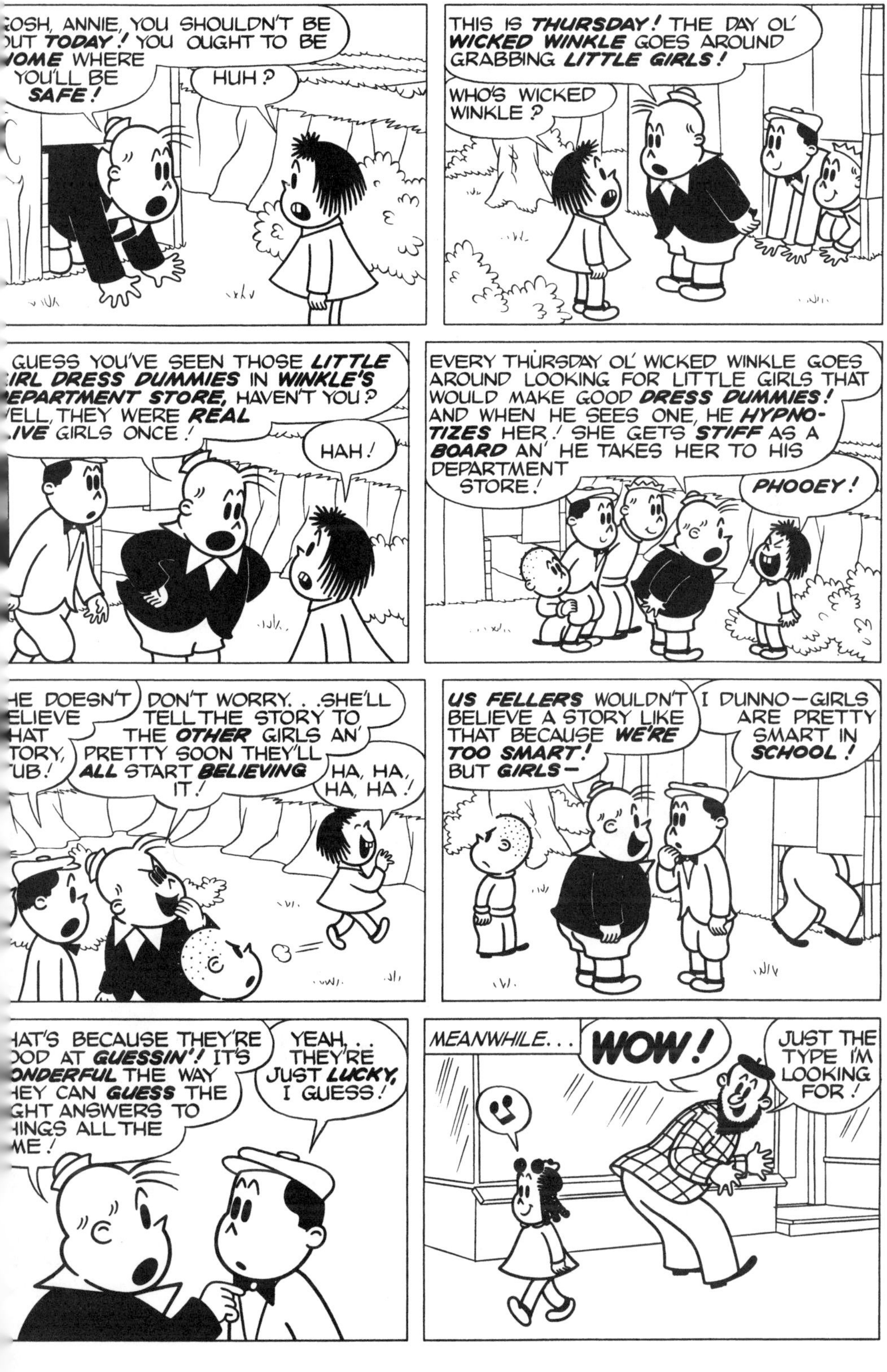

OSH, ANNIE, YOU SHOULDN'T BE UT TODAY! YOU OUGHT TO BE OME WHERE YOU'LL BE SAFE!
HUH?
THIS IS THURSDAY! THE DAY OL' WICKED WINKLE GOES AROUND GRABBING LITTLE GIRLS!
WHO'S WICKED WINKLE?
GUESS YOU'VE SEEN THOSE LITTLE IRL DRESS DUMMIES IN WINKLE'S EPARTMENT STORE, HAVEN'T YOU? ELL, THEY WERE REAL IVE GIRLS ONCE!
HAH!
EVERY THURSDAY OL' WICKED WINKLE GOES AROUND LOOKING FOR LITTLE GIRLS THAT WOULD MAKE GOOD DRESS DUMMIES! AND WHEN HE SEES ONE, HE HYPNOTIZES HER! SHE GETS STIFF AS A BOARD AN' HE TAKES HER TO HIS DEPARTMENT STORE!
PHOOEY!
E DOESN'T ELIEVE HAT TORY, UB!
DON'T WORRY. . .SHE'LL TELL THE STORY TO THE OTHER GIRLS AN' PRETTY SOON THEY'LL ALL START BELIEVING IT!
HA, HA, HA, HA!
US FELLERS WOULDN'T BELIEVE A STORY LIKE THAT BECAUSE WE'RE TOO SMART! BUT GIRLS—
I DUNNO—GIRLS ARE PRETTY SMART IN SCHOOL!
HAT'S BECAUSE THEY'RE OOD AT GUESSIN'! IT'S ONDERFUL THE WAY HEY CAN GUESS THE GHT ANSWERS TO HINGS ALL THE ME!
YEAH. . THEY'RE JUST LUCKY, I GUESS!
MEANWHILE. . .
WOW!
JUST THE TYPE I'M LOOKING FOR!

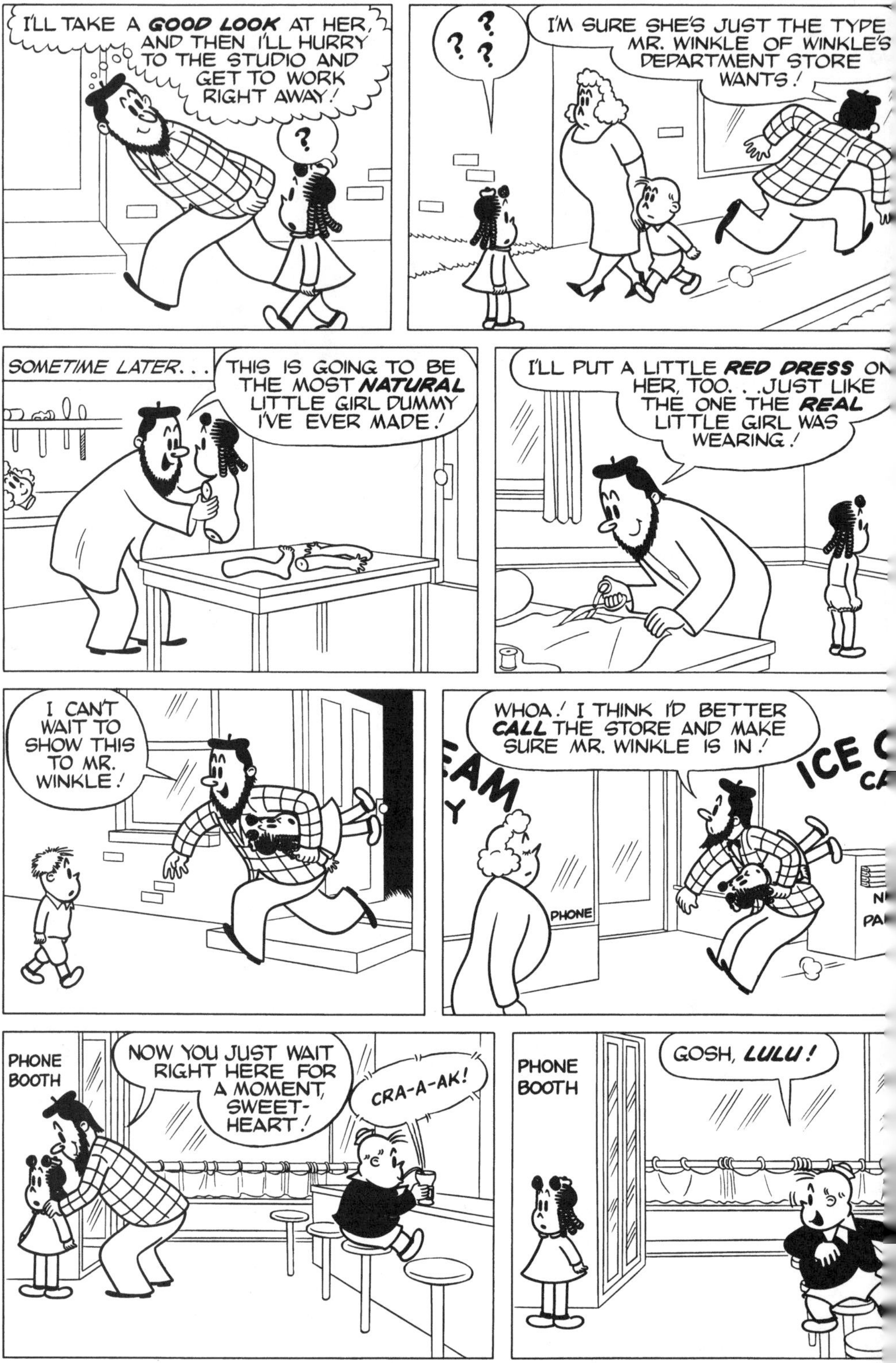
I'LL TAKE A **GOOD LOOK** AT HER, AND THEN I'LL HURRY TO THE STUDIO AND GET TO WORK RIGHT AWAY!
?
? ? ?
I'M SURE SHE'S JUST THE TYPE MR. WINKLE OF WINKLE'S DEPARTMENT STORE WANTS!
SOMETIME LATER. . .
THIS IS GOING TO BE THE MOST **NATURAL** LITTLE GIRL DUMMY I'VE EVER MADE!
I'LL PUT A LITTLE **RED DRESS** ON HER, TOO. . .JUST LIKE THE ONE THE **REAL** LITTLE GIRL WAS WEARING!
I CAN'T WAIT TO SHOW THIS TO MR. WINKLE!
WHOA! I THINK I'D BETTER **CALL** THE STORE AND MAKE SURE MR. WINKLE IS IN!
PHONE
PHONE BOOTH
NOW YOU JUST WAIT RIGHT HERE FOR A MOMENT, SWEET-HEART!
CRA-A-AK!
PHONE BOOTH
GOSH, **LULU**!

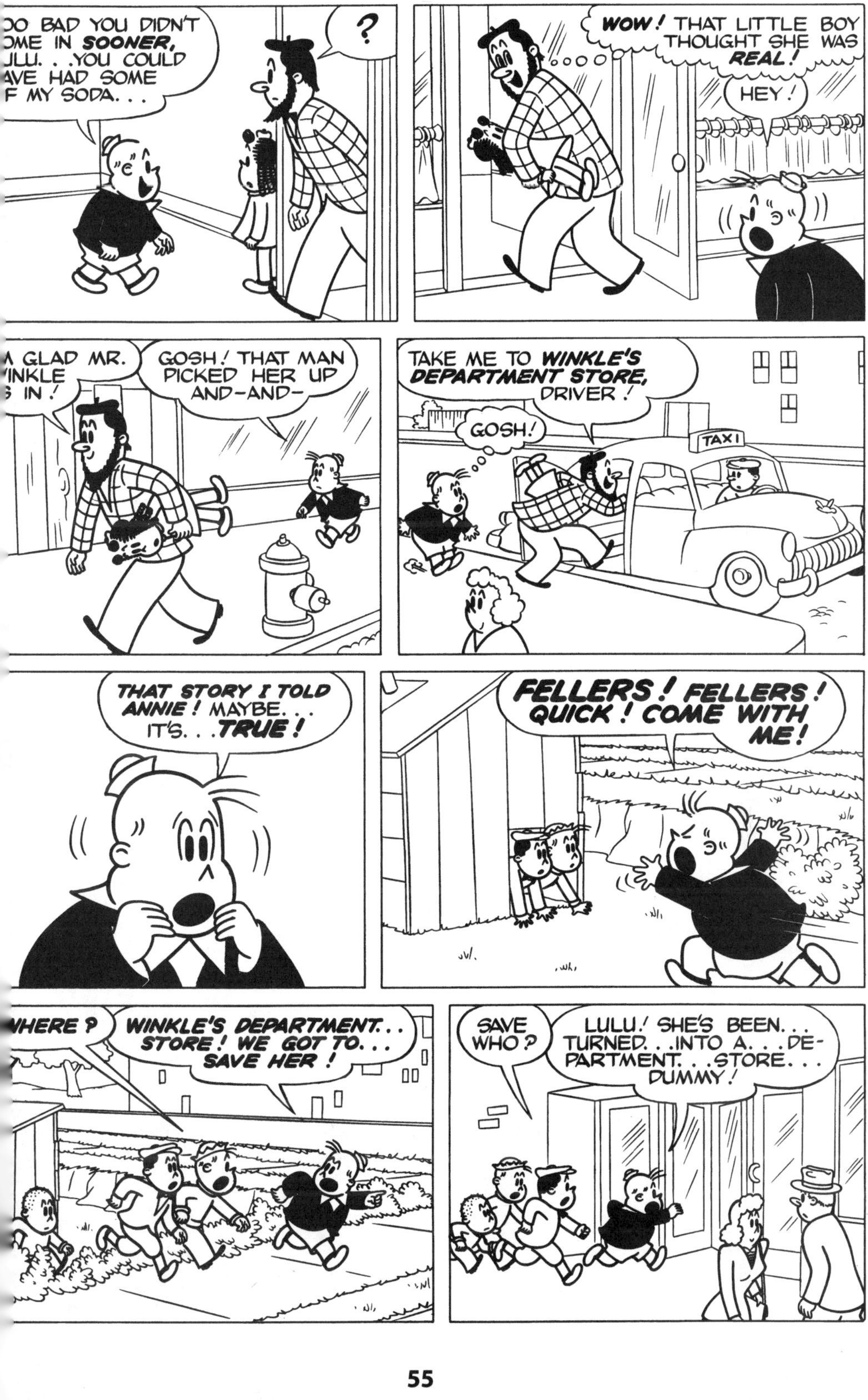

OO BAD YOU DIDN'T OME IN SOONER, LULU. . .YOU COULD AVE HAD SOME F MY SODA. . .
?
WOW! THAT LITTLE BOY THOUGHT SHE WAS REAL!
HEY!
A GLAD MR. INKLE S IN!
GOSH! THAT MAN PICKED HER UP AND-AND-
TAKE ME TO WINKLE'S DEPARTMENT STORE, DRIVER!
GOSH!
TAXI
THAT STORY I TOLD ANNIE! MAYBE. . . IT'S. . .TRUE!
FELLERS! FELLERS! QUICK! COME WITH ME!
WHERE?
WINKLE'S DEPARTMENT. . . STORE! WE GOT TO. . . SAVE HER!
SAVE WHO?
LULU! SHE'S BEEN. . . TURNED. . .INTO A. . .DE-PARTMENT. . .STORE. . . DUMMY!

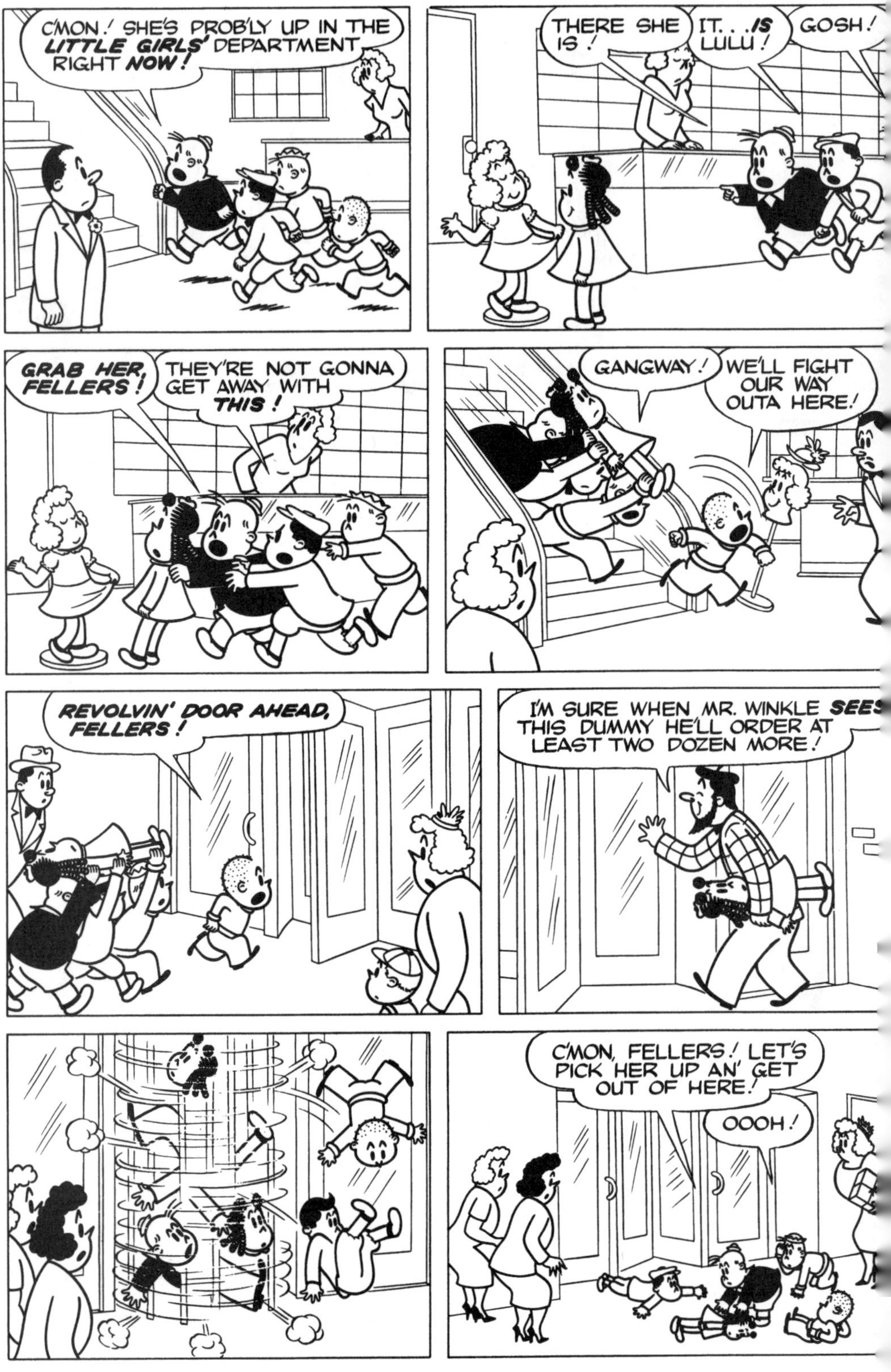
C'MON! SHE'S PROB'LY UP IN THE LITTLE GIRLS' DEPARTMENT RIGHT NOW!
THERE SHE IS!
IT. . .IS LULU!
GOSH!
GRAB HER, FELLERS!
THEY'RE NOT GONNA GET AWAY WITH THIS!
GANGWAY!
WE'LL FIGHT OUR WAY OUTA HERE!
REVOLVIN' DOOR AHEAD, FELLERS!
I'M SURE WHEN MR. WINKLE SEES THIS DUMMY HE'LL ORDER AT LEAST TWO DOZEN MORE!
C'MON, FELLERS! LET'S PICK HER UP AN' GET OUT OF HERE!
OOOH!

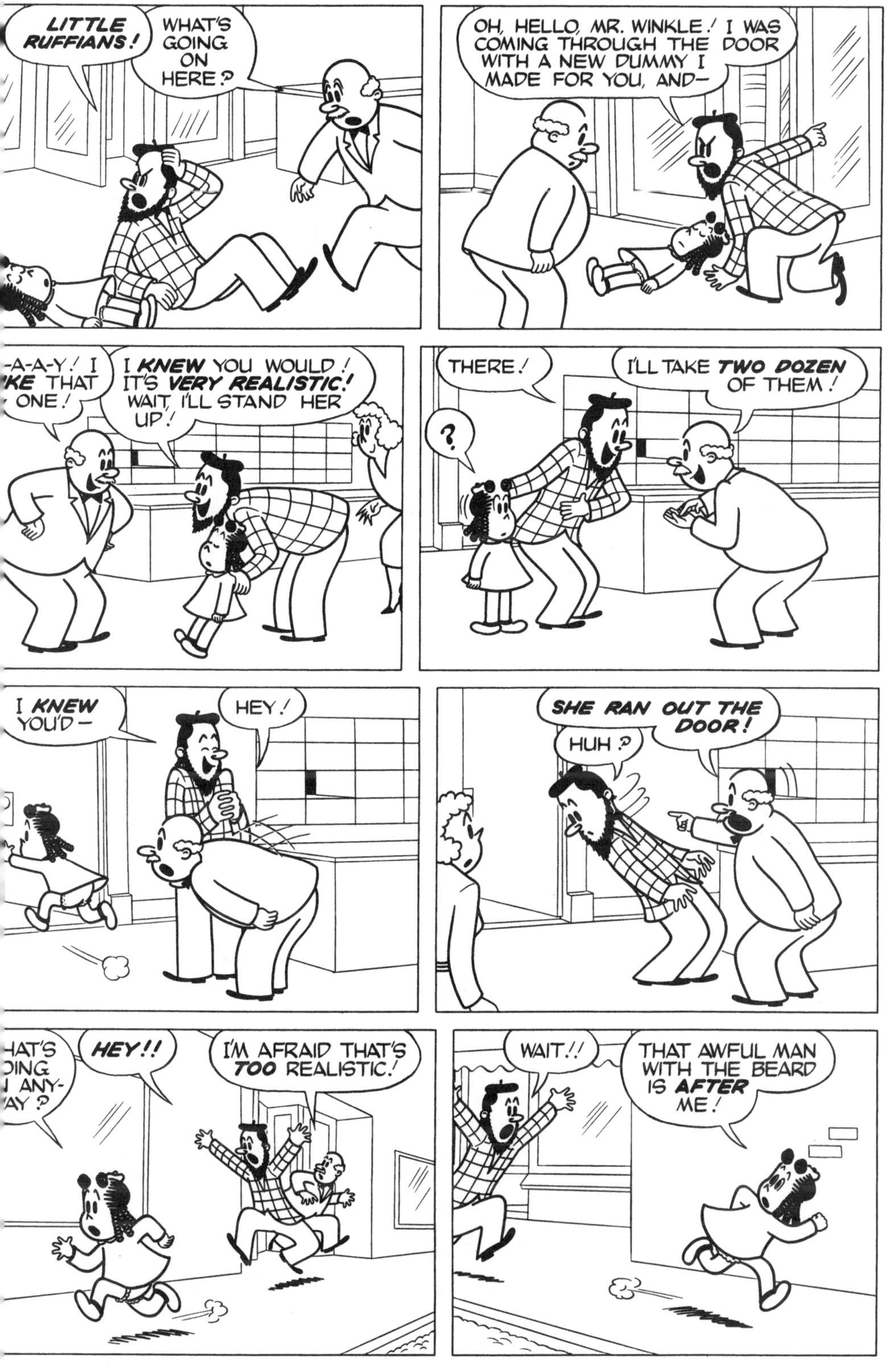
LITTLE RUFFIANS!
WHAT'S GOING ON HERE?
OH, HELLO, MR. WINKLE! I WAS COMING THROUGH THE DOOR WITH A NEW DUMMY I MADE FOR YOU, AND—
-A-A-Y! I KE THAT ONE!
I KNEW YOU WOULD! IT'S VERY REALISTIC! WAIT, I'LL STAND HER UP!
THERE!
?
I'LL TAKE TWO DOZEN OF THEM!
I KNEW YOU'D—
HEY!
SHE RAN OUT THE DOOR!
HUH?
HAT'S OING ANY- AY?
HEY!!
I'M AFRAID THAT'S TOO REALISTIC!
WAIT!!
THAT AWFUL MAN WITH THE BEARD IS AFTER ME!

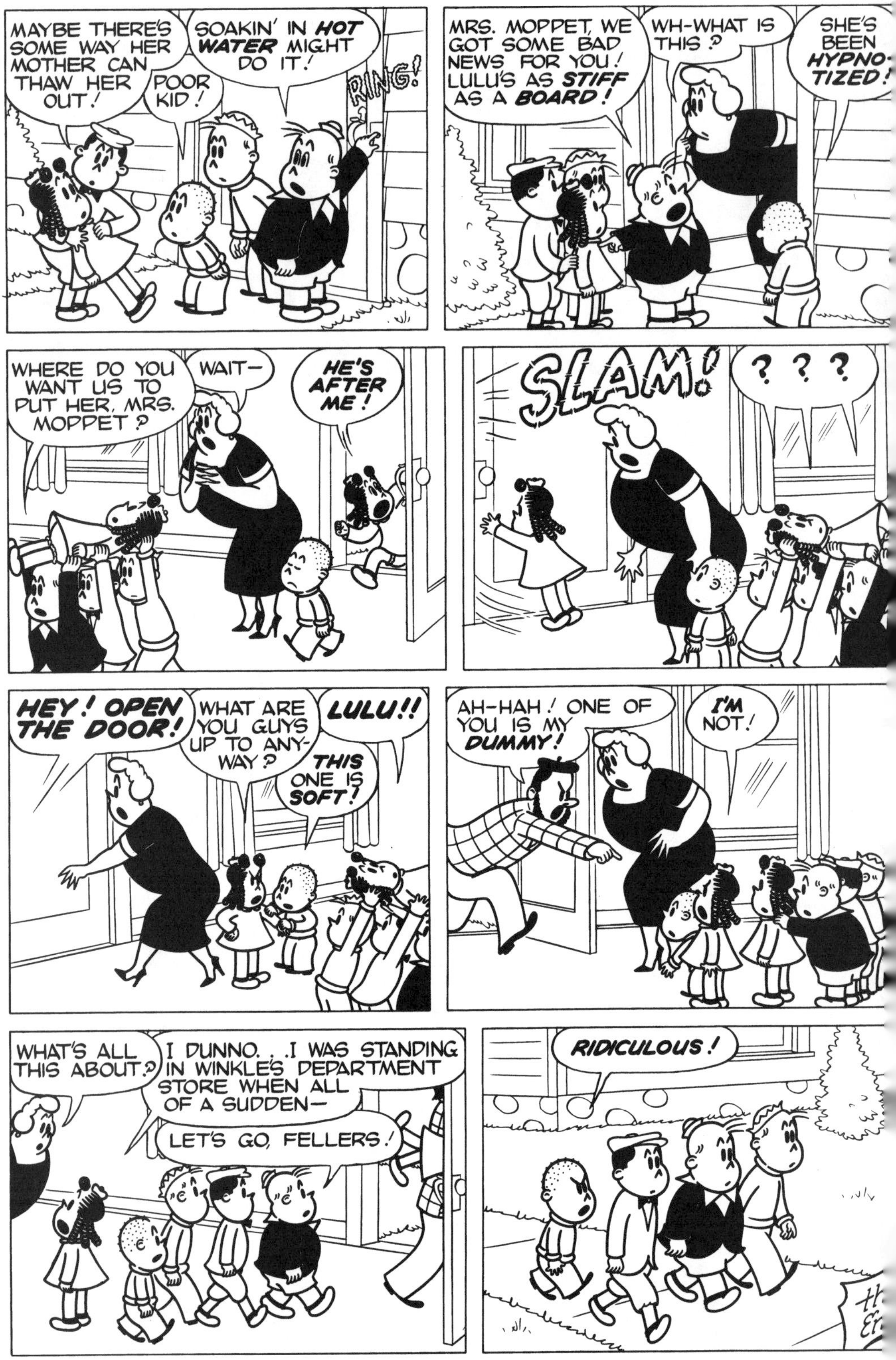
MAYBE THERE'S SOME WAY HER MOTHER CAN THAW HER OUT!
SOAKIN' IN HOT WATER MIGHT DO IT!
POOR KID!
RING!
MRS. MOPPET, WE GOT SOME BAD NEWS FOR YOU! LULU'S AS STIFF AS A BOARD!
WH-WHAT IS THIS?
SHE'S BEEN HYPNOTIZED!
WHERE DO YOU WANT US TO PUT HER, MRS. MOPPET?
WAIT—
HE'S AFTER ME!
SLAM!
? ? ?
HEY! OPEN THE DOOR!
WHAT ARE YOU GUYS UP TO ANYWAY?
LULU!!
THIS ONE IS SOFT!
AH-HAH! ONE OF YOU IS MY DUMMY!
I'M NOT!
WHAT'S ALL THIS ABOUT?
I DUNNO. . .I WAS STANDING IN WINKLE'S DEPARTMENT STORE WHEN ALL OF A SUDDEN—
LET'S GO, FELLERS!
RIDICULOUS!

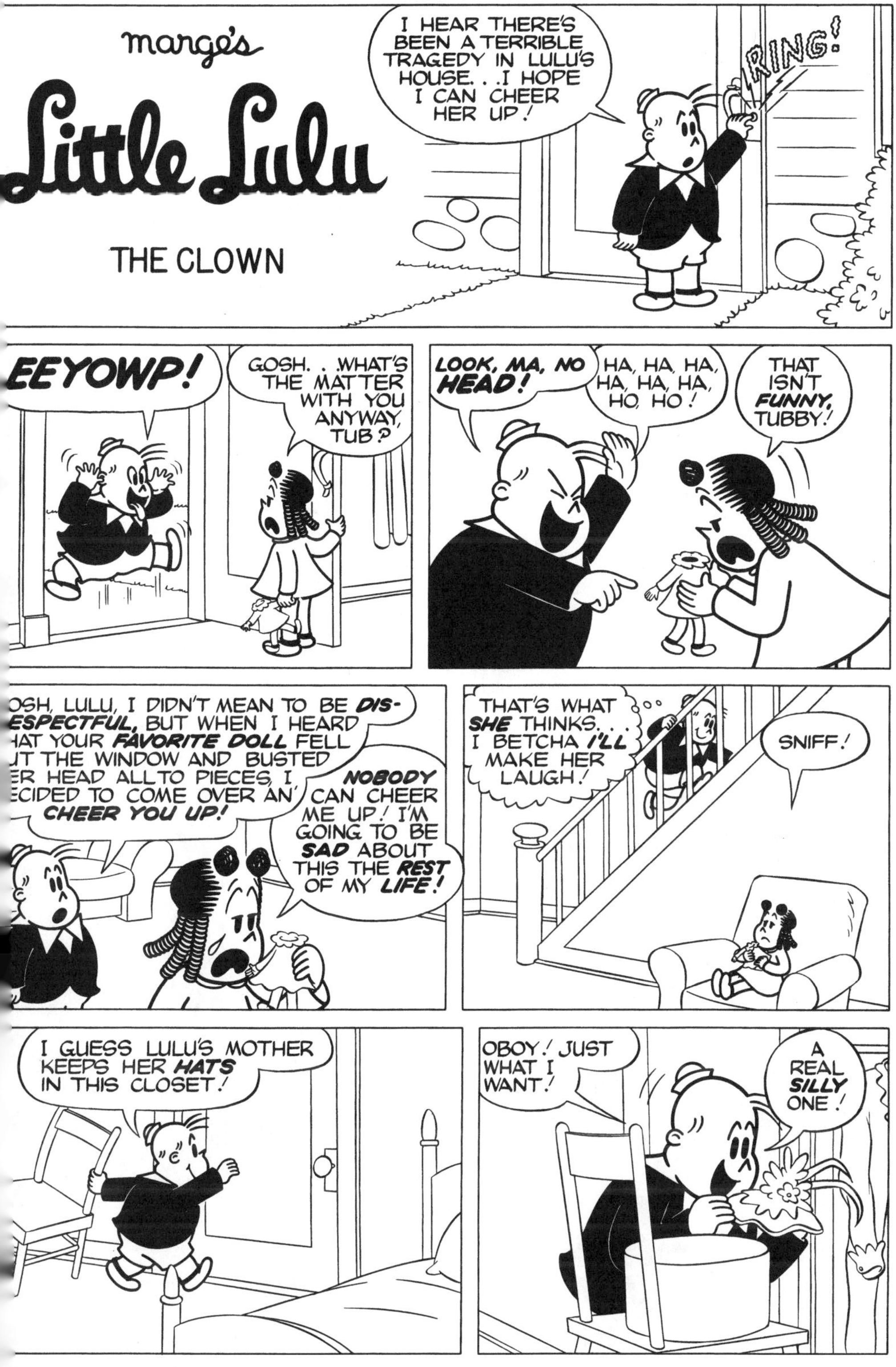
marge's
Little Lulu
THE CLOWN
I HEAR THERE'S BEEN A TERRIBLE TRAGEDY IN LULU'S HOUSE. . .I HOPE I CAN CHEER HER UP!
RING!
EEYOWP!
GOSH. . .WHAT'S THE MATTER WITH YOU ANYWAY, TUB?
LOOK, MA, NO HEAD!
HA, HA, HA, HA, HA, HA, HO, HO!
THAT ISN'T FUNNY, TUBBY!
OSH, LULU, I DIDN'T MEAN TO BE DIS-
ESPECTFUL, BUT WHEN I HEARD
HAT YOUR FAVORITE DOLL FELL
UT THE WINDOW AND BUSTED
ER HEAD ALL TO PIECES, I
ECIDED TO COME OVER AN'
CHEER YOU UP!
NOBODY CAN CHEER ME UP! I'M GOING TO BE SAD ABOUT THIS THE REST OF MY LIFE!
THAT'S WHAT SHE THINKS. . . I BETCHA I'LL MAKE HER LAUGH!
SNIFF!
I GUESS LULU'S MOTHER KEEPS HER HATS IN THIS CLOSET!
OBOY! JUST WHAT I WANT!
A REAL SILLY ONE!

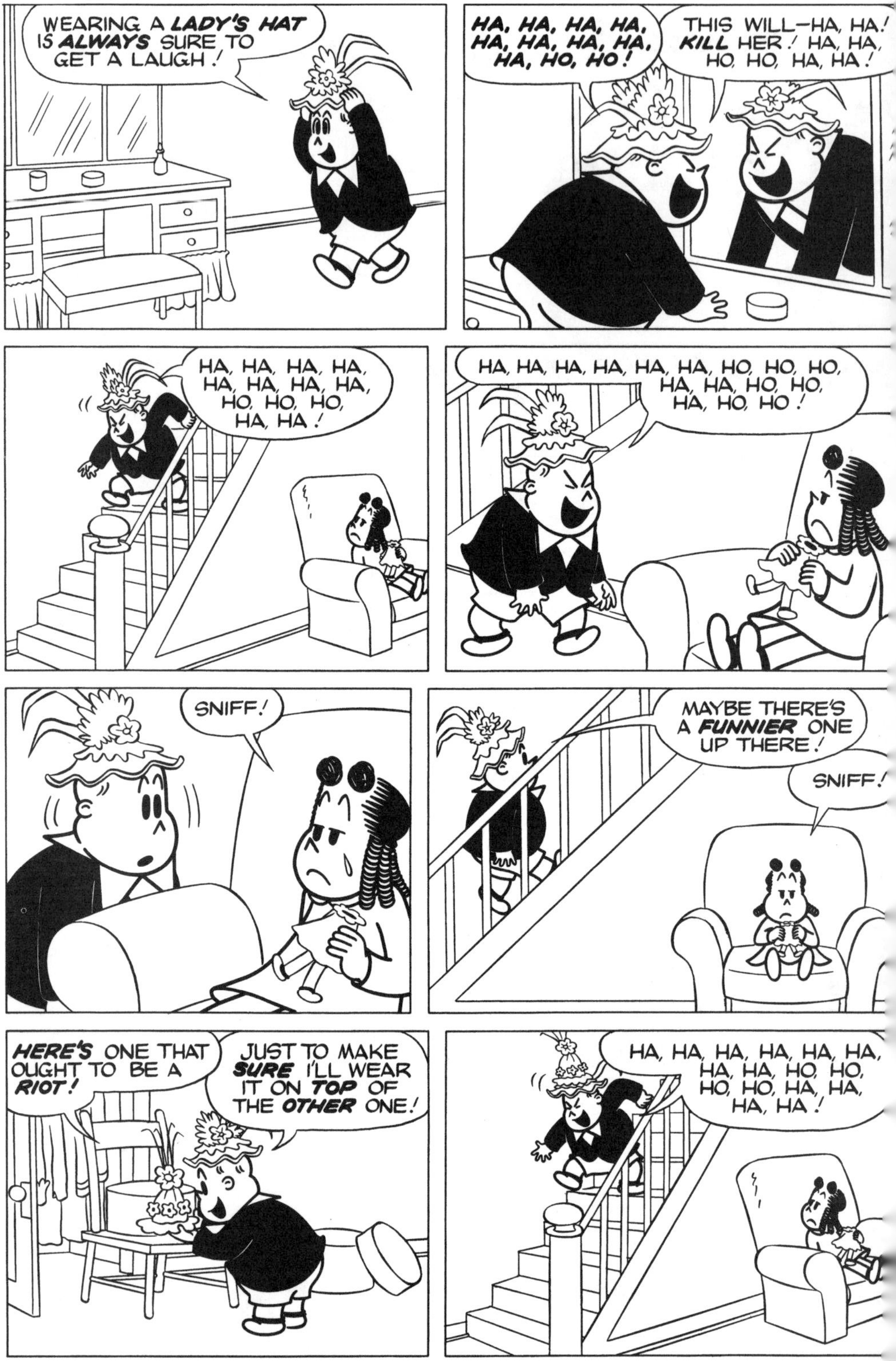
WEARING A LADY'S HAT IS ALWAYS SURE TO GET A LAUGH!
HA, HA, HA, HA, HA, HA, HA, HA, HA, HO, HO!
THIS WILL—HA, HA! KILL HER! HA, HA, HO, HO, HA, HA!
HA, HA, HA, HA, HA, HA, HA, HA, HO, HO, HO, HA, HA!
HA, HA, HA, HA, HA, HA, HO, HO, HO, HA, HA, HO, HO, HA, HO, HO!
SNIFF!
MAYBE THERE'S A FUNNIER ONE UP THERE!
SNIFF!
HERE'S ONE THAT OUGHT TO BE A RIOT!
JUST TO MAKE SURE I'LL WEAR IT ON TOP OF THE OTHER ONE!
HA, HA, HA, HA, HA, HA, HA, HA, HO, HO, HO, HO, HA, HA, HA, HA!

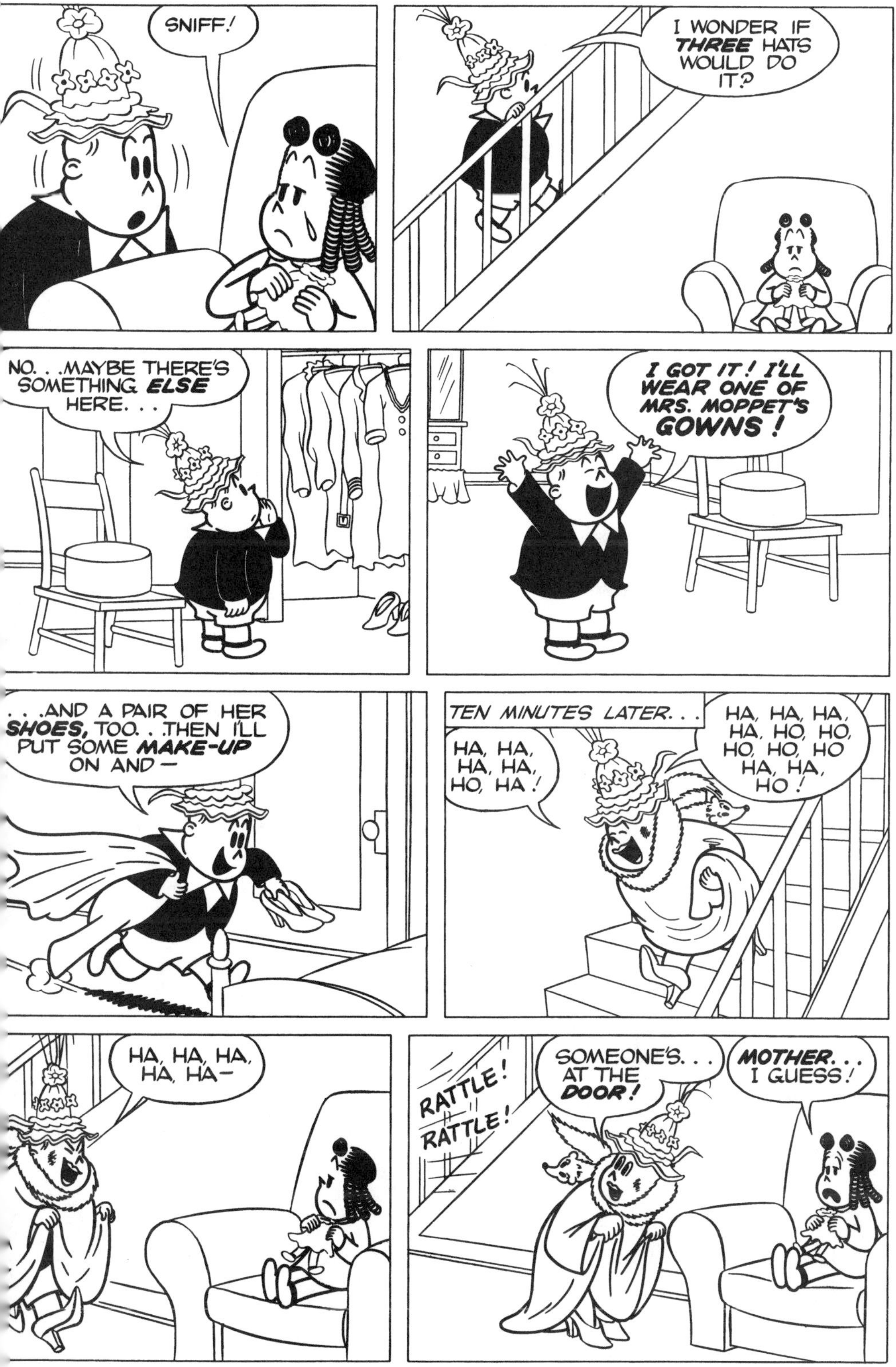
SNIFF!
I WONDER IF THREE HATS WOULD DO IT?
NO. . .MAYBE THERE'S SOMETHING ELSE HERE. . .
I GOT IT! I'LL WEAR ONE OF MRS. MOPPET'S GOWNS!
. . .AND A PAIR OF HER SHOES, TOO. . THEN I'LL PUT SOME MAKE-UP ON AND—
TEN MINUTES LATER. . .
HA, HA, HA, HA, HA, HO, HA!
HA, HA, HA, HA, HO, HO, HO, HO, HO HA, HA, HO!
HA, HA, HA, HA, HA—
RATTLE! RATTLE!
SOMEONE'S. . . AT THE DOOR!
MOTHER. . . I GUESS!

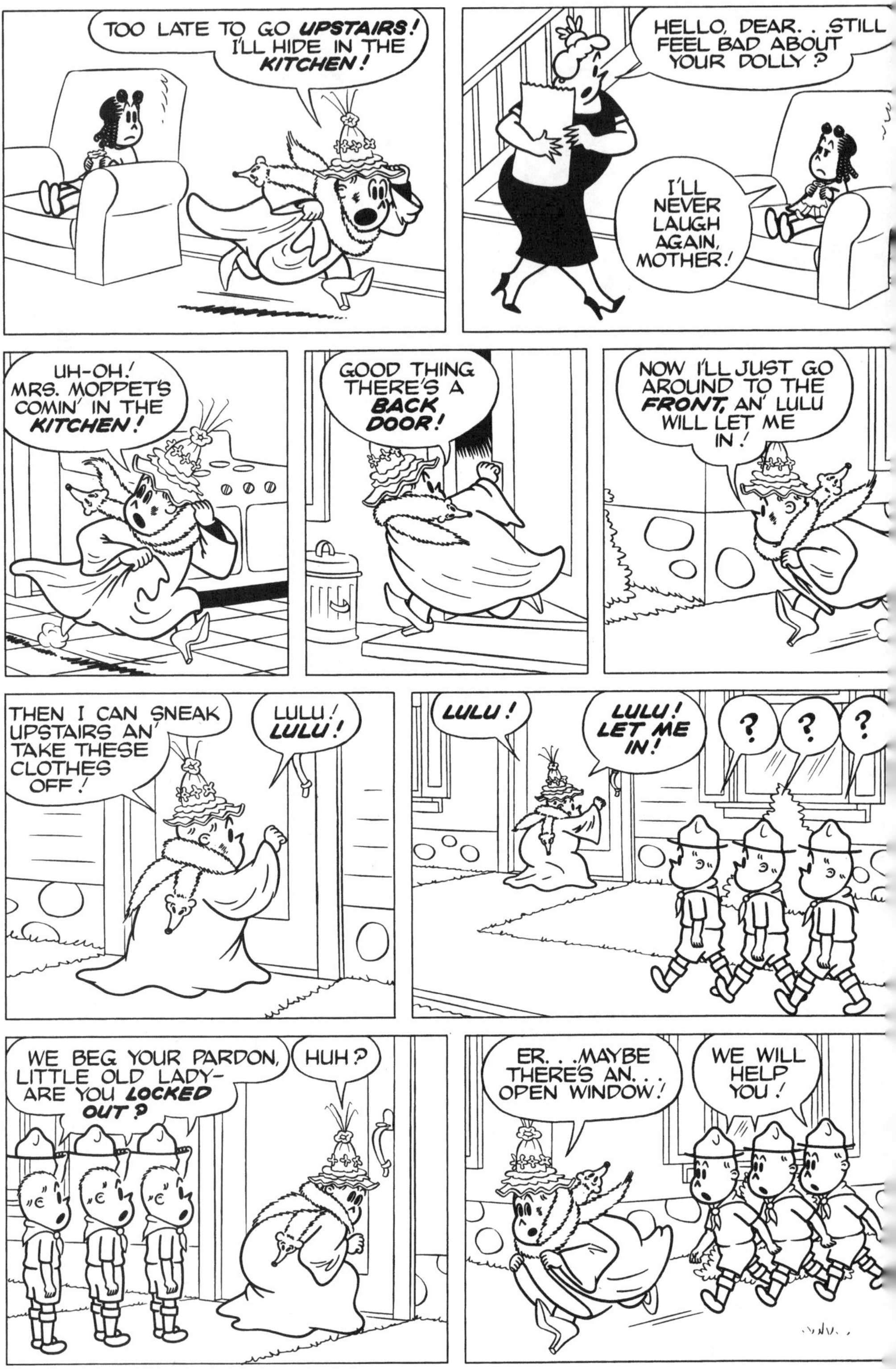
TOO LATE TO GO UPSTAIRS! I'LL HIDE IN THE KITCHEN!
HELLO, DEAR. . .STILL FEEL BAD ABOUT YOUR DOLLY?
I'LL NEVER LAUGH AGAIN, MOTHER!
UH-OH! MRS. MOPPET'S COMIN' IN THE KITCHEN!
GOOD THING THERE'S A BACK DOOR!
NOW I'LL JUST GO AROUND TO THE FRONT, AN' LULU WILL LET ME IN!
THEN I CAN SNEAK UPSTAIRS AN' TAKE THESE CLOTHES OFF!
LULU! LULU!
LULU!
LULU! LET ME IN!
?
?
?
WE BEG YOUR PARDON, LITTLE OLD LADY-ARE YOU LOCKED OUT?
HUH?
ER. . .MAYBE THERE'S AN. . . OPEN WINDOW!
WE WILL HELP YOU!

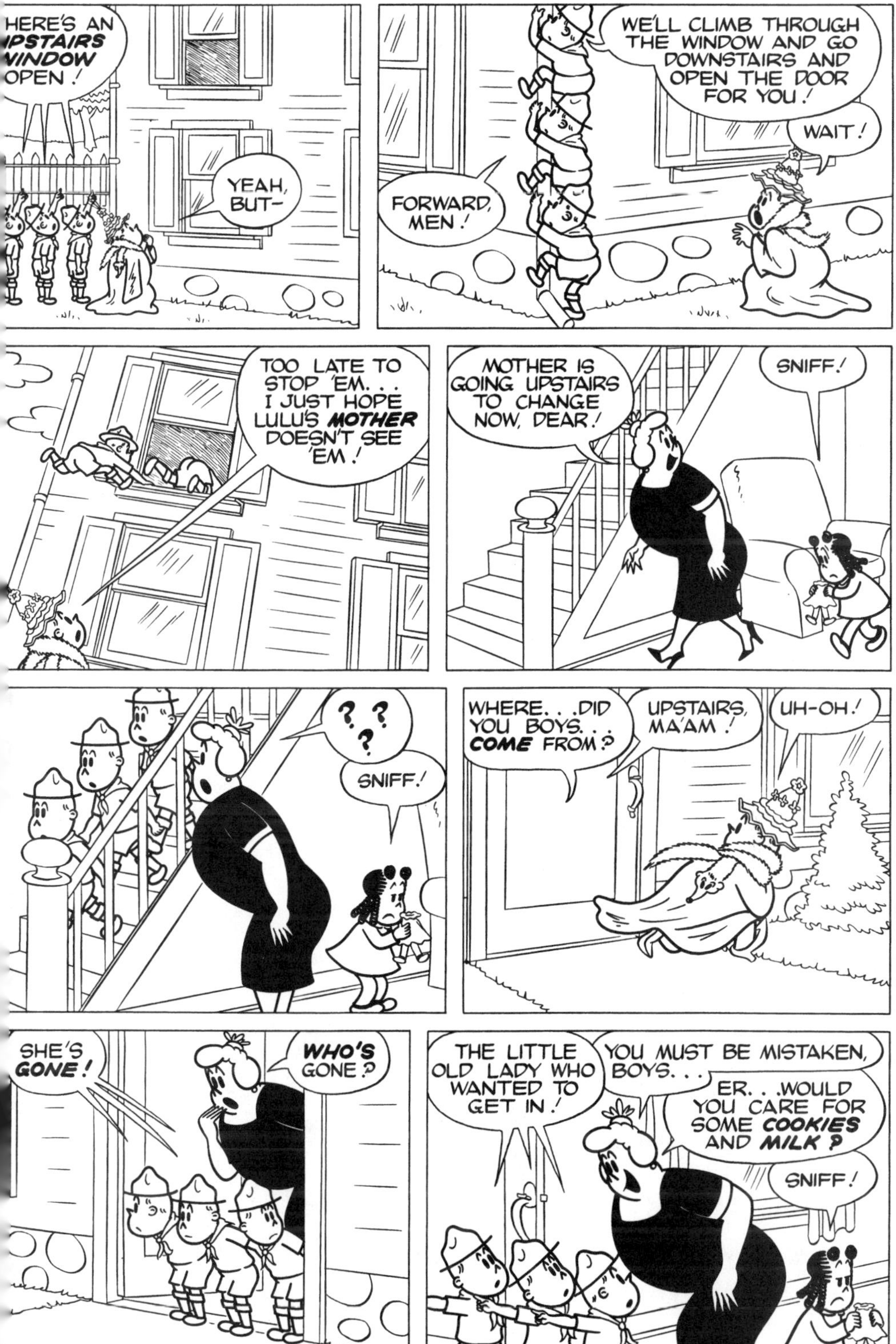
HERE'S AN UPSTAIRS WINDOW OPEN!
YEAH, BUT-
WE'LL CLIMB THROUGH THE WINDOW AND GO DOWNSTAIRS AND OPEN THE DOOR FOR YOU!
FORWARD, MEN!
WAIT!
TOO LATE TO STOP 'EM. . . I JUST HOPE LULU'S MOTHER DOESN'T SEE 'EM!
MOTHER IS GOING UPSTAIRS TO CHANGE NOW, DEAR!
SNIFF!
? ? ?
SNIFF!
WHERE. . .DID YOU BOYS. . . COME FROM?
UPSTAIRS, MA'AM!
UH-OH!
SHE'S GONE!
WHO'S GONE?
THE LITTLE OLD LADY WHO WANTED TO GET IN!
YOU MUST BE MISTAKEN, BOYS. . .
ER. . .WOULD YOU CARE FOR SOME COOKIES AND MILK?
SNIFF!

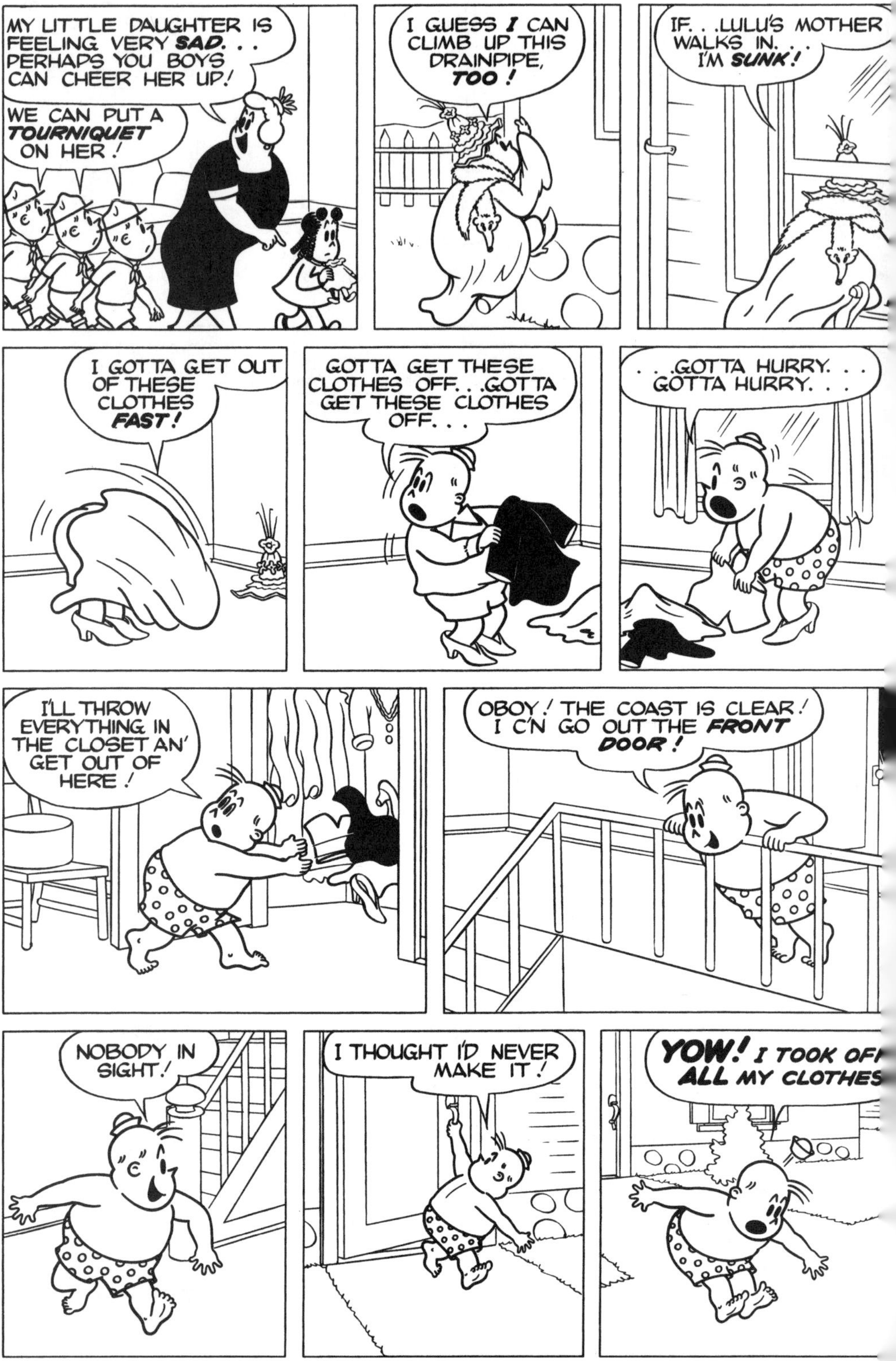
MY LITTLE DAUGHTER IS FEELING VERY SAD. . . PERHAPS YOU BOYS CAN CHEER HER UP!
WE CAN PUT A TOURNIQUET ON HER!
I GUESS I CAN CLIMB UP THIS DRAINPIPE, TOO!
IF. . .LULU'S MOTHER WALKS IN. . . I'M SUNK!
I GOTTA GET OUT OF THESE CLOTHES FAST!
GOTTA GET THESE CLOTHES OFF. . .GOTTA GET THESE CLOTHES OFF. . .
. . .GOTTA HURRY. . . GOTTA HURRY. . .
I'LL THROW EVERYTHING IN THE CLOSET AN' GET OUT OF HERE!
OBOY! THE COAST IS CLEAR! I C'N GO OUT THE FRONT DOOR!
NOBODY IN SIGHT!
I THOUGHT I'D NEVER MAKE IT!
YOW! I TOOK OFF ALL MY CLOTHES

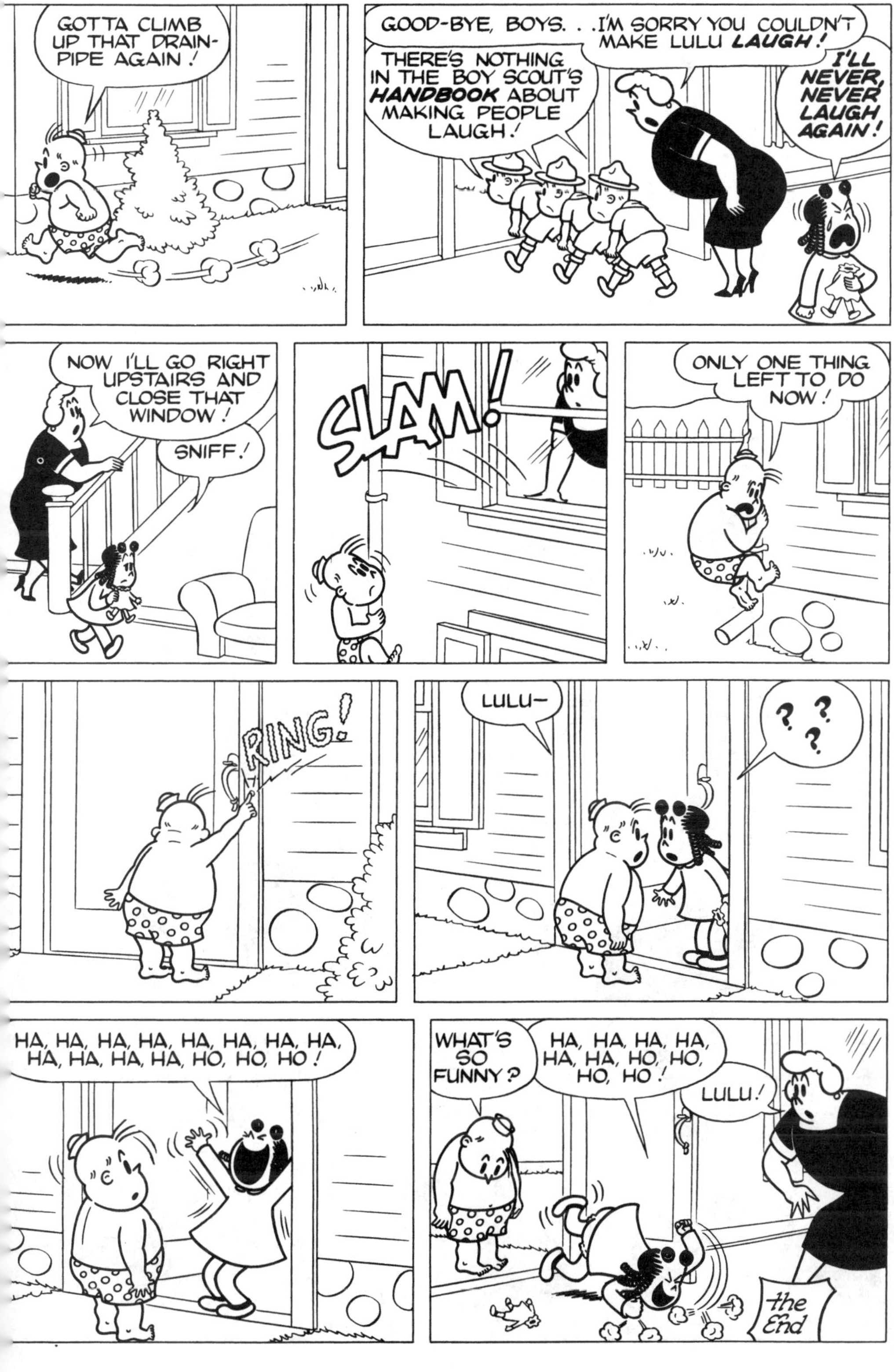

GOTTA CLIMB UP THAT DRAIN-PIPE AGAIN!
GOOD-BYE, BOYS. . .I'M SORRY YOU COULDN'T MAKE LULU LAUGH!
THERE'S NOTHING IN THE BOY SCOUT'S HANDBOOK ABOUT MAKING PEOPLE LAUGH!
I'LL NEVER, NEVER LAUGH AGAIN!
NOW I'LL GO RIGHT UPSTAIRS AND CLOSE THAT WINDOW!
SNIFF!
SLAM!
ONLY ONE THING LEFT TO DO NOW!
RING!
LULU—
? ? ?
HA, HA, HA, HA, HA, HA, HA, HA, HA, HA, HA, HA, HO, HO, HO!
WHAT'S SO FUNNY?
HA, HA, HA, HA, HA, HA, HO, HO, HO, HO!
LULU!
the End

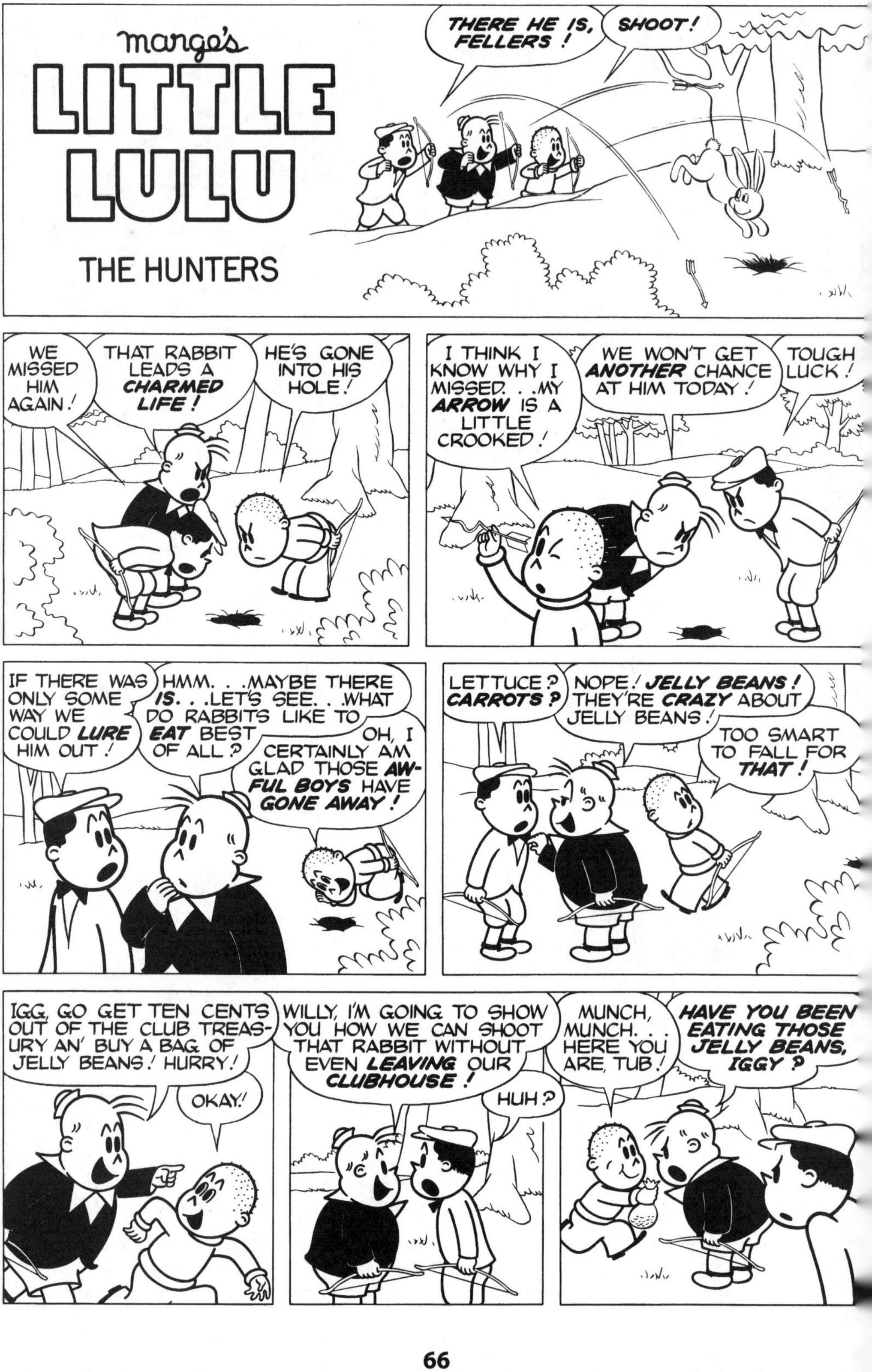
marge's
LITTLE LULU
THE HUNTERS
THERE HE IS, FELLERS!
SHOOT!
WE MISSED HIM AGAIN!
THAT RABBIT LEADS A CHARMED LIFE!
HE'S GONE INTO HIS HOLE!
I THINK I KNOW WHY I MISSED. . .MY ARROW IS A LITTLE CROOKED!
WE WON'T GET ANOTHER CHANCE AT HIM TODAY!
TOUGH LUCK!
IF THERE WAS ONLY SOME WAY WE COULD LURE HIM OUT!
HMM. . .MAYBE THERE IS. . .LET'S SEE. . .WHAT DO RABBITS LIKE TO EAT BEST OF ALL?
OH, I CERTAINLY AM GLAD THOSE AWFUL BOYS HAVE GONE AWAY!
LETTUCE? CARROTS?
NOPE! JELLY BEANS! THEY'RE CRAZY ABOUT JELLY BEANS!
TOO SMART TO FALL FOR THAT!
IGG, GO GET TEN CENTS OUT OF THE CLUB TREASURY AN' BUY A BAG OF JELLY BEANS! HURRY!
OKAY!
WILLY, I'M GOING TO SHOW YOU HOW WE CAN SHOOT THAT RABBIT WITHOUT EVEN LEAVING OUR CLUBHOUSE!
HUH?
MUNCH, MUNCH. . . HERE YOU ARE, TUB!
HAVE YOU BEEN EATING THOSE JELLY BEANS, IGGY?

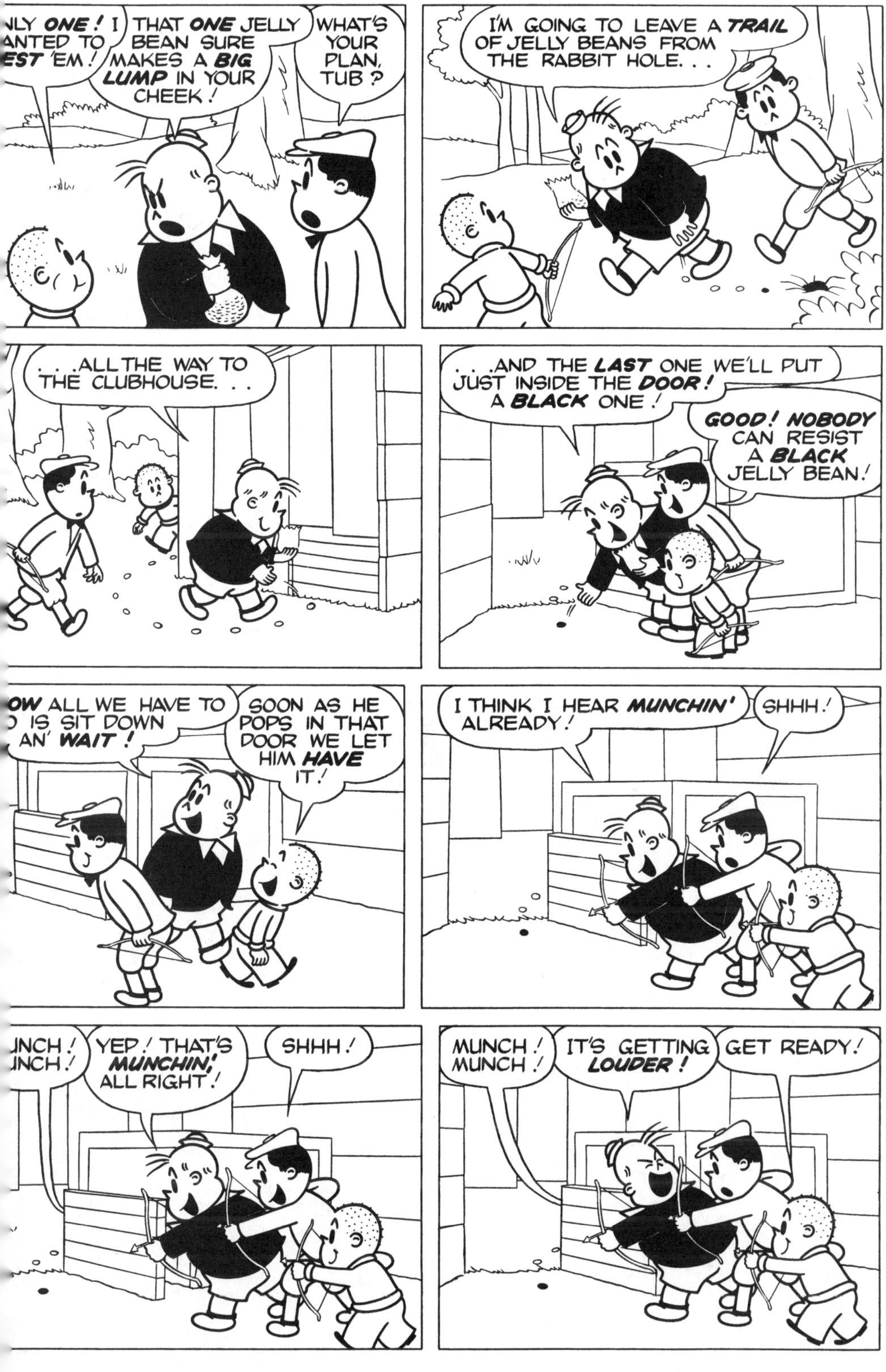
NLY ONE! I ANTED TO EST 'EM!
THAT ONE JELLY BEAN SURE MAKES A BIG LUMP IN YOUR CHEEK!
WHAT'S YOUR PLAN, TUB?
I'M GOING TO LEAVE A TRAIL OF JELLY BEANS FROM THE RABBIT HOLE. . .
. . .ALL THE WAY TO THE CLUBHOUSE. . .
. . .AND THE LAST ONE WE'LL PUT JUST INSIDE THE DOOR! A BLACK ONE!
GOOD! NOBODY CAN RESIST A BLACK JELLY BEAN!
OW ALL WE HAVE TO) IS SIT DOWN AN' WAIT!
SOON AS HE POPS IN THAT DOOR WE LET HIM HAVE IT!
I THINK I HEAR MUNCHIN' ALREADY!
SHHH!
UNCH! UNCH!
YEP! THAT'S MUNCHIN' ALL RIGHT!
SHHH!
MUNCH! MUNCH!
IT'S GETTING LOUDER!
GET READY!

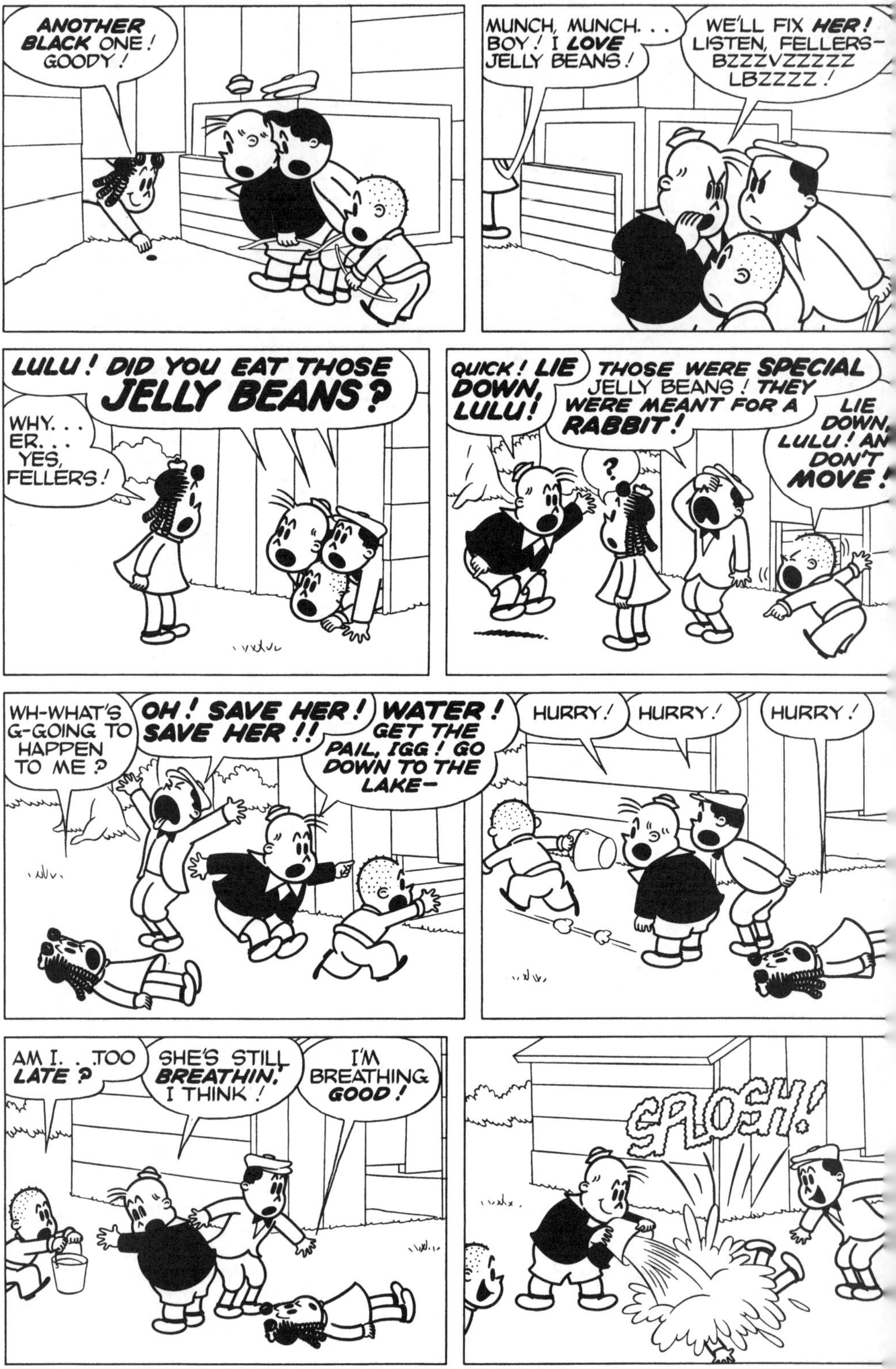
ANOTHER BLACK ONE! GOODY!
MUNCH, MUNCH... BOY! I LOVE JELLY BEANS!
WE'LL FIX HER! LISTEN, FELLERS- BZZZVZZZZZ LBZZZZ!
LULU! DID YOU EAT THOSE JELLY BEANS?
WHY... ER... YES, FELLERS!
QUICK! LIE DOWN, LULU!
THOSE WERE SPECIAL JELLY BEANS! THEY WERE MEANT FOR A RABBIT!
?
WH-WHAT'S G-GOING TO HAPPEN TO ME?
OH! SAVE HER! SAVE HER!!
WATER! GET THE PAIL, IGG! GO DOWN TO THE LAKE-
HURRY!
HURRY!
HURRY!
AM I...TOO LATE?
SHE'S STILL BREATHIN', I THINK!
I'M BREATHING GOOD!
SPLOSH!

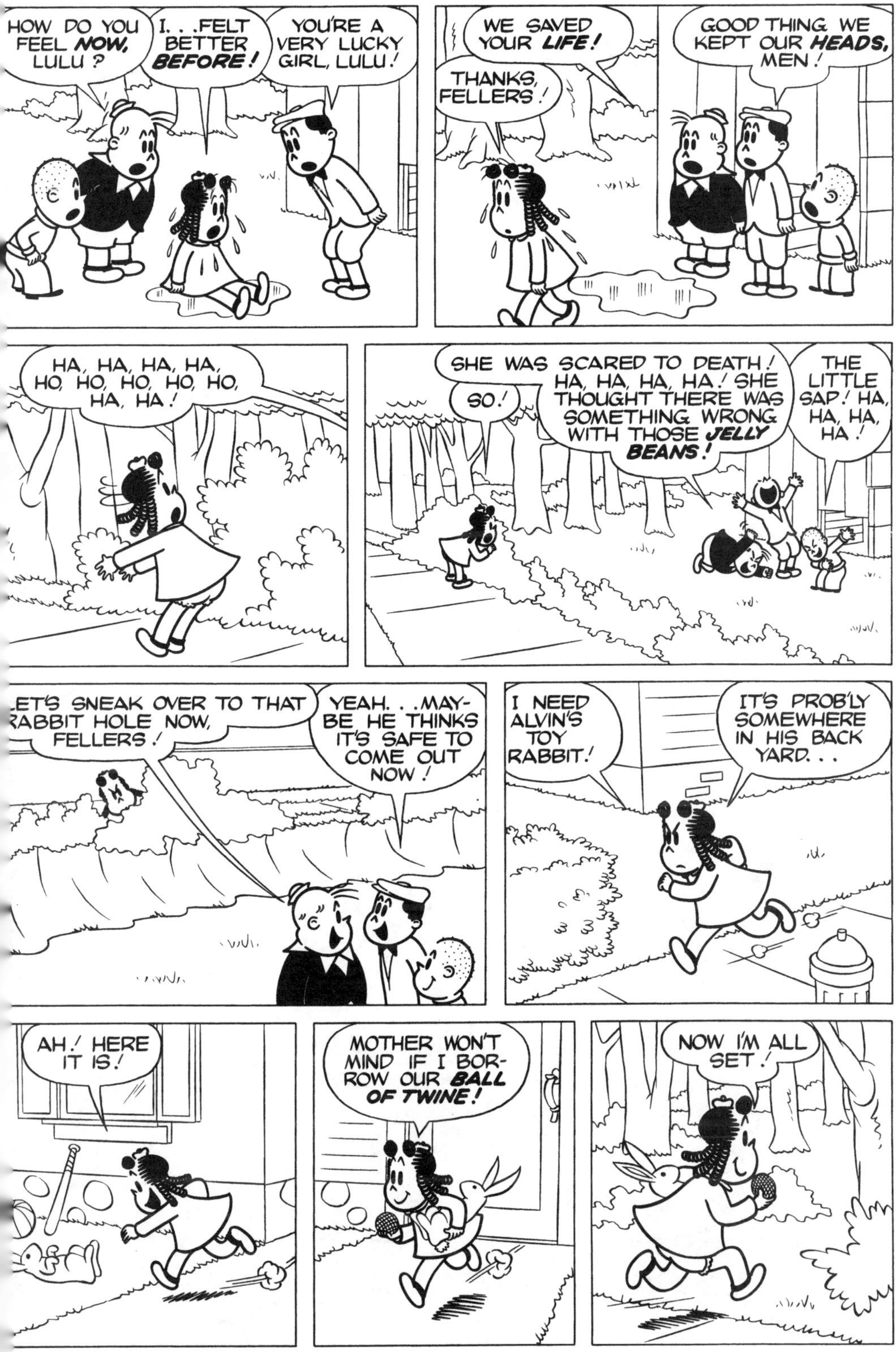
HOW DO YOU FEEL *NOW,* LULU ?
I. . .FELT BETTER *BEFORE!*
YOU'RE A VERY LUCKY GIRL, LULU!
WE SAVED YOUR *LIFE!*
THANKS, FELLERS!
GOOD THING WE KEPT OUR *HEADS,* MEN!
HA, HA, HA, HA, HO, HO, HO, HO, HO, HA, HA!
SHE WAS SCARED TO DEATH! HA, HA, HA, HA! SHE THOUGHT THERE WAS SOMETHING WRONG WITH THOSE *JELLY BEANS!*
SO!
THE LITTLE SAP! HA, HA, HA, HA!
LET'S SNEAK OVER TO THAT RABBIT HOLE NOW, FELLERS!
YEAH. . .MAY-BE HE THINKS IT'S SAFE TO COME OUT NOW!
I NEED ALVIN'S TOY RABBIT!
IT'S PROB'LY SOMEWHERE IN HIS BACK YARD. . .
AH! HERE IT IS!
MOTHER WON'T MIND IF I BOR-ROW OUR *BALL OF TWINE!*
NOW I'M ALL SET!

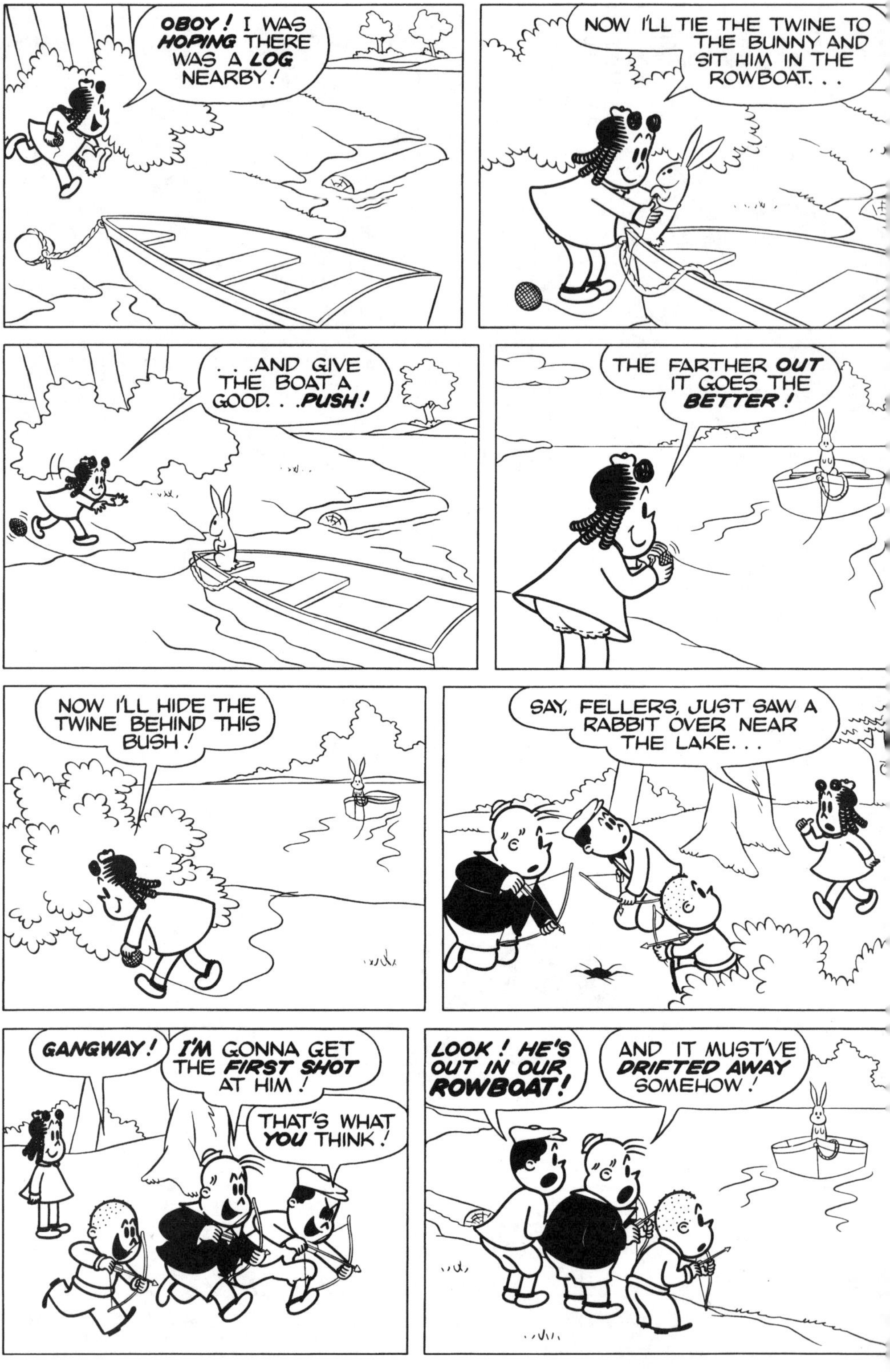

OBOY! I WAS HOPING THERE WAS A LOG NEARBY!
NOW I'LL TIE THE TWINE TO THE BUNNY AND SIT HIM IN THE ROWBOAT. . .
. . .AND GIVE THE BOAT A GOOD. . .PUSH!
THE FARTHER OUT IT GOES THE BETTER!
NOW I'LL HIDE THE TWINE BEHIND THIS BUSH!
SAY, FELLERS, JUST SAW A RABBIT OVER NEAR THE LAKE. . .
GANGWAY!
I'M GONNA GET THE FIRST SHOT AT HIM!
THAT'S WHAT YOU THINK!
LOOK! HE'S OUT IN OUR ROWBOAT!
AND IT MUST'VE DRIFTED AWAY SOMEHOW!

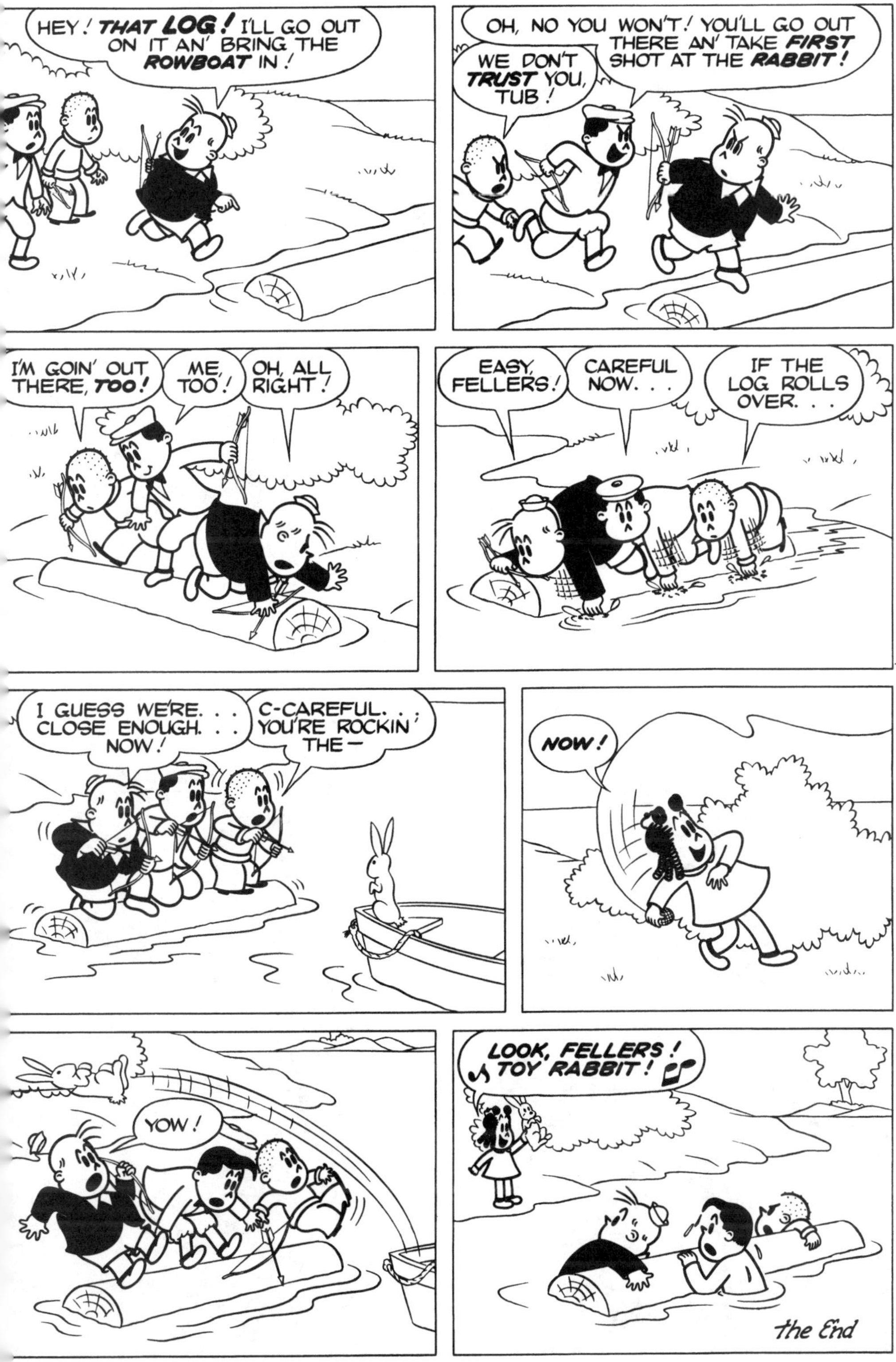
HEY! THAT LOG! I'LL GO OUT ON IT AN' BRING THE ROWBOAT IN!
OH, NO YOU WON'T! YOU'LL GO OUT THERE AN' TAKE FIRST SHOT AT THE RABBIT!
WE DON'T TRUST YOU, TUB!
I'M GOIN' OUT THERE, TOO!
ME, TOO!
OH, ALL RIGHT!
EASY, FELLERS!
CAREFUL NOW. . .
IF THE LOG ROLLS OVER. . .
I GUESS WE'RE. . . CLOSE ENOUGH. . . NOW!
C-CAREFUL. . . YOU'RE ROCKIN' THE—
NOW!
YOW!
LOOK, FELLERS! TOY RABBIT!
the End

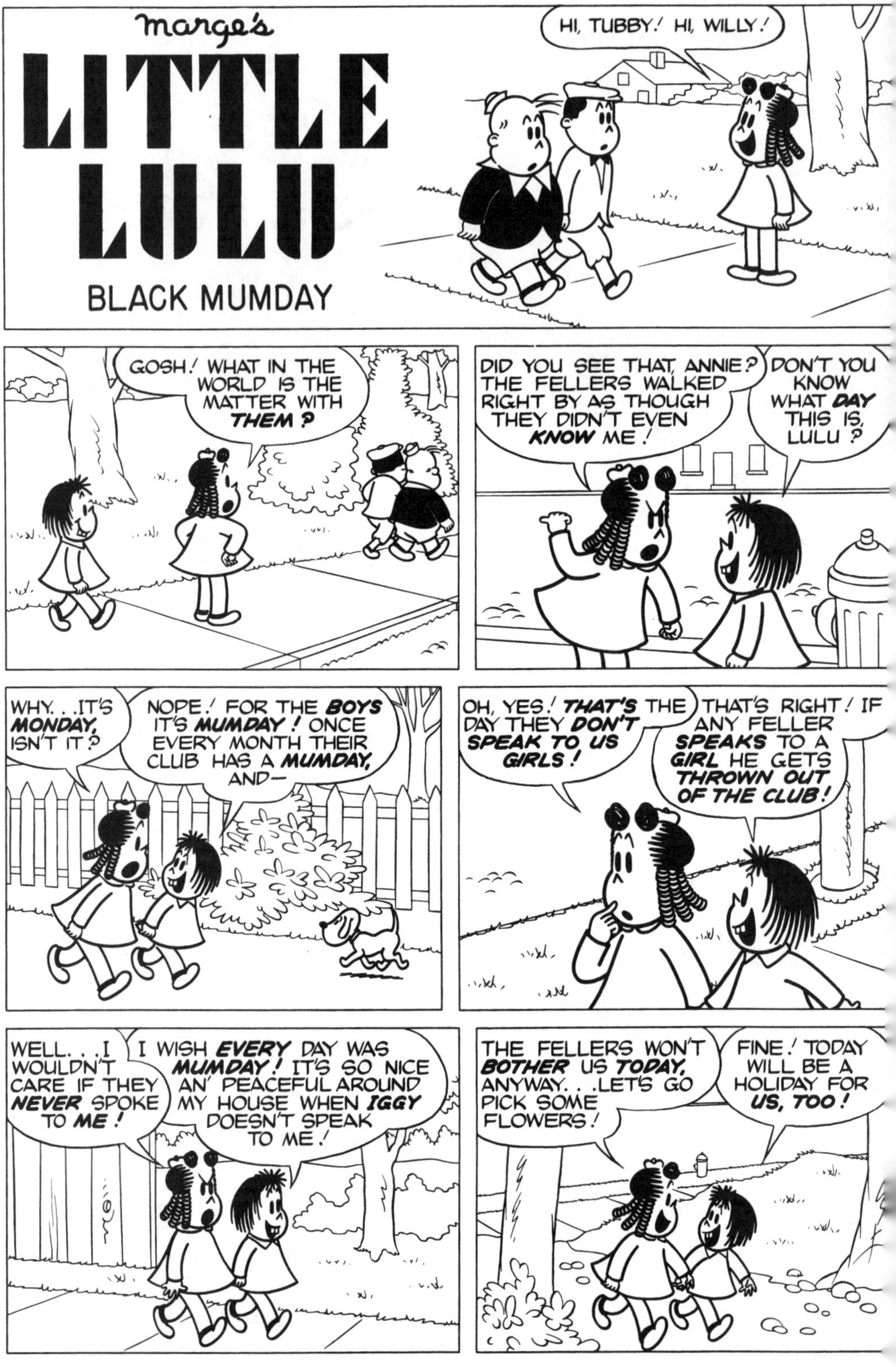

marge's
LITTLE LULU
BLACK MUMDAY
HI, TUBBY! HI, WILLY!
GOSH! WHAT IN THE WORLD IS THE MATTER WITH THEM?
DID YOU SEE THAT, ANNIE? THE FELLERS WALKED RIGHT BY AS THOUGH THEY DIDN'T EVEN KNOW ME!
DON'T YOU KNOW WHAT DAY THIS IS, LULU?
WHY. . .IT'S MONDAY, ISN'T IT?
NOPE! FOR THE BOYS IT'S MUMDAY! ONCE EVERY MONTH THEIR CLUB HAS A MUMDAY, AND—
OH, YES! THAT'S THE DAY THEY DON'T SPEAK TO US GIRLS!
THAT'S RIGHT! IF ANY FELLER SPEAKS TO A GIRL HE GETS THROWN OUT OF THE CLUB!
WELL. . .I WOULDN'T CARE IF THEY NEVER SPOKE TO ME!
I WISH EVERY DAY WAS MUMDAY! IT'S SO NICE AN' PEACEFUL AROUND MY HOUSE WHEN IGGY DOESN'T SPEAK TO ME!
THE FELLERS WON'T BOTHER US TODAY, ANYWAY. . .LET'S GO PICK SOME FLOWERS!
FINE! TODAY WILL BE A HOLIDAY FOR US, TOO!

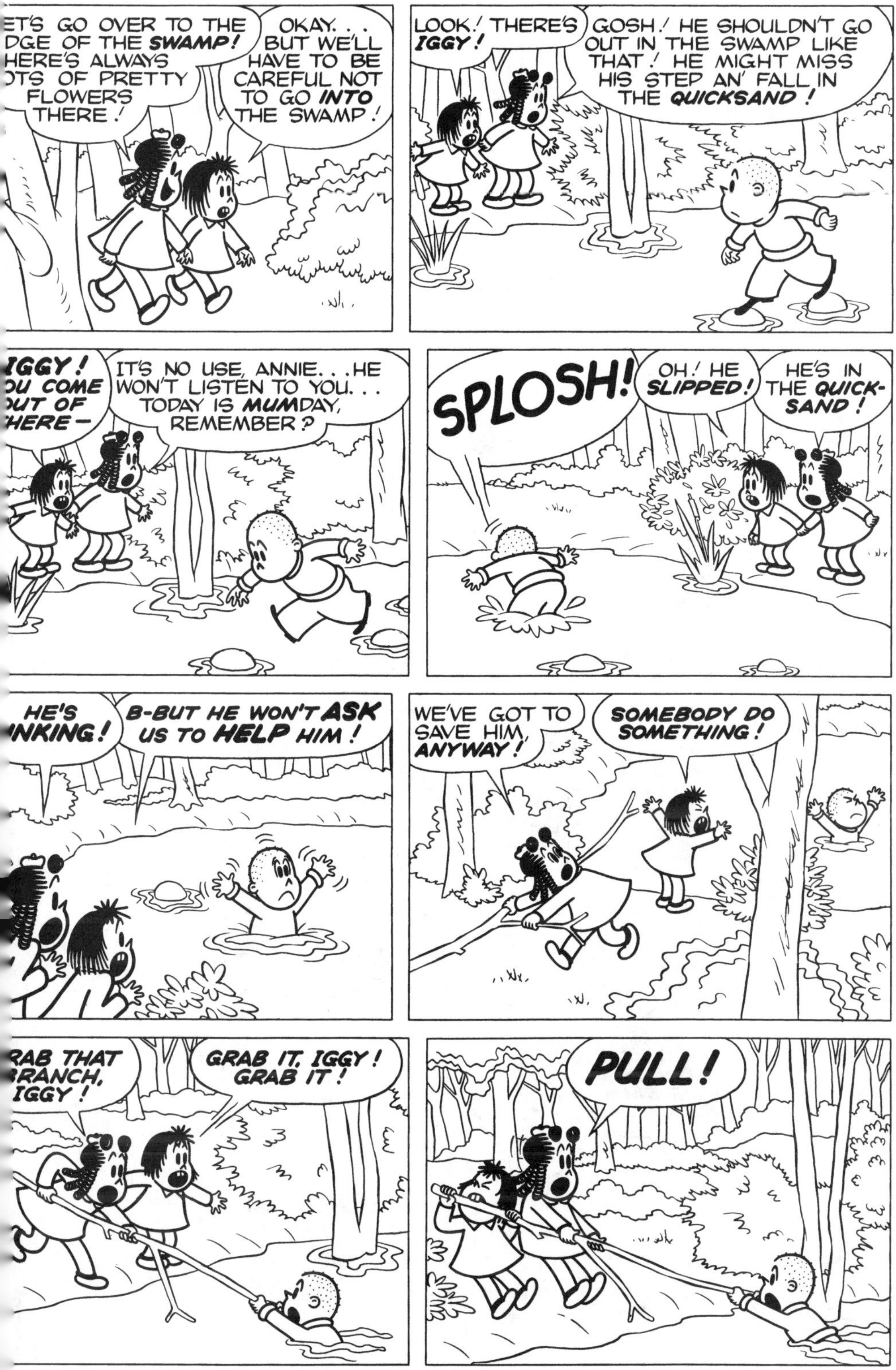
ET'S GO OVER TO THE DGE OF THE SWAMP! HERE'S ALWAYS OTS OF PRETTY FLOWERS THERE!
OKAY. . . BUT WE'LL HAVE TO BE CAREFUL NOT TO GO INTO THE SWAMP!
LOOK! THERE'S IGGY!
GOSH! HE SHOULDN'T GO OUT IN THE SWAMP LIKE THAT! HE MIGHT MISS HIS STEP AN' FALL IN THE QUICKSAND!
IGGY! OU COME UT OF HERE—
IT'S NO USE, ANNIE. . . HE WON'T LISTEN TO YOU. . . TODAY IS MUMDAY, REMEMBER?
SPLOSH!
OH! HE SLIPPED!
HE'S IN THE QUICK-SAND!
HE'S NKING!
B-BUT HE WON'T ASK US TO HELP HIM!
WE'VE GOT TO SAVE HIM, ANYWAY!
SOMEBODY DO SOMETHING!
RAB THAT RANCH, IGGY!
GRAB IT, IGGY! GRAB IT!
PULL!

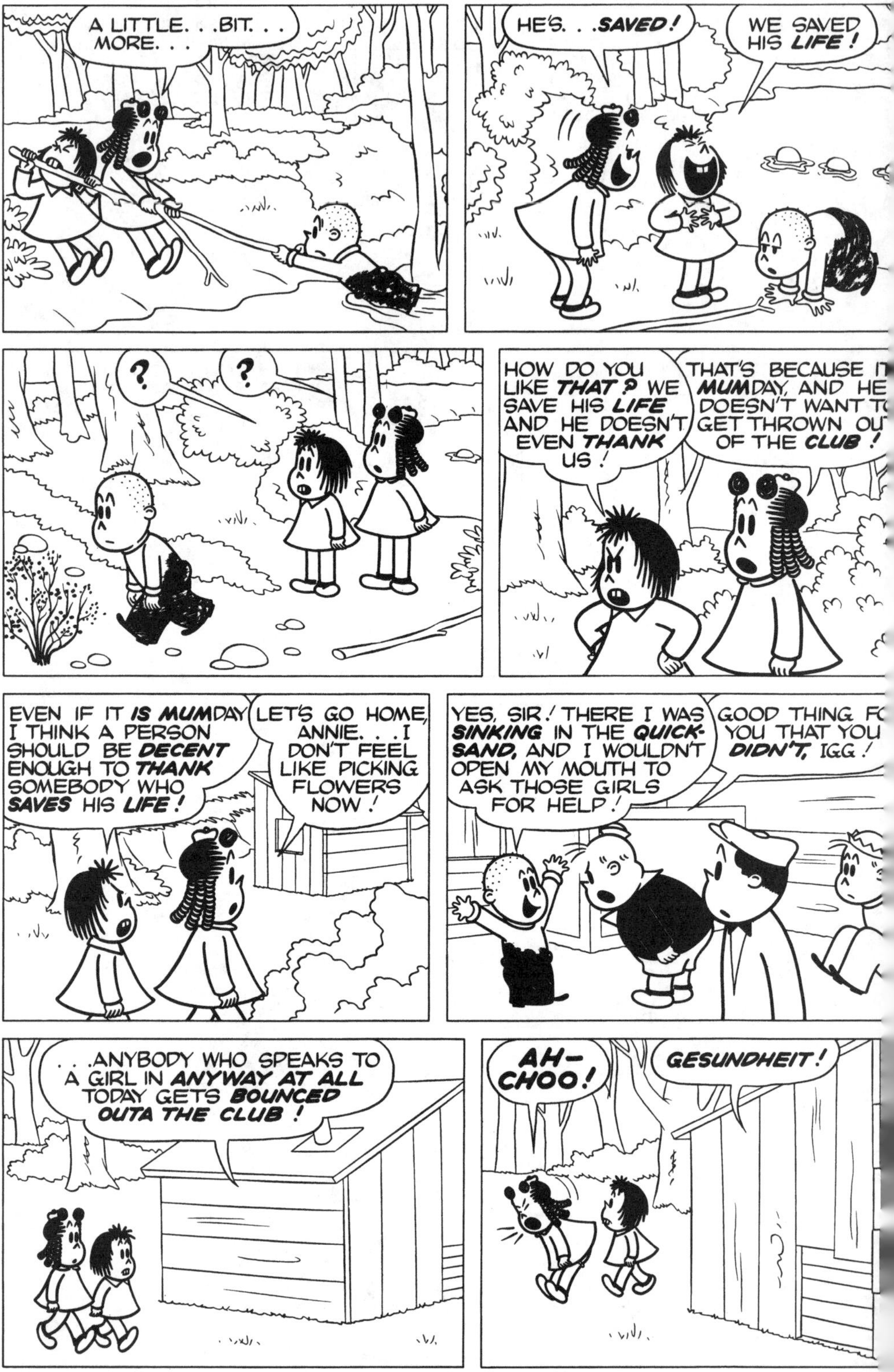

A LITTLE. . .BIT. . . MORE. . .
HE'S. . .SAVED!
WE SAVED HIS LIFE!
?
?
HOW DO YOU LIKE THAT? WE SAVE HIS LIFE AND HE DOESN'T EVEN THANK US!
THAT'S BECAUSE IT MUMDAY, AND HE DOESN'T WANT T GET THROWN OU OF THE CLUB!
EVEN IF IT IS MUMDAY I THINK A PERSON SHOULD BE DECENT ENOUGH TO THANK SOMEBODY WHO SAVES HIS LIFE!
LET'S GO HOME, ANNIE. . .I DON'T FEEL LIKE PICKING FLOWERS NOW!
YES, SIR! THERE I WAS SINKING IN THE QUICK-SAND, AND I WOULDN'T OPEN MY MOUTH TO ASK THOSE GIRLS FOR HELP!
GOOD THING F YOU THAT YOU DIDN'T, IGG!
. . .ANYBODY WHO SPEAKS TO A GIRL IN ANYWAY AT ALL TODAY GETS BOUNCED OUTA THE CLUB!
AH-CHOO!
GESUNDHEIT!

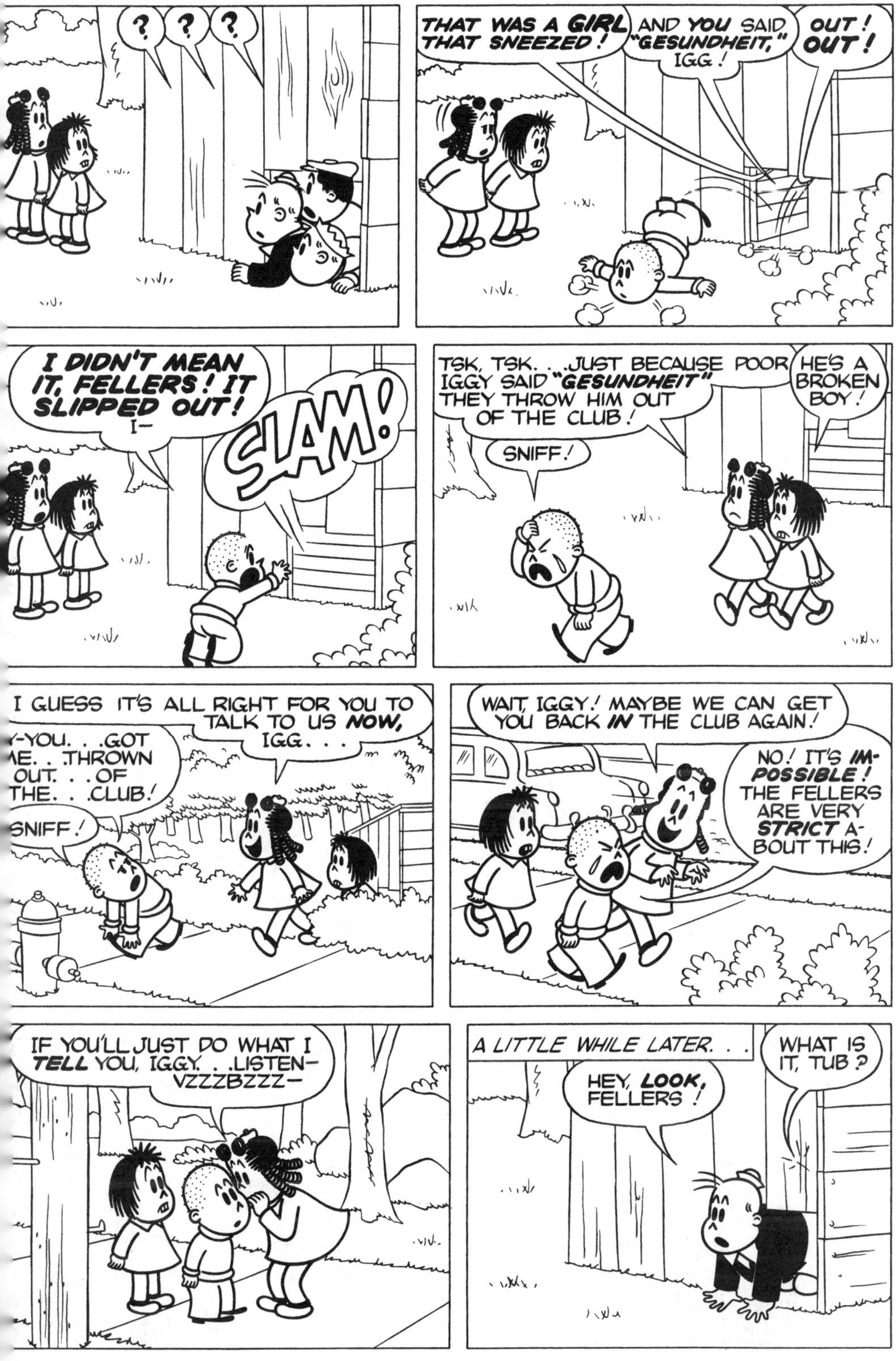
?
?
?
THAT WAS A GIRL THAT SNEEZED!
AND YOU SAID "GESUNDHEIT," IGG!
OUT! OUT!
I DIDN'T MEAN IT, FELLERS! IT SLIPPED OUT! I—
SLAM!
TSK, TSK. . .JUST BECAUSE POOR IGGY SAID "GESUNDHEIT" THEY THROW HIM OUT OF THE CLUB!
HE'S A BROKEN BOY!
SNIFF!
I GUESS IT'S ALL RIGHT FOR YOU TO TALK TO US NOW, IGG. . .
-YOU. . .GOT ME. . .THROWN OUT. . .OF THE. . .CLUB!
SNIFF!
WAIT, IGGY! MAYBE WE CAN GET YOU BACK IN THE CLUB AGAIN!
NO! IT'S IMPOSSIBLE! THE FELLERS ARE VERY STRICT ABOUT THIS!
IF YOU'LL JUST DO WHAT I TELL YOU, IGGY. . .LISTEN— VZZZBZZZ—
A LITTLE WHILE LATER. . .
HEY, LOOK, FELLERS!
WHAT IS IT, TUB?

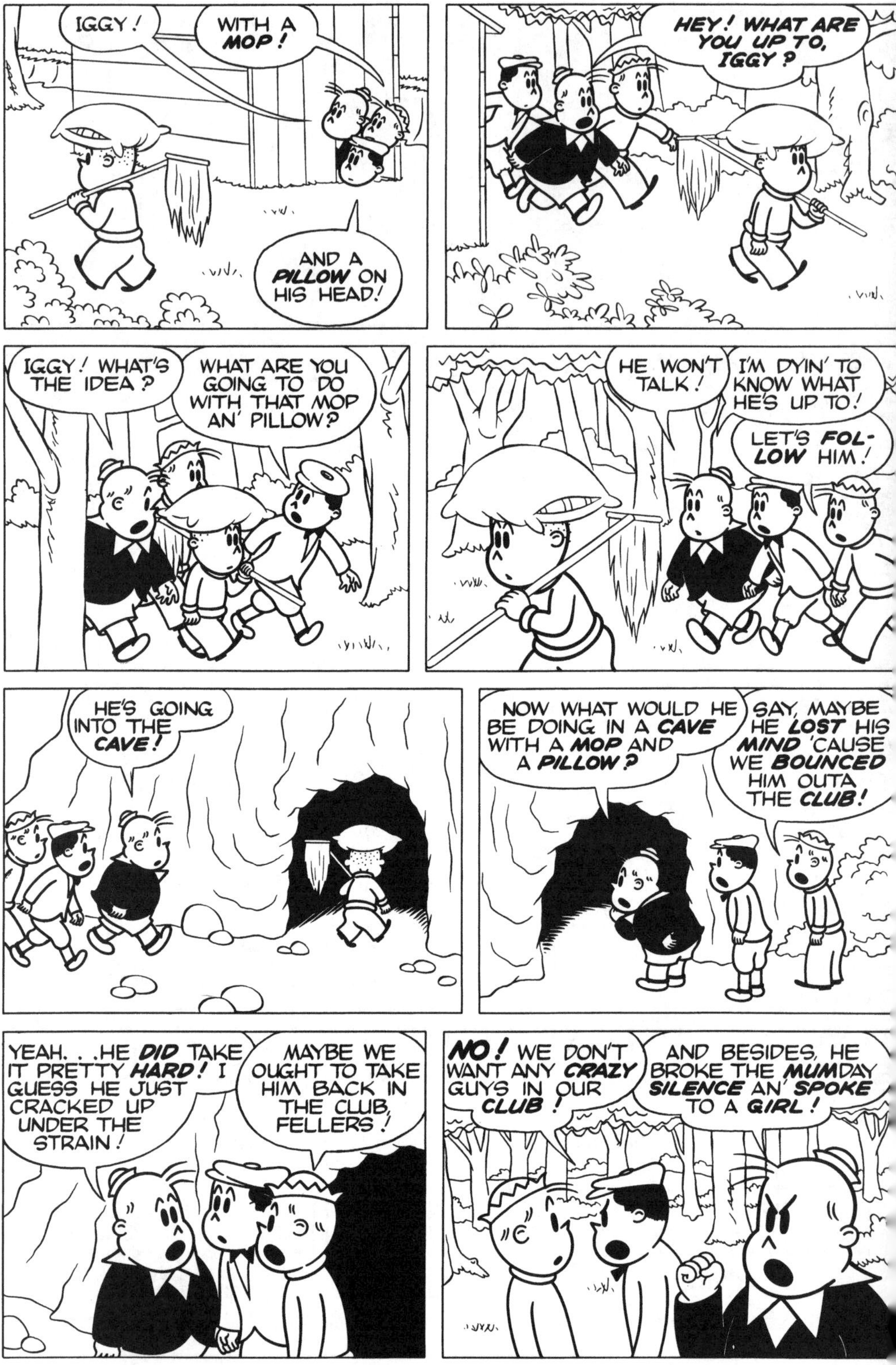
IGGY!
WITH A MOP!
AND A PILLOW ON HIS HEAD!
HEY! WHAT ARE YOU UP TO, IGGY?
IGGY! WHAT'S THE IDEA?
WHAT ARE YOU GOING TO DO WITH THAT MOP AN' PILLOW?
HE WON'T TALK!
I'M DYIN' TO KNOW WHAT HE'S UP TO!
LET'S FOL-LOW HIM!
HE'S GOING INTO THE CAVE!
NOW WHAT WOULD HE BE DOING IN A CAVE WITH A MOP AND A PILLOW?
SAY, MAYBE HE LOST HIS MIND 'CAUSE WE BOUNCED HIM OUTA THE CLUB!
YEAH. . .HE DID TAKE IT PRETTY HARD! I GUESS HE JUST CRACKED UP UNDER THE STRAIN!
MAYBE WE OUGHT TO TAKE HIM BACK IN THE CLUB, FELLERS!
NO! WE DON'T WANT ANY CRAZY GUYS IN OUR CLUB!
AND BESIDES, HE BROKE THE MUMDAY SILENCE AN' SPOKE TO A GIRL!

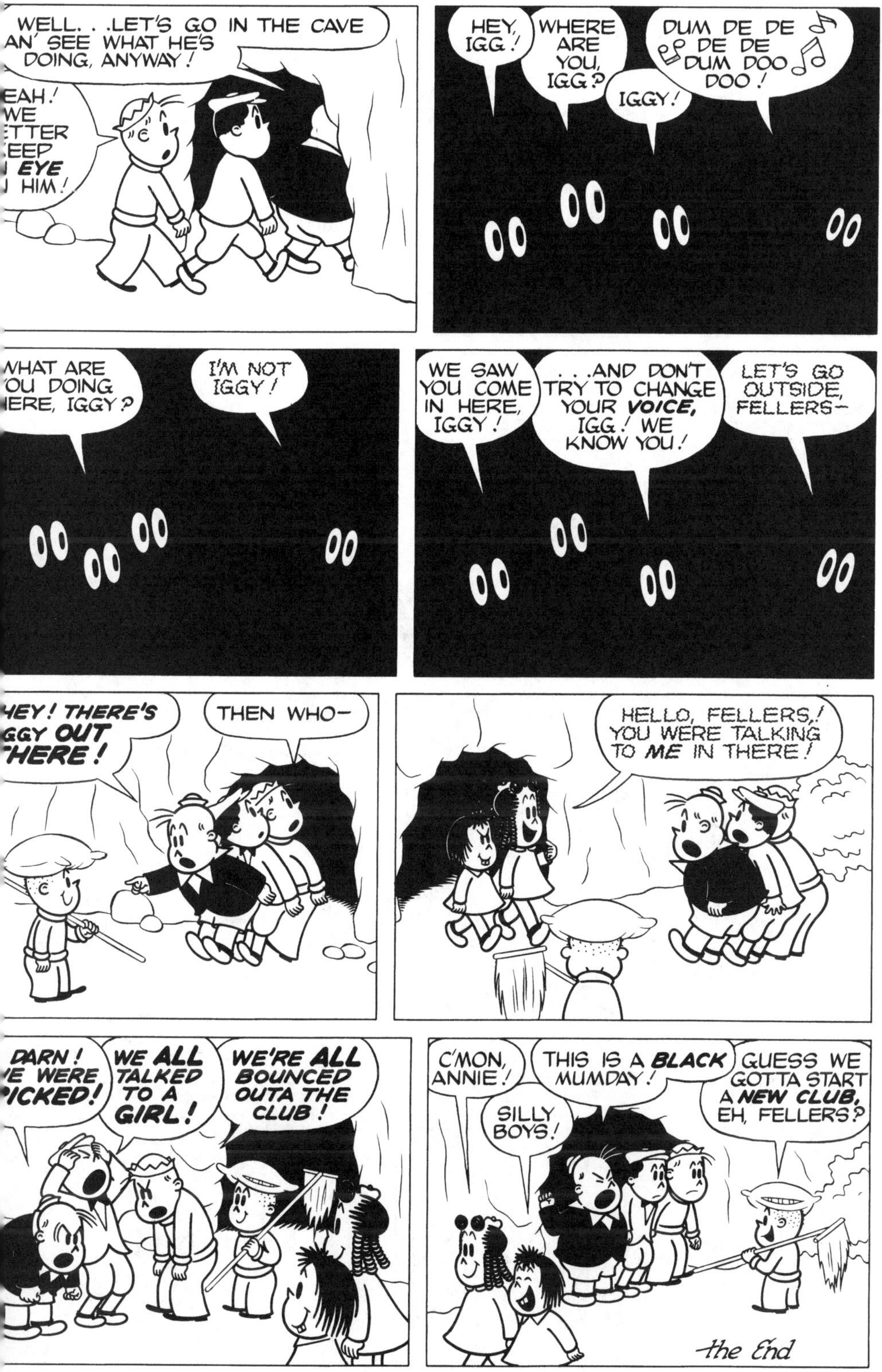

WELL. . .LET'S GO IN THE CAVE AN' SEE WHAT HE'S DOING, ANYWAY!
EAH! WE ETTER EEP EYE HIM!
HEY, IGG!
WHERE ARE YOU, IGG?
IGGY!
DUM DE DE DE DE DUM DOO DOO!
WHAT ARE OU DOING IERE, IGGY?
I'M NOT IGGY!
WE SAW YOU COME IN HERE, IGGY!
. . .AND DON'T TRY TO CHANGE YOUR VOICE, IGG! WE KNOW YOU!
LET'S GO OUTSIDE, FELLERS—
HEY! THERE'S GGY OUT THERE!
THEN WHO—
HELLO, FELLERS! YOU WERE TALKING TO ME IN THERE!
DARN! E WERE ICKED!
WE ALL TALKED TO A GIRL!
WE'RE ALL BOUNCED OUTA THE CLUB!
C'MON, ANNIE!
SILLY BOYS!
THIS IS A BLACK MUMDAY!
GUESS WE GOTTA START A NEW CLUB, EH, FELLERS?
the End

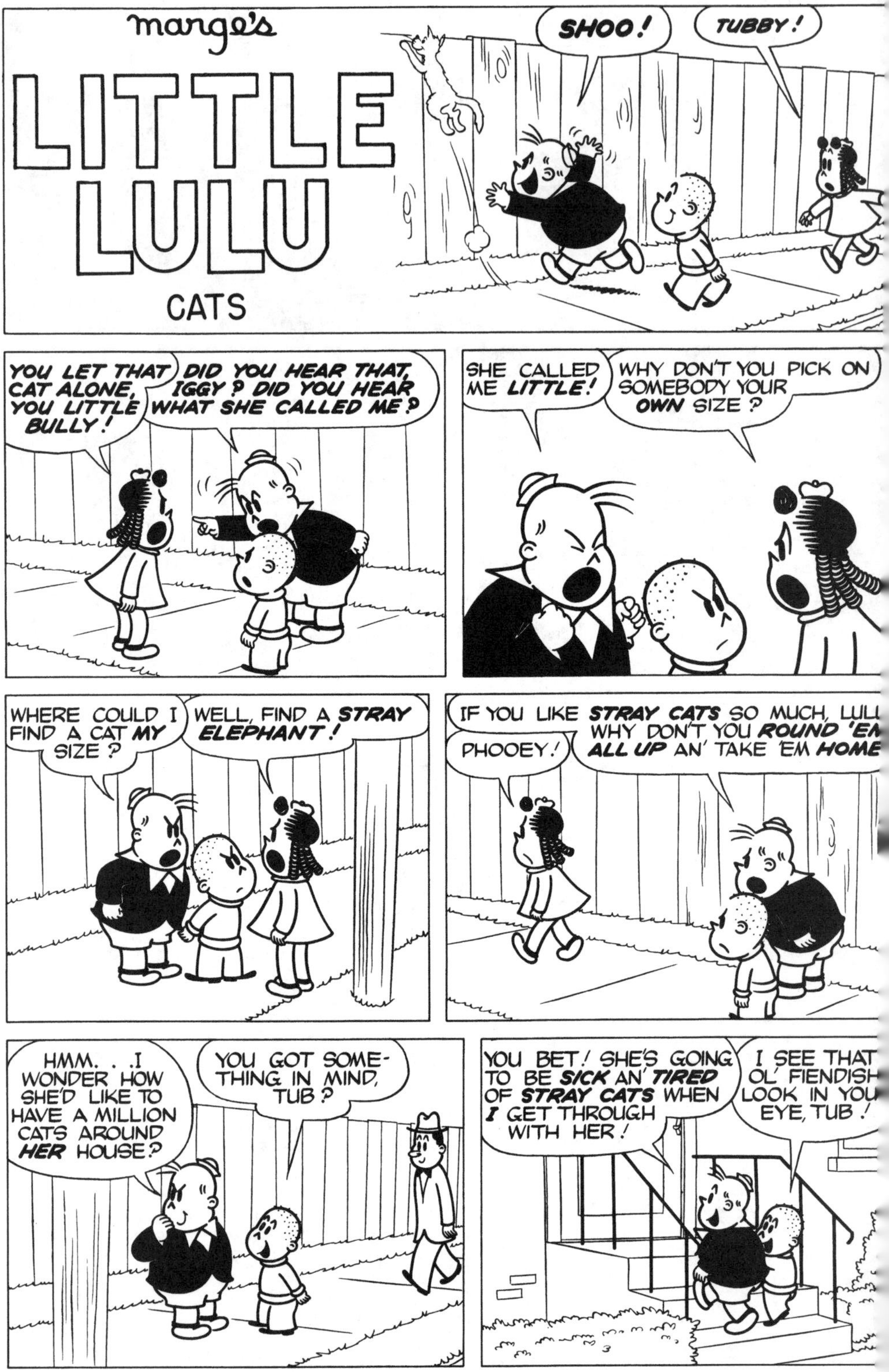
marge's
LITTLE LULU
CATS
SHOO!
TUBBY!
YOU LET THAT CAT ALONE, YOU LITTLE BULLY!
DID YOU HEAR THAT, IGGY? DID YOU HEAR WHAT SHE CALLED ME?
SHE CALLED ME LITTLE!
WHY DON'T YOU PICK ON SOMEBODY YOUR OWN SIZE?
WHERE COULD I FIND A CAT MY SIZE?
WELL, FIND A STRAY ELEPHANT!
IF YOU LIKE STRAY CATS SO MUCH, LULU WHY DON'T YOU ROUND 'EM ALL UP AN' TAKE 'EM HOME
PHOOEY!
HMM. . .I WONDER HOW SHE'D LIKE TO HAVE A MILLION CATS AROUND HER HOUSE?
YOU GOT SOME-THING IN MIND, TUB?
YOU BET! SHE'S GOING TO BE SICK AN' TIRED OF STRAY CATS WHEN I GET THROUGH WITH HER!
I SEE THAT OL' FIENDISH LOOK IN YOU EYE, TUB!

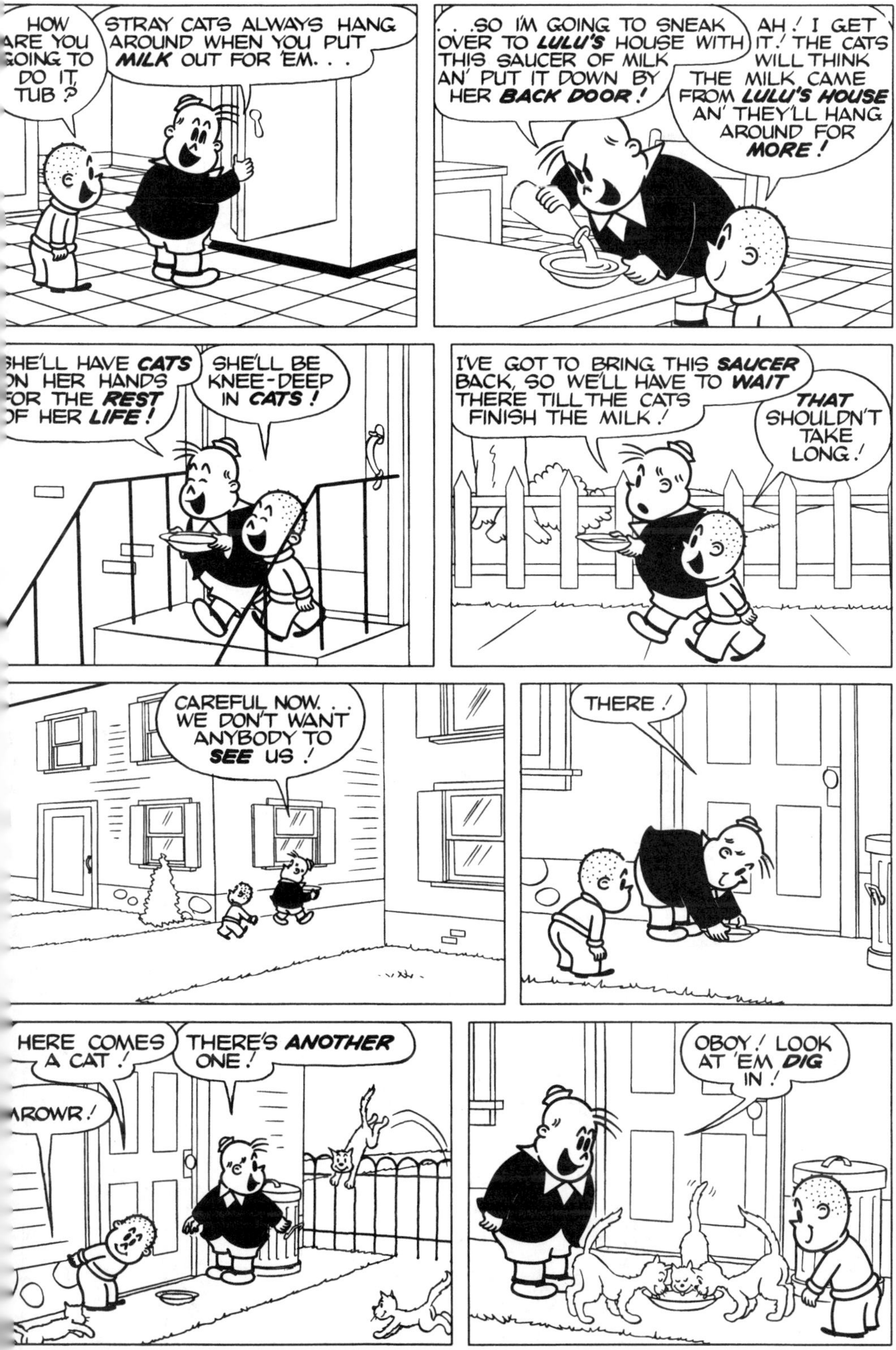
HOW ARE YOU GOING TO DO IT, TUB ?
STRAY CATS ALWAYS HANG AROUND WHEN YOU PUT **MILK** OUT FOR 'EM. . .
. . .SO I'M GOING TO SNEAK OVER TO **LULU'S** HOUSE WITH THIS SAUCER OF MILK AN' PUT IT DOWN BY HER **BACK DOOR** !
AH ! I GET IT ! THE CATS WILL THINK THE MILK CAME FROM **LULU'S HOUSE** AN' THEY'LL HANG AROUND FOR **MORE** !
SHE'LL HAVE **CATS** ON HER HANDS FOR THE **REST** OF HER **LIFE** !
SHE'LL BE KNEE-DEEP IN **CATS** !
I'VE GOT TO BRING THIS **SAUCER** BACK, SO WE'LL HAVE TO **WAIT** THERE TILL THE CATS FINISH THE MILK !
THAT SHOULDN'T TAKE LONG !
CAREFUL NOW. . . WE DON'T WANT ANYBODY TO **SEE** US !
THERE !
HERE COMES A CAT !
THERE'S **ANOTHER** ONE !
ROWR !
OBOY ! LOOK AT 'EM **DIG** IN !

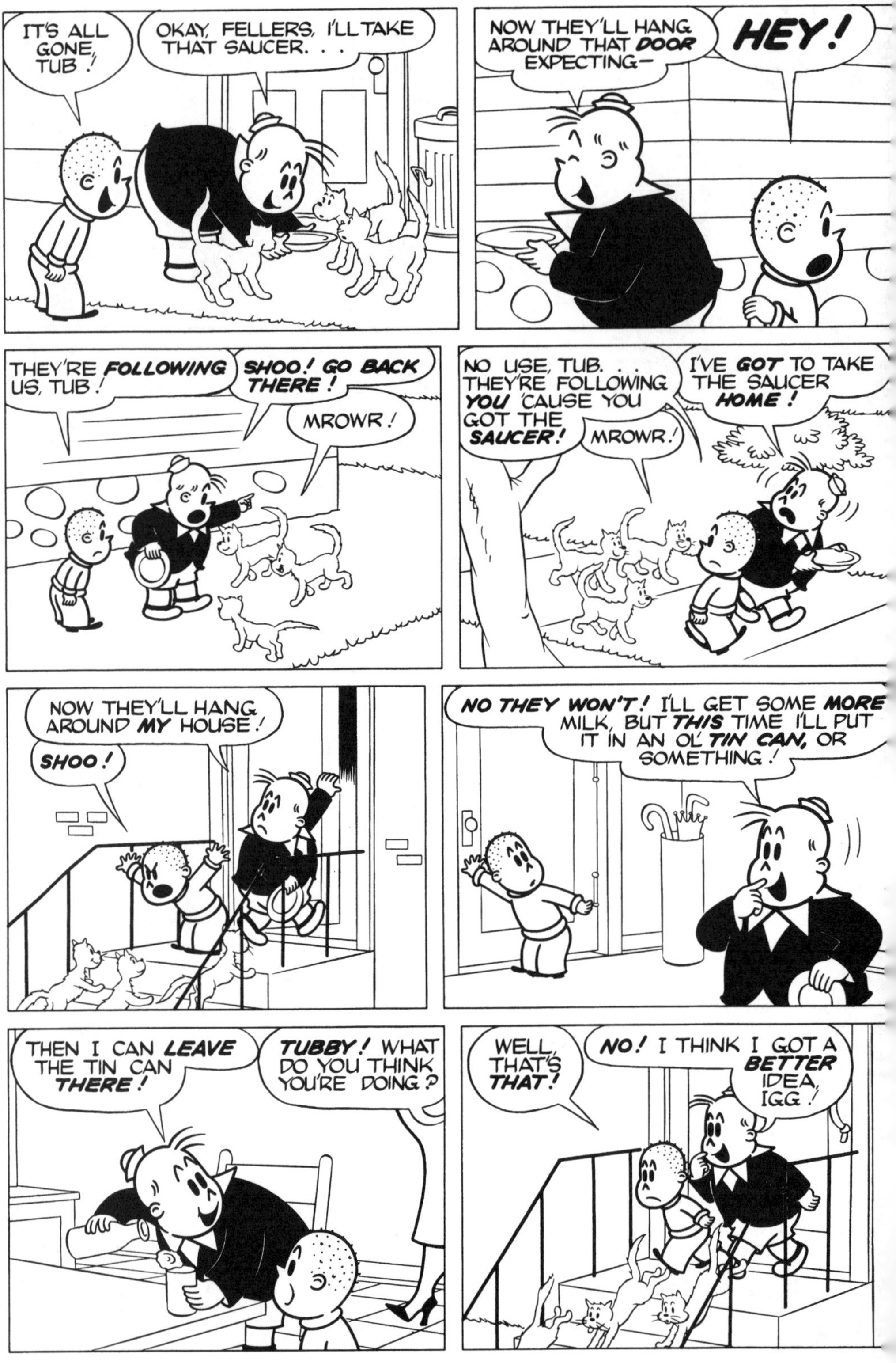
IT'S ALL GONE, TUB!
OKAY, FELLERS, I'LL TAKE THAT SAUCER. . .
NOW THEY'LL HANG AROUND THAT DOOR EXPECTING—
HEY!
THEY'RE FOLLOWING US, TUB!
SHOO! GO BACK THERE!
MROWR!
NO USE, TUB. . . THEY'RE FOLLOWING YOU 'CAUSE YOU GOT THE SAUCER!
MROWR!
I'VE GOT TO TAKE THE SAUCER HOME!
NOW THEY'LL HANG AROUND MY HOUSE!
SHOO!
NO THEY WON'T! I'LL GET SOME MORE MILK, BUT THIS TIME I'LL PUT IT IN AN OL' TIN CAN, OR SOMETHING!
THEN I CAN LEAVE THE TIN CAN THERE!
TUBBY! WHAT DO YOU THINK YOU'RE DOING?
WELL, THAT'S THAT!
NO! I THINK I GOT A BETTER IDEA, IGG!

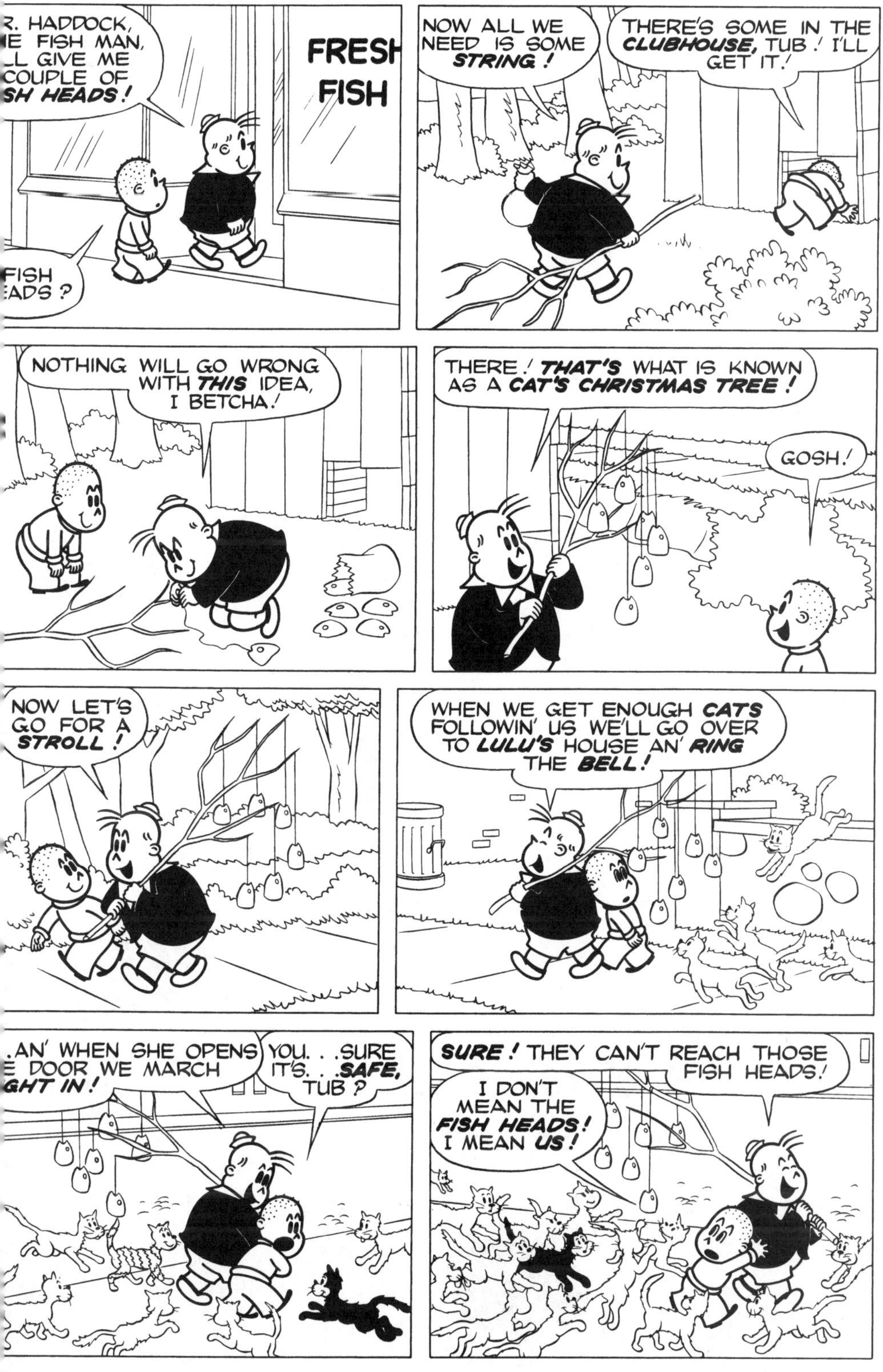
R. HADDOCK, E FISH MAN, LL GIVE ME COUPLE OF SH HEADS!
FRESH FISH
FISH EADS?
NOW ALL WE NEED IS SOME STRING!
THERE'S SOME IN THE CLUBHOUSE, TUB! I'LL GET IT!
NOTHING WILL GO WRONG WITH THIS IDEA, I BETCHA!
THERE! THAT'S WHAT IS KNOWN AS A CAT'S CHRISTMAS TREE!
GOSH!
NOW LET'S GO FOR A STROLL!
WHEN WE GET ENOUGH CATS FOLLOWIN' US WE'LL GO OVER TO LULU'S HOUSE AN' RING THE BELL!
..AN' WHEN SHE OPENS E DOOR WE MARCH GHT IN!
YOU. . .SURE IT'S. . .SAFE, TUB?
SURE! THEY CAN'T REACH THOSE FISH HEADS!
I DON'T MEAN THE FISH HEADS! I MEAN US!

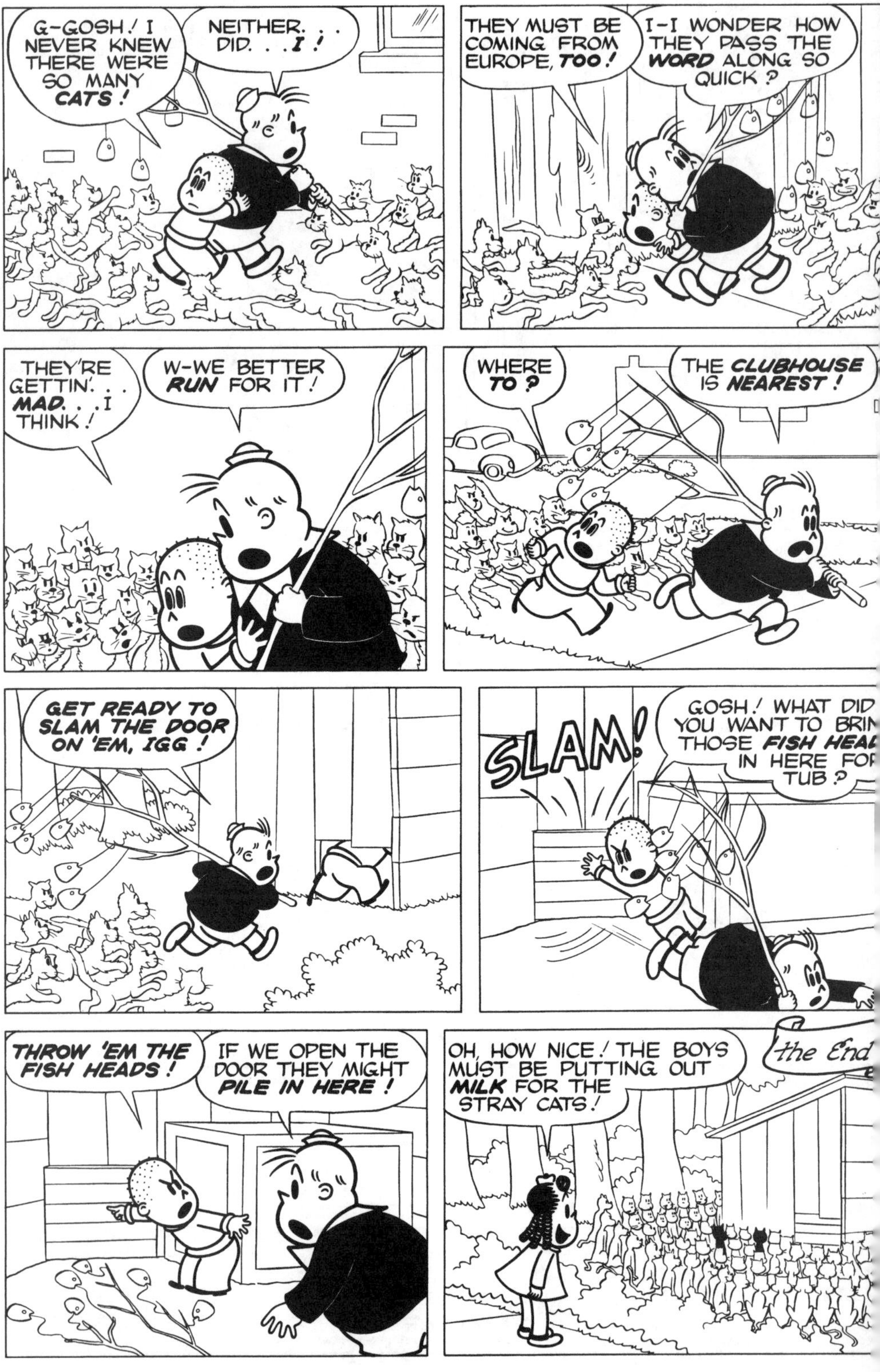
G-GOSH! I NEVER KNEW THERE WERE SO MANY CATS!
NEITHER. . . DID. . . I!
THEY MUST BE COMING FROM EUROPE, TOO!
I-I WONDER HOW THEY PASS THE WORD ALONG SO QUICK?
THEY'RE GETTIN'. . . MAD. . . I THINK!
W-WE BETTER RUN FOR IT!
WHERE TO?
THE CLUBHOUSE IS NEAREST!
GET READY TO SLAM THE DOOR ON 'EM, IGG!
SLAM!
GOSH! WHAT DID YOU WANT TO BRIN THOSE FISH HEAD IN HERE FOR TUB?
THROW 'EM THE FISH HEADS!
IF WE OPEN THE DOOR THEY MIGHT PILE IN HERE!
OH, HOW NICE! THE BOYS MUST BE PUTTING OUT MILK FOR THE STRAY CATS!
the End

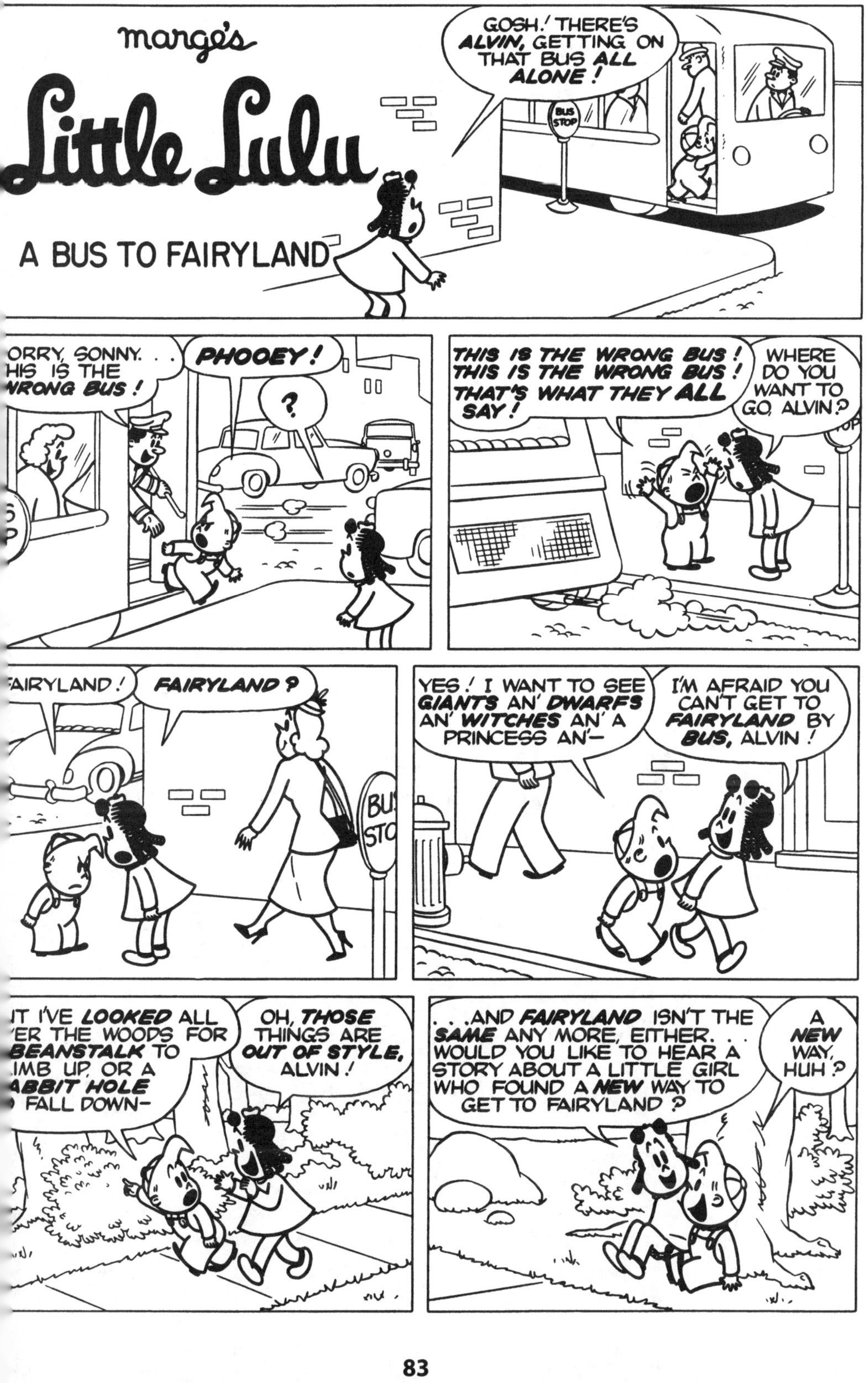
marge's
Little Lulu
A BUS TO FAIRYLAND
GOSH! THERE'S ALVIN, GETTING ON THAT BUS ALL ALONE!
BUS STOP
ORRY, SONNY. . . HIS IS THE WRONG BUS!
PHOOEY!
?
THIS IS THE WRONG BUS! THIS IS THE WRONG BUS! THAT'S WHAT THEY ALL SAY!
WHERE DO YOU WANT TO GO, ALVIN?
FAIRYLAND!
FAIRYLAND?
BUS STO
YES! I WANT TO SEE GIANTS AN' DWARFS AN' WITCHES AN' A PRINCESS AN'—
I'M AFRAID YOU CAN'T GET TO FAIRYLAND BY BUS, ALVIN!
IT I'VE LOOKED ALL 'ER THE WOODS FOR BEANSTALK TO IMB UP, OR A ABBIT HOLE FALL DOWN—
OH, THOSE THINGS ARE OUT OF STYLE, ALVIN!
. . . AND FAIRYLAND ISN'T THE SAME ANY MORE, EITHER. . . WOULD YOU LIKE TO HEAR A STORY ABOUT A LITTLE GIRL WHO FOUND A NEW WAY TO GET TO FAIRYLAND?
A NEW WAY, HUH?

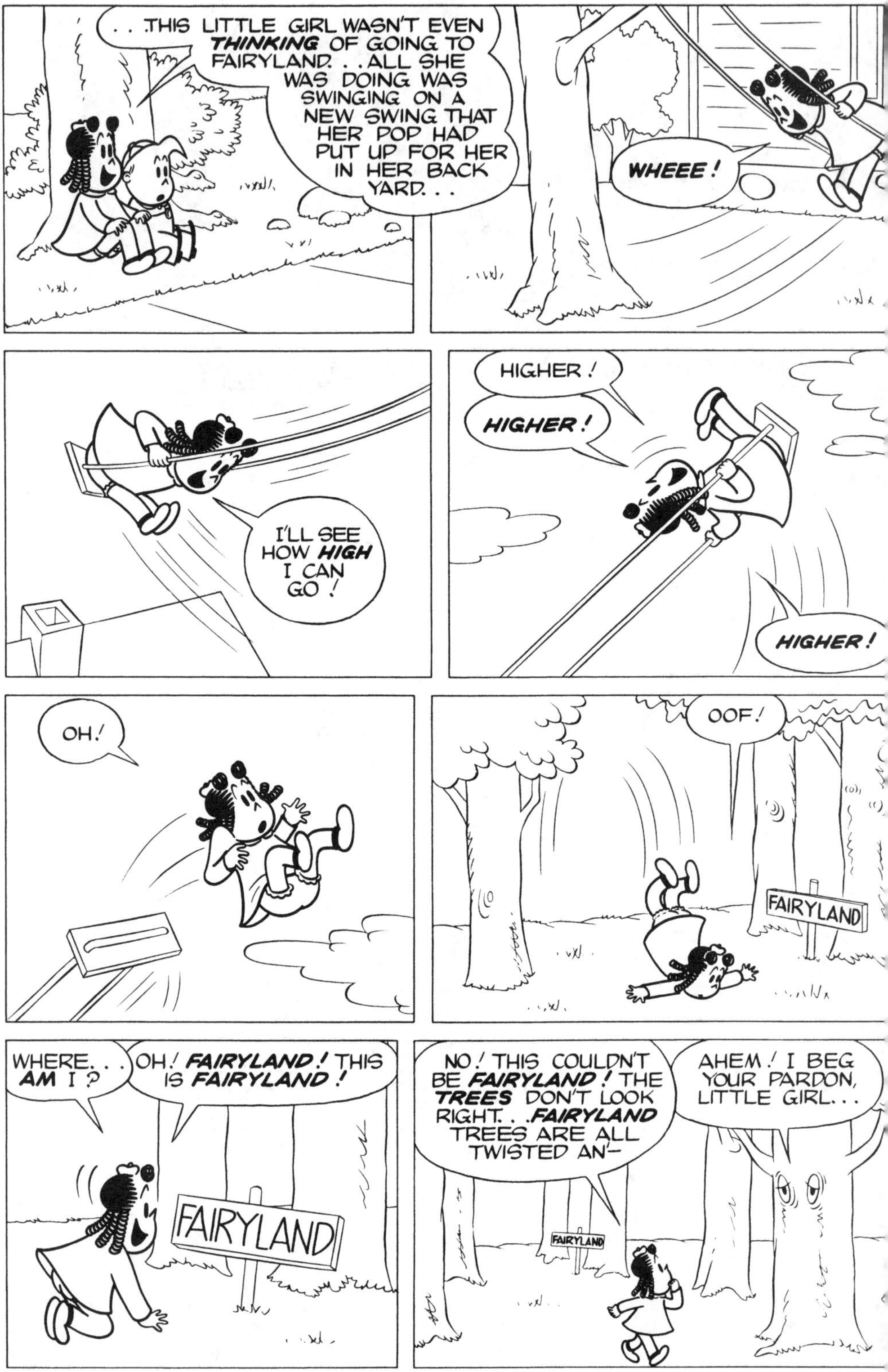

. . THIS LITTLE GIRL WASN'T EVEN *THINKING* OF GOING TO FAIRYLAND. . .ALL SHE WAS DOING WAS SWINGING ON A NEW SWING THAT HER POP HAD PUT UP FOR HER IN HER BACK YARD. . .
WHEEE!
I'LL SEE HOW *HIGH* I CAN GO!
HIGHER!
HIGHER!
HIGHER!
OH!
OOF!
FAIRYLAND
WHERE. . . *AM* I?
OH! *FAIRYLAND!* THIS IS *FAIRYLAND!*
FAIRYLAND
NO! THIS COULDN'T BE *FAIRYLAND!* THE *TREES* DON'T LOOK RIGHT. . .*FAIRYLAND* TREES ARE ALL TWISTED AN'—
AHEM! I BEG YOUR PARDON, LITTLE GIRL. . .
FAIRYLAND

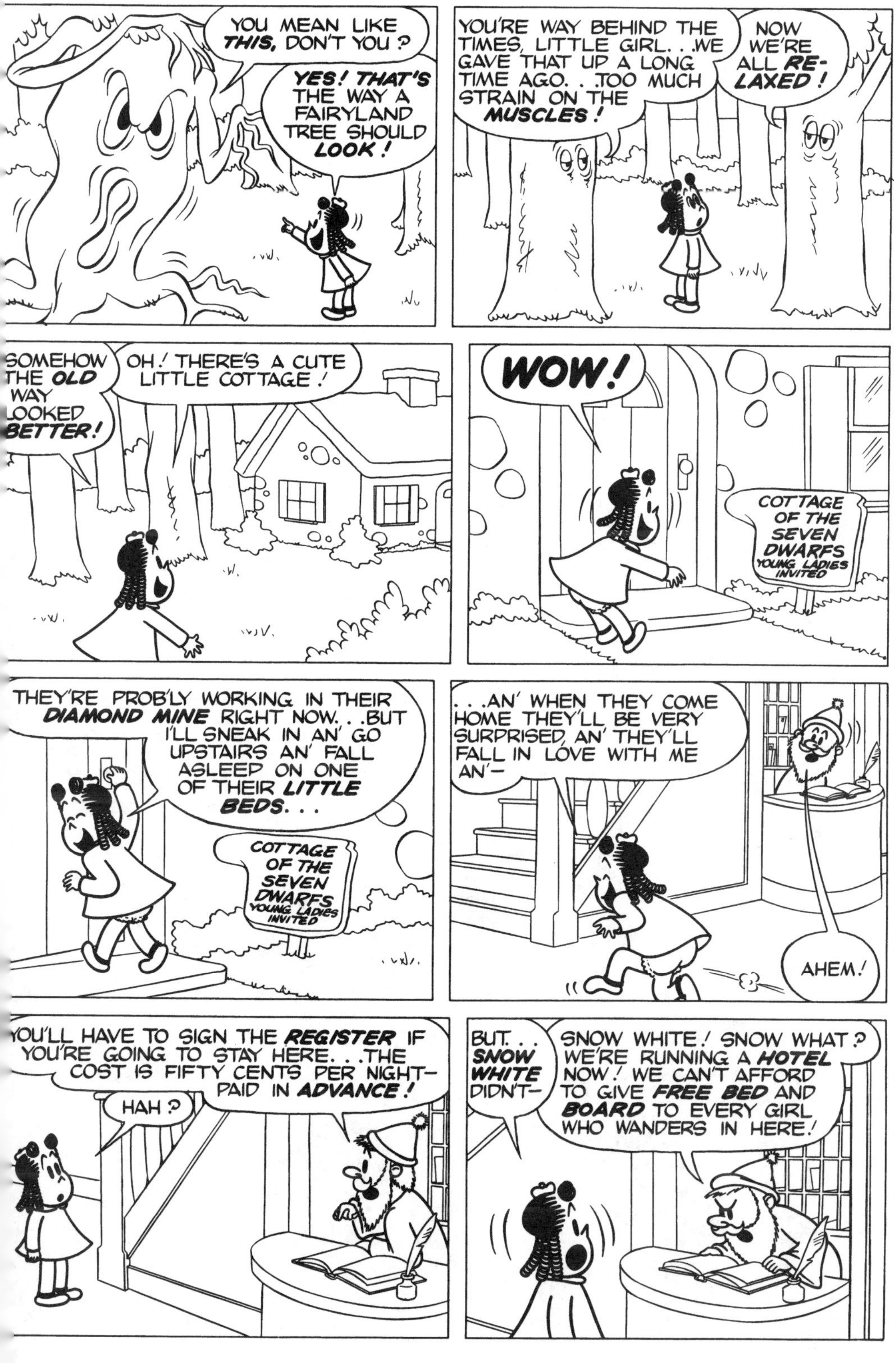
YOU MEAN LIKE THIS, DON'T YOU ?
YES! THAT'S THE WAY A FAIRYLAND TREE SHOULD LOOK!
YOU'RE WAY BEHIND THE TIMES, LITTLE GIRL. . .WE GAVE THAT UP A LONG TIME AGO. . .TOO MUCH STRAIN ON THE MUSCLES!
NOW WE'RE ALL RE-LAXED!
SOMEHOW THE OLD WAY LOOKED BETTER!
OH! THERE'S A CUTE LITTLE COTTAGE!
WOW!
COTTAGE OF THE SEVEN DWARFS YOUNG LADIES INVITED
THEY'RE PROB'LY WORKING IN THEIR DIAMOND MINE RIGHT NOW. . .BUT I'LL SNEAK IN AN' GO UPSTAIRS AN' FALL ASLEEP ON ONE OF THEIR LITTLE BEDS. . .
COTTAGE OF THE SEVEN DWARFS YOUNG LADIES INVITED
. . .AN' WHEN THEY COME HOME THEY'LL BE VERY SURPRISED AN' THEY'LL FALL IN LOVE WITH ME AN'—
AHEM!
YOU'LL HAVE TO SIGN THE REGISTER IF YOU'RE GOING TO STAY HERE. . .THE COST IS FIFTY CENTS PER NIGHT— PAID IN ADVANCE!
HAH ?
BUT. . . SNOW WHITE DIDN'T—
SNOW WHITE! SNOW WHAT? WE'RE RUNNING A HOTEL NOW! WE CAN'T AFFORD TO GIVE FREE BED AND BOARD TO EVERY GIRL WHO WANDERS IN HERE!

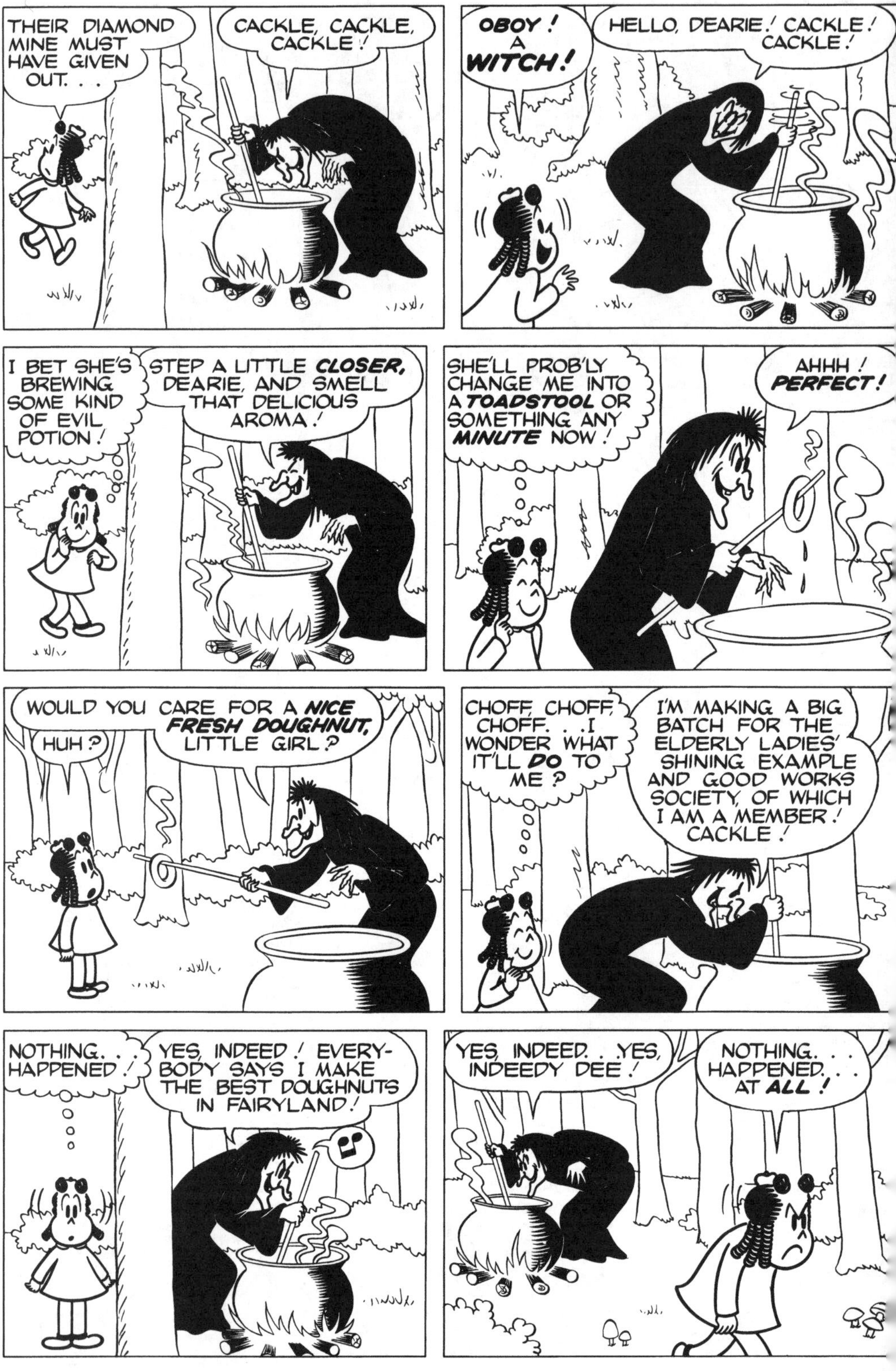
THEIR DIAMOND MINE MUST HAVE GIVEN OUT. . .
CACKLE, CACKLE, CACKLE!
OBOY! A WITCH!
HELLO, DEARIE! CACKLE! CACKLE!
I BET SHE'S BREWING SOME KIND OF EVIL POTION!
STEP A LITTLE CLOSER, DEARIE, AND SMELL THAT DELICIOUS AROMA!
SHE'LL PROB'LY CHANGE ME INTO A TOADSTOOL OR SOMETHING ANY MINUTE NOW!
AHHH! PERFECT!
WOULD YOU CARE FOR A NICE FRESH DOUGHNUT, LITTLE GIRL?
HUH?
CHOFF, CHOFF, CHOFF. . .I WONDER WHAT IT'LL DO TO ME?
I'M MAKING A BIG BATCH FOR THE ELDERLY LADIES' SHINING EXAMPLE AND GOOD WORKS SOCIETY, OF WHICH I AM A MEMBER! CACKLE!
NOTHING. . . HAPPENED!
YES, INDEED! EVERY-BODY SAYS I MAKE THE BEST DOUGHNUTS IN FAIRYLAND!
YES, INDEED. . .YES, INDEEDY DEE!
NOTHING. . . HAPPENED. . . AT ALL!

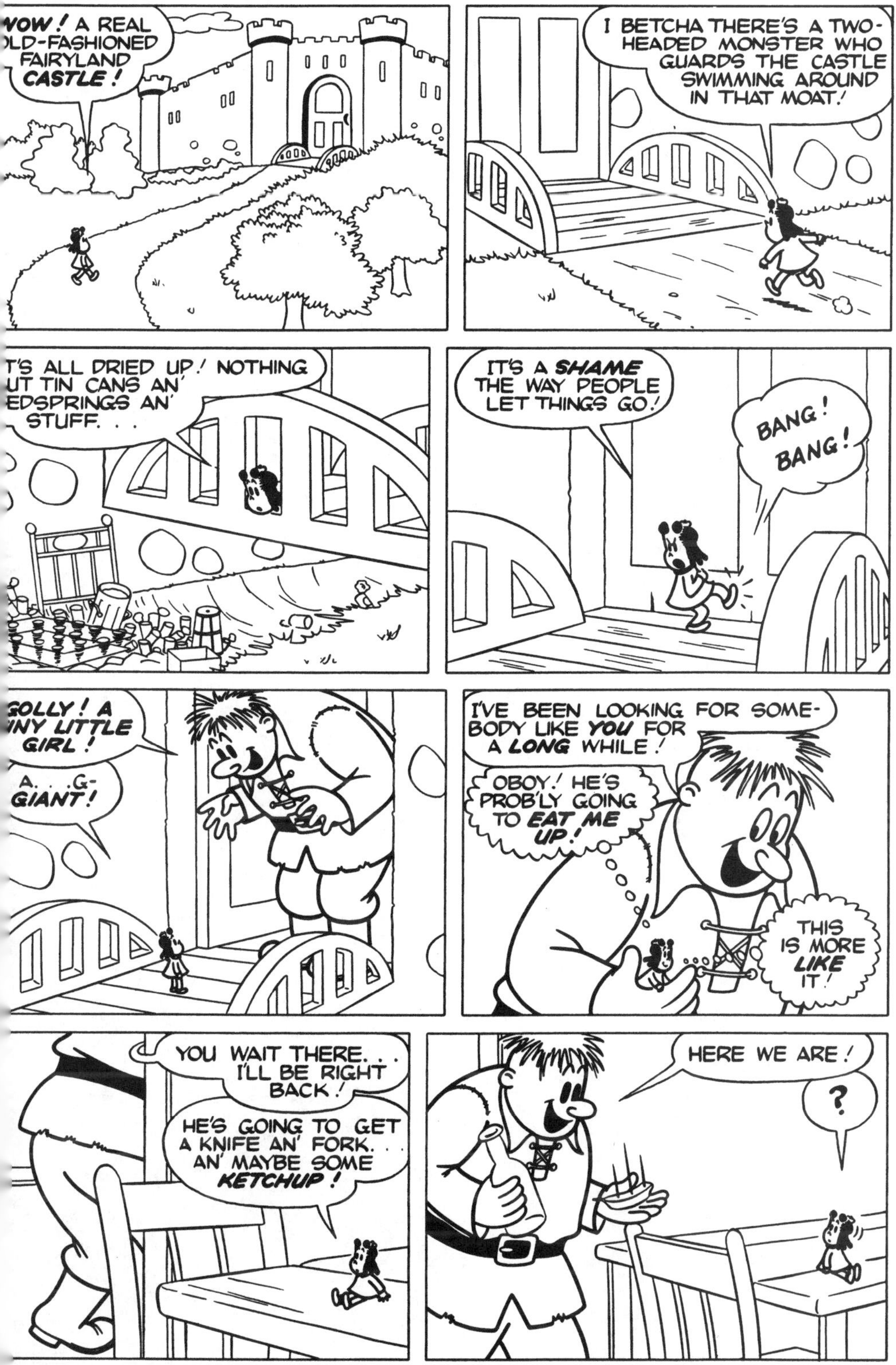
WOW! A REAL LD-FASHIONED FAIRYLAND CASTLE!
I BETCHA THERE'S A TWO-HEADED MONSTER WHO GUARDS THE CASTLE SWIMMING AROUND IN THAT MOAT!
T'S ALL DRIED UP! NOTHING UT TIN CANS AN' EDSPRINGS AN' STUFF. . .
IT'S A SHAME THE WAY PEOPLE LET THINGS GO!
BANG! BANG!
GOLLY! A INY LITTLE GIRL!
A. . .G-GIANT!
I'VE BEEN LOOKING FOR SOMEBODY LIKE YOU FOR A LONG WHILE!
OBOY! HE'S PROB'LY GOING TO EAT ME UP!
THIS IS MORE LIKE IT!
YOU WAIT THERE. . . I'LL BE RIGHT BACK!
HE'S GOING TO GET A KNIFE AN' FORK. . . AN' MAYBE SOME KETCHUP!
HERE WE ARE!
?

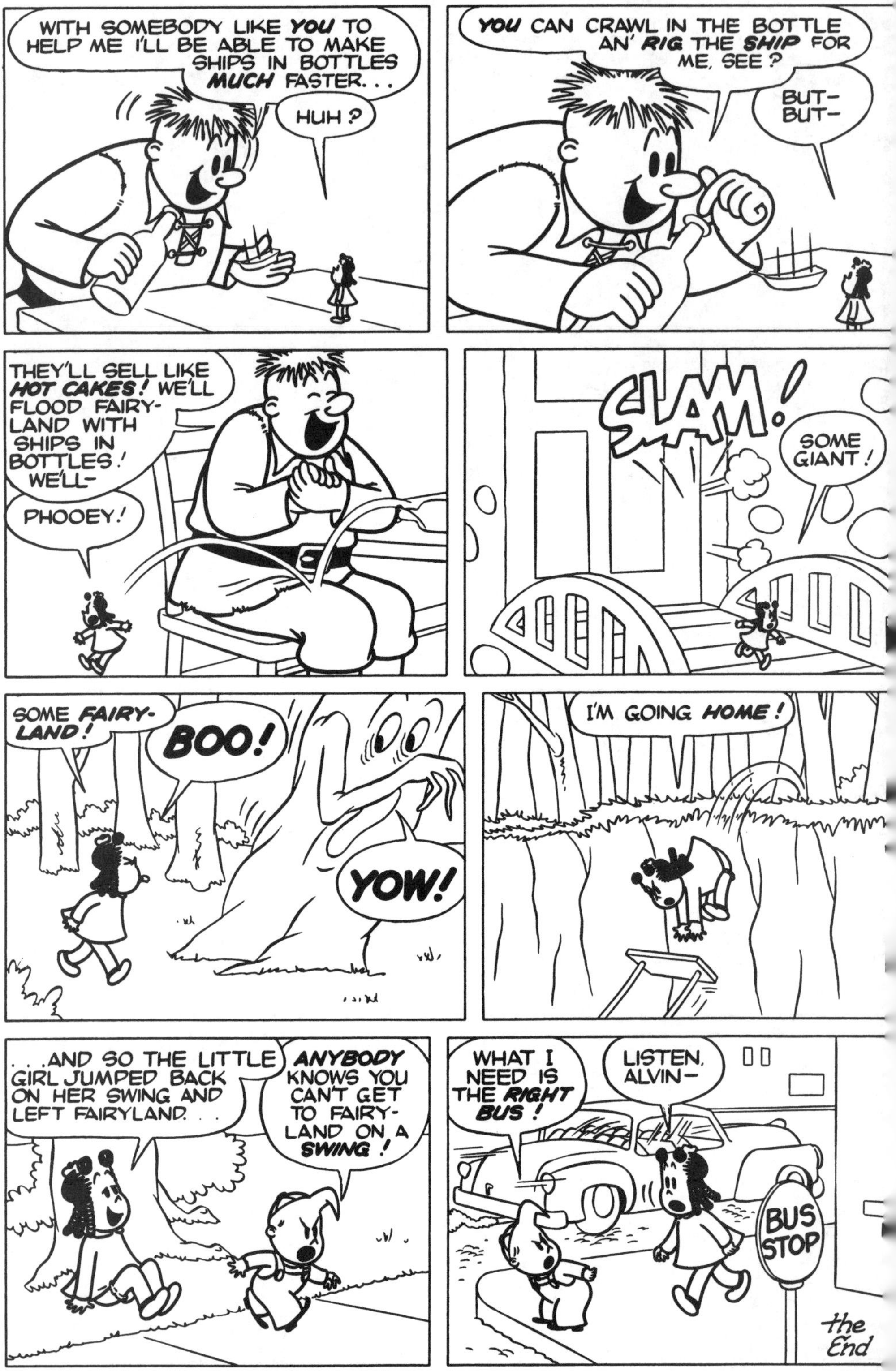
WITH SOMEBODY LIKE YOU TO HELP ME I'LL BE ABLE TO MAKE SHIPS IN BOTTLES MUCH FASTER. . .
HUH ?
YOU CAN CRAWL IN THE BOTTLE AN' RIG THE SHIP FOR ME, SEE ?
BUT- BUT-
THEY'LL SELL LIKE HOT CAKES! WE'LL FLOOD FAIRY-LAND WITH SHIPS IN BOTTLES! WE'LL-
PHOOEY!
SLAM!
SOME GIANT!
SOME FAIRY-LAND!
BOO!
YOW!
I'M GOING HOME!
. . .AND SO THE LITTLE GIRL JUMPED BACK ON HER SWING AND LEFT FAIRYLAND. . .
ANYBODY KNOWS YOU CAN'T GET TO FAIRY-LAND ON A SWING!
WHAT I NEED IS THE RIGHT BUS!
LISTEN, ALVIN-
BUS STOP
the End

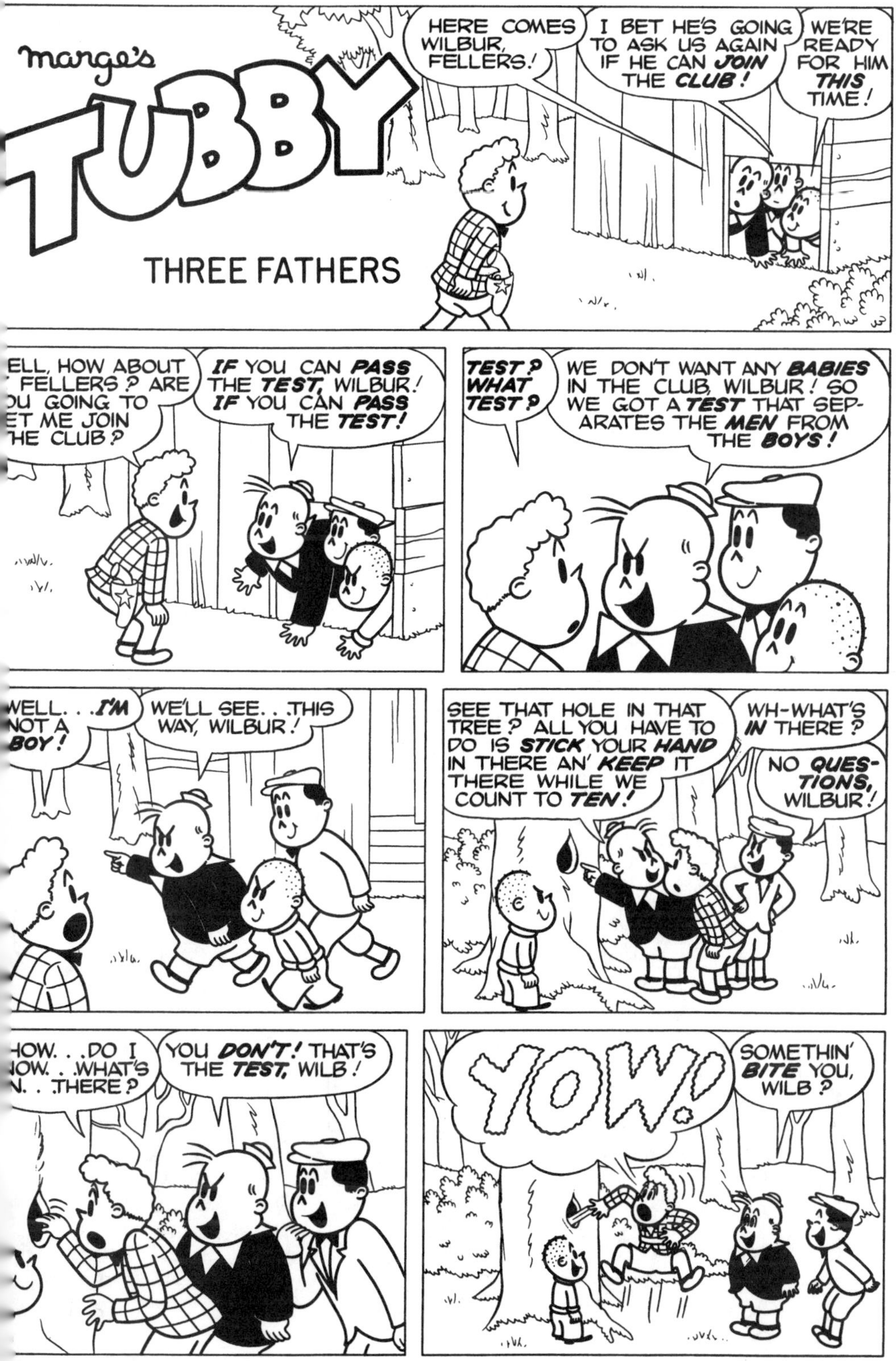
marge's
TUBBY
THREE FATHERS
HERE COMES WILBUR, FELLERS!
I BET HE'S GOING TO ASK US AGAIN IF HE CAN JOIN THE CLUB!
WE'RE READY FOR HIM THIS TIME!
ELL, HOW ABOUT FELLERS? ARE OU GOING TO ET ME JOIN HE CLUB?
IF YOU CAN PASS THE TEST, WILBUR! IF YOU CAN PASS THE TEST!
TEST? WHAT TEST?
WE DON'T WANT ANY BABIES IN THE CLUB, WILBUR! SO WE GOT A TEST THAT SEPARATES THE MEN FROM THE BOYS!
WELL. . .I'M NOT A BOY!
WE'LL SEE. . .THIS WAY, WILBUR!
SEE THAT HOLE IN THAT TREE? ALL YOU HAVE TO DO IS STICK YOUR HAND IN THERE AN' KEEP IT THERE WHILE WE COUNT TO TEN!
WH-WHAT'S IN THERE?
NO QUESTIONS, WILBUR!
HOW. . .DO I NOW. . .WHAT'S N. . .THERE?
YOU DON'T! THAT'S THE TEST, WILB!
YOW!
SOMETHIN' BITE YOU, WILB?

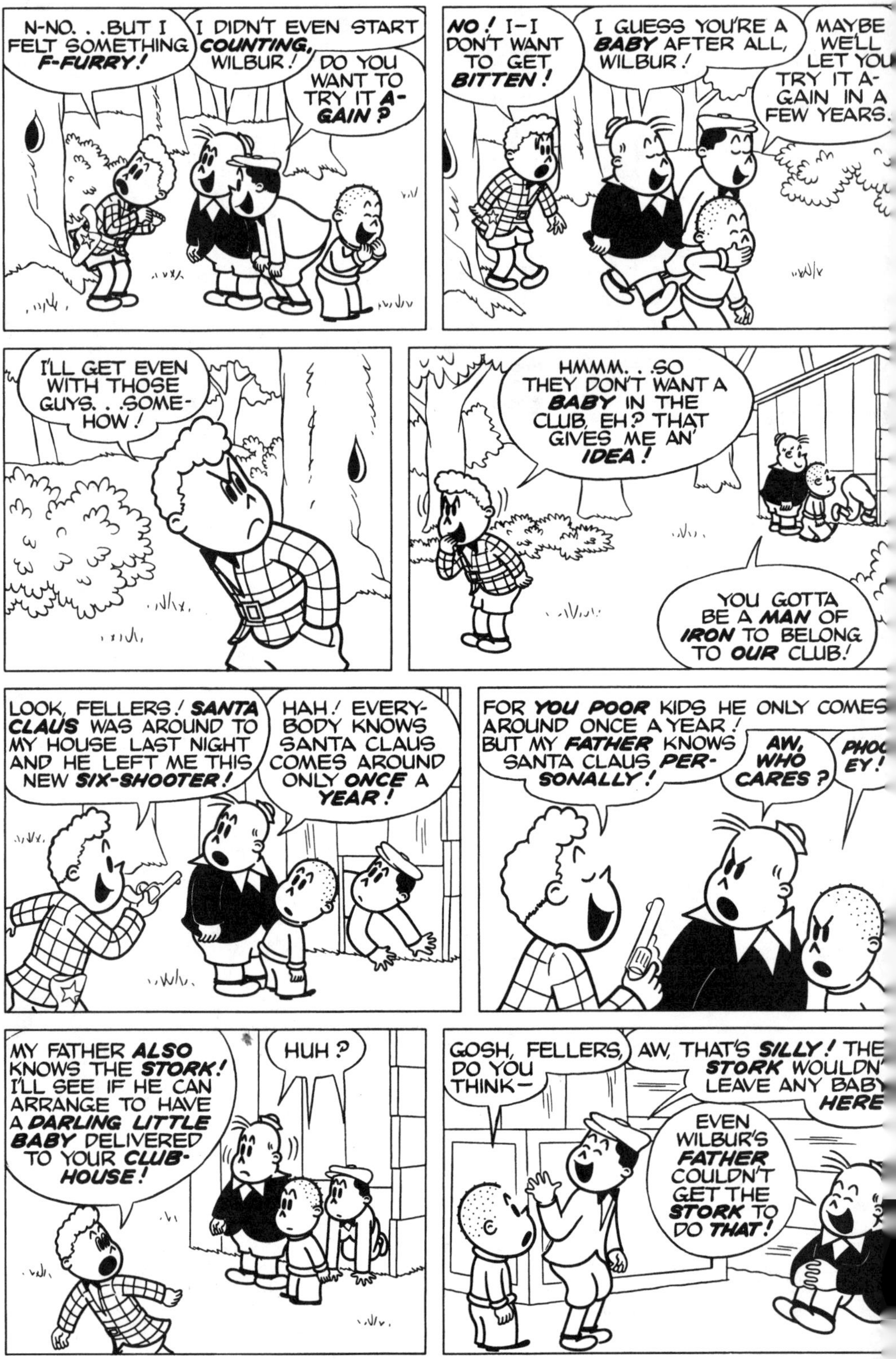
N-NO. . .BUT I FELT SOMETHING F-FURRY!
I DIDN'T EVEN START COUNTING, WILBUR!
DO YOU WANT TO TRY IT A-GAIN?
NO! I-I DON'T WANT TO GET BITTEN!
I GUESS YOU'RE A BABY AFTER ALL, WILBUR!
MAYBE WE'LL LET YOU TRY IT A-GAIN IN A FEW YEARS.
I'LL GET EVEN WITH THOSE GUYS. . .SOME-HOW!
HMMM. . .SO THEY DON'T WANT A BABY IN THE CLUB, EH? THAT GIVES ME AN' IDEA!
YOU GOTTA BE A MAN OF IRON TO BELONG TO OUR CLUB!
LOOK, FELLERS! SANTA CLAUS WAS AROUND TO MY HOUSE LAST NIGHT AND HE LEFT ME THIS NEW SIX-SHOOTER!
HAH! EVERY-BODY KNOWS SANTA CLAUS COMES AROUND ONLY ONCE A YEAR!
FOR YOU POOR KIDS HE ONLY COMES AROUND ONCE A YEAR! BUT MY FATHER KNOWS SANTA CLAUS PER-SONALLY!
AW, WHO CARES?
PHOO EY!
MY FATHER ALSO KNOWS THE STORK! I'LL SEE IF HE CAN ARRANGE TO HAVE A DARLING LITTLE BABY DELIVERED TO YOUR CLUB-HOUSE!
HUH?
GOSH, FELLERS, DO YOU THINK—
AW, THAT'S SILLY! THE STORK WOULDN' LEAVE ANY BABY HERE
EVEN WILBUR'S FATHER COULDN'T GET THE STORK TO DO THAT!

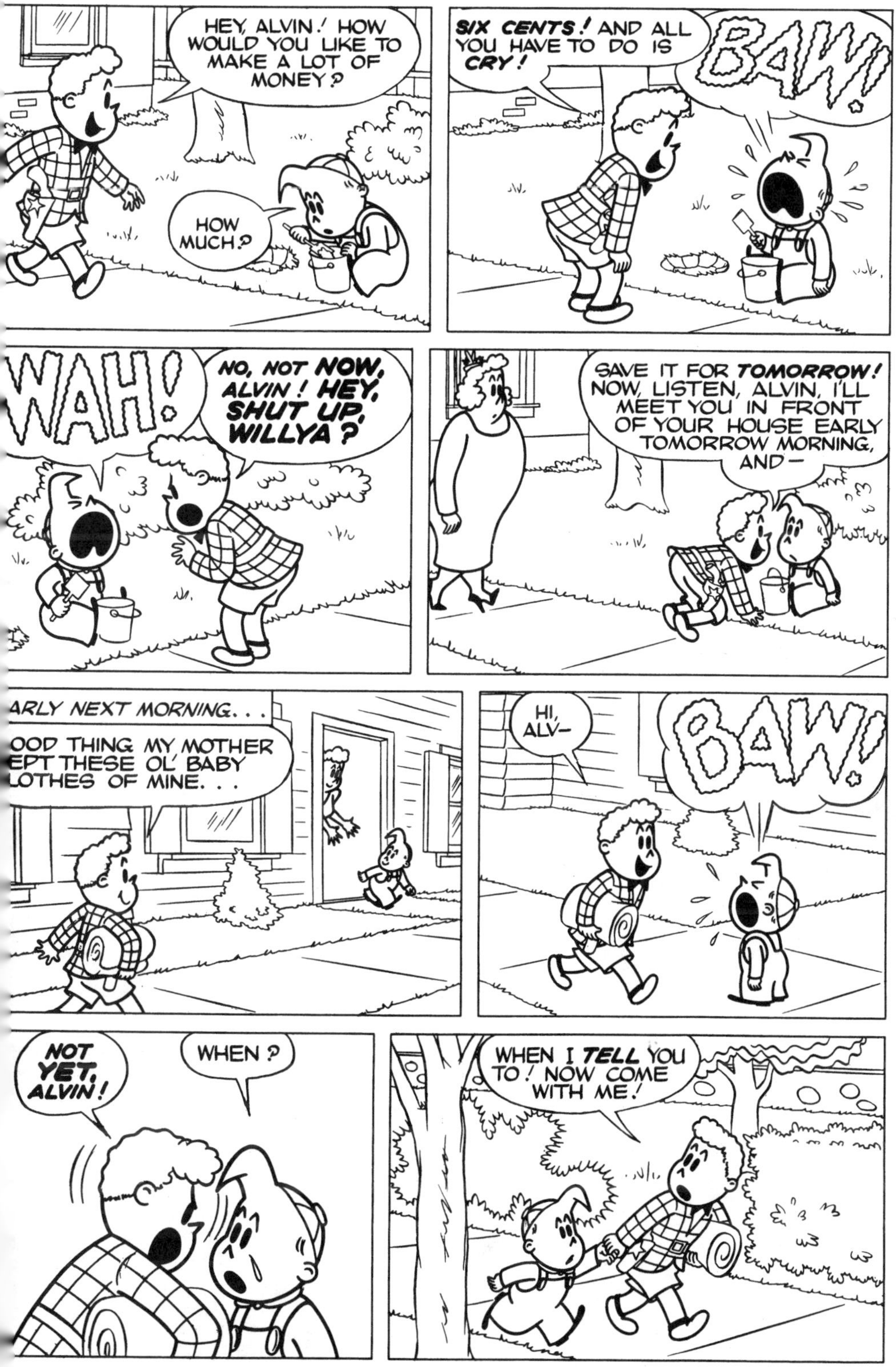
HEY, ALVIN! HOW WOULD YOU LIKE TO MAKE A LOT OF MONEY?
HOW MUCH?
SIX CENTS! AND ALL YOU HAVE TO DO IS CRY!
BAW!
WAH!
NO, NOT NOW, ALVIN! HEY, SHUT UP, WILLYA?
SAVE IT FOR TOMORROW! NOW, LISTEN, ALVIN, I'LL MEET YOU IN FRONT OF YOUR HOUSE EARLY TOMORROW MORNING, AND—
ARLY NEXT MORNING. . .
OOD THING MY MOTHER EPT THESE OL' BABY LOTHES OF MINE. . .
HI, ALV—
BAW!
NOT YET, ALVIN!
WHEN?
WHEN I TELL YOU TO! NOW COME WITH ME!

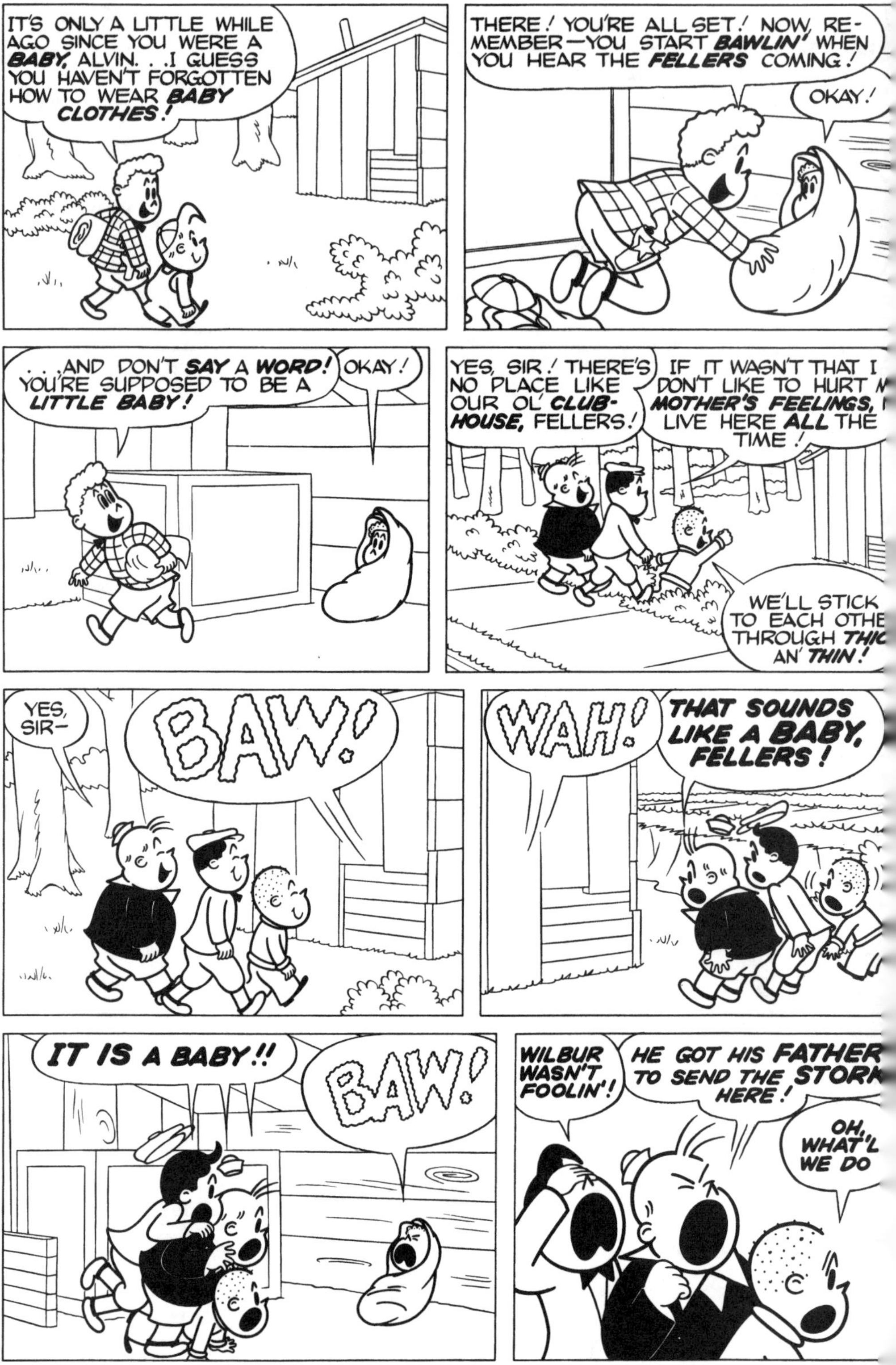
IT'S ONLY A LITTLE WHILE AGO SINCE YOU WERE A BABY, ALVIN. . .I GUESS YOU HAVEN'T FORGOTTEN HOW TO WEAR BABY CLOTHES!
THERE! YOU'RE ALL SET! NOW, RE-MEMBER—YOU START BAWLIN' WHEN YOU HEAR THE FELLERS COMING!
OKAY!
. . .AND DON'T SAY A WORD! YOU'RE SUPPOSED TO BE A LITTLE BABY!
OKAY!
YES, SIR! THERE'S NO PLACE LIKE OUR OL' CLUB-HOUSE, FELLERS!
IF IT WASN'T THAT I DON'T LIKE TO HURT M MOTHER'S FEELINGS, I LIVE HERE ALL THE TIME!
WE'LL STICK TO EACH OTHE THROUGH THIC AN' THIN!
YES, SIR—
BAW!
WAH!
THAT SOUNDS LIKE A BABY, FELLERS!
IT IS A BABY!!
BAW!
WILBUR WASN'T FOOLIN'!
HE GOT HIS FATHER TO SEND THE STORK HERE!
OH, WHAT'L WE DO

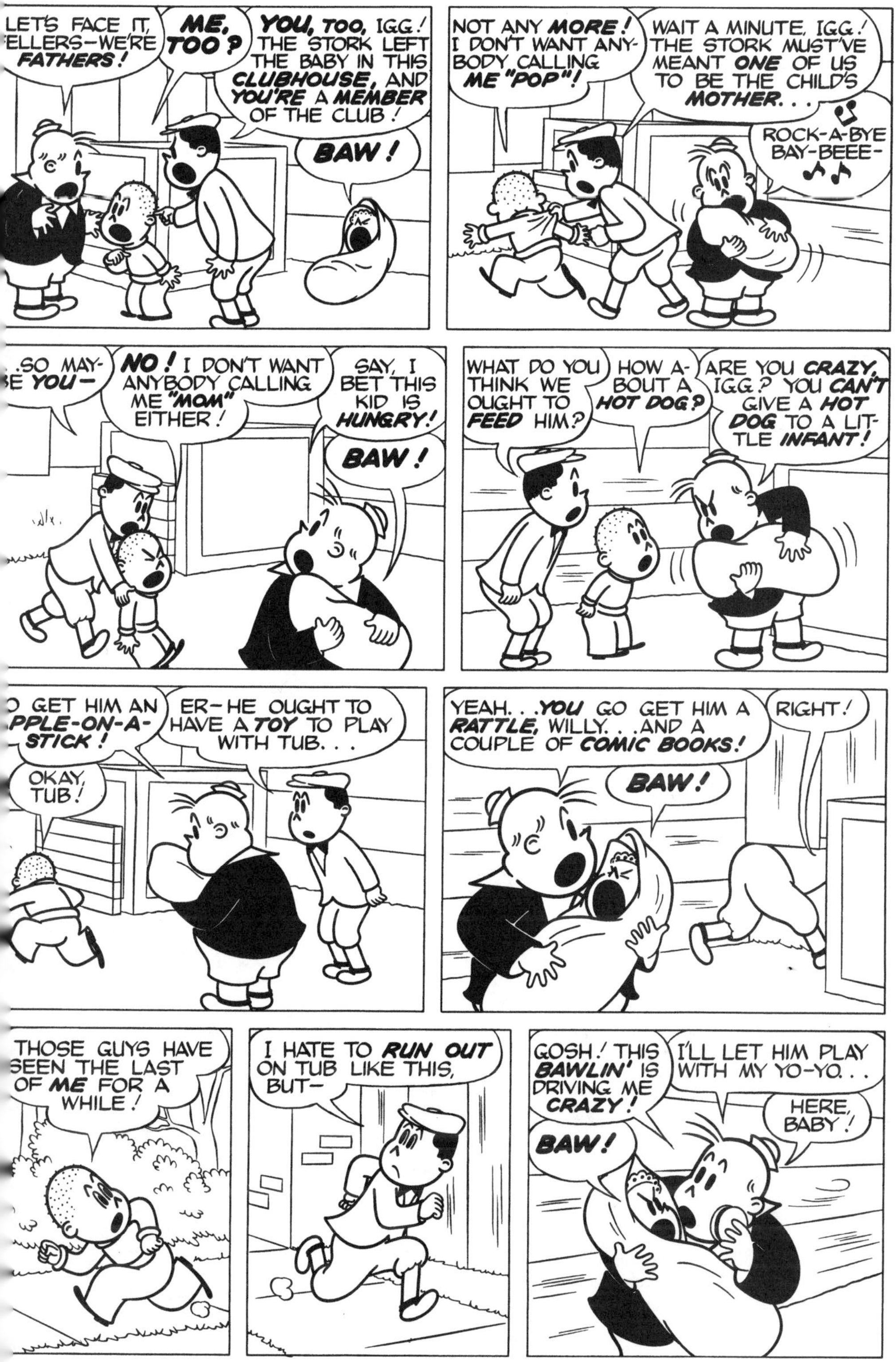

LET'S FACE IT, FELLERS—WE'RE FATHERS!
ME, TOO?
YOU, TOO, IGG! THE STORK LEFT THE BABY IN THIS CLUBHOUSE, AND YOU'RE A MEMBER OF THE CLUB!
BAW!
NOT ANY MORE! I DON'T WANT ANYBODY CALLING ME "POP"!
WAIT A MINUTE, IGG! THE STORK MUST'VE MEANT ONE OF US TO BE THE CHILD'S MOTHER. . .
ROCK-A-BYE BAY-BEEE-
. .SO MAYBE YOU—
NO! I DON'T WANT ANYBODY CALLING ME "MOM" EITHER!
SAY, I BET THIS KID IS HUNGRY!
BAW!
WHAT DO YOU THINK WE OUGHT TO FEED HIM?
HOW ABOUT A HOT DOG?
ARE YOU CRAZY, IGG? YOU CAN'T GIVE A HOT DOG TO A LITTLE INFANT!
O GET HIM AN PPLE-ON-A-STICK!
ER—HE OUGHT TO HAVE A TOY TO PLAY WITH TUB. . .
OKAY, TUB!
YEAH. . .YOU GO GET HIM A RATTLE, WILLY. . .AND A COUPLE OF COMIC BOOKS!
RIGHT!
BAW!
THOSE GUYS HAVE SEEN THE LAST OF ME FOR A WHILE!
I HATE TO RUN OUT ON TUB LIKE THIS, BUT—
GOSH! THIS BAWLIN' IS DRIVING ME CRAZY!
I'LL LET HIM PLAY WITH MY YO-YO. . .
HERE, BABY!
BAW!

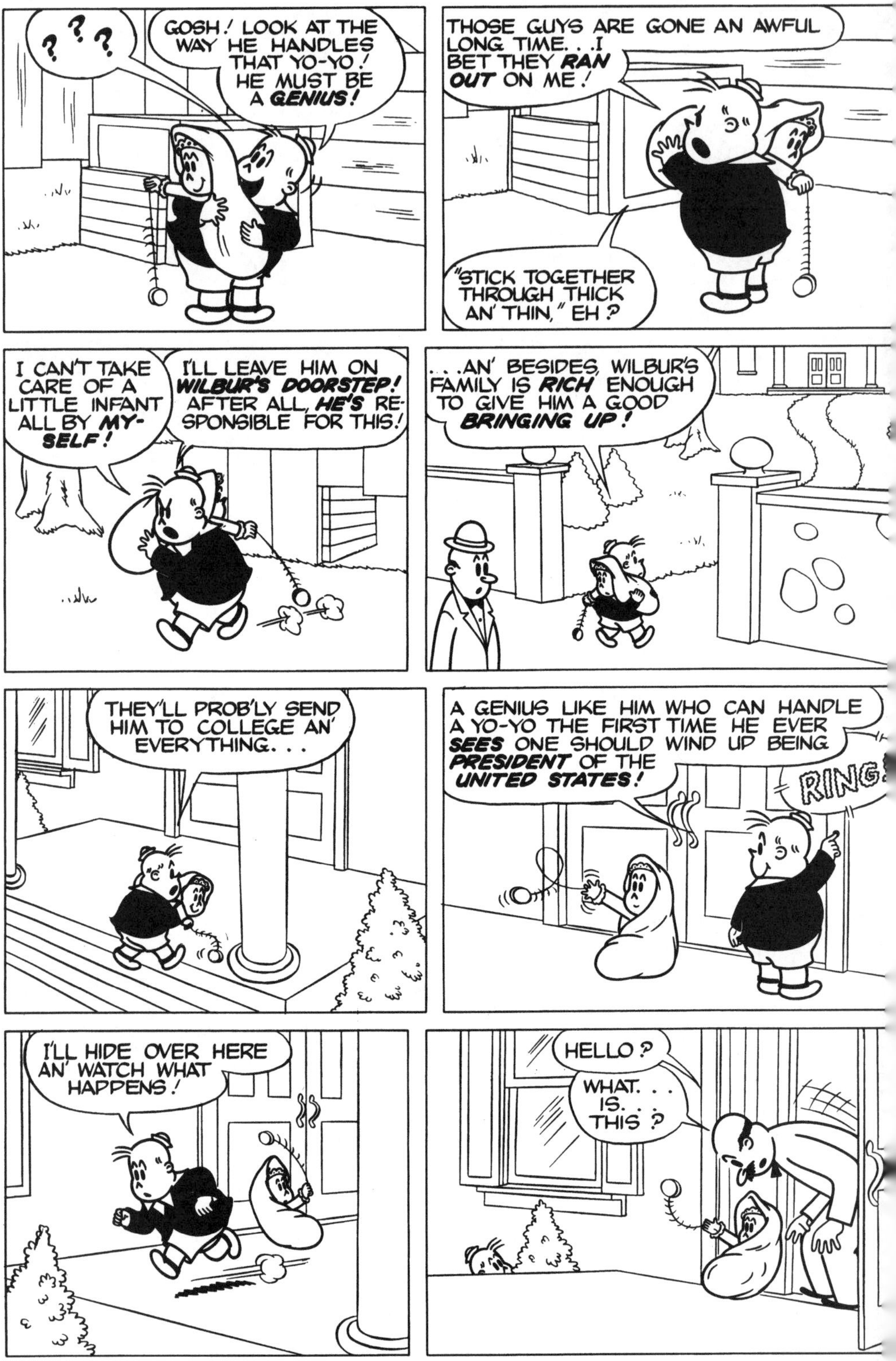
? ? ?
GOSH! LOOK AT THE WAY HE HANDLES THAT YO-YO! HE MUST BE A GENIUS!
THOSE GUYS ARE GONE AN AWFUL LONG TIME. . .I BET THEY RAN OUT ON ME!
"STICK TOGETHER THROUGH THICK AN' THIN," EH?
I CAN'T TAKE CARE OF A LITTLE INFANT ALL BY MY-SELF!
I'LL LEAVE HIM ON WILBUR'S DOORSTEP! AFTER ALL, HE'S RE-SPONSIBLE FOR THIS!
. . .AN' BESIDES, WILBUR'S FAMILY IS RICH ENOUGH TO GIVE HIM A GOOD BRINGING UP!
THEY'LL PROB'LY SEND HIM TO COLLEGE AN' EVERYTHING. . .
A GENIUS LIKE HIM WHO CAN HANDLE A YO-YO THE FIRST TIME HE EVER SEES ONE SHOULD WIND UP BEING PRESIDENT OF THE UNITED STATES!
RING
I'LL HIDE OVER HERE AN' WATCH WHAT HAPPENS!
HELLO?
WHAT. . . IS. . . THIS?

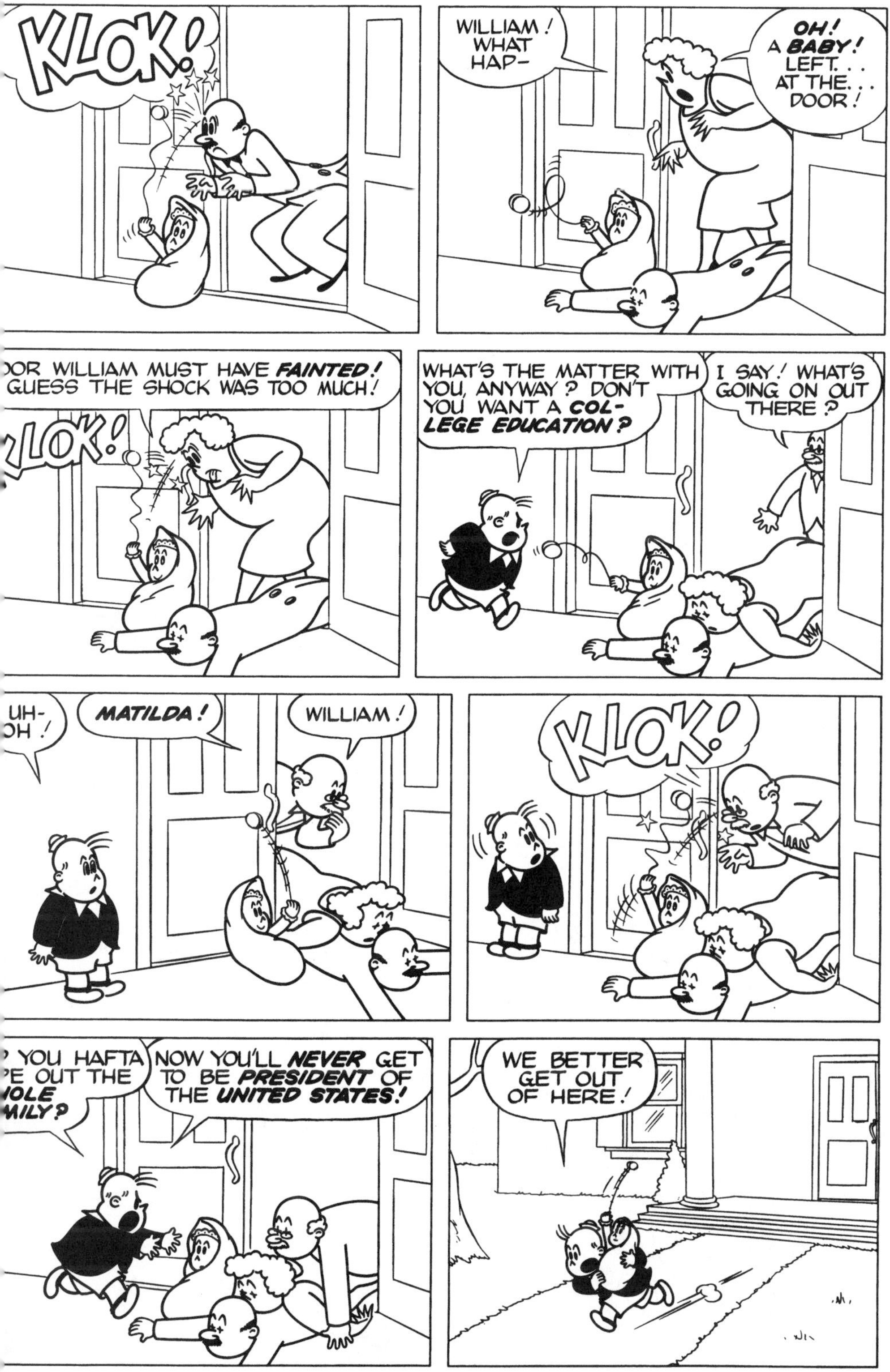

KLOK!
WILLIAM! WHAT HAP–
OH! A BABY! LEFT... AT THE... DOOR!
OOR WILLIAM MUST HAVE FAINTED! GUESS THE SHOCK WAS TOO MUCH!
KLOK!
WHAT'S THE MATTER WITH YOU, ANYWAY? DON'T YOU WANT A COLLEGE EDUCATION?
I SAY! WHAT'S GOING ON OUT THERE?
UH-OH!
MATILDA!
WILLIAM!
KLOK!
YOU HAFTA PE OUT THE HOLE MILY?
NOW YOU'LL NEVER GET TO BE PRESIDENT OF THE UNITED STATES!
WE BETTER GET OUT OF HERE!

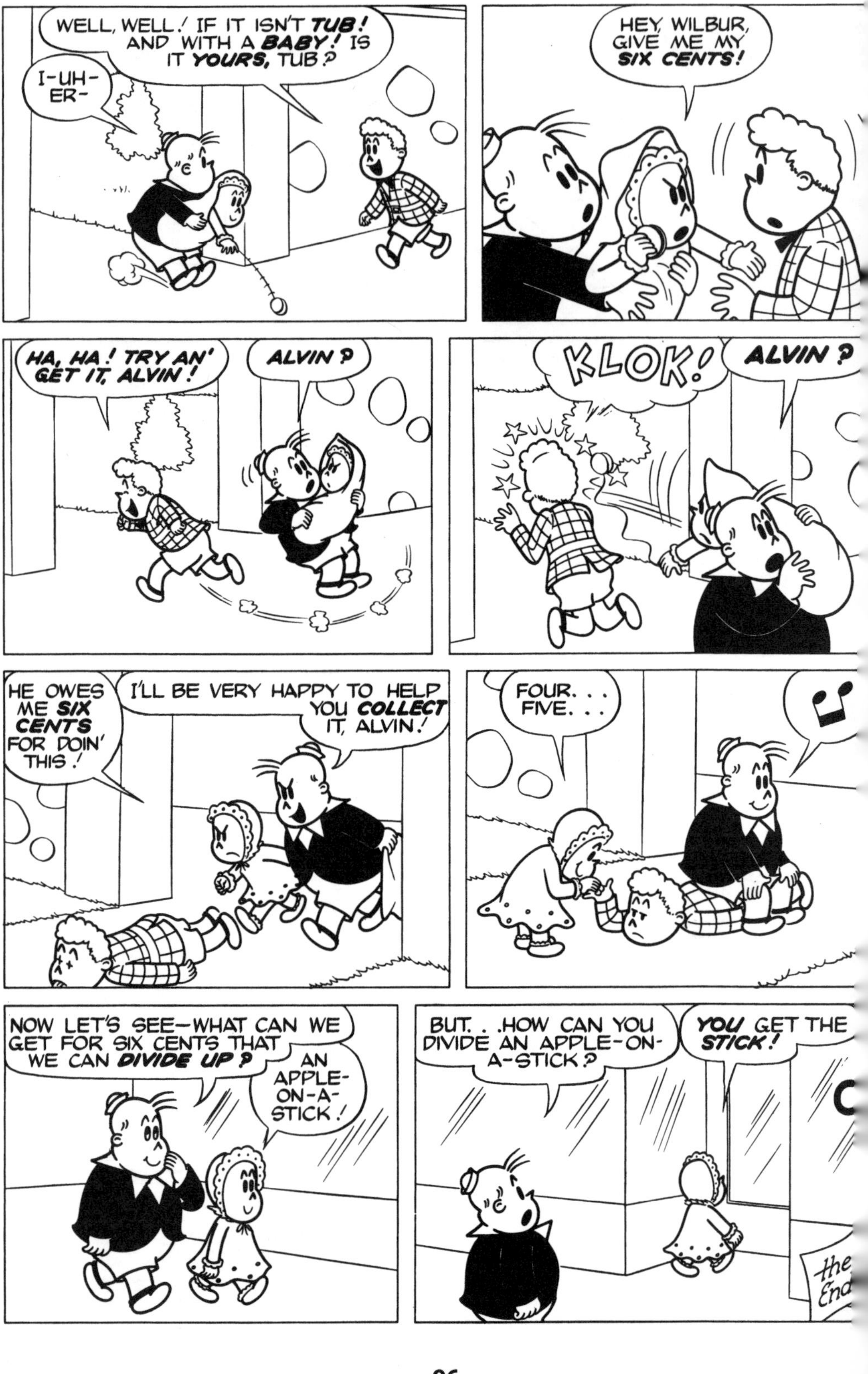
WELL, WELL! IF IT ISN'T TUB! AND WITH A BABY! IS IT YOURS, TUB?
I-UH-ER-
HEY, WILBUR, GIVE ME MY SIX CENTS!
HA, HA! TRY AN' GET IT, ALVIN!
ALVIN?
KLOK!
ALVIN?
HE OWES ME SIX CENTS FOR DOIN' THIS!
I'LL BE VERY HAPPY TO HELP YOU COLLECT IT, ALVIN!
FOUR... FIVE...
NOW LET'S SEE—WHAT CAN WE GET FOR SIX CENTS THAT WE CAN DIVIDE UP?
AN APPLE-ON-A-STICK!
BUT...HOW CAN YOU DIVIDE AN APPLE-ON-A-STICK?
YOU GET THE STICK!
the End

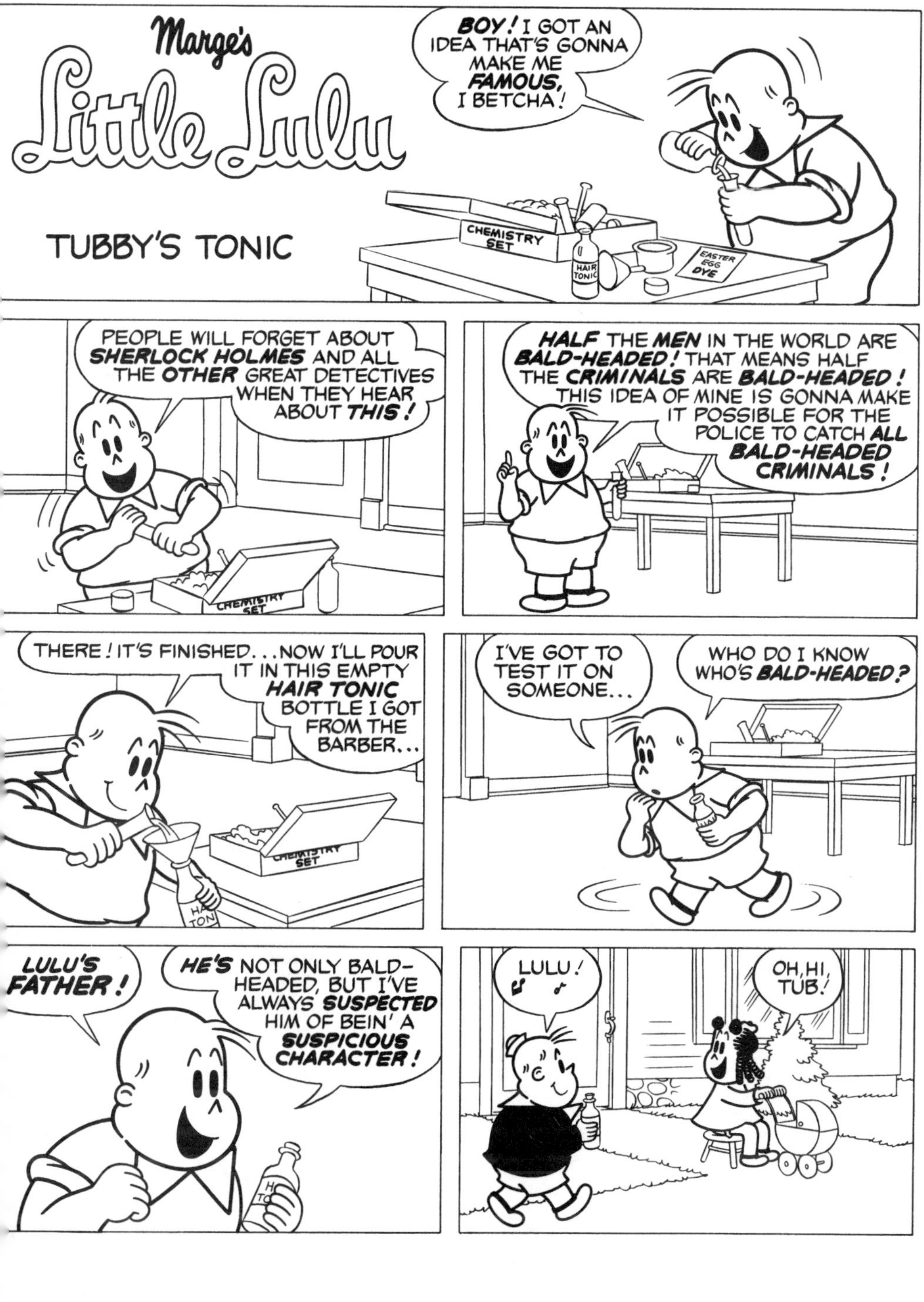
Marge's Little Lulu
TUBBY'S TONIC
BOY! I GOT AN IDEA THAT'S GONNA MAKE ME FAMOUS, I BETCHA!
CHEMISTRY SET
HAIR TONIC
EASTER EGG DYE
PEOPLE WILL FORGET ABOUT SHERLOCK HOLMES AND ALL THE OTHER GREAT DETECTIVES WHEN THEY HEAR ABOUT THIS!
CHEMISTRY SET
HALF THE MEN IN THE WORLD ARE BALD-HEADED! THAT MEANS HALF THE CRIMINALS ARE BALD-HEADED! THIS IDEA OF MINE IS GONNA MAKE IT POSSIBLE FOR THE POLICE TO CATCH ALL BALD-HEADED CRIMINALS!
THERE! IT'S FINISHED...NOW I'LL POUR IT IN THIS EMPTY HAIR TONIC BOTTLE I GOT FROM THE BARBER...
CHEMISTRY SET
I'VE GOT TO TEST IT ON SOMEONE...
WHO DO I KNOW WHO'S BALD-HEADED?
LULU'S FATHER!
HE'S NOT ONLY BALD-HEADED, BUT I'VE ALWAYS SUSPECTED HIM OF BEIN' A SUSPICIOUS CHARACTER!
LULU!
OH, HI, TUB!

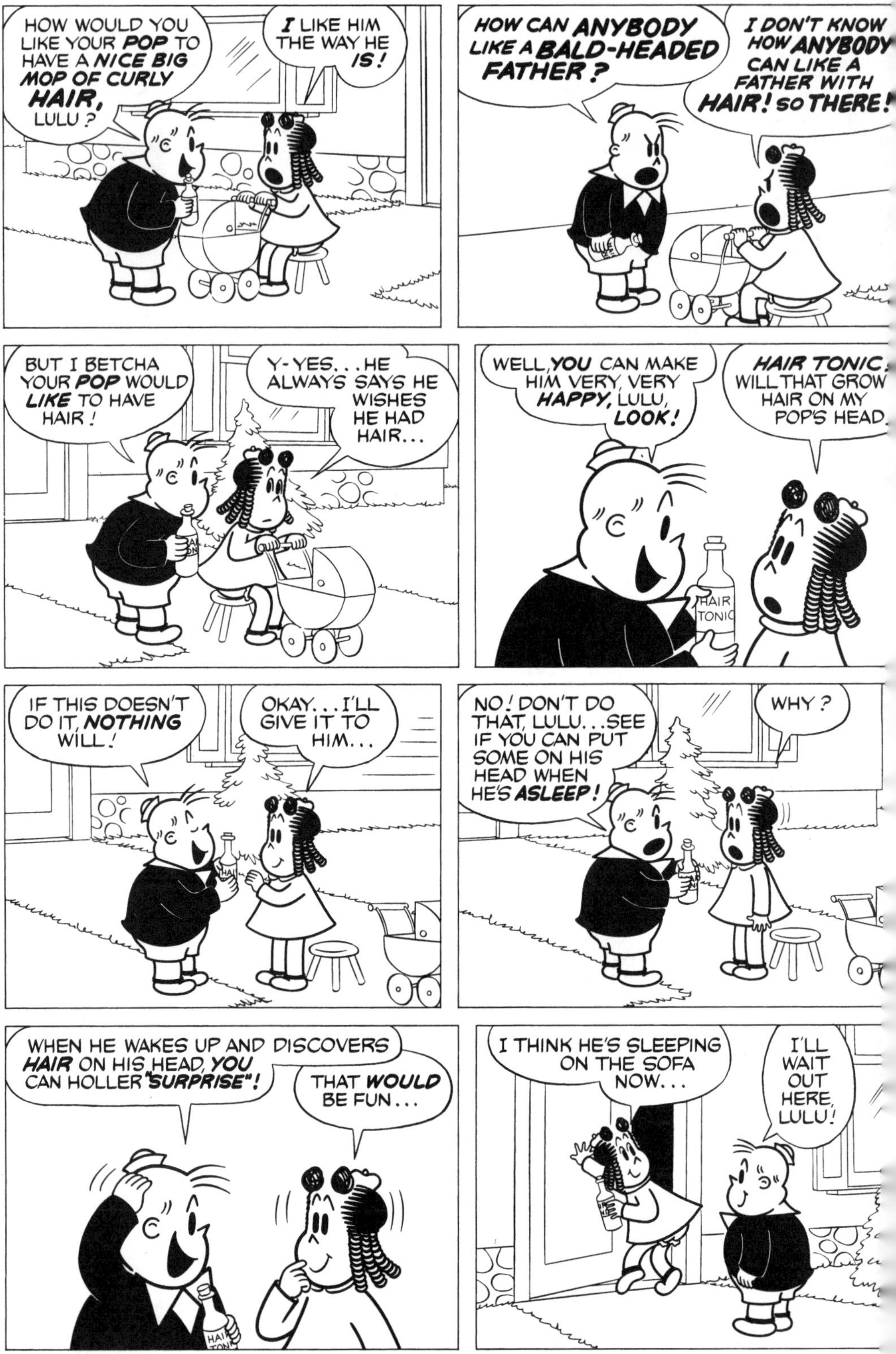
HOW WOULD YOU LIKE YOUR POP TO HAVE A NICE BIG MOP OF CURLY HAIR, LULU?
I LIKE HIM THE WAY HE IS!
HOW CAN ANYBODY LIKE A BALD-HEADED FATHER?
I DON'T KNOW HOW ANYBODY CAN LIKE A FATHER WITH HAIR! SO THERE!
BUT I BETCHA YOUR POP WOULD LIKE TO HAVE HAIR!
Y-YES...HE ALWAYS SAYS HE WISHES HE HAD HAIR...
WELL, YOU CAN MAKE HIM VERY, VERY HAPPY, LULU, LOOK!
HAIR TONIC
HAIR TONIC! WILL THAT GROW HAIR ON MY POP'S HEAD?
IF THIS DOESN'T DO IT, NOTHING WILL!
OKAY...I'LL GIVE IT TO HIM...
NO! DON'T DO THAT, LULU...SEE IF YOU CAN PUT SOME ON HIS HEAD WHEN HE'S ASLEEP!
WHY?
WHEN HE WAKES UP AND DISCOVERS HAIR ON HIS HEAD, YOU CAN HOLLER "SURPRISE"!
THAT WOULD BE FUN...
I THINK HE'S SLEEPING ON THE SOFA NOW...
I'LL WAIT OUT HERE, LULU!

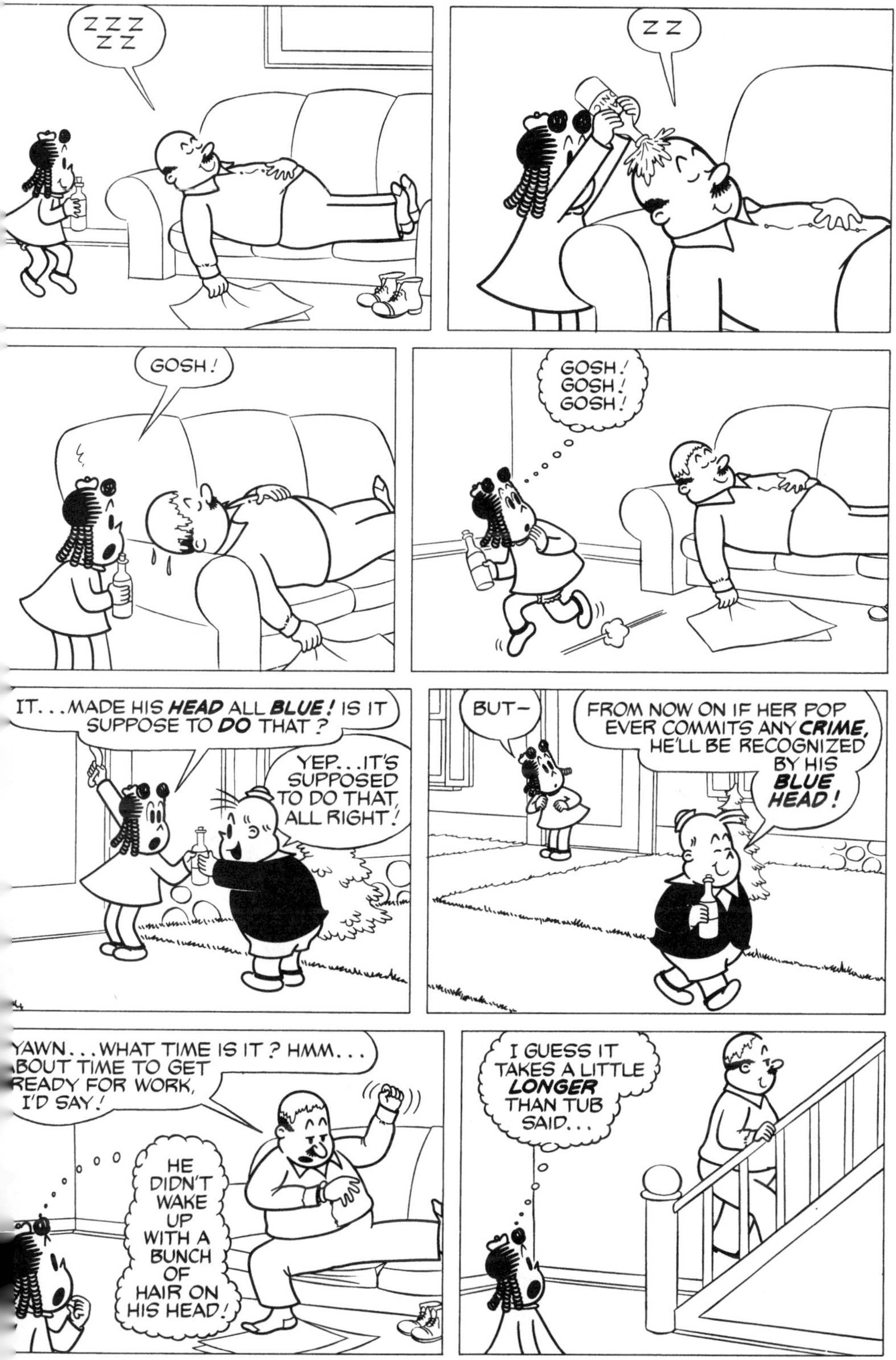
Z Z Z
Z Z
Z Z
GOSH!
GOSH! GOSH! GOSH!
IT...MADE HIS HEAD ALL BLUE! IS IT SUPPOSE TO DO THAT?
YEP...IT'S SUPPOSED TO DO THAT, ALL RIGHT!
BUT–
FROM NOW ON IF HER POP EVER COMMITS ANY CRIME, HE'LL BE RECOGNIZED BY HIS BLUE HEAD!
YAWN...WHAT TIME IS IT? HMM... ABOUT TIME TO GET READY FOR WORK, I'D SAY!
HE DIDN'T WAKE UP WITH A BUNCH OF HAIR ON HIS HEAD!
I GUESS IT TAKES A LITTLE LONGER THAN TUB SAID...

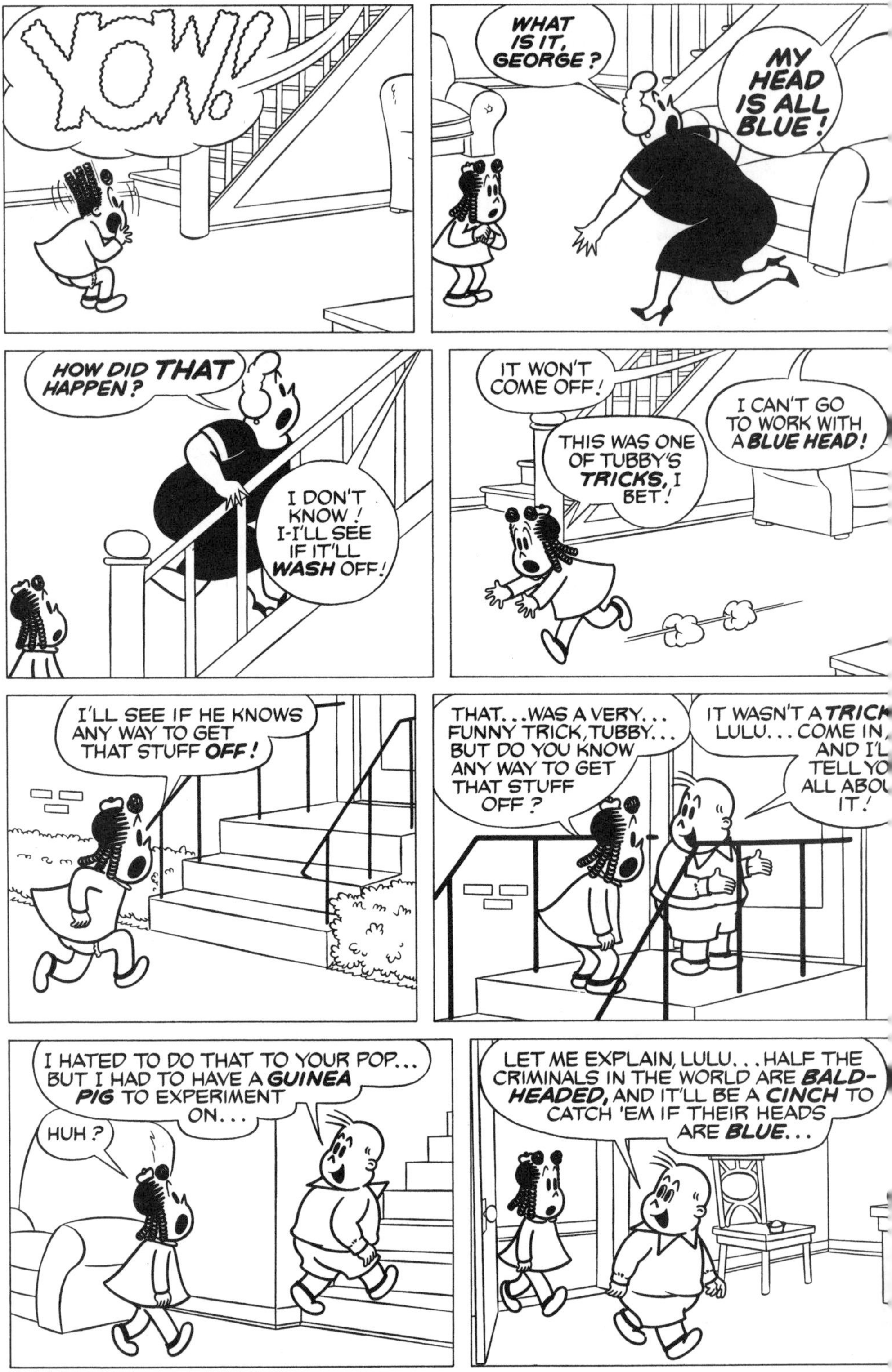
YOW!
WHAT IS IT, GEORGE?
MY HEAD IS ALL BLUE!
HOW DID THAT HAPPEN?
I DON'T KNOW! I-I'LL SEE IF IT'LL WASH OFF!
IT WON'T COME OFF!
I CAN'T GO TO WORK WITH A BLUE HEAD!
THIS WAS ONE OF TUBBY'S TRICKS, I BET!
I'LL SEE IF HE KNOWS ANY WAY TO GET THAT STUFF OFF!
THAT...WAS A VERY... FUNNY TRICK, TUBBY... BUT DO YOU KNOW ANY WAY TO GET THAT STUFF OFF?
I HATED TO DO THAT TO YOUR POP... BUT I HAD TO HAVE A GUINEA PIG TO EXPERIMENT ON...
HUH?
LET ME EXPLAIN, LULU... HALF THE CRIMINALS IN THE WORLD ARE BALD-HEADED, AND IT'LL BE A CINCH TO CATCH 'EM IF THEIR HEADS ARE BLUE...

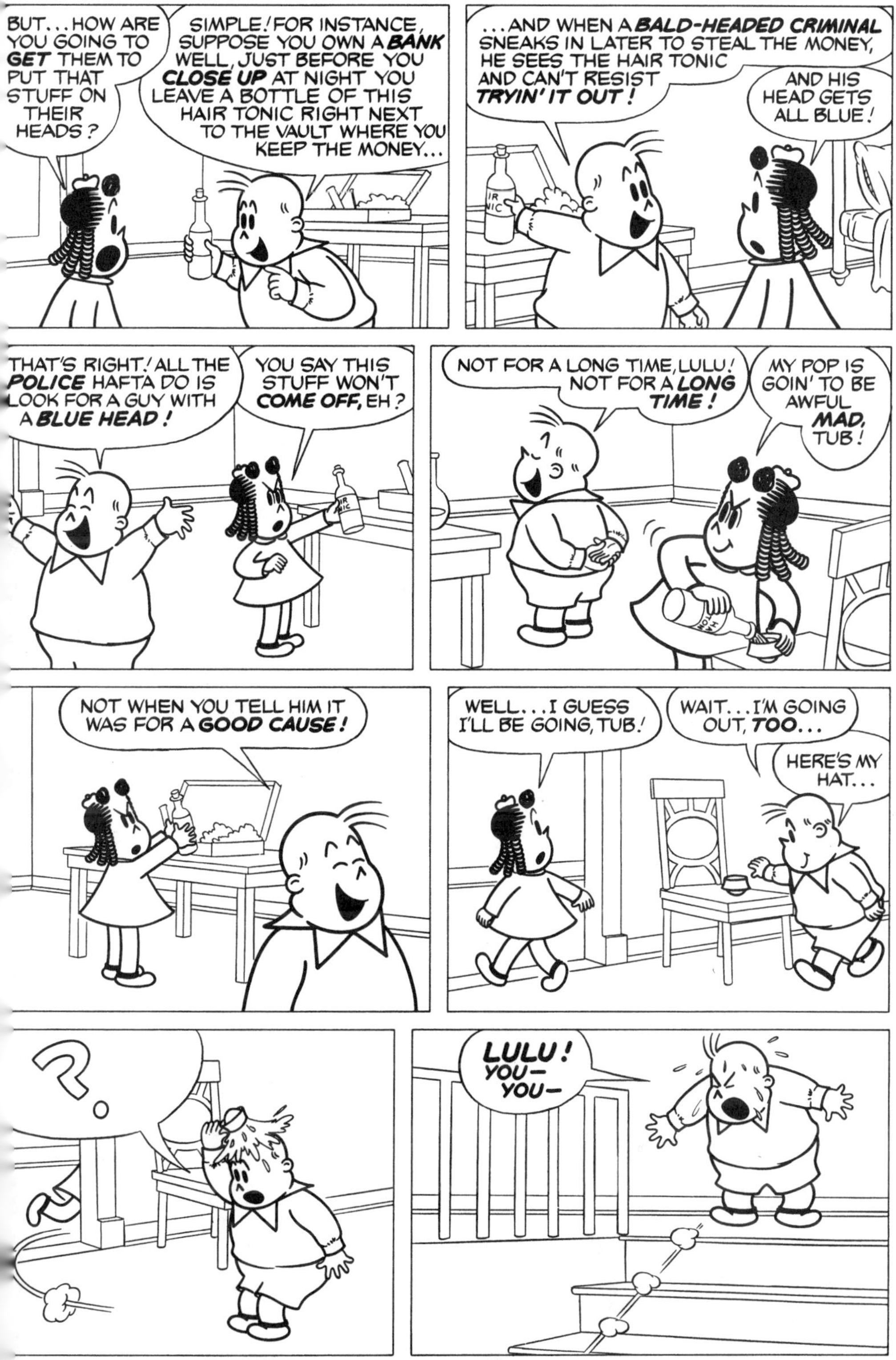
BUT...HOW ARE YOU GOING TO **GET** THEM TO PUT THAT STUFF ON THEIR HEADS?
SIMPLE! FOR INSTANCE, SUPPOSE YOU OWN A **BANK** WELL, JUST BEFORE YOU **CLOSE UP** AT NIGHT YOU LEAVE A BOTTLE OF THIS HAIR TONIC RIGHT NEXT TO THE VAULT WHERE YOU KEEP THE MONEY...
...AND WHEN A **BALD-HEADED CRIMINAL** SNEAKS IN LATER TO STEAL THE MONEY, HE SEES THE HAIR TONIC AND CAN'T RESIST **TRYIN' IT OUT!**
AND HIS HEAD GETS ALL BLUE!
THAT'S RIGHT! ALL THE **POLICE** HAFTA DO IS LOOK FOR A GUY WITH A **BLUE HEAD!**
YOU SAY THIS STUFF WON'T **COME OFF,** EH?
NOT FOR A LONG TIME, LULU! NOT FOR A **LONG TIME!**
MY POP IS GOIN' TO BE AWFUL **MAD,** TUB!
NOT WHEN YOU TELL HIM IT WAS FOR A **GOOD CAUSE!**
WELL...I GUESS I'LL BE GOING, TUB!
WAIT...I'M GOING OUT, **TOO...**
HERE'S MY HAT...
?
LULU! YOU— YOU—

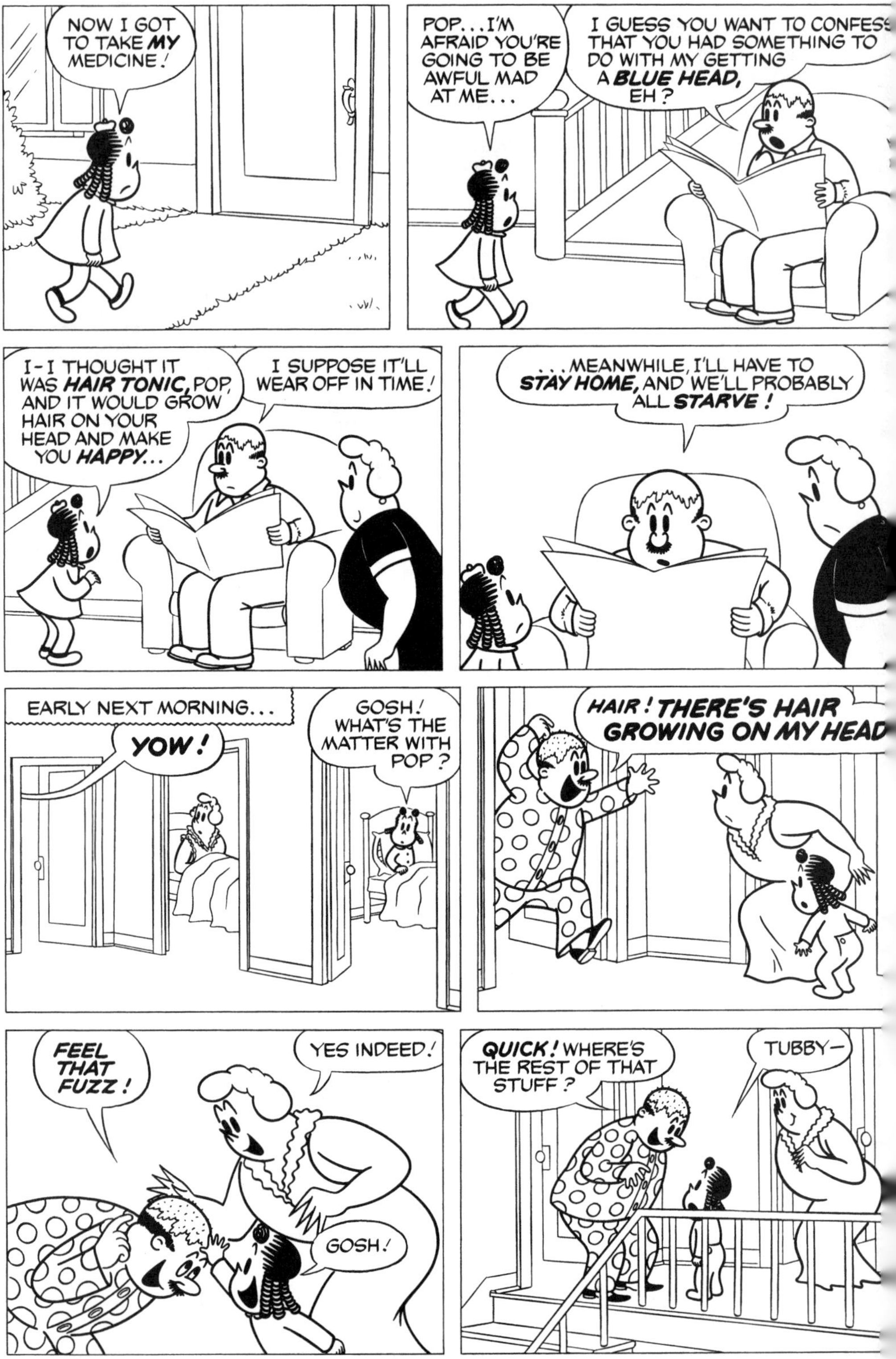
NOW I GOT TO TAKE MY MEDICINE!
POP...I'M AFRAID YOU'RE GOING TO BE AWFUL MAD AT ME...
I GUESS YOU WANT TO CONFESS THAT YOU HAD SOMETHING TO DO WITH MY GETTING A BLUE HEAD, EH?
I-I THOUGHT IT WAS HAIR TONIC, POP, AND IT WOULD GROW HAIR ON YOUR HEAD AND MAKE YOU HAPPY...
I SUPPOSE IT'LL WEAR OFF IN TIME!
...MEANWHILE, I'LL HAVE TO STAY HOME, AND WE'LL PROBABLY ALL STARVE!
EARLY NEXT MORNING...
YOW!
GOSH! WHAT'S THE MATTER WITH POP?
HAIR! THERE'S HAIR GROWING ON MY HEAD
FEEL THAT FUZZ!
YES INDEED!
GOSH!
QUICK! WHERE'S THE REST OF THAT STUFF?
TUBBY—

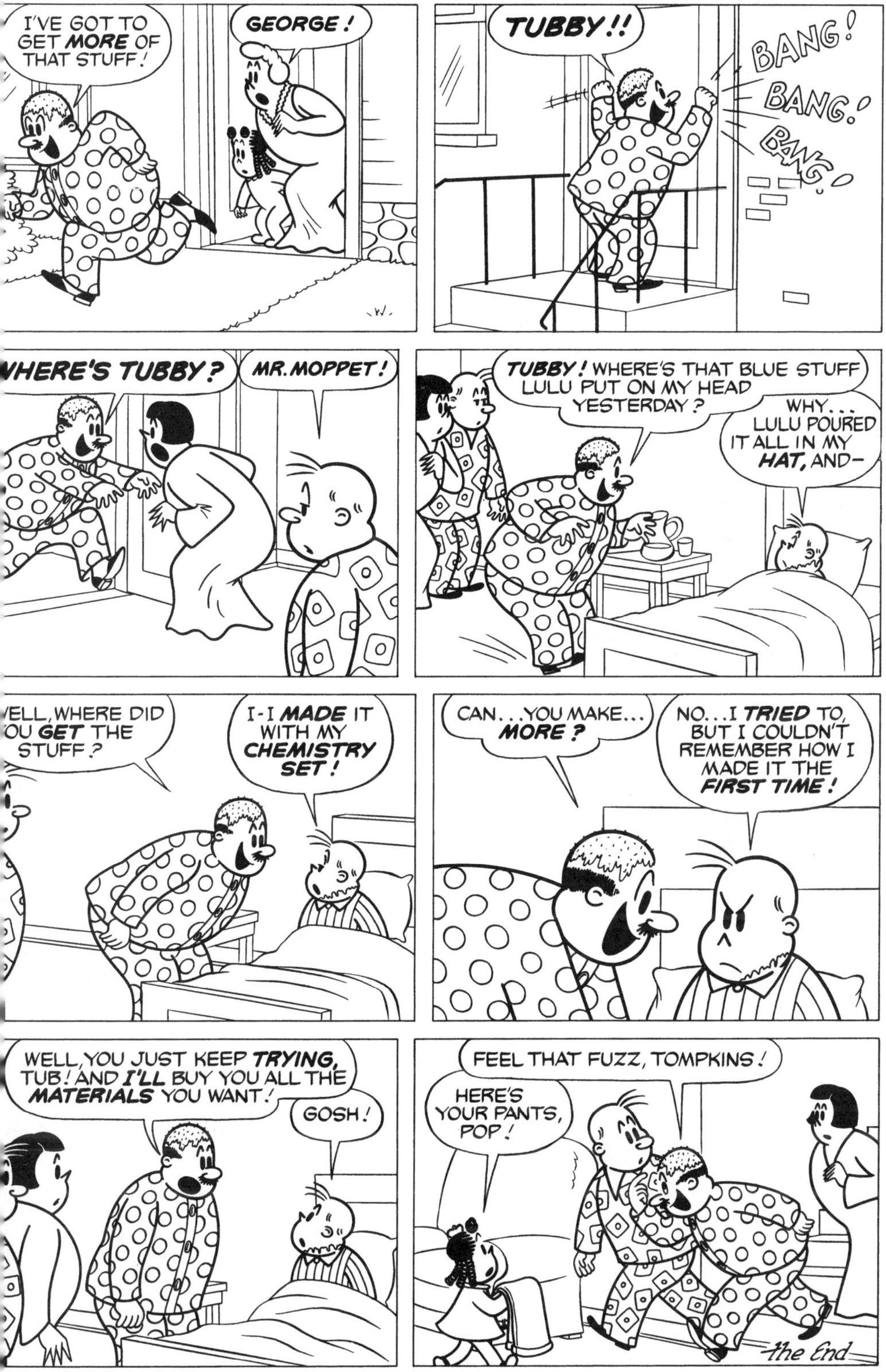
I'VE GOT TO GET MORE OF THAT STUFF!
GEORGE!
TUBBY!!
BANG!
BANG!
BANG!
WHERE'S TUBBY?
MR. MOPPET!
TUBBY! WHERE'S THAT BLUE STUFF LULU PUT ON MY HEAD YESTERDAY?
WHY... LULU POURED IT ALL IN MY HAT, AND–
WELL, WHERE DID YOU GET THE STUFF?
I-I MADE IT WITH MY CHEMISTRY SET!
CAN... YOU MAKE... MORE?
NO... I TRIED TO, BUT I COULDN'T REMEMBER HOW I MADE IT THE FIRST TIME!
WELL, YOU JUST KEEP TRYING, TUB! AND I'LL BUY YOU ALL THE MATERIALS YOU WANT!
GOSH!
FEEL THAT FUZZ, TOMPKINS!
HERE'S YOUR PANTS, POP!
The End

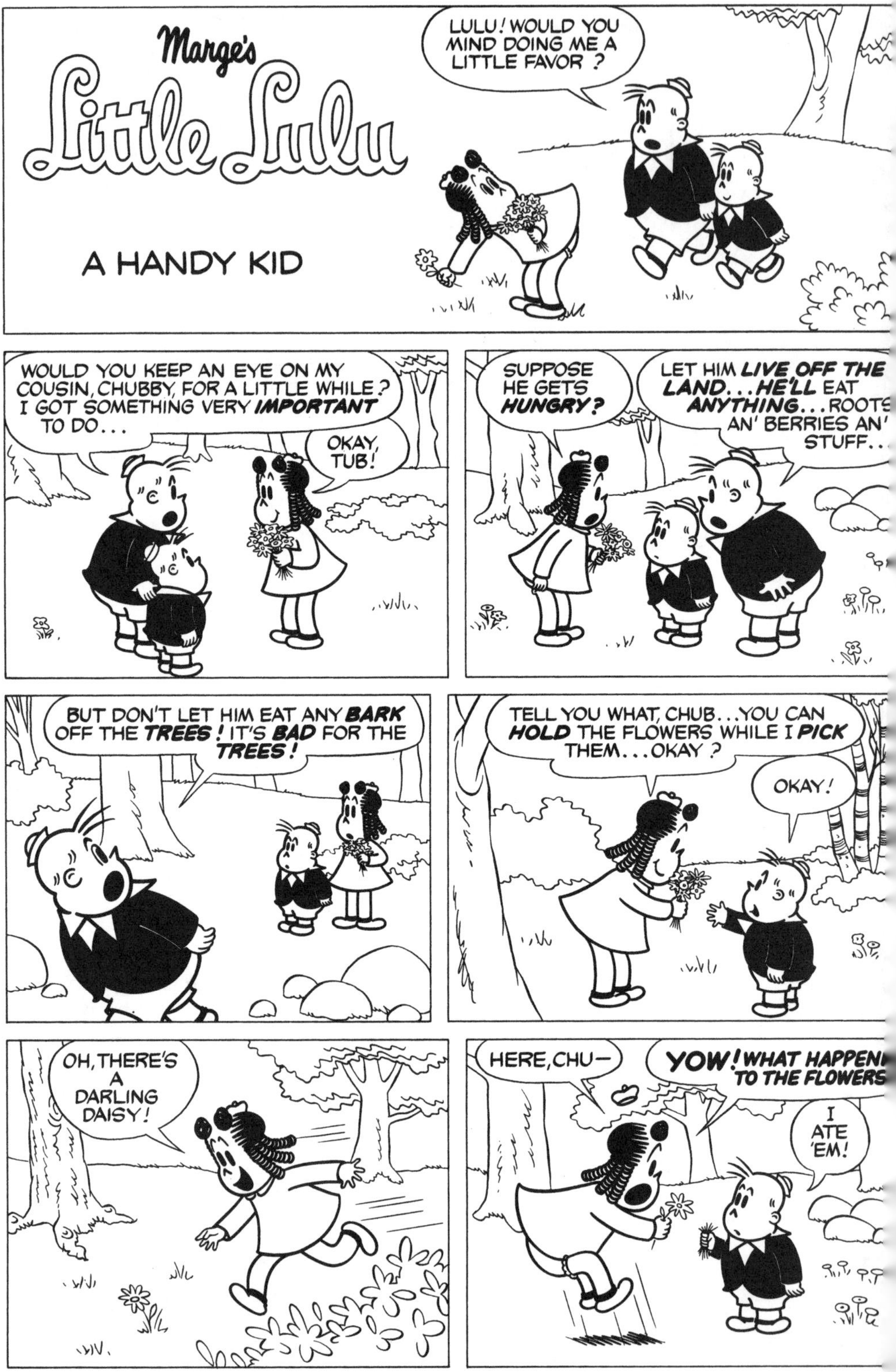
Marge's
Little Lulu
A HANDY KID
LULU! WOULD YOU MIND DOING ME A LITTLE FAVOR ?
WOULD YOU KEEP AN EYE ON MY COUSIN, CHUBBY, FOR A LITTLE WHILE? I GOT SOMETHING VERY IMPORTANT TO DO...
OKAY, TUB!
SUPPOSE HE GETS HUNGRY?
LET HIM LIVE OFF THE LAND...HE'LL EAT ANYTHING...ROOTS AN' BERRIES AN' STUFF...
BUT DON'T LET HIM EAT ANY BARK OFF THE TREES! IT'S BAD FOR THE TREES!
TELL YOU WHAT, CHUB...YOU CAN HOLD THE FLOWERS WHILE I PICK THEM...OKAY ?
OKAY!
OH, THERE'S A DARLING DAISY!
HERE, CHU—
YOW! WHAT HAPPEN TO THE FLOWERS
I ATE 'EM!

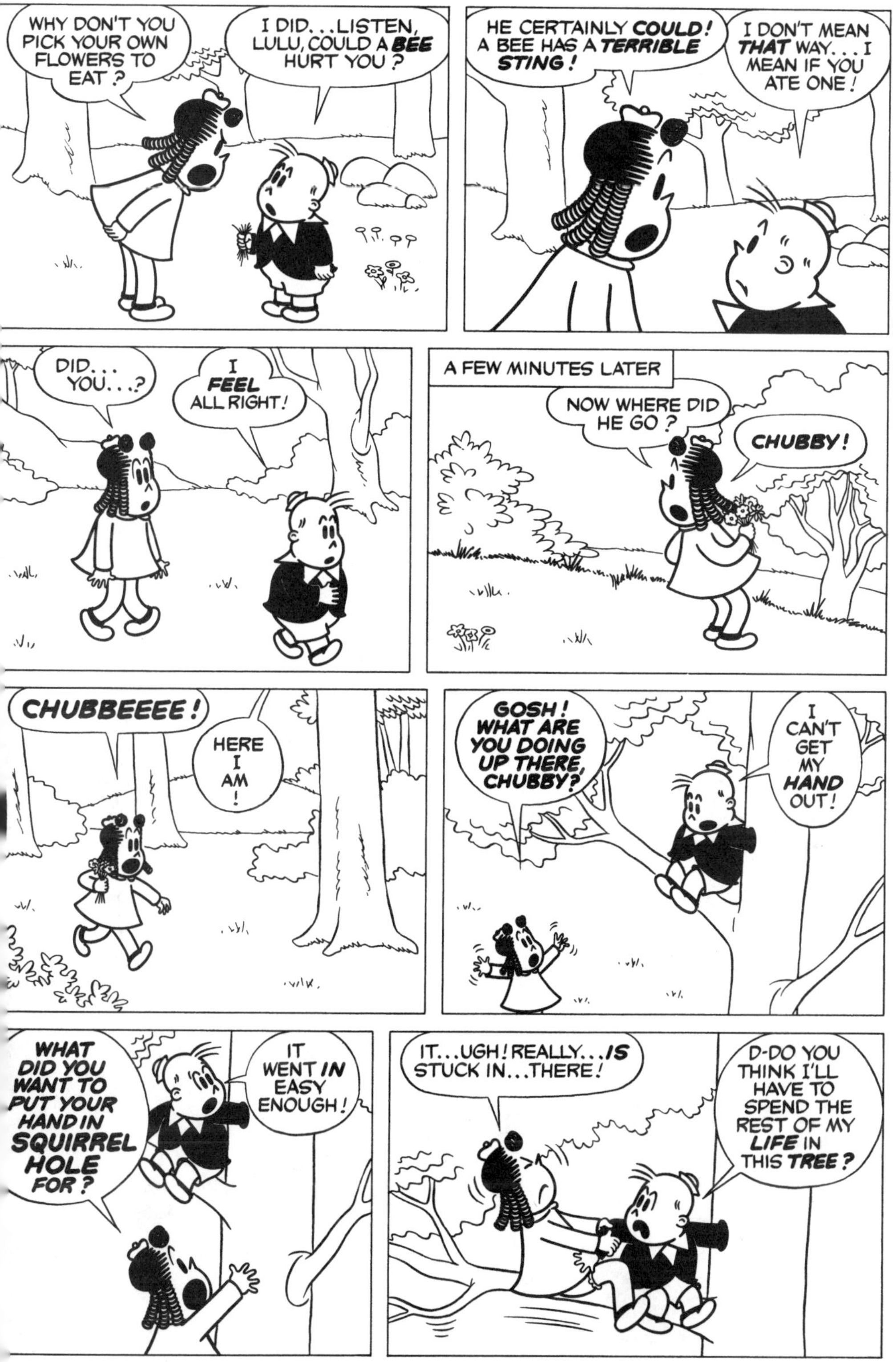
WHY DON'T YOU PICK YOUR OWN FLOWERS TO EAT ?
I DID...LISTEN, LULU, COULD A **BEE** HURT YOU ?
HE CERTAINLY **COULD!** A BEE HAS A **TERRIBLE STING!**
I DON'T MEAN **THAT** WAY...I MEAN IF YOU ATE ONE!
DID... YOU...?
I **FEEL** ALL RIGHT!
A FEW MINUTES LATER
NOW WHERE DID HE GO ?
CHUBBY!
CHUBBEEEE!
HERE I AM !
GOSH! WHAT ARE YOU DOING UP THERE, CHUBBY?
I CAN'T GET MY **HAND** OUT!
WHAT DID YOU WANT TO PUT YOUR HAND IN SQUIRREL HOLE FOR?
IT WENT **IN** EASY ENOUGH!
IT...UGH! REALLY...**IS** STUCK IN...THERE!
D-DO YOU THINK I'LL HAVE TO SPEND THE REST OF MY **LIFE** IN THIS **TREE?**

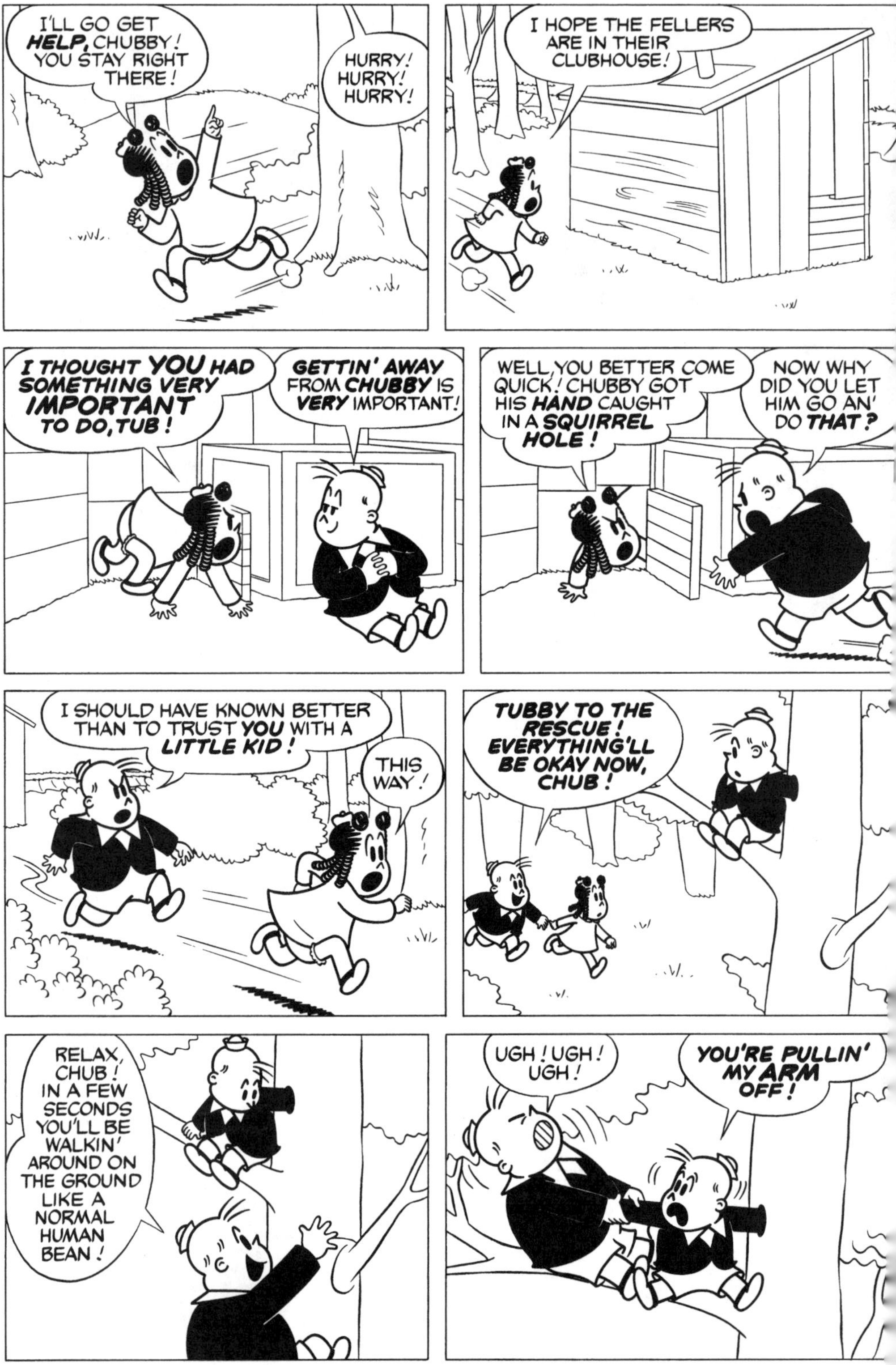
I'LL GO GET HELP, CHUBBY! YOU STAY RIGHT THERE!
HURRY! HURRY! HURRY!
I HOPE THE FELLERS ARE IN THEIR CLUBHOUSE!
I THOUGHT YOU HAD SOMETHING VERY IMPORTANT TO DO, TUB!
GETTIN' AWAY FROM CHUBBY IS VERY IMPORTANT!
WELL, YOU BETTER COME QUICK! CHUBBY GOT HIS HAND CAUGHT IN A SQUIRREL HOLE!
NOW WHY DID YOU LET HIM GO AN' DO THAT?
I SHOULD HAVE KNOWN BETTER THAN TO TRUST YOU WITH A LITTLE KID!
THIS WAY!
TUBBY TO THE RESCUE! EVERYTHING'LL BE OKAY NOW, CHUB!
RELAX, CHUB! IN A FEW SECONDS YOU'LL BE WALKIN' AROUND ON THE GROUND LIKE A NORMAL HUMAN BEAN!
UGH! UGH! UGH!
YOU'RE PULLIN' MY ARM OFF!

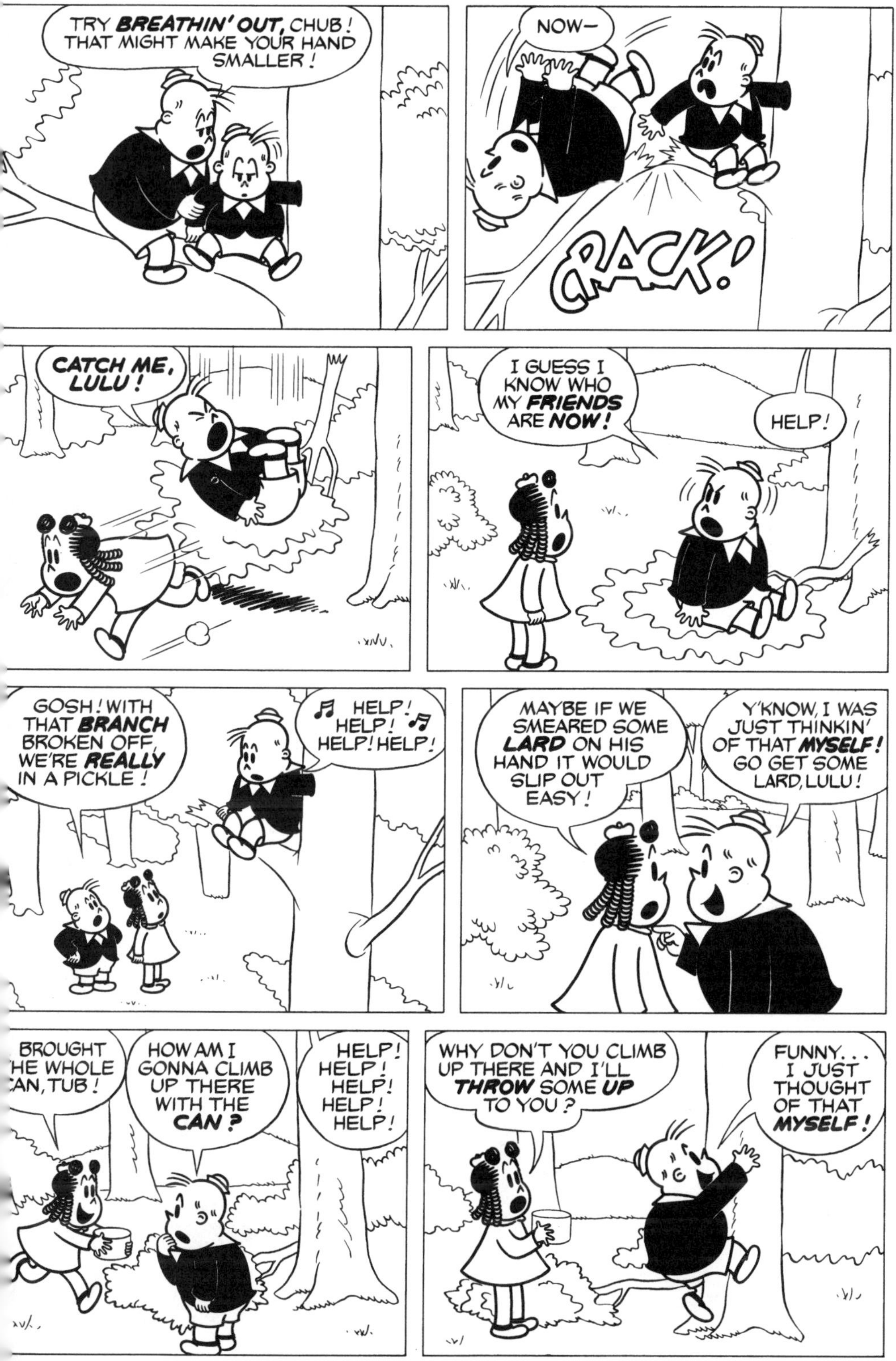
TRY BREATHIN' OUT, CHUB! THAT MIGHT MAKE YOUR HAND SMALLER!
NOW—
CRACK!
CATCH ME, LULU!
I GUESS I KNOW WHO MY FRIENDS ARE NOW!
HELP!
GOSH! WITH THAT BRANCH BROKEN OFF, WE'RE REALLY IN A PICKLE!
HELP! HELP! HELP! HELP!
MAYBE IF WE SMEARED SOME LARD ON HIS HAND IT WOULD SLIP OUT EASY!
Y'KNOW, I WAS JUST THINKIN' OF THAT MYSELF! GO GET SOME LARD, LULU!
BROUGHT HE WHOLE AN, TUB!
HOW AM I GONNA CLIMB UP THERE WITH THE CAN?
HELP! HELP! HELP! HELP! HELP!
WHY DON'T YOU CLIMB UP THERE AND I'LL THROW SOME UP TO YOU?
FUNNY... I JUST THOUGHT OF THAT MYSELF!

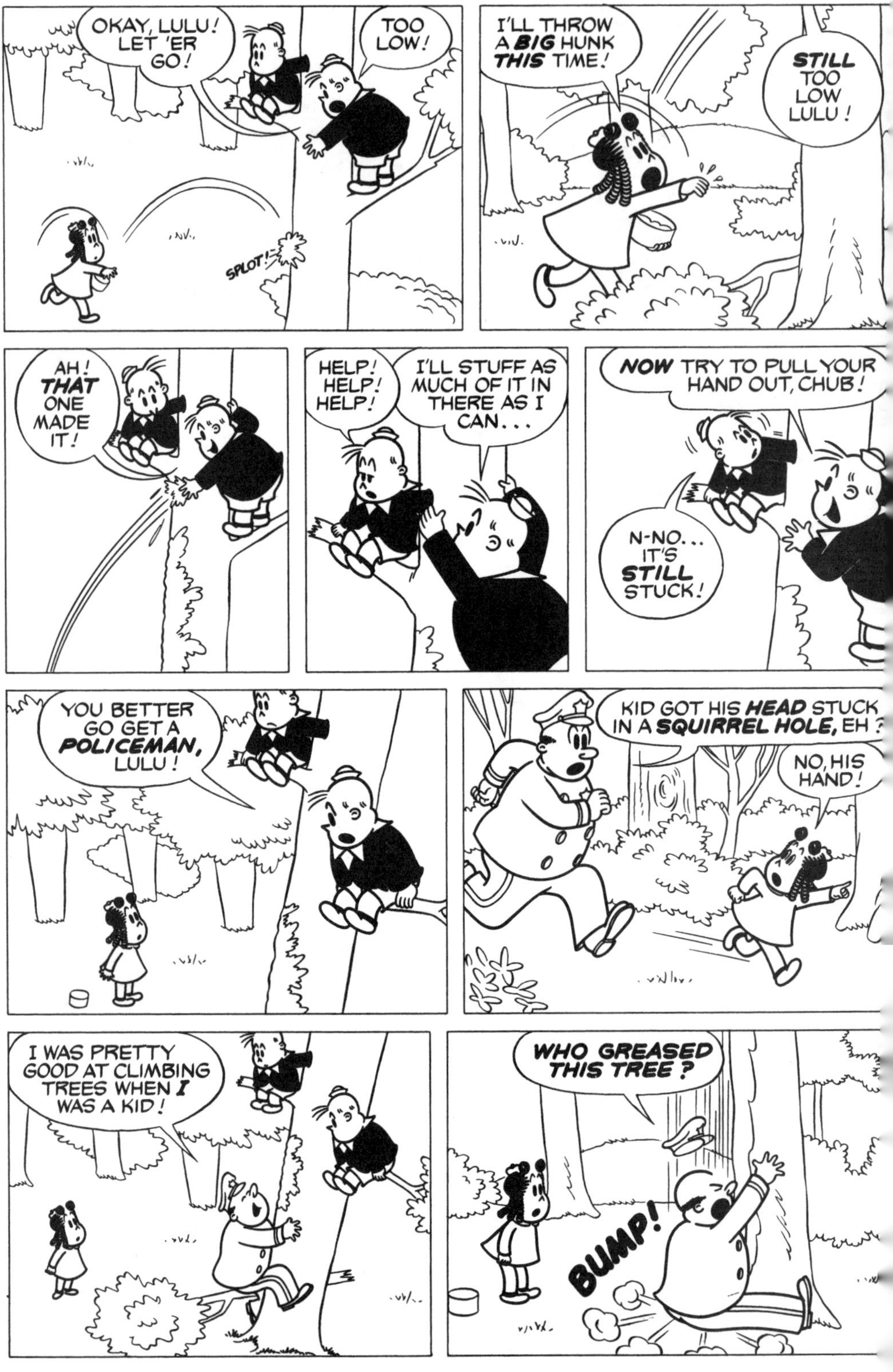
OKAY, LULU! LET 'ER GO!
TOO LOW!
SPLOT!
I'LL THROW A **BIG** HUNK **THIS** TIME!
STILL TOO LOW LULU!
AH! **THAT** ONE MADE IT!
HELP! HELP! HELP!
I'LL STUFF AS MUCH OF IT IN THERE AS I CAN...
NOW TRY TO PULL YOUR HAND OUT, CHUB!
N-NO... IT'S **STILL** STUCK!
YOU BETTER GO GET A **POLICEMAN,** LULU!
KID GOT HIS **HEAD** STUCK IN A **SQUIRREL HOLE,** EH?
NO, HIS HAND!
I WAS PRETTY GOOD AT CLIMBING TREES WHEN **I** WAS A KID!
WHO GREASED THIS TREE?
BUMP!

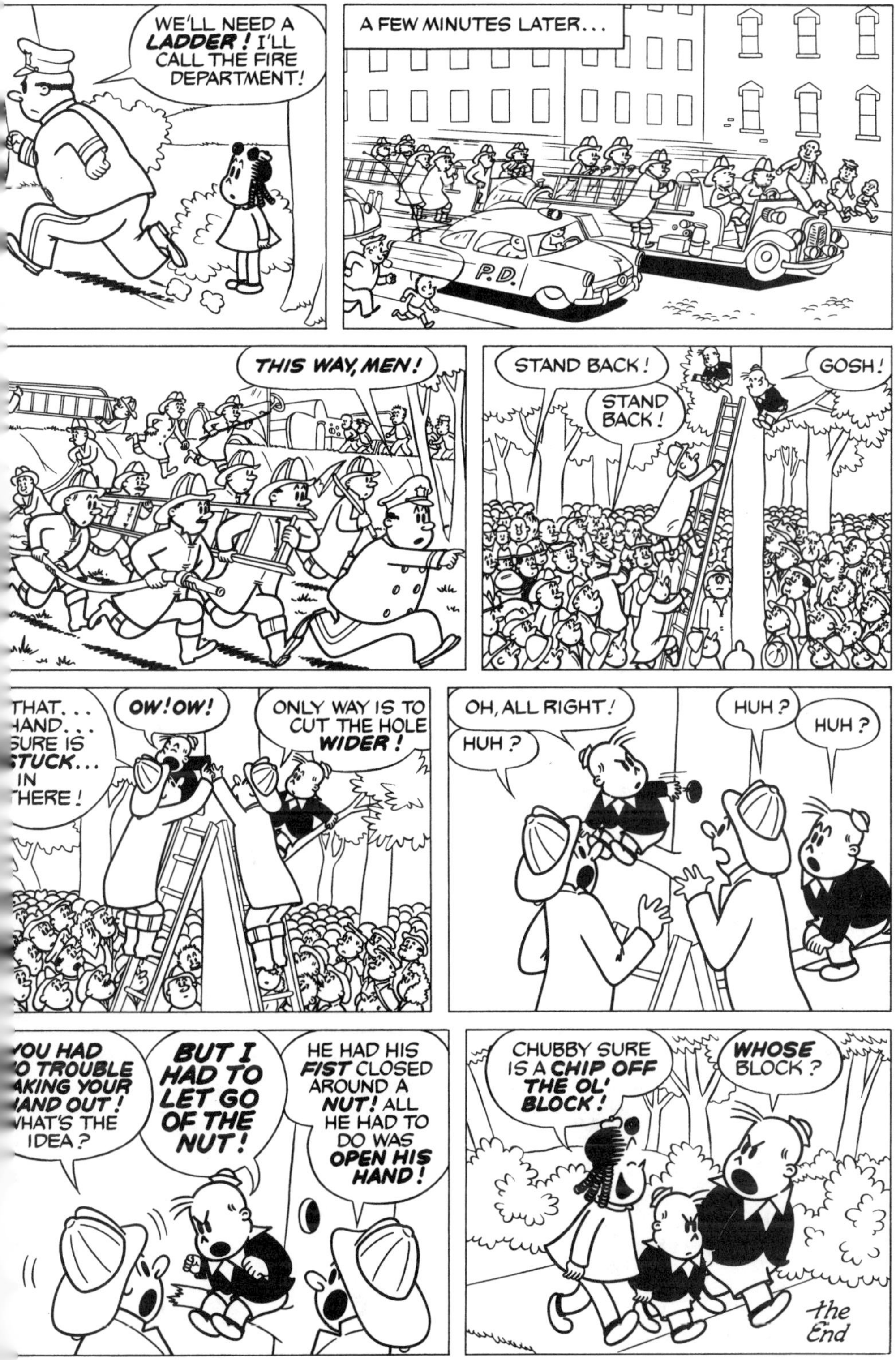
WE'LL NEED A LADDER! I'LL CALL THE FIRE DEPARTMENT!
A FEW MINUTES LATER...
P.D.
THIS WAY, MEN!
STAND BACK!
STAND BACK!
GOSH!
THAT... HAND... SURE IS STUCK... IN THERE!
OW! OW!
ONLY WAY IS TO CUT THE HOLE WIDER!
OH, ALL RIGHT!
HUH?
HUH?
HUH?
BUT I HAD TO LET GO OF THE NUT!
HE HAD HIS FIST CLOSED AROUND A NUT! ALL HE HAD TO DO WAS OPEN HIS HAND!
CHUBBY SURE IS A CHIP OFF THE OL' BLOCK!
WHOSE BLOCK?
the End

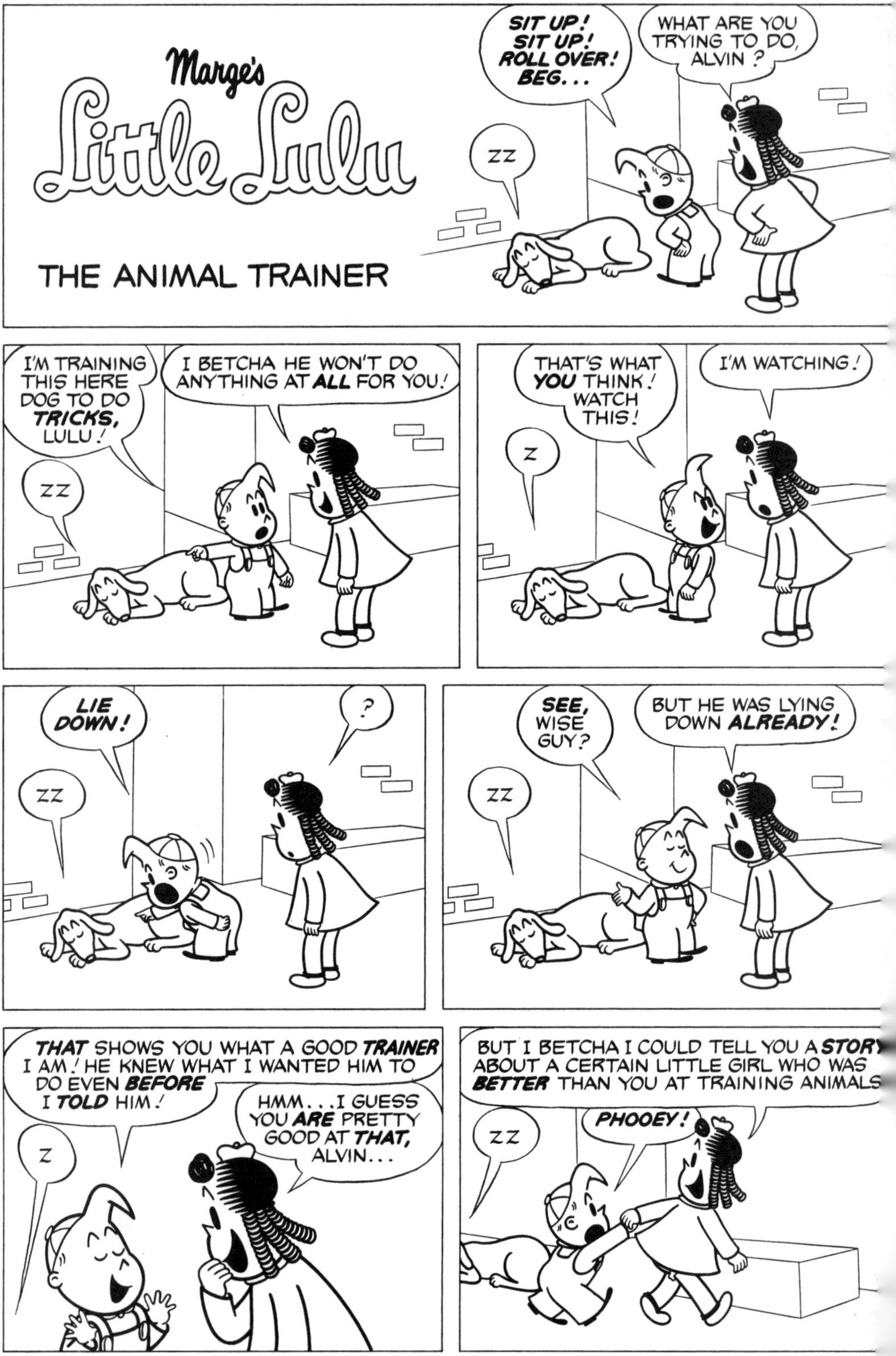

Marge's Little Lulu
THE ANIMAL TRAINER
SIT UP! SIT UP! ROLL OVER! BEG...
WHAT ARE YOU TRYING TO DO, ALVIN?
ZZ
I'M TRAINING THIS HERE DOG TO DO TRICKS, LULU!
I BETCHA HE WON'T DO ANYTHING AT ALL FOR YOU!
ZZ
THAT'S WHAT YOU THINK! WATCH THIS!
I'M WATCHING!
Z
LIE DOWN!
?
ZZ
SEE, WISE GUY?
BUT HE WAS LYING DOWN ALREADY!
ZZ
THAT SHOWS YOU WHAT A GOOD TRAINER I AM! HE KNEW WHAT I WANTED HIM TO DO EVEN BEFORE I TOLD HIM!
HMM...I GUESS YOU ARE PRETTY GOOD AT THAT, ALVIN...
Z
BUT I BETCHA I COULD TELL YOU A STORY ABOUT A CERTAIN LITTLE GIRL WHO WAS BETTER THAN YOU AT TRAINING ANIMALS
PHOOEY!
ZZ

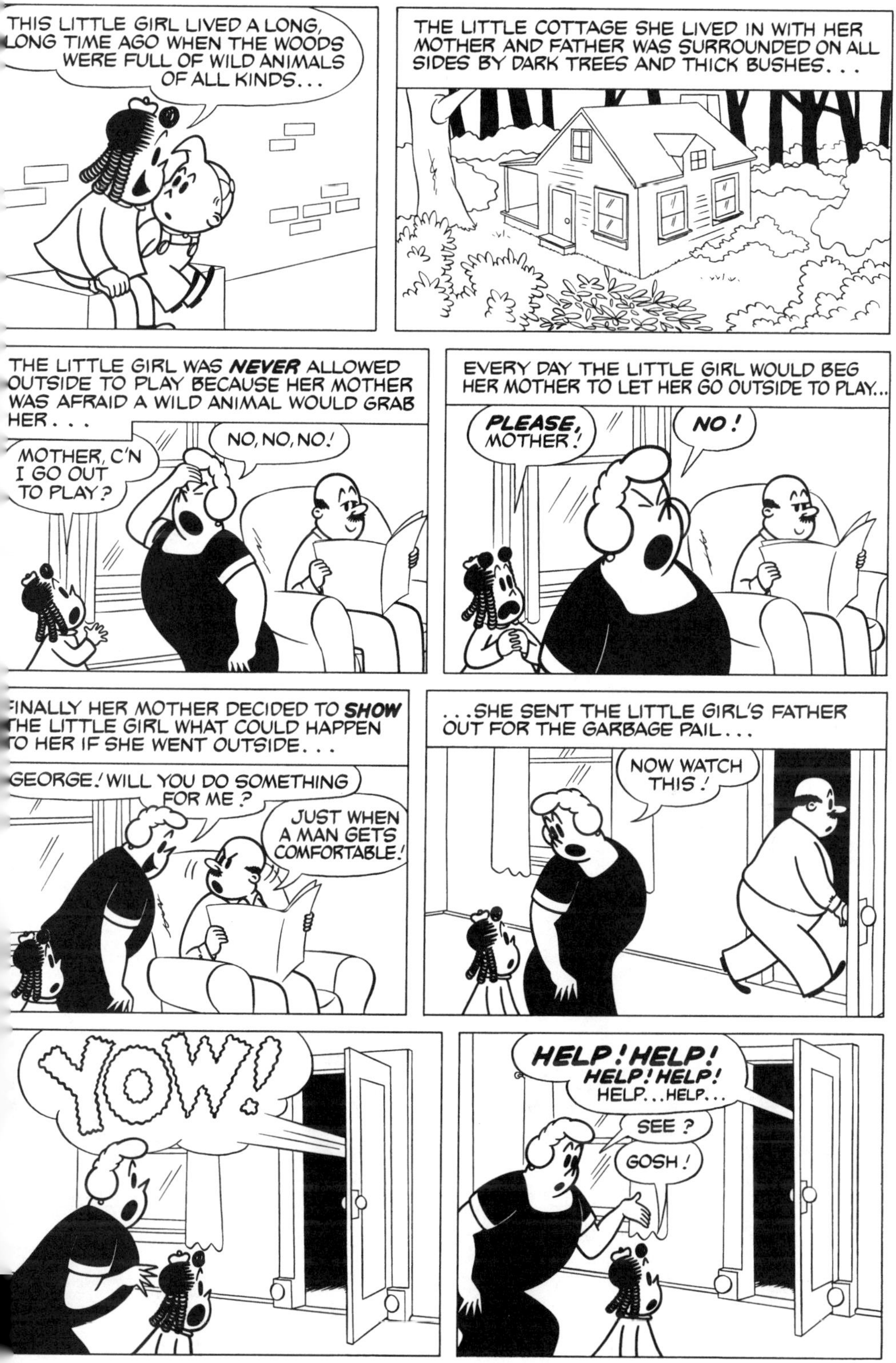

THIS LITTLE GIRL LIVED A LONG, LONG TIME AGO WHEN THE WOODS WERE FULL OF WILD ANIMALS OF ALL KINDS...
THE LITTLE COTTAGE SHE LIVED IN WITH HER MOTHER AND FATHER WAS SURROUNDED ON ALL SIDES BY DARK TREES AND THICK BUSHES...
THE LITTLE GIRL WAS NEVER ALLOWED OUTSIDE TO PLAY BECAUSE HER MOTHER WAS AFRAID A WILD ANIMAL WOULD GRAB HER...
MOTHER, C'N I GO OUT TO PLAY?
NO, NO, NO!
EVERY DAY THE LITTLE GIRL WOULD BEG HER MOTHER TO LET HER GO OUTSIDE TO PLAY...
PLEASE, MOTHER!
NO!
FINALLY HER MOTHER DECIDED TO SHOW THE LITTLE GIRL WHAT COULD HAPPEN TO HER IF SHE WENT OUTSIDE...
GEORGE! WILL YOU DO SOMETHING FOR ME?
JUST WHEN A MAN GETS COMFORTABLE!
...SHE SENT THE LITTLE GIRL'S FATHER OUT FOR THE GARBAGE PAIL...
NOW WATCH THIS!
YOW!
HELP! HELP! HELP! HELP! HELP... HELP...
SEE?
GOSH!

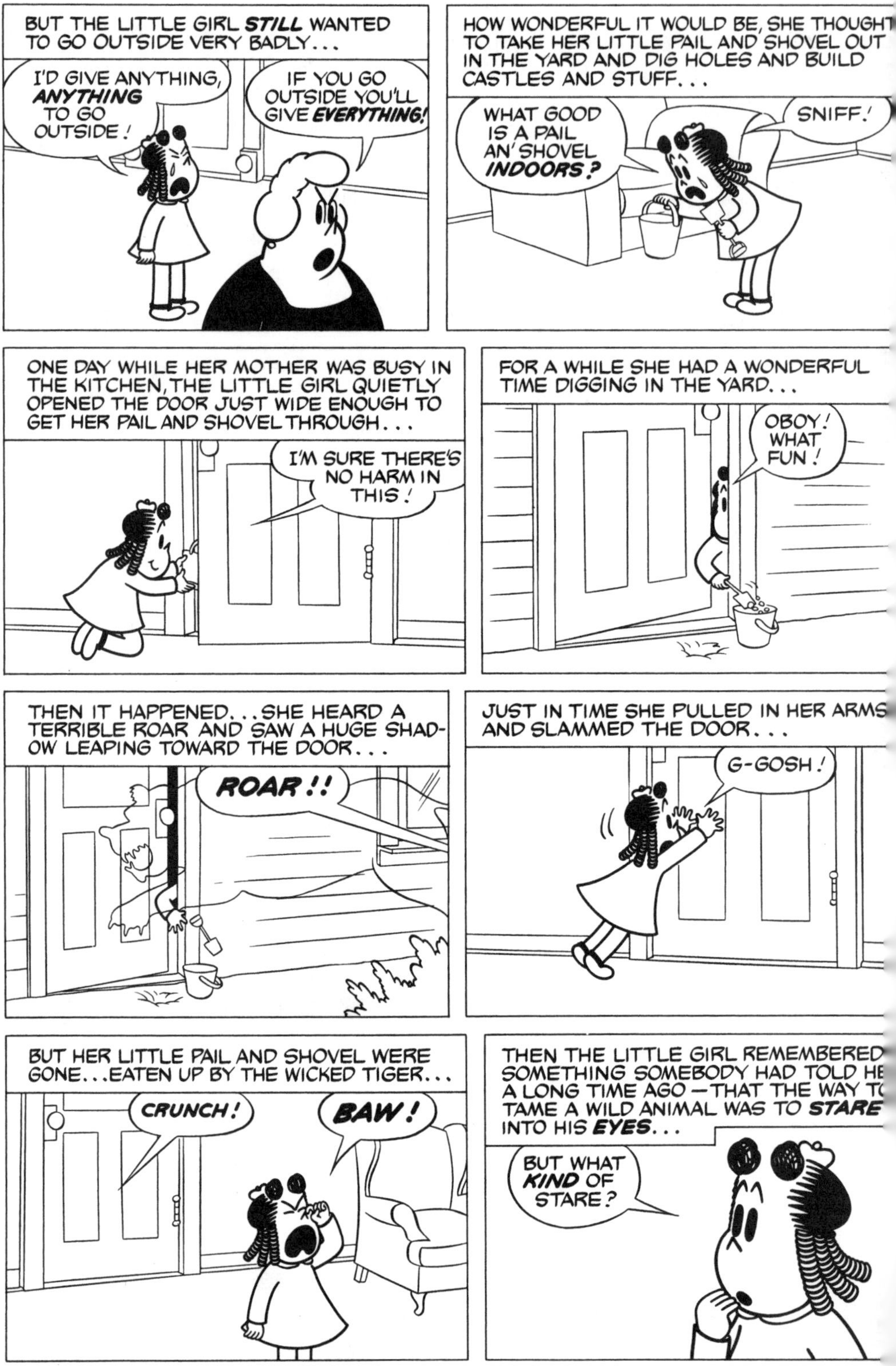
BUT THE LITTLE GIRL STILL WANTED TO GO OUTSIDE VERY BADLY...
I'D GIVE ANYTHING, ANYTHING TO GO OUTSIDE!
IF YOU GO OUTSIDE YOU'LL GIVE EVERYTHING!
HOW WONDERFUL IT WOULD BE, SHE THOUGHT TO TAKE HER LITTLE PAIL AND SHOVEL OUT IN THE YARD AND DIG HOLES AND BUILD CASTLES AND STUFF...
WHAT GOOD IS A PAIL AN' SHOVEL INDOORS?
SNIFF!
ONE DAY WHILE HER MOTHER WAS BUSY IN THE KITCHEN, THE LITTLE GIRL QUIETLY OPENED THE DOOR JUST WIDE ENOUGH TO GET HER PAIL AND SHOVEL THROUGH...
I'M SURE THERE'S NO HARM IN THIS!
FOR A WHILE SHE HAD A WONDERFUL TIME DIGGING IN THE YARD...
OBOY! WHAT FUN!
THEN IT HAPPENED...SHE HEARD A TERRIBLE ROAR AND SAW A HUGE SHADOW LEAPING TOWARD THE DOOR...
ROAR!!
JUST IN TIME SHE PULLED IN HER ARMS AND SLAMMED THE DOOR...
G-GOSH!
BUT HER LITTLE PAIL AND SHOVEL WERE GONE...EATEN UP BY THE WICKED TIGER...
CRUNCH!
BAW!
THEN THE LITTLE GIRL REMEMBERED SOMETHING SOMEBODY HAD TOLD HE A LONG TIME AGO—THAT THE WAY T TAME A WILD ANIMAL WAS TO STARE INTO HIS EYES...
BUT WHAT KIND OF STARE?

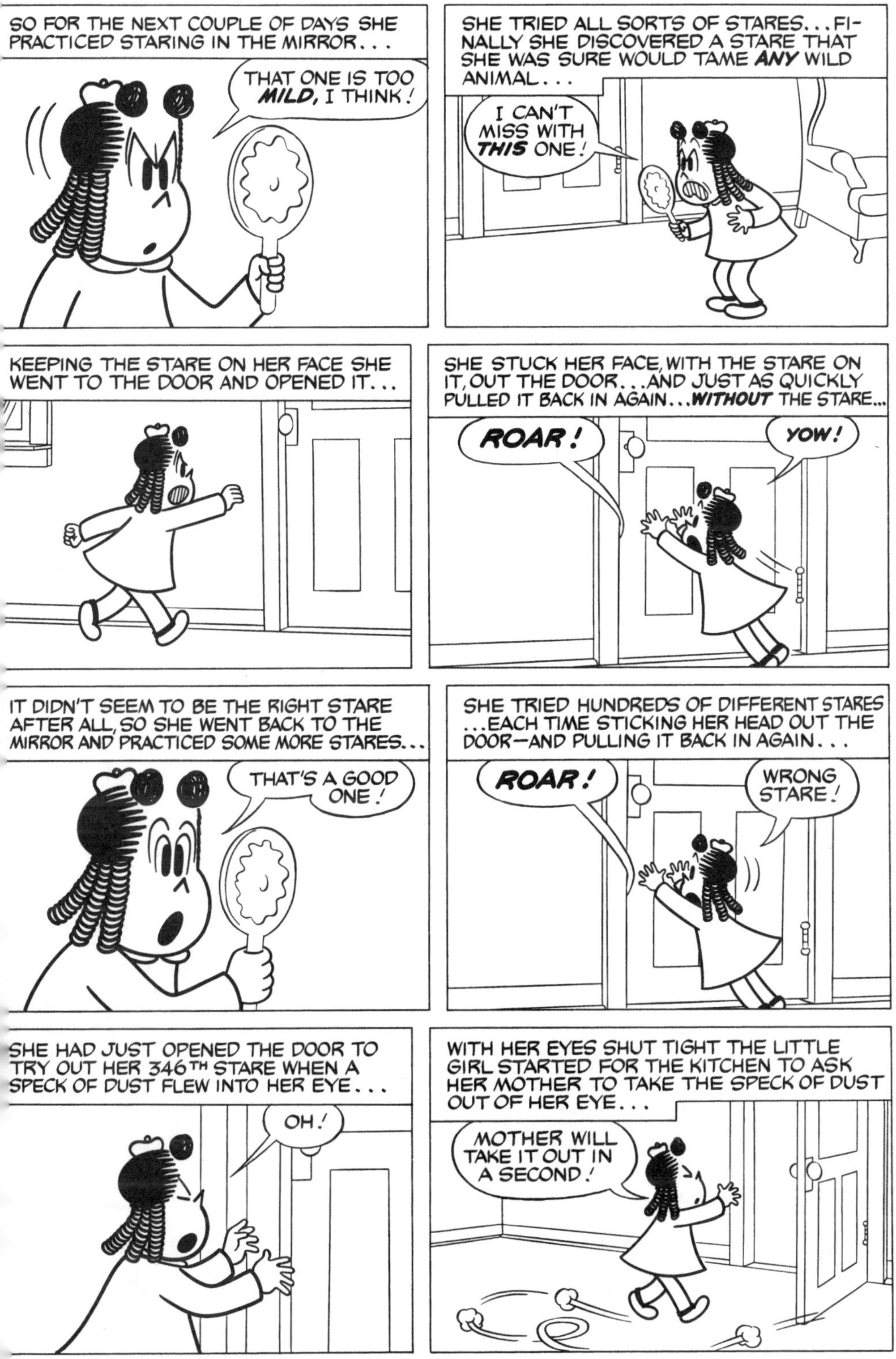
SO FOR THE NEXT COUPLE OF DAYS SHE PRACTICED STARING IN THE MIRROR. . .
THAT ONE IS TOO MILD, I THINK!
SHE TRIED ALL SORTS OF STARES. . . FINALLY SHE DISCOVERED A STARE THAT SHE WAS SURE WOULD TAME ANY WILD ANIMAL. . .
I CAN'T MISS WITH THIS ONE!
KEEPING THE STARE ON HER FACE SHE WENT TO THE DOOR AND OPENED IT. . .
SHE STUCK HER FACE, WITH THE STARE ON IT, OUT THE DOOR. . . AND JUST AS QUICKLY PULLED IT BACK IN AGAIN. . . WITHOUT THE STARE...
ROAR!
YOW!
IT DIDN'T SEEM TO BE THE RIGHT STARE AFTER ALL, SO SHE WENT BACK TO THE MIRROR AND PRACTICED SOME MORE STARES. . .
THAT'S A GOOD ONE!
SHE TRIED HUNDREDS OF DIFFERENT STARES . . . EACH TIME STICKING HER HEAD OUT THE DOOR—AND PULLING IT BACK IN AGAIN. . .
ROAR!
WRONG STARE!
SHE HAD JUST OPENED THE DOOR TO TRY OUT HER 346TH STARE WHEN A SPECK OF DUST FLEW INTO HER EYE. . .
OH!
WITH HER EYES SHUT TIGHT THE LITTLE GIRL STARTED FOR THE KITCHEN TO ASK HER MOTHER TO TAKE THE SPECK OF DUST OUT OF HER EYE. . .
MOTHER WILL TAKE IT OUT IN A SECOND!

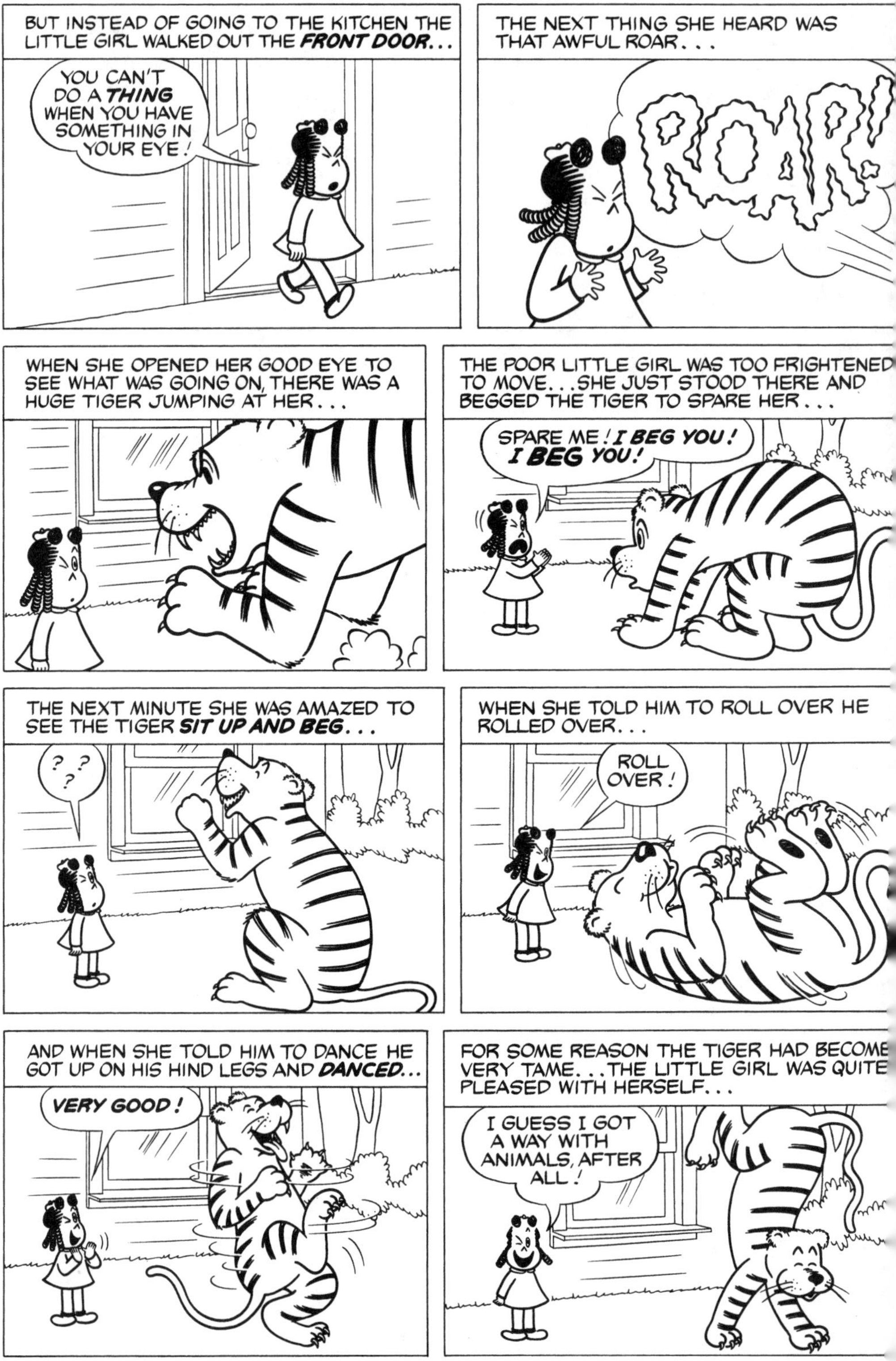
BUT INSTEAD OF GOING TO THE KITCHEN THE LITTLE GIRL WALKED OUT THE FRONT DOOR...
YOU CAN'T DO A THING WHEN YOU HAVE SOMETHING IN YOUR EYE!
THE NEXT THING SHE HEARD WAS THAT AWFUL ROAR...
ROAR!
WHEN SHE OPENED HER GOOD EYE TO SEE WHAT WAS GOING ON, THERE WAS A HUGE TIGER JUMPING AT HER...
THE POOR LITTLE GIRL WAS TOO FRIGHTENED TO MOVE...SHE JUST STOOD THERE AND BEGGED THE TIGER TO SPARE HER...
SPARE ME! I BEG YOU! I BEG YOU!
THE NEXT MINUTE SHE WAS AMAZED TO SEE THE TIGER SIT UP AND BEG...
? ? ?
WHEN SHE TOLD HIM TO ROLL OVER HE ROLLED OVER...
ROLL OVER!
AND WHEN SHE TOLD HIM TO DANCE HE GOT UP ON HIS HIND LEGS AND DANCED...
VERY GOOD!
FOR SOME REASON THE TIGER HAD BECOME VERY TAME...THE LITTLE GIRL WAS QUITE PLEASED WITH HERSELF...
I GUESS I GOT A WAY WITH ANIMALS, AFTER ALL!

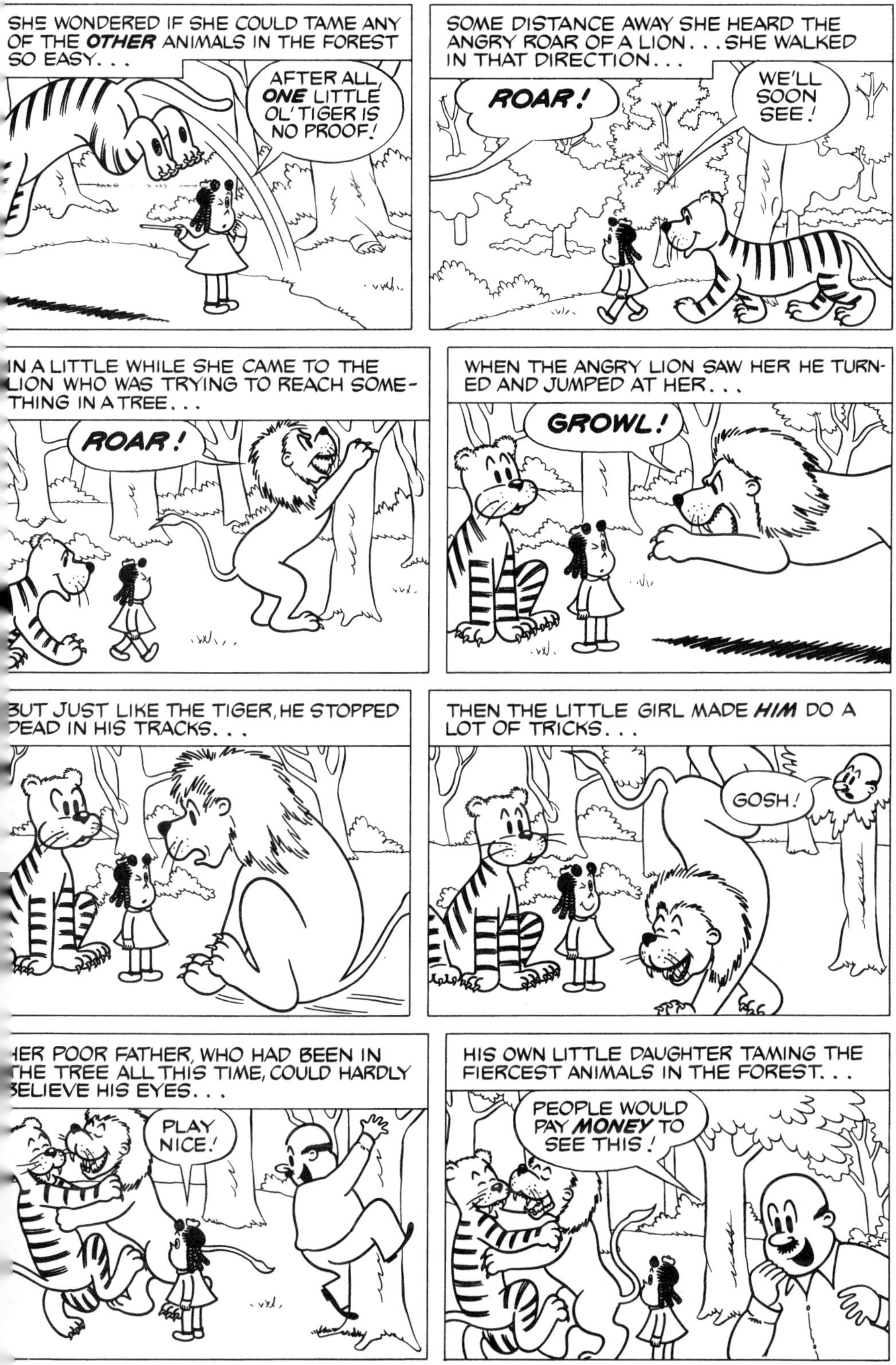
SHE WONDERED IF SHE COULD TAME ANY OF THE OTHER ANIMALS IN THE FOREST SO EASY. . .
AFTER ALL, ONE LITTLE OL' TIGER IS NO PROOF!
SOME DISTANCE AWAY SHE HEARD THE ANGRY ROAR OF A LION. . . SHE WALKED IN THAT DIRECTION. . .
ROAR!
WE'LL SOON SEE!
IN A LITTLE WHILE SHE CAME TO THE LION WHO WAS TRYING TO REACH SOMETHING IN A TREE. . .
ROAR!
WHEN THE ANGRY LION SAW HER HE TURNED AND JUMPED AT HER. . .
GROWL!
BUT JUST LIKE THE TIGER, HE STOPPED DEAD IN HIS TRACKS. . .
THEN THE LITTLE GIRL MADE HIM DO A LOT OF TRICKS. . .
GOSH!
HER POOR FATHER, WHO HAD BEEN IN THE TREE ALL THIS TIME, COULD HARDLY BELIEVE HIS EYES. . .
PLAY NICE!
HIS OWN LITTLE DAUGHTER TAMING THE FIERCEST ANIMALS IN THE FOREST. . .
PEOPLE WOULD PAY MONEY TO SEE THIS!

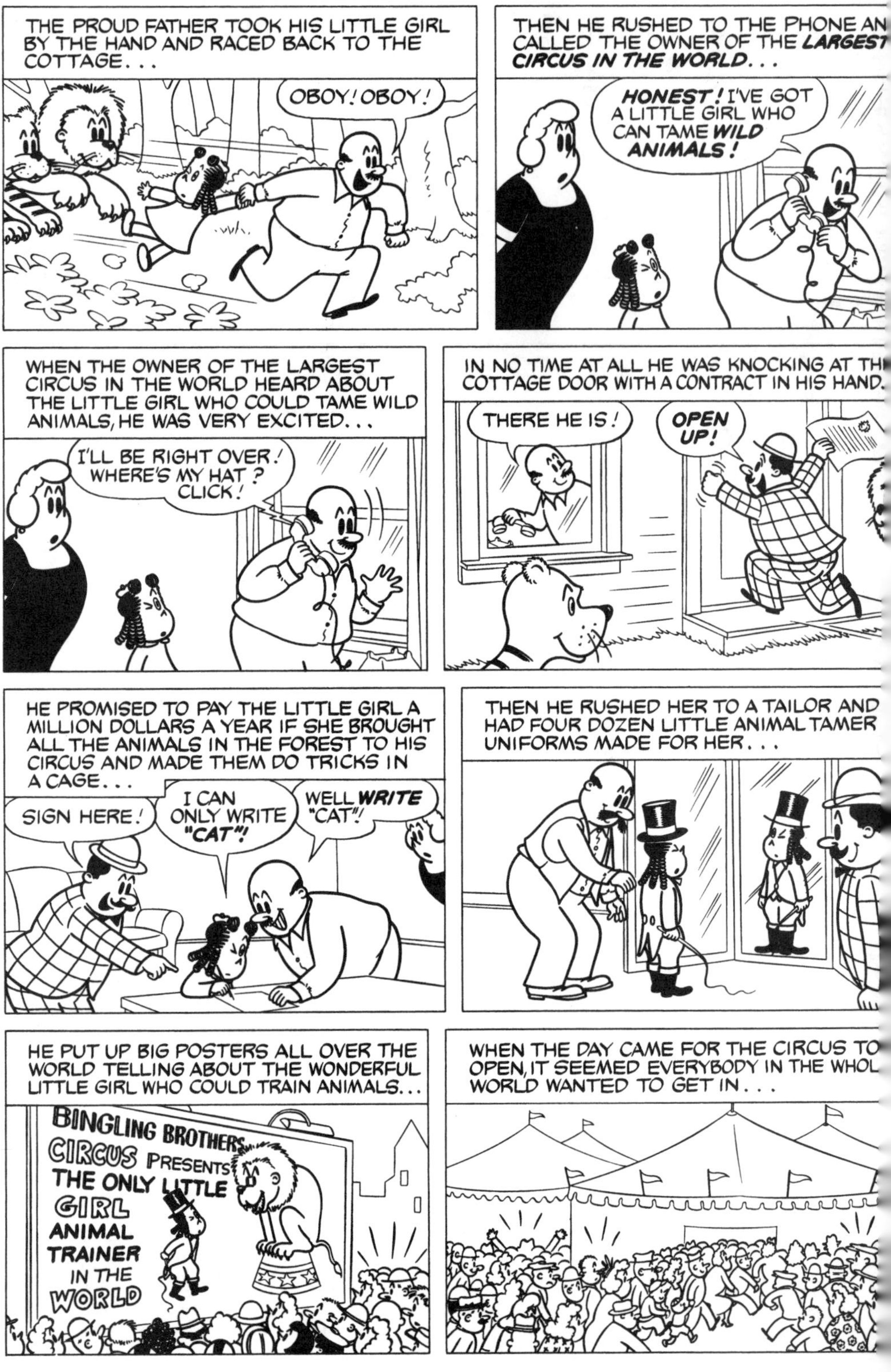
THE PROUD FATHER TOOK HIS LITTLE GIRL BY THE HAND AND RACED BACK TO THE COTTAGE...
OBOY! OBOY!
THEN HE RUSHED TO THE PHONE AN CALLED THE OWNER OF THE LARGEST CIRCUS IN THE WORLD...
HONEST! I'VE GOT A LITTLE GIRL WHO CAN TAME WILD ANIMALS!
WHEN THE OWNER OF THE LARGEST CIRCUS IN THE WORLD HEARD ABOUT THE LITTLE GIRL WHO COULD TAME WILD ANIMALS, HE WAS VERY EXCITED...
I'LL BE RIGHT OVER! WHERE'S MY HAT? CLICK!
IN NO TIME AT ALL HE WAS KNOCKING AT TH COTTAGE DOOR WITH A CONTRACT IN HIS HAND.
THERE HE IS!
OPEN UP!
HE PROMISED TO PAY THE LITTLE GIRL A MILLION DOLLARS A YEAR IF SHE BROUGHT ALL THE ANIMALS IN THE FOREST TO HIS CIRCUS AND MADE THEM DO TRICKS IN A CAGE...
SIGN HERE!
I CAN ONLY WRITE "CAT"!
WELL WRITE "CAT"!
THEN HE RUSHED HER TO A TAILOR AND HAD FOUR DOZEN LITTLE ANIMAL TAMER UNIFORMS MADE FOR HER...
HE PUT UP BIG POSTERS ALL OVER THE WORLD TELLING ABOUT THE WONDERFUL LITTLE GIRL WHO COULD TRAIN ANIMALS...
BINGLING BROTHERS CIRCUS PRESENTS THE ONLY LITTLE GIRL ANIMAL TRAINER IN THE WORLD
WHEN THE DAY CAME FOR THE CIRCUS TO OPEN, IT SEEMED EVERYBODY IN THE WHOL WORLD WANTED TO GET IN...

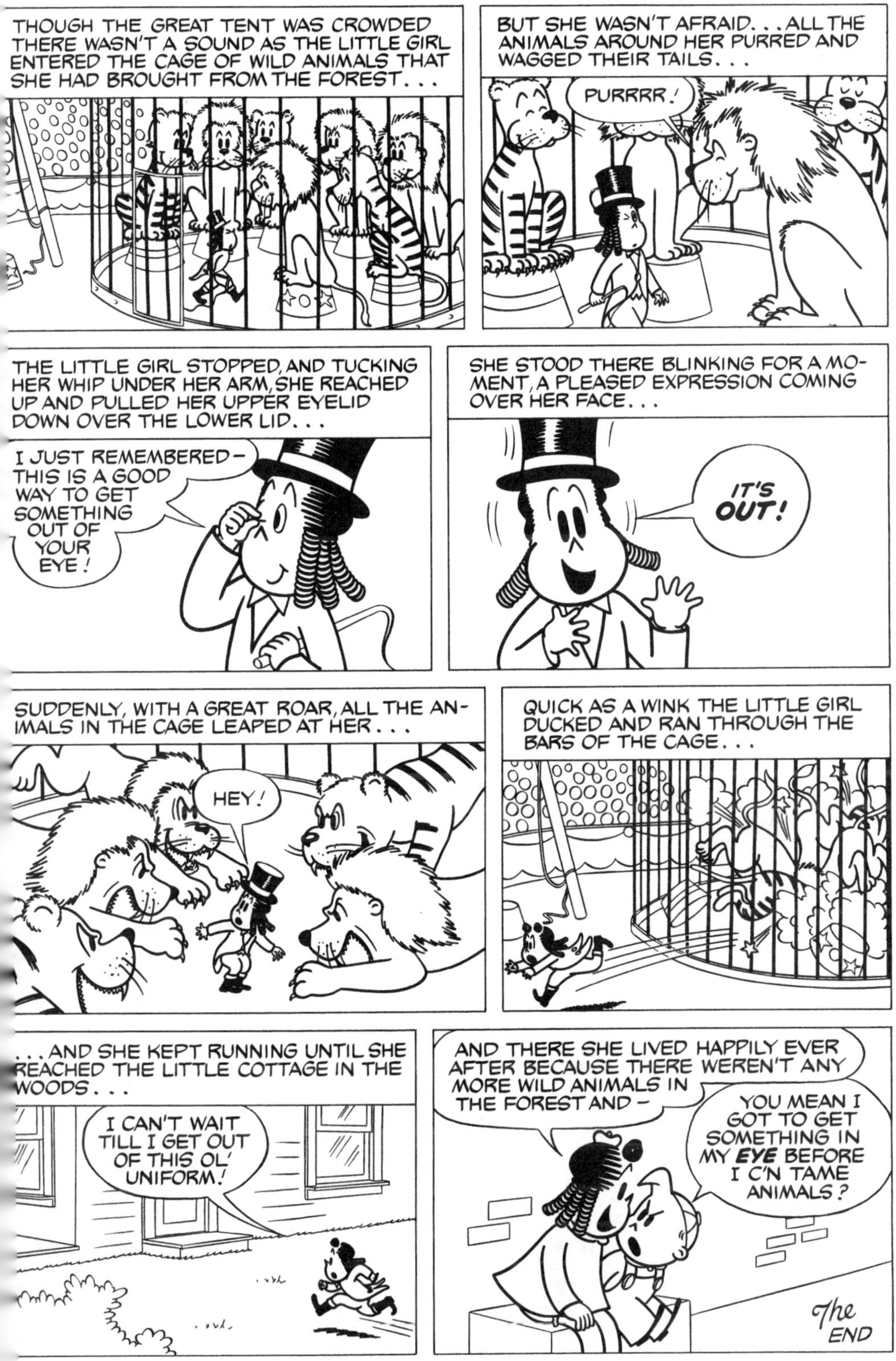
THOUGH THE GREAT TENT WAS CROWDED THERE WASN'T A SOUND AS THE LITTLE GIRL ENTERED THE CAGE OF WILD ANIMALS THAT SHE HAD BROUGHT FROM THE FOREST...
BUT SHE WASN'T AFRAID...ALL THE ANIMALS AROUND HER PURRED AND WAGGED THEIR TAILS...
PURRRR!
THE LITTLE GIRL STOPPED, AND TUCKING HER WHIP UNDER HER ARM, SHE REACHED UP AND PULLED HER UPPER EYELID DOWN OVER THE LOWER LID...
I JUST REMEMBERED— THIS IS A GOOD WAY TO GET SOMETHING OUT OF YOUR EYE!
SHE STOOD THERE BLINKING FOR A MOMENT, A PLEASED EXPRESSION COMING OVER HER FACE...
IT'S OUT!
SUDDENLY, WITH A GREAT ROAR, ALL THE ANIMALS IN THE CAGE LEAPED AT HER...
HEY!
QUICK AS A WINK THE LITTLE GIRL DUCKED AND RAN THROUGH THE BARS OF THE CAGE...
...AND SHE KEPT RUNNING UNTIL SHE REACHED THE LITTLE COTTAGE IN THE WOODS...
I CAN'T WAIT TILL I GET OUT OF THIS OL' UNIFORM!
AND THERE SHE LIVED HAPPILY EVER AFTER BECAUSE THERE WEREN'T ANY MORE WILD ANIMALS IN THE FOREST AND—
YOU MEAN I GOT TO GET SOMETHING IN MY EYE BEFORE I C'N TAME ANIMALS?
The END

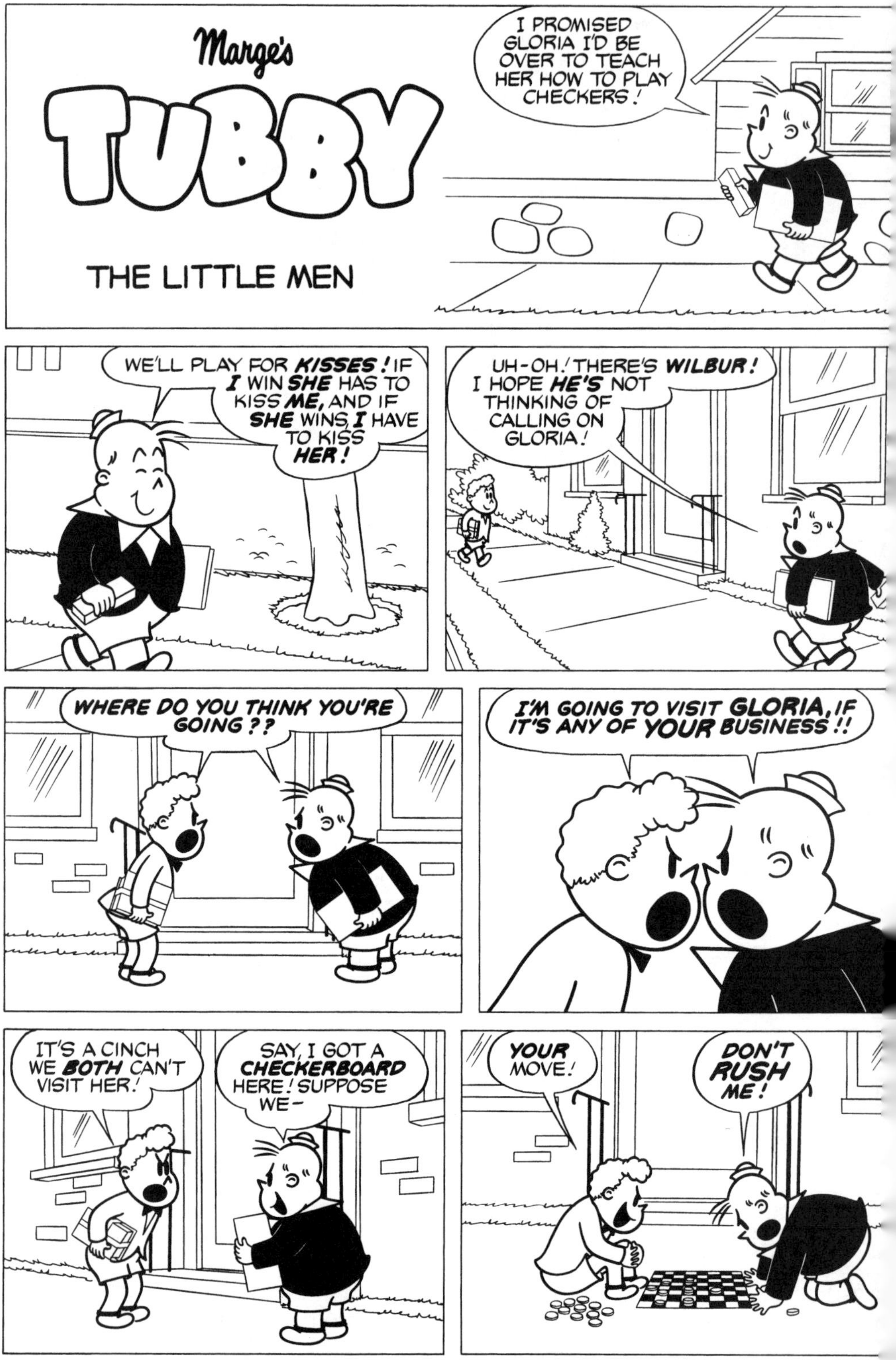
Marge's
TUBBY
THE LITTLE MEN
I PROMISED GLORIA I'D BE OVER TO TEACH HER HOW TO PLAY CHECKERS!
WE'LL PLAY FOR KISSES! IF I WIN SHE HAS TO KISS ME, AND IF SHE WINS, I HAVE TO KISS HER!
UH-OH! THERE'S WILBUR! I HOPE HE'S NOT THINKING OF CALLING ON GLORIA!
WHERE DO YOU THINK YOU'RE GOING??
I'M GOING TO VISIT GLORIA, IF IT'S ANY OF YOUR BUSINESS!!
IT'S A CINCH WE BOTH CAN'T VISIT HER!
SAY, I GOT A CHECKERBOARD HERE! SUPPOSE WE-
YOUR MOVE!
DON'T RUSH ME!

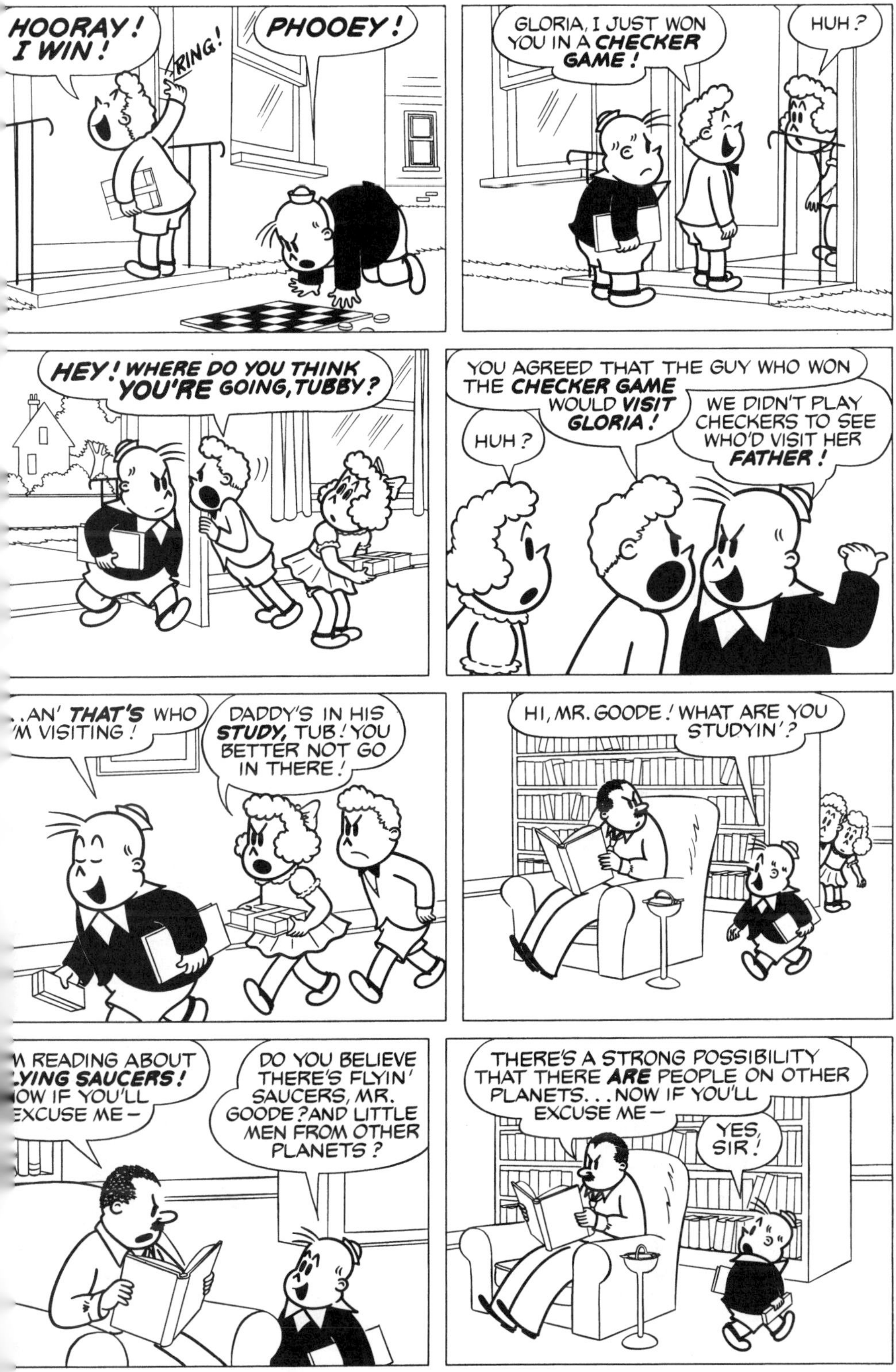
HOORAY! I WIN!
RING!
PHOOEY!
GLORIA, I JUST WON YOU IN A CHECKER GAME!
HUH?
HEY! WHERE DO YOU THINK YOU'RE GOING, TUBBY?
YOU AGREED THAT THE GUY WHO WON THE CHECKER GAME WOULD VISIT GLORIA!
HUH?
WE DIDN'T PLAY CHECKERS TO SEE WHO'D VISIT HER FATHER!
..AN' THAT'S WHO 'M VISITING!
DADDY'S IN HIS STUDY, TUB! YOU BETTER NOT GO IN THERE!
HI, MR. GOODE! WHAT ARE YOU STUDYIN'?
'M READING ABOUT FLYING SAUCERS! NOW IF YOU'LL EXCUSE ME—
DO YOU BELIEVE THERE'S FLYIN' SAUCERS, MR. GOODE? AND LITTLE MEN FROM OTHER PLANETS?
THERE'S A STRONG POSSIBILITY THAT THERE ARE PEOPLE ON OTHER PLANETS... NOW IF YOU'LL EXCUSE ME—
YES, SIR!

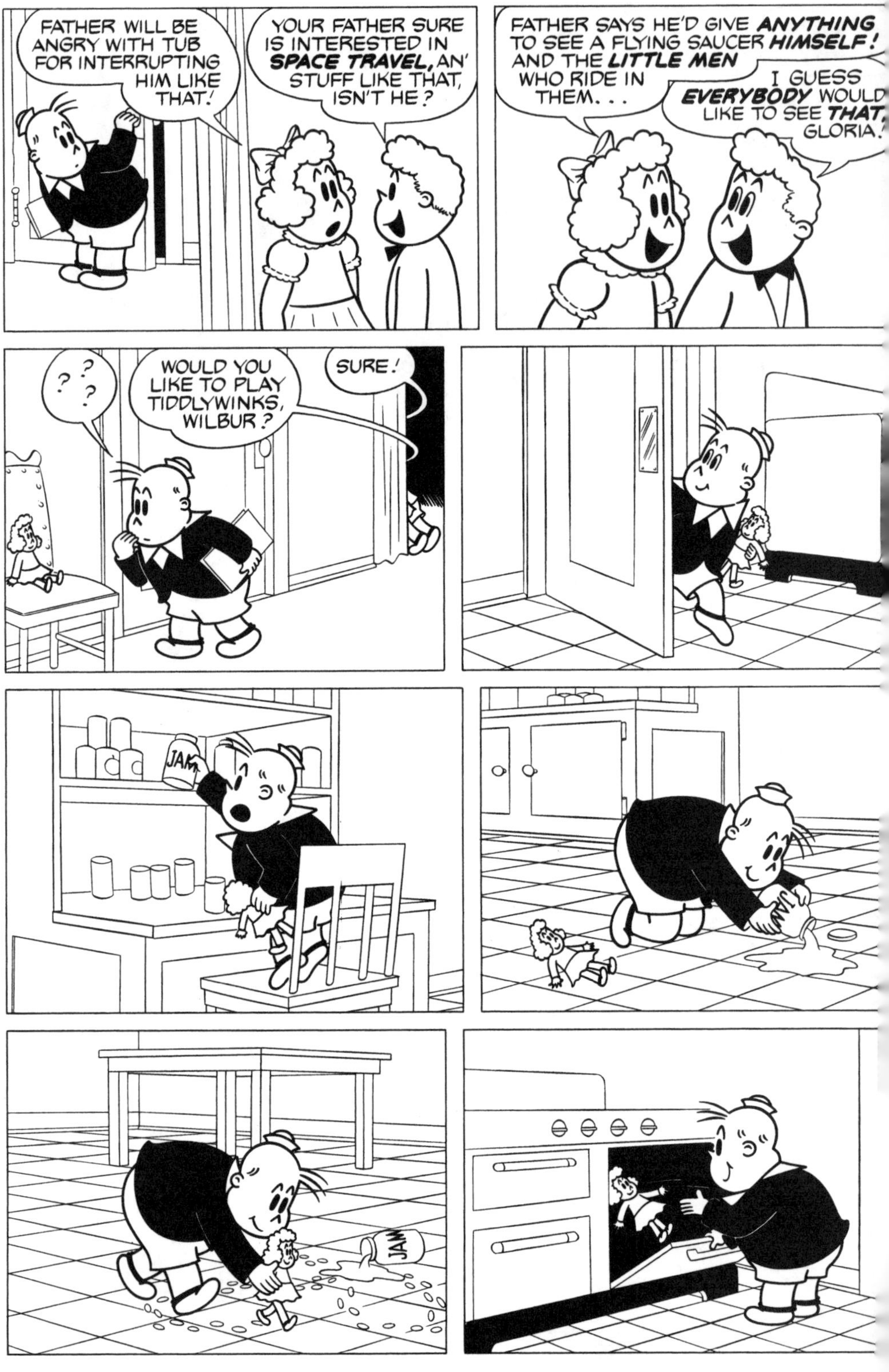
FATHER WILL BE ANGRY WITH TUB FOR INTERRUPTING HIM LIKE THAT!
YOUR FATHER SURE IS INTERESTED IN **SPACE TRAVEL,** AN' STUFF LIKE THAT, ISN'T HE?
FATHER SAYS HE'D GIVE **ANYTHING** TO SEE A FLYING SAUCER **HIMSELF!** AND THE **LITTLE MEN** WHO RIDE IN THEM. . .
I GUESS **EVERYBODY** WOULD LIKE TO SEE **THAT,** GLORIA!
? ? ?
WOULD YOU LIKE TO PLAY TIDDLYWINKS, WILBUR?
SURE!
JAM
JAM

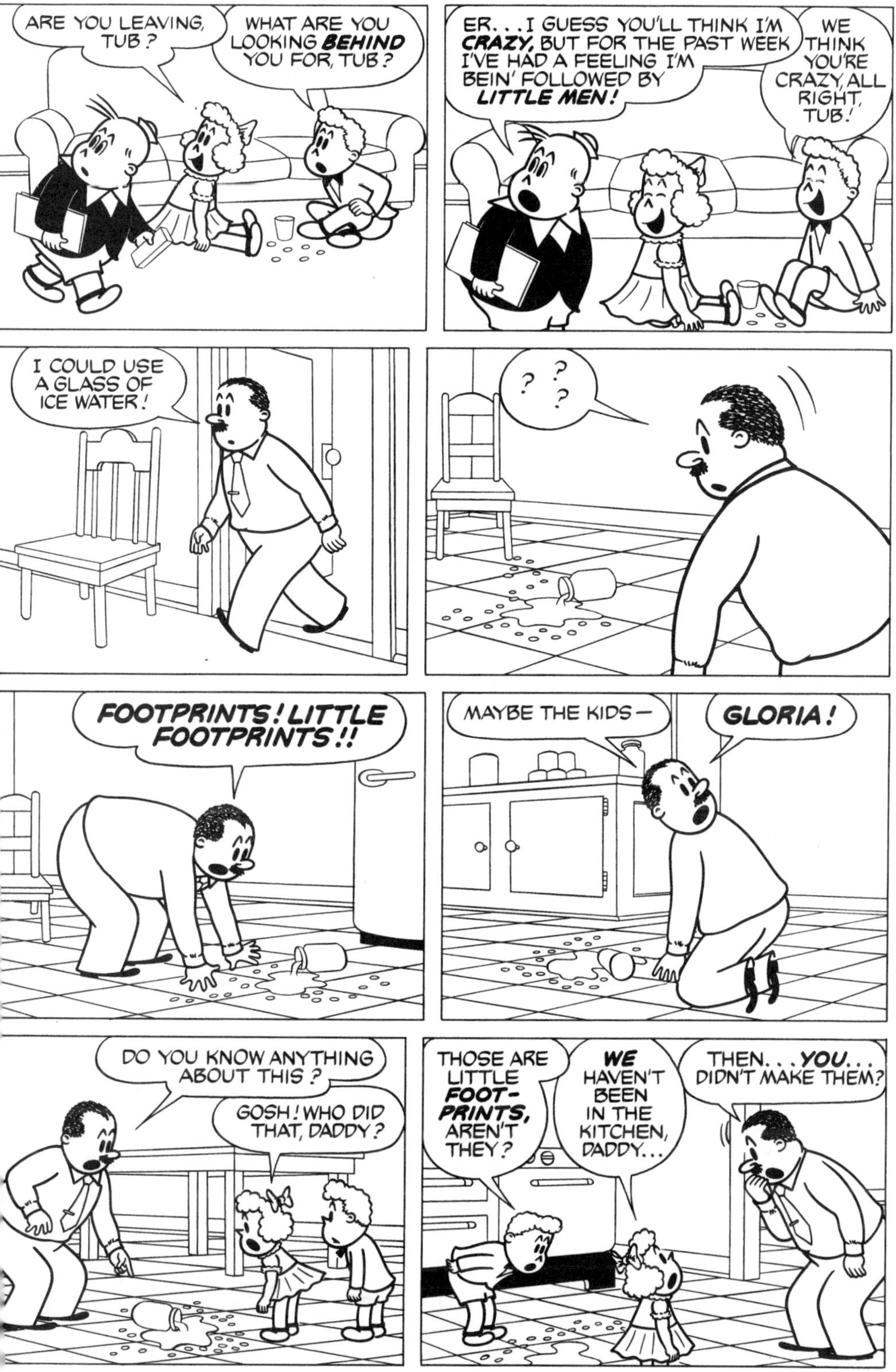
ARE YOU LEAVING, TUB?
WHAT ARE YOU LOOKING BEHIND YOU FOR, TUB?
ER...I GUESS YOU'LL THINK I'M CRAZY, BUT FOR THE PAST WEEK I'VE HAD A FEELING I'M BEIN' FOLLOWED BY LITTLE MEN!
WE THINK YOU'RE CRAZY, ALL RIGHT, TUB!
I COULD USE A GLASS OF ICE WATER!
? ? ?
FOOTPRINTS! LITTLE FOOTPRINTS!!
MAYBE THE KIDS—
GLORIA!
DO YOU KNOW ANYTHING ABOUT THIS?
GOSH! WHO DID THAT, DADDY?
THOSE ARE LITTLE FOOT-PRINTS, AREN'T THEY?
WE HAVEN'T BEEN IN THE KITCHEN, DADDY...
THEN...YOU... DIDN'T MAKE THEM?

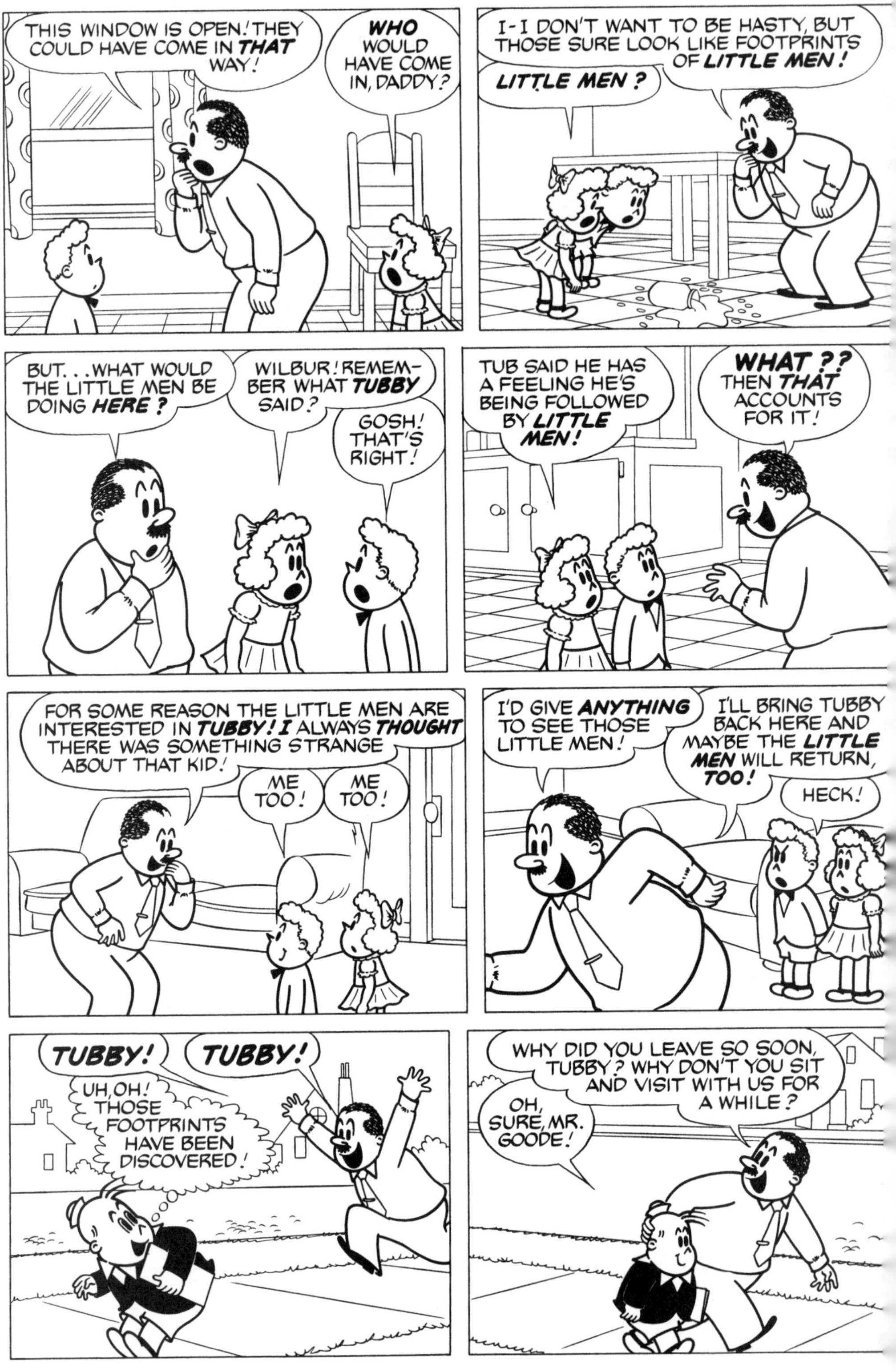
THIS WINDOW IS OPEN! THEY COULD HAVE COME IN THAT WAY!
WHO WOULD HAVE COME IN, DADDY?
I-I DON'T WANT TO BE HASTY, BUT THOSE SURE LOOK LIKE FOOTPRINTS OF LITTLE MEN!
LITTLE MEN?
BUT...WHAT WOULD THE LITTLE MEN BE DOING HERE?
WILBUR! REMEMBER WHAT TUBBY SAID?
GOSH! THAT'S RIGHT!
TUB SAID HE HAS A FEELING HE'S BEING FOLLOWED BY LITTLE MEN!
WHAT?? THEN THAT ACCOUNTS FOR IT!
FOR SOME REASON THE LITTLE MEN ARE INTERESTED IN TUBBY! I ALWAYS THOUGHT THERE WAS SOMETHING STRANGE ABOUT THAT KID!
ME TOO!
ME TOO!
I'D GIVE ANYTHING TO SEE THOSE LITTLE MEN!
I'LL BRING TUBBY BACK HERE AND MAYBE THE LITTLE MEN WILL RETURN, TOO!
HECK!
TUBBY!
TUBBY!
UH, OH! THOSE FOOTPRINTS HAVE BEEN DISCOVERED!
WHY DID YOU LEAVE SO SOON, TUBBY? WHY DON'T YOU SIT AND VISIT WITH US FOR A WHILE?
OH, SURE, MR. GOODE!

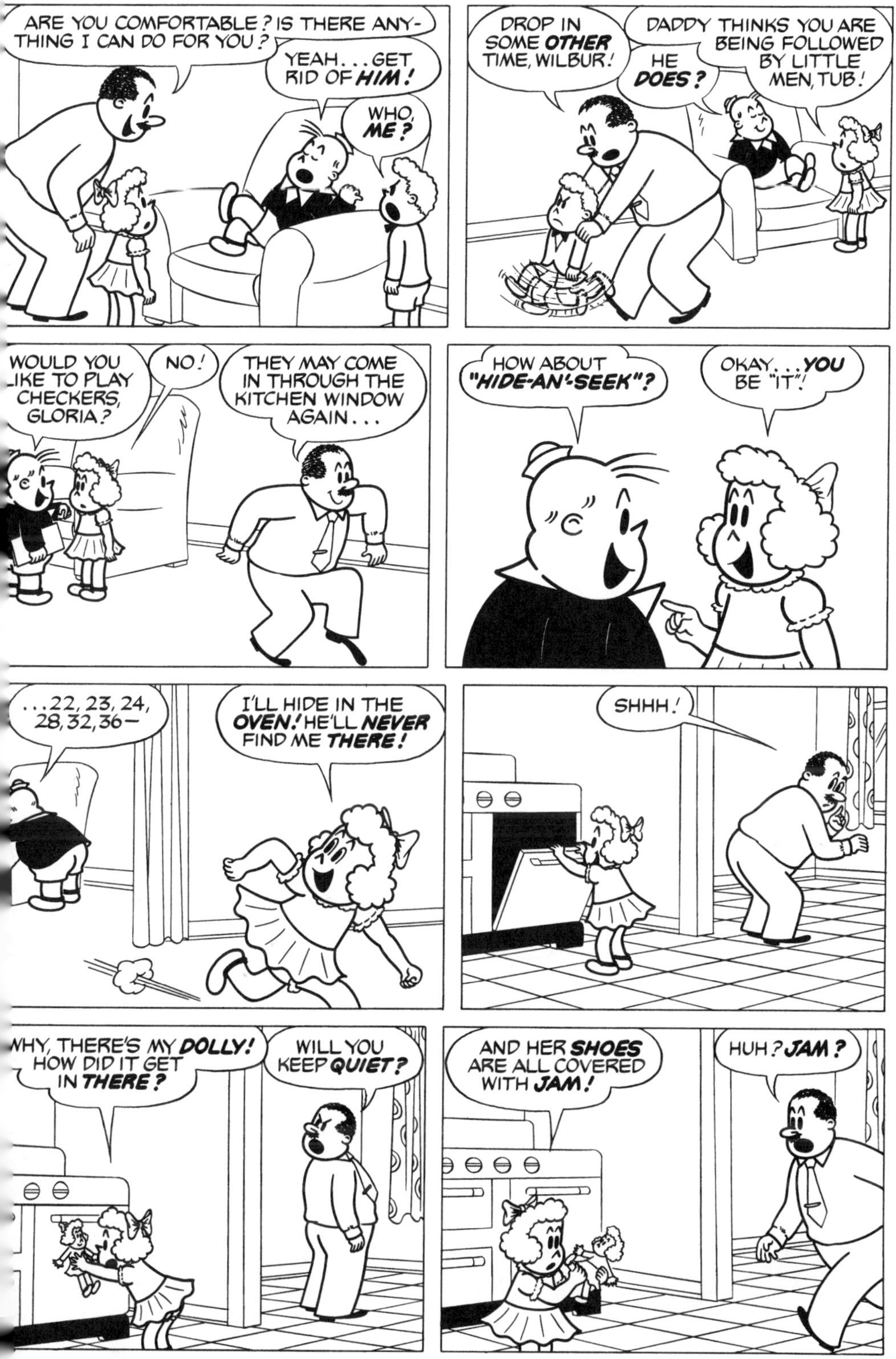
ARE YOU COMFORTABLE? IS THERE ANYTHING I CAN DO FOR YOU?
YEAH...GET RID OF HIM!
WHO, ME?
DROP IN SOME OTHER TIME, WILBUR!
DADDY THINKS YOU ARE BEING FOLLOWED BY LITTLE MEN, TUB!
HE DOES?
WOULD YOU LIKE TO PLAY CHECKERS, GLORIA?
NO!
THEY MAY COME IN THROUGH THE KITCHEN WINDOW AGAIN...
HOW ABOUT "HIDE-AN'-SEEK"?
OKAY...YOU BE "IT"!
...22, 23, 24, 28, 32, 36—
I'LL HIDE IN THE OVEN! HE'LL NEVER FIND ME THERE!
SHHH!
WHY, THERE'S MY DOLLY! HOW DID IT GET IN THERE?
WILL YOU KEEP QUIET?
AND HER SHOES ARE ALL COVERED WITH JAM!
HUH? JAM?

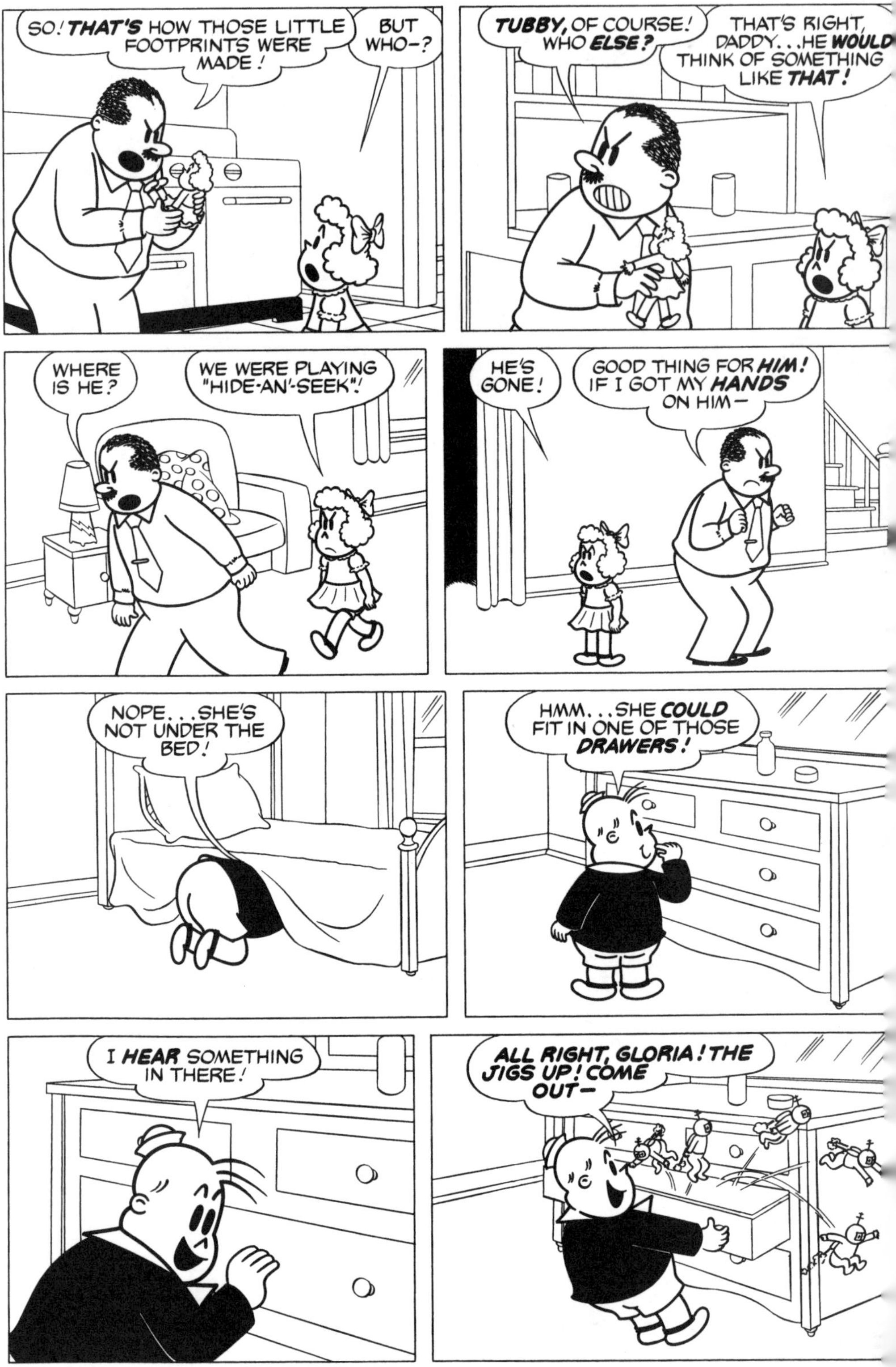
SO! THAT'S HOW THOSE LITTLE FOOTPRINTS WERE MADE!
BUT WHO–?
TUBBY, OF COURSE! WHO ELSE?
THAT'S RIGHT, DADDY...HE WOULD THINK OF SOMETHING LIKE THAT!
WHERE IS HE?
WE WERE PLAYING "HIDE-AN'-SEEK"!
HE'S GONE!
GOOD THING FOR HIM! IF I GOT MY HANDS ON HIM—
NOPE...SHE'S NOT UNDER THE BED!
HMM...SHE COULD FIT IN ONE OF THOSE DRAWERS!
I HEAR SOMETHING IN THERE!
ALL RIGHT, GLORIA! THE JIGS UP! COME OUT—

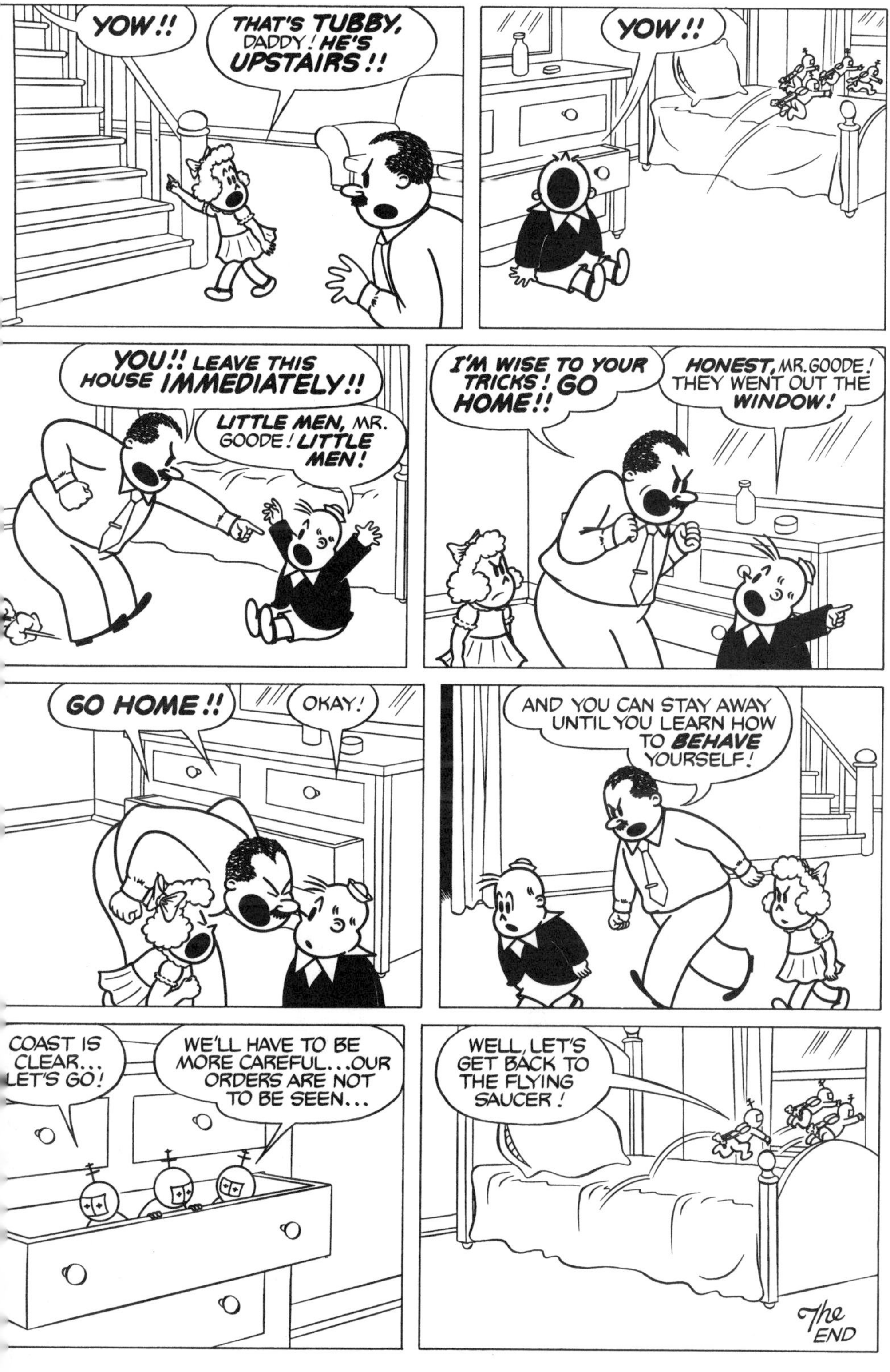
YOW!!
THAT'S TUBBY, DADDY! HE'S UPSTAIRS!!
YOW!!
YOU!! LEAVE THIS HOUSE IMMEDIATELY!!
LITTLE MEN, MR. GOODE! LITTLE MEN!
I'M WISE TO YOUR TRICKS! GO HOME!!
HONEST, MR. GOODE! THEY WENT OUT THE WINDOW!
GO HOME!!
OKAY!
AND YOU CAN STAY AWAY UNTIL YOU LEARN HOW TO BEHAVE YOURSELF!
COAST IS CLEAR... LET'S GO!
WE'LL HAVE TO BE MORE CAREFUL...OUR ORDERS ARE NOT TO BE SEEN...
WELL, LET'S GET BACK TO THE FLYING SAUCER!
The END

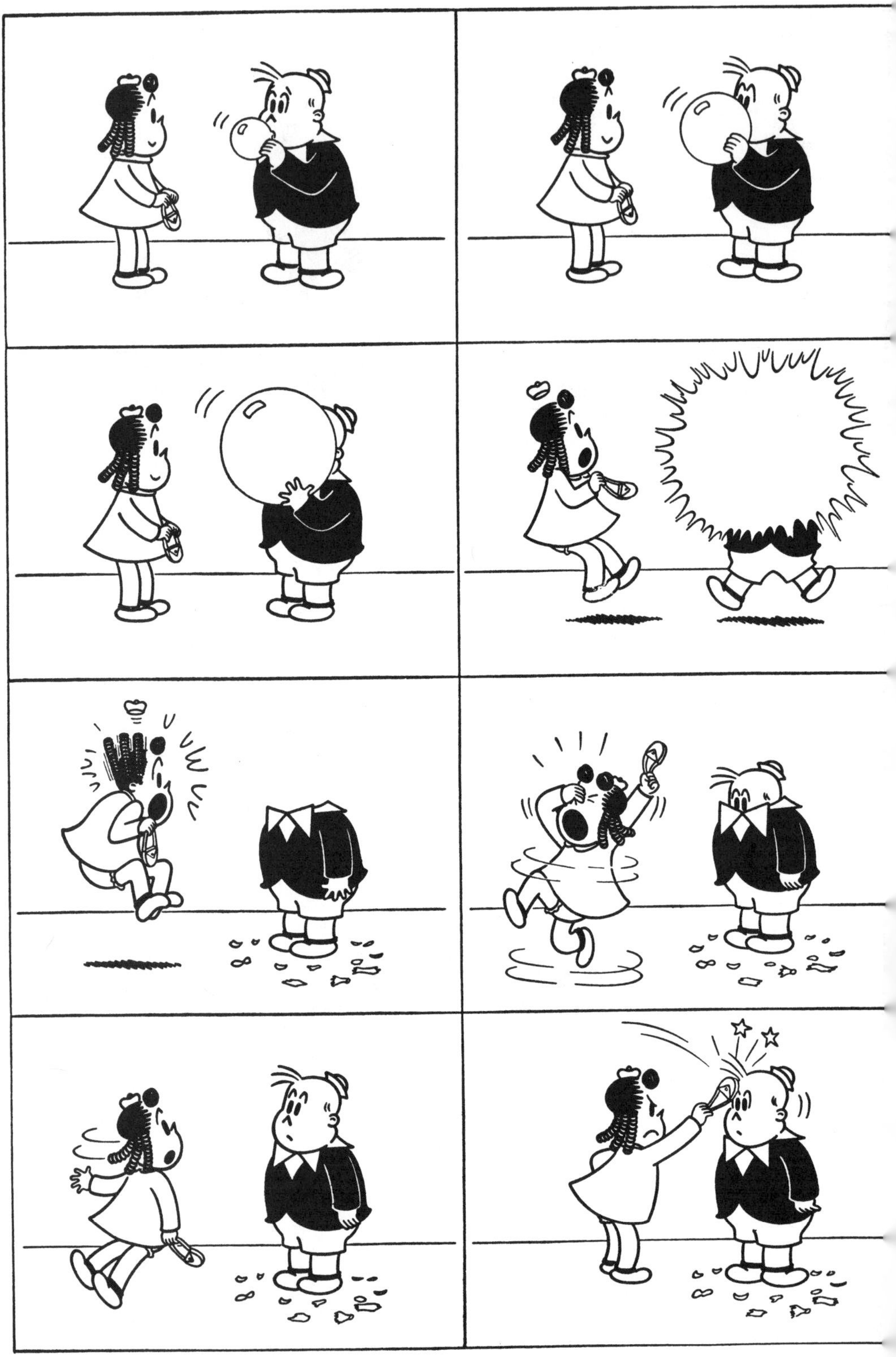

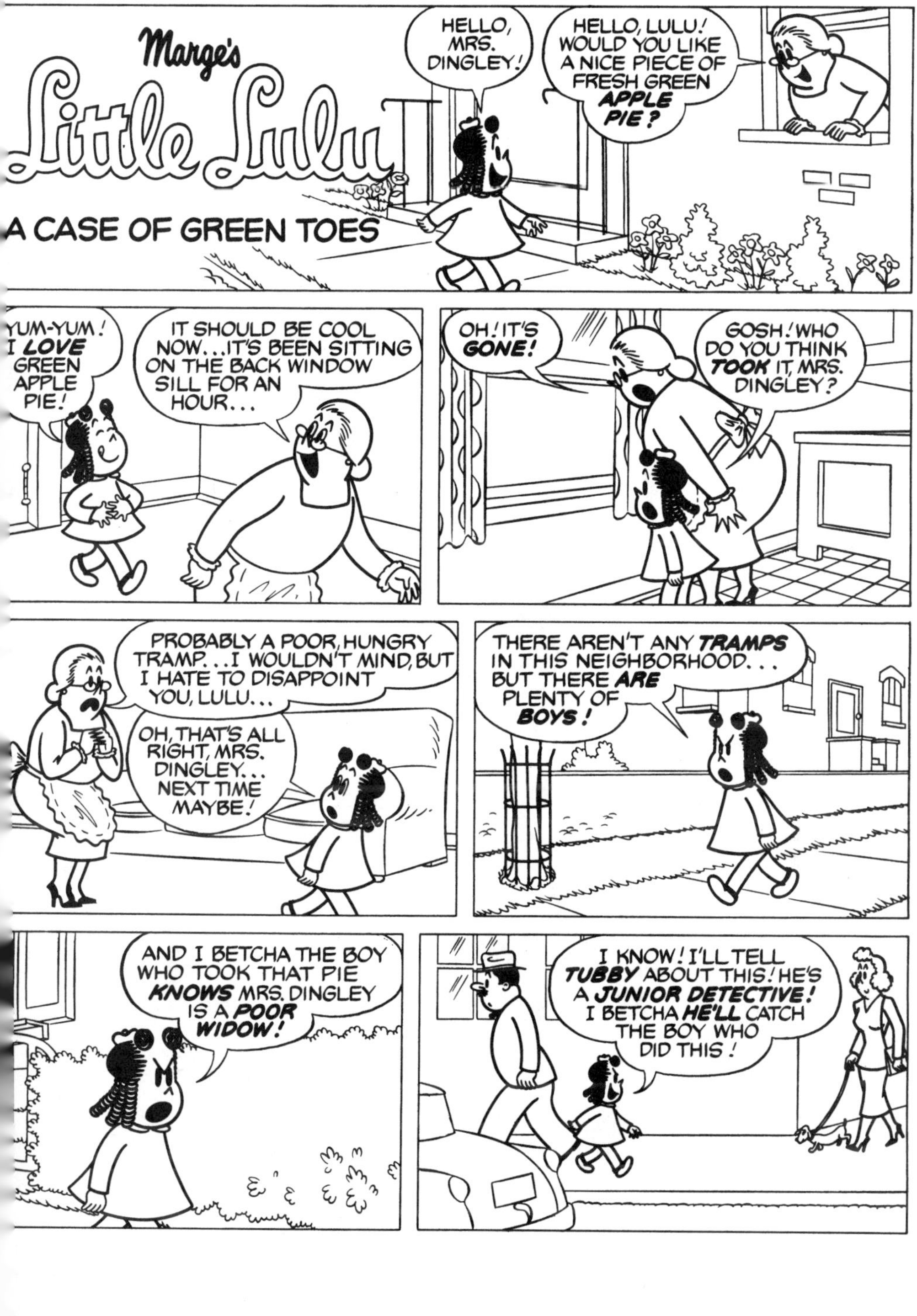
Marge's
Little Lulu
A CASE OF GREEN TOES
HELLO, MRS. DINGLEY!
HELLO, LULU! WOULD YOU LIKE A NICE PIECE OF FRESH GREEN APPLE PIE?
YUM-YUM! I LOVE GREEN APPLE PIE!
IT SHOULD BE COOL NOW...IT'S BEEN SITTING ON THE BACK WINDOW SILL FOR AN HOUR...
OH! IT'S GONE!
GOSH! WHO DO YOU THINK TOOK IT, MRS. DINGLEY?
PROBABLY A POOR, HUNGRY TRAMP...I WOULDN'T MIND, BUT I HATE TO DISAPPOINT YOU, LULU...
OH, THAT'S ALL RIGHT, MRS. DINGLEY... NEXT TIME MAYBE!
THERE AREN'T ANY TRAMPS IN THIS NEIGHBORHOOD... BUT THERE ARE PLENTY OF BOYS!
AND I BETCHA THE BOY WHO TOOK THAT PIE KNOWS MRS. DINGLEY IS A POOR WIDOW!
I KNOW! I'LL TELL TUBBY ABOUT THIS! HE'S A JUNIOR DETECTIVE! I BETCHA HE'LL CATCH THE BOY WHO DID THIS!

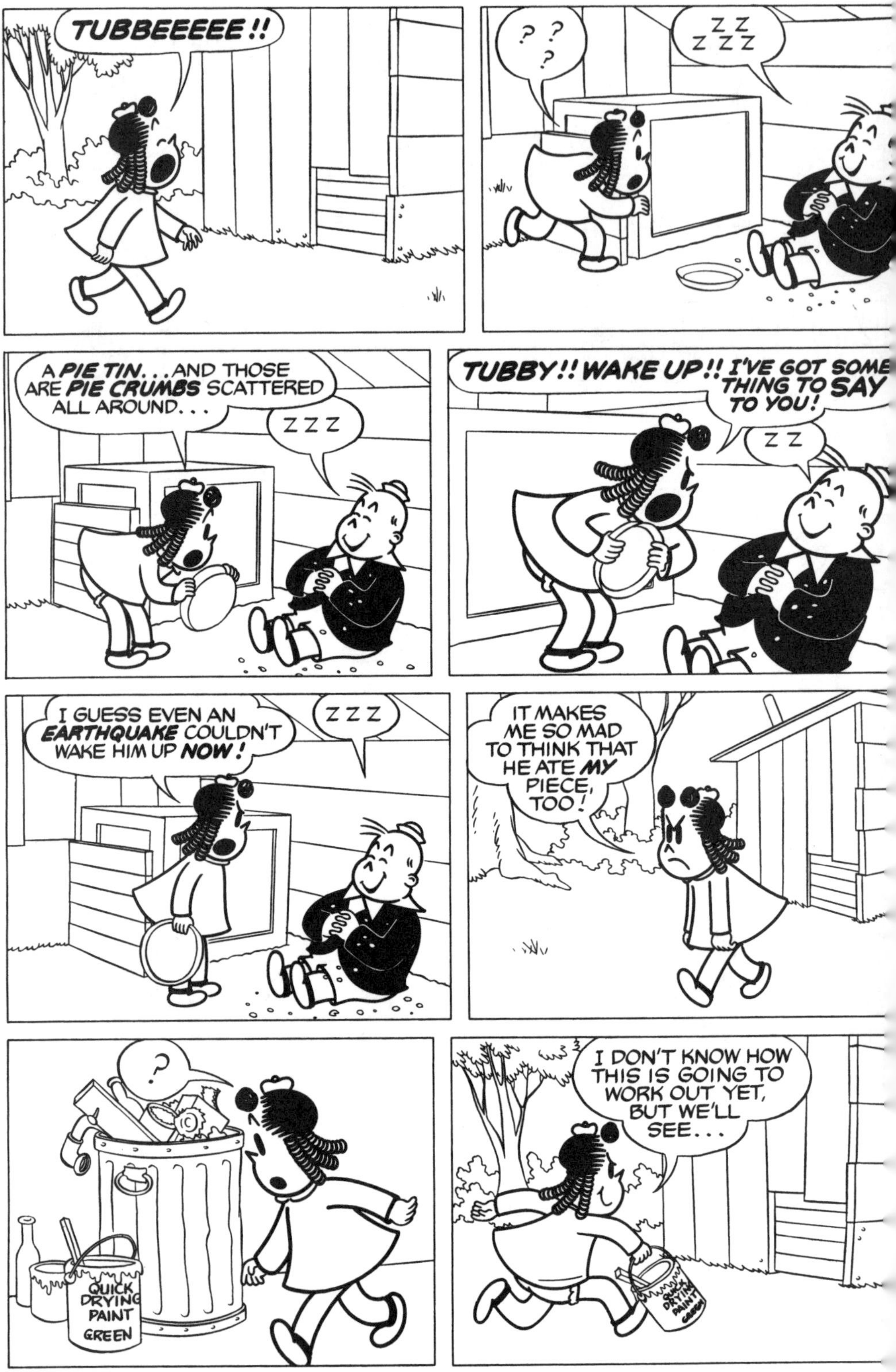
TUBBEEEEEE!!
? ? ?
Z Z Z Z Z
A PIE TIN...AND THOSE ARE PIE CRUMBS SCATTERED ALL AROUND...
Z Z Z
TUBBY!! WAKE UP!! I'VE GOT SOME THING TO SAY TO YOU!
Z Z
I GUESS EVEN AN EARTHQUAKE COULDN'T WAKE HIM UP NOW!
Z Z Z
IT MAKES ME SO MAD TO THINK THAT HE ATE MY PIECE, TOO!
?
QUICK DRYING PAINT GREEN
I DON'T KNOW HOW THIS IS GOING TO WORK OUT YET, BUT WE'LL SEE...
QUICK DRYING PAINT GREEN

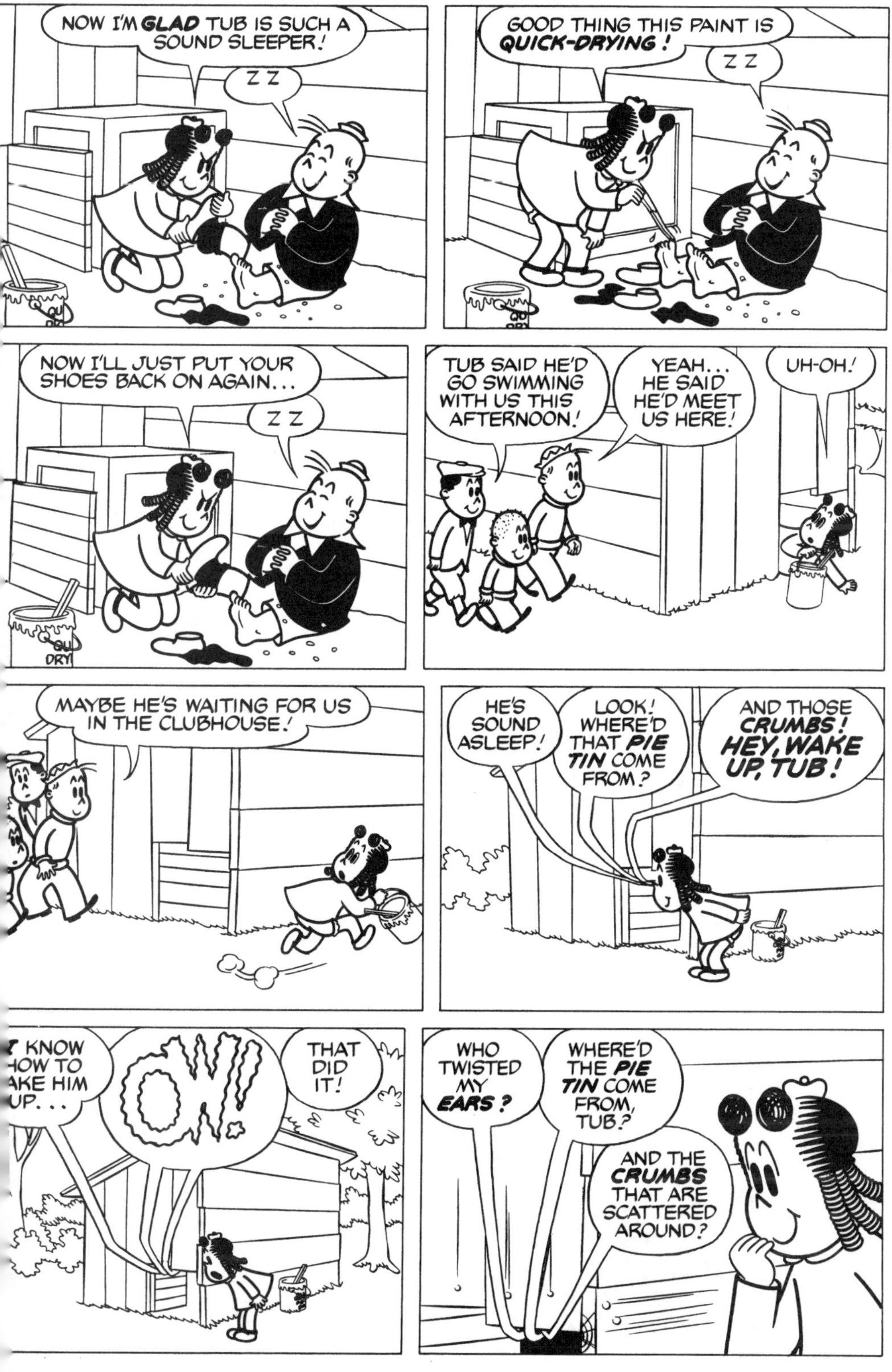
NOW I'M **GLAD** TUB IS SUCH A SOUND SLEEPER!
Z Z
GOOD THING THIS PAINT IS **QUICK-DRYING!**
Z Z
NOW I'LL JUST PUT YOUR SHOES BACK ON AGAIN...
Z Z
TUB SAID HE'D GO SWIMMING WITH US THIS AFTERNOON!
YEAH... HE SAID HE'D MEET US HERE!
UH-OH!
MAYBE HE'S WAITING FOR US IN THE CLUBHOUSE!
HE'S SOUND ASLEEP!
LOOK! WHERE'D THAT **PIE TIN** COME FROM?
AND THOSE **CRUMBS! HEY, WAKE UP, TUB!**
KNOW HOW TO AKE HIM UP...
OW!
THAT DID IT!
WHO TWISTED MY **EARS?**
WHERE'D THE **PIE TIN** COME FROM, TUB?
AND THE **CRUMBS** THAT ARE SCATTERED AROUND?

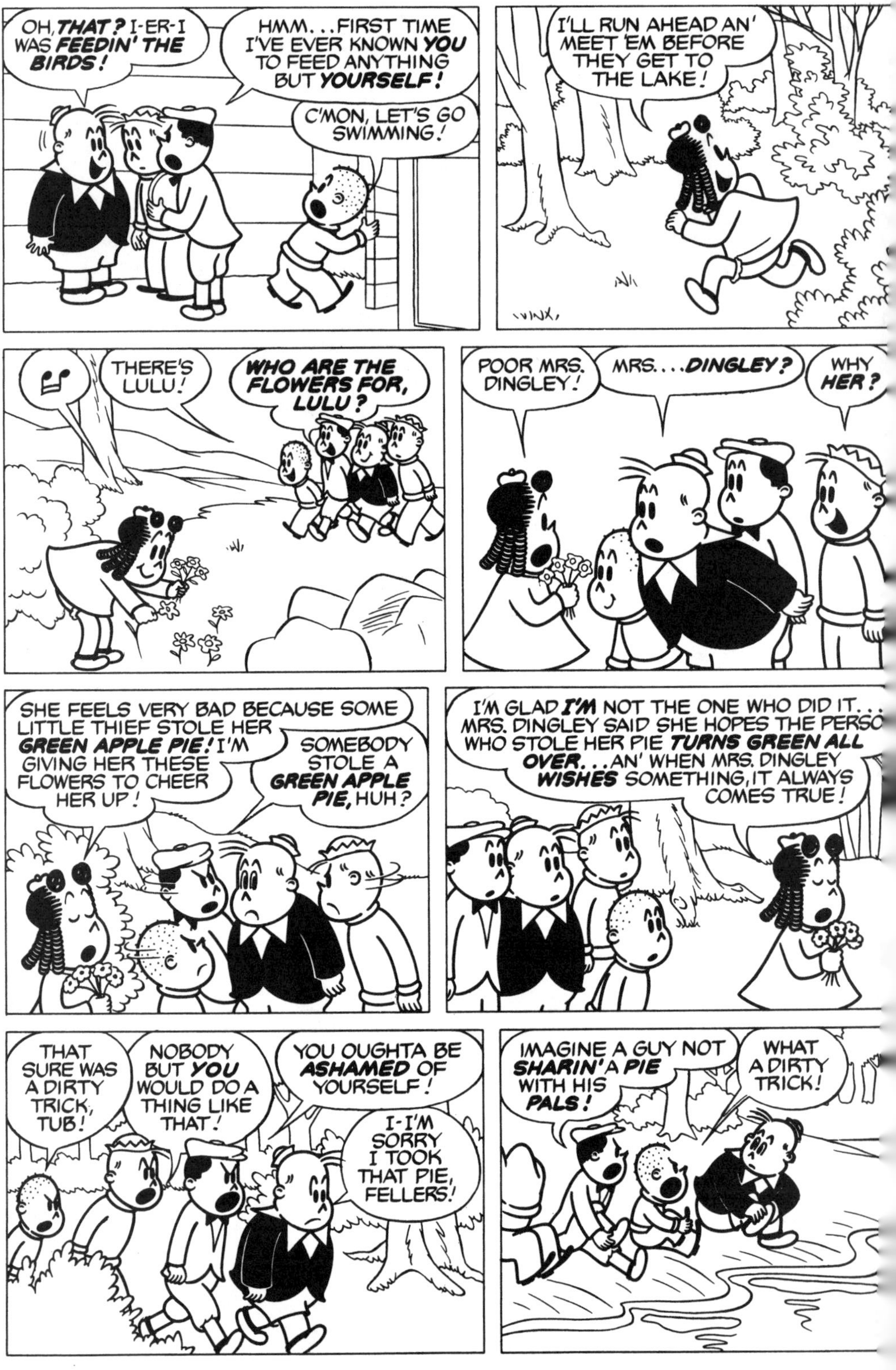
OH, THAT? I-ER-I WAS FEEDIN' THE BIRDS!
HMM...FIRST TIME I'VE EVER KNOWN YOU TO FEED ANYTHING BUT YOURSELF!
C'MON, LET'S GO SWIMMING!
I'LL RUN AHEAD AN' MEET 'EM BEFORE THEY GET TO THE LAKE!
THERE'S LULU!
WHO ARE THE FLOWERS FOR, LULU?
POOR MRS. DINGLEY!
MRS....DINGLEY?
WHY HER?
SHE FEELS VERY BAD BECAUSE SOME LITTLE THIEF STOLE HER GREEN APPLE PIE! I'M GIVING HER THESE FLOWERS TO CHEER HER UP!
SOMEBODY STOLE A GREEN APPLE PIE, HUH?
I'M GLAD I'M NOT THE ONE WHO DID IT... MRS. DINGLEY SAID SHE HOPES THE PERSO WHO STOLE HER PIE TURNS GREEN ALL OVER...AN' WHEN MRS. DINGLEY WISHES SOMETHING, IT ALWAYS COMES TRUE!
THAT SURE WAS A DIRTY TRICK, TUB!
NOBODY BUT YOU WOULD DO A THING LIKE THAT!
YOU OUGHTA BE ASHAMED OF YOURSELF!
I-I'M SORRY I TOOK THAT PIE, FELLERS!
IMAGINE A GUY NOT SHARIN' A PIE WITH HIS PALS!
WHAT A DIRTY TRICK!

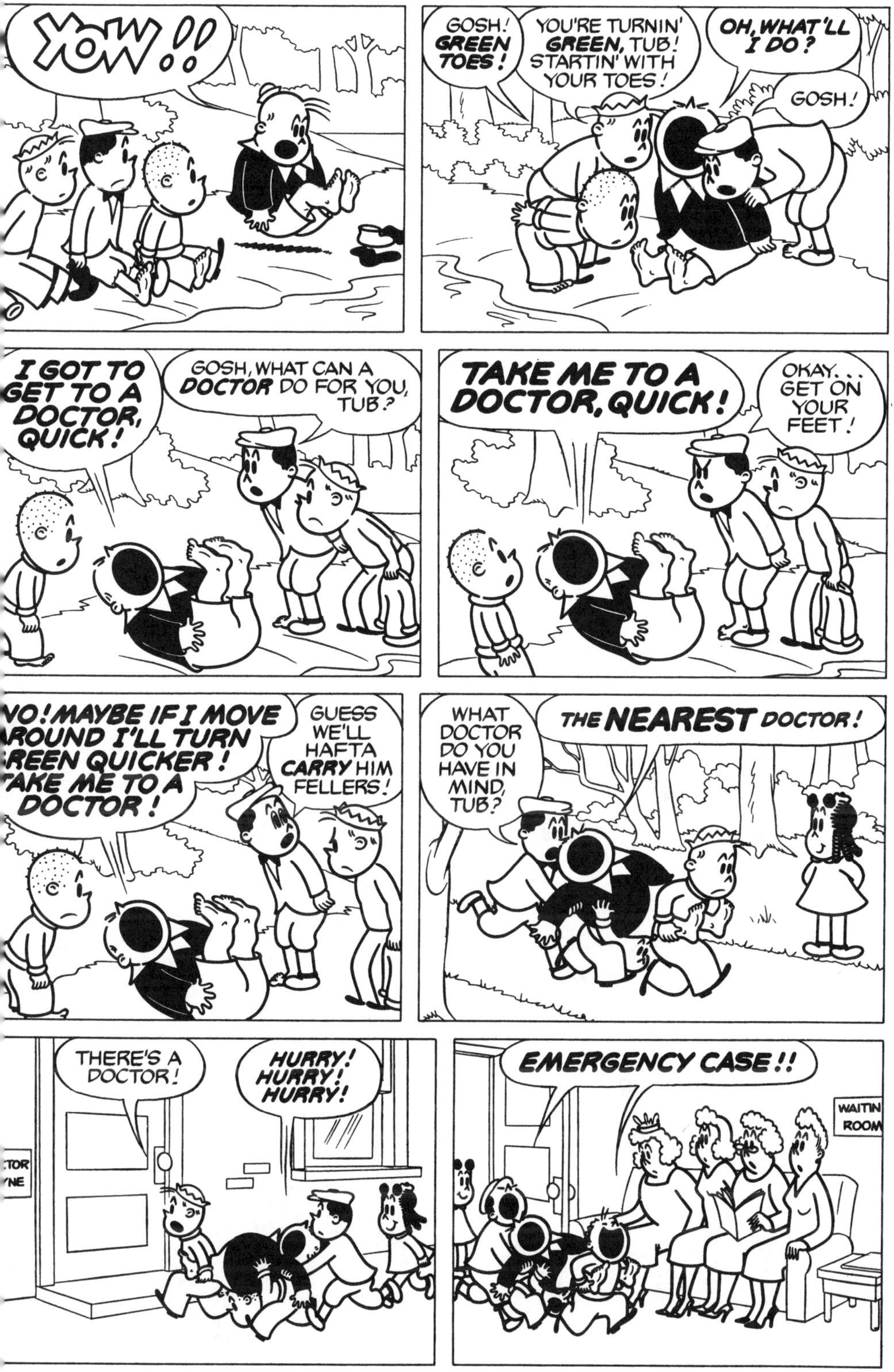
YOW!!!
GOSH! GREEN TOES!
YOU'RE TURNIN' GREEN, TUB! STARTIN' WITH YOUR TOES!
OH, WHAT'LL I DO?
GOSH!
I GOT TO GET TO A DOCTOR, QUICK!
GOSH, WHAT CAN A DOCTOR DO FOR YOU, TUB?
TAKE ME TO A DOCTOR, QUICK!
OKAY... GET ON YOUR FEET!
NO! MAYBE IF I MOVE AROUND I'LL TURN GREEN QUICKER! TAKE ME TO A DOCTOR!
GUESS WE'LL HAFTA CARRY HIM FELLERS!
WHAT DOCTOR DO YOU HAVE IN MIND, TUB?
THE NEAREST DOCTOR!
THERE'S A DOCTOR!
HURRY! HURRY! HURRY!
EMERGENCY CASE!!
WAITIN ROOM

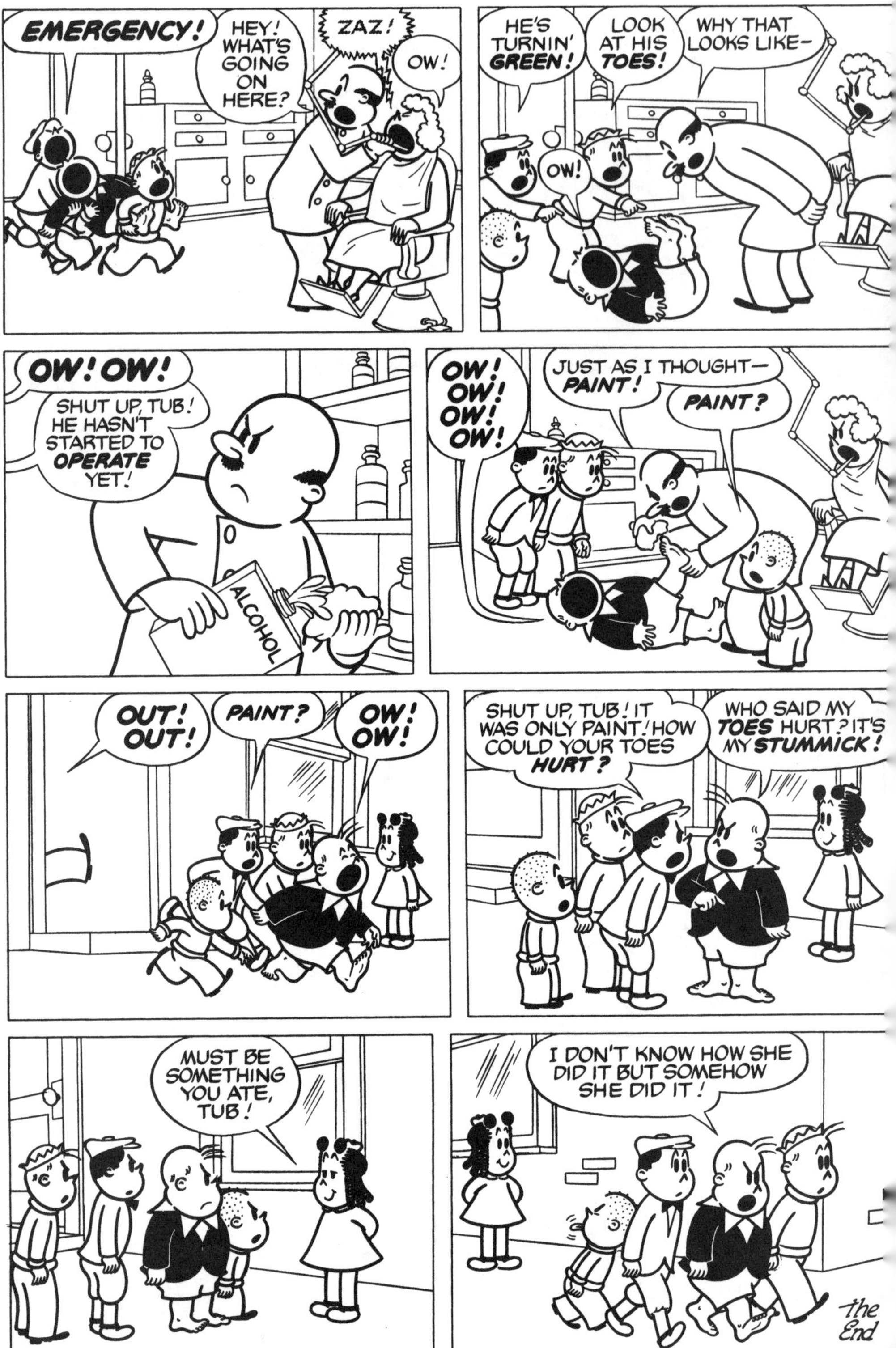
EMERGENCY!
HEY! WHAT'S GOING ON HERE?
ZAZ!
OW!
HE'S TURNIN' GREEN!
LOOK AT HIS TOES!
WHY THAT LOOKS LIKE—
OW!
OW! OW!
SHUT UP, TUB! HE HASN'T STARTED TO OPERATE YET!
ALCOHOL
OW! OW! OW! OW!
JUST AS I THOUGHT— PAINT!
PAINT?
OUT! OUT!
PAINT?
OW! OW!
SHUT UP, TUB! IT WAS ONLY PAINT! HOW COULD YOUR TOES HURT?
WHO SAID MY TOES HURT? IT'S MY STUMMICK!
MUST BE SOMETHING YOU ATE, TUB!
I DON'T KNOW HOW SHE DID IT BUT SOMEHOW SHE DID IT!
the End

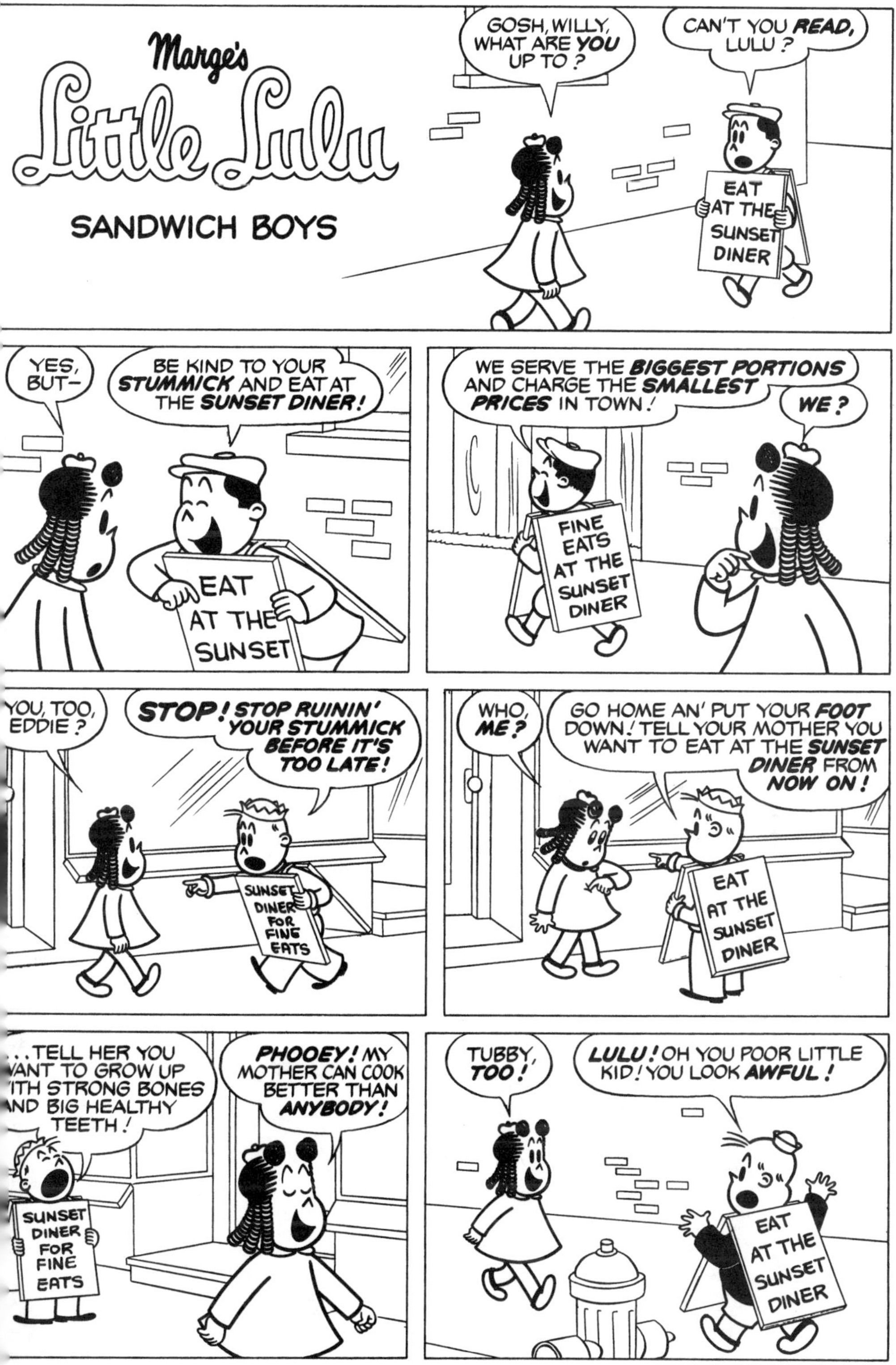

Marge's Little Lulu
SANDWICH BOYS
GOSH, WILLY, WHAT ARE YOU UP TO ?
CAN'T YOU READ, LULU ?
EAT AT THE SUNSET DINER
YES, BUT–
BE KIND TO YOUR STUMMICK AND EAT AT THE SUNSET DINER!
EAT AT THE SUNSET
WE SERVE THE BIGGEST PORTIONS AND CHARGE THE SMALLEST PRICES IN TOWN!
WE ?
FINE EATS AT THE SUNSET DINER
YOU, TOO, EDDIE ?
STOP! STOP RUININ' YOUR STUMMICK BEFORE IT'S TOO LATE!
SUNSET DINER FOR FINE EATS
WHO, ME ?
GO HOME AN' PUT YOUR FOOT DOWN! TELL YOUR MOTHER YOU WANT TO EAT AT THE SUNSET DINER FROM NOW ON!
EAT AT THE SUNSET DINER
...TELL HER YOU WANT TO GROW UP WITH STRONG BONES AND BIG HEALTHY TEETH!
PHOOEY! MY MOTHER CAN COOK BETTER THAN ANYBODY!
SUNSET DINER FOR FINE EATS
TUBBY, TOO!
LULU! OH YOU POOR LITTLE KID! YOU LOOK AWFUL!
EAT AT THE SUNSET DINER

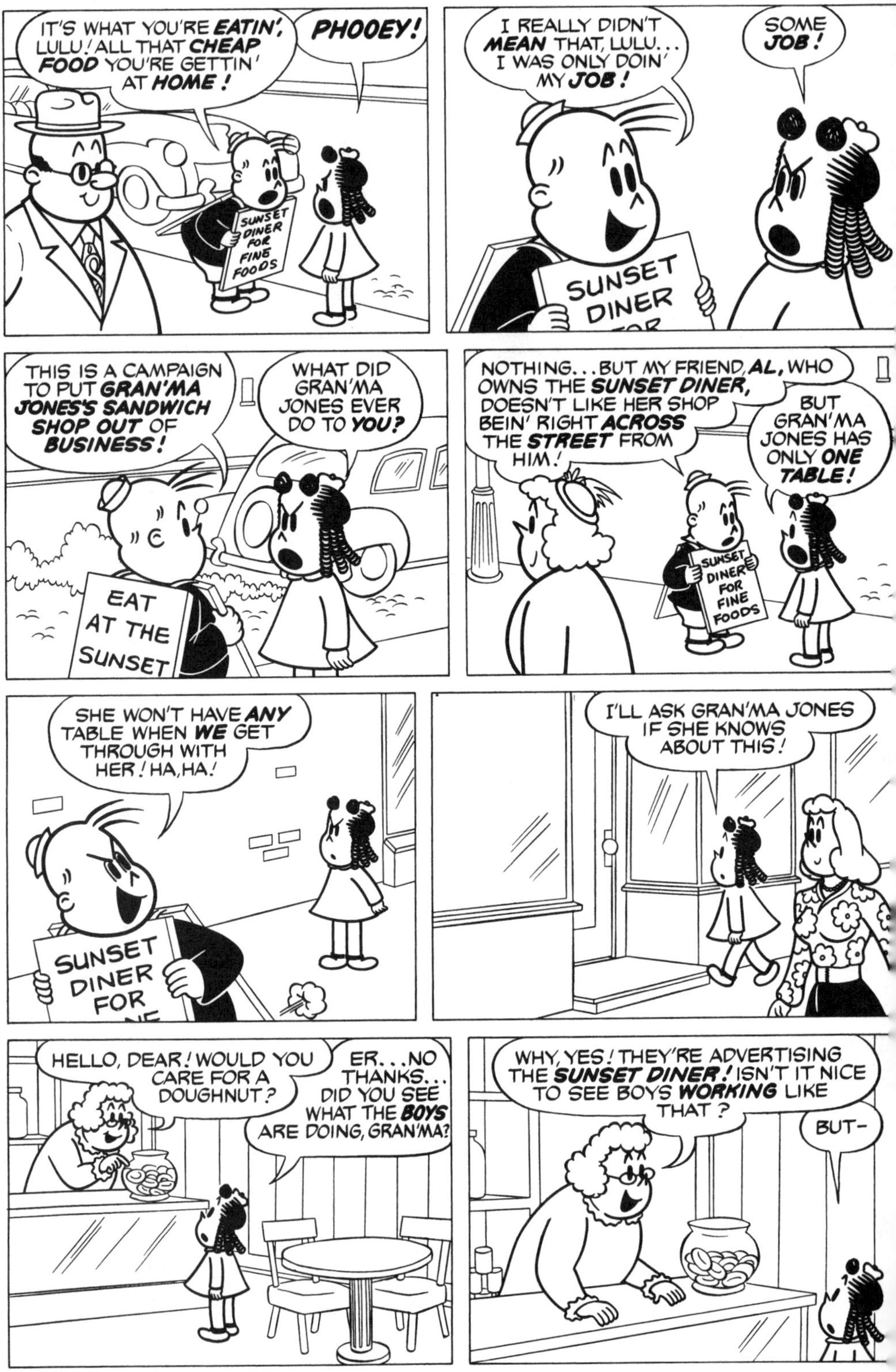
IT'S WHAT YOU'RE EATIN', LULU! ALL THAT CHEAP FOOD YOU'RE GETTIN' AT HOME!
PHOOEY!
SUNSET DINER FOR FINE FOODS
I REALLY DIDN'T MEAN THAT, LULU... I WAS ONLY DOIN' MY JOB!
SOME JOB!
SUNSET DINER
THIS IS A CAMPAIGN TO PUT GRAN'MA JONES'S SANDWICH SHOP OUT OF BUSINESS!
WHAT DID GRAN'MA JONES EVER DO TO YOU?
EAT AT THE SUNSET
NOTHING...BUT MY FRIEND, AL, WHO OWNS THE SUNSET DINER, DOESN'T LIKE HER SHOP BEIN' RIGHT ACROSS THE STREET FROM HIM!
BUT GRAN'MA JONES HAS ONLY ONE TABLE!
SUNSET DINER FOR FINE FOODS
SHE WON'T HAVE ANY TABLE WHEN WE GET THROUGH WITH HER! HA, HA!
SUNSET DINER FOR
I'LL ASK GRAN'MA JONES IF SHE KNOWS ABOUT THIS!
HELLO, DEAR! WOULD YOU CARE FOR A DOUGHNUT?
ER...NO THANKS... DID YOU SEE WHAT THE BOYS ARE DOING, GRAN'MA?
WHY, YES! THEY'RE ADVERTISING THE SUNSET DINER! ISN'T IT NICE TO SEE BOYS WORKING LIKE THAT?
BUT-

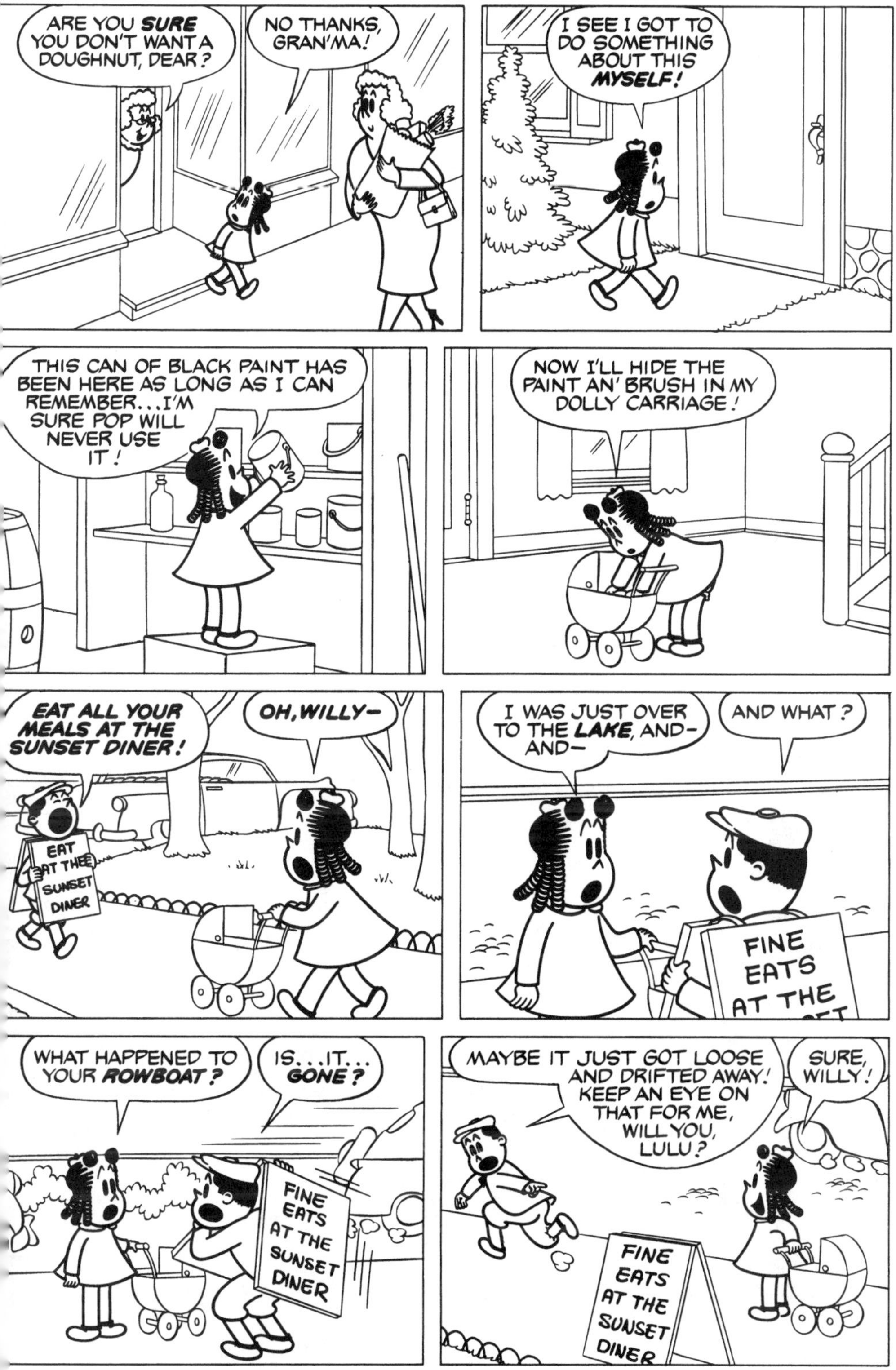

ARE YOU **SURE** YOU DON'T WANT A DOUGHNUT, DEAR?
NO THANKS, GRAN'MA!
I SEE I GOT TO DO SOMETHING ABOUT THIS **MYSELF!**
THIS CAN OF BLACK PAINT HAS BEEN HERE AS LONG AS I CAN REMEMBER...I'M SURE POP WILL NEVER USE IT!
NOW I'LL HIDE THE PAINT AN' BRUSH IN MY DOLLY CARRIAGE!
EAT ALL YOUR MEALS AT THE SUNSET DINER!
EAT AT THE SUNSET DINER
OH, WILLY—
I WAS JUST OVER TO THE **LAKE**, AND—AND—
AND WHAT?
FINE EATS AT THE
WHAT HAPPENED TO YOUR **ROWBOAT?**
IS...IT...**GONE?**
FINE EATS AT THE SUNSET DINER
MAYBE IT JUST GOT LOOSE AND DRIFTED AWAY! KEEP AN EYE ON THAT FOR ME, WILL YOU, LULU?
SURE, WILLY!
FINE EATS AT THE SUNSET DINER

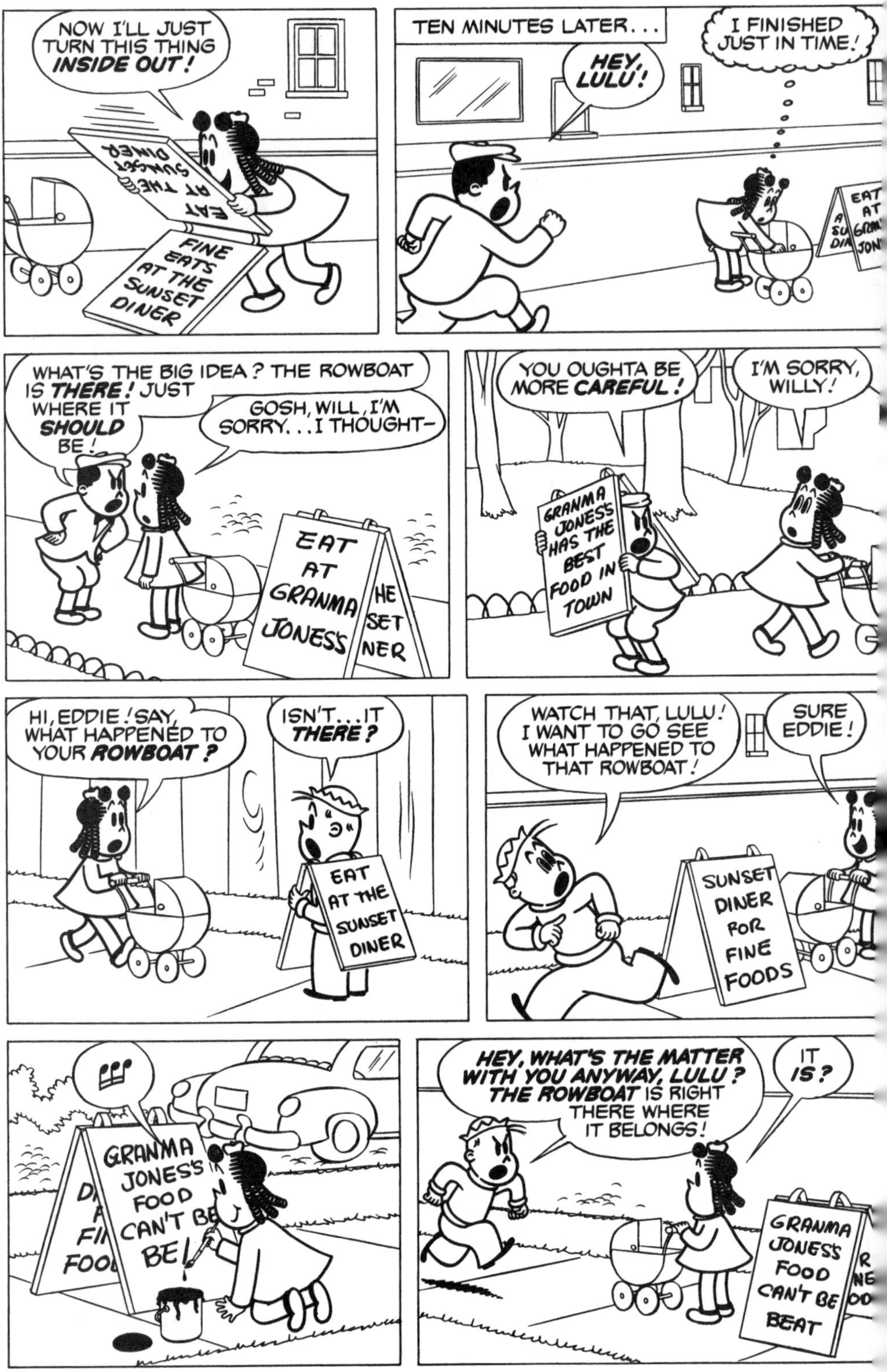
NOW I'LL JUST TURN THIS THING **INSIDE OUT!**
FINE EATS AT THE SUNSET DINER
TEN MINUTES LATER...
HEY, LULU!
I FINISHED JUST IN TIME!
WHAT'S THE BIG IDEA? THE ROWBOAT IS **THERE!** JUST WHERE IT **SHOULD** BE!
GOSH, WILL, I'M SORRY... I THOUGHT—
EAT AT GRANMA JONES'S
YOU OUGHTA BE MORE **CAREFUL!**
I'M SORRY, WILLY!
GRANMA JONES'S HAS THE BEST FOOD IN TOWN
HI, EDDIE! SAY, WHAT HAPPENED TO YOUR **ROWBOAT?**
ISN'T... IT **THERE?**
EAT AT THE SUNSET DINER
WATCH THAT, LULU! I WANT TO GO SEE WHAT HAPPENED TO THAT ROWBOAT!
SURE EDDIE!
SUNSET DINER FOR FINE FOODS
GRANMA JONES'S FOOD CAN'T BE BE
HEY, WHAT'S THE MATTER WITH YOU ANYWAY, LULU? THE ROWBOAT IS RIGHT THERE WHERE IT BELONGS!
IT **IS?**
GRANMA JONES'S FOOD CAN'T BE BEAT

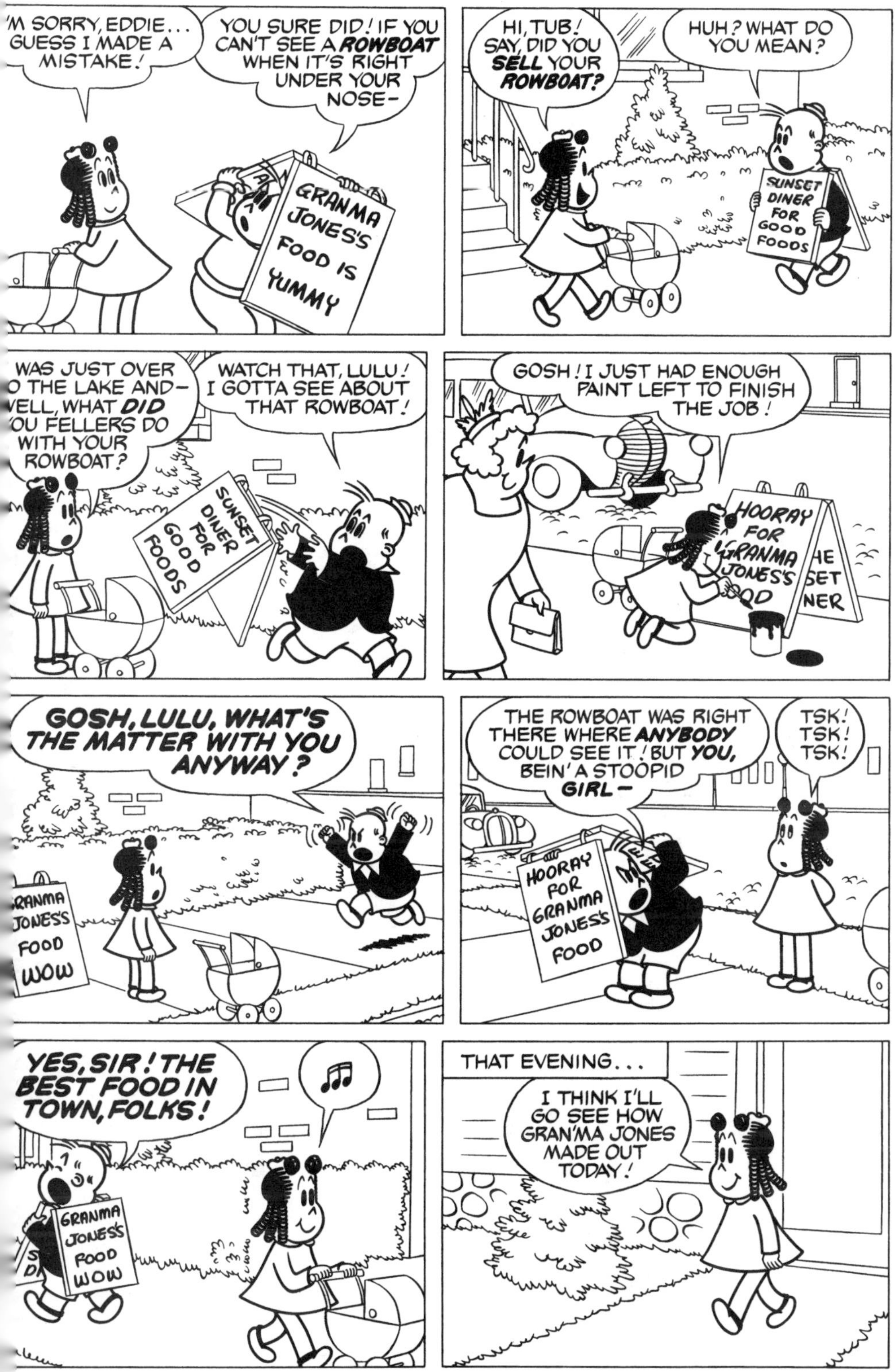
'M SORRY, EDDIE... GUESS I MADE A MISTAKE!
YOU SURE DID! IF YOU CAN'T SEE A ROWBOAT WHEN IT'S RIGHT UNDER YOUR NOSE–
GRANMA JONES'S FOOD IS YUMMY
HI, TUB! SAY, DID YOU SELL YOUR ROWBOAT?
HUH? WHAT DO YOU MEAN?
SUNSET DINER FOR GOOD FOODS
WAS JUST OVER
O THE LAKE AND–
VELL, WHAT DID
'OU FELLERS DO
WITH YOUR ROWBOAT?
WATCH THAT, LULU! I GOTTA SEE ABOUT THAT ROWBOAT!
SUNSET DINER FOR GOOD FOODS
GOSH! I JUST HAD ENOUGH PAINT LEFT TO FINISH THE JOB!
HOORAY FOR GRANMA JONES'S
GOSH, LULU, WHAT'S THE MATTER WITH YOU ANYWAY?
GRANMA JONES'S FOOD WOW
THE ROWBOAT WAS RIGHT THERE WHERE ANYBODY COULD SEE IT! BUT YOU, BEIN' A STOOPID GIRL–
TSK! TSK! TSK!
HOORAY FOR GRANMA JONES'S FOOD
YES, SIR! THE BEST FOOD IN TOWN, FOLKS!
GRANMA JONES'S FOOD WOW
THAT EVENING...
I THINK I'LL GO SEE HOW GRAN'MA JONES MADE OUT TODAY!

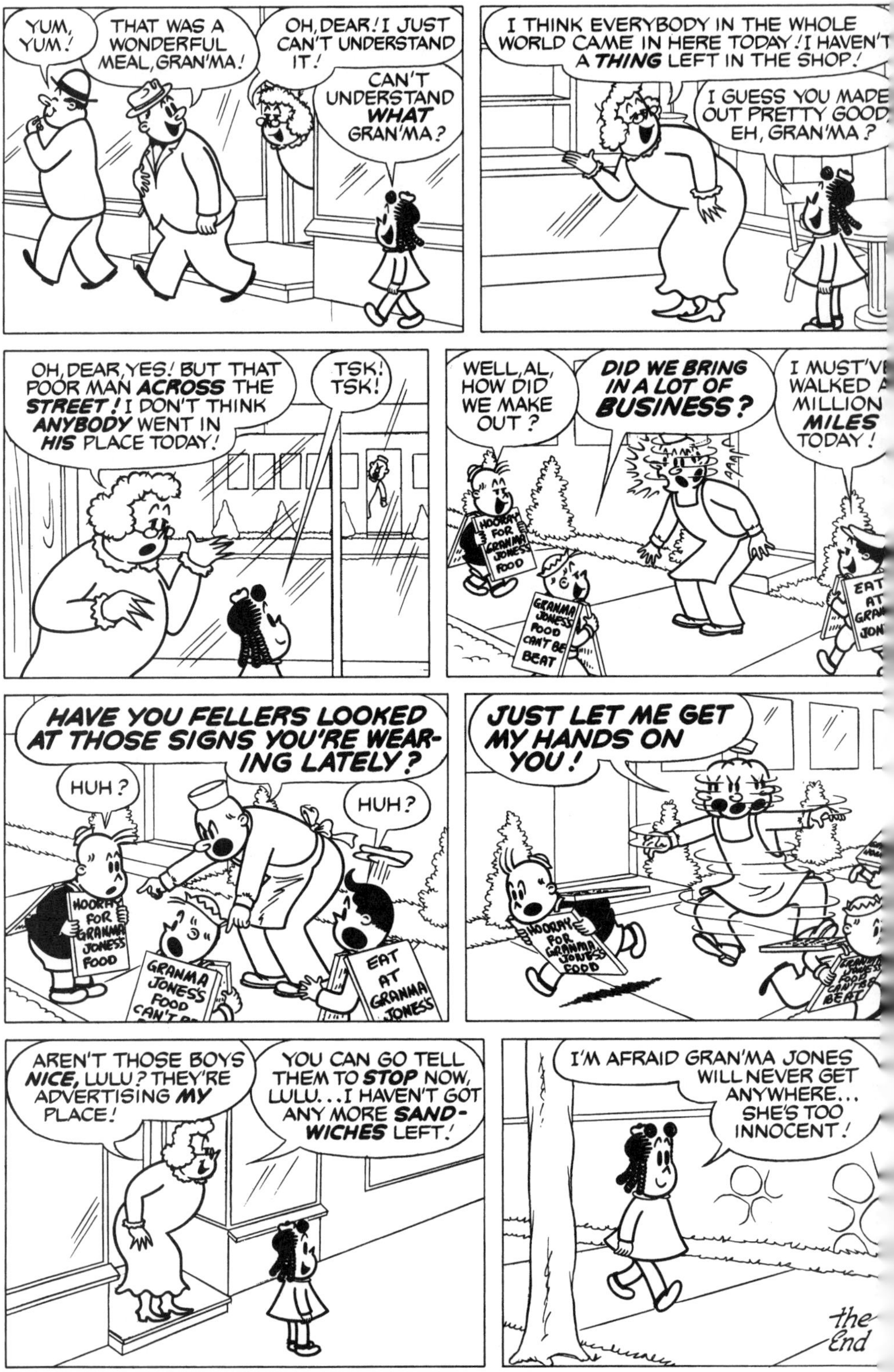
YUM, YUM!
THAT WAS A WONDERFUL MEAL, GRAN'MA!
OH, DEAR! I JUST CAN'T UNDERSTAND IT!
CAN'T UNDERSTAND WHAT GRAN'MA?
I THINK EVERYBODY IN THE WHOLE WORLD CAME IN HERE TODAY! I HAVEN'T A THING LEFT IN THE SHOP!
I GUESS YOU MADE OUT PRETTY GOOD, EH, GRAN'MA?
OH, DEAR, YES! BUT THAT POOR MAN ACROSS THE STREET! I DON'T THINK ANYBODY WENT IN HIS PLACE TODAY!
TSK! TSK!
WELL, AL, HOW DID WE MAKE OUT?
DID WE BRING IN A LOT OF BUSINESS?
I MUST'VE WALKED A MILLION MILES TODAY!
HOORAY FOR GRANMA JONES'S FOOD
GRANMA JONES'S FOOD CAN'T BE BEAT
HAVE YOU FELLERS LOOKED AT THOSE SIGNS YOU'RE WEARING LATELY?
HUH?
HUH?
HOORAY FOR GRANMA JONES'S FOOD
GRANMA JONES'S FOOD
EAT AT GRANMA JONES'S
JUST LET ME GET MY HANDS ON YOU!
HOORAY FOR GRANMA JONES'S FOOD
AREN'T THOSE BOYS NICE, LULU? THEY'RE ADVERTISING MY PLACE!
YOU CAN GO TELL THEM TO STOP NOW, LULU...I HAVEN'T GOT ANY MORE SANDWICHES LEFT!
I'M AFRAID GRAN'MA JONES WILL NEVER GET ANYWHERE... SHE'S TOO INNOCENT!
the End

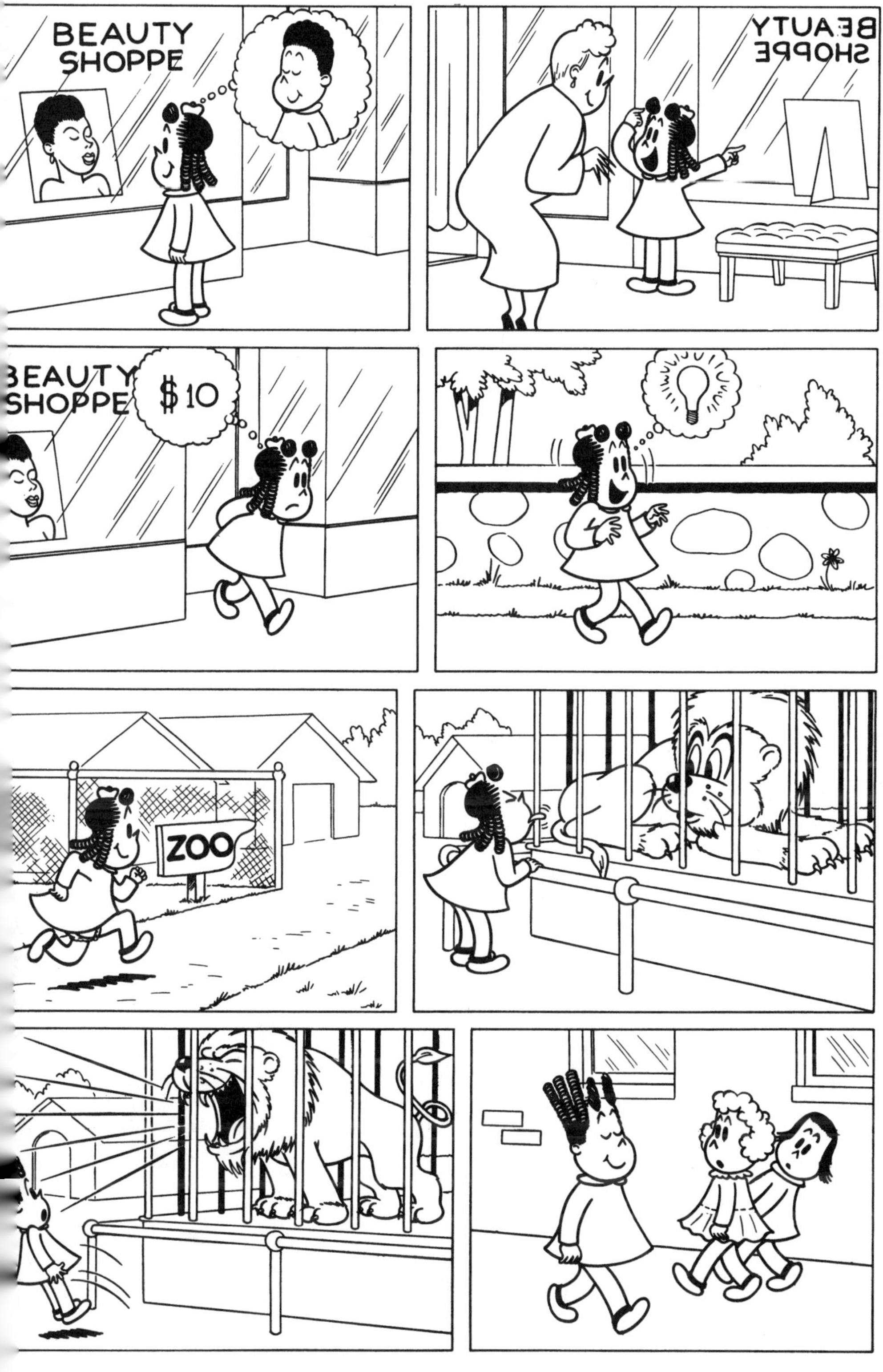
BEAUTY
SHOPPE
BEAUTY
SHOPPE
BEAUTY
SHOPPE
$10
ZOO

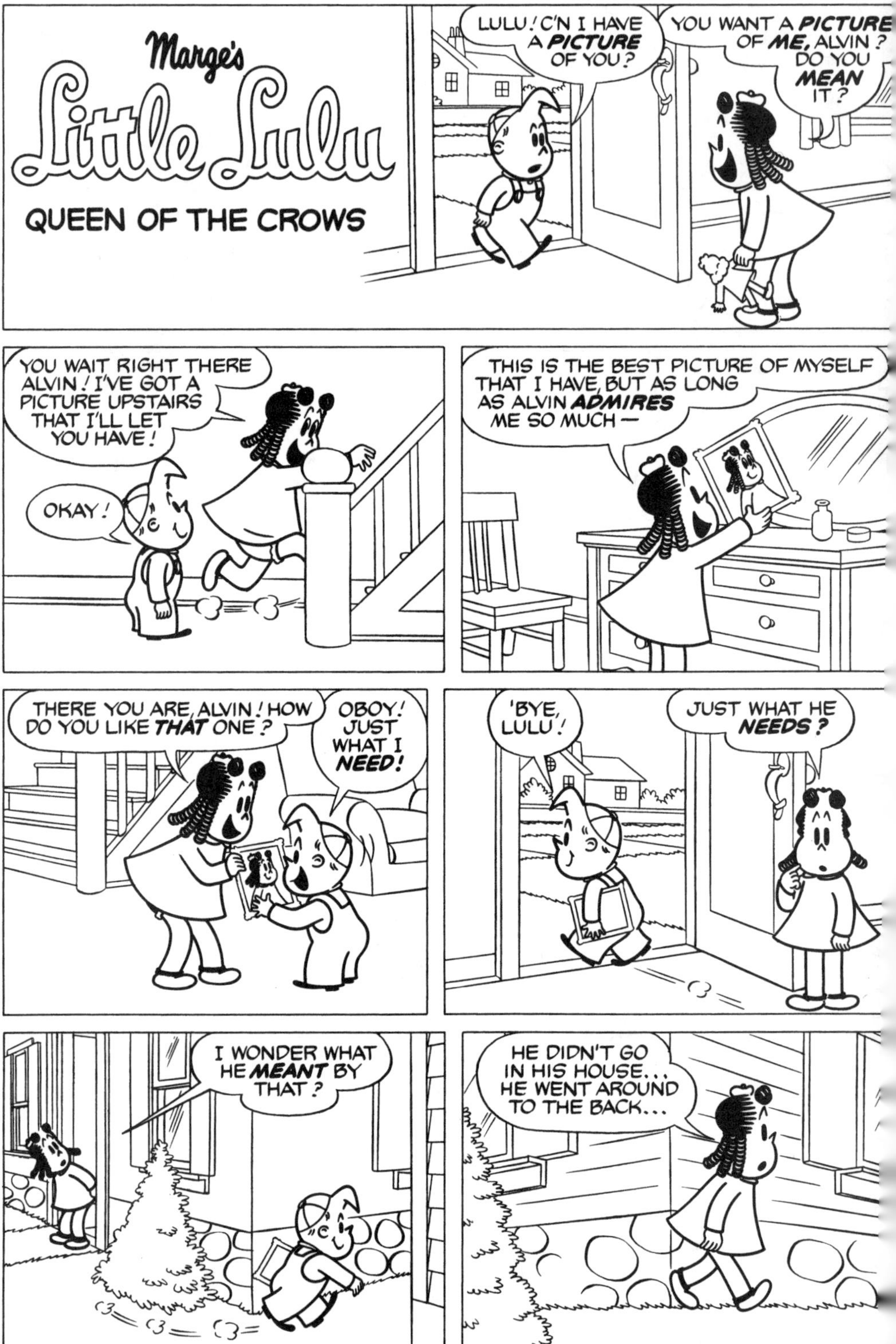
Marge's
Little Lulu
QUEEN OF THE CROWS
LULU! C'N I HAVE A PICTURE OF YOU?
YOU WANT A PICTURE OF ME, ALVIN? DO YOU MEAN IT?
YOU WAIT RIGHT THERE ALVIN! I'VE GOT A PICTURE UPSTAIRS THAT I'LL LET YOU HAVE!
OKAY!
THIS IS THE BEST PICTURE OF MYSELF THAT I HAVE, BUT AS LONG AS ALVIN ADMIRES ME SO MUCH —
THERE YOU ARE, ALVIN! HOW DO YOU LIKE THAT ONE?
OBOY! JUST WHAT I NEED!
'BYE, LULU!
JUST WHAT HE NEEDS?
I WONDER WHAT HE MEANT BY THAT?
HE DIDN'T GO IN HIS HOUSE... HE WENT AROUND TO THE BACK...

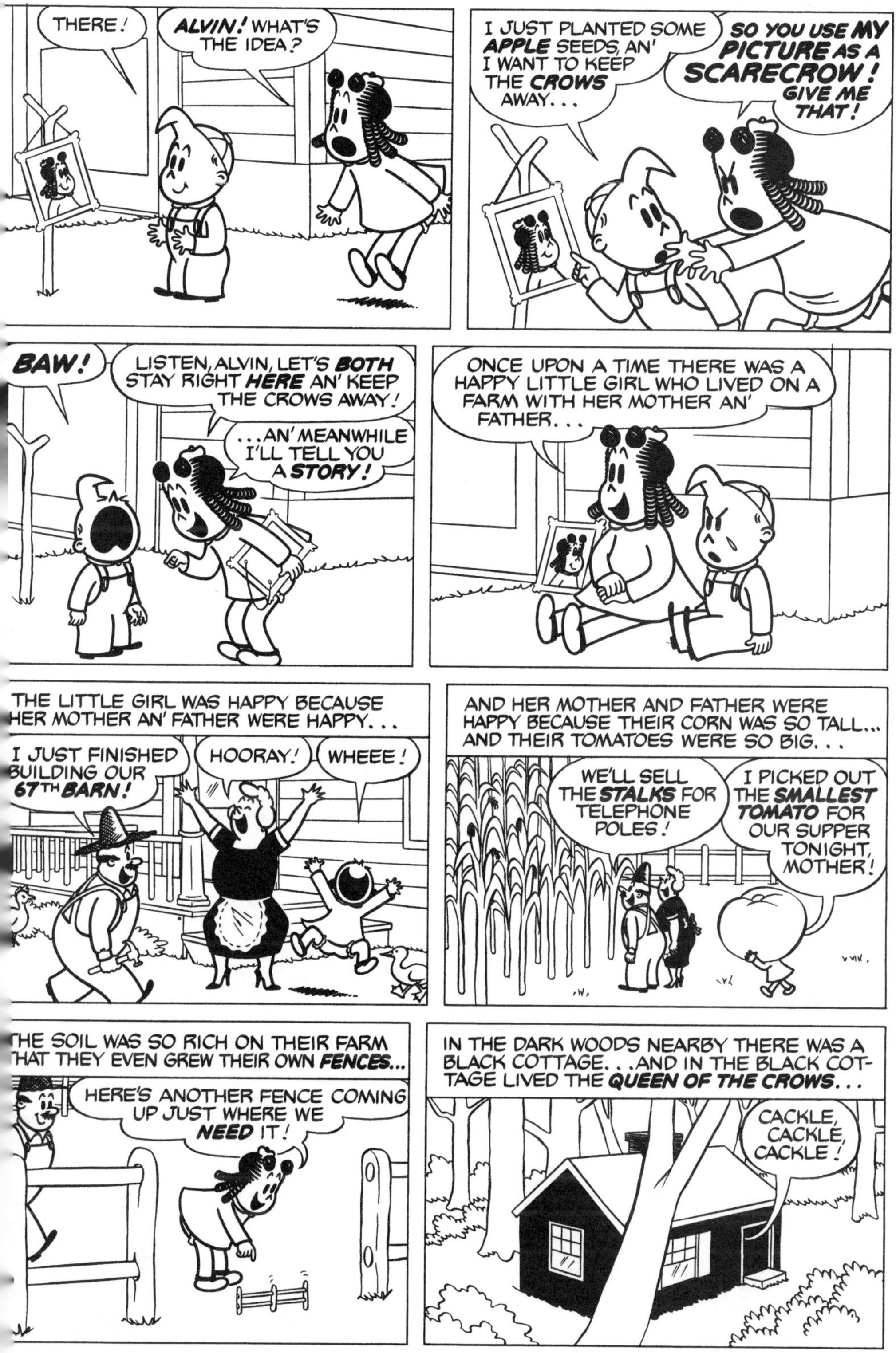

THERE!
ALVIN! WHAT'S THE IDEA?
I JUST PLANTED SOME APPLE SEEDS, AN' I WANT TO KEEP THE CROWS AWAY...
SO YOU USE MY PICTURE AS A SCARECROW! GIVE ME THAT!
BAW!
LISTEN, ALVIN, LET'S BOTH STAY RIGHT HERE AN' KEEP THE CROWS AWAY!
...AN' MEANWHILE I'LL TELL YOU A STORY!
ONCE UPON A TIME THERE WAS A HAPPY LITTLE GIRL WHO LIVED ON A FARM WITH HER MOTHER AN' FATHER...
THE LITTLE GIRL WAS HAPPY BECAUSE HER MOTHER AN' FATHER WERE HAPPY...
I JUST FINISHED BUILDING OUR 67TH BARN!
HOORAY!
WHEEE!
AND HER MOTHER AND FATHER WERE HAPPY BECAUSE THEIR CORN WAS SO TALL... AND THEIR TOMATOES WERE SO BIG...
WE'LL SELL THE STALKS FOR TELEPHONE POLES!
I PICKED OUT THE SMALLEST TOMATO FOR OUR SUPPER TONIGHT, MOTHER!
THE SOIL WAS SO RICH ON THEIR FARM THAT THEY EVEN GREW THEIR OWN FENCES...
HERE'S ANOTHER FENCE COMING UP JUST WHERE WE NEED IT!
IN THE DARK WOODS NEARBY THERE WAS A BLACK COTTAGE...AND IN THE BLACK COTTAGE LIVED THE QUEEN OF THE CROWS...
CACKLE, CACKLE, CACKLE!

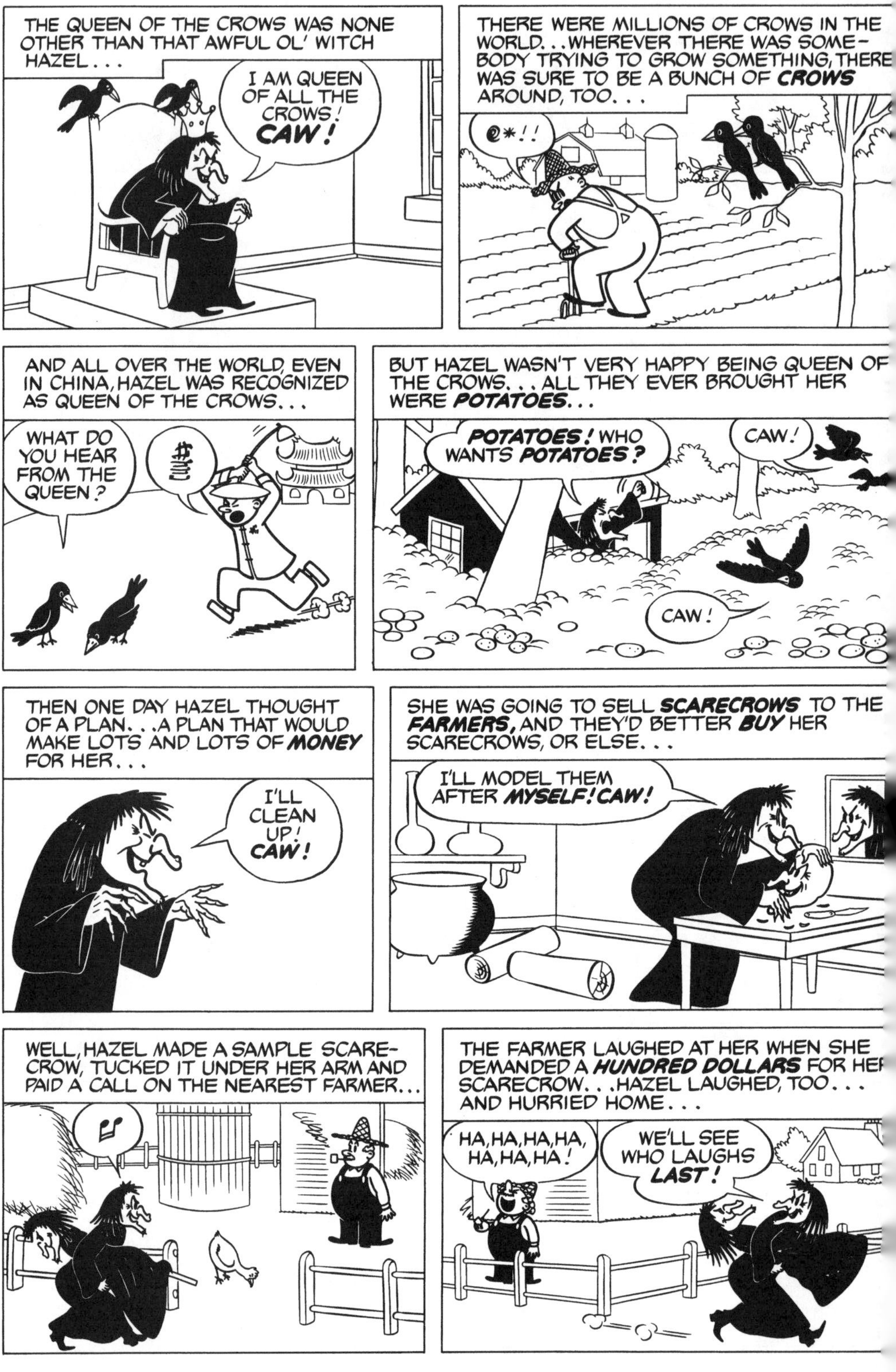
THE QUEEN OF THE CROWS WAS NONE OTHER THAN THAT AWFUL OL' WITCH HAZEL...
I AM QUEEN OF ALL THE CROWS! CAW!
THERE WERE MILLIONS OF CROWS IN THE WORLD...WHEREVER THERE WAS SOMEBODY TRYING TO GROW SOMETHING, THERE WAS SURE TO BE A BUNCH OF CROWS AROUND, TOO...
@*!!
AND ALL OVER THE WORLD, EVEN IN CHINA, HAZEL WAS RECOGNIZED AS QUEEN OF THE CROWS...
WHAT DO YOU HEAR FROM THE QUEEN?
BUT HAZEL WASN'T VERY HAPPY BEING QUEEN OF THE CROWS...ALL THEY EVER BROUGHT HER WERE POTATOES...
POTATOES! WHO WANTS POTATOES?
CAW!
CAW!
THEN ONE DAY HAZEL THOUGHT OF A PLAN...A PLAN THAT WOULD MAKE LOTS AND LOTS OF MONEY FOR HER...
I'LL CLEAN UP! CAW!
SHE WAS GOING TO SELL SCARECROWS TO THE FARMERS, AND THEY'D BETTER BUY HER SCARECROWS, OR ELSE...
I'LL MODEL THEM AFTER MYSELF! CAW!
WELL, HAZEL MADE A SAMPLE SCARECROW, TUCKED IT UNDER HER ARM AND PAID A CALL ON THE NEAREST FARMER...
THE FARMER LAUGHED AT HER WHEN SHE DEMANDED A HUNDRED DOLLARS FOR HER SCARECROW...HAZEL LAUGHED, TOO...AND HURRIED HOME...
HA, HA, HA, HA, HA, HA, HA!
WE'LL SEE WHO LAUGHS LAST!

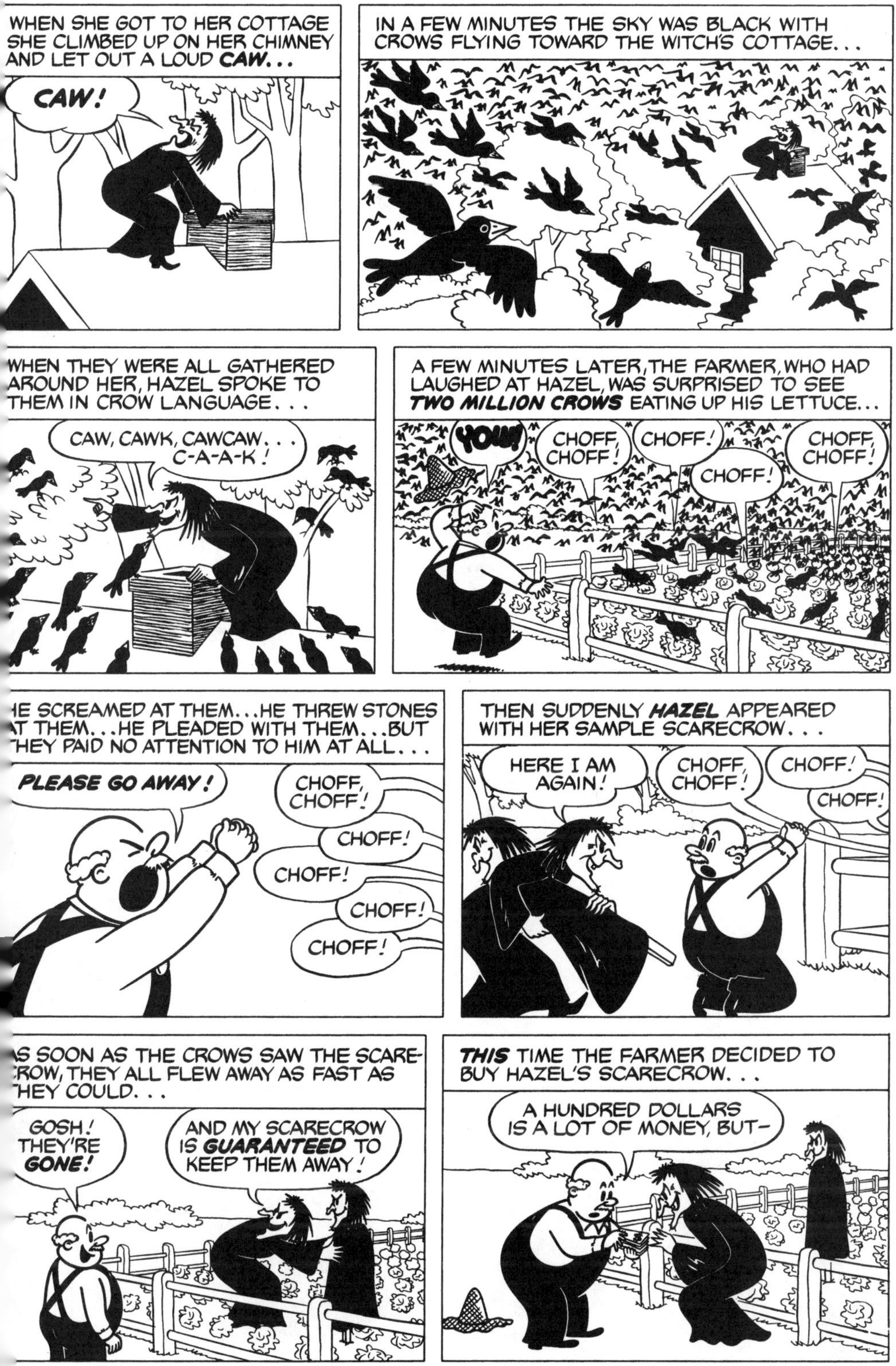
WHEN SHE GOT TO HER COTTAGE SHE CLIMBED UP ON HER CHIMNEY AND LET OUT A LOUD CAW...
CAW!
IN A FEW MINUTES THE SKY WAS BLACK WITH CROWS FLYING TOWARD THE WITCH'S COTTAGE...
WHEN THEY WERE ALL GATHERED AROUND HER, HAZEL SPOKE TO THEM IN CROW LANGUAGE...
CAW, CAWK, CAWCAW... C-A-A-K!
A FEW MINUTES LATER, THE FARMER, WHO HAD LAUGHED AT HAZEL, WAS SURPRISED TO SEE TWO MILLION CROWS EATING UP HIS LETTUCE...
YOW!
CHOFF, CHOFF!
CHOFF!
CHOFF!
CHOFF, CHOFF!
IE SCREAMED AT THEM...HE THREW STONES T THEM...HE PLEADED WITH THEM...BUT HEY PAID NO ATTENTION TO HIM AT ALL...
PLEASE GO AWAY!
CHOFF, CHOFF!
CHOFF!
CHOFF!
CHOFF!
CHOFF!
THEN SUDDENLY HAZEL APPEARED WITH HER SAMPLE SCARECROW...
HERE I AM AGAIN!
CHOFF, CHOFF!
CHOFF!
CHOFF!
S SOON AS THE CROWS SAW THE SCARE-ROW, THEY ALL FLEW AWAY AS FAST AS HEY COULD...
GOSH! THEY'RE GONE!
AND MY SCARECROW IS GUARANTEED TO KEEP THEM AWAY!
THIS TIME THE FARMER DECIDED TO BUY HAZEL'S SCARECROW...
A HUNDRED DOLLARS IS A LOT OF MONEY, BUT-

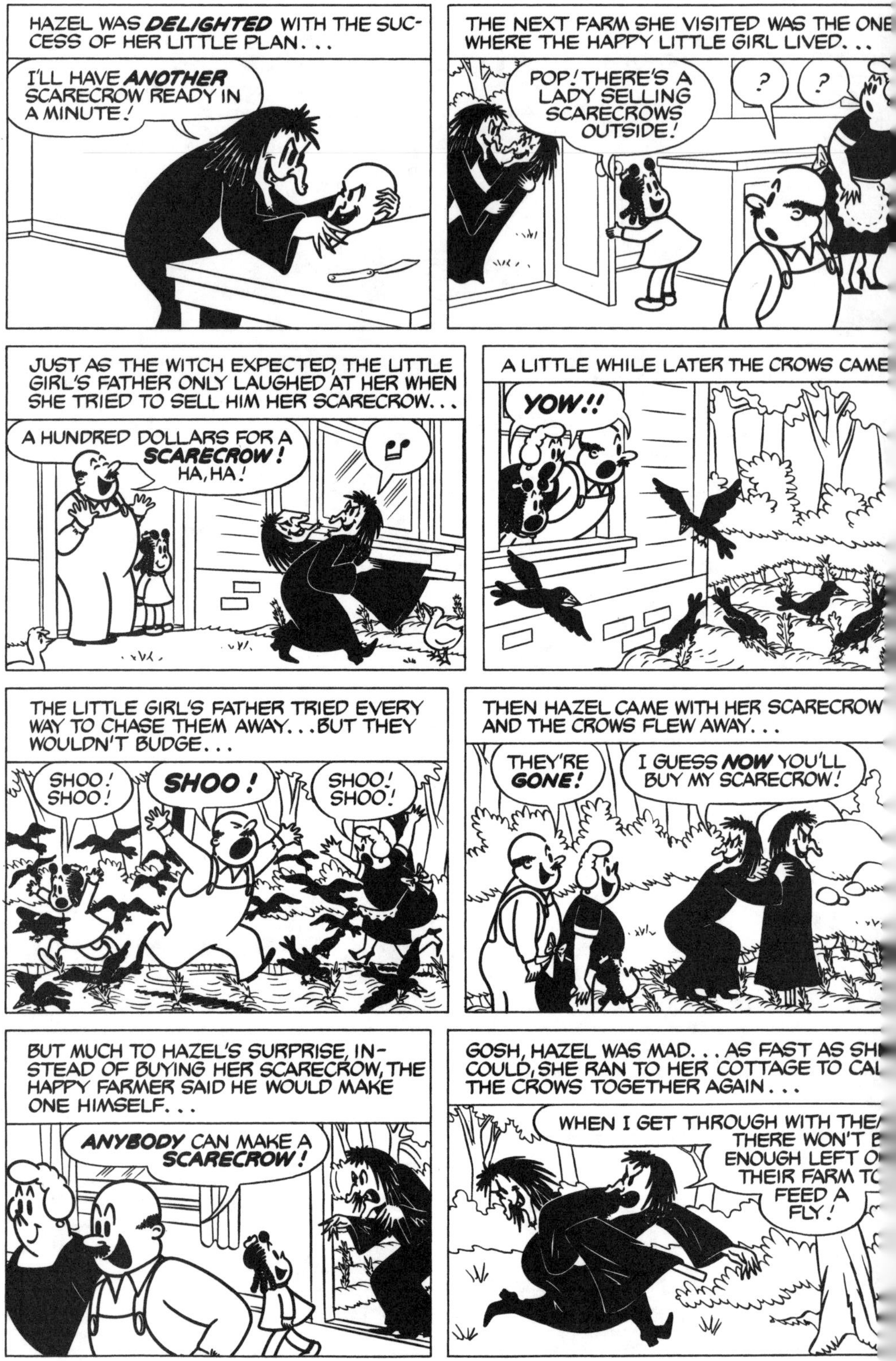
HAZEL WAS DELIGHTED WITH THE SUCCESS OF HER LITTLE PLAN...
I'LL HAVE ANOTHER SCARECROW READY IN A MINUTE!
THE NEXT FARM SHE VISITED WAS THE ONE WHERE THE HAPPY LITTLE GIRL LIVED...
POP! THERE'S A LADY SELLING SCARECROWS OUTSIDE!
?
?
JUST AS THE WITCH EXPECTED, THE LITTLE GIRL'S FATHER ONLY LAUGHED AT HER WHEN SHE TRIED TO SELL HIM HER SCARECROW...
A HUNDRED DOLLARS FOR A SCARECROW! HA, HA!
A LITTLE WHILE LATER THE CROWS CAME
YOW!!
THE LITTLE GIRL'S FATHER TRIED EVERY WAY TO CHASE THEM AWAY...BUT THEY WOULDN'T BUDGE...
SHOO! SHOO!
SHOO!
SHOO! SHOO!
THEN HAZEL CAME WITH HER SCARECROW AND THE CROWS FLEW AWAY...
THEY'RE GONE!
I GUESS NOW YOU'LL BUY MY SCARECROW!
BUT MUCH TO HAZEL'S SURPRISE, INSTEAD OF BUYING HER SCARECROW, THE HAPPY FARMER SAID HE WOULD MAKE ONE HIMSELF...
ANYBODY CAN MAKE A SCARECROW!
GOSH, HAZEL WAS MAD...AS FAST AS SH COULD, SHE RAN TO HER COTTAGE TO CAL THE CROWS TOGETHER AGAIN...
WHEN I GET THROUGH WITH THE THERE WON'T B ENOUGH LEFT O THEIR FARM T FEED A FLY!

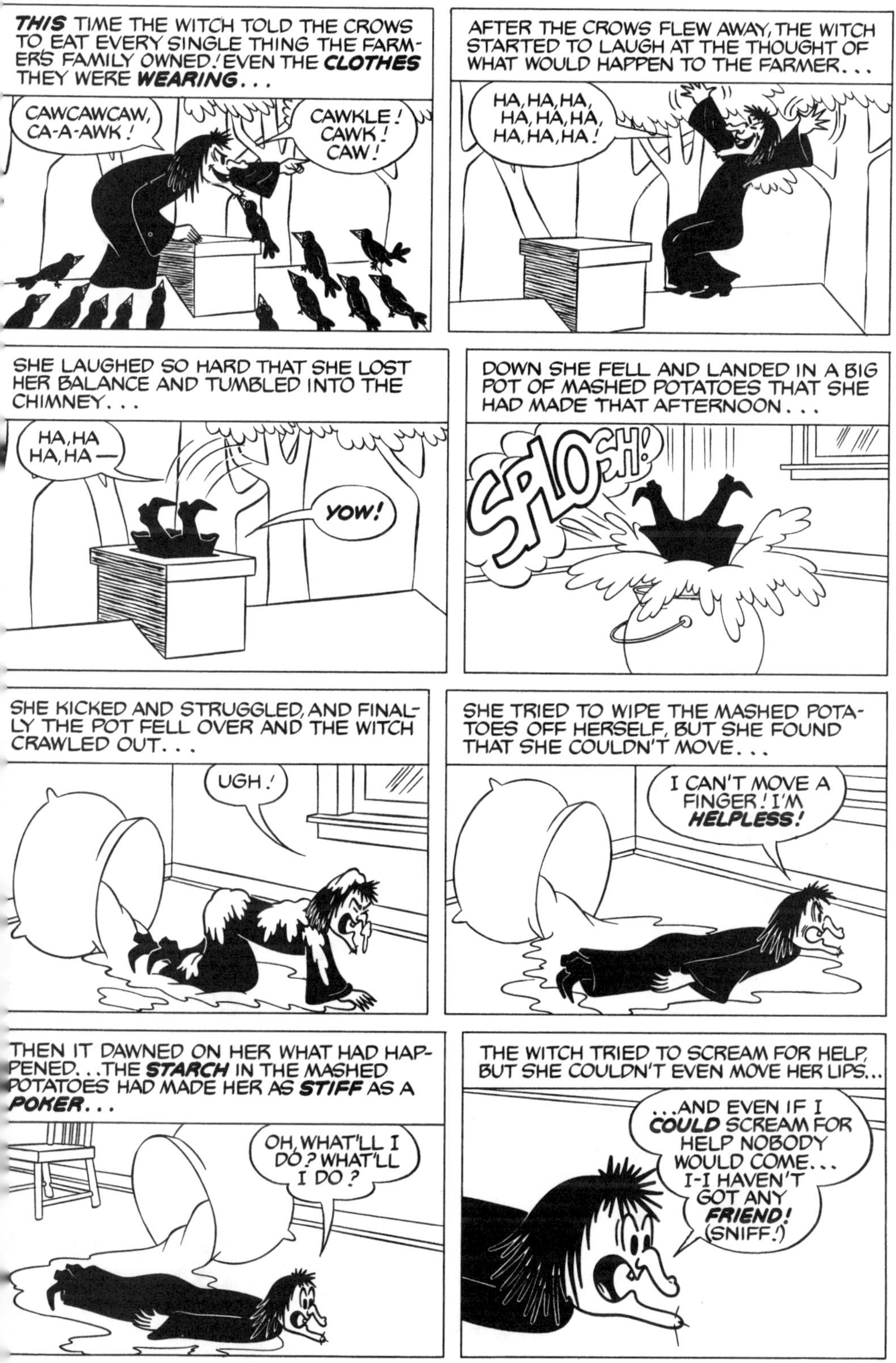
THIS TIME THE WITCH TOLD THE CROWS TO EAT EVERY SINGLE THING THE FARMER'S FAMILY OWNED! EVEN THE CLOTHES THEY WERE WEARING...
CAWCAWCAW, CA-A-AWK!
CAWKLE! CAWK! CAW!
AFTER THE CROWS FLEW AWAY, THE WITCH STARTED TO LAUGH AT THE THOUGHT OF WHAT WOULD HAPPEN TO THE FARMER...
HA, HA, HA, HA, HA, HA, HA, HA, HA!
SHE LAUGHED SO HARD THAT SHE LOST HER BALANCE AND TUMBLED INTO THE CHIMNEY...
HA, HA HA, HA—
YOW!
DOWN SHE FELL AND LANDED IN A BIG POT OF MASHED POTATOES THAT SHE HAD MADE THAT AFTERNOON...
SPLOSH!
SHE KICKED AND STRUGGLED, AND FINALLY THE POT FELL OVER AND THE WITCH CRAWLED OUT...
UGH!
SHE TRIED TO WIPE THE MASHED POTATOES OFF HERSELF, BUT SHE FOUND THAT SHE COULDN'T MOVE...
I CAN'T MOVE A FINGER! I'M HELPLESS!
THEN IT DAWNED ON HER WHAT HAD HAPPENED... THE STARCH IN THE MASHED POTATOES HAD MADE HER AS STIFF AS A POKER...
OH, WHAT'LL I DO? WHAT'LL I DO?
THE WITCH TRIED TO SCREAM FOR HELP, BUT SHE COULDN'T EVEN MOVE HER LIPS...
...AND EVEN IF I COULD SCREAM FOR HELP NOBODY WOULD COME... I-I HAVEN'T GOT ANY FRIEND! (SNIFF!)

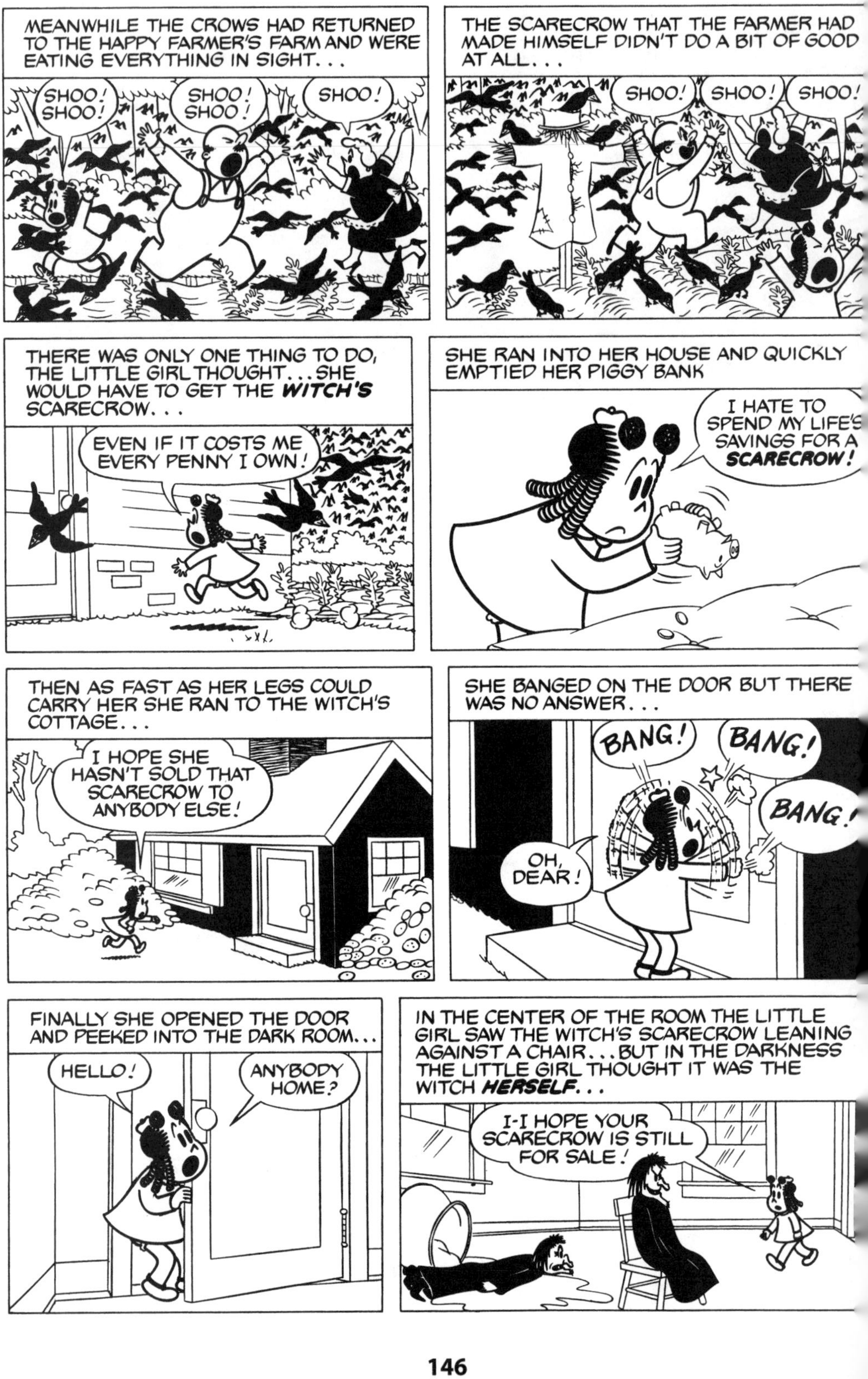
MEANWHILE THE CROWS HAD RETURNED TO THE HAPPY FARMER'S FARM AND WERE EATING EVERYTHING IN SIGHT...
SHOO! SHOO!
SHOO! SHOO!
SHOO!
THE SCARECROW THAT THE FARMER HAD MADE HIMSELF DIDN'T DO A BIT OF GOOD AT ALL...
SHOO!
SHOO!
SHOO!
THERE WAS ONLY ONE THING TO DO, THE LITTLE GIRL THOUGHT...SHE WOULD HAVE TO GET THE WITCH'S SCARECROW...
EVEN IF IT COSTS ME EVERY PENNY I OWN!
SHE RAN INTO HER HOUSE AND QUICKLY EMPTIED HER PIGGY BANK
I HATE TO SPEND MY LIFE'S SAVINGS FOR A SCARECROW!
THEN AS FAST AS HER LEGS COULD CARRY HER SHE RAN TO THE WITCH'S COTTAGE...
I HOPE SHE HASN'T SOLD THAT SCARECROW TO ANYBODY ELSE!
SHE BANGED ON THE DOOR BUT THERE WAS NO ANSWER...
BANG!
BANG!
BANG!
OH, DEAR!
FINALLY SHE OPENED THE DOOR AND PEEKED INTO THE DARK ROOM...
HELLO!
ANYBODY HOME?
IN THE CENTER OF THE ROOM THE LITTLE GIRL SAW THE WITCH'S SCARECROW LEANING AGAINST A CHAIR...BUT IN THE DARKNESS THE LITTLE GIRL THOUGHT IT WAS THE WITCH HERSELF...
I-I HOPE YOUR SCARECROW IS STILL FOR SALE!

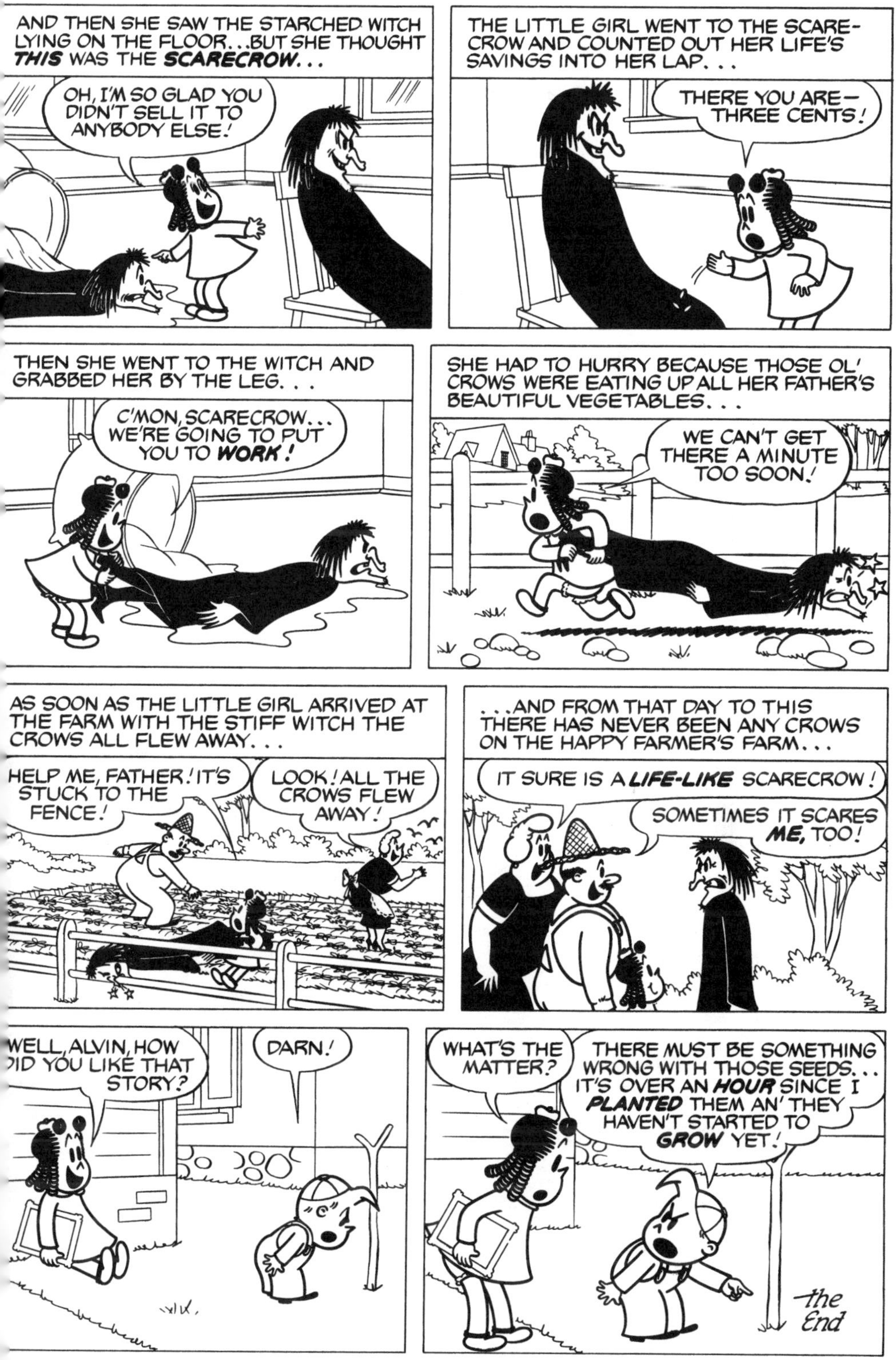
AND THEN SHE SAW THE STARCHED WITCH LYING ON THE FLOOR...BUT SHE THOUGHT THIS WAS THE SCARECROW...
OH, I'M SO GLAD YOU DIDN'T SELL IT TO ANYBODY ELSE!
THE LITTLE GIRL WENT TO THE SCARE-CROW AND COUNTED OUT HER LIFE'S SAVINGS INTO HER LAP...
THERE YOU ARE— THREE CENTS!
THEN SHE WENT TO THE WITCH AND GRABBED HER BY THE LEG...
C'MON, SCARECROW... WE'RE GOING TO PUT YOU TO WORK!
SHE HAD TO HURRY BECAUSE THOSE OL' CROWS WERE EATING UP ALL HER FATHER'S BEAUTIFUL VEGETABLES...
WE CAN'T GET THERE A MINUTE TOO SOON!
AS SOON AS THE LITTLE GIRL ARRIVED AT THE FARM WITH THE STIFF WITCH THE CROWS ALL FLEW AWAY...
HELP ME, FATHER! IT'S STUCK TO THE FENCE!
LOOK! ALL THE CROWS FLEW AWAY!
...AND FROM THAT DAY TO THIS THERE HAS NEVER BEEN ANY CROWS ON THE HAPPY FARMER'S FARM...
IT SURE IS A LIFE-LIKE SCARECROW!
SOMETIMES IT SCARES ME, TOO!
WELL, ALVIN, HOW DID YOU LIKE THAT STORY?
DARN!
WHAT'S THE MATTER?
THERE MUST BE SOMETHING WRONG WITH THOSE SEEDS... IT'S OVER AN HOUR SINCE I PLANTED THEM AN' THEY HAVEN'T STARTED TO GROW YET!
the End

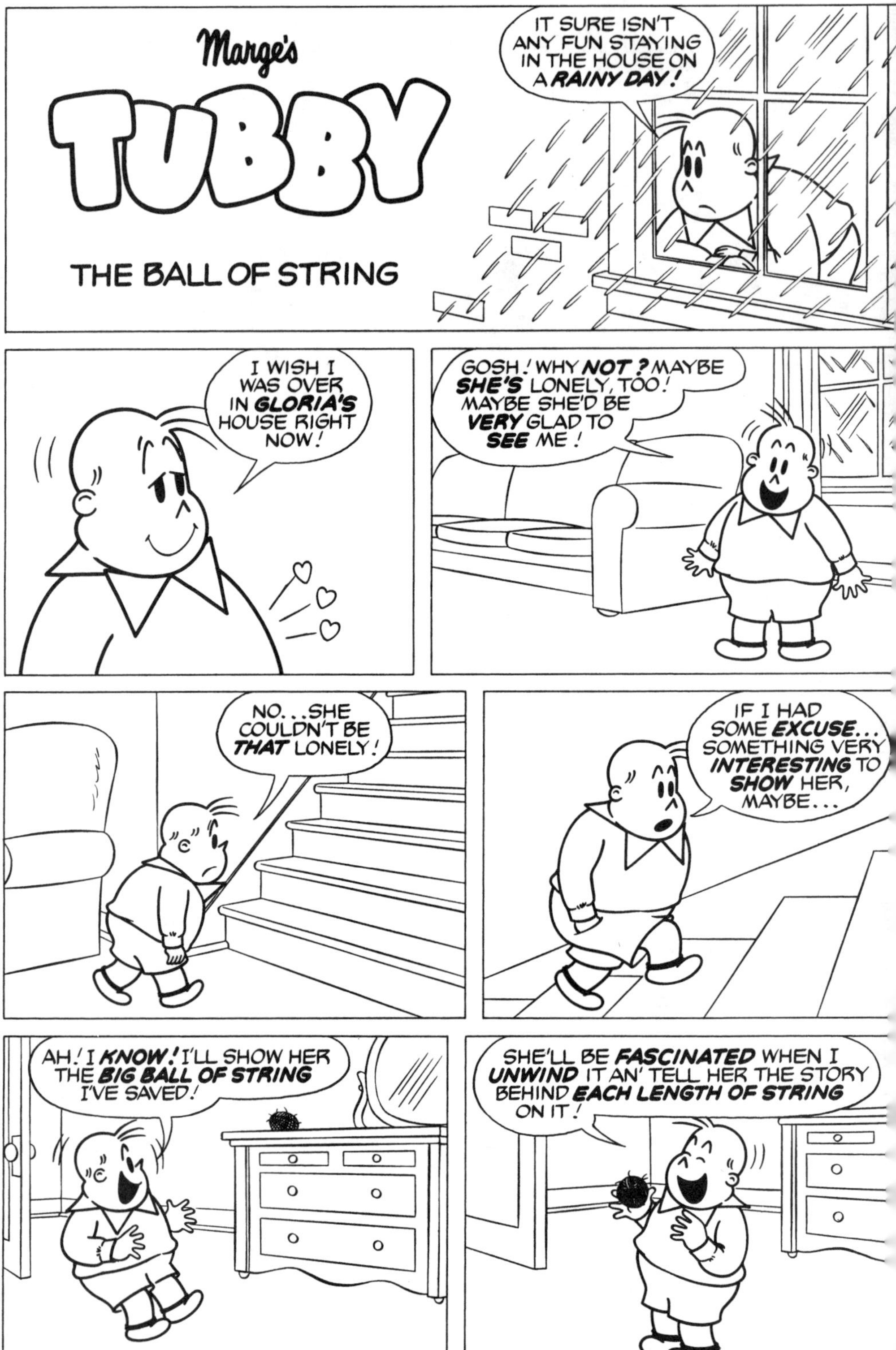
Marge's
TUBBY
THE BALL OF STRING
IT SURE ISN'T ANY FUN STAYING IN THE HOUSE ON A RAINY DAY!
I WISH I WAS OVER IN GLORIA'S HOUSE RIGHT NOW!
GOSH! WHY NOT? MAYBE SHE'S LONELY, TOO! MAYBE SHE'D BE VERY GLAD TO SEE ME!
NO...SHE COULDN'T BE THAT LONELY!
IF I HAD SOME EXCUSE... SOMETHING VERY INTERESTING TO SHOW HER, MAYBE...
AH! I KNOW! I'LL SHOW HER THE BIG BALL OF STRING I'VE SAVED!
SHE'LL BE FASCINATED WHEN I UNWIND IT AN' TELL HER THE STORY BEHIND EACH LENGTH OF STRING ON IT!

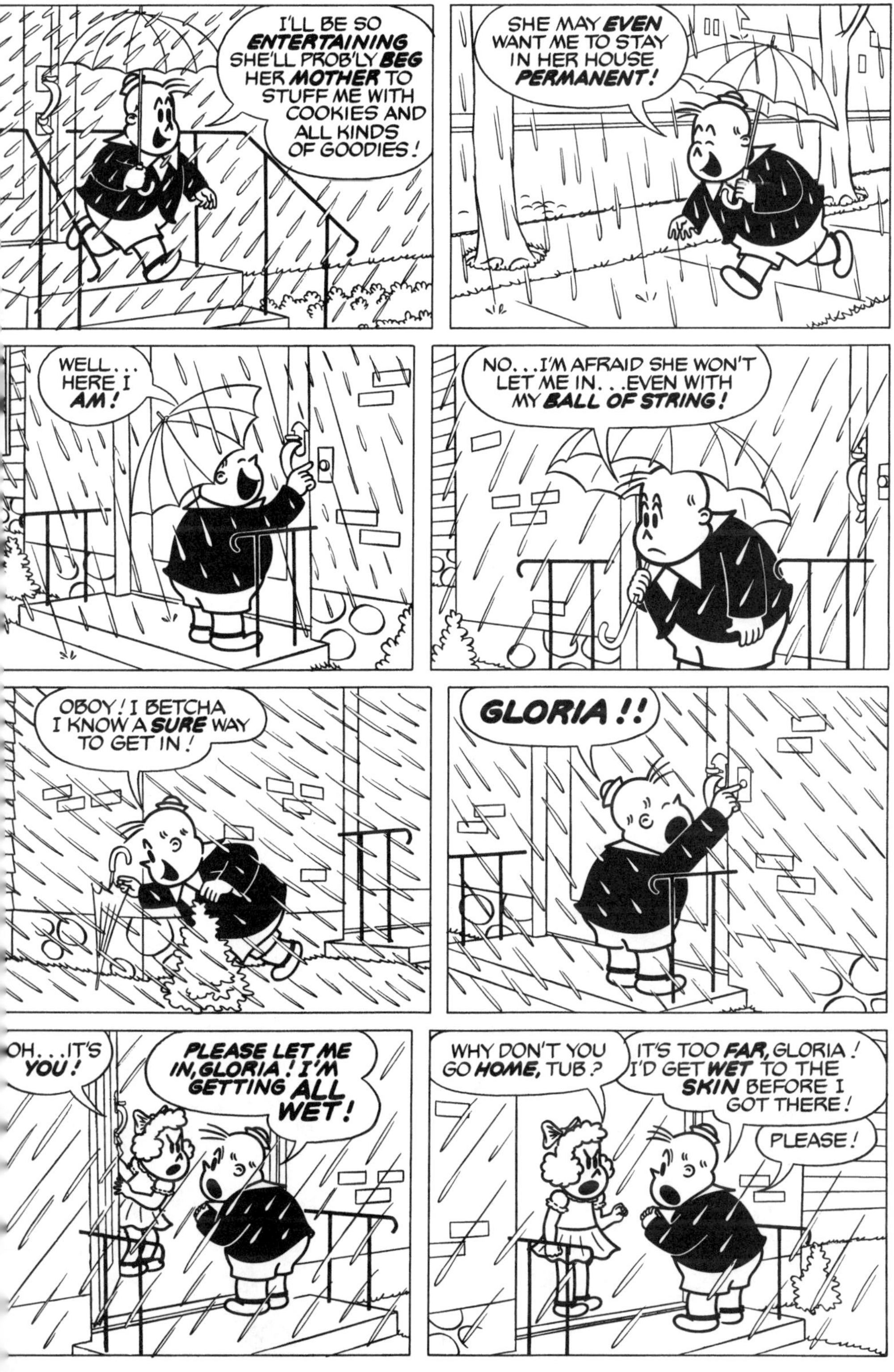
I'LL BE SO ENTERTAINING SHE'LL PROB'LY BEG HER MOTHER TO STUFF ME WITH COOKIES AND ALL KINDS OF GOODIES!
SHE MAY EVEN WANT ME TO STAY IN HER HOUSE PERMANENT!
WELL... HERE I AM!
NO...I'M AFRAID SHE WON'T LET ME IN...EVEN WITH MY BALL OF STRING!
OBOY! I BETCHA I KNOW A SURE WAY TO GET IN!
GLORIA!!
OH...IT'S YOU!
PLEASE LET ME IN, GLORIA! I'M GETTING ALL WET!
WHY DON'T YOU GO HOME, TUB?
IT'S TOO FAR, GLORIA! I'D GET WET TO THE SKIN BEFORE I GOT THERE!
PLEASE!

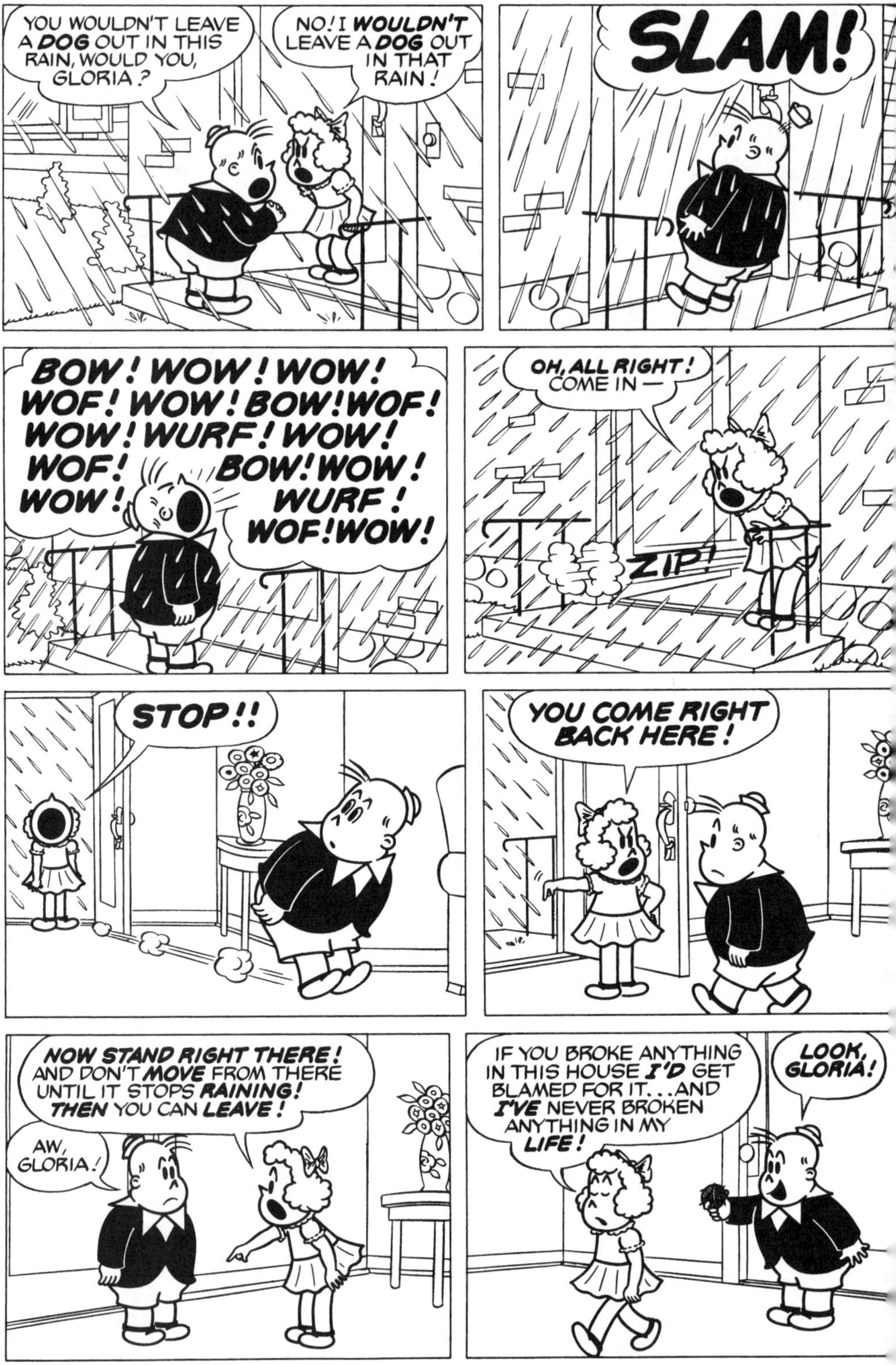
YOU WOULDN'T LEAVE A DOG OUT IN THIS RAIN, WOULD YOU, GLORIA?
NO! I WOULDN'T LEAVE A DOG OUT IN THAT RAIN!
SLAM!
BOW! WOW! WOW! WOF! WOW! BOW! WOF! WOW! WURF! WOW! WOF! WOW! BOW! WOW! WURF! WOF! WOW!
OH, ALL RIGHT! COME IN —
ZIP!
STOP!!
YOU COME RIGHT BACK HERE!
NOW STAND RIGHT THERE! AND DON'T MOVE FROM THERE UNTIL IT STOPS RAINING! THEN YOU CAN LEAVE!
AW, GLORIA!
IF YOU BROKE ANYTHING IN THIS HOUSE I'D GET BLAMED FOR IT...AND I'VE NEVER BROKEN ANYTHING IN MY LIFE!
LOOK, GLORIA!

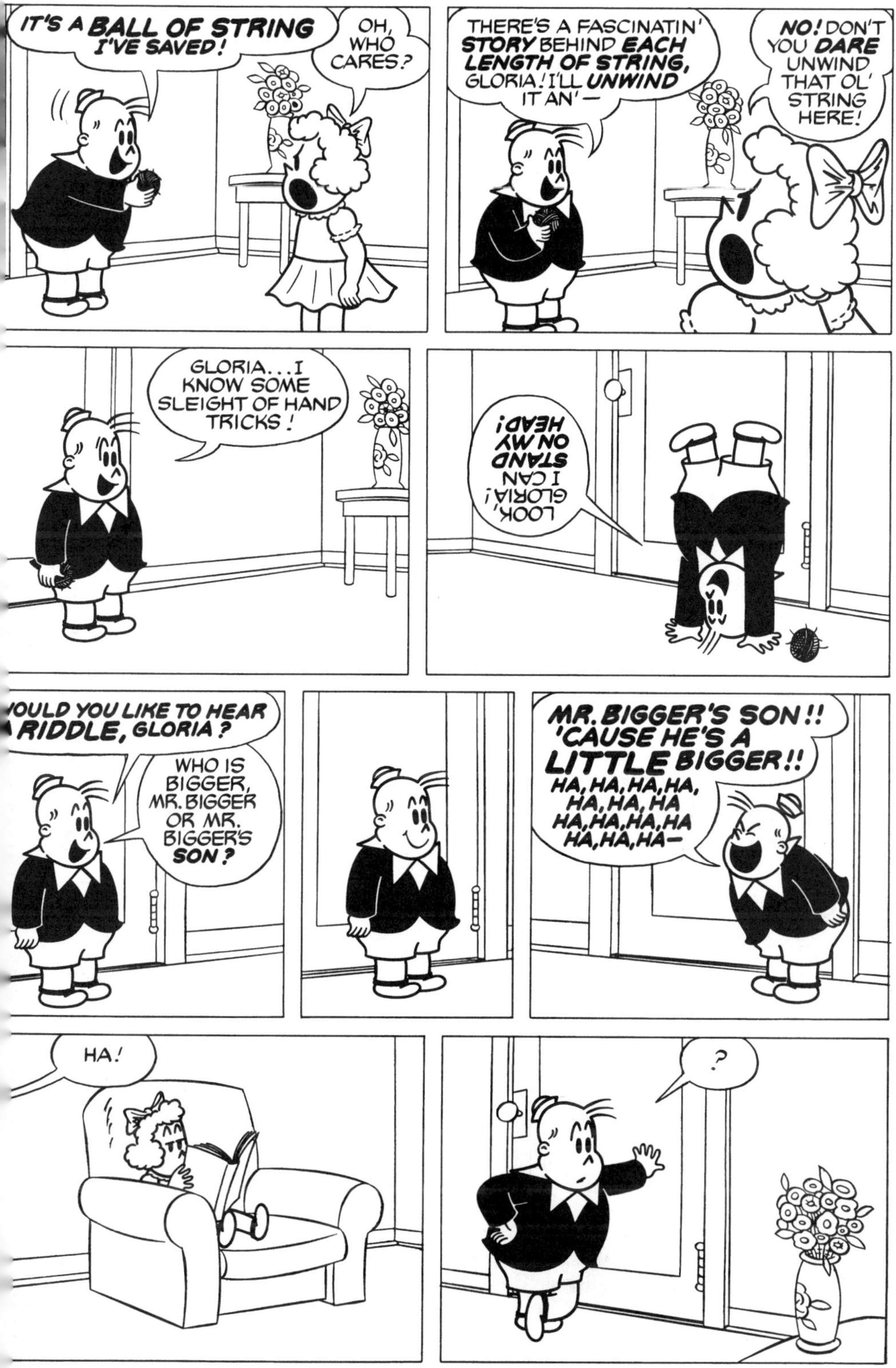

IT'S A BALL OF STRING I'VE SAVED!
OH, WHO CARES?
THERE'S A FASCINATIN' STORY BEHIND EACH LENGTH OF STRING, GLORIA! I'LL UNWIND IT AN'—
NO! DON'T YOU DARE UNWIND THAT OL' STRING HERE!
GLORIA...I KNOW SOME SLEIGHT OF HAND TRICKS!
LOOK, GLORIA! I CAN STAND ON MY HEAD!
OULD YOU LIKE TO HEAR RIDDLE, GLORIA?
WHO IS BIGGER, MR. BIGGER OR MR. BIGGER'S SON?
MR. BIGGER'S SON!! 'CAUSE HE'S A LITTLE BIGGER!!
HA, HA, HA, HA, HA, HA, HA HA, HA, HA, HA HA, HA, HA—
HA!
?

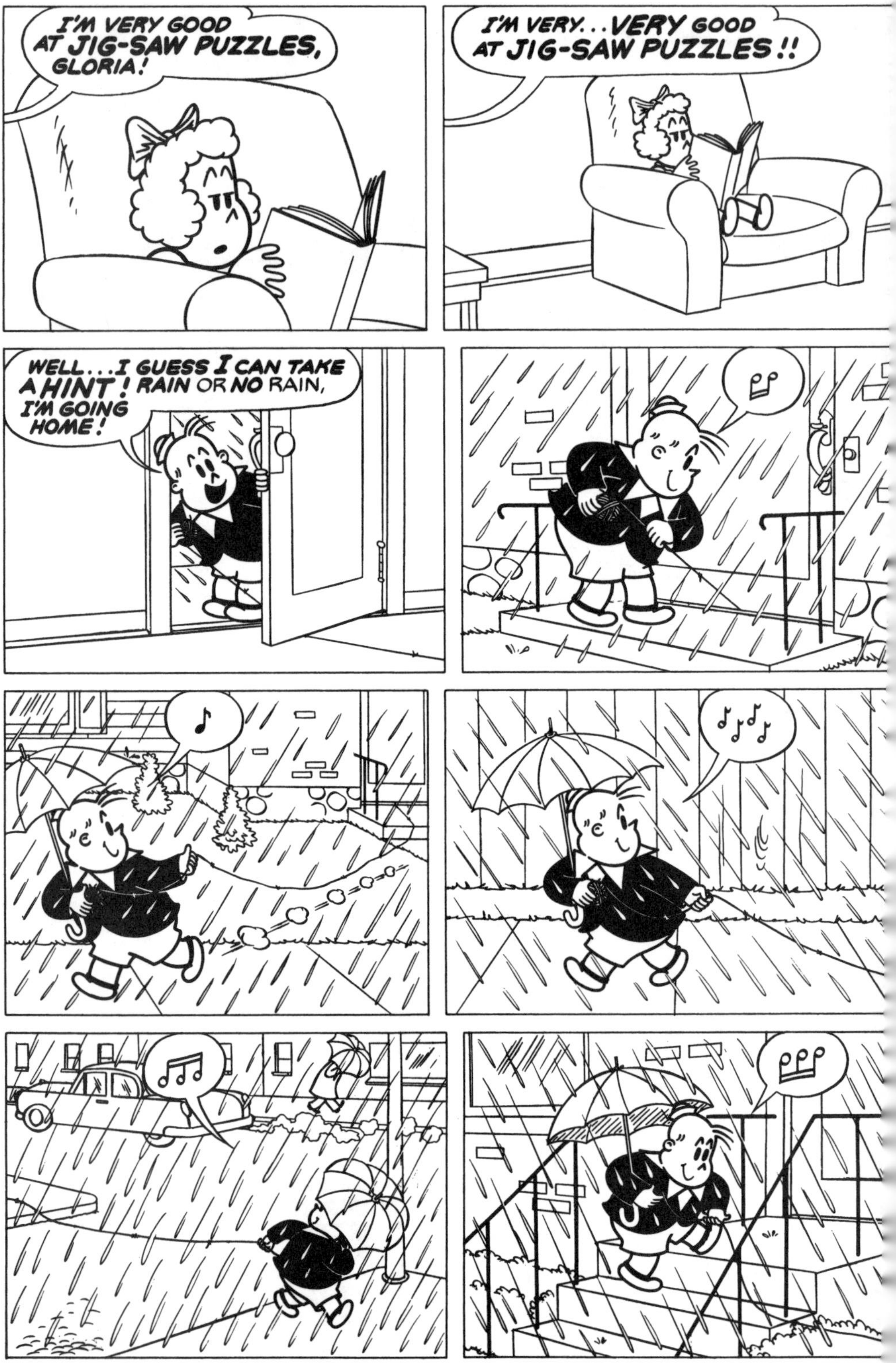
I'M VERY GOOD AT JIG-SAW PUZZLES, GLORIA!
I'M VERY...VERY GOOD AT JIG-SAW PUZZLES!!
WELL...I GUESS I CAN TAKE A HINT! RAIN OR NO RAIN, I'M GOING HOME!

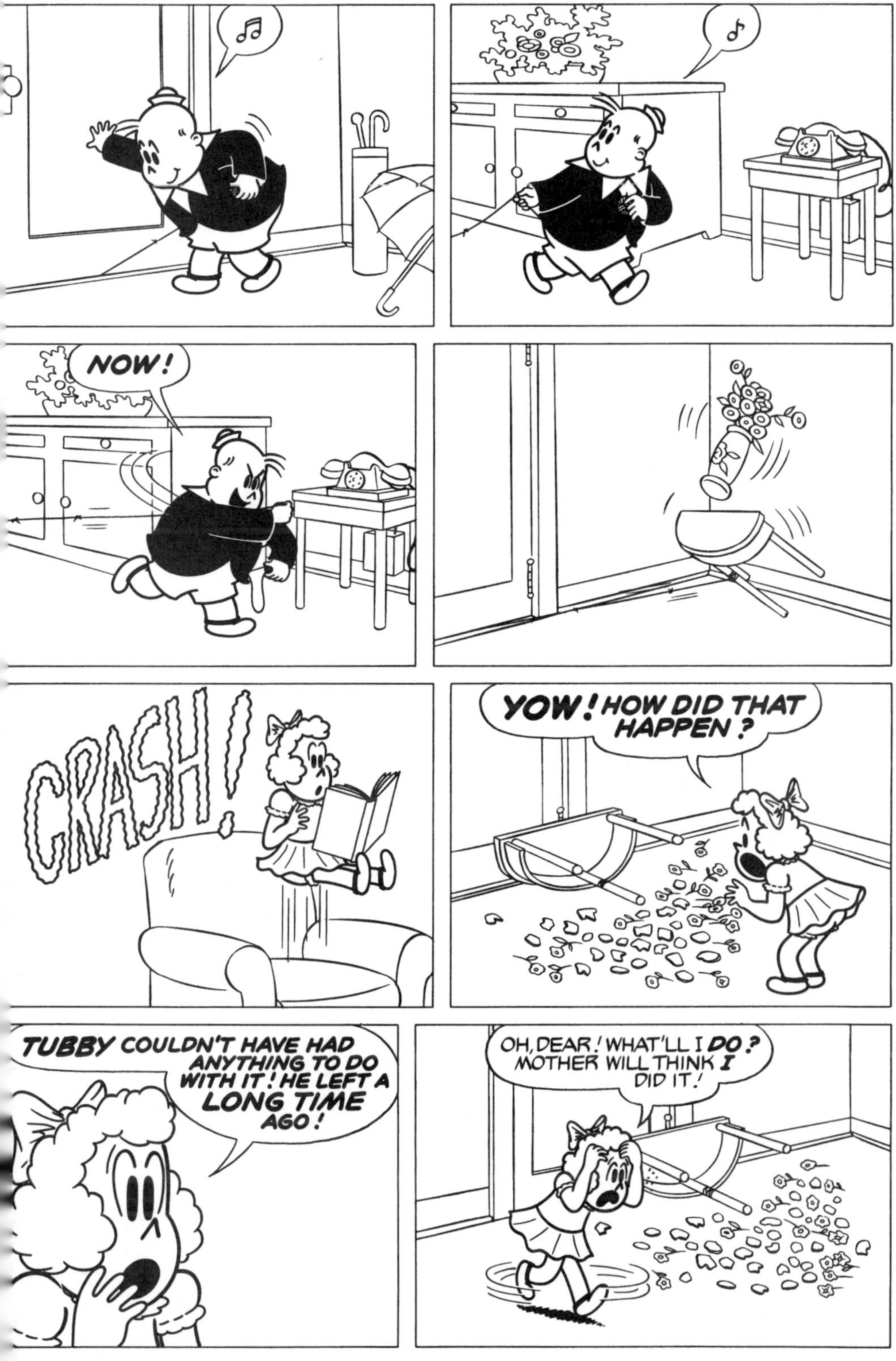
NOW!
CRASH!
YOW! HOW DID THAT HAPPEN?
TUBBY COULDN'T HAVE HAD ANYTHING TO DO WITH IT! HE LEFT A LONG TIME AGO!
OH, DEAR! WHAT'LL I DO? MOTHER WILL THINK I DID IT!

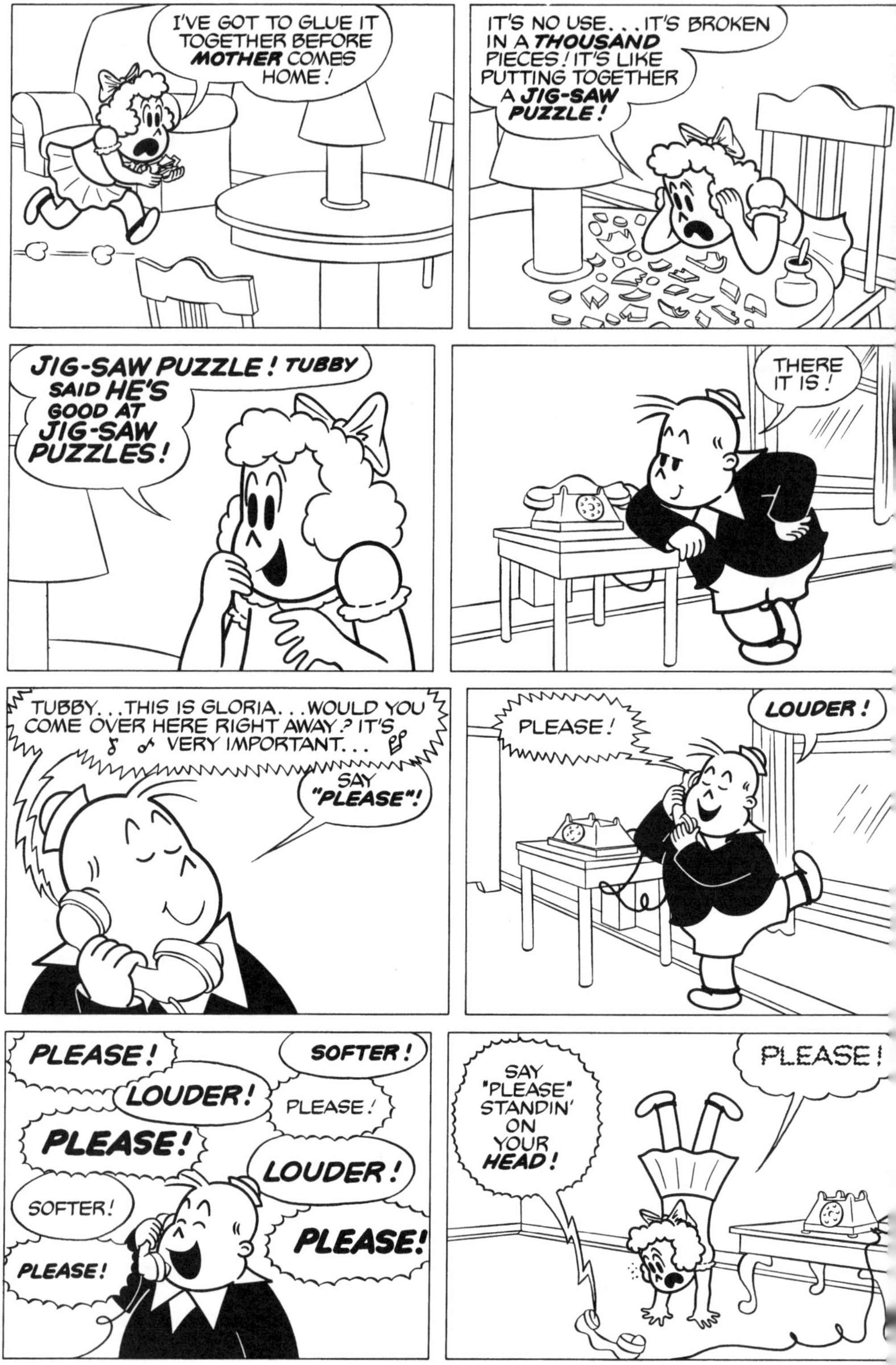
I'VE GOT TO GLUE IT TOGETHER BEFORE MOTHER COMES HOME!
IT'S NO USE...IT'S BROKEN IN A THOUSAND PIECES! IT'S LIKE PUTTING TOGETHER A JIG-SAW PUZZLE!
JIG-SAW PUZZLE! TUBBY SAID HE'S GOOD AT JIG-SAW PUZZLES!
THERE IT IS!
TUBBY...THIS IS GLORIA...WOULD YOU COME OVER HERE RIGHT AWAY? IT'S VERY IMPORTANT...
SAY "PLEASE"!
PLEASE!
LOUDER!
PLEASE!
SOFTER!
LOUDER!
PLEASE!
PLEASE!
LOUDER!
SOFTER!
PLEASE!
PLEASE!
SAY "PLEASE" STANDIN' ON YOUR HEAD!
PLEASE!

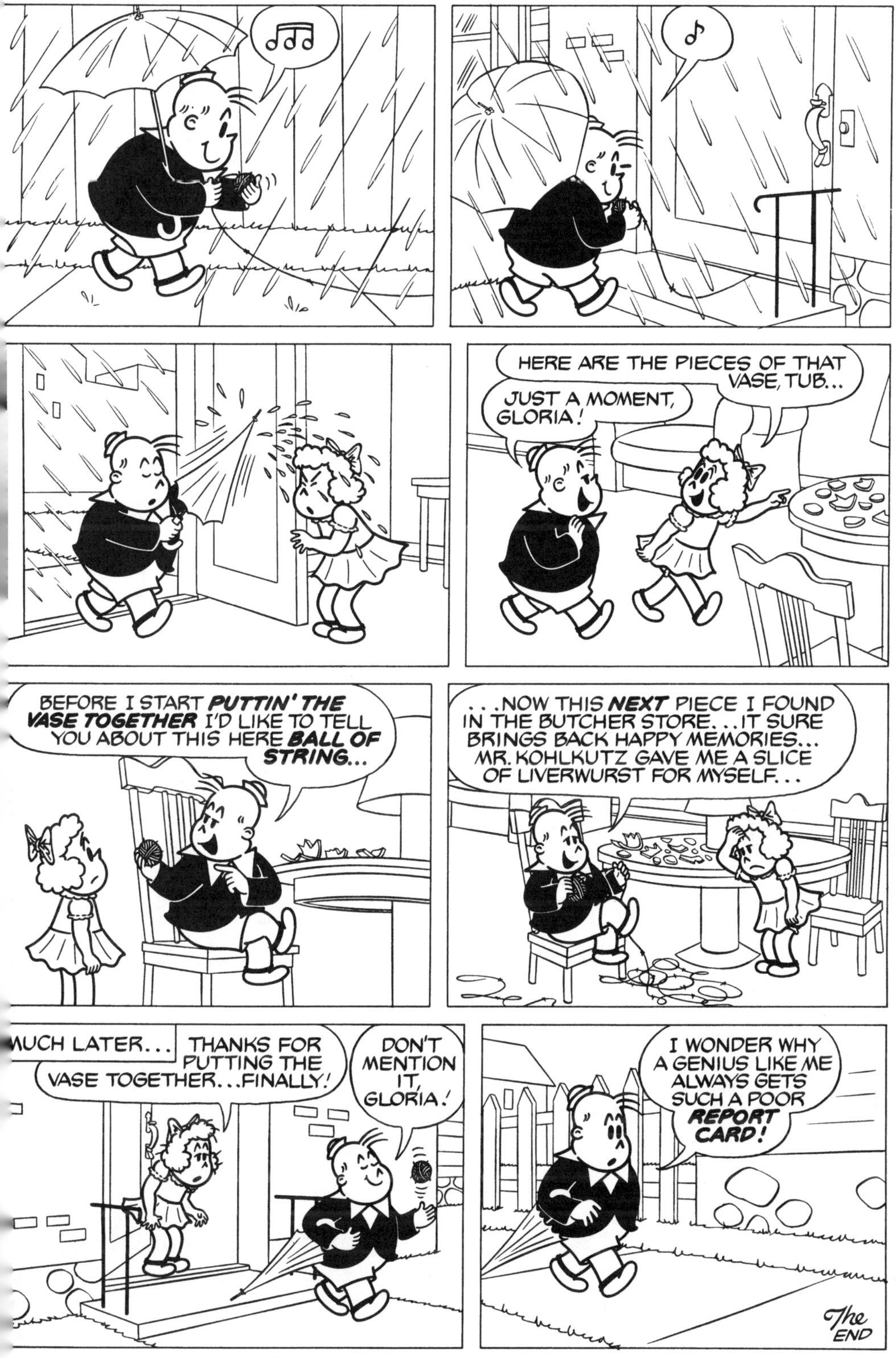
HERE ARE THE PIECES OF THAT VASE, TUB...
JUST A MOMENT, GLORIA!
BEFORE I START **PUTTIN' THE VASE TOGETHER** I'D LIKE TO TELL YOU ABOUT THIS HERE **BALL OF STRING**...
...NOW THIS **NEXT** PIECE I FOUND IN THE BUTCHER STORE...IT SURE BRINGS BACK HAPPY MEMORIES... MR. KOHLKUTZ GAVE ME A SLICE OF LIVERWURST FOR MYSELF...
MUCH LATER...
THANKS FOR PUTTING THE VASE TOGETHER...FINALLY!
DON'T MENTION IT, GLORIA!
I WONDER WHY A GENIUS LIKE ME ALWAYS GETS SUCH A POOR **REPORT CARD**!
The END

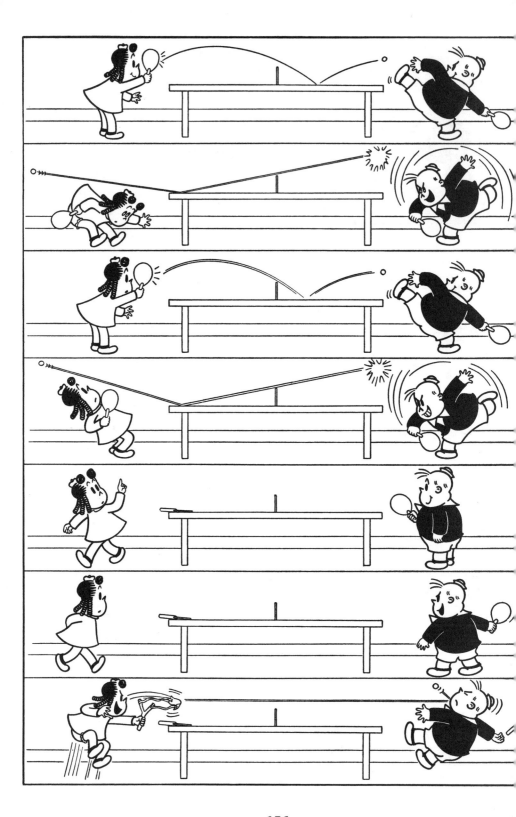

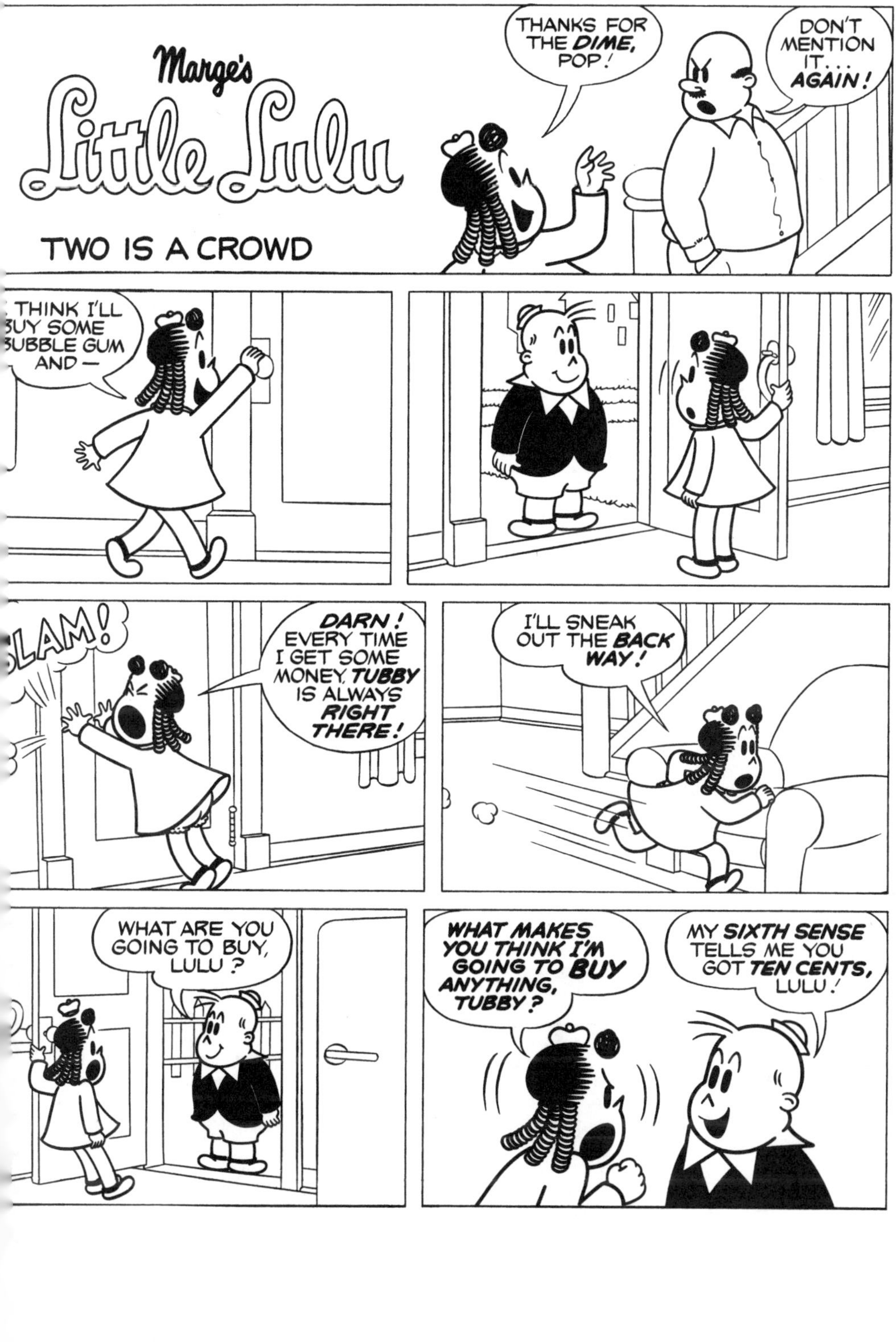
Marge's
Little Lulu
TWO IS A CROWD
THANKS FOR THE DIME, POP!
DON'T MENTION IT... AGAIN!
THINK I'LL BUY SOME BUBBLE GUM AND —
SLAM!
DARN! EVERY TIME I GET SOME MONEY, TUBBY IS ALWAYS RIGHT THERE!
I'LL SNEAK OUT THE BACK WAY!
WHAT ARE YOU GOING TO BUY, LULU?
WHAT MAKES YOU THINK I'M GOING TO BUY ANYTHING, TUBBY?
MY SIXTH SENSE TELLS ME YOU GOT TEN CENTS, LULU!

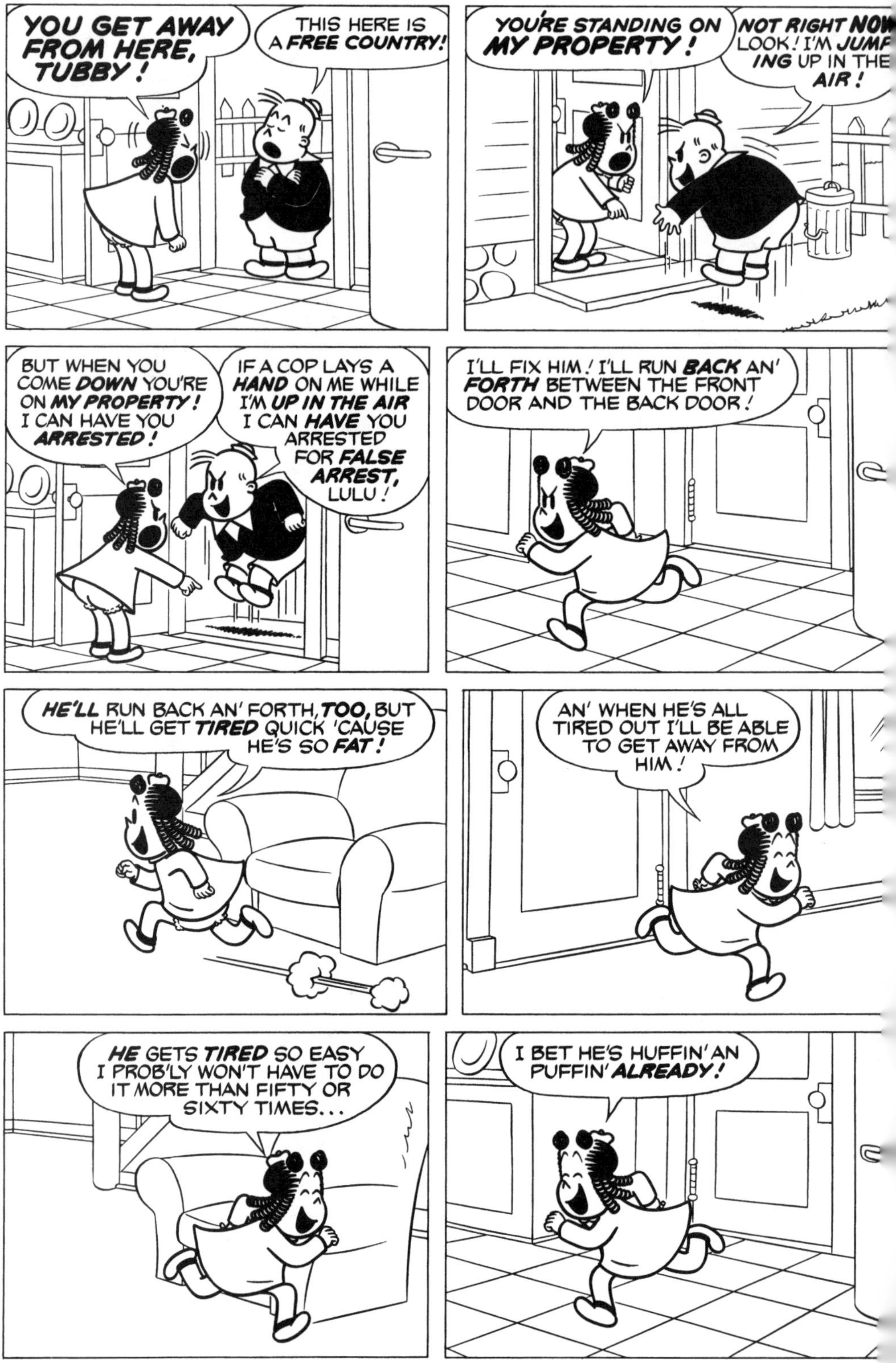
YOU GET AWAY FROM HERE, TUBBY!
THIS HERE IS A FREE COUNTRY!
YOU'RE STANDING ON MY PROPERTY!
NOT RIGHT NOW LOOK! I'M JUMPING UP IN THE AIR!
BUT WHEN YOU COME DOWN YOU'RE ON MY PROPERTY! I CAN HAVE YOU ARRESTED!
IF A COP LAYS A HAND ON ME WHILE I'M UP IN THE AIR I CAN HAVE YOU ARRESTED FOR FALSE ARREST, LULU!
I'LL FIX HIM! I'LL RUN BACK AN' FORTH BETWEEN THE FRONT DOOR AND THE BACK DOOR!
HE'LL RUN BACK AN' FORTH, TOO, BUT HE'LL GET TIRED QUICK 'CAUSE HE'S SO FAT!
AN' WHEN HE'S ALL TIRED OUT I'LL BE ABLE TO GET AWAY FROM HIM!
HE GETS TIRED SO EASY I PROB'LY WON'T HAVE TO DO IT MORE THAN FIFTY OR SIXTY TIMES...
I BET HE'S HUFFIN' AN PUFFIN' ALREADY!

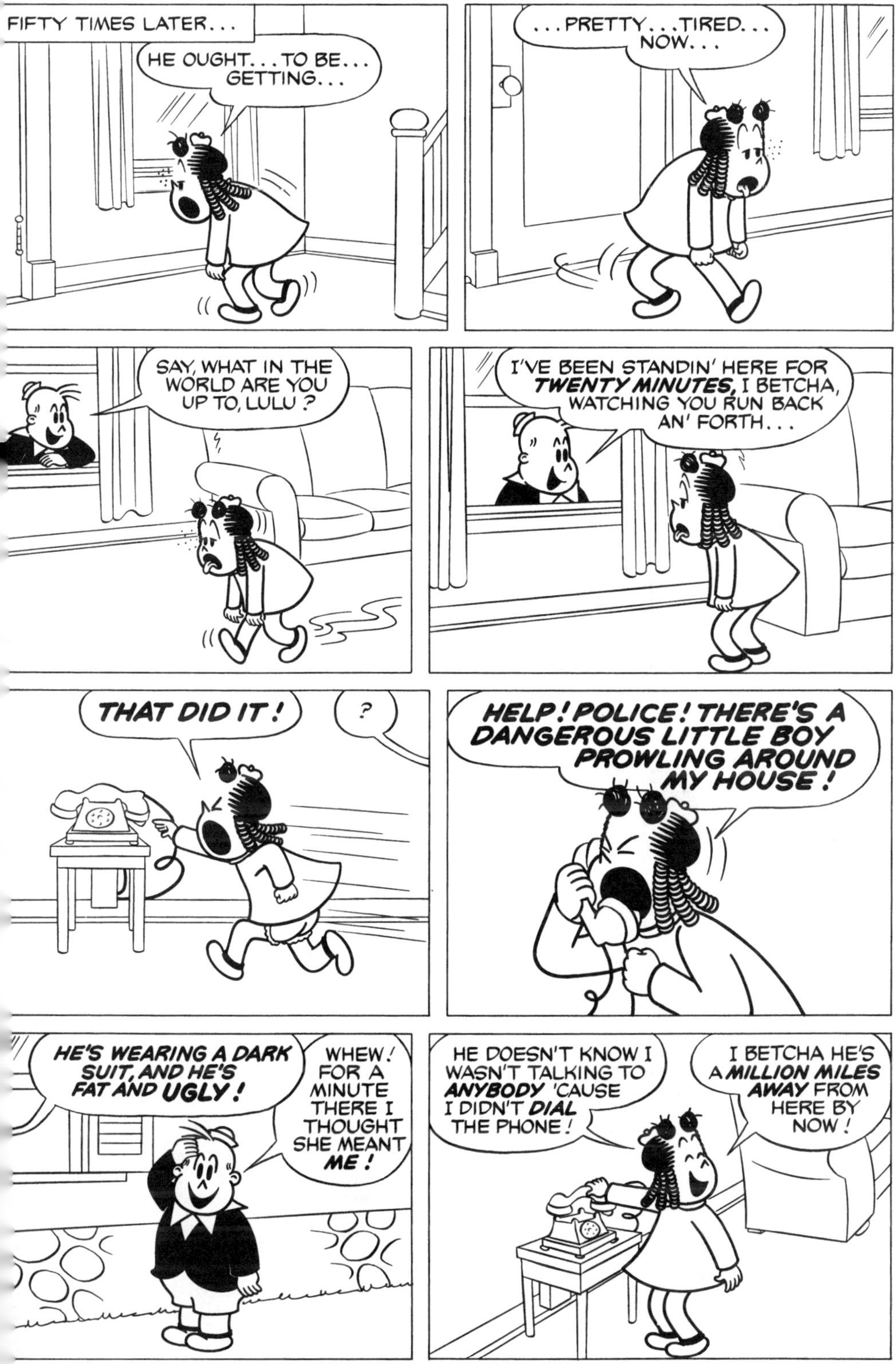
FIFTY TIMES LATER...
HE OUGHT...TO BE... GETTING...
...PRETTY...TIRED... NOW...
SAY, WHAT IN THE WORLD ARE YOU UP TO, LULU?
I'VE BEEN STANDIN' HERE FOR TWENTY MINUTES, I BETCHA, WATCHING YOU RUN BACK AN' FORTH...
THAT DID IT!
?
HELP! POLICE! THERE'S A DANGEROUS LITTLE BOY PROWLING AROUND MY HOUSE!
HE'S WEARING A DARK SUIT, AND HE'S FAT AND UGLY!
WHEW! FOR A MINUTE THERE I THOUGHT SHE MEANT ME!
HE DOESN'T KNOW I WASN'T TALKING TO ANYBODY 'CAUSE I DIDN'T DIAL THE PHONE!
I BETCHA HE'S A MILLION MILES AWAY FROM HERE BY NOW!

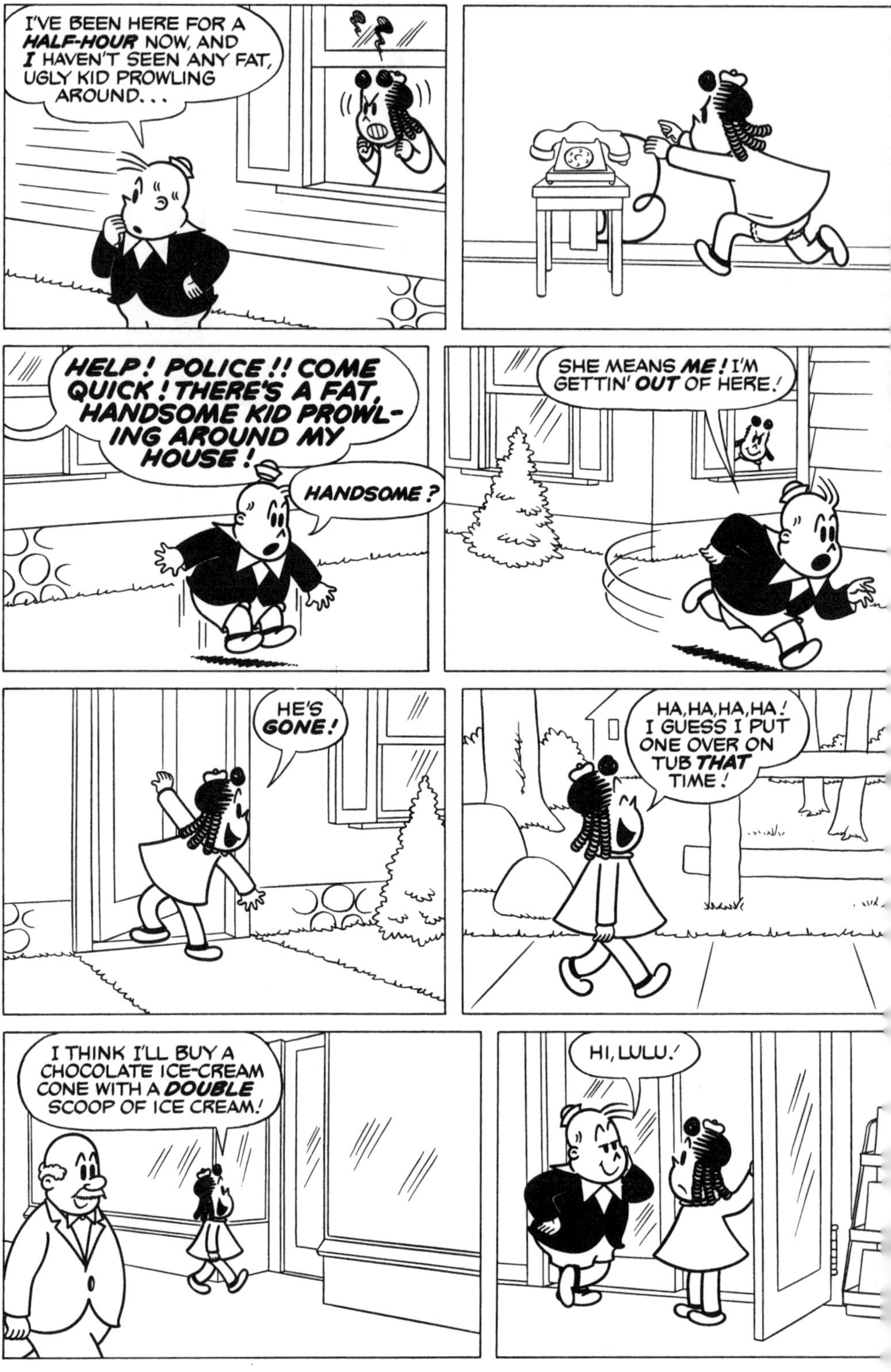
I'VE BEEN HERE FOR A **HALF-HOUR** NOW, AND **I** HAVEN'T SEEN ANY FAT, UGLY KID PROWLING AROUND...
HELP! POLICE!! COME QUICK! THERE'S A FAT, HANDSOME KID PROWLING AROUND MY HOUSE!
HANDSOME?
SHE MEANS **ME!** I'M GETTIN' **OUT** OF HERE!
HE'S **GONE!**
HA, HA, HA, HA! I GUESS I PUT ONE OVER ON TUB **THAT** TIME!
I THINK I'LL BUY A CHOCOLATE ICE-CREAM CONE WITH A **DOUBLE** SCOOP OF ICE CREAM!
HI, LULU!

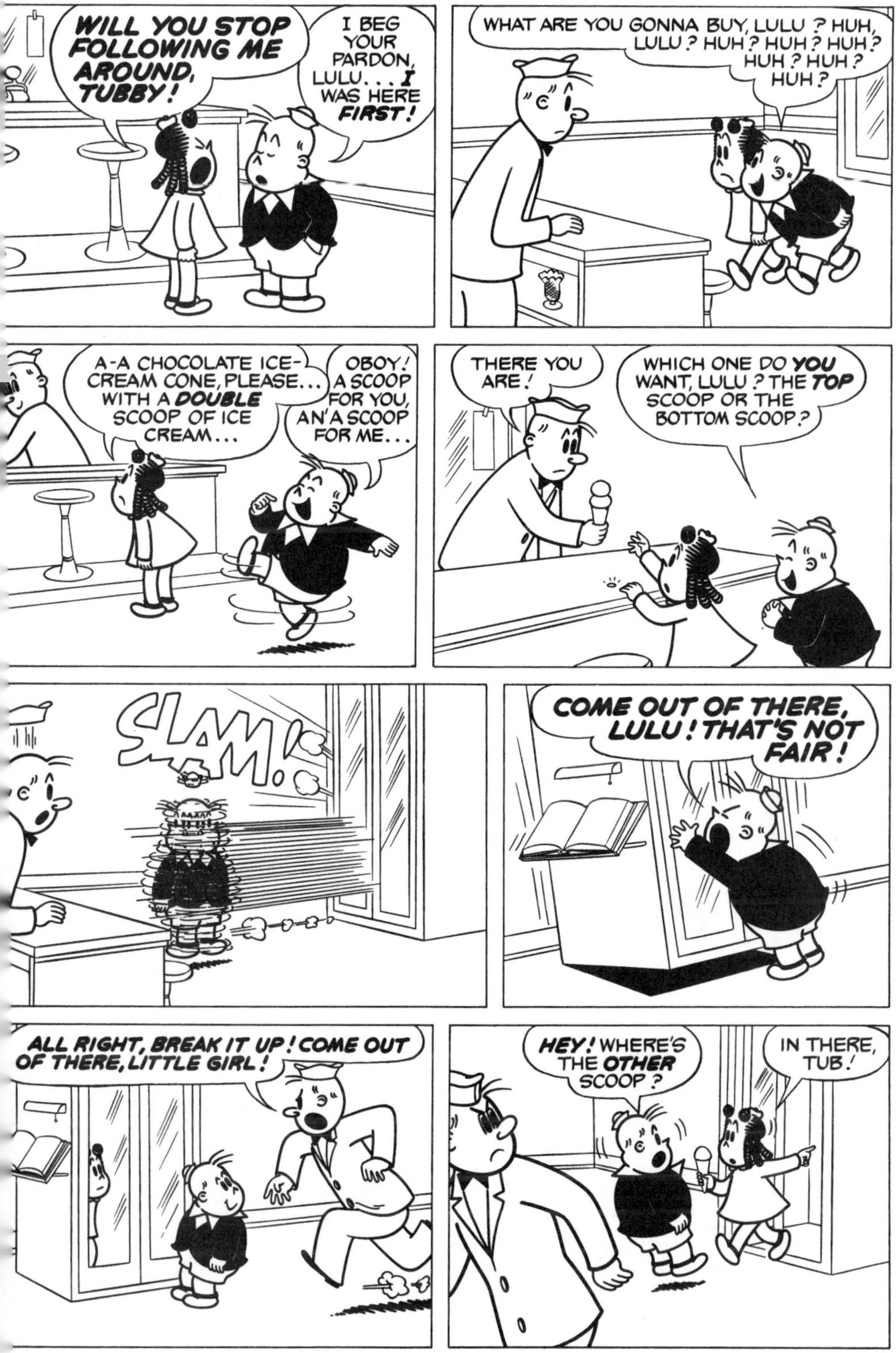
WILL YOU STOP FOLLOWING ME AROUND, TUBBY!
I BEG YOUR PARDON, LULU... I WAS HERE FIRST!
WHAT ARE YOU GONNA BUY, LULU? HUH, LULU? HUH? HUH? HUH? HUH? HUH? HUH?
A-A CHOCOLATE ICE-CREAM CONE, PLEASE... WITH A DOUBLE SCOOP OF ICE CREAM...
OBOY! A SCOOP FOR YOU, AN' A SCOOP FOR ME...
THERE YOU ARE!
WHICH ONE DO YOU WANT, LULU? THE TOP SCOOP OR THE BOTTOM SCOOP?
SLAM!
COME OUT OF THERE, LULU! THAT'S NOT FAIR!
ALL RIGHT, BREAK IT UP! COME OUT OF THERE, LITTLE GIRL!
HEY! WHERE'S THE OTHER SCOOP?
IN THERE, TUB!

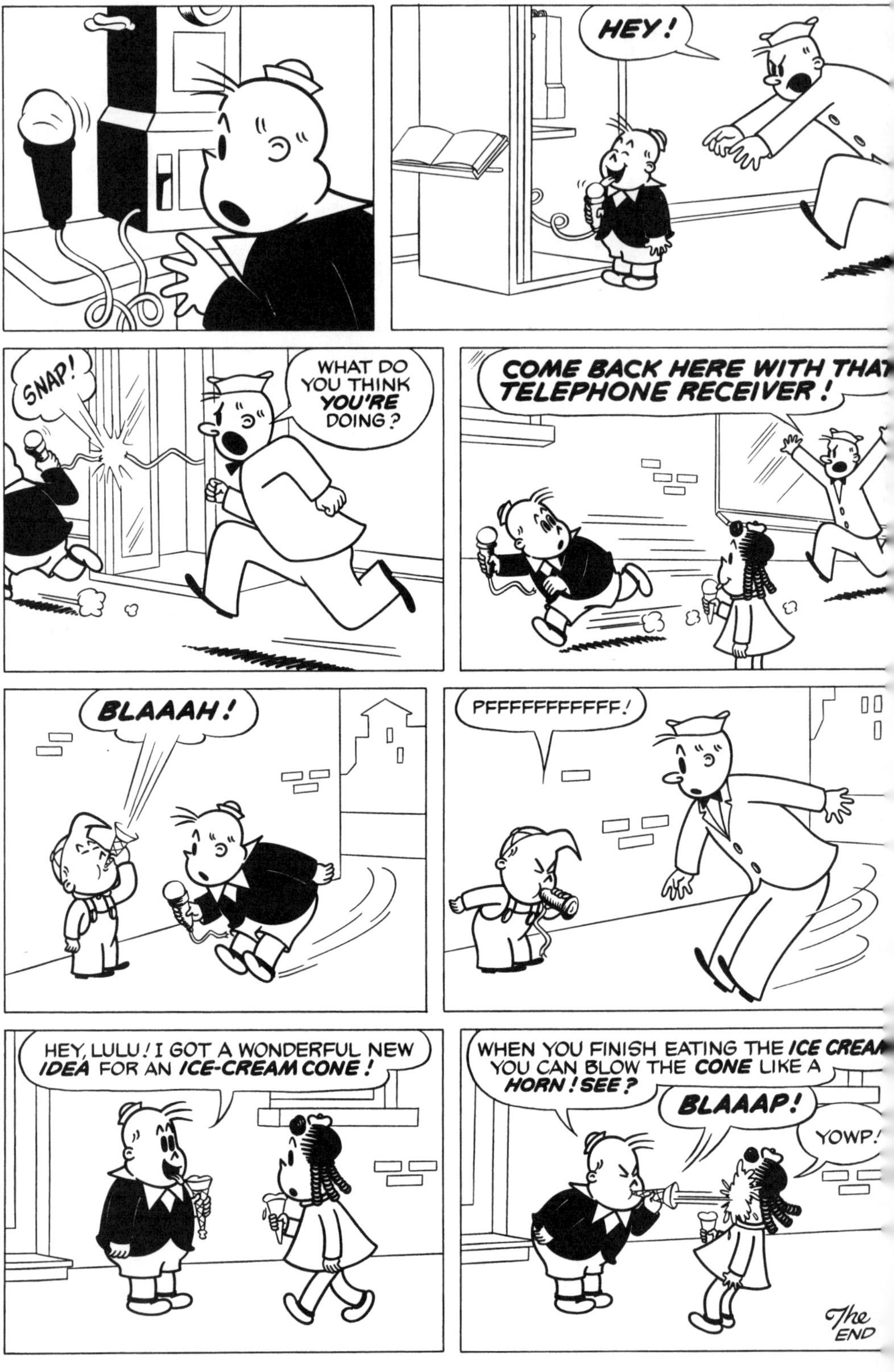

HEY!
SNAP!
WHAT DO YOU THINK YOU'RE DOING?
COME BACK HERE WITH THAT TELEPHONE RECEIVER!
BLAAAH!
PFFFFFFFFFFFF!
HEY, LULU! I GOT A WONDERFUL NEW IDEA FOR AN ICE-CREAM CONE!
WHEN YOU FINISH EATING THE ICE CREAM YOU CAN BLOW THE CONE LIKE A HORN! SEE?
BLAAAP!
YOWP!
The END

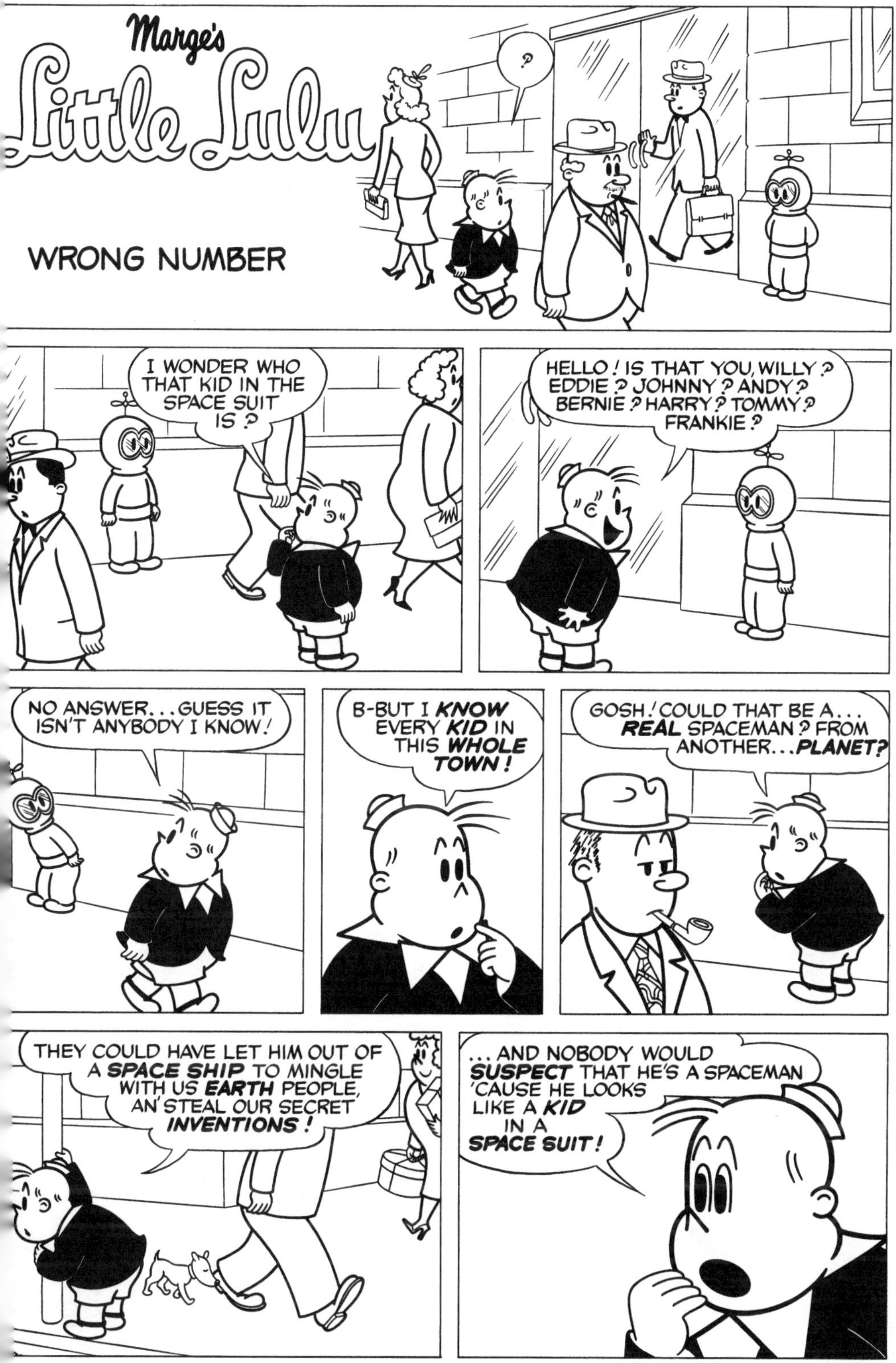
Marge's Little Lulu
WRONG NUMBER
?
I WONDER WHO THAT KID IN THE SPACE SUIT IS ?
HELLO ! IS THAT YOU, WILLY ? EDDIE ? JOHNNY ? ANDY ? BERNIE ? HARRY ? TOMMY ? FRANKIE ?
NO ANSWER. . . GUESS IT ISN'T ANYBODY I KNOW !
B-BUT I KNOW EVERY KID IN THIS WHOLE TOWN !
GOSH ! COULD THAT BE A. . . REAL SPACEMAN ? FROM ANOTHER. . . PLANET?
THEY COULD HAVE LET HIM OUT OF A SPACE SHIP TO MINGLE WITH US EARTH PEOPLE, AN' STEAL OUR SECRET INVENTIONS !
. . . AND NOBODY WOULD SUSPECT THAT HE'S A SPACEMAN 'CAUSE HE LOOKS LIKE A KID IN A SPACE SUIT !

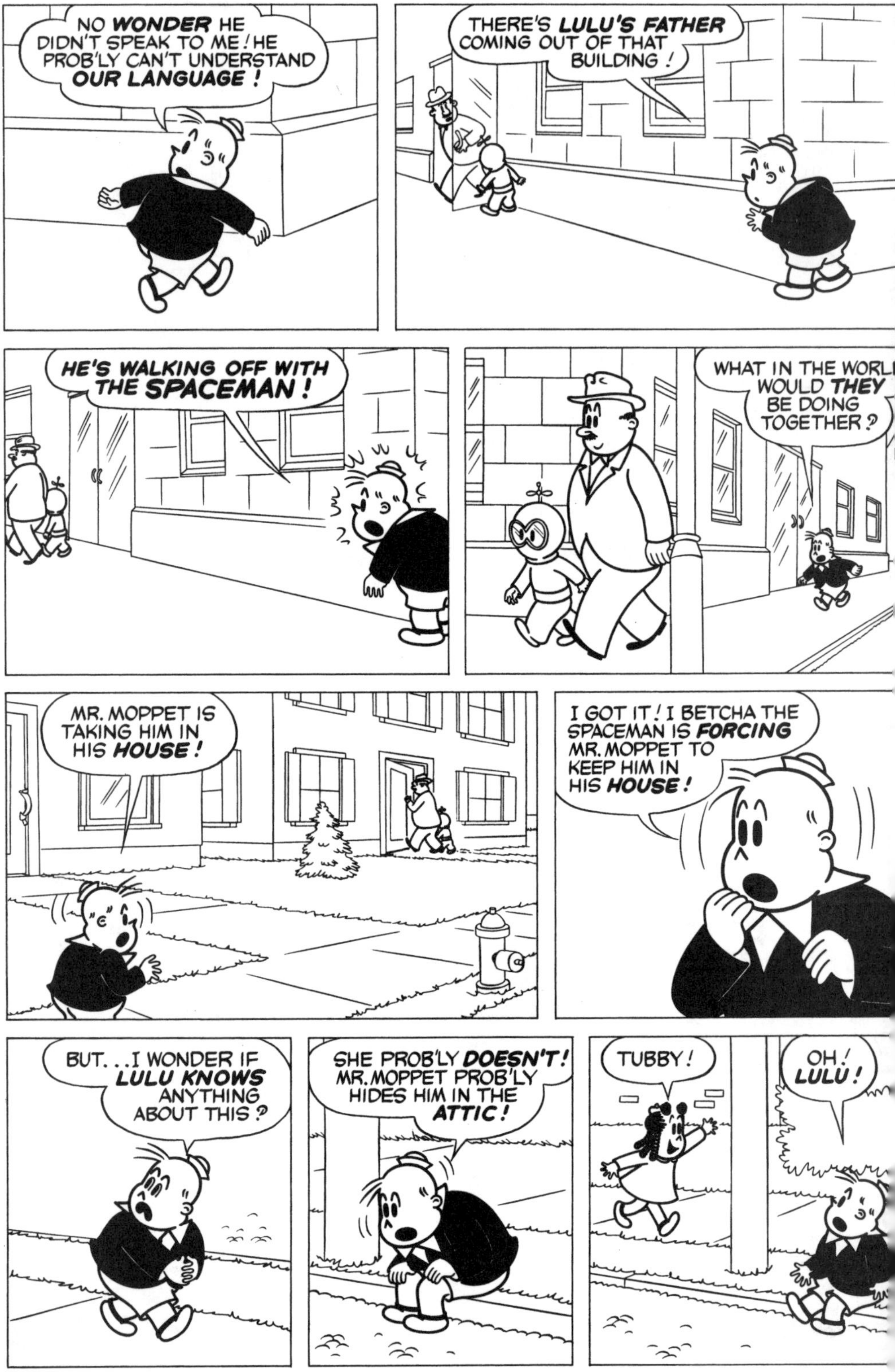
NO WONDER HE DIDN'T SPEAK TO ME! HE PROB'LY CAN'T UNDERSTAND OUR LANGUAGE!
THERE'S LULU'S FATHER COMING OUT OF THAT BUILDING!
HE'S WALKING OFF WITH THE SPACEMAN!
WHAT IN THE WORLD WOULD THEY BE DOING TOGETHER?
MR. MOPPET IS TAKING HIM IN HIS HOUSE!
I GOT IT! I BETCHA THE SPACEMAN IS FORCING MR. MOPPET TO KEEP HIM IN HIS HOUSE!
BUT...I WONDER IF LULU KNOWS ANYTHING ABOUT THIS?
SHE PROB'LY DOESN'T! MR. MOPPET PROB'LY HIDES HIM IN THE ATTIC!
TUBBY!
OH! LULU!

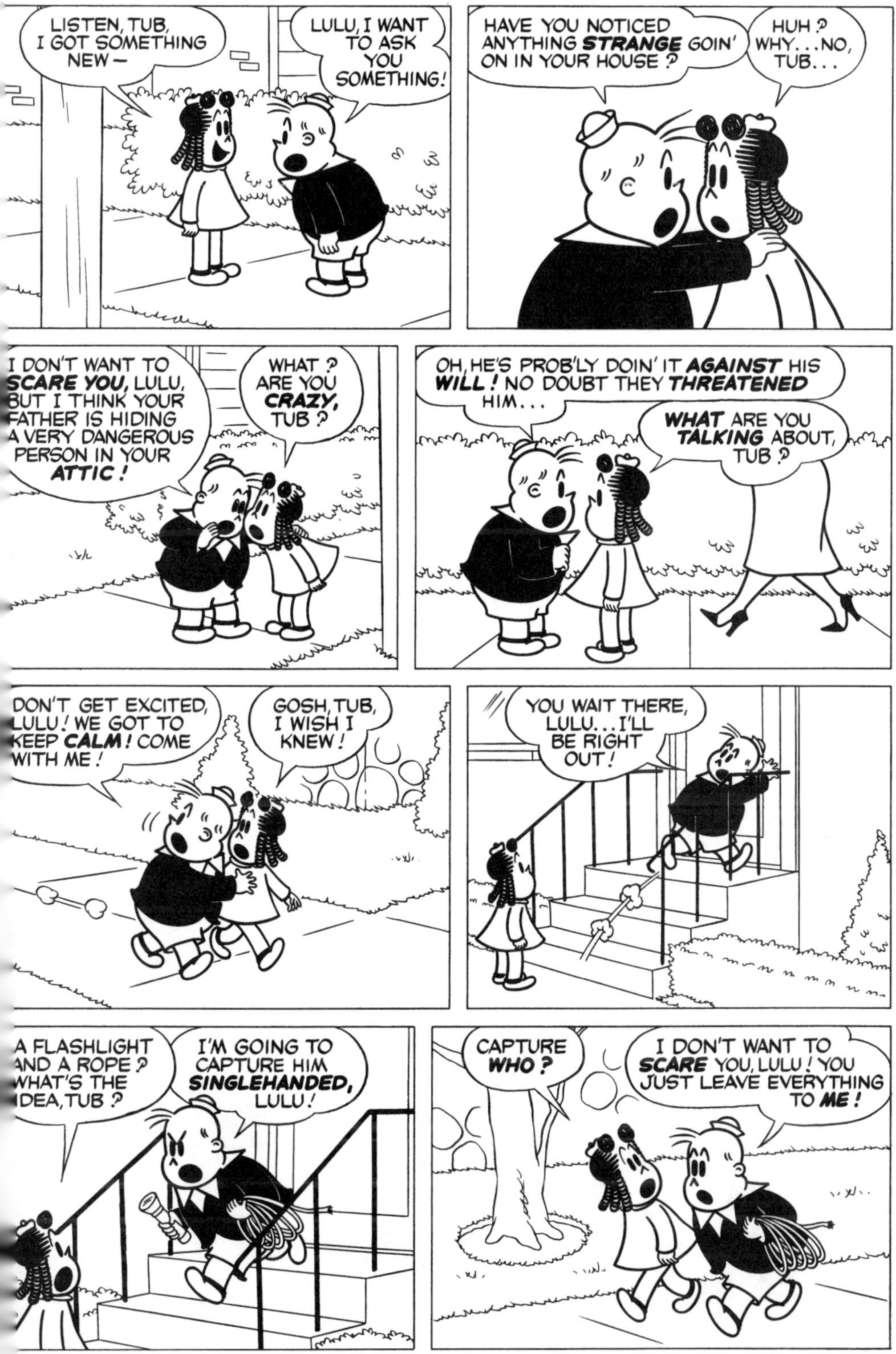
LISTEN, TUB, I GOT SOMETHING NEW—
LULU, I WANT TO ASK YOU SOMETHING!
HAVE YOU NOTICED ANYTHING STRANGE GOIN' ON IN YOUR HOUSE?
HUH? WHY...NO, TUB...
I DON'T WANT TO SCARE YOU, LULU, BUT I THINK YOUR FATHER IS HIDING A VERY DANGEROUS PERSON IN YOUR ATTIC!
WHAT? ARE YOU CRAZY, TUB?
OH, HE'S PROB'LY DOIN' IT AGAINST HIS WILL! NO DOUBT THEY THREATENED HIM...
WHAT ARE YOU TALKING ABOUT, TUB?
DON'T GET EXCITED, LULU! WE GOT TO KEEP CALM! COME WITH ME!
GOSH, TUB, I WISH I KNEW!
YOU WAIT THERE, LULU...I'LL BE RIGHT OUT!
A FLASHLIGHT AND A ROPE? WHAT'S THE IDEA, TUB?
I'M GOING TO CAPTURE HIM SINGLEHANDED, LULU!
CAPTURE WHO?
I DON'T WANT TO SCARE YOU, LULU! YOU JUST LEAVE EVERYTHING TO ME!

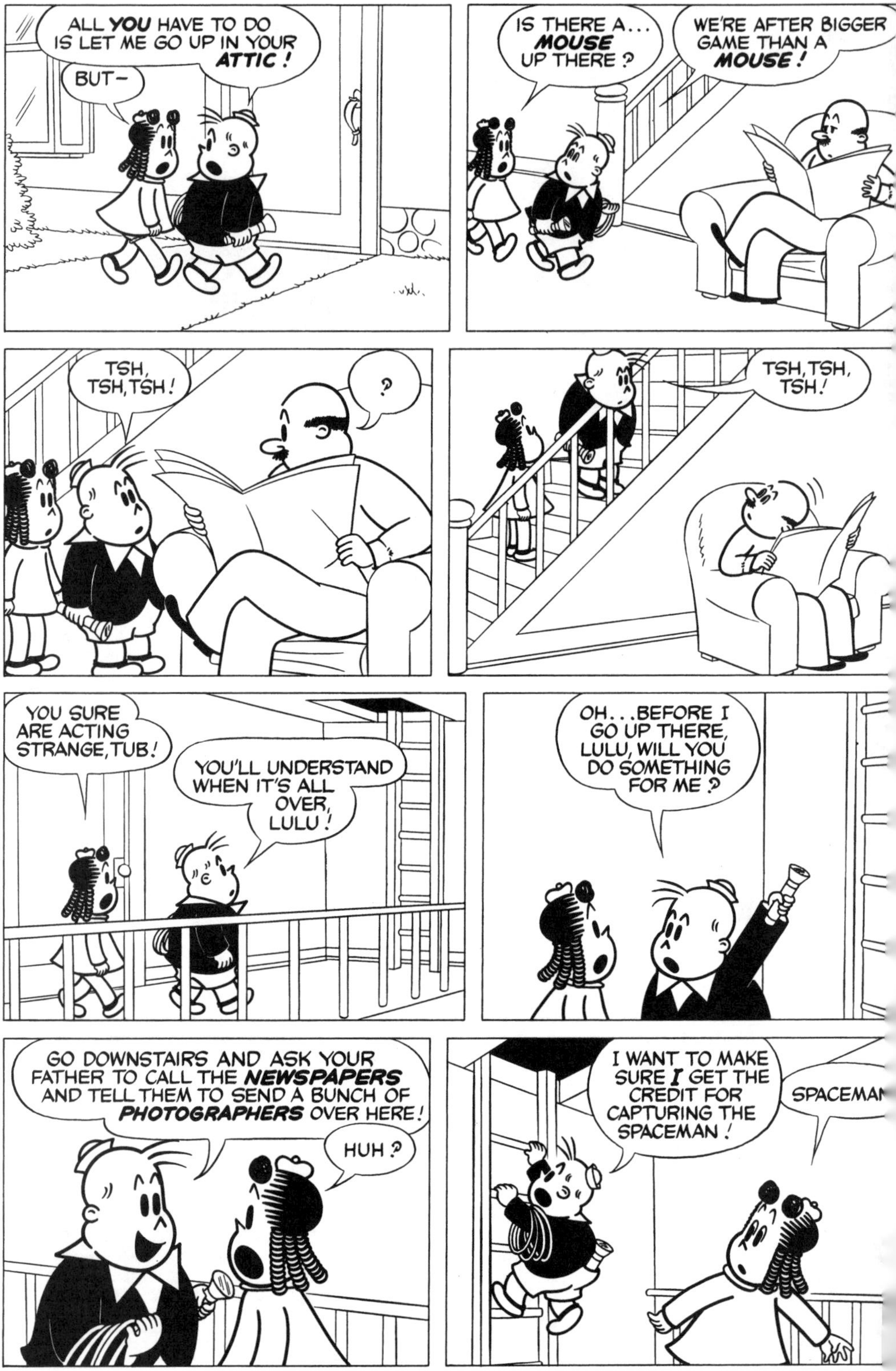
ALL YOU HAVE TO DO IS LET ME GO UP IN YOUR ATTIC!
BUT–
IS THERE A... MOUSE UP THERE?
WE'RE AFTER BIGGER GAME THAN A MOUSE!
TSH, TSH, TSH!
?
TSH, TSH, TSH!
YOU SURE ARE ACTING STRANGE, TUB!
YOU'LL UNDERSTAND WHEN IT'S ALL OVER, LULU!
OH...BEFORE I GO UP THERE, LULU, WILL YOU DO SOMETHING FOR ME?
GO DOWNSTAIRS AND ASK YOUR FATHER TO CALL THE NEWSPAPERS AND TELL THEM TO SEND A BUNCH OF PHOTOGRAPHERS OVER HERE!
HUH?
I WANT TO MAKE SURE I GET THE CREDIT FOR CAPTURING THE SPACEMAN!

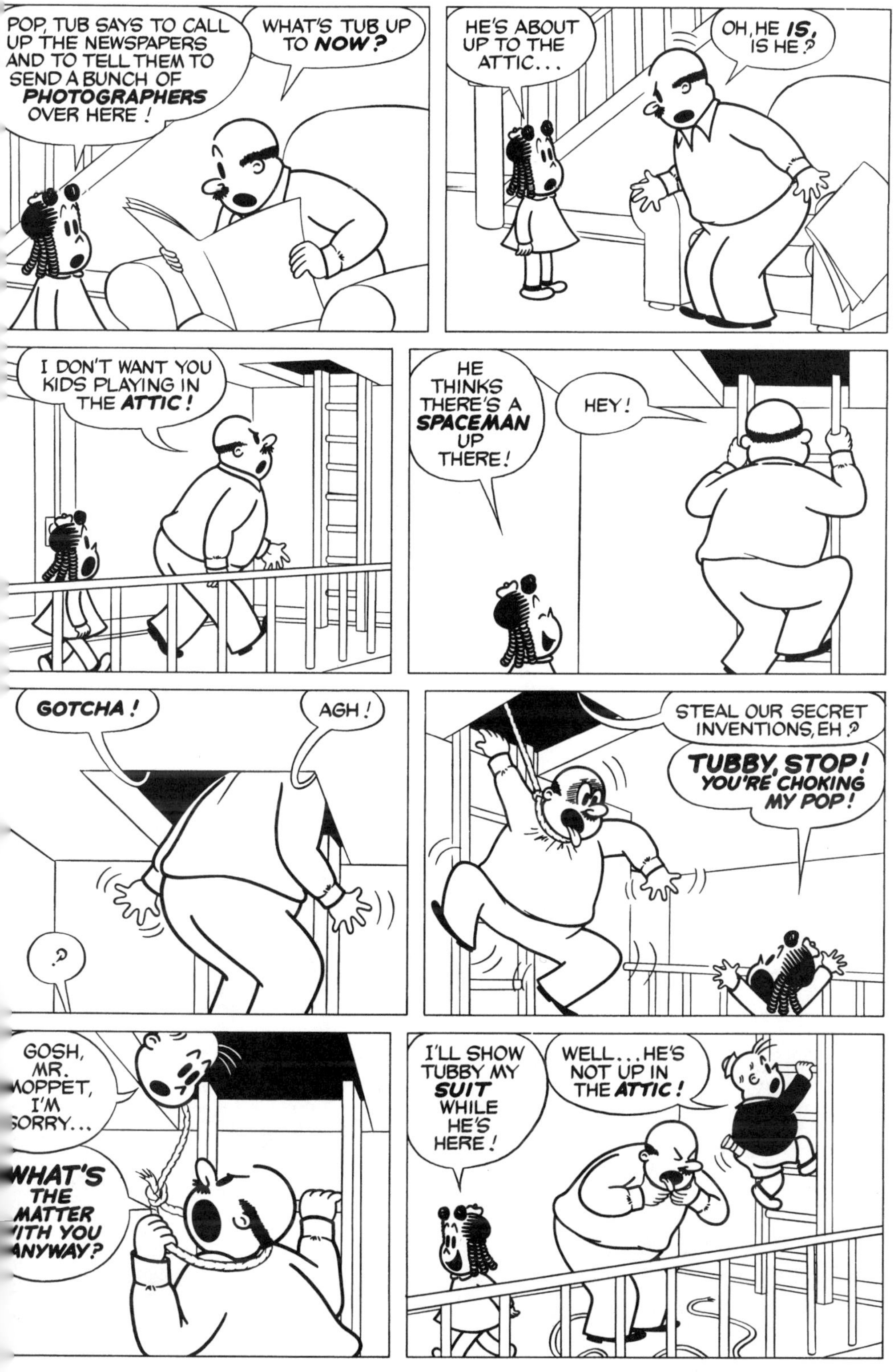

POP, TUB SAYS TO CALL UP THE NEWSPAPERS AND TO TELL THEM TO SEND A BUNCH OF PHOTOGRAPHERS OVER HERE!
WHAT'S TUB UP TO NOW?
HE'S ABOUT UP TO THE ATTIC...
OH, HE IS, IS HE?
I DON'T WANT YOU KIDS PLAYING IN THE ATTIC!
HE THINKS THERE'S A SPACEMAN UP THERE!
HEY!
GOTCHA!
AGH!
?
STEAL OUR SECRET INVENTIONS, EH?
TUBBY, STOP! YOU'RE CHOKING MY POP!
GOSH, MR. MOPPET, I'M SORRY...
WHAT'S THE MATTER WITH YOU ANYWAY?
I'LL SHOW TUBBY MY SUIT WHILE HE'S HERE!
WELL...HE'S NOT UP IN THE ATTIC!

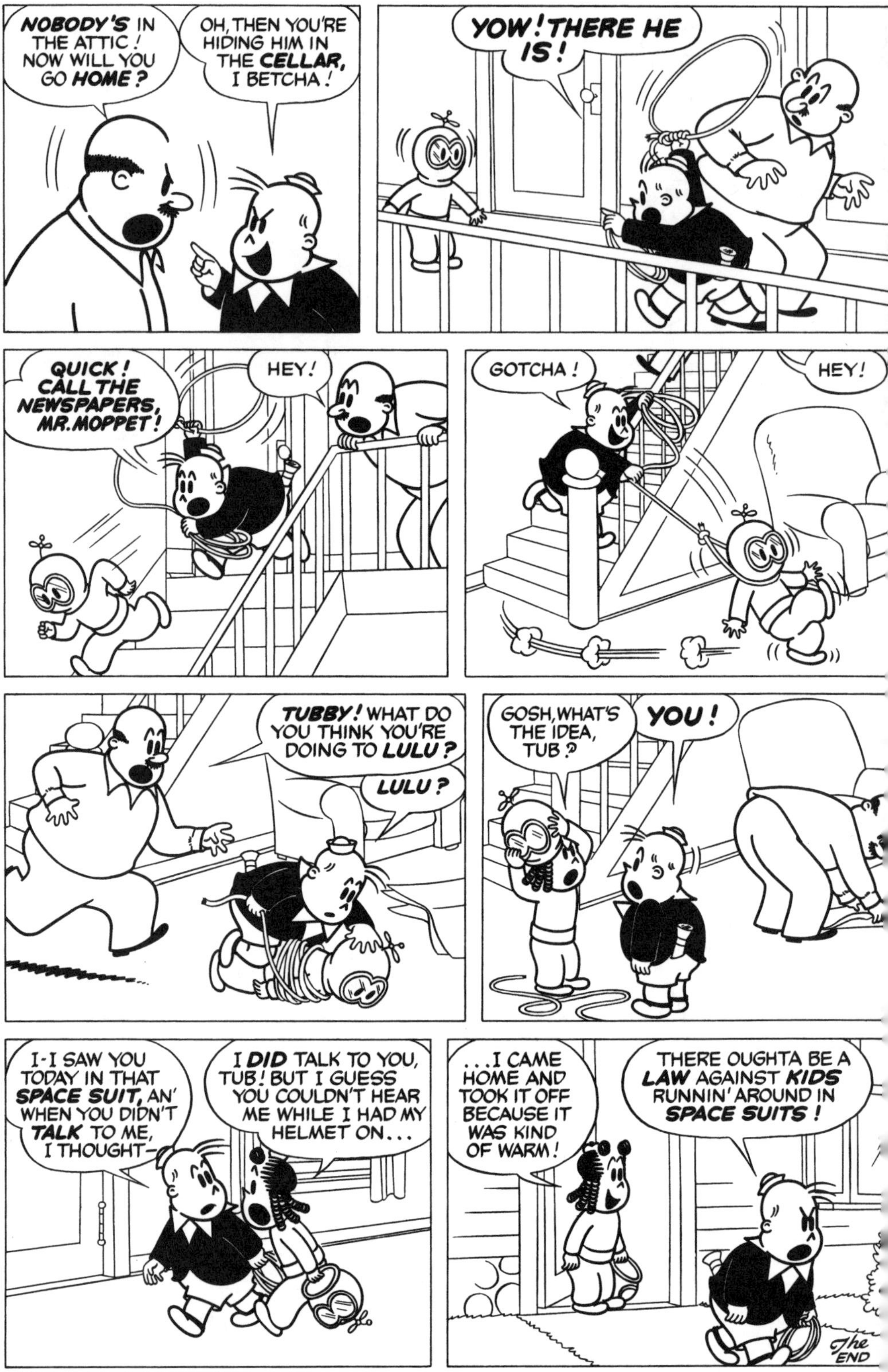
NOBODY'S IN THE ATTIC! NOW WILL YOU GO HOME?
OH, THEN YOU'RE HIDING HIM IN THE CELLAR, I BETCHA!
YOW! THERE HE IS!
QUICK! CALL THE NEWSPAPERS, MR. MOPPET!
HEY!
GOTCHA!
HEY!
TUBBY! WHAT DO YOU THINK YOU'RE DOING TO LULU?
LULU?
GOSH, WHAT'S THE IDEA, TUB?
YOU!
I-I SAW YOU TODAY IN THAT SPACE SUIT, AN' WHEN YOU DIDN'T TALK TO ME, I THOUGHT—
I DID TALK TO YOU, TUB! BUT I GUESS YOU COULDN'T HEAR ME WHILE I HAD MY HELMET ON...
...I CAME HOME AND TOOK IT OFF BECAUSE IT WAS KIND OF WARM!
THERE OUGHTA BE A LAW AGAINST KIDS RUNNIN' AROUND IN SPACE SUITS!
The END

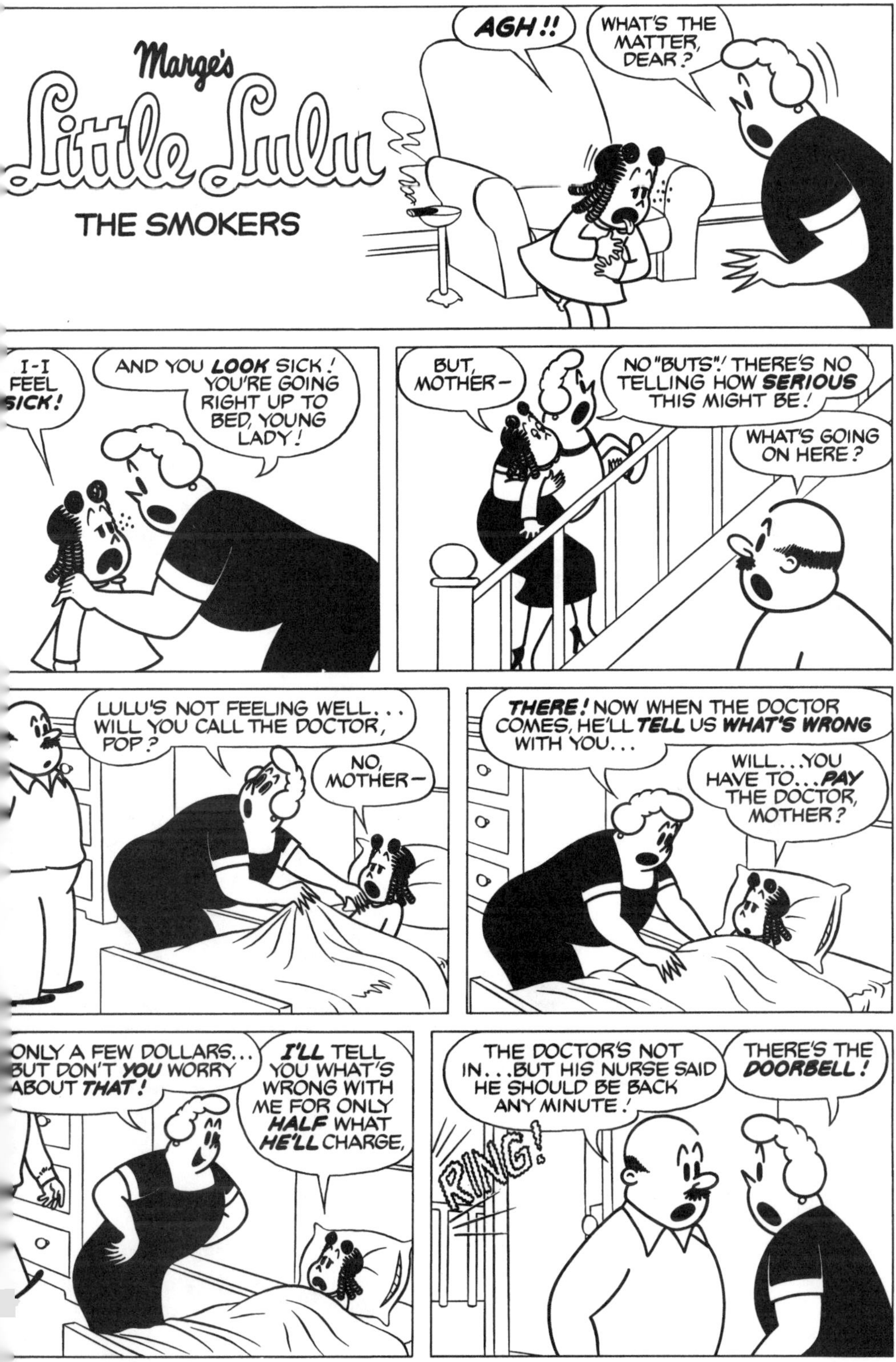
Marge's
Little Lulu
THE SMOKERS
AGH!!
WHAT'S THE MATTER, DEAR?
I-I FEEL SICK!
AND YOU LOOK SICK! YOU'RE GOING RIGHT UP TO BED, YOUNG LADY!
BUT, MOTHER—
NO "BUTS"! THERE'S NO TELLING HOW SERIOUS THIS MIGHT BE!
WHAT'S GOING ON HERE?
LULU'S NOT FEELING WELL... WILL YOU CALL THE DOCTOR, POP?
NO, MOTHER—
THERE! NOW WHEN THE DOCTOR COMES, HE'LL TELL US WHAT'S WRONG WITH YOU...
WILL...YOU HAVE TO...PAY THE DOCTOR, MOTHER?
ONLY A FEW DOLLARS... BUT DON'T YOU WORRY ABOUT THAT!
I'LL TELL YOU WHAT'S WRONG WITH ME FOR ONLY HALF WHAT HE'LL CHARGE,
THE DOCTOR'S NOT IN...BUT HIS NURSE SAID HE SHOULD BE BACK ANY MINUTE!
THERE'S THE DOORBELL!
RING!

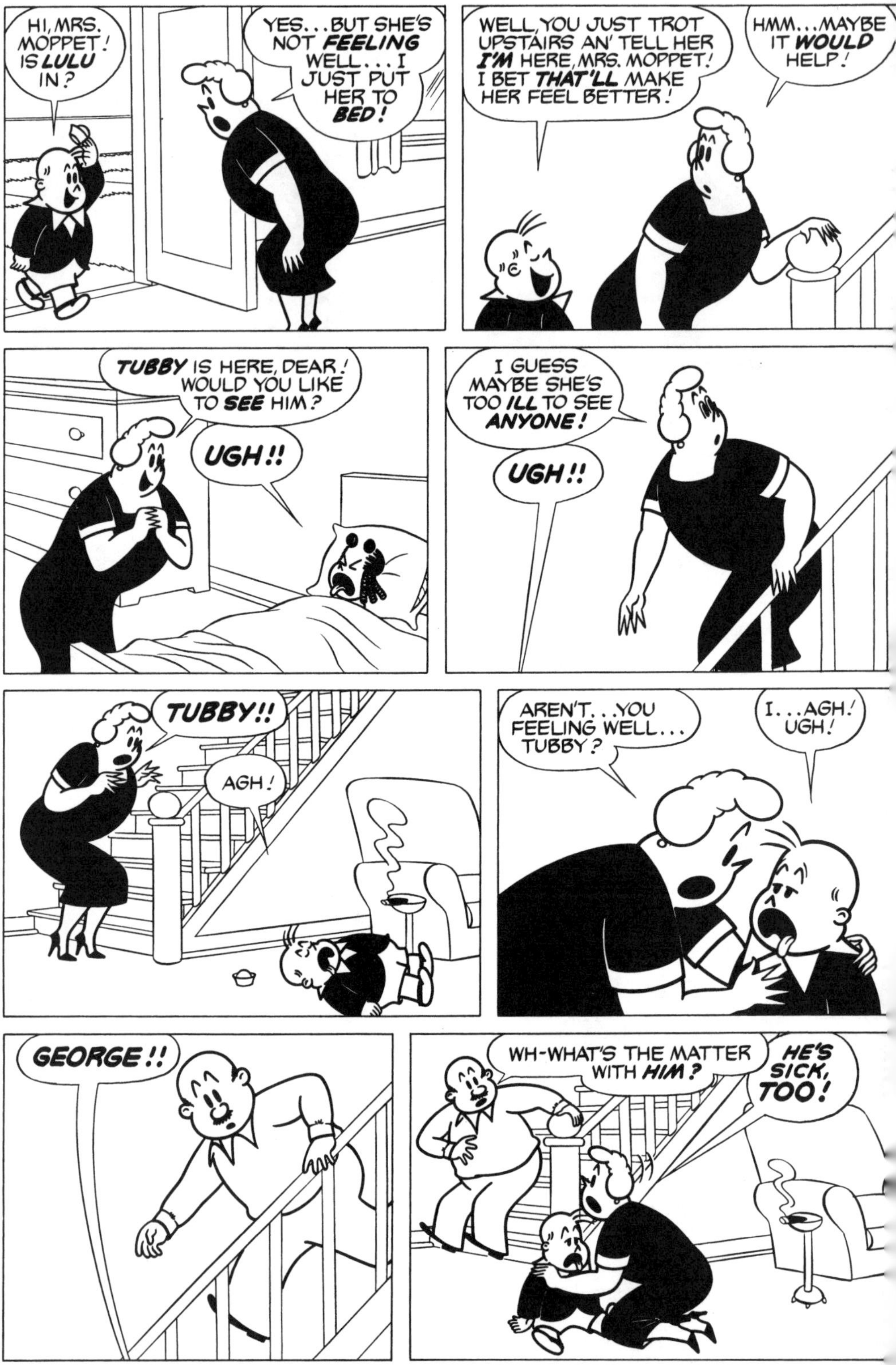
HI, MRS. MOPPET! IS LULU IN?
YES...BUT SHE'S NOT FEELING WELL...I JUST PUT HER TO BED!
WELL, YOU JUST TROT UPSTAIRS AN' TELL HER I'M HERE, MRS. MOPPET! I BET THAT'LL MAKE HER FEEL BETTER!
HMM...MAYBE IT WOULD HELP!
TUBBY IS HERE, DEAR! WOULD YOU LIKE TO SEE HIM?
UGH!!
I GUESS MAYBE SHE'S TOO ILL TO SEE ANYONE!
UGH!!
TUBBY!!
AGH!
AREN'T...YOU FEELING WELL...TUBBY?
I...AGH! UGH!
GEORGE!!
WH-WHAT'S THE MATTER WITH HIM?
HE'S SICK, TOO!

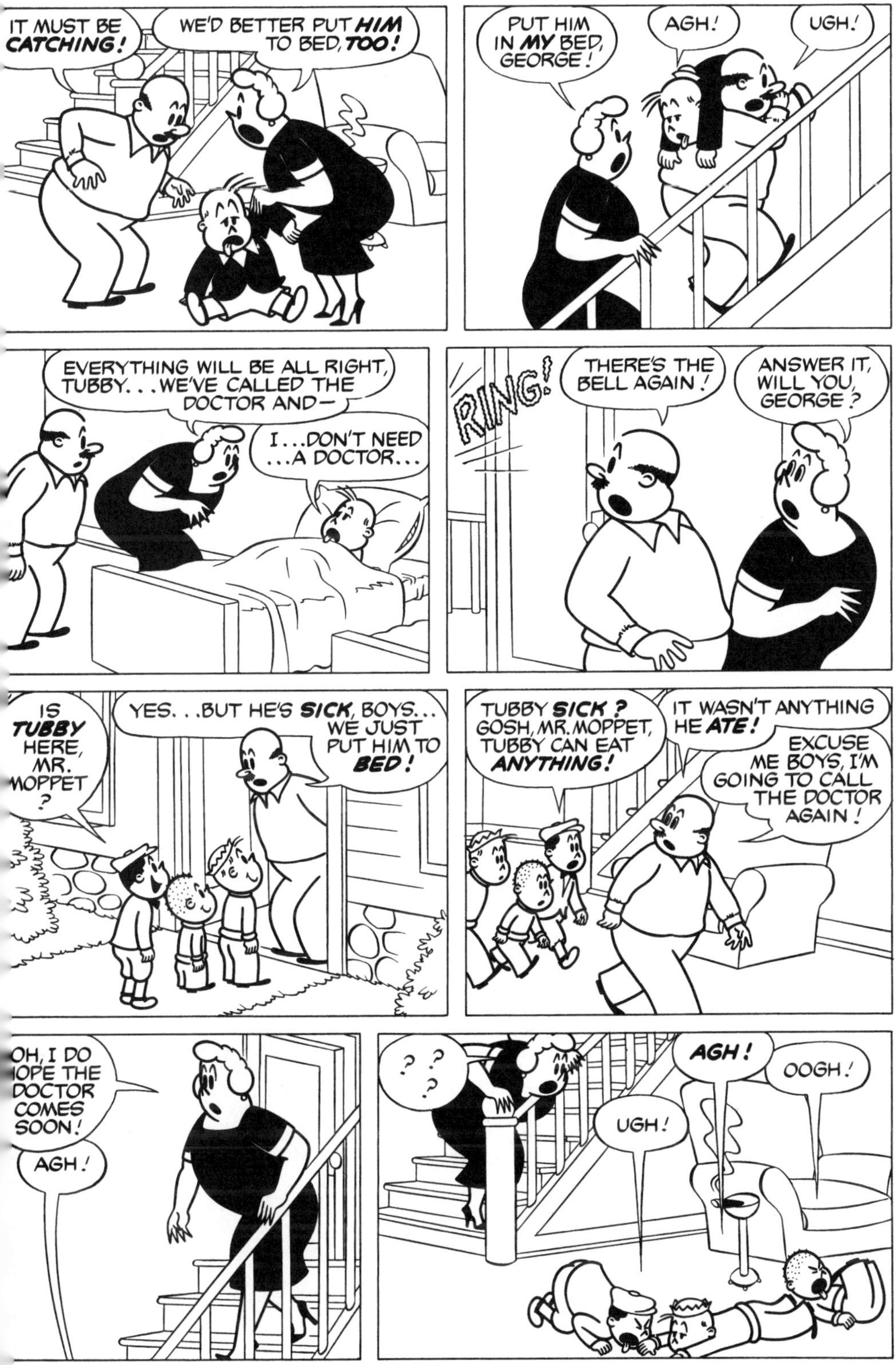
IT MUST BE CATCHING!
WE'D BETTER PUT HIM TO BED, TOO!
PUT HIM IN MY BED, GEORGE!
AGH!
UGH!
EVERYTHING WILL BE ALL RIGHT, TUBBY. . . WE'VE CALLED THE DOCTOR AND—
I. . .DON'T NEED . . .A DOCTOR. . .
RING!
THERE'S THE BELL AGAIN!
ANSWER IT, WILL YOU, GEORGE?
IS TUBBY HERE, MR. MOPPET?
YES. . .BUT HE'S SICK, BOYS. . . WE JUST PUT HIM TO BED!
TUBBY SICK? GOSH, MR. MOPPET, TUBBY CAN EAT ANYTHING!
IT WASN'T ANYTHING HE ATE!
EXCUSE ME BOYS, I'M GOING TO CALL THE DOCTOR AGAIN!
OH, I DO HOPE THE DOCTOR COMES SOON!
AGH!
? ? ?
AGH!
OOGH!
UGH!

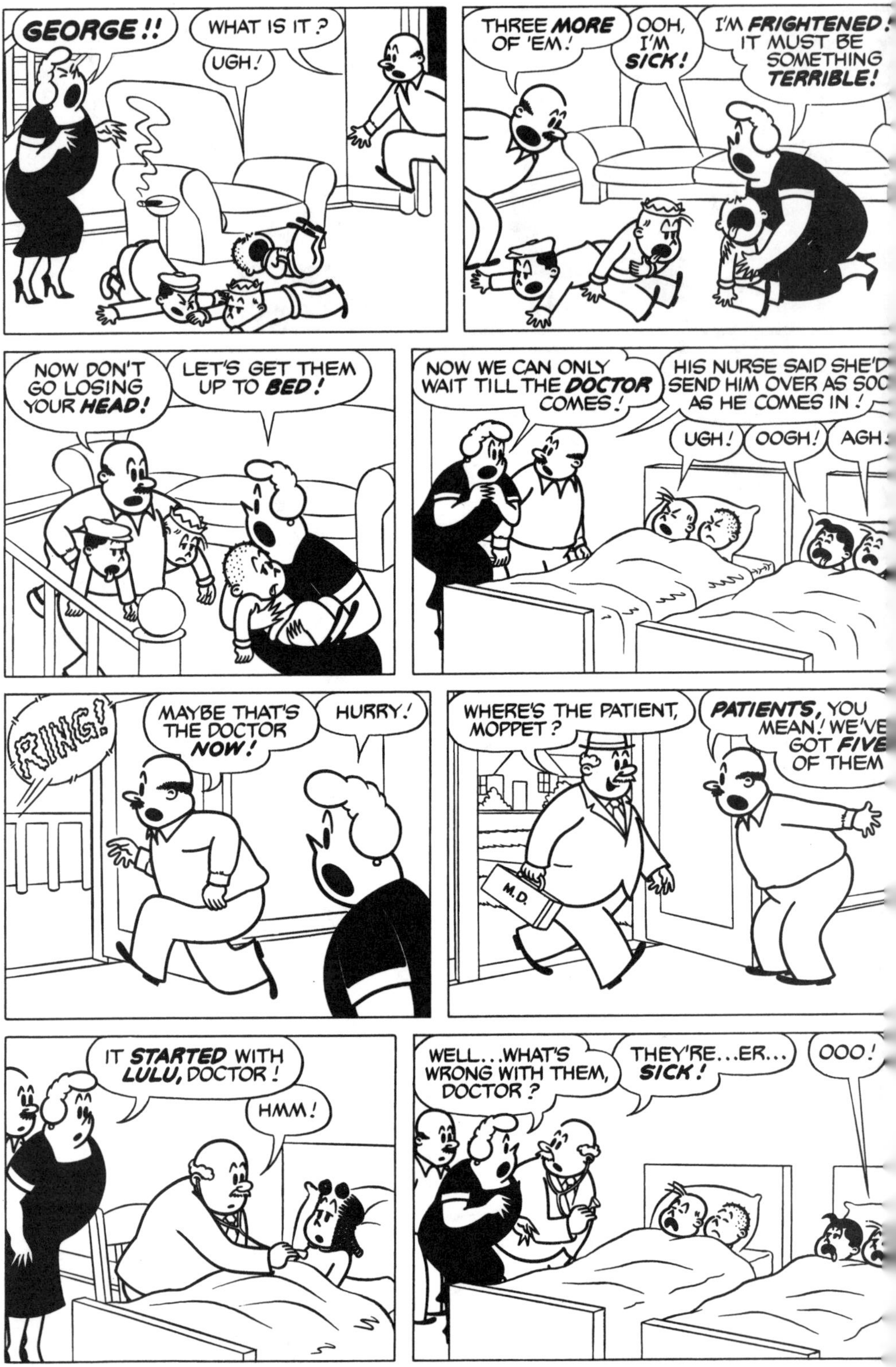
GEORGE!!
WHAT IS IT?
UGH!
THREE MORE OF 'EM!
OOH, I'M SICK!
I'M FRIGHTENED! IT MUST BE SOMETHING TERRIBLE!
NOW DON'T GO LOSING YOUR HEAD!
LET'S GET THEM UP TO BED!
NOW WE CAN ONLY WAIT TILL THE DOCTOR COMES!
HIS NURSE SAID SHE'D SEND HIM OVER AS SOO AS HE COMES IN!
UGH!
OOGH!
AGH
RING!
MAYBE THAT'S THE DOCTOR NOW!
HURRY!
WHERE'S THE PATIENT, MOPPET?
PATIENTS, YOU MEAN! WE'VE GOT FIVE OF THEM
M.D.
IT STARTED WITH LULU, DOCTOR!
HMM!
WELL...WHAT'S WRONG WITH THEM, DOCTOR?
THEY'RE...ER... SICK!
OOO!

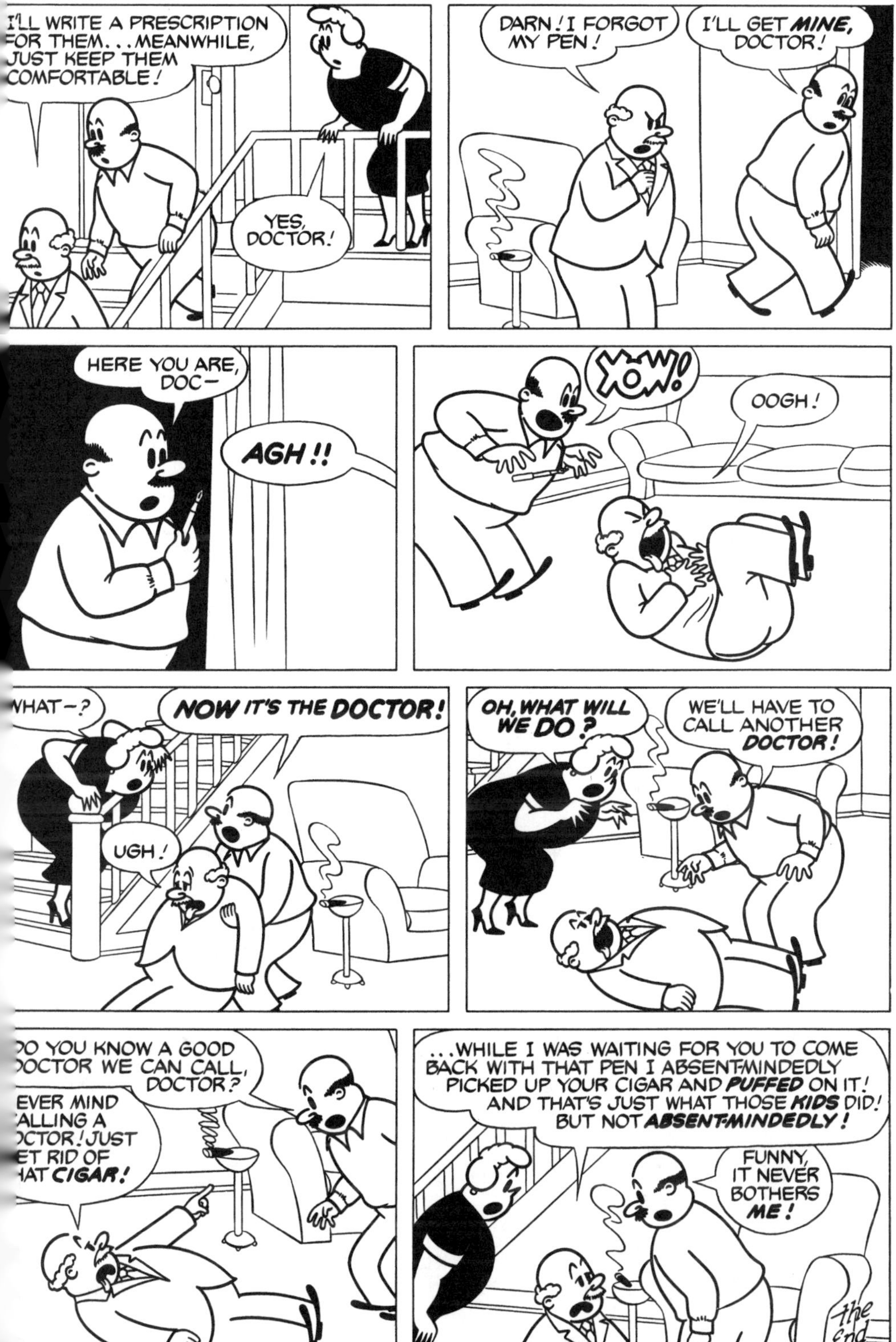
I'LL WRITE A PRESCRIPTION FOR THEM... MEANWHILE, JUST KEEP THEM COMFORTABLE!
YES, DOCTOR!
DARN! I FORGOT MY PEN!
I'LL GET MINE, DOCTOR!
HERE YOU ARE, DOC—
AGH!!
YOW!
OOGH!
WHAT—?
NOW IT'S THE DOCTOR!
UGH!
OH, WHAT WILL WE DO?
WE'LL HAVE TO CALL ANOTHER DOCTOR!
DO YOU KNOW A GOOD DOCTOR WE CAN CALL, DOCTOR?
EVER MIND CALLING A OCTOR! JUST ET RID OF HAT CIGAR!
...WHILE I WAS WAITING FOR YOU TO COME BACK WITH THAT PEN I ABSENT-MINDEDLY PICKED UP YOUR CIGAR AND PUFFED ON IT! AND THAT'S JUST WHAT THOSE KIDS DID! BUT NOT ABSENT-MINDEDLY!
FUNNY, IT NEVER BOTHERS ME!
the End

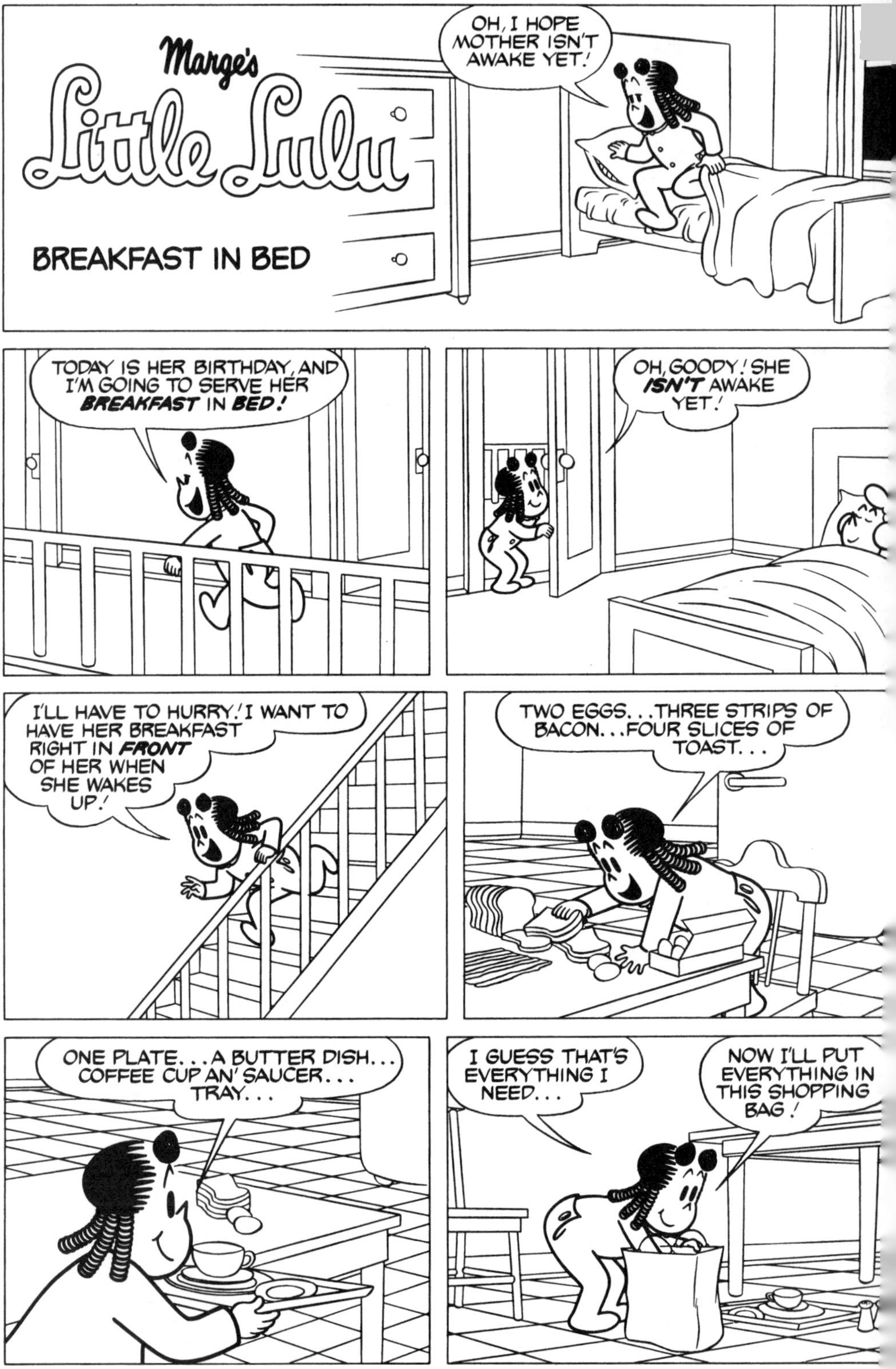
Marge's Little Lulu
BREAKFAST IN BED
OH, I HOPE MOTHER ISN'T AWAKE YET!
TODAY IS HER BIRTHDAY, AND I'M GOING TO SERVE HER BREAKFAST IN BED!
OH, GOODY! SHE ISN'T AWAKE YET!
I'LL HAVE TO HURRY! I WANT TO HAVE HER BREAKFAST RIGHT IN FRONT OF HER WHEN SHE WAKES UP!
TWO EGGS...THREE STRIPS OF BACON...FOUR SLICES OF TOAST...
ONE PLATE...A BUTTER DISH... COFFEE CUP AN' SAUCER... TRAY...
I GUESS THAT'S EVERYTHING I NEED...
NOW I'LL PUT EVERYTHING IN THIS SHOPPING BAG!

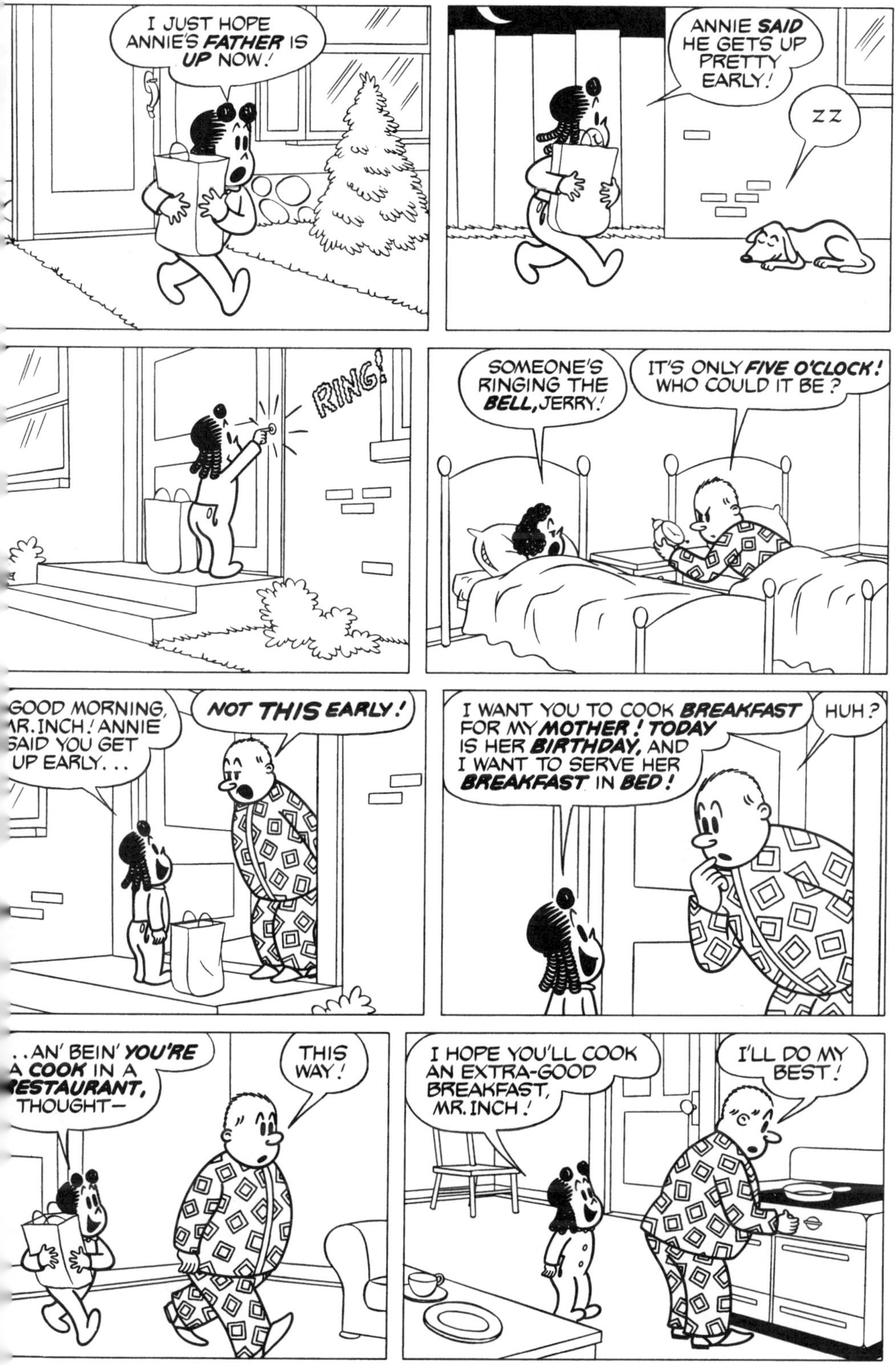
I JUST HOPE ANNIE'S FATHER IS UP NOW!
ANNIE SAID HE GETS UP PRETTY EARLY!
ZZ
RING!
SOMEONE'S RINGING THE BELL, JERRY!
IT'S ONLY FIVE O'CLOCK! WHO COULD IT BE?
GOOD MORNING, MR. INCH! ANNIE SAID YOU GET UP EARLY...
NOT THIS EARLY!
I WANT YOU TO COOK BREAKFAST FOR MY MOTHER! TODAY IS HER BIRTHDAY, AND I WANT TO SERVE HER BREAKFAST IN BED!
HUH?
..AN' BEIN' YOU'RE A COOK IN A RESTAURANT, THOUGHT—
THIS WAY!
I HOPE YOU'LL COOK AN EXTRA-GOOD BREAKFAST, MR. INCH!
I'LL DO MY BEST!

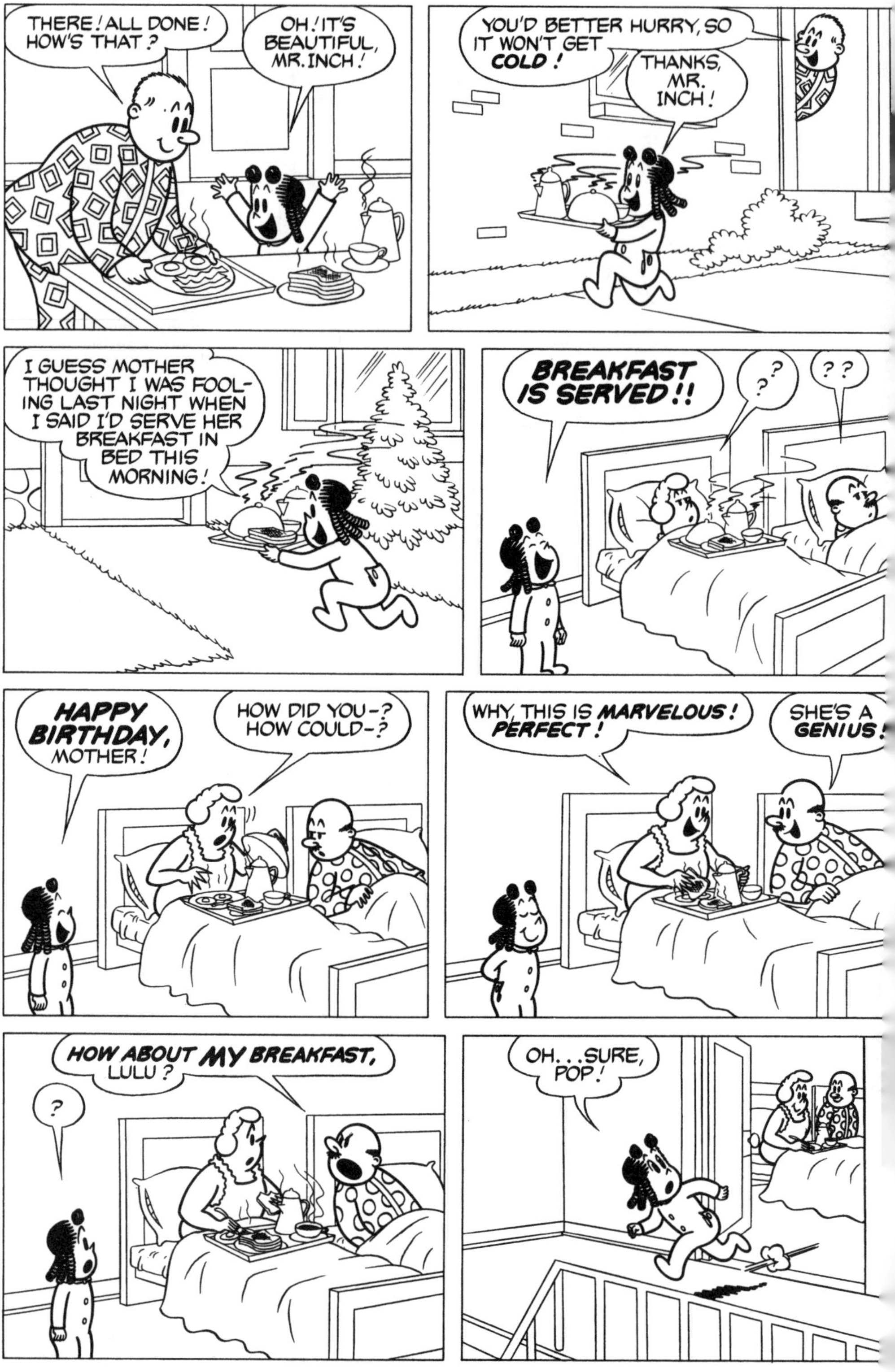
THERE! ALL DONE! HOW'S THAT?
OH! IT'S BEAUTIFUL, MR. INCH!
YOU'D BETTER HURRY, SO IT WON'T GET COLD!
THANKS, MR. INCH!
I GUESS MOTHER THOUGHT I WAS FOOLING LAST NIGHT WHEN I SAID I'D SERVE HER BREAKFAST IN BED THIS MORNING!
BREAKFAST IS SERVED!!
???
??
HAPPY BIRTHDAY, MOTHER!
HOW DID YOU-? HOW COULD-?
WHY, THIS IS MARVELOUS! PERFECT!
SHE'S A GENIUS!
HOW ABOUT MY BREAKFAST, LULU?
?
OH...SURE, POP!

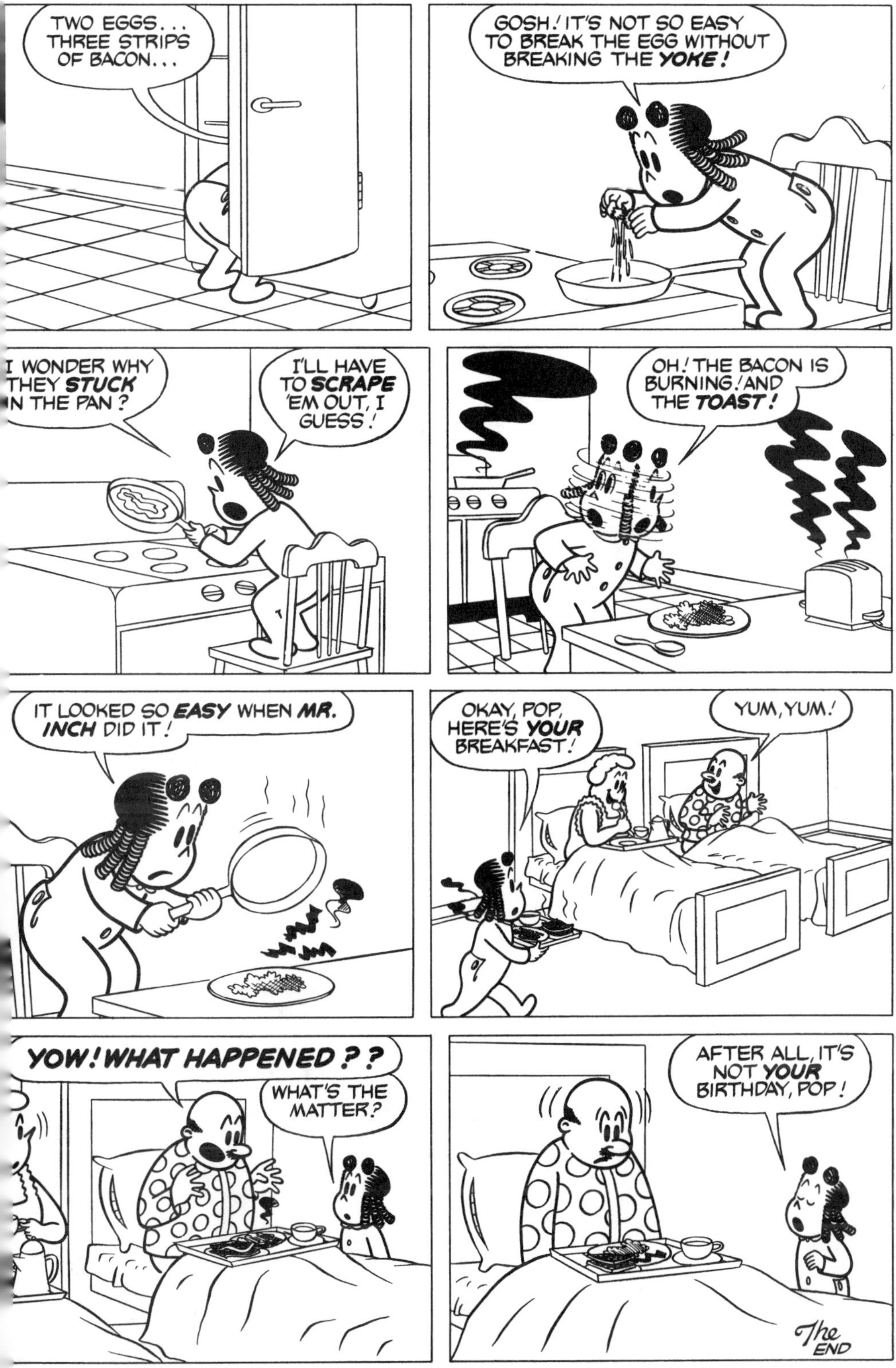

TWO EGGS... THREE STRIPS OF BACON...
GOSH! IT'S NOT SO EASY TO BREAK THE EGG WITHOUT BREAKING THE YOKE!
I WONDER WHY THEY STUCK IN THE PAN?
I'LL HAVE TO SCRAPE 'EM OUT, I GUESS!
OH! THE BACON IS BURNING! AND THE TOAST!
IT LOOKED SO EASY WHEN MR. INCH DID IT!
OKAY, POP, HERE'S YOUR BREAKFAST!
YUM, YUM!
YOW! WHAT HAPPENED??
WHAT'S THE MATTER?
AFTER ALL, IT'S NOT YOUR BIRTHDAY, POP!
The END

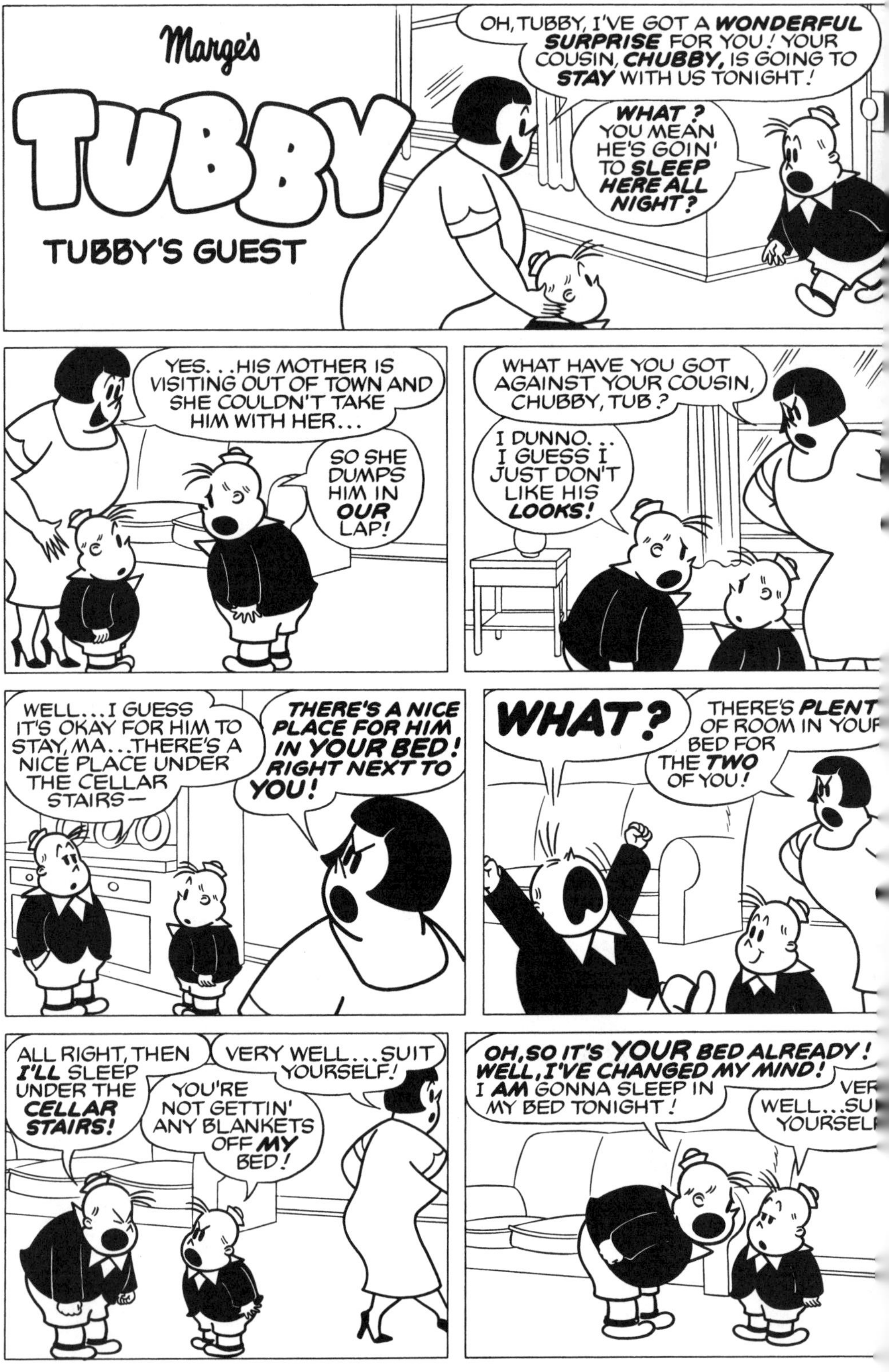
Marge's
TUBBY
TUBBY'S GUEST
OH, TUBBY, I'VE GOT A WONDERFUL SURPRISE FOR YOU! YOUR COUSIN, CHUBBY, IS GOING TO STAY WITH US TONIGHT!
WHAT? YOU MEAN HE'S GOIN' TO SLEEP HERE ALL NIGHT?
YES...HIS MOTHER IS VISITING OUT OF TOWN AND SHE COULDN'T TAKE HIM WITH HER...
SO SHE DUMPS HIM IN OUR LAP!
WHAT HAVE YOU GOT AGAINST YOUR COUSIN, CHUBBY, TUB?
I DUNNO... I GUESS I JUST DON'T LIKE HIS LOOKS!
WELL...I GUESS IT'S OKAY FOR HIM TO STAY, MA...THERE'S A NICE PLACE UNDER THE CELLAR STAIRS—
THERE'S A NICE PLACE FOR HIM IN YOUR BED! RIGHT NEXT TO YOU!
WHAT?
THERE'S PLENT
OF ROOM IN YOU
BED FOR THE TWO OF YOU!
ALL RIGHT, THEN I'LL SLEEP UNDER THE CELLAR STAIRS!
VERY WELL...SUIT YOURSELF!
YOU'RE NOT GETTIN' ANY BLANKETS OFF MY BED!
OH, SO IT'S YOUR BED ALREADY! WELL, I'VE CHANGED MY MIND! I AM GONNA SLEEP IN MY BED TONIGHT!
VER
WELL...SU
YOURSEL

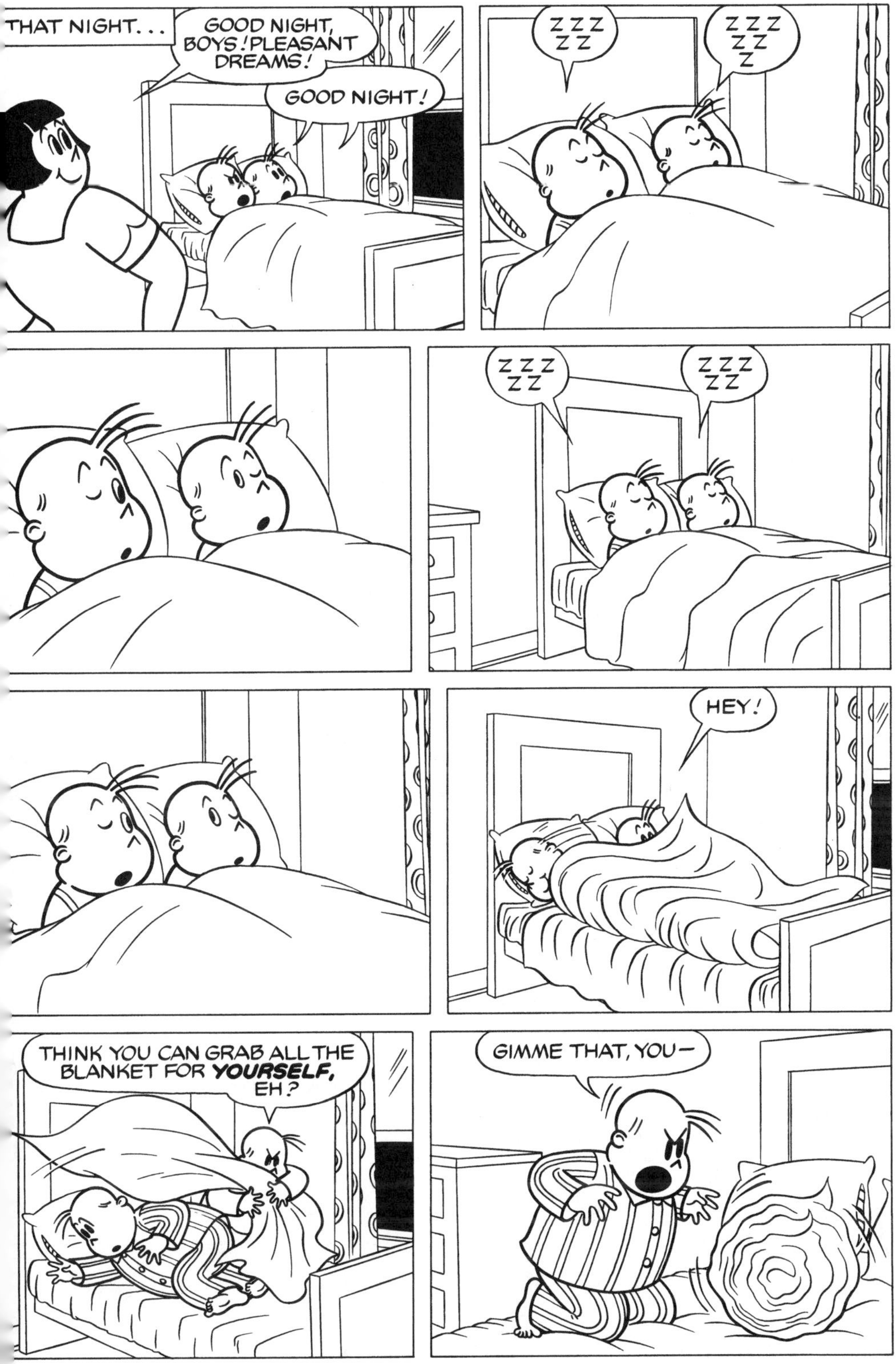
THAT NIGHT...
GOOD NIGHT, BOYS! PLEASANT DREAMS!
GOOD NIGHT!
Z Z Z
Z Z
Z Z Z
Z Z
Z
Z Z Z
Z Z
Z Z Z
Z Z
HEY!
THINK YOU CAN GRAB ALL THE BLANKET FOR **YOURSELF,** EH?
GIMME THAT, YOU—

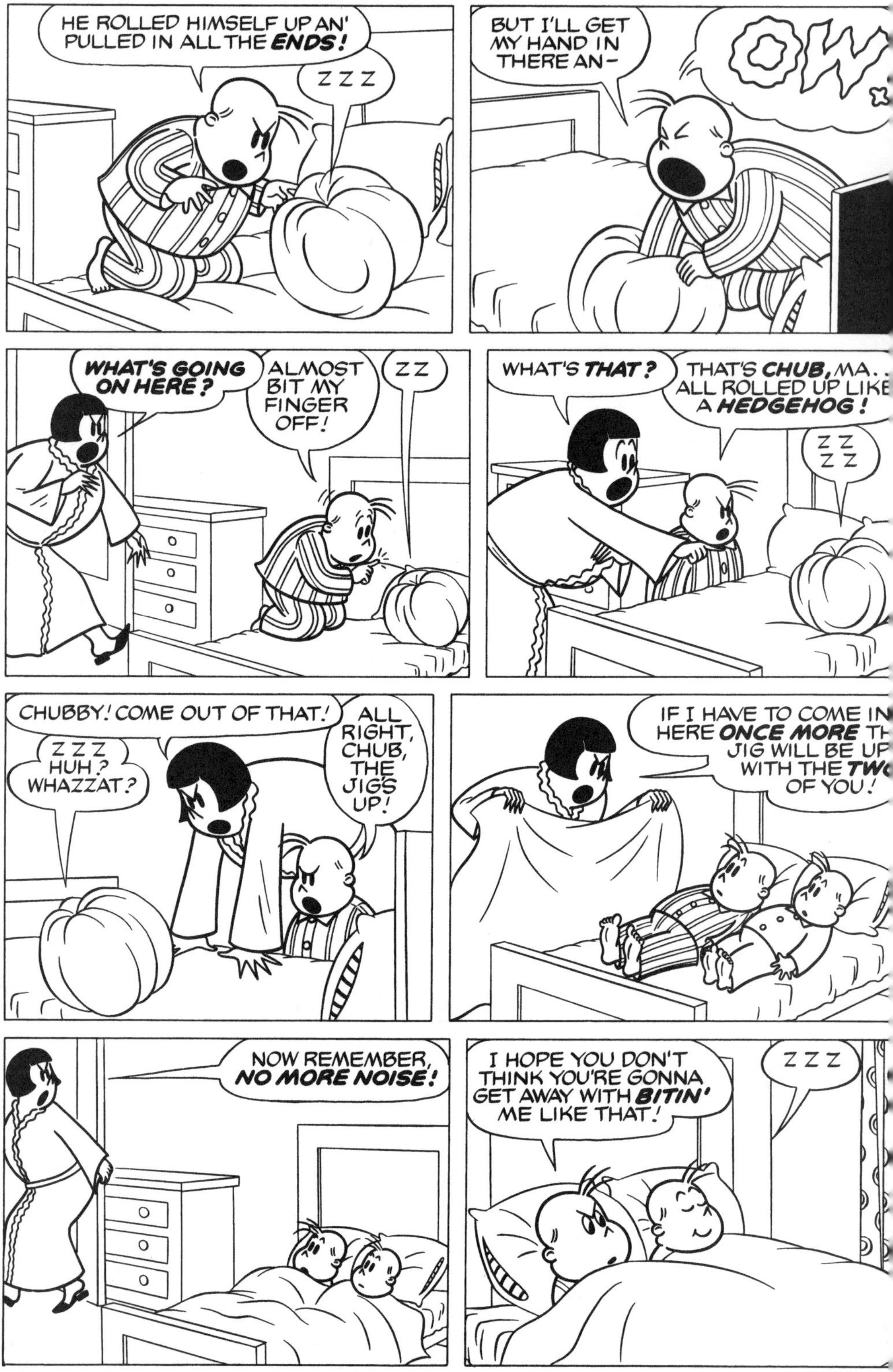
HE ROLLED HIMSELF UP AN' PULLED IN ALL THE ENDS!
Z Z Z
BUT I'LL GET MY HAND IN THERE AN—
OW
WHAT'S GOING ON HERE?
ALMOST BIT MY FINGER OFF!
Z Z
WHAT'S THAT?
THAT'S CHUB, MA... ALL ROLLED UP LIKE A HEDGEHOG!
Z Z Z Z
CHUBBY! COME OUT OF THAT!
Z Z Z HUH? WHAZZAT?
ALL RIGHT, CHUB, THE JIG'S UP!
IF I HAVE TO COME IN HERE ONCE MORE TH JIG WILL BE UP WITH THE TWO OF YOU!
NOW REMEMBER, NO MORE NOISE!
I HOPE YOU DON'T THINK YOU'RE GONNA GET AWAY WITH BITIN' ME LIKE THAT!
Z Z Z

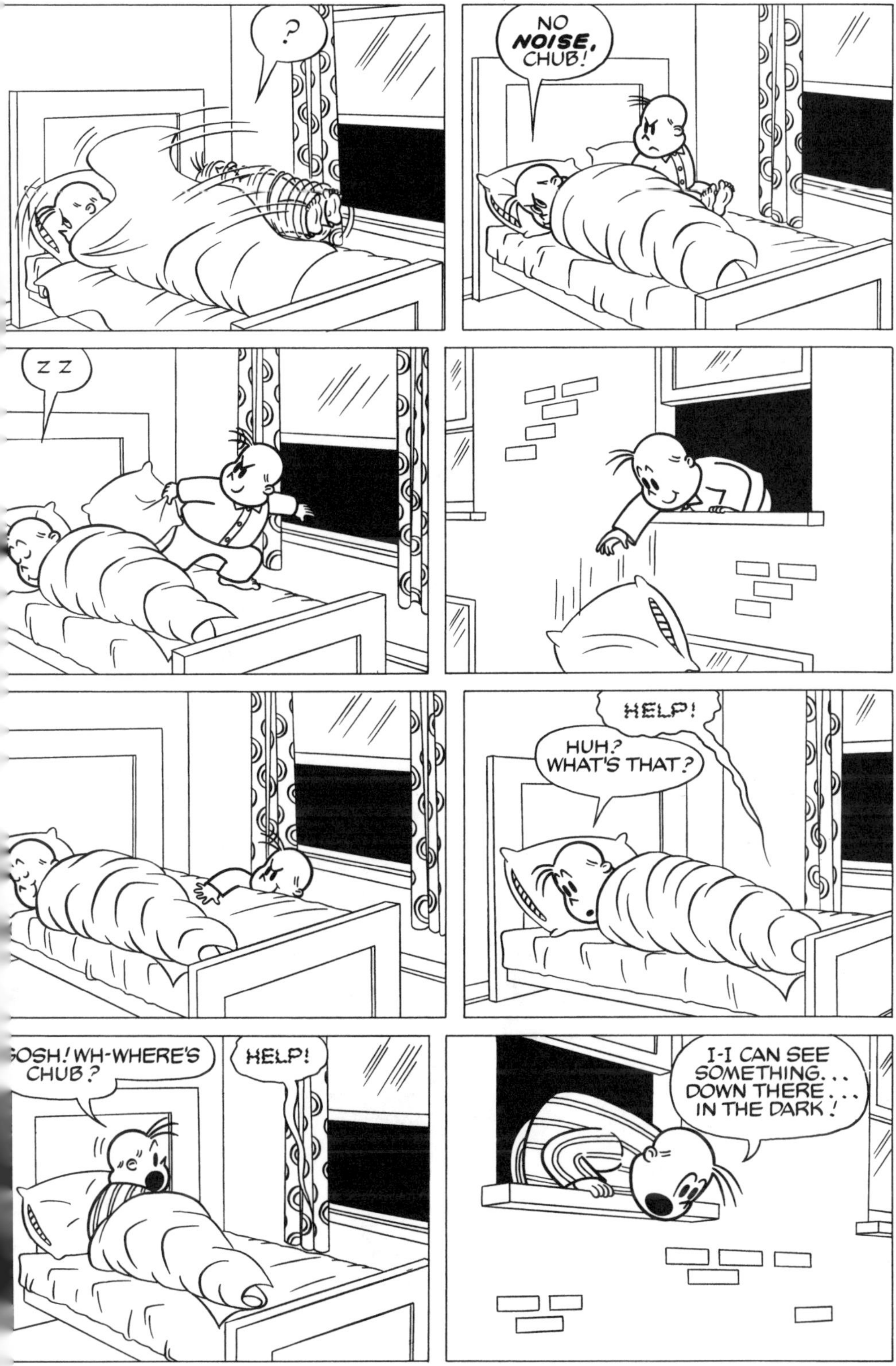
?
NO NOISE, CHUB!
Z Z
HELP!
HUH? WHAT'S THAT?
GOSH! WH-WHERE'S CHUB?
HELP!
I-I CAN SEE SOMETHING... DOWN THERE... IN THE DARK!

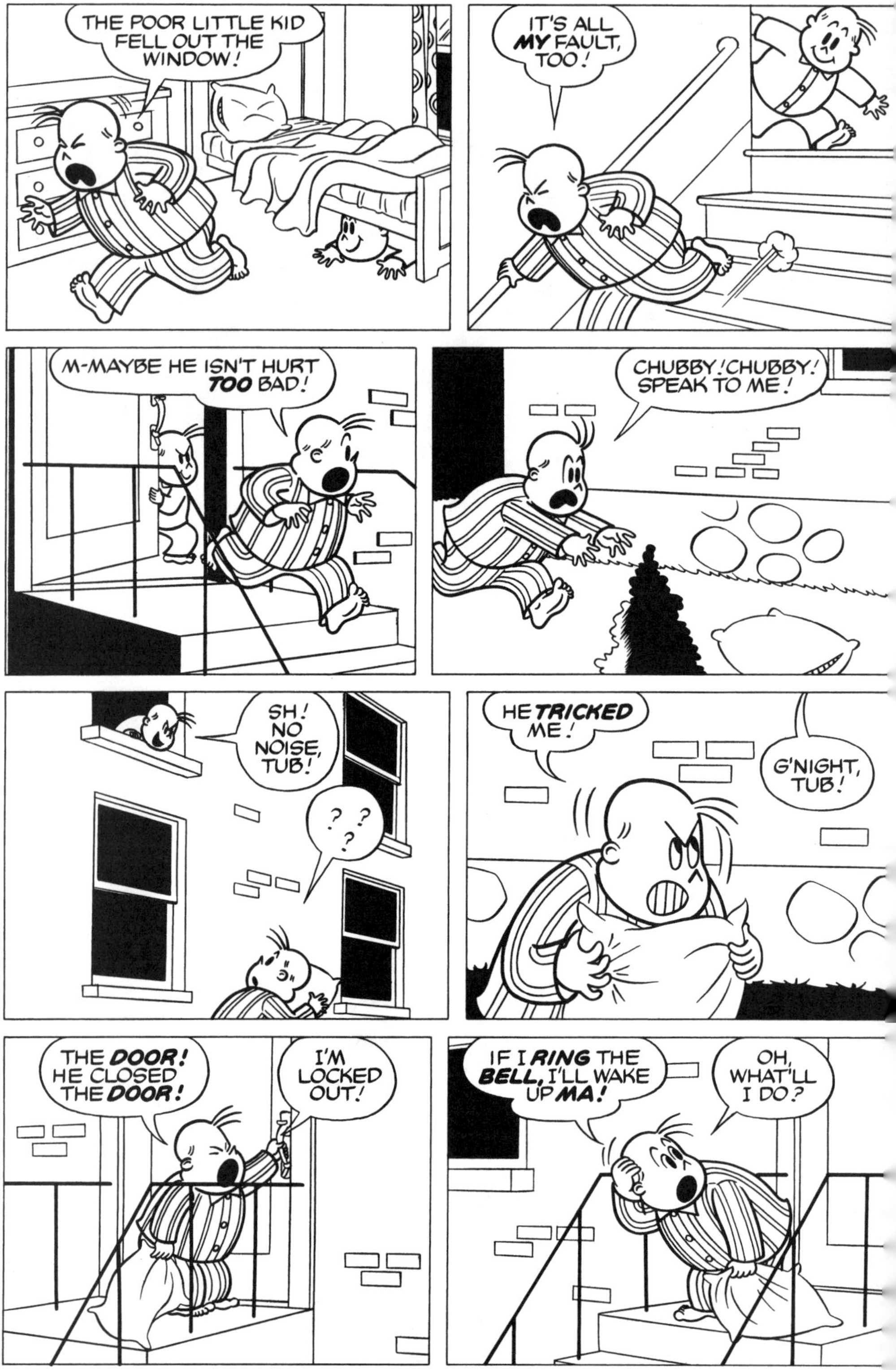
THE POOR LITTLE KID FELL OUT THE WINDOW!
IT'S ALL MY FAULT, TOO!
M-MAYBE HE ISN'T HURT TOO BAD!
CHUBBY! CHUBBY! SPEAK TO ME!
SH! NO NOISE, TUB!
? ? ?
HE TRICKED ME!
G'NIGHT, TUB!
THE DOOR! HE CLOSED THE DOOR!
I'M LOCKED OUT!
IF I RING THE BELL, I'LL WAKE UP MA!
OH, WHAT'LL I DO?

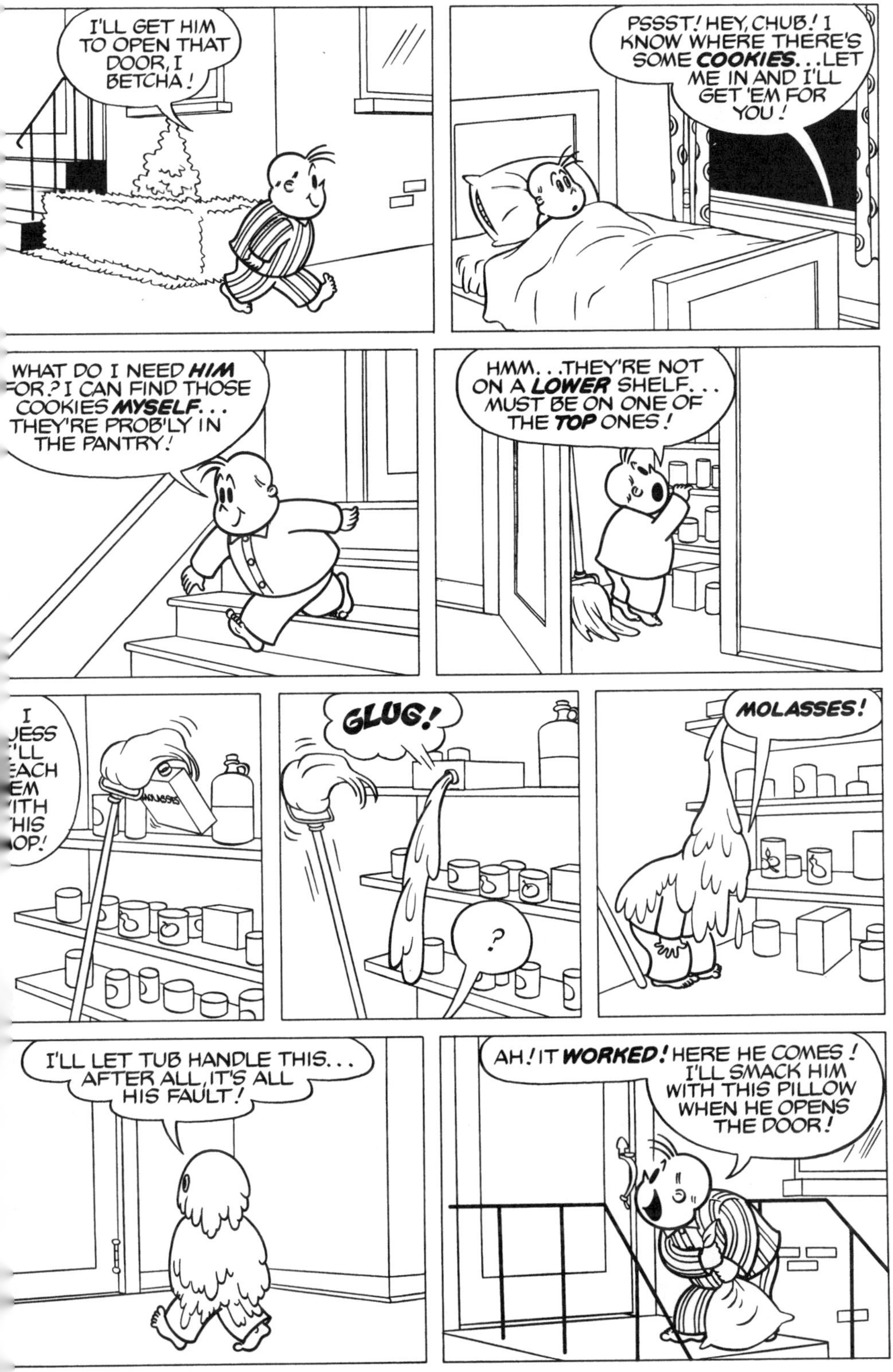

I'LL GET HIM TO OPEN THAT DOOR, I BETCHA!
PSSST! HEY, CHUB! I KNOW WHERE THERE'S SOME COOKIES...LET ME IN AND I'LL GET 'EM FOR YOU!
WHAT DO I NEED HIM FOR? I CAN FIND THOSE COOKIES MYSELF... THEY'RE PROB'LY IN THE PANTRY!
HMM...THEY'RE NOT ON A LOWER SHELF... MUST BE ON ONE OF THE TOP ONES!
MOLASSES
GLUG!
?
MOLASSES!
I'LL LET TUB HANDLE THIS... AFTER ALL, IT'S ALL HIS FAULT!
AH! IT WORKED! HERE HE COMES! I'LL SMACK HIM WITH THIS PILLOW WHEN HE OPENS THE DOOR!

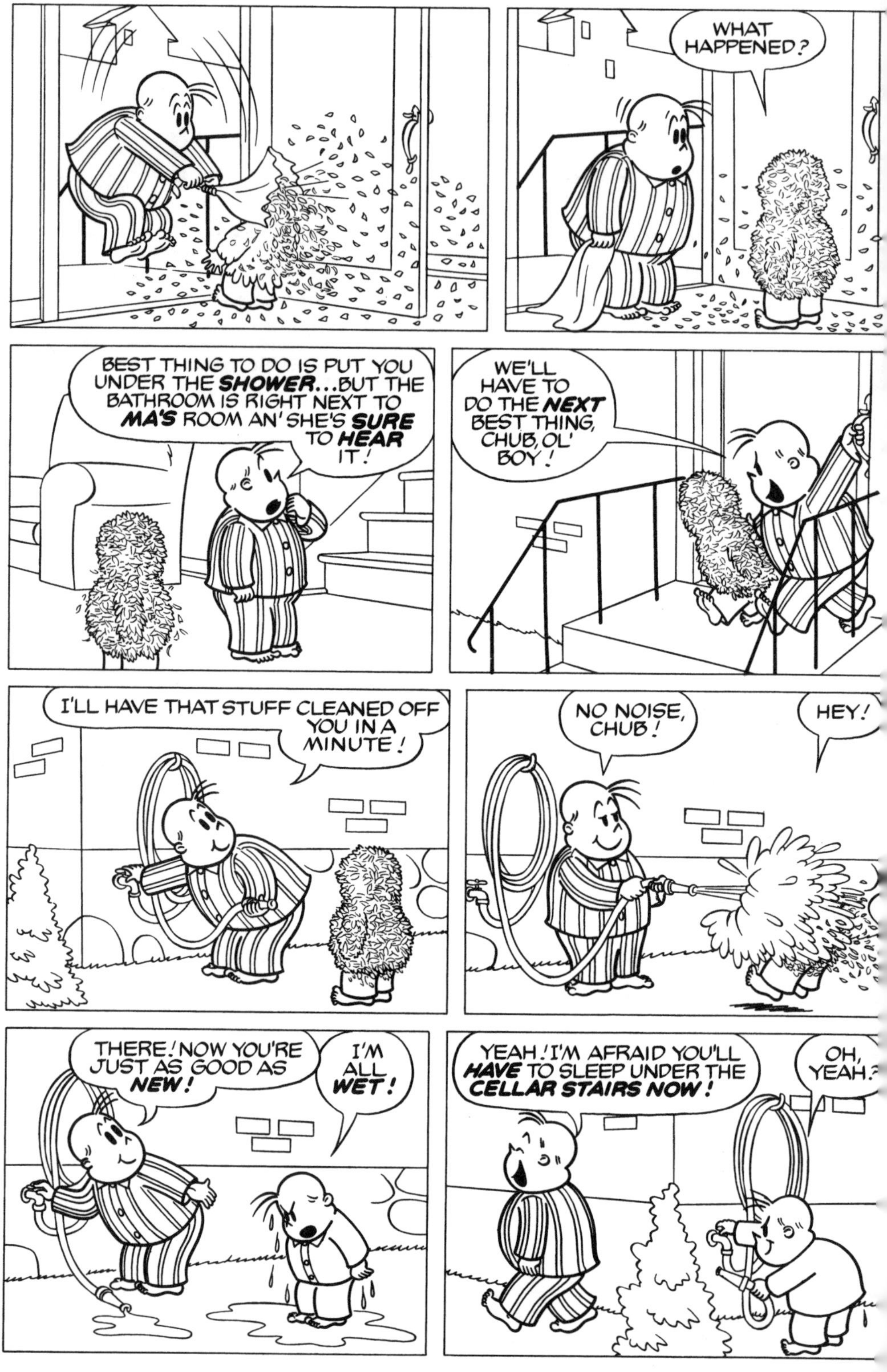
WHAT HAPPENED?
BEST THING TO DO IS PUT YOU UNDER THE SHOWER...BUT THE BATHROOM IS RIGHT NEXT TO MA'S ROOM AN' SHE'S SURE TO HEAR IT!
WE'LL HAVE TO DO THE NEXT BEST THING, CHUB, OL' BOY!
I'LL HAVE THAT STUFF CLEANED OFF YOU IN A MINUTE!
NO NOISE, CHUB!
HEY!
THERE! NOW YOU'RE JUST AS GOOD AS NEW!
I'M ALL WET!
YEAH! I'M AFRAID YOU'LL HAVE TO SLEEP UNDER THE CELLAR STAIRS NOW!
OH, YEAH?

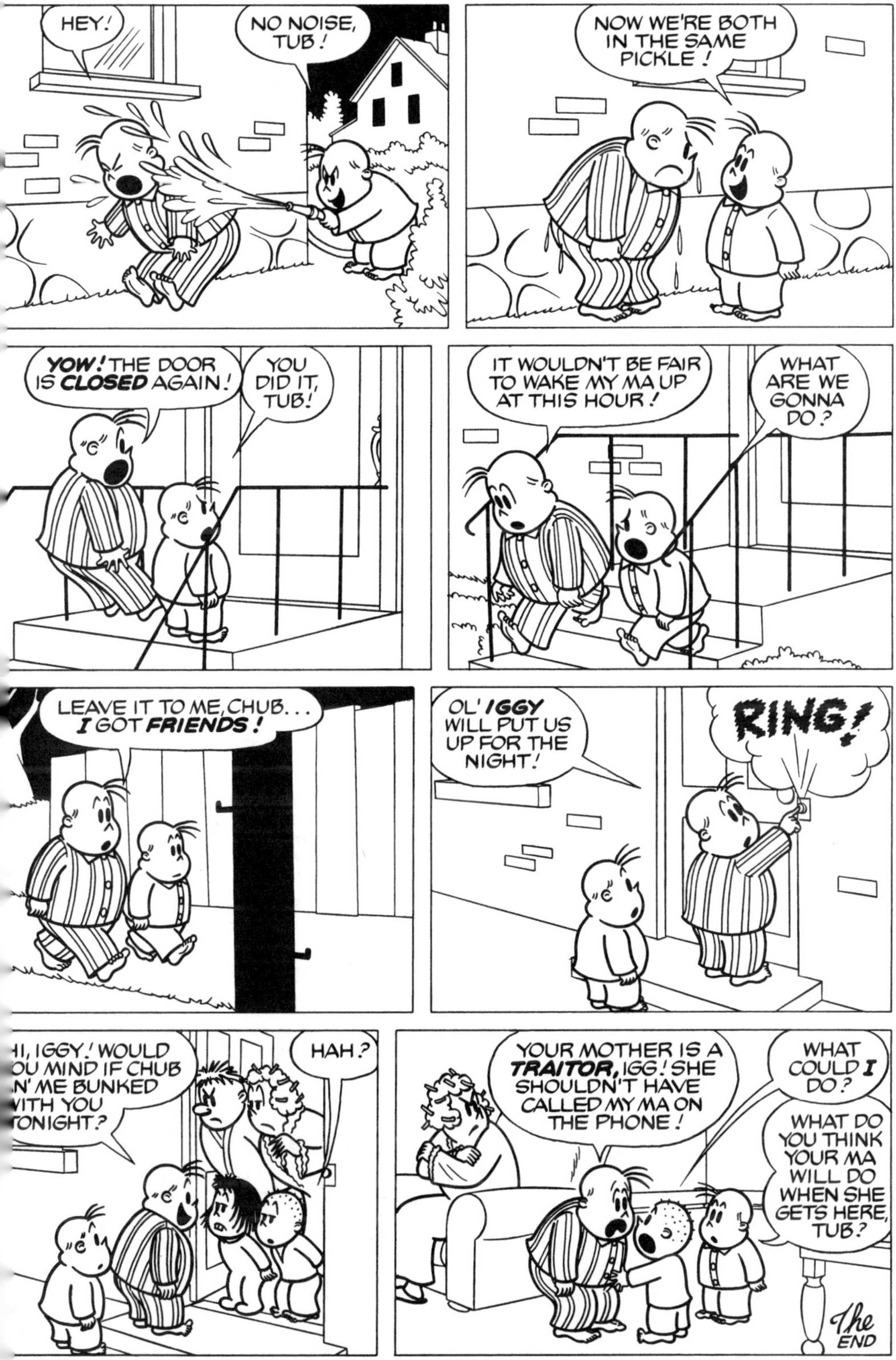
HEY!
NO NOISE, TUB!
NOW WE'RE BOTH IN THE SAME PICKLE!
YOW! THE DOOR IS CLOSED AGAIN!
YOU DID IT, TUB!
IT WOULDN'T BE FAIR TO WAKE MY MA UP AT THIS HOUR!
WHAT ARE WE GONNA DO?
LEAVE IT TO ME, CHUB... I GOT FRIENDS!
OL' IGGY WILL PUT US UP FOR THE NIGHT!
RING!
HI, IGGY! WOULD YOU MIND IF CHUB AN' ME BUNKED WITH YOU TONIGHT?
HAH?
YOUR MOTHER IS A TRAITOR, IGG! SHE SHOULDN'T HAVE CALLED MY MA ON THE PHONE!
WHAT COULD I DO?
WHAT DO YOU THINK YOUR MA WILL DO WHEN SHE GETS HERE, TUB?
The END

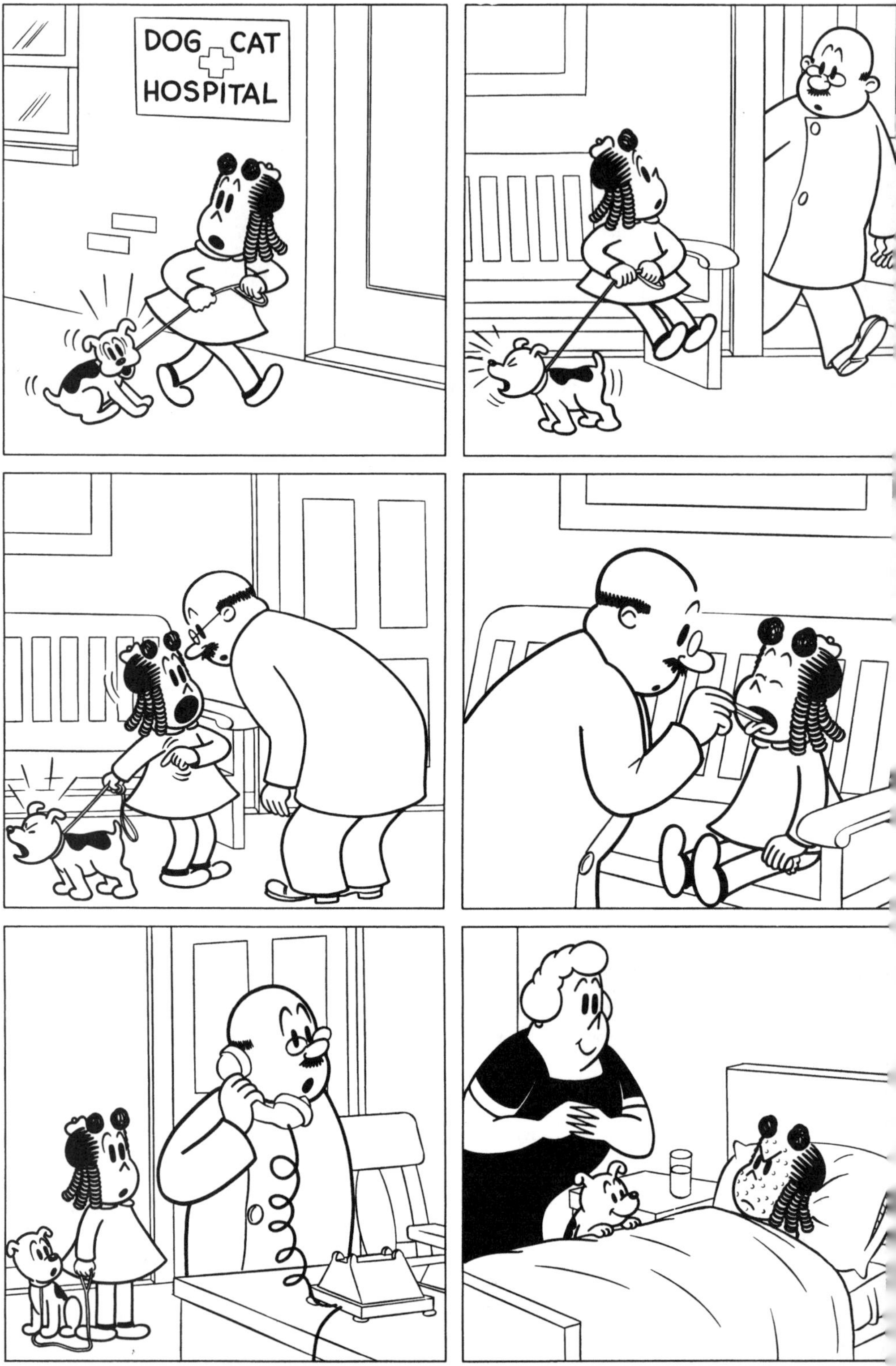
DOG CAT
HOSPITAL

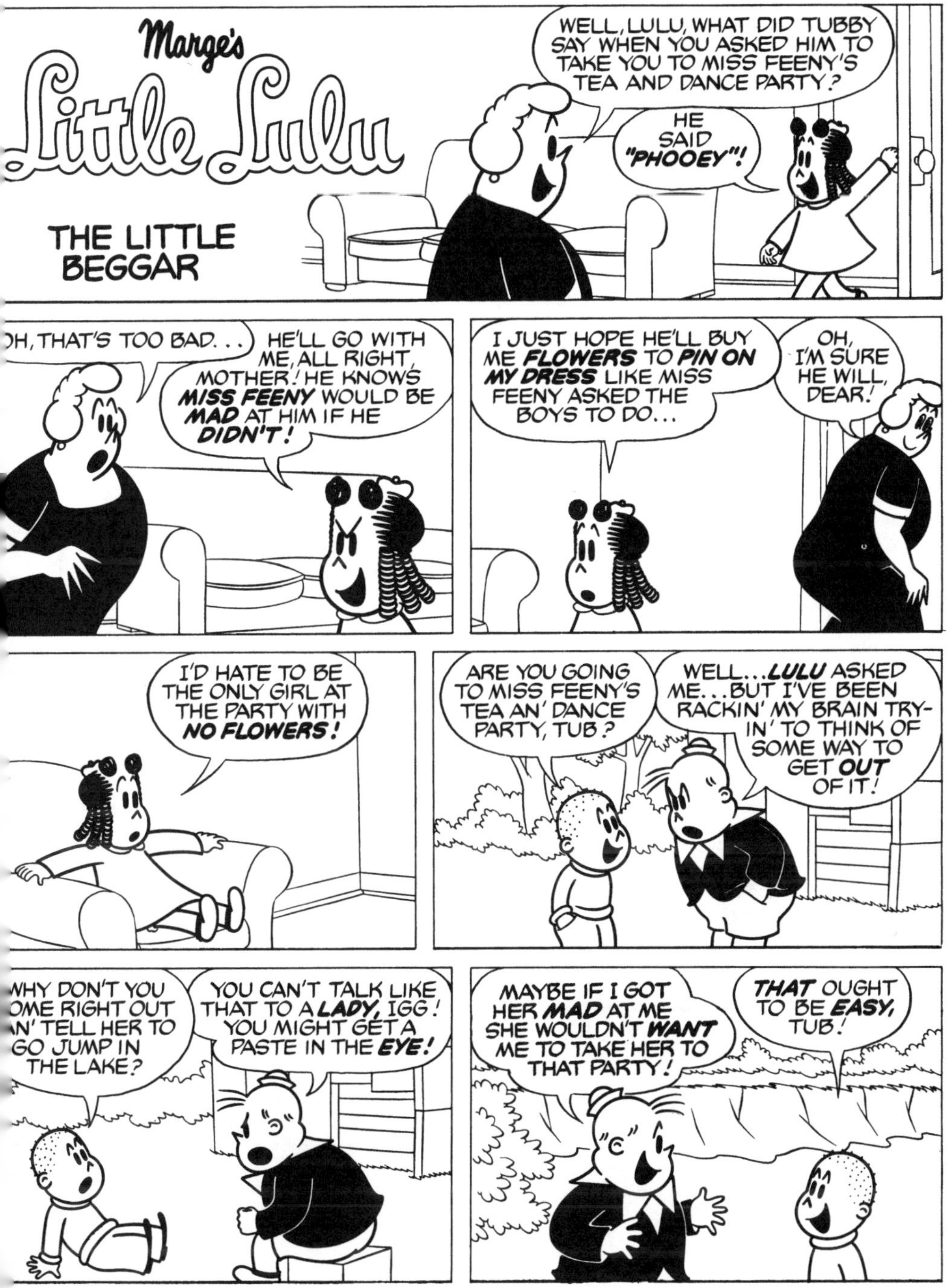
Marge's Little Lulu
THE LITTLE BEGGAR
WELL, LULU, WHAT DID TUBBY SAY WHEN YOU ASKED HIM TO TAKE YOU TO MISS FEENY'S TEA AND DANCE PARTY?
HE SAID "PHOOEY"!
OH, THAT'S TOO BAD...
HE'LL GO WITH ME, ALL RIGHT, MOTHER! HE KNOWS MISS FEENY WOULD BE MAD AT HIM IF HE DIDN'T!
I JUST HOPE HE'LL BUY ME FLOWERS TO PIN ON MY DRESS LIKE MISS FEENY ASKED THE BOYS TO DO...
OH, I'M SURE HE WILL, DEAR!
I'D HATE TO BE THE ONLY GIRL AT THE PARTY WITH NO FLOWERS!
ARE YOU GOING TO MISS FEENY'S TEA AN' DANCE PARTY, TUB?
WELL...LULU ASKED ME...BUT I'VE BEEN RACKIN' MY BRAIN TRY-IN' TO THINK OF SOME WAY TO GET OUT OF IT!
WHY DON'T YOU OME RIGHT OUT N' TELL HER TO GO JUMP IN THE LAKE?
YOU CAN'T TALK LIKE THAT TO A LADY, IGG! YOU MIGHT GET A PASTE IN THE EYE!
MAYBE IF I GOT HER MAD AT ME SHE WOULDN'T WANT ME TO TAKE HER TO THAT PARTY!
THAT OUGHT TO BE EASY, TUB!

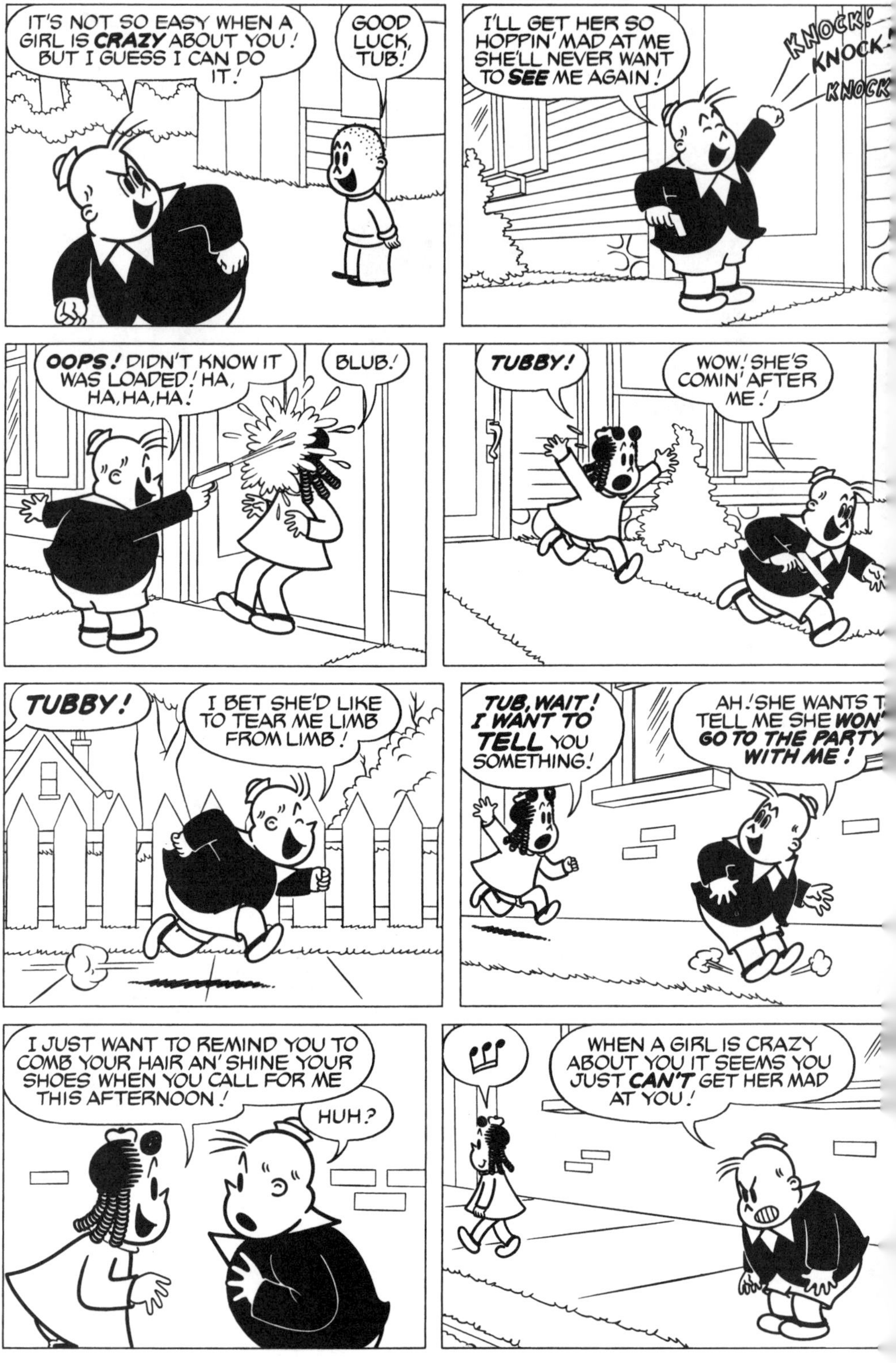
IT'S NOT SO EASY WHEN A GIRL IS CRAZY ABOUT YOU! BUT I GUESS I CAN DO IT!
GOOD LUCK, TUB!
I'LL GET HER SO HOPPIN' MAD AT ME SHE'LL NEVER WANT TO SEE ME AGAIN!
KNOCK!
KNOCK
KNOCK
OOPS! DIDN'T KNOW IT WAS LOADED! HA, HA, HA, HA!
BLUB!
TUBBY!
WOW! SHE'S COMIN' AFTER ME!
TUBBY!
I BET SHE'D LIKE TO TEAR ME LIMB FROM LIMB!
TUB, WAIT! I WANT TO TELL YOU SOMETHING!
AH! SHE WANTS T TELL ME SHE WON GO TO THE PARTY WITH ME!
I JUST WANT TO REMIND YOU TO COMB YOUR HAIR AN' SHINE YOUR SHOES WHEN YOU CALL FOR ME THIS AFTERNOON!
HUH?
WHEN A GIRL IS CRAZY ABOUT YOU IT SEEMS YOU JUST CAN'T GET HER MAD AT YOU!

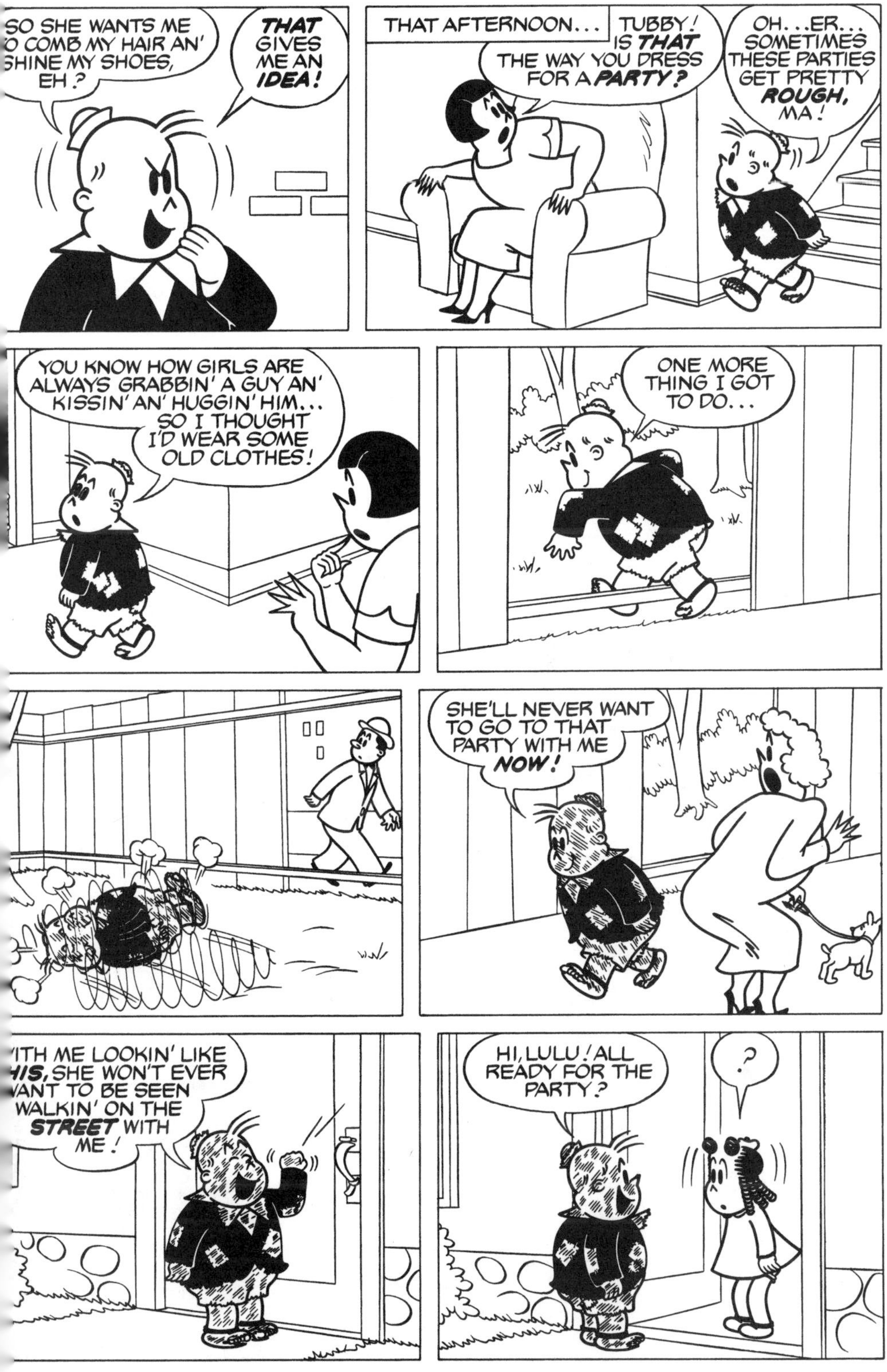
SO SHE WANTS ME
O COMB MY HAIR AN'
SHINE MY SHOES,
EH ?
THAT GIVES ME AN IDEA!
THAT AFTERNOON...
TUBBY! IS THAT THE WAY YOU DRESS FOR A PARTY?
OH...ER... SOMETIMES THESE PARTIES GET PRETTY ROUGH, MA!
YOU KNOW HOW GIRLS ARE ALWAYS GRABBIN' A GUY AN' KISSIN' AN' HUGGIN' HIM... SO I THOUGHT I'D WEAR SOME OLD CLOTHES!
ONE MORE THING I GOT TO DO...
SHE'LL NEVER WANT TO GO TO THAT PARTY WITH ME NOW!
ITH ME LOOKIN' LIKE HIS, SHE WON'T EVER ANT TO BE SEEN WALKIN' ON THE STREET WITH ME!
HI, LULU! ALL READY FOR THE PARTY?
?

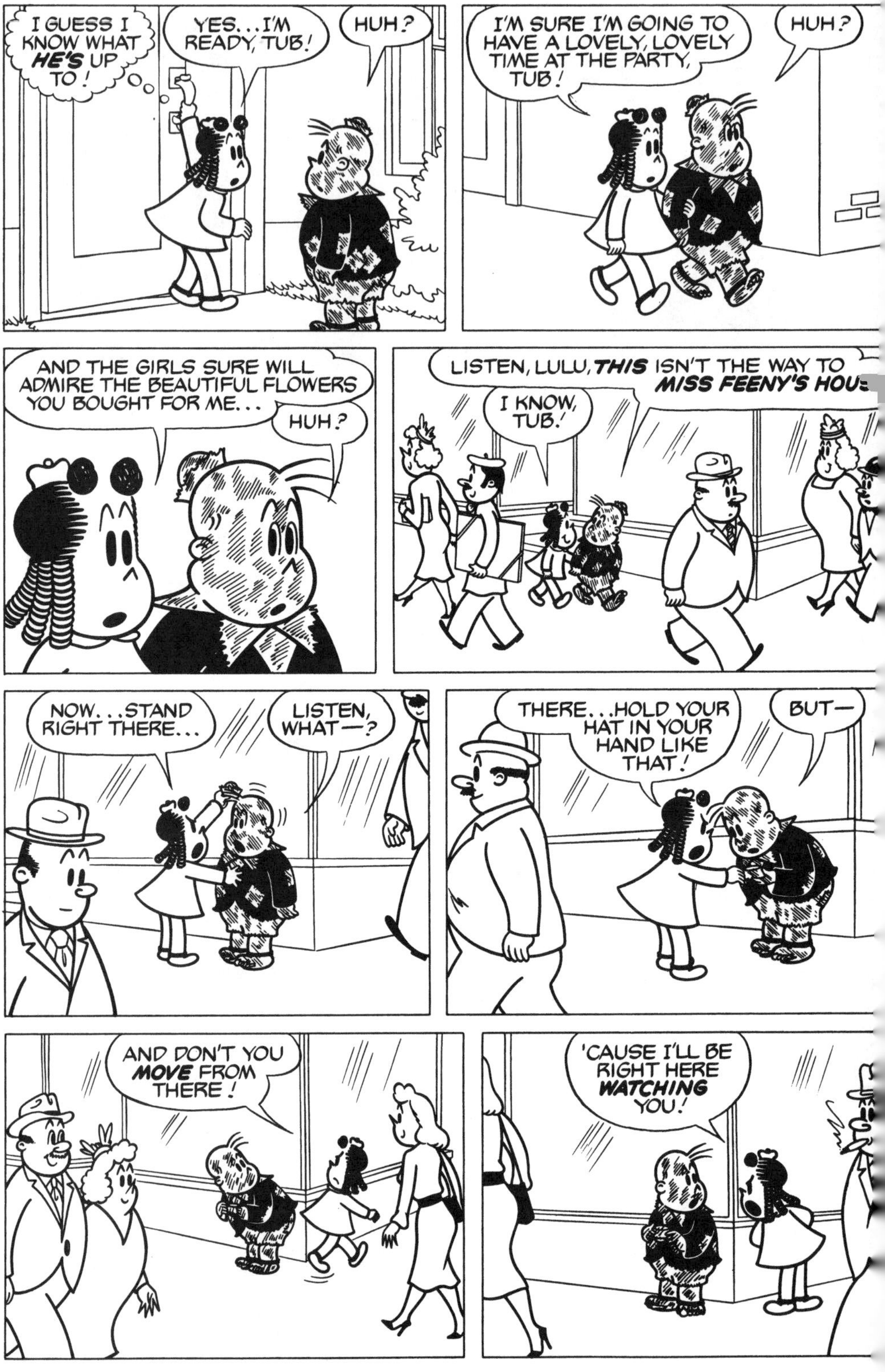

I GUESS I KNOW WHAT HE'S UP TO!
YES...I'M READY, TUB!
HUH?
I'M SURE I'M GOING TO HAVE A LOVELY, LOVELY TIME AT THE PARTY, TUB!
HUH?
AND THE GIRLS SURE WILL ADMIRE THE BEAUTIFUL FLOWERS YOU BOUGHT FOR ME...
HUH?
LISTEN, LULU, THIS ISN'T THE WAY TO MISS FEENY'S HOUS
I KNOW, TUB!
NOW...STAND RIGHT THERE...
LISTEN, WHAT—?
THERE...HOLD YOUR HAT IN YOUR HAND LIKE THAT!
BUT—
AND DON'T YOU MOVE FROM THERE!
'CAUSE I'LL BE RIGHT HERE WATCHING YOU!

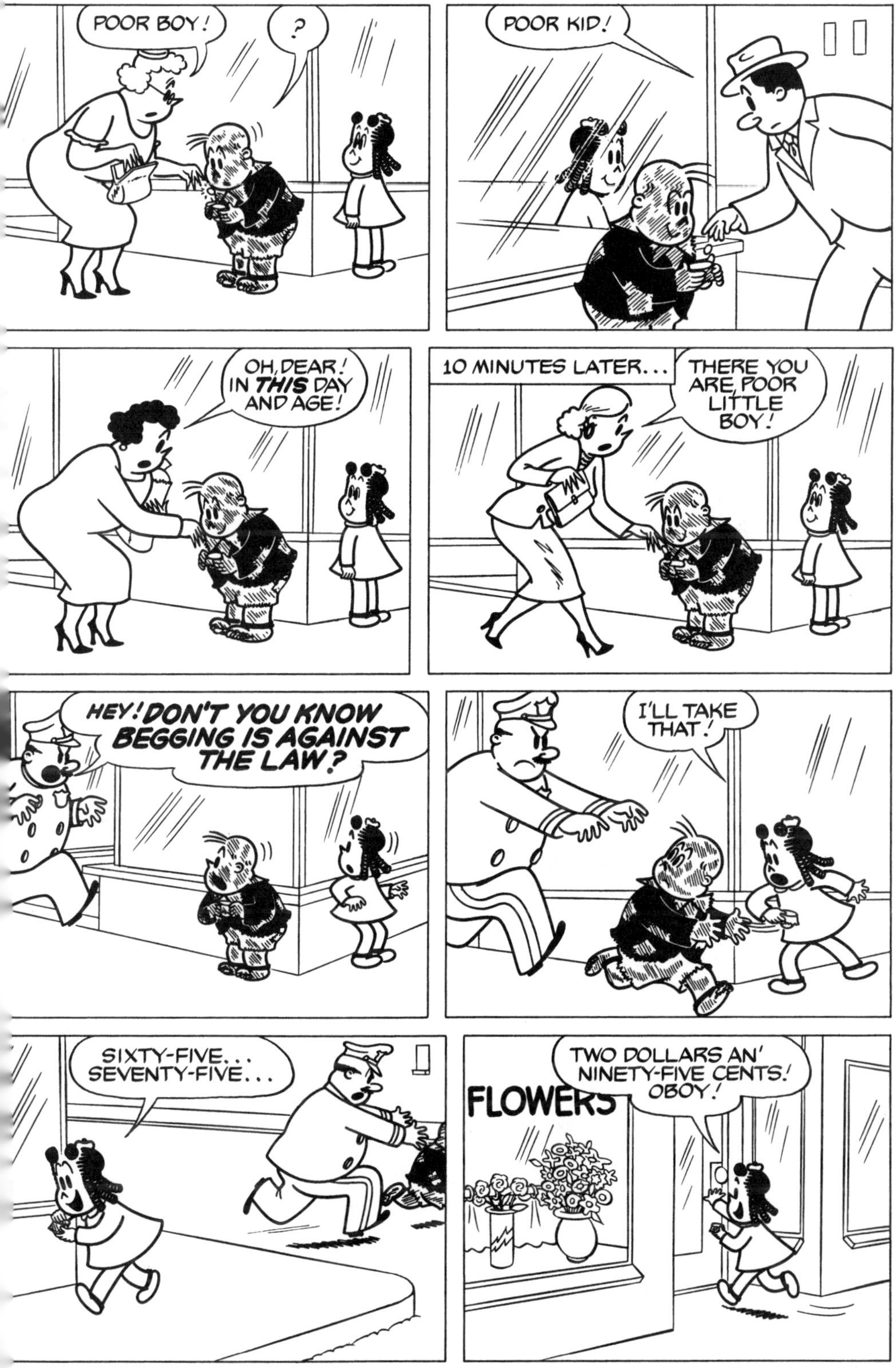
POOR BOY!
?
POOR KID!
OH, DEAR! IN THIS DAY AND AGE!
10 MINUTES LATER...
THERE YOU ARE, POOR LITTLE BOY!
HEY! DON'T YOU KNOW BEGGING IS AGAINST THE LAW?
I'LL TAKE THAT!
SIXTY-FIVE... SEVENTY-FIVE...
FLOWERS
TWO DOLLARS AN' NINETY-FIVE CENTS! OBOY!

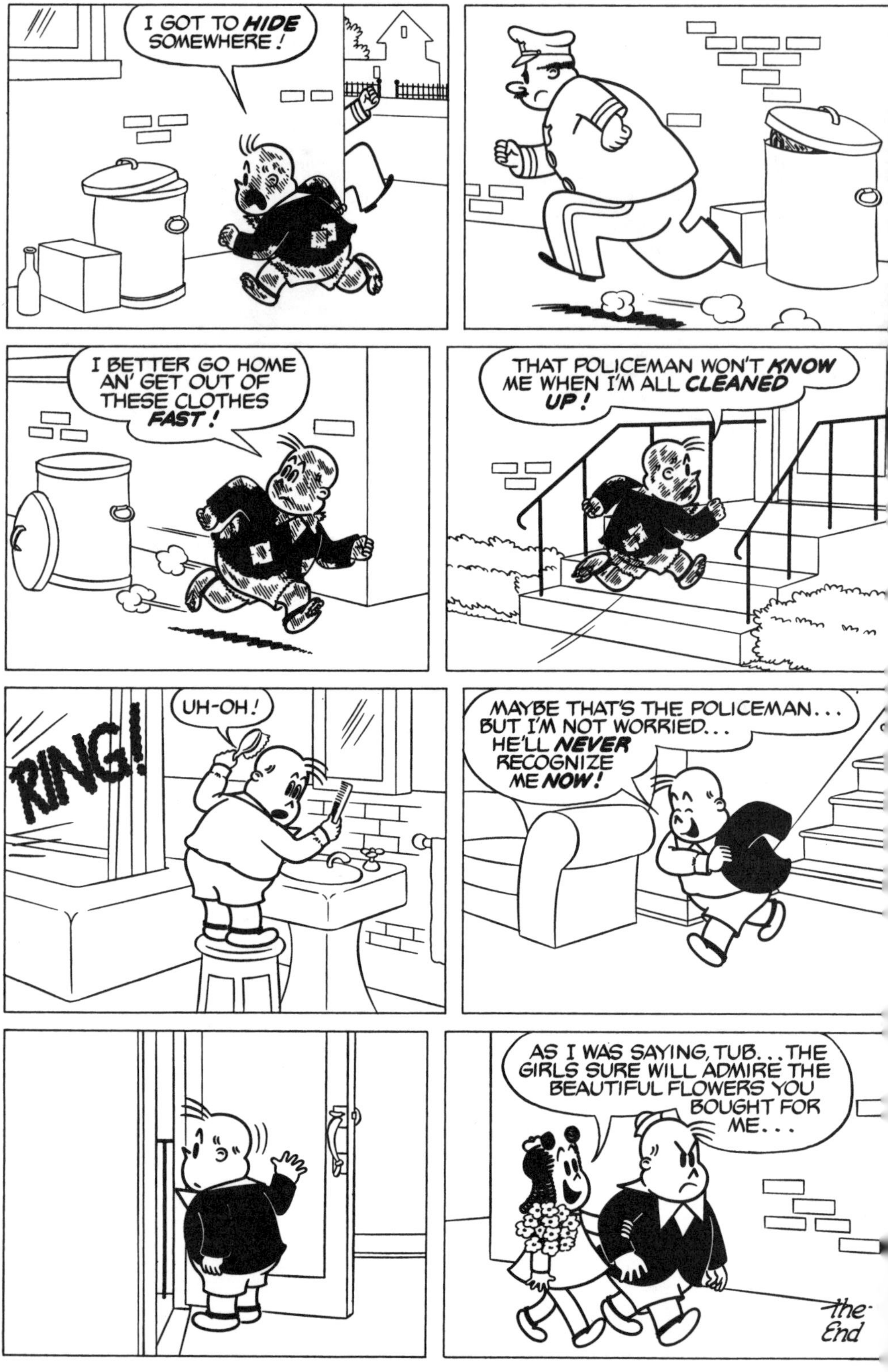
I GOT TO HIDE SOMEWHERE!
I BETTER GO HOME AN' GET OUT OF THESE CLOTHES FAST!
THAT POLICEMAN WON'T KNOW ME WHEN I'M ALL CLEANED UP!
RING!
UH-OH!
MAYBE THAT'S THE POLICEMAN... BUT I'M NOT WORRIED... HE'LL NEVER RECOGNIZE ME NOW!
AS I WAS SAYING, TUB... THE GIRLS SURE WILL ADMIRE THE BEAUTIFUL FLOWERS YOU BOUGHT FOR ME...
the End

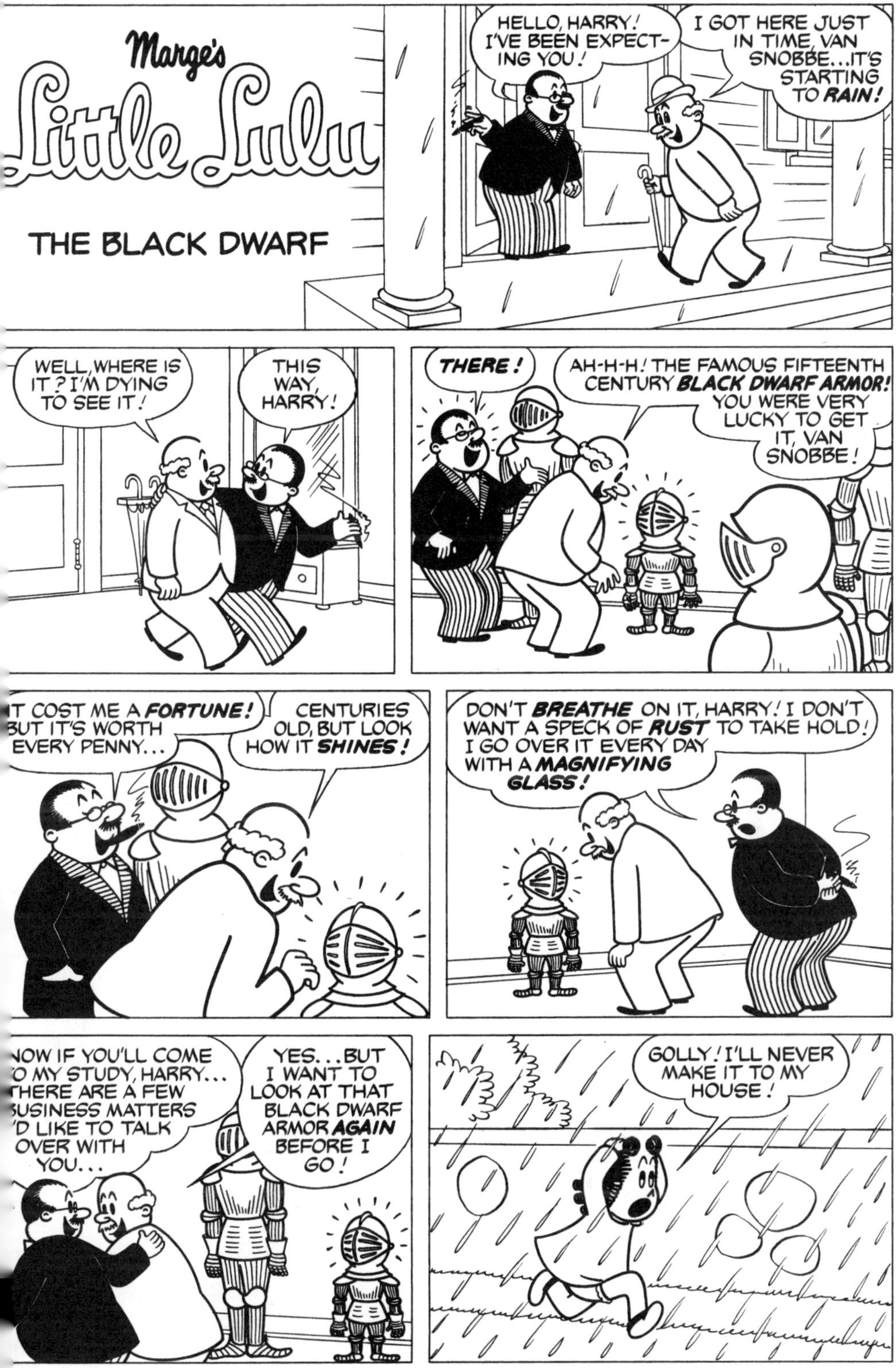

Marge's
Little Lulu
THE BLACK DWARF
HELLO, HARRY! I'VE BEEN EXPECTING YOU!
I GOT HERE JUST IN TIME, VAN SNOBBE...IT'S STARTING TO RAIN!
WELL, WHERE IS IT? I'M DYING TO SEE IT!
THIS WAY, HARRY!
THERE!
AH-H-H! THE FAMOUS FIFTEENTH CENTURY BLACK DWARF ARMOR! YOU WERE VERY LUCKY TO GET IT, VAN SNOBBE!
IT COST ME A FORTUNE! BUT IT'S WORTH EVERY PENNY...
CENTURIES OLD, BUT LOOK HOW IT SHINES!
DON'T BREATHE ON IT, HARRY! I DON'T WANT A SPECK OF RUST TO TAKE HOLD! I GO OVER IT EVERY DAY WITH A MAGNIFYING GLASS!
NOW IF YOU'LL COME TO MY STUDY, HARRY... THERE ARE A FEW BUSINESS MATTERS I'D LIKE TO TALK OVER WITH YOU...
YES...BUT I WANT TO LOOK AT THAT BLACK DWARF ARMOR AGAIN BEFORE I GO!
GOLLY! I'LL NEVER MAKE IT TO MY HOUSE!

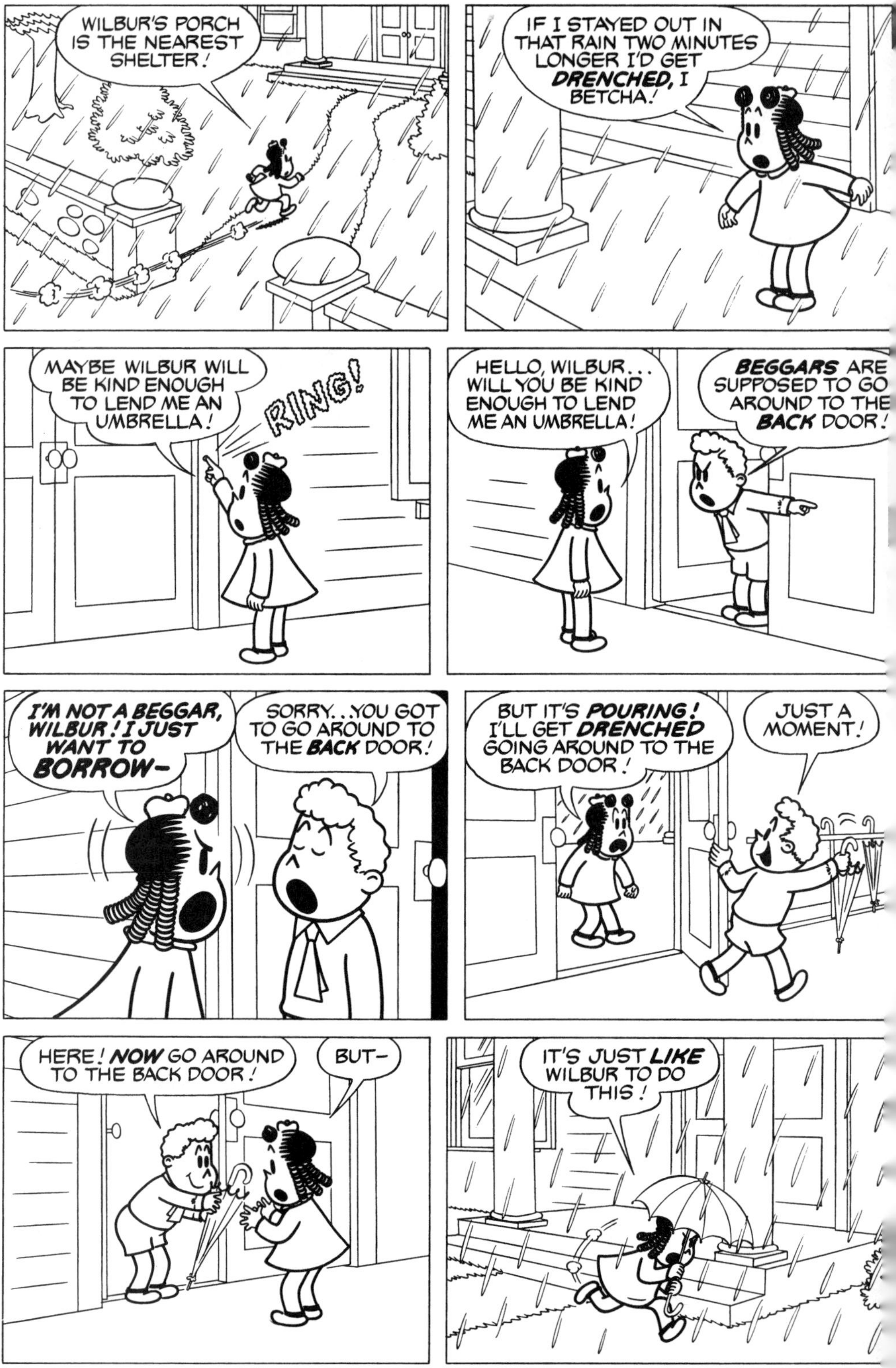
WILBUR'S PORCH IS THE NEAREST SHELTER!
IF I STAYED OUT IN THAT RAIN TWO MINUTES LONGER I'D GET **DRENCHED,** I BETCHA!
MAYBE WILBUR WILL BE KIND ENOUGH TO LEND ME AN UMBRELLA!
RING!
HELLO, WILBUR... WILL YOU BE KIND ENOUGH TO LEND ME AN UMBRELLA!
BEGGARS ARE SUPPOSED TO GO AROUND TO THE **BACK** DOOR!
I'M NOT A BEGGAR, WILBUR! I JUST WANT TO BORROW—
SORRY...YOU GOT TO GO AROUND TO THE **BACK** DOOR!
BUT IT'S **POURING!** I'LL GET **DRENCHED** GOING AROUND TO THE BACK DOOR!
JUST A MOMENT!
HERE! **NOW** GO AROUND TO THE BACK DOOR!
BUT—
IT'S JUST **LIKE** WILBUR TO DO THIS!

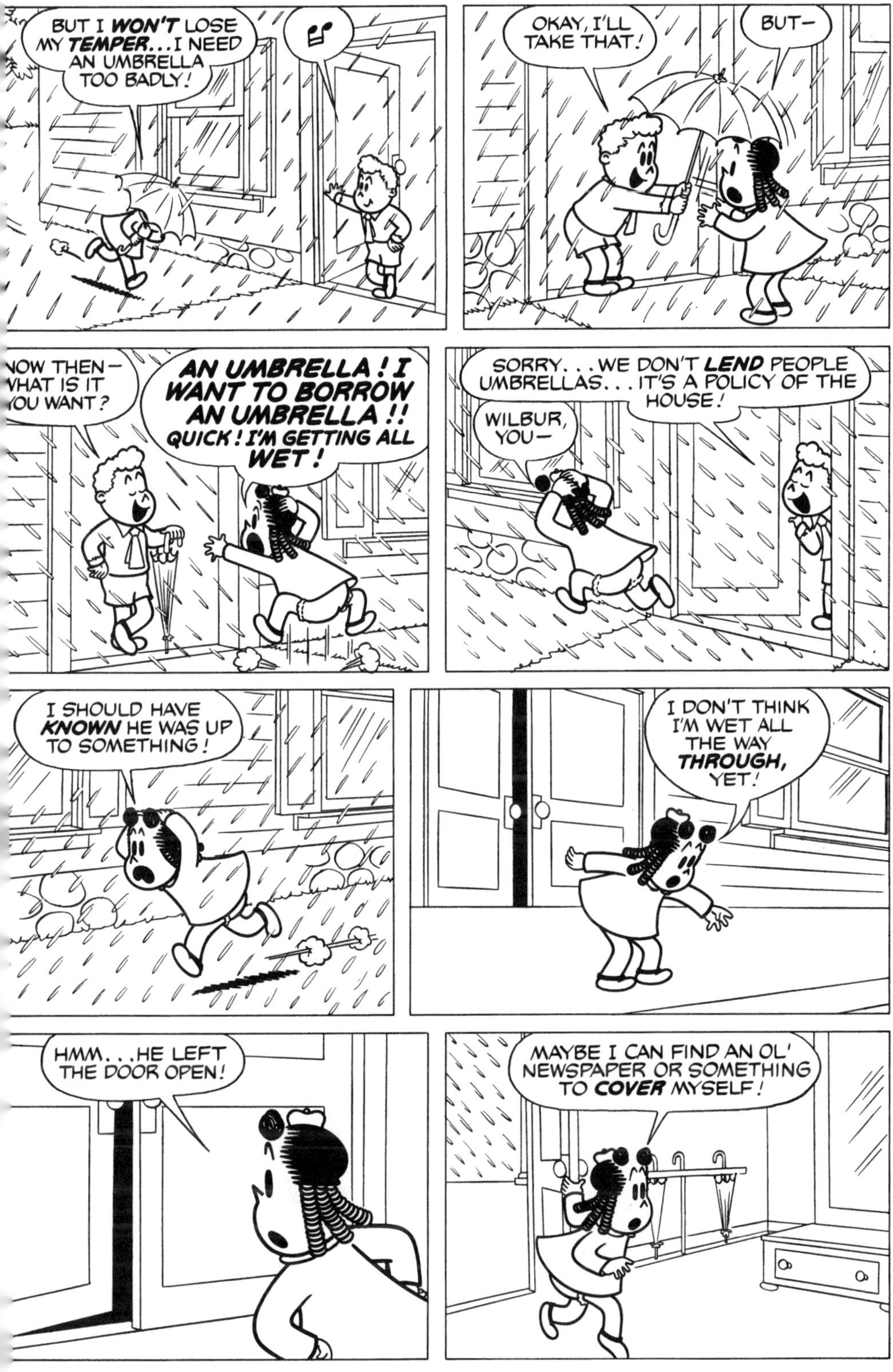
BUT I WON'T LOSE MY TEMPER...I NEED AN UMBRELLA TOO BADLY!
OKAY, I'LL TAKE THAT!
BUT—
NOW THEN—WHAT IS IT YOU WANT?
AN UMBRELLA! I WANT TO BORROW AN UMBRELLA!! QUICK! I'M GETTING ALL WET!
SORRY...WE DON'T LEND PEOPLE UMBRELLAS...IT'S A POLICY OF THE HOUSE!
WILBUR, YOU—
I SHOULD HAVE KNOWN HE WAS UP TO SOMETHING!
I DON'T THINK I'M WET ALL THE WAY THROUGH, YET!
HMM...HE LEFT THE DOOR OPEN!
MAYBE I CAN FIND AN OL' NEWSPAPER OR SOMETHING TO COVER MYSELF!

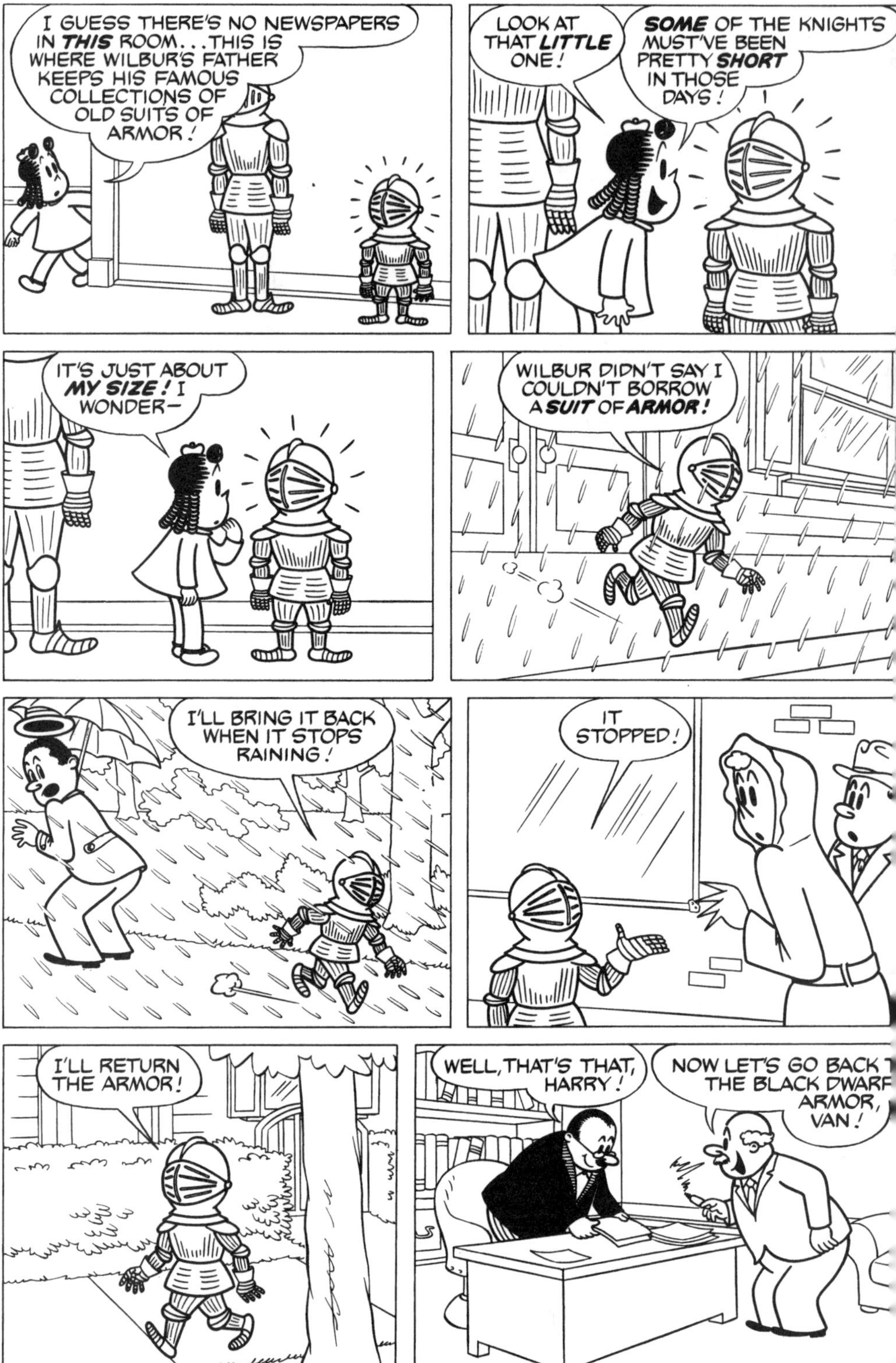
I GUESS THERE'S NO NEWSPAPERS IN THIS ROOM...THIS IS WHERE WILBUR'S FATHER KEEPS HIS FAMOUS COLLECTIONS OF OLD SUITS OF ARMOR!
LOOK AT THAT LITTLE ONE!
SOME OF THE KNIGHTS MUST'VE BEEN PRETTY SHORT IN THOSE DAYS!
IT'S JUST ABOUT MY SIZE! I WONDER—
WILBUR DIDN'T SAY I COULDN'T BORROW A SUIT OF ARMOR!
I'LL BRING IT BACK WHEN IT STOPS RAINING!
IT STOPPED!
I'LL RETURN THE ARMOR!
WELL, THAT'S THAT, HARRY!
NOW LET'S GO BACK T
THE BLACK DWARF
ARMOR,
VAN!

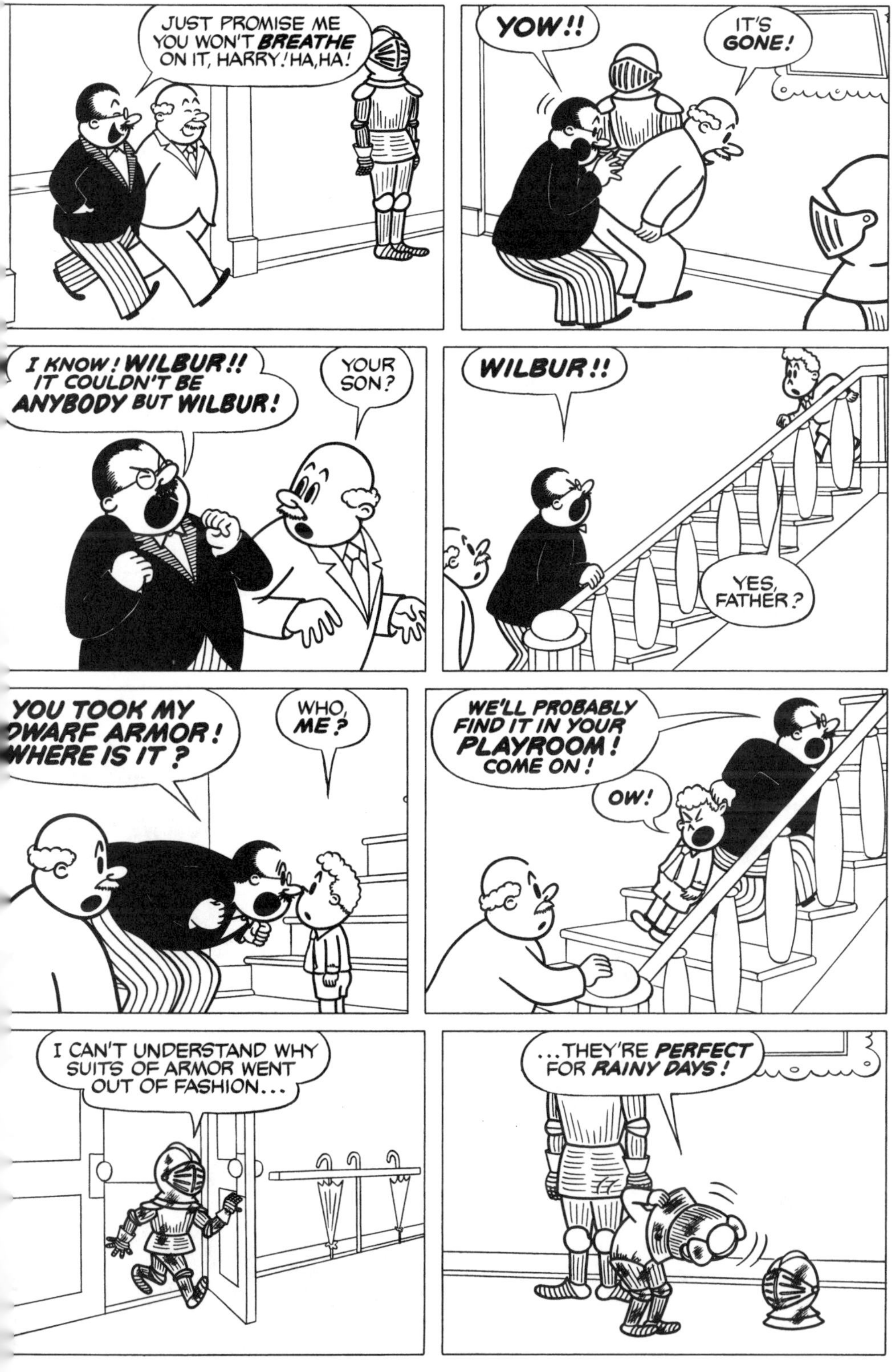
JUST PROMISE ME YOU WON'T BREATHE ON IT, HARRY! HA,HA!
YOW!!
IT'S GONE!
I KNOW! WILBUR!! IT COULDN'T BE ANYBODY BUT WILBUR!
YOUR SON?
WILBUR!!
YES, FATHER?
YOU TOOK MY DWARF ARMOR! WHERE IS IT?
WHO, ME?
WE'LL PROBABLY FIND IT IN YOUR PLAYROOM! COME ON!
OW!
I CAN'T UNDERSTAND WHY SUITS OF ARMOR WENT OUT OF FASHION...
...THEY'RE PERFECT FOR RAINY DAYS!

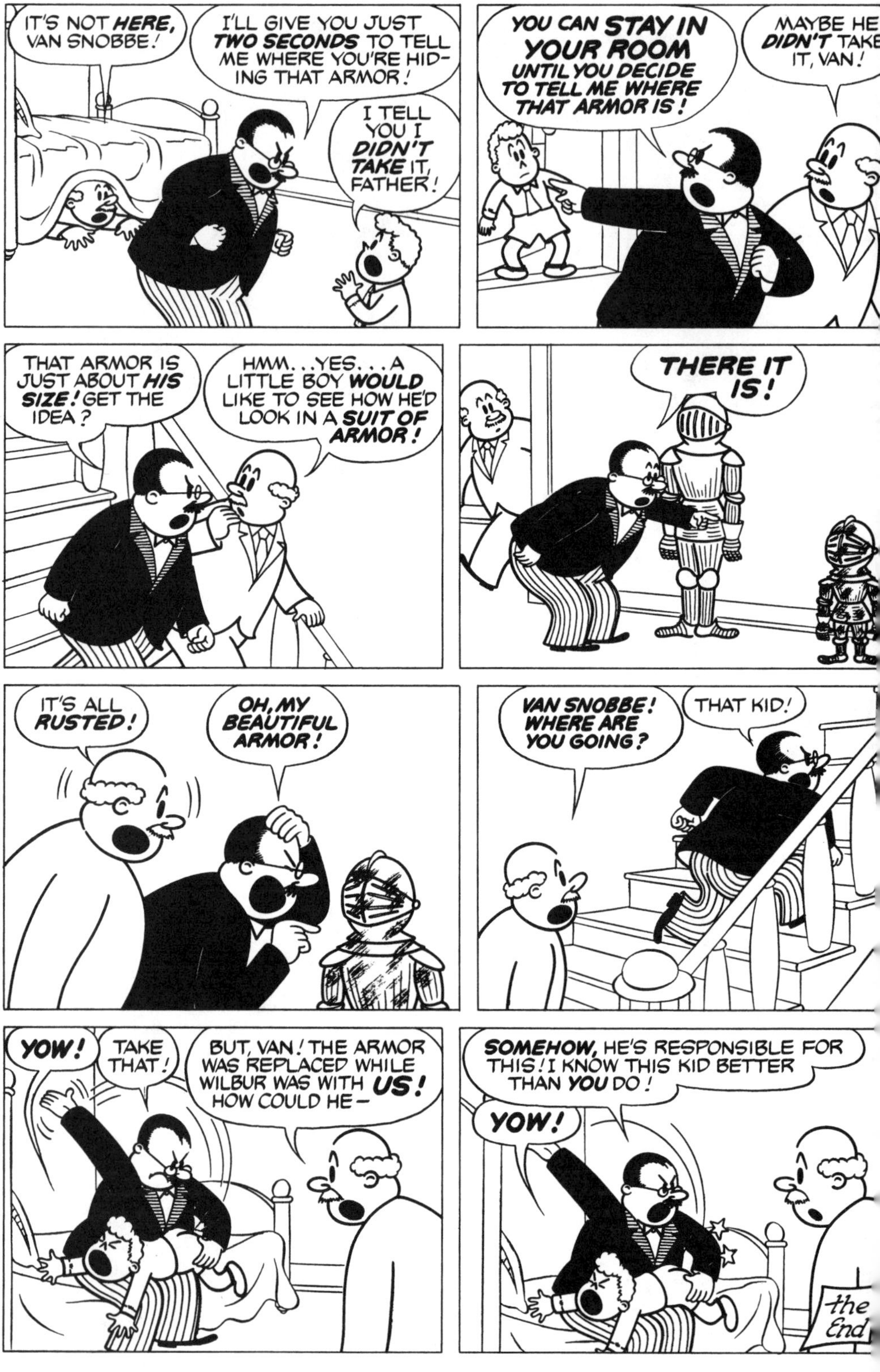
IT'S NOT HERE, VAN SNOBBE!
I'LL GIVE YOU JUST TWO SECONDS TO TELL ME WHERE YOU'RE HIDING THAT ARMOR!
I TELL YOU I DIDN'T TAKE IT, FATHER!
YOU CAN STAY IN YOUR ROOM UNTIL YOU DECIDE TO TELL ME WHERE THAT ARMOR IS!
MAYBE HE DIDN'T TAKE IT, VAN!
THAT ARMOR IS JUST ABOUT HIS SIZE! GET THE IDEA?
HMM...YES...A LITTLE BOY WOULD LIKE TO SEE HOW HE'D LOOK IN A SUIT OF ARMOR!
THERE IT IS!
IT'S ALL RUSTED!
OH, MY BEAUTIFUL ARMOR!
VAN SNOBBE! WHERE ARE YOU GOING?
THAT KID!
YOW!
TAKE THAT!
BUT, VAN! THE ARMOR WAS REPLACED WHILE WILBUR WAS WITH US! HOW COULD HE—
SOMEHOW, HE'S RESPONSIBLE FOR THIS! I KNOW THIS KID BETTER THAN YOU DO!
YOW!
the End

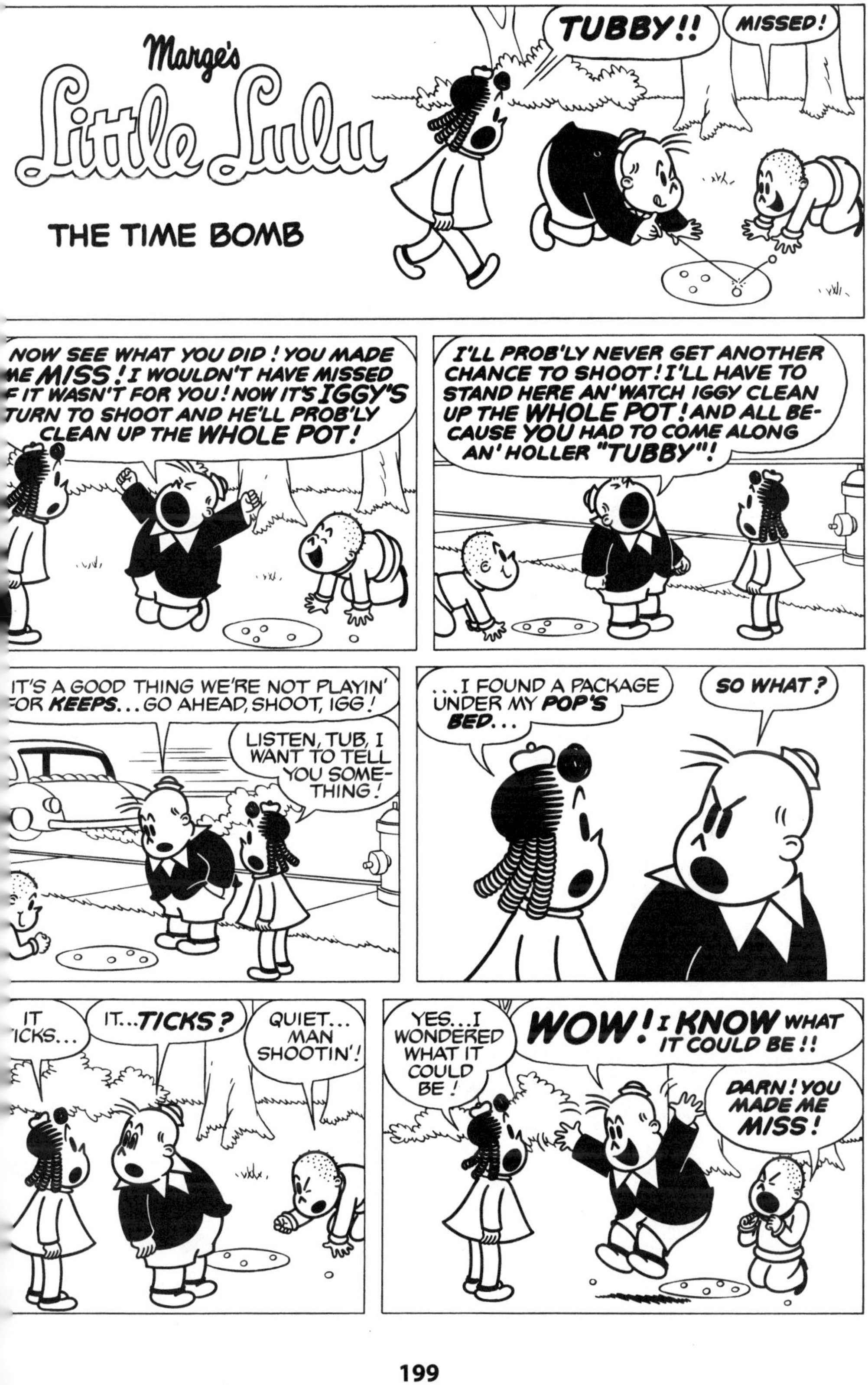
Marge's
Little Lulu
THE TIME BOMB
TUBBY!!
MISSED!
NOW SEE WHAT YOU DID! YOU MADE ME MISS! I WOULDN'T HAVE MISSED IF IT WASN'T FOR YOU! NOW IT'S IGGY'S TURN TO SHOOT AND HE'LL PROB'LY CLEAN UP THE WHOLE POT!
I'LL PROB'LY NEVER GET ANOTHER CHANCE TO SHOOT! I'LL HAVE TO STAND HERE AN' WATCH IGGY CLEAN UP THE WHOLE POT! AND ALL BECAUSE YOU HAD TO COME ALONG AN' HOLLER "TUBBY"!
IT'S A GOOD THING WE'RE NOT PLAYIN' FOR KEEPS... GO AHEAD, SHOOT, IGG!
LISTEN, TUB, I WANT TO TELL YOU SOMETHING!
...I FOUND A PACKAGE UNDER MY POP'S BED...
SO WHAT?
IT TICKS...
IT...TICKS?
QUIET... MAN SHOOTIN'!
YES...I WONDERED WHAT IT COULD BE!
WOW! I KNOW WHAT IT COULD BE!!
DARN! YOU MADE ME MISS!

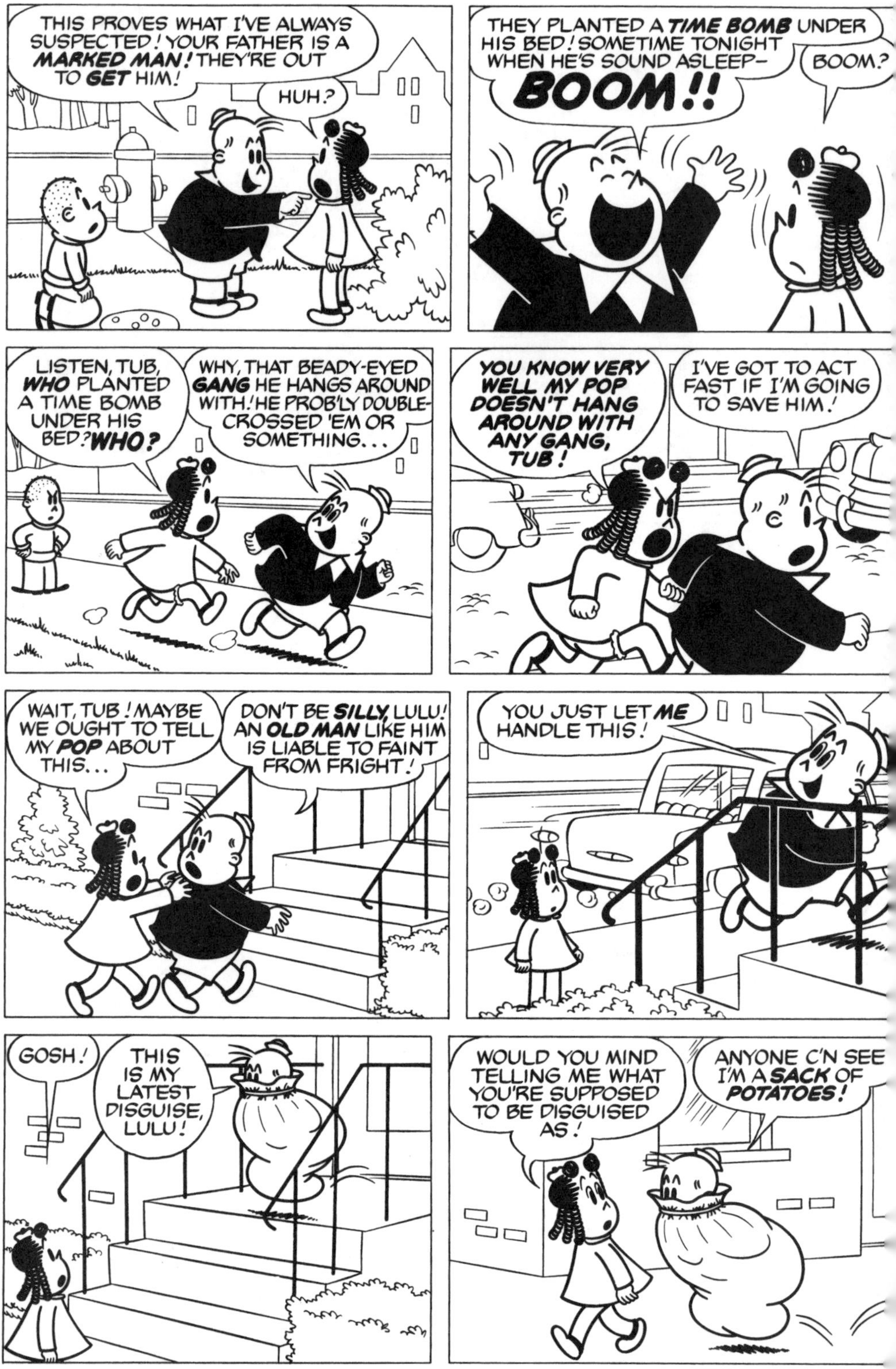
THIS PROVES WHAT I'VE ALWAYS SUSPECTED! YOUR FATHER IS A MARKED MAN! THEY'RE OUT TO GET HIM!
HUH?
THEY PLANTED A TIME BOMB UNDER HIS BED! SOMETIME TONIGHT WHEN HE'S SOUND ASLEEP—
BOOM!!
BOOM?
LISTEN, TUB, WHO PLANTED A TIME BOMB UNDER HIS BED? WHO?
WHY, THAT BEADY-EYED GANG HE HANGS AROUND WITH! HE PROB'LY DOUBLE-CROSSED 'EM OR SOMETHING...
YOU KNOW VERY WELL MY POP DOESN'T HANG AROUND WITH ANY GANG, TUB!
I'VE GOT TO ACT FAST IF I'M GOING TO SAVE HIM!
WAIT, TUB! MAYBE WE OUGHT TO TELL MY POP ABOUT THIS...
DON'T BE SILLY, LULU! AN OLD MAN LIKE HIM IS LIABLE TO FAINT FROM FRIGHT!
YOU JUST LET ME HANDLE THIS!
GOSH!
THIS IS MY LATEST DISGUISE, LULU!
WOULD YOU MIND TELLING ME WHAT YOU'RE SUPPOSED TO BE DISGUISED AS!
ANYONE C'N SEE I'M A SACK OF POTATOES!

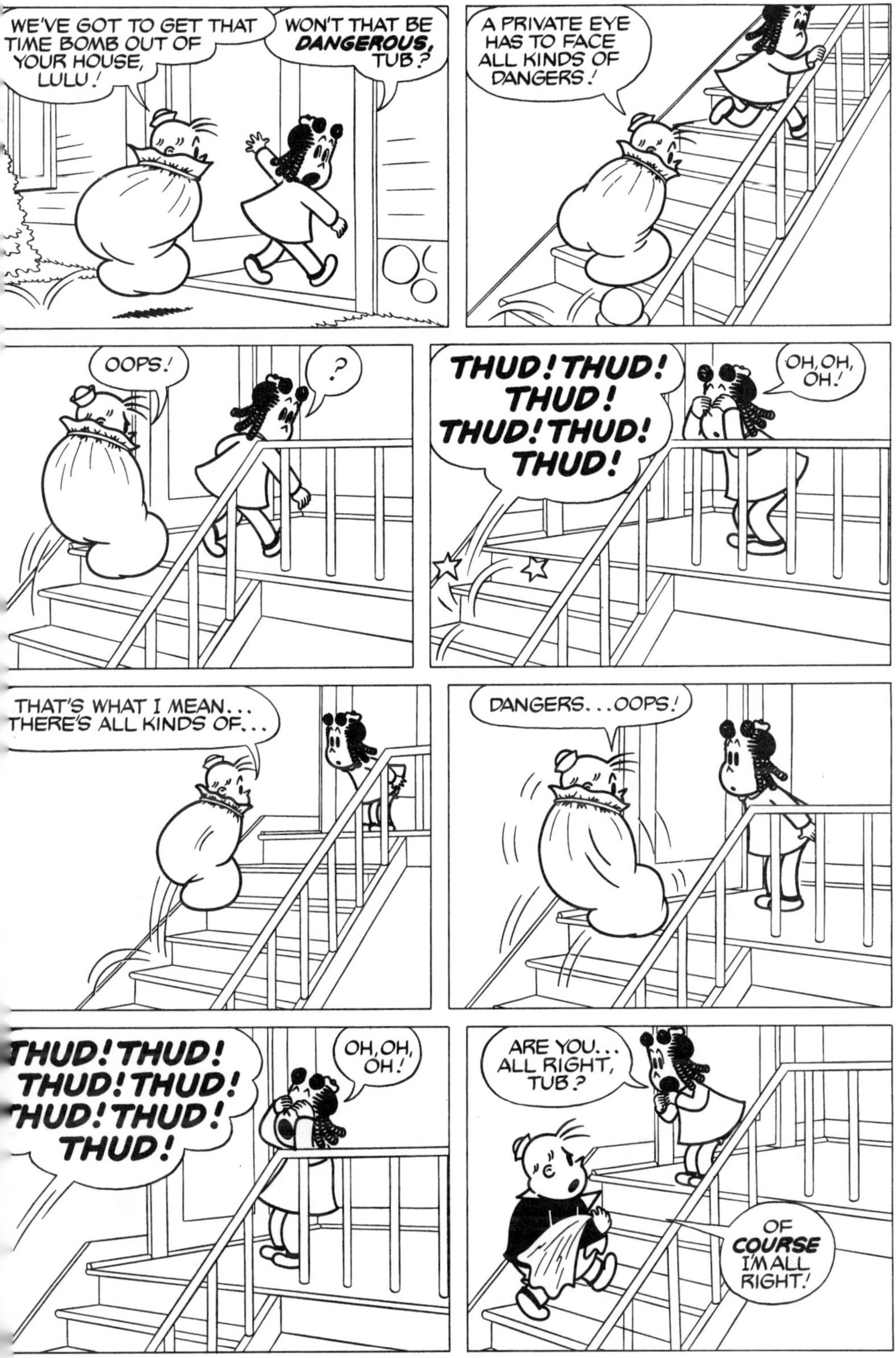
WE'VE GOT TO GET THAT TIME BOMB OUT OF YOUR HOUSE, LULU!
WON'T THAT BE DANGEROUS, TUB?
A PRIVATE EYE HAS TO FACE ALL KINDS OF DANGERS!
OOPS!
?
THUD! THUD! THUD! THUD! THUD! THUD!
OH, OH, OH!
THAT'S WHAT I MEAN... THERE'S ALL KINDS OF...
DANGERS...OOPS!
THUD! THUD! THUD! THUD! THUD! THUD! THUD!
OH, OH, OH!
ARE YOU... ALL RIGHT, TUB?
OF COURSE I'M ALL RIGHT!

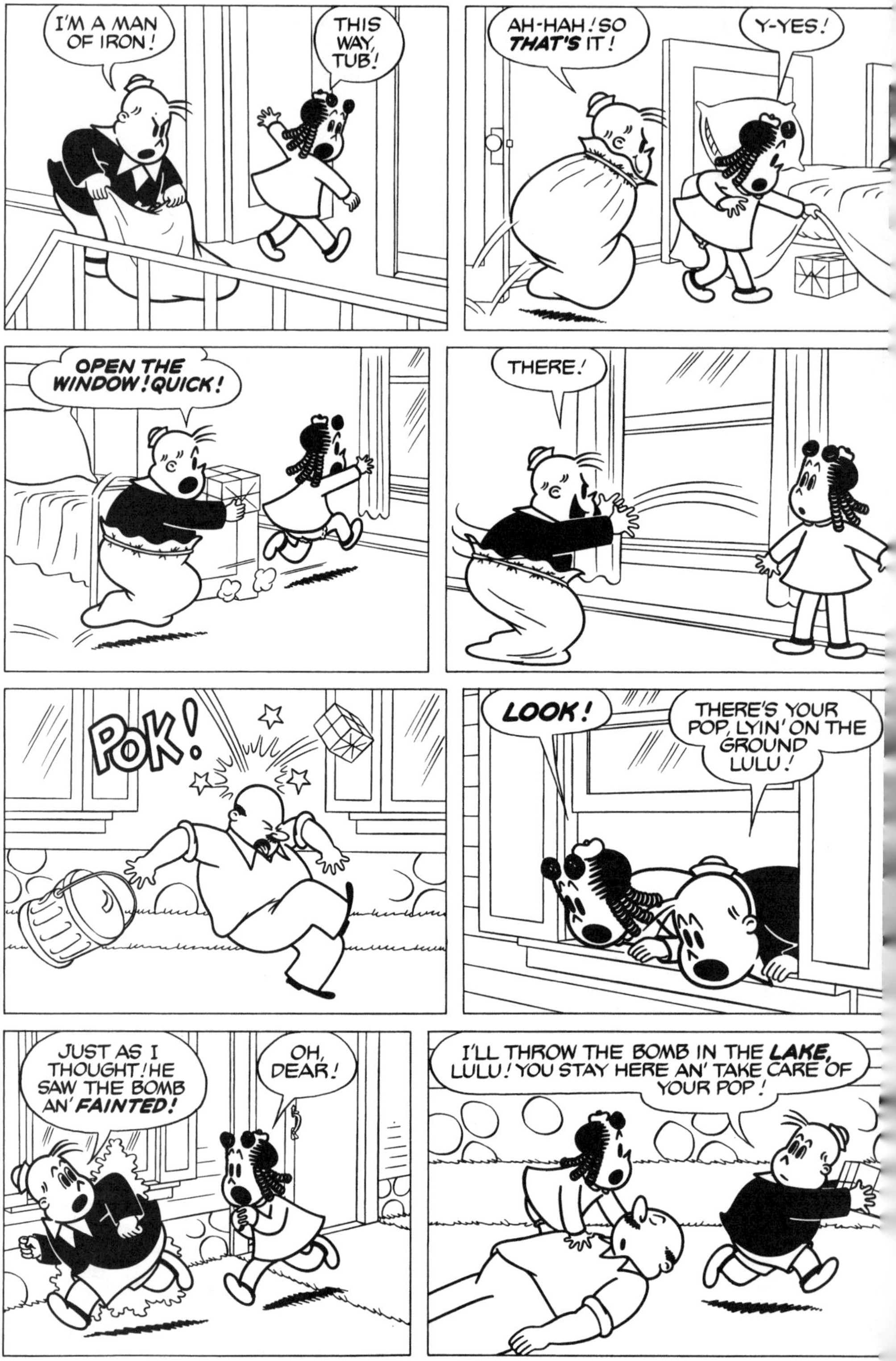
I'M A MAN OF IRON!
THIS WAY, TUB!
AH-HAH! SO THAT'S IT!
Y-YES!
OPEN THE WINDOW! QUICK!
THERE!
POK!
LOOK!
THERE'S YOUR POP, LYIN' ON THE GROUND LULU!
JUST AS I THOUGHT! HE SAW THE BOMB AN' FAINTED!
OH, DEAR!
I'LL THROW THE BOMB IN THE LAKE, LULU! YOU STAY HERE AN' TAKE CARE OF YOUR POP!

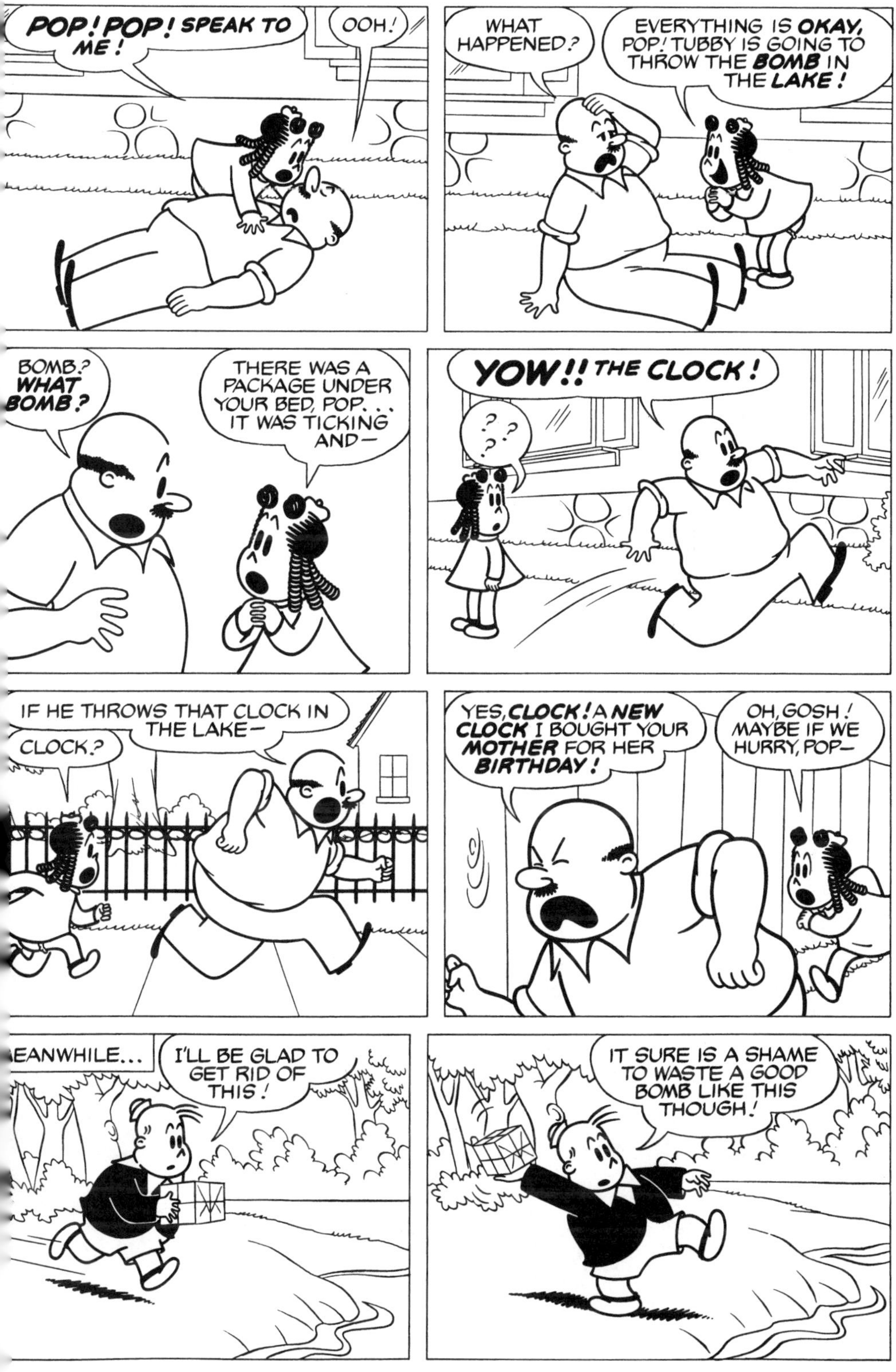
POP! POP! SPEAK TO ME!
OOH!
WHAT HAPPENED?
EVERYTHING IS OKAY, POP! TUBBY IS GOING TO THROW THE BOMB IN THE LAKE!
BOMB? WHAT BOMB?
THERE WAS A PACKAGE UNDER YOUR BED, POP. . . IT WAS TICKING AND—
YOW!! THE CLOCK!
? ? ?
IF HE THROWS THAT CLOCK IN THE LAKE—
CLOCK?
YES, CLOCK! A NEW CLOCK I BOUGHT YOUR MOTHER FOR HER BIRTHDAY!
OH, GOSH! MAYBE IF WE HURRY, POP—
EANWHILE...
I'LL BE GLAD TO GET RID OF THIS!
IT SURE IS A SHAME TO WASTE A GOOD BOMB LIKE THIS THOUGH!

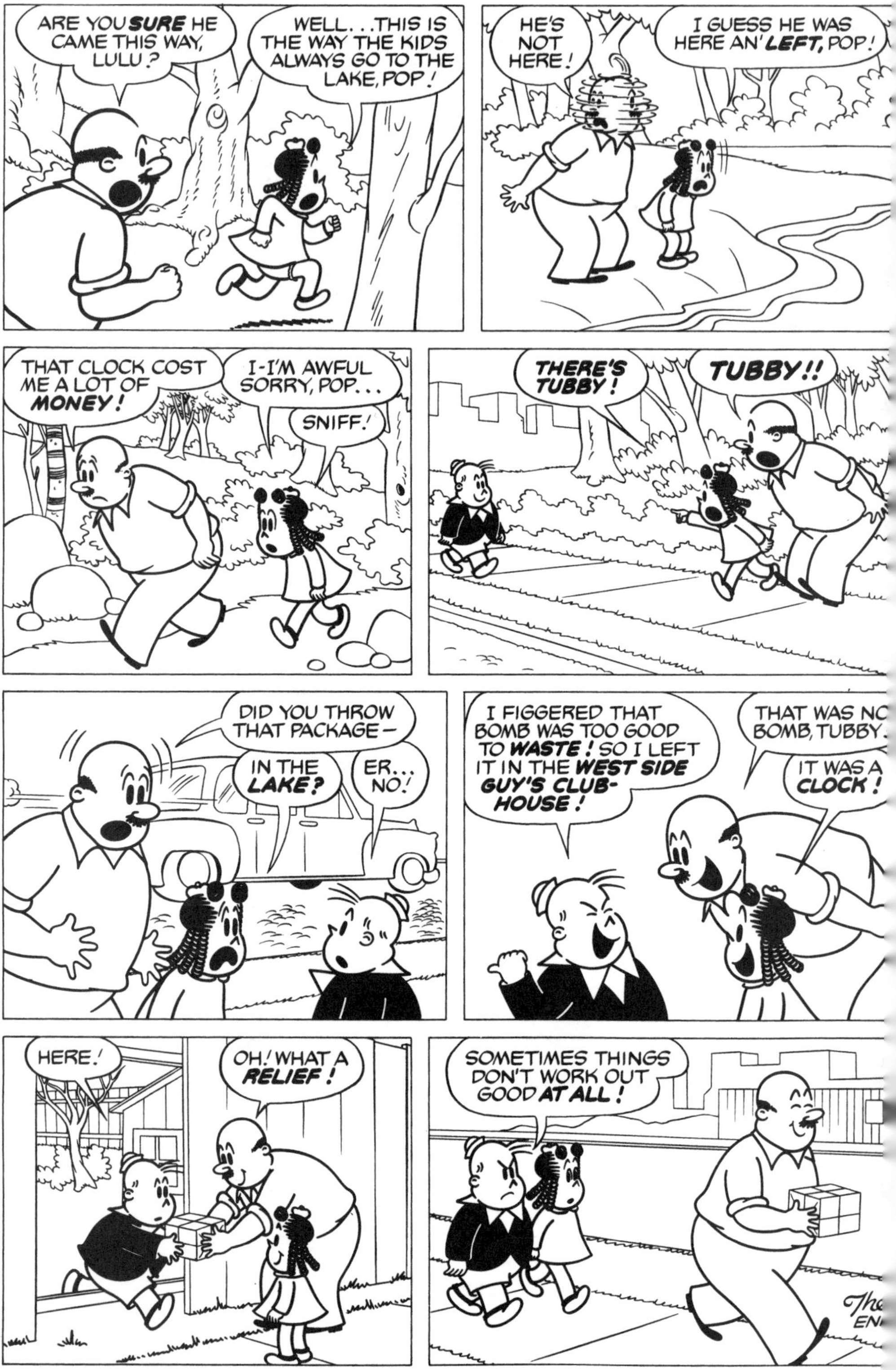
ARE YOU **SURE** HE CAME THIS WAY, LULU?
WELL...THIS IS THE WAY THE KIDS ALWAYS GO TO THE LAKE, POP!
HE'S NOT HERE!
I GUESS HE WAS HERE AN' **LEFT,** POP!
THAT CLOCK COST ME A LOT OF **MONEY!**
I-I'M AWFUL SORRY, POP...
SNIFF!
THERE'S TUBBY!
TUBBY!!
DID YOU THROW THAT PACKAGE—
IN THE **LAKE?**
ER... NO!
I FIGGERED THAT BOMB WAS TOO GOOD TO **WASTE!** SO I LEFT IT IN THE **WEST SIDE GUY'S CLUB-HOUSE!**
THAT WAS NO BOMB, TUBBY.
IT WAS A **CLOCK!**
HERE!
OH! WHAT A **RELIEF!**
SOMETIMES THINGS DON'T WORK OUT GOOD **AT ALL!**

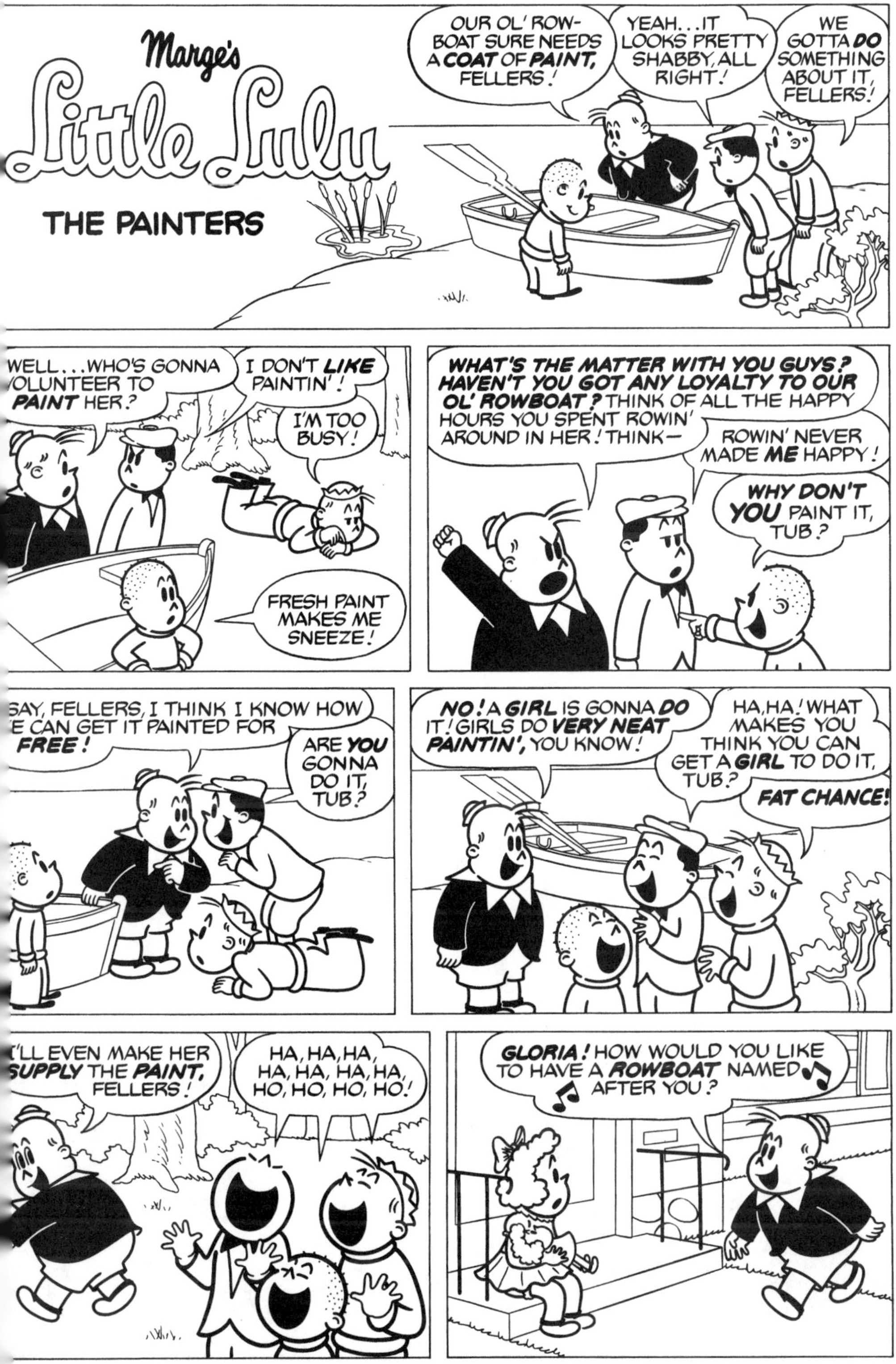
Marge's Little Lulu
THE PAINTERS
OUR OL' ROW-BOAT SURE NEEDS A COAT OF PAINT, FELLERS!
YEAH...IT LOOKS PRETTY SHABBY, ALL RIGHT!
WE GOTTA DO SOMETHING ABOUT IT, FELLERS!
WELL...WHO'S GONNA VOLUNTEER TO PAINT HER?
I DON'T LIKE PAINTIN'!
I'M TOO BUSY!
FRESH PAINT MAKES ME SNEEZE!
WHAT'S THE MATTER WITH YOU GUYS? HAVEN'T YOU GOT ANY LOYALTY TO OUR OL' ROWBOAT? THINK OF ALL THE HAPPY HOURS YOU SPENT ROWIN' AROUND IN HER! THINK—
ROWIN' NEVER MADE ME HAPPY!
WHY DON'T YOU PAINT IT, TUB?
SAY, FELLERS, I THINK I KNOW HOW WE CAN GET IT PAINTED FOR FREE!
ARE YOU GONNA DO IT, TUB?
NO! A GIRL IS GONNA DO IT! GIRLS DO VERY NEAT PAINTIN', YOU KNOW!
HA, HA! WHAT MAKES YOU THINK YOU CAN GET A GIRL TO DO IT, TUB?
FAT CHANCE!
I'LL EVEN MAKE HER SUPPLY THE PAINT, FELLERS!
HA, HA, HA, HA, HA, HA, HA, HO, HO, HO, HO!
GLORIA! HOW WOULD YOU LIKE TO HAVE A ROWBOAT NAMED AFTER YOU?

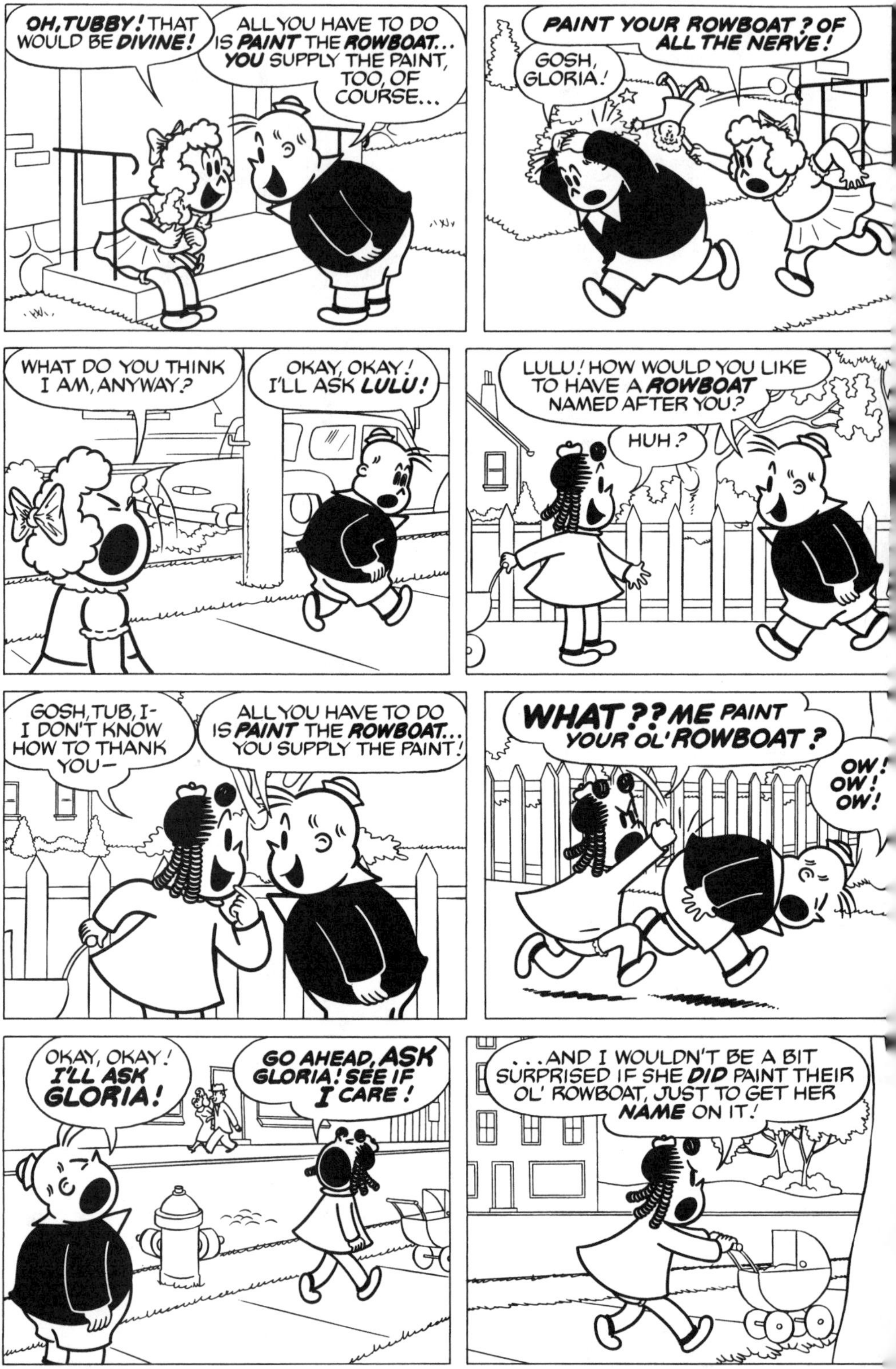
OH, TUBBY! THAT WOULD BE DIVINE!
ALL YOU HAVE TO DO IS PAINT THE ROWBOAT... YOU SUPPLY THE PAINT, TOO, OF COURSE...
PAINT YOUR ROWBOAT? OF ALL THE NERVE!
GOSH, GLORIA!
WHAT DO YOU THINK I AM, ANYWAY?
OKAY, OKAY! I'LL ASK LULU!
LULU! HOW WOULD YOU LIKE TO HAVE A ROWBOAT NAMED AFTER YOU?
HUH?
GOSH, TUB, I- I DON'T KNOW HOW TO THANK YOU—
ALL YOU HAVE TO DO IS PAINT THE ROWBOAT... YOU SUPPLY THE PAINT!
WHAT?? ME PAINT YOUR OL' ROWBOAT?
OW! OW! OW!
OKAY, OKAY! I'LL ASK GLORIA!
GO AHEAD, ASK GLORIA! SEE IF I CARE!
...AND I WOULDN'T BE A BIT SURPRISED IF SHE DID PAINT THEIR OL' ROWBOAT, JUST TO GET HER NAME ON IT!

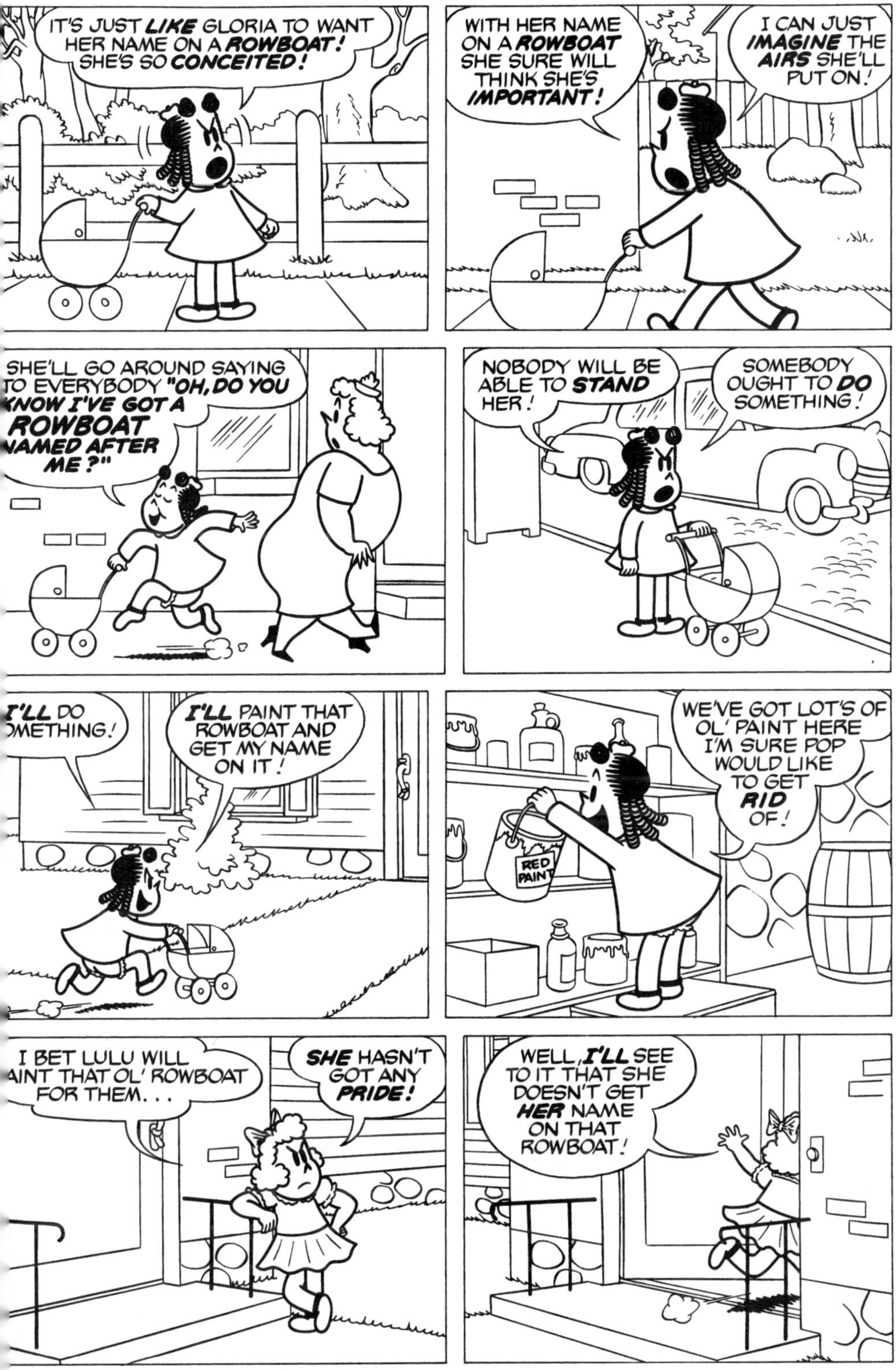
IT'S JUST LIKE GLORIA TO WANT HER NAME ON A ROWBOAT! SHE'S SO CONCEITED!
WITH HER NAME ON A ROWBOAT SHE SURE WILL THINK SHE'S IMPORTANT!
I CAN JUST IMAGINE THE AIRS SHE'LL PUT ON!
SHE'LL GO AROUND SAYING TO EVERYBODY "OH, DO YOU NOW I'VE GOT A ROWBOAT AMED AFTER ME?"
NOBODY WILL BE ABLE TO STAND HER!
SOMEBODY OUGHT TO DO SOMETHING!
'LL DO OMETHING!
I'LL PAINT THAT ROWBOAT AND GET MY NAME ON IT!
WE'VE GOT LOT'S OF OL' PAINT HERE I'M SURE POP WOULD LIKE TO GET RID OF!
RED PAINT
I BET LULU WILL AINT THAT OL' ROWBOAT FOR THEM...
SHE HASN'T GOT ANY PRIDE!
WELL, I'LL SEE TO IT THAT SHE DOESN'T GET HER NAME ON THAT ROWBOAT!

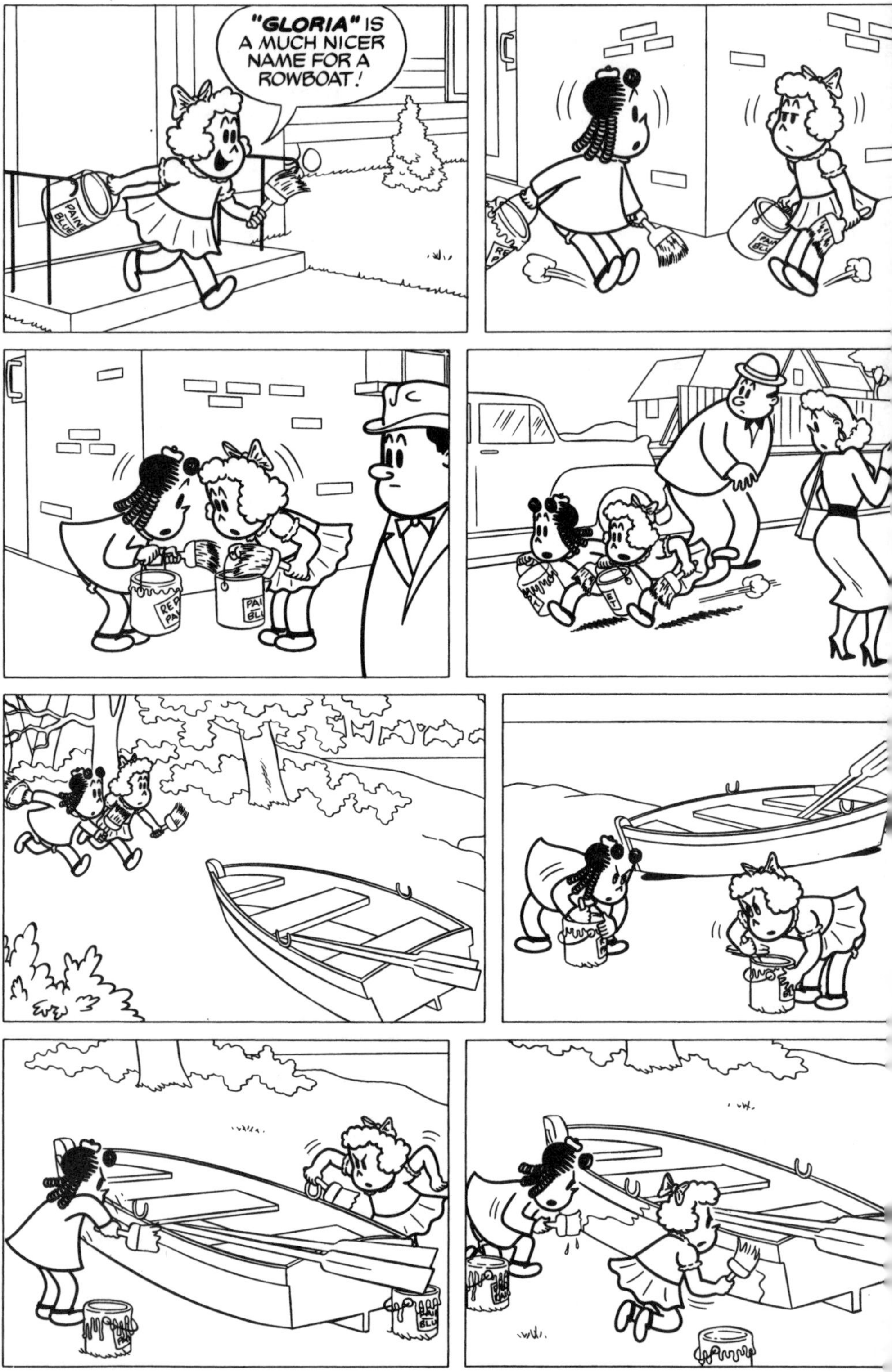
"GLORIA" IS A MUCH NICER NAME FOR A ROWBOAT!

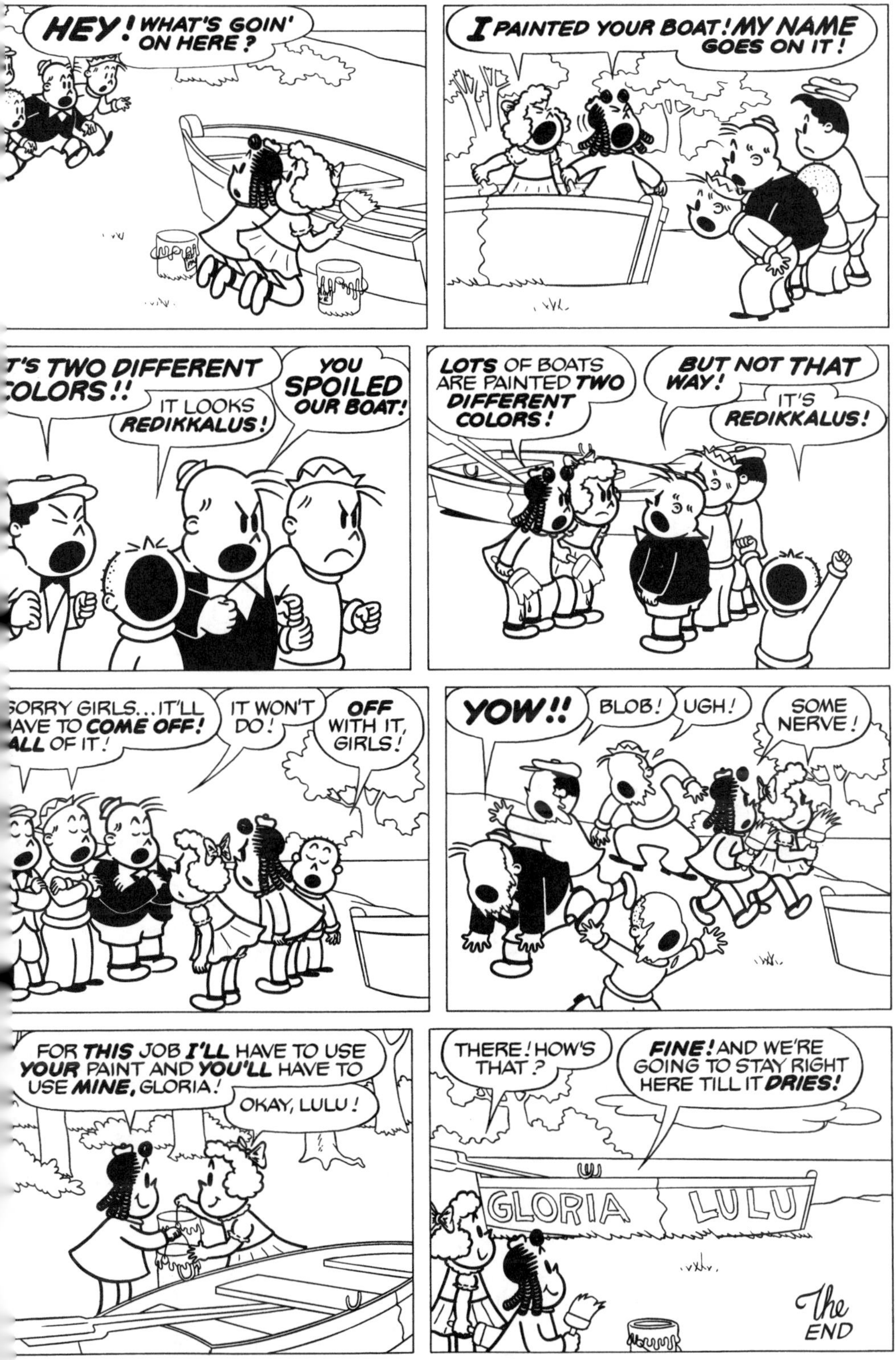
HEY! WHAT'S GOIN' ON HERE?
I PAINTED YOUR BOAT! MY NAME GOES ON IT!
T'S TWO DIFFERENT COLORS!!
IT LOOKS REDIKKALUS!
YOU SPOILED OUR BOAT!
LOTS OF BOATS ARE PAINTED TWO DIFFERENT COLORS!
BUT NOT THAT WAY!
IT'S REDIKKALUS!
SORRY GIRLS...IT'LL AVE TO COME OFF! ALL OF IT!
IT WON'T DO!
OFF WITH IT, GIRLS!
YOW!!
BLOB!
UGH!
SOME NERVE!
FOR THIS JOB I'LL HAVE TO USE YOUR PAINT AND YOU'LL HAVE TO USE MINE, GLORIA!
OKAY, LULU!
THERE! HOW'S THAT?
FINE! AND WE'RE GOING TO STAY RIGHT HERE TILL IT DRIES!
GLORIA
LULU
The END

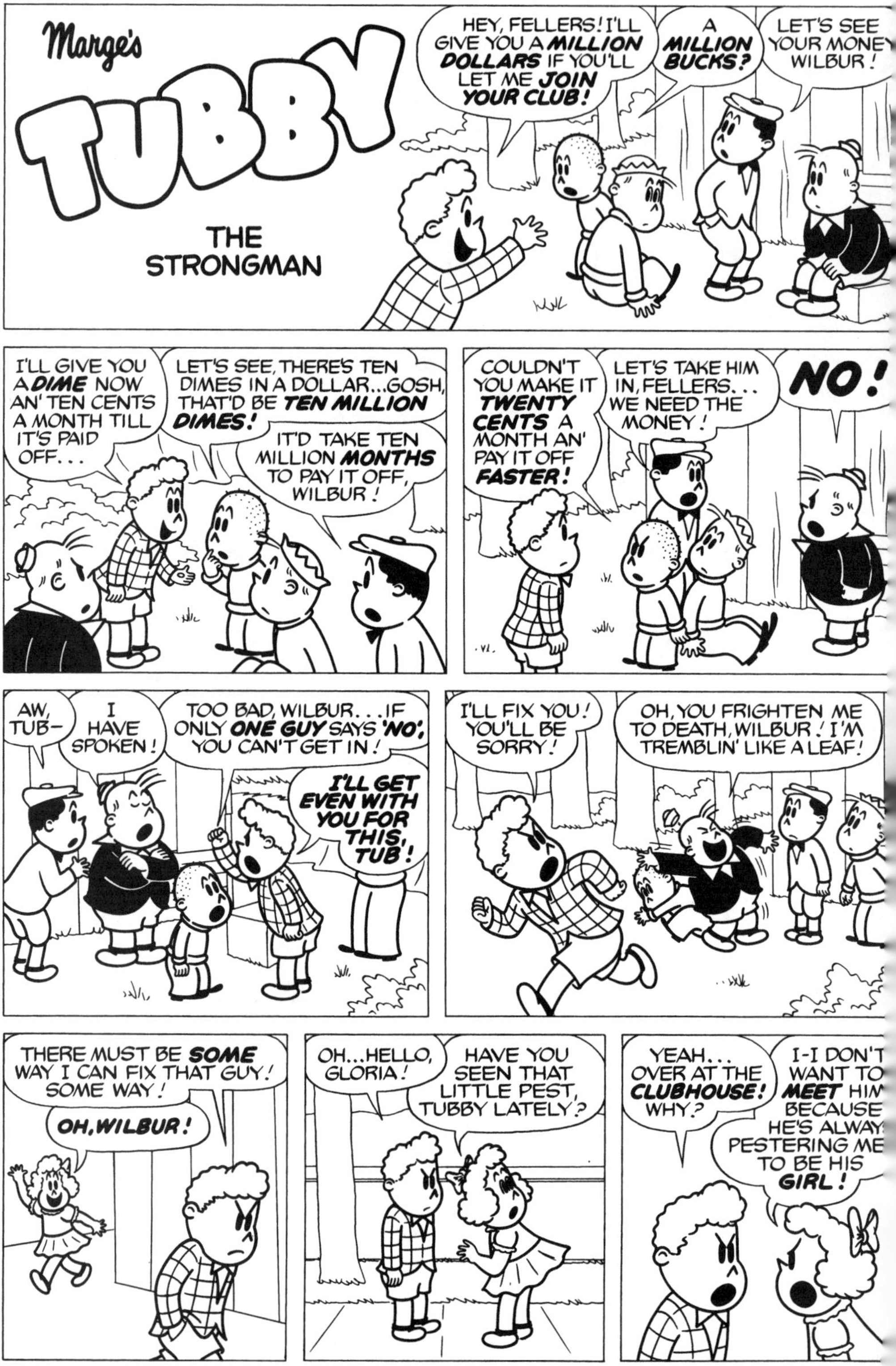
Marge's
TUBBY
THE STRONGMAN
HEY, FELLERS! I'LL GIVE YOU A MILLION DOLLARS IF YOU'LL LET ME JOIN YOUR CLUB!
A MILLION BUCKS?
LET'S SEE YOUR MONEY WILBUR!
I'LL GIVE YOU A DIME NOW AN' TEN CENTS A MONTH TILL IT'S PAID OFF...
LET'S SEE, THERE'S TEN DIMES IN A DOLLAR...GOSH, THAT'D BE TEN MILLION DIMES!
IT'D TAKE TEN MILLION MONTHS TO PAY IT OFF, WILBUR!
COULDN'T YOU MAKE IT TWENTY CENTS A MONTH AN' PAY IT OFF FASTER!
LET'S TAKE HIM IN, FELLERS... WE NEED THE MONEY!
NO!
AW, TUB—
I HAVE SPOKEN!
TOO BAD, WILBUR...IF ONLY ONE GUY SAYS 'NO', YOU CAN'T GET IN!
I'LL GET EVEN WITH YOU FOR THIS, TUB!
I'LL FIX YOU! YOU'LL BE SORRY!
OH, YOU FRIGHTEN ME TO DEATH, WILBUR! I'M TREMBLIN' LIKE A LEAF!
THERE MUST BE SOME WAY I CAN FIX THAT GUY! SOME WAY!
OH, WILBUR!
OH...HELLO, GLORIA!
HAVE YOU SEEN THAT LITTLE PEST, TUBBY LATELY?
YEAH... OVER AT THE CLUBHOUSE! WHY?
I-I DON'T WANT TO MEET HIM BECAUSE HE'S ALWAYS PESTERING ME TO BE HIS GIRL!

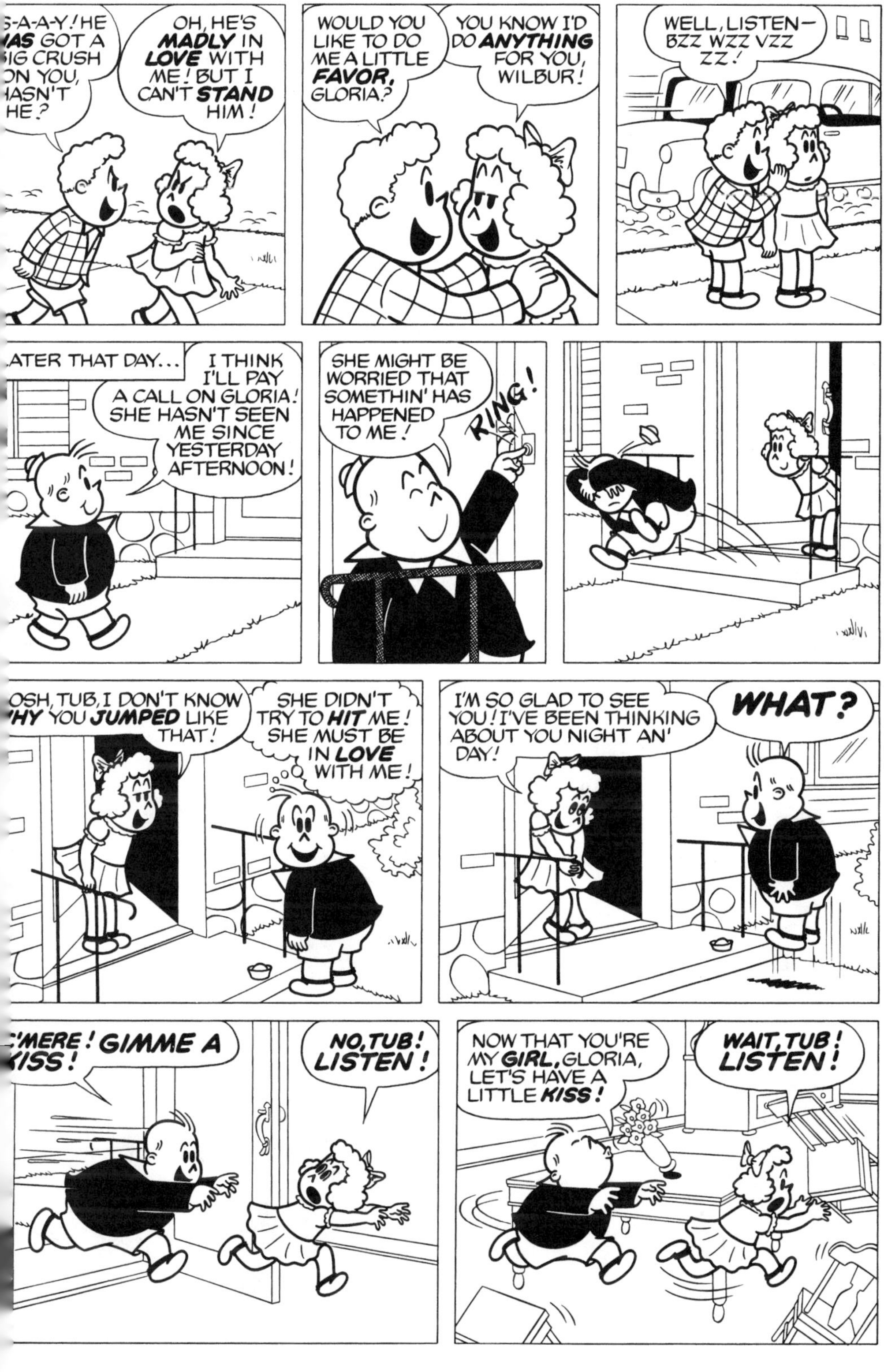
S-A-A-Y! HE HAS GOT A BIG CRUSH ON YOU, HASN'T HE?
OH, HE'S MADLY IN LOVE WITH ME! BUT I CAN'T STAND HIM!
WOULD YOU LIKE TO DO ME A LITTLE FAVOR, GLORIA?
YOU KNOW I'D DO ANYTHING FOR YOU, WILBUR!
WELL, LISTEN— BZZ WZZ VZZ ZZ!
LATER THAT DAY...
I THINK I'LL PAY A CALL ON GLORIA! SHE HASN'T SEEN ME SINCE YESTERDAY AFTERNOON!
SHE MIGHT BE WORRIED THAT SOMETHIN' HAS HAPPENED TO ME!
RING!
GOSH, TUB, I DON'T KNOW WHY YOU JUMPED LIKE THAT!
SHE DIDN'T TRY TO HIT ME! SHE MUST BE IN LOVE WITH ME!
I'M SO GLAD TO SEE YOU! I'VE BEEN THINKING ABOUT YOU NIGHT AN' DAY!
WHAT?
C'MERE! GIMME A KISS!
NO, TUB! LISTEN!
NOW THAT YOU'RE MY GIRL, GLORIA, LET'S HAVE A LITTLE KISS!
WAIT, TUB! LISTEN!

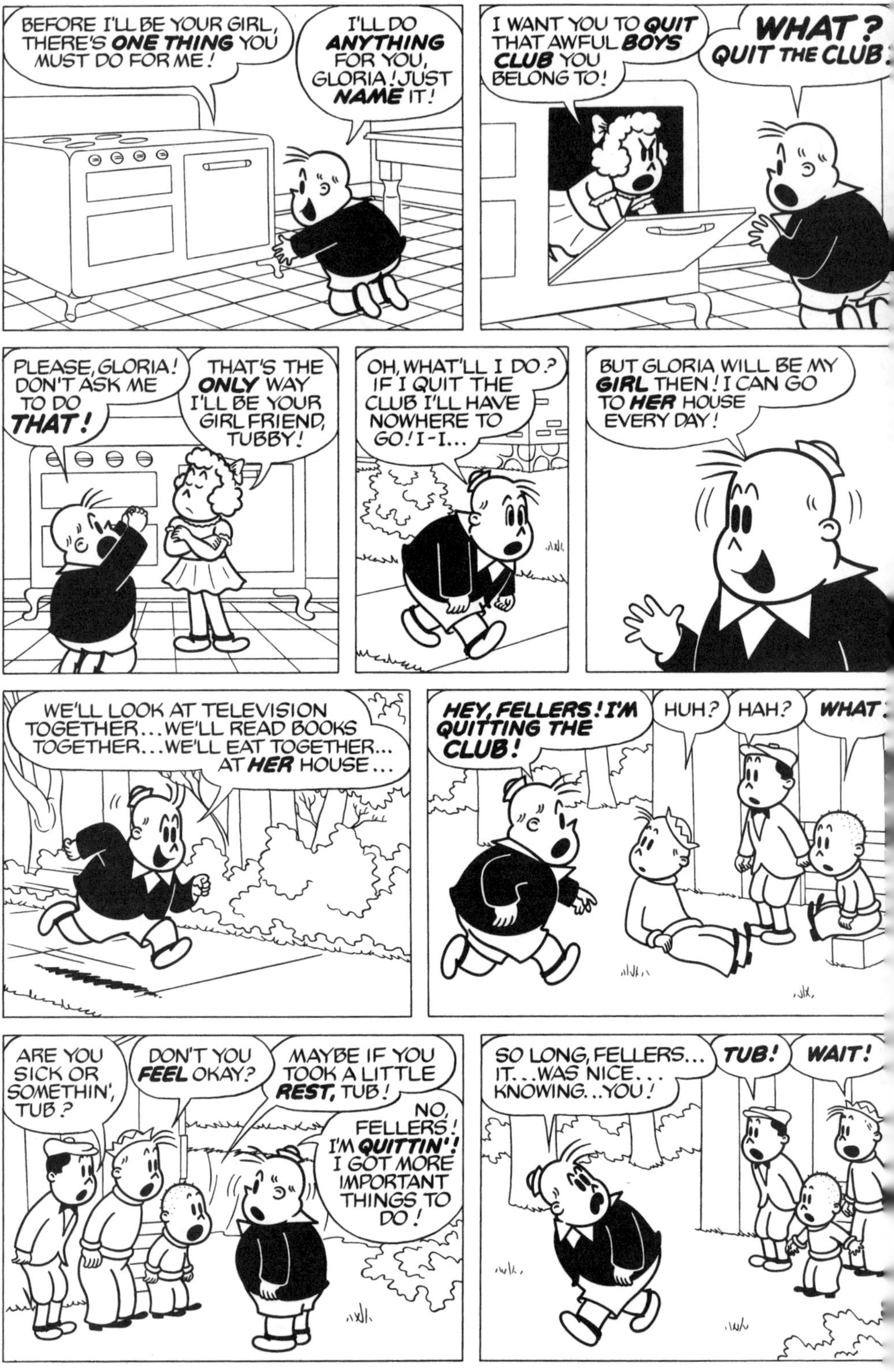
BEFORE I'LL BE YOUR GIRL, THERE'S ONE THING YOU MUST DO FOR ME!
I'LL DO ANYTHING FOR YOU, GLORIA! JUST NAME IT!
I WANT YOU TO QUIT THAT AWFUL BOYS CLUB YOU BELONG TO!
WHAT? QUIT THE CLUB?
PLEASE, GLORIA! DON'T ASK ME TO DO THAT!
THAT'S THE ONLY WAY I'LL BE YOUR GIRL FRIEND, TUBBY!
OH, WHAT'LL I DO? IF I QUIT THE CLUB I'LL HAVE NOWHERE TO GO! I-I...
BUT GLORIA WILL BE MY GIRL THEN! I CAN GO TO HER HOUSE EVERY DAY!
WE'LL LOOK AT TELEVISION TOGETHER... WE'LL READ BOOKS TOGETHER... WE'LL EAT TOGETHER... AT HER HOUSE...
HEY, FELLERS! I'M QUITTING THE CLUB!
HUH?
HAH?
WHAT
ARE YOU SICK OR SOMETHIN', TUB?
DON'T YOU FEEL OKAY?
MAYBE IF YOU TOOK A LITTLE REST, TUB!
NO, FELLERS! I'M QUITTIN'! I GOT MORE IMPORTANT THINGS TO DO!
SO LONG, FELLERS... IT... WAS NICE... KNOWING... YOU!
TUB!
WAIT!

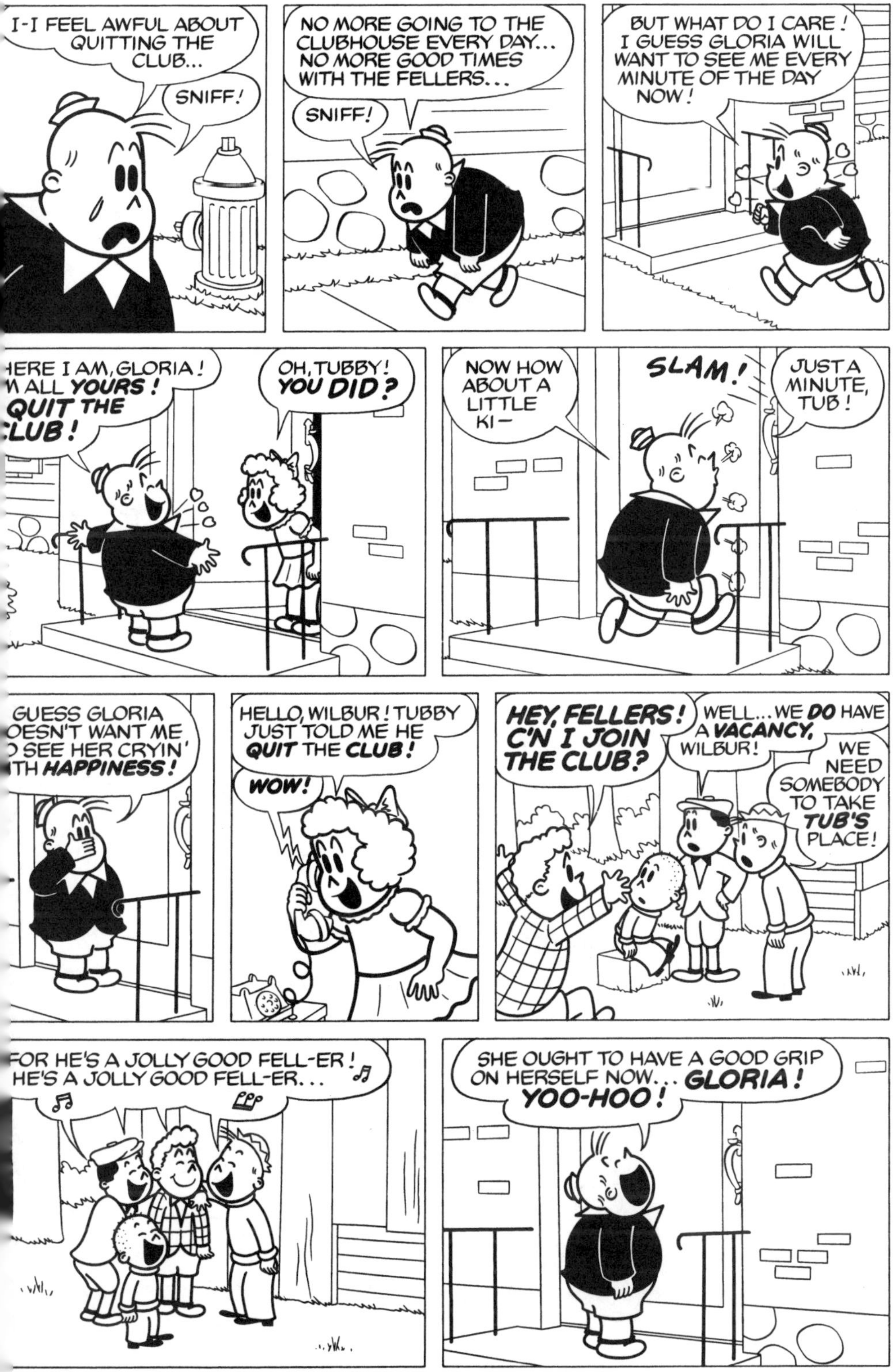
I-I FEEL AWFUL ABOUT QUITTING THE CLUB...
SNIFF!
NO MORE GOING TO THE CLUBHOUSE EVERY DAY... NO MORE GOOD TIMES WITH THE FELLERS...
SNIFF!
BUT WHAT DO I CARE! I GUESS GLORIA WILL WANT TO SEE ME EVERY MINUTE OF THE DAY NOW!
HERE I AM, GLORIA! I'M ALL YOURS! I QUIT THE CLUB!
OH, TUBBY! YOU DID?
NOW HOW ABOUT A LITTLE KI—
SLAM!
JUST A MINUTE, TUB!
I GUESS GLORIA DOESN'T WANT ME TO SEE HER CRYIN' WITH HAPPINESS!
HELLO, WILBUR! TUBBY JUST TOLD ME HE QUIT THE CLUB!
WOW!
HEY, FELLERS! C'N I JOIN THE CLUB?
WELL... WE DO HAVE A VACANCY, WILBUR!
WE NEED SOMEBODY TO TAKE TUB'S PLACE!
FOR HE'S A JOLLY GOOD FELL-ER! HE'S A JOLLY GOOD FELL-ER...
SHE OUGHT TO HAVE A GOOD GRIP ON HERSELF NOW... GLORIA! YOO-HOO!

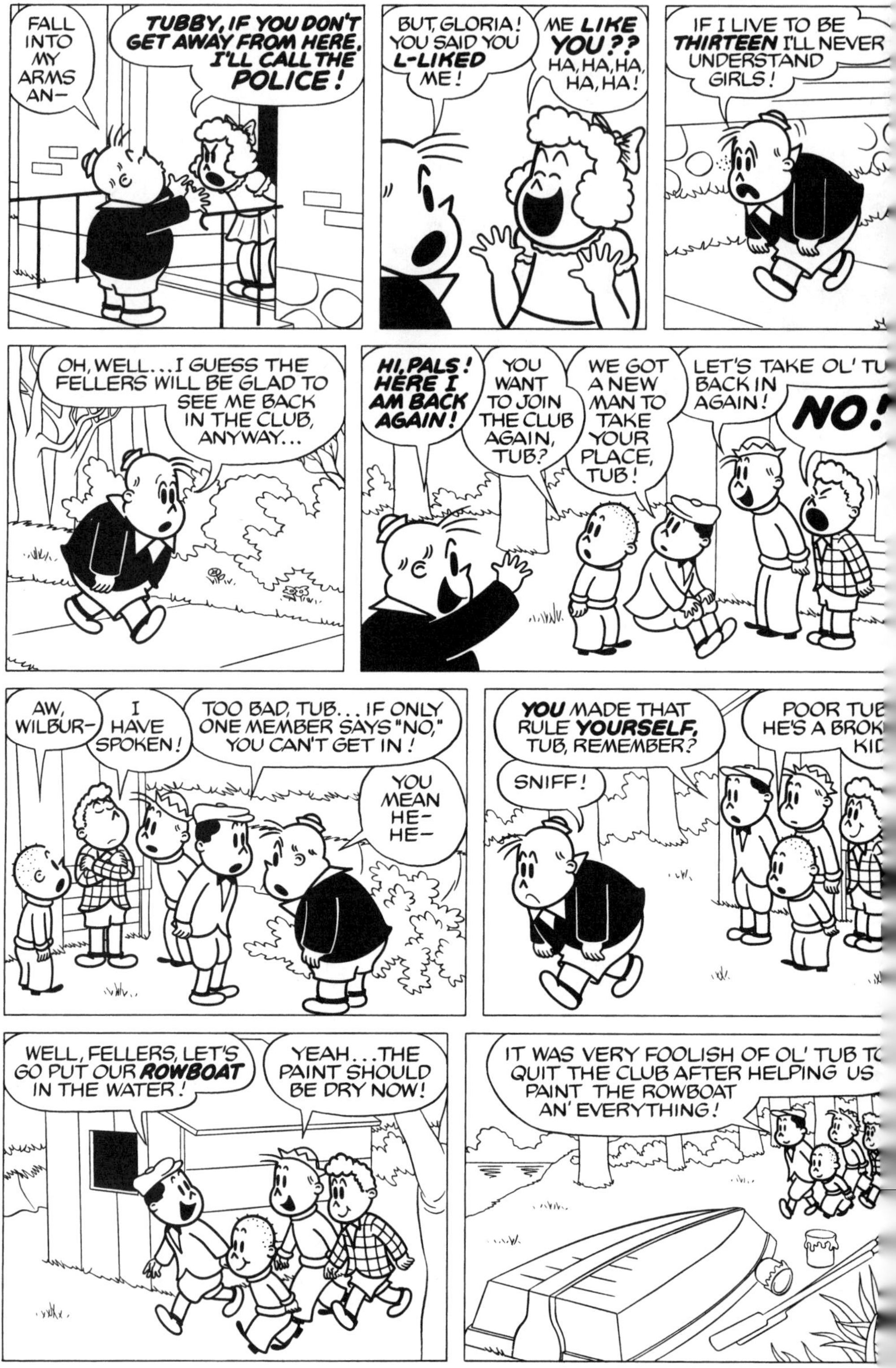
FALL INTO MY ARMS AN—
TUBBY, IF YOU DON'T GET AWAY FROM HERE, I'LL CALL THE POLICE!
BUT, GLORIA! YOU SAID YOU L-LIKED ME!
ME LIKE YOU?? HA, HA, HA, HA, HA!
IF I LIVE TO BE THIRTEEN I'LL NEVER UNDERSTAND GIRLS!
OH, WELL... I GUESS THE FELLERS WILL BE GLAD TO SEE ME BACK IN THE CLUB, ANYWAY...
HI, PALS! HERE I AM BACK AGAIN!
YOU WANT TO JOIN THE CLUB AGAIN, TUB?
WE GOT A NEW MAN TO TAKE YOUR PLACE, TUB!
LET'S TAKE OL' TU BACK IN AGAIN!
NO!
AW, WILBUR—
I HAVE SPOKEN!
TOO BAD, TUB... IF ONLY ONE MEMBER SAYS "NO," YOU CAN'T GET IN!
YOU MEAN HE-HE—
YOU MADE THAT RULE YOURSELF, TUB, REMEMBER?
SNIFF!
POOR TUB HE'S A BROK KID
WELL, FELLERS, LET'S GO PUT OUR ROWBOAT IN THE WATER!
YEAH... THE PAINT SHOULD BE DRY NOW!
IT WAS VERY FOOLISH OF OL' TUB TO QUIT THE CLUB AFTER HELPING US PAINT THE ROWBOAT AN' EVERYTHING!

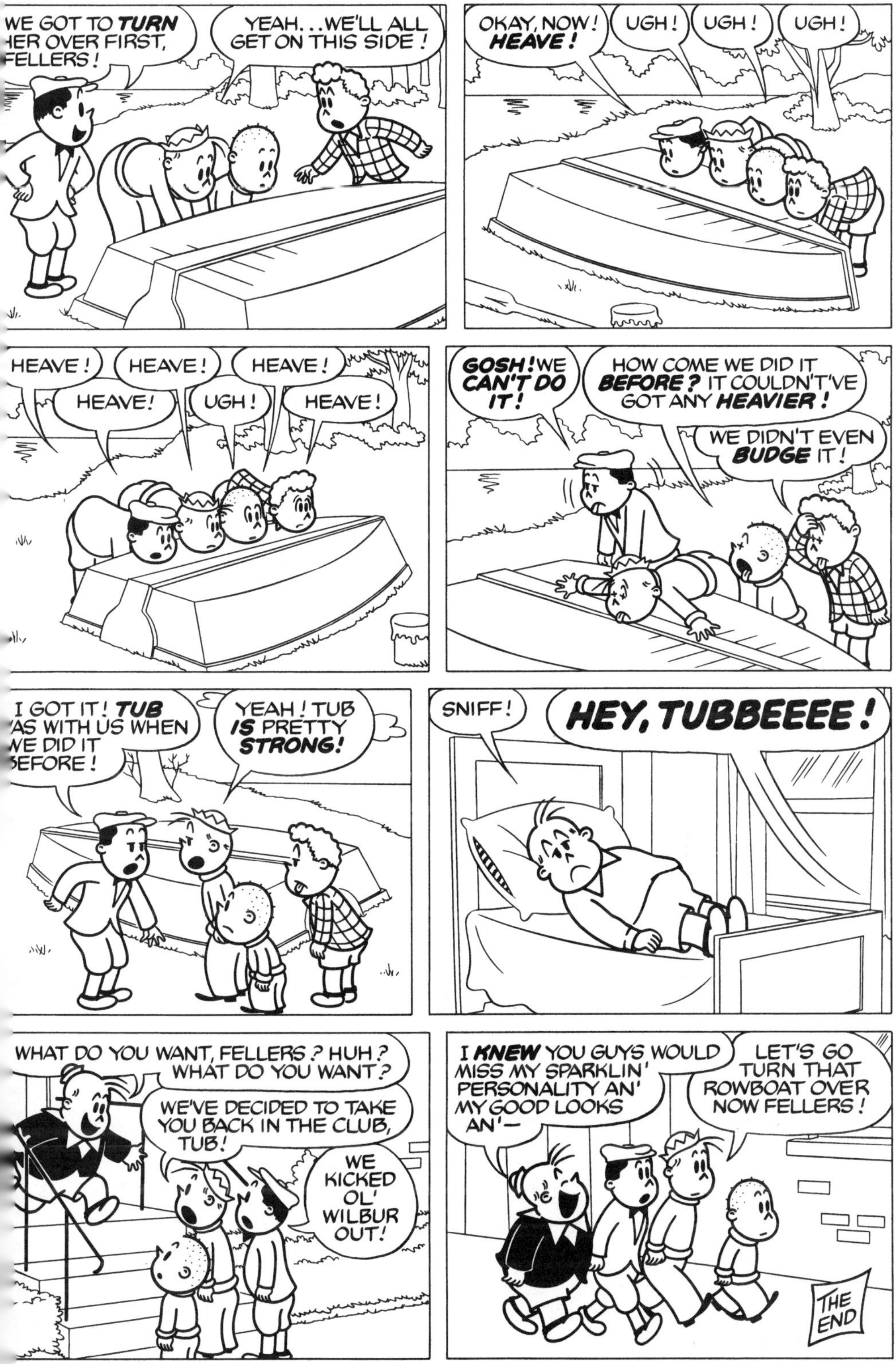
WE GOT TO TURN HER OVER FIRST, FELLERS!
YEAH...WE'LL ALL GET ON THIS SIDE!
OKAY, NOW! HEAVE!
UGH!
UGH!
UGH!
HEAVE!
HEAVE!
HEAVE!
HEAVE!
UGH!
HEAVE!
GOSH! WE CAN'T DO IT!
HOW COME WE DID IT BEFORE? IT COULDN'T'VE GOT ANY HEAVIER!
WE DIDN'T EVEN BUDGE IT!
I GOT IT! TUB WAS WITH US WHEN WE DID IT BEFORE!
YEAH! TUB IS PRETTY STRONG!
SNIFF!
HEY, TUBBEEEE!
WHAT DO YOU WANT, FELLERS? HUH? WHAT DO YOU WANT?
WE'VE DECIDED TO TAKE YOU BACK IN THE CLUB, TUB!
WE KICKED OL' WILBUR OUT!
I KNEW YOU GUYS WOULD MISS MY SPARKLIN' PERSONALITY AN' MY GOOD LOOKS AN'—
LET'S GO TURN THAT ROWBOAT OVER NOW FELLERS!
THE END

Little Lulu®

Volume 1:
My Dinner with Lulu
ISBN-10: 1-59307-318-6
ISBN-13: 978-1-59307-318-3
$9.95

Volume 2:
Sunday Afternoon
ISBN-10: 1-59307-345-3
ISBN-13: 978-1-59307-345-9
$9.95

Volume 3:
Lulu in the Doghouse
ISBN-10: 1-59307-346-1
ISBN-13: 978-1-59307-346-6
$9.95

Volume 4:
Lulu Goes Shopping
ISBN-10: 1-59307-270-8
ISBN-13: 978-1-59307-270-4
$9.95

Volume 5:
Lulu Takes a Trip
ISBN-10: 1-59307-317-8
ISBN-13: 978-1-59307-317-6
$9.95

Volume 6:
Letters to Santa
ISBN-10: 1-59307-386-0
ISBN-13: 978-1-59307-386-2
$9.95

Volume 7:
Lulu's Umbrella Service
ISBN-10: 1-59307-399-2
ISBN-13: 978-1-59307-399-2
$9.95

Volume 8:
Late for School
ISBN-10: 1-59307-453-0
ISBN-13: 978-1-59307-453-1
$9.95

Volume 9:
Lucky Lulu
ISBN-10: 1-59307-471-9
ISBN-13: 978-1-59307-471-5
$9.95

Volume 10:
All Dressed Up
ISBN-10: 1-59307-534-0
ISBN-13: 978-1-59307-534-7
$9.95

Volume 11:
April Fools
ISBN-10: 1-59307-557-X
ISBN-13: 978-1-59307-557-6
$9.95

Volume 12:
Leave It to Lulu
ISBN-10: 1-59307-620-7
ISBN-13: 978-1-59307-620-7
$9.95

Volume 13:
Too Much Fun
ISBN-10: 1-59307-621-5
ISBN-13: 978-1-59307-621-4
$9.95

Volume 14:
Queen Lulu
ISBN-10: 1-59307-683-5
ISBN-13: 978-1-59307-683-2
$9.95

Volume 15:
The Explorers
ISBN-10: 1-59307-684-3
ISBN-13: 978-1-59307-684-9
$9.95

Volume 16:
A Handy Kid
ISBN-10: 1-59307-685-1
ISBN-13: 978-1-59307-685-6
$10.95

COMING IN OCTOBER!
Volume 17:
The Valentine
ISBN-10: 1-59307-686-X
ISBN-13: 978-1-59307-686-3
$10.95

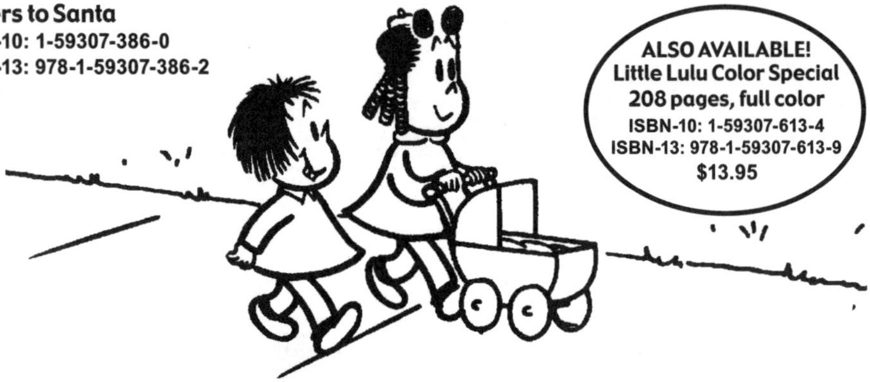

ALSO AVAILABLE!
Little Lulu Color Special
208 pages, full color
ISBN-10: 1-59307-613-4
ISBN-13: 978-1-59307-613-9
$13.95

AVAILABLE AT YOUR LOCAL COMICS SHOP OR BOOKSTORE!
To find a comics shop in your area, call 1-888-266-4226
For more information or to order direct, visit darkhorse.com or call 1-800-862-0052
Mon.-Fri. 9 A.M. to 5 P.M. Pacific Time *Prices and availability subject to change without notice